Connections: A World History

Volume One: To 1650

D1398704

Edward H. Judge

Le Moyne College

John W. Langdon

Le Moyne College

vango books | Read it. Get it.

New York   San Francisco   Boston   Upper Saddle River
London   Toronto   Sydney   Tokyo   Singapore   Madrid
Mexico City   Munich   Paris   Cape Town   Hong Kong   Montreal

Library of Congress Cataloging-in-Publication Data

Judge, Edward H.
   Connections : a world history / Edward H. Judge, John W. Langdon.
     p. cm.
   Includes bibliographical references and index.
   ISBN-13: 978-0-321-10782-4 (set)
   ISBN-10: 0-321-10782-9 (set)
   ISBN-10: 0-321-10796-9 (v. 1)
   ISBN-10: 0-321-10797-7 (v. 2)
   1. World history.   I. Langdon, John W.   II. Title.
   D21.J73 2009
   909—dc22

Executive Editor: Charles Cavaliere
Editor in Chief, History: Priscilla McGeehon
Assistant Development Manager: David B. Kear
Production Project Manager: Lynn Savino Wendel
Associate Editor: Emsal Hasan
Editorial Assistant: Lauren Aylward
Director of Marketing: Brandy Dawson
Senior Marketing Manager: Laura Lee Manley
Marketing Assistant: Athena Moore
Senior Managing Editor: Ann Marie McCarthy
Senior Operations Supervisor: Mary Ann Gloriande
Media Project Manager: Brian Hyland
Senior Art Director: Maria Lange
Manager, Rights and Permissions: Zina Arabia
Manager, Visual Research: Beth Brenzel
Image Permission Coordinator: Richard Rodriques
A/V Project Manager: Mirella Signoretto
Permissions Coordinator: Marcy Lunetta
Cover Illustration/Photo credits: Ronald Walko
Full Service Project Management: Kristy Zamagni, Pre-Press PMG

Copyright © 2009 by Pearson Education, Inc., Upper Saddle River, New Jersey 07458

All rights reserved. Printed in the United States of America. This publication is protected by Copyright and permission should be obtained from the publisher prior to any prohibited reproduction, storage in a retrieval system, or transmission in any form or by any means, electronic, mechanical, photocopying, recording, or likewise. For information regarding permission(s), write to: Rights and Permissions Department.

VangoBooks™ is an imprint of Pearson Education
Pearson® is a registered trademark of Pearson plc

Pearson Education LTD
Pearson Education Singapore, Pte. Ltd
Pearson Education Canada, Inc.
Pearson Education–Japan
Pearson Education Australia PTY, Limited

Pearson Education North Asia, Ltd., Hong Kong
Pearson Educación de Mexico, S.A. de C.V.
Pearson Education Malaysia, Pte. Ltd
Pearson Education Upper Saddle River, New Jersey

10 9 8 7 6 5 4 3 2

ISBN 13: 978-0-32-110796-1
ISBN 10:   0-32-110796-9

To Susan and Janice

CONTENTS

PART III Cross-Cultural Conflicts and Commercial Connections, 1000–1650

CHAPTER 15
Nomadic Conquests and Eurasian Connections, 1000–1400   354

CHAPTER 16
The Resurgence of the Christian West, 1050–1530   382

CHAPTER 20

The West in an Age of Religious Conflict and Global Expansion, 1500–1650

MAPS

We are two professors who love teaching world history. For the past two decades, at our middle-sized college, we have team-taught a two-semester world history course that first-year students take to fulfill a college-wide requirement. Our students have very diverse backgrounds and interests. Most take world history only because it is required, and many find it very challenging. Helping them to understand it and infecting them with our enthusiasm for it are our main purposes and passions.

This is an exciting time to be teaching world history. In an age of growing global interconnectedness, an understanding of diverse world cultures and their histories has never been more essential. Indeed, it is increasingly apparent that students who lack this understanding will be poorly prepared to function in modern society or even to comprehend the daily news.

At the same time, the teaching of world history has never seemed more challenging. As the amount and complexity of the material increases, students can get bogged down in details and inundated with information, losing sight of the overall scope and significance of the human experience. Conveying world history to college students in a comprehensible and appealing way, without leaving them confused and overwhelmed, is one of the toughest challenges we face.

To help meet this challenge and better connect with our students, we have written a compact, affordable world history text that is tailored to meet their needs. In developing this text, we pursued several main goals:

First, because students often find it difficult to read and process lengthy, detailed chapters, we sought to write a text that is concise and engaging, with short, interesting chapters that focus on major trends and developments.

Second, since students often see history as a bewildering array of details, dates, and events, we chose a unifying theme—connections among world societies—and grouped our chapters to reflect the growth of such connections from regional to global.

Third, having seen many students struggle because they lack a good sense of geography, we included 223 maps—far more than most other texts—and provided a number of other features designed to help readers better understand and process the material.

A Concise and Readable Text

Since even the best text does little good if students do not read it, we endeavored above all to produce one that is concise and readable. We addressed ourselves to first-year college students, using a simple, straightforward narrative that tells the compelling story of the peoples and societies that preceded us and how they shaped the world. To avoid drowning our readers in a welter of details, we chose to take an introductory approach rather than an encyclopedic one. With this text, students will become familiar with the most important trends, developments, and issues in world history, and they will gain an appreciation for the vast diversity of human societies and endeavors.

To make our book less overwhelming and more accessible to students, we have limited most chapters to about 10,000 words, and divided each chapter into short topical subsections. By writing concise chapters, we have enabled average students to read them in an hour or so. By keeping subsections short, we have partitioned the text into manageable segments, so that readers can process material before they move on. By furnishing an outline at the start of each chapter, marginal notes that highlight our main theme, and a perspective section at the end, we have kept in sight the overall trends and developments, without interrupting the narrative's basic flow.

Connections in World History

In our teaching we have found that many students find world history confusing and overwhelming, in part because they have no overall framework for understanding it. To help them sort things out, we have focused our text on a central theme of connections among world societies. By stressing this theme, we have sought to maintain a sense of coherence and purpose, and to give our readers a framework that will help them to make sense of history.

Rather than dividing our text into ancient, medieval, and modern eras, an arrangement that works for Europe but has limited value elsewhere, we have instead grouped our chapters into two overlapping ages: an Age of Regional Connections, lasting until about 1650 C.E., and an Age of Global Connections, dating from roughly 1500 to the present. Each age is then subdivided into three sections, reflecting the expansion of connections from regional to global levels. This framework, summarized in our table of contents, is designed to give students the "big picture" of world history that they often lack.

Within each section are chapters that provide both regional and global perspectives, stressing not only each culture's distinct features but also its connections with other regions and cultures. Readers thus can readily appreciate both the diversity and the interconnectedness of human societies.

Within each chapter, on almost every page, are marginal notations that summarize material and highlight our connections theme. Readers thus can easily keep sight of the overall context.

An Extensive and Consistent Map Program

Many students approach world history with only a rudimentary understanding of world geography, and maps are a crucial tool in understanding world history. Our text contains a copious abundance of carefully crafted maps, designed within each chapter to build one upon another. With over 220 maps throughout the book, *Connections* offers one of the most extensive map programs of any world history survey textbook.

Each chapter begins with a **foundation map**, positioning chapter events in global context or highlighting a key part of the world under discussion.

We have worked very hard to make the maps clear and to place them where readers can refer to them without turning pages. As much as possible, the maps use colors, fonts, labels, and other markers consistently, so that students will find these features familiar from one map to the next.

Finally, the map captions were carefully written to clarify the maps, to connect them with surrounding text, and to guide the students' attention to the most important elements in that map. Each map caption includes a question to help students consider critical issues.

Features

We have incorporated in our text a carefully selected set of features, each chosen with this basic guideline in mind: Will it help students to better envision, understand, and process the material they are reading?

VISUALS   We provide an ample array of photos and other visuals, selected to illustrate developments explicitly discussed in the text. To ensure that students will connect the text with the images, we have placed them in the margins near the passages that they illustrate.

PRONUNCIATION GUIDES   Since students often struggle to pronounce unfamiliar names and places, we have placed parenthetical pronunciation guides immediately following first use of such names and places in the text.

CHAPTER-OPENING VIGNETTES   Each chapter opens with a vignette designed to capture the reader's interest and introduce the chapter's main themes.

PRIMARY SOURCE DOCUMENT EXCERPTS   To acquaint students with primary sources and illuminate materials covered in our text, we have provided concise excerpts from selected historical sources, in feature boxes placed where the document is discussed in the text.

CHAPTER REVIEW SECTIONS   Each chapter has a comprehensive end-of-chapter review section that incorporates the following features:

- **Putting It in Perspective.** This feature provides a concise overview of the chapter's main themes, highlights key connections, and puts them in historical perspective.
- **Key Concepts.** Key concepts are highlighted in boldface in the text, defined in the text when first discussed and also in an alphabetic glossary, and listed at the end of each chapter with page references to facilitate review.
- **Key People.** Important individuals mentioned in the text are also listed at the end of each chapter, followed by page references to facilitate review.
- **Ask Yourself.** A set of questions at the end of every chapter encourages further reflection and analysis of topics, issues, and connections considered in the chapter.
- **Going Further.** A list of books at the end of each chapter provides resources for teachers and students interested in delving more deeply into topics covered.
- **Key Dates and Developments.** Each chapter contains a comprehensive chronology that lists the key dates and developments, helping students to see at a glance sequence of important events.

A Student-Centered Textbook

For several years, we and our colleagues have used a draft version of our text, with highly encouraging results. Since the book is affordable and portable, we find that most students buy it and bring it to class. Since chapters are concise and engaging, we find that students actually read them before coming to class and thus are better prepared to understand and discuss key issues. Students who completed questionnaires or wrote reviews of our chapters said they found them clear and compelling. By pointing out passages they found dry or confusing, these students also helped make the book more readable. We went to great lengths to create a text that is useful, accessible, and attractive to our students. For they, after all, are the reasons we wrote this book.

Ed Judge and John Langdon

VangoBooks are innovative course materials created to better meet the needs of today's college students. They are portable, convenient, student-oriented texts that present essential information and issues in a compact form at a much lower price than traditional textbooks. Designed to make world history more meaningful and accessible, this VangoBook comes with an extensive package of support materials for instructors and students.

For Instructors

INSTRUCTOR'S MANUAL   For each chapter of the text, the Instructor's Manual provides lecture outlines, chapter summaries, learning objectives, discussion questions, Connection Questions, and suggestions for audio-visual materials.

TEST-ITEM FILE   Written and extensively class-tested by Connie Brand of Meridian Community College, the Test-Item File includes over 3000 questions (multiple choice, essay, short answer, true/false, and map questions).

TEST GEN   is a computerized test-management program for Windows and Macintosh computers that allows users to customize their own tests, for both traditional and online classrooms. The user-friendly interface enables instructors to view, edit, and add questions. Search and sort features allow instructors to locate questions quickly and arrange them in preferred order. Available online at www.pearsonhighered.com/irc. Contact your local Pearson representative for an access code.

POWERPOINT SLIDES AND DIGITAL TRANSPARENCIES   are available for downloading to adopters of *Connections* from the Pearson instructor resource center (www.pearsonhighered.com/irc). Contact your Pearson representative for an access code.

For Students

VANGOBOOKS.COM   VangoBooks.com/judge offers educational tools specifically designed to help students fully understand world history and study smarter. Resources such as documents, audio, video and images are correlated to each chapter in *Connections*. Interactive maps feature engaging simulations to enrich the maps from the text. Multiple Choice and True/False questions from the Chapter Exams provide a great way to prepare for tests, while the Essay section offers a variety of sample essay questions. Test questions and essays can be submitted online for immediate grading.

VANGOCARD FOR WORLD HISTORY   Colorful, affordable, and packed with useful information, Pearson's VangoCard for World History makes studying easier, more efficient, and more enjoyable. Course information is distilled down to the basics, helping students quickly master fundamentals, review a subject for understanding, or prepare for an exam. And because Cards are laminated, they are a durable reference tool. VangoCards can be packaged with the text. Contact your local Pearson representative for details.

RESEARCH NAVIGATOR™   *Available when bundled with the text.* **Make the most of your research time with Research Navigator.** Understanding the research process is important to success in college. Pearson's

Research Navigator is the easiest way to start a research assignment or research paper. With access to exclusive databases of credible and reliable source material, including the EBSCO Academic Journal and Abstract Database, The *New York Times* Search by Subject Archive, "Best of the Web" Link Library, and *Financial Times* Article Archive and Company Financials, **Research Navigator** gives students all the tools they need to conduct online research for projects and papers.

- Extensively revised and updated, the **Primary Source: Documents in Global History DVD** is both a rich collection of textual and visual documents in world history and an indispensable tool for working with sources. Extensively developed with the guidance of historians and teachers, the revised and updated DVD version includes over 800 sources in world history—from cave art to satellite images of the Earth from space. More sources from Africa, Latin America, and southeast Asia have been added to this revised and updated DVD version. All sources are accompanied by headnotes, focus questions, and are searchable by topic or region.

- Penguin logo TK) Titles from the renowned **Penguin Classics** series can be bundled with *Connections: A World History* for a nominal charge. Please contact your Pearson Arts and Sciences sales representative for details.

- ***The Prentice Hall Atlas in World History, Second Edition*** includes over 100 full-color maps in world history, drawn by Dorling Kindersley, one of the world's most respected cartographic publishers. Copies of the Atlas can be bundled with *Connections: A World History* for a nominal charge. Contact your Pearson Arts and Sciences sales representative for details.

- **CourseSmart Textbooks Online** is an exciting new choice for students looking to save money. As an alternative to purchasing the print textbook, students can subscribe to the same content online and save up to 50% off the suggested list price of the print text. With a CourseSmart eTextbook, students can search the text, make notes online, print out reading assignments that incorporate lecture notes, and bookmark important passages for later review. For more information, or to subscribe to the CourseSmart eTextbook, visit www.coursesmart.com.

In conceiving, composing, and bringing out this book, we are deeply grateful to the many people who helped us along the way. Our senior colleagues Bill Telesca and Fr. Bill Bosch, with whom we first taught world history, shared with us their many decades of experience as teachers and scholars. Our current colleagues, Doug Egerton, Holly Rine, Yamin Xu, and Bob Zens have class-tested a preliminary version of our book, and have provided us with feedback from their students and insights from their expertise in Atlantic World, Amerind, East Asian, and Islamic history. Yamin Xu has also been particularly helpful with the spelling and pronunciation of East Asian names. Connie Brand and her colleagues at Meridian Community College have likewise class-tested our book with their students, and Connie has written an extremely useful test bank.

Expert Content Reviewers

We are teachers of world history, but we are not experts in every area of history. For that reason, we acknowledge with profound gratitude the insightful and thorough critiques provided by a panel of expert reviewers, who read and commented on the following chapters:

David Christian, San Diego State University (Human Origins and Early Societies: Chapter 1)

Karl Galinsky, University of Texas (Greece and Rome: Chapters 6–10)

Leonard Gordon, Columbia University (Southeast Asia: Chapters 3, 12, 17, 22, 29, 32, 35)

Megan Greene, The University of Kansas (Asia: Chapters 4, 14, 15, 21, 25, 29, 32, 33, 35)

William Ochsenwalk, Virginia Polytechnic Institute and State University (the Muslim world: Chapters 11, 12, 13, 15, 17, 22, 30, 37)

Jeffrey Pilcher, University of Minnesota (Latin America: Chapters 5, 18, 19, 26, 28, 36)

Sean Redding, Amherst College (Africa: Chapters 2, 13, 23, 30, 37)

Advisory Council

We greatly appreciate the edifying suggestions offered to us by an Advisory Council of our colleagues and peers that Pearson brought together:

Sanjam Ahluwalia, Northern Arizona University

Robert Becker, Gainesville State College

Brett Berliner, Morgan State University

Rebecca Berry, Wake Tech Community College

David Blaylock, Eastern Kentucky

Beau Bowers, Central Piedmont CC

Ras Michael Brown, Southern Illinois University

Brian Bunk, University of Massachusetts—Amherst

Harry Carpenter III, Western Piedmont Community College

Charles Crouch, Georgia Southern University

Lisa Edwards, University of Massachusetts—Lowell

John Frederick, South Louisiana Community College

Patricia Gajda, The University of Texas at Tyler

Donald Grinde, SUNY, Buffalo

Anthony Gulig, University of Wisconsin Whitewater

Brian Gurian, Harrisburg Area Community College

Anne Hardgrove, University of Texas at San Antonio

Donald Harreld, Brigham Young University

Randolph Head, University of California, Riverside

Padhraig Higgins, Mercer County Community College

Marie Hooper, Oklahoma City University

Michael Houf, Texas A&M University—Kingsville

Michael Jacobs, University of Wisconsin—Baraboo

Ellen Jenkins, Arkansas Tech University

Timothy Jenks, East Carolina University

Robert Kunath, Illinois College

Ben Lieberman, Fitchburg State College

Susan Maneck, Jackson State University

David John Marley, Vanguard University

Joel McMahon, Georgia Perimeter College

David McQuilken, Bridgewater College

Cristina Mehrtens, University of Massachusetts—Dartmouth

Scott More, Indiana University of Pennsylvania

Luke Nichter, Bowling Green State University

Robert Parkinson, Shepherd University

Tracie Provost, Middle Georgia College

David Rayson, Normandale Community College

Scott Reese, Northern Arizona University

Maria Teresa Romero, Saddleback College

Steven Salm, Xavier University of Louisiana

Linda Scherr, Mercer County Community College

David Simonelli, Youngstown State University

Govind Sreenivasan, Brandeis University

Rachel Stocking, Southern Illinois University Carbondale

Michael Swope, Schoolcraft College

Joseph Tse-Hei, Pace University

John Van Sant, University of Alabama

Charles Weber, Wheaton College

Theodore Jun Yoo, University of Hawaii at Manoa

Alex Zukas, National University

Patricia Ali, Morris College

Stanley Arnold, Northern Illinois University

Mary Gross, Marian College of Fond du Lac

Michael Jacobs, University of Wisconsin—Baraboo

Lester Lee, Salem State College

Farid Mahdavi, San Diego State University

Laura Mitchell, UC Irvine

Pamela Sayre, Henry Ford Community College

Gordon Thomasson, Broome Community College (SUNY)

Khodr Zaarour, Shaw University

Reviewers

We also thank the many scholars and teachers whose thoughtful and often detailed comments helped improve our book. Whatever errors remain are, of course, our own:

Sanjam Ahluwalia, Northern Arizona University

Robert Becker, Gainesville State College

Brett Berliner, Morgan State University

Rebecca Berry, Wake Technical Community College

David Blaylock, Eastern Kentucky University

Connie Brand, Mississippi Community College

Beau Browers, Central Piedmont Community College

Ras Michael Brown, Southern Illinois University

Robert W. Brown, University of North Carolina, Pembroke

Brian Bunk, University of Massachusetts—Amherst

Fred Burkhard, University of Maryland, University College

Robert J. Caputi, Erie Community College

Harry E. Carpenter III, Western Piedmont Community College

Abdin Chande, Adelphi University

Nupur Chandhuri, Texas Southern University

Ken Chauvin, Appalachian State University

Yinghong Cheng, Delaware State University

Charles Crouch, Georgia Southern University

Lisa M. Edwards, University of Massachusetts—Lowell

Charles H. Ford, Norfolk State University

John H. Frederick, South Louisiana Community College

Patricia A. Gajda, The University of Texas at Tyler

Donald A. Grinde, Jr., SUNY, Buffalo

Anthony Gulig, University of Washington, Whitewater

Mark Gunn, Meridian Community College

Brian Gurian, Harrisburg Area Community College

Edward M. Hanlon, John Jay College

Donald J. Harreld, Brigham Young University

Paul Hatley, Rogers State University

Randolph Head, University of California, Riverside

Padhraig Higgins, Mercer County Community College

Marie Hooper, Oklahoma City University

Michael Houf, Texas A&M University—Kingsville

Clark Hultquist, University of Montevallo

Ellen J. Jenkins, Arkansas Tech University

Timothy Jenks, East Carolina University

Rhea S. Klenovich, Lakeland College

Robert Kunath, Illinois College

Joseph Tse-Hei Lee, Pace University

Yi Li, Tacoma Community College

Benjamin Lieberman, Fitchburg State College

Valdis Lumans, University of South Carolina, Aiken

Susan Maneck, Jackson State University

Cathlyn Mariscotti, Holy Family University

David John Marley, Vanguard University

Joel McMahon, Georgia Perimeter College

David K. McQuilkin, Bridgewater College

Cristina Mehrtens, University of Massachusetts—Dartmouth

David Meier, Dickinson State University

Greg Miller, Hillsborough Community College

Robert Scott Moore, Indiana University of Pennsylvania

Luke A. Nichter, Bowling Green State University

Chris Padgett, American River College

Van Plexico, Georgia Perimeter College

Tracie Provost, Middle Georgia College

David Rayson, Normandale Community College

Scott S. Reese, Northern Arizona University

Maria Theresa Romero, Saddleback College

Steven J. Salm, Xavier University of Louisiana

Linda Scherr, Mercer County Community College

David Simonelli, Youngstown State University

Govind P. Sreenivasan, Brandeis University

Anthony J. Steinhoff, University of Tennessee, Chattanooga

Elizabeth Stice, University of Hawaii, Hilo

Rachel Stocking, Southern Illinois University, Carbondale

William Van Norman, James Madison University

John Van Sant, University of Alabama, Birmingham

Charles Weber, Wheaton College

Theodore Yoo, University of Hawaii at Manoa

Qiang Zhai, Auburn University

Alex Zukas, National University

Numerous others have contributed immensely to this work. Kathryn Buturla, Gwen Morgan, Dan Nieciecki, Adam Zaremba, and the late Marc Ball assisted us with various aspects of our research and writing. Jaime Wadowiec and Vicky Green each read our work in its early stages and supplied us with a student's perspective on its clarity, structure, coherence, and appeal to readers. Erika Gutierrez, Lisa Pinto, and Janet Lanphier challenged us, believed in us, supported us, and pushed us to expand our vision and our goals. Phil Herbst poured his heart into editing our work, correcting our mistakes, improving our style, sharpening our insights, enlivening our narrative, clarifying our explanations, and pressing us to excel. David Kear further refined our work, strengthened our writing, highlighted our connections theme, and worked assiduously to make our numerous maps the best in the business. Charles Cavaliere likewise worked carefully on our visuals and photos, locating appropriate images to illustrate certain passages and placing these images near the passages they illustrate.

Our biggest debt of gratitude is the one that we owe to our wives. Sue Judge and Jan Langdon sustained, encouraged, and supported us, especially when the going got tough, enduring numerous sacrifices as they shared both our burdens and our joys. We owe them far more than words can express or than we can ever repay. This book is rightfully theirs as much as it is ours.

A Note on Dates and Spellings

In labeling dates, like many other world history teachers, we use the initials B.C.E. (Before the Common Era) and C.E. (Common Era), which correspond respectively to the labels B.C. (Before Christ) and A.D. (*Anno Domini*, "The Year of the Lord"), long used in Western societies. In spelling Chinese names we use the Pinyin system, internationally adopted in 1979, but we sometimes also give other spellings that were widely used before then. (In Chapters 32 and 35, for example, Chinese Nationalist leader Jiang Jieshi is also identified as Chiang Kaishek.) Our spelling of names and terms from other languages follows standard usage, with alternative versions given where appropriate. (Chapter 17, for example, notes that Central Asian warrior Timur Lenk was also called Tamerlane in Europe.)

The Emergence of Human Societies, to 3000 B.C.E.

- Our Earliest Ancestors
- The Origins and Impact of Agriculture
- The Emergence of Complex Societies
- Chapter Review

Early Human Cave Art

Fossils and cultural artifacts, such as these dramatic paintings on cave walls in southern France, provide us with insights into the lives and societies of early humans (pages 8-9).

In July 2001, in a desolate, sun-baked region of the north-central African nation of Chad, a group of professional fossil-hunters, searching for remnants of life in past ages, made an astonishing discovery. There, in the windswept, shifting sands, they came upon a small crusty object that appeared to have teeth. At first they thought it was the fossilized jaw of a pig, but on further examination they concluded that it was the flat-faced skull of a **hominid** (*HAH-mih-nid*), a term scientists apply to human beings and their two-legged pre-human predecessors. Later testing showed that the skull was seven million years old—the oldest hominid fossil yet discovered.

Early Farming and Herding Areas

This discovery, which created great excitement, illustrates both the allure and challenge of studying the distant past. Although hominids have existed for millions of years, humans have left behind written records only for about 5,000 years. Recorded history thus covers only a small fraction of human experience. The preceding ages, encompassing all human existence before the emergence of writing, are often called the prehistoric era, despite the probability that people who lived then kept track of their history by passing on oral accounts. Since these early people left no surviving written records, however, modern scholars who study this era must rely mainly on analysis of fossils and cultural artifacts, augmented by enlightened speculation subject to scholarly debate. Several scholars, for instance, challenged the Chad discovery, claiming that the skull might belong to an ancient gorilla rather than a hominid.

Despite such disputes, the general outlines of our ancestry are reasonably clear. Hominids first emerged in Africa at least five million years ago, and for millions of years most likely survived by eating wild plants. Over many generations, they learned to communicate by spoken language, form small nomadic groups for cooperation and protection, fashion stone tools, hunt wild animals, and use fire, passing on their knowledge and skills to their young. In their quest for food, some hominid groups migrated from Africa to parts of Eurasia. Over time, most early hominid species died out, but one branch of the hominid family survived, evolving within the past half million years into modern humans like ourselves.

Equipped with greater intelligence and communication skills than their hominid forerunners, humans formed larger communities, devised better tools and weapons, learned to hunt more effectively, and occasionally fought with other groups vying for food. Some communities, seeking new food sources, migrated to Australia and the Americas. Some eventually figured out how to raise food, by growing crops and domesticating certain animals. Farming and herding made possible even larger communities, such as cities and states, that established commercial, cultural, and political connections, inaugurating the historical era.

Our Earliest Ancestors

Since no historical records survive from before five thousand years ago, most of what we know of the prehistoric era is based on the work of archeologists and anthropologists, who study early hominids through fossils, cultural artifacts, and genetic comparisons with other animals. Using such sources, scholars surmise that humans are descended from hominids who lived in east-central Africa millions of years ago (and hence that we all have African ancestry). By modern human standards, early hominids were small, standing only three or four feet tall, with brains that were smaller and less complex than ours. But hominids had larger brains than other animals, and voice boxes that could make more complex sounds, enabling them to better communicate what they learned with each other and with their offspring. And hominids walked on two feet rather than four, enabling them to use their arms and hands for creative purposes, such as fashioning and using tools and weapons.

About two million years ago, as hominids grew in dexterity and brainpower, some began to chip and shape pieces of stone into rough-hewn tools. Modern researchers have characterized this activity—the first indication of conscious cultural behavior—as the onset of the Old Stone Age or **Paleolithic** (*pā-lē-ō-LITH-ik*) period, the earliest and longest stage of cultural development, lasting from approximately 2,000,000 B.C.E. until about 10,000 B.C.E. During this extended period, hominids vastly improved their social and communicative skills, learned to hunt in groups that pursued prey from one region to another, and migrated to diverse regions, including northern Africa and parts of Eurasia. In the process they developed diverse ways of life.

Hominids, with improved communication, hunt and migrate in groups

Hominids and Cultural Adaptation

Beginning in the Paleolithic period, hominids diverged from other animals in a significant way. Rather than adjusting to their environment mainly through biological evolution, as most other organisms did, hominids also developed through **cultural adaptation**, the process of using their intellectual and social skills to adjust to their surroundings and improve their chances for survival. Organized into small kinship groups that traveled from place to place, they developed a number of new techniques that they shared with each other and their young, thus transmitting their knowledge and skills to future generations.

With their growing intellectual capacities, hominids increasingly found better ways to make use of and adapt to their environment. From long and sometimes bitter experience, for example, they learned which plants were digestible, which could be harmful or lethal, and which had certain medicinal or intoxicative properties. In time some hominid groups learned how to hunt with the use of crude stone axes, which they used to hurl at their prey and then to strip away the hides for clothing and the meat for food. Later, they learned to use fire for cooking meats and plants to make them more digestible, for warding off wild animals, and for providing nighttime warmth and light.

Hominids use their intelligence to adapt to their surroundings

Furthermore, as their powers of memory and speech improved, hominids transmitted their discoveries to each other and their offspring by sharing ideas and learning from one another. A hominid woman who learned to build a fire, for example, could share

Hominids pass on what they learn to each other and their young

Early hominid tools.

this knowledge with the rest of her group, and also teach it to her children. A hominid band returning from the hunt could sit around the fire, cook their meat, share their experiences, and pass on wisdom and practices from earlier generations. One result was that hominids could build upon their knowledge from one generation to the next, and thus could adapt more quickly than other animals. Another result was that separate human societies eventually developed their own **cultures**: unique combinations of customs, beliefs, and practices—including languages, arts, rituals, institutions, and technologies—that distinguished these societies from each other.

Foraging, Family, and Gender

Early hominids apparently were scavengers, moving about in small nomadic groups that survived mainly by gathering wild nuts and berries, feeding occasionally on the carcasses of dead animals. Then, after exhausting the readily accessible food resources in a particular region, the hominid groups moved on. As they learned to hunt they not only increased their consumption of meat, but also killed or drove away their prey, so they still relocated periodically to find new sources of game. Since these groups survived by searching for and scouring food, they are often called **foragers**—those who subsist by gathering wild plant foods and hunting wild animals.

Hominids, connected by kinship, travel in foraging bands

Having no written records of these early foraging societies, modern scholars study them by examining archeological remains, comparing what they learn with the practices of the few foraging cultures that still exist today in Siberia, South Africa, Australia, and the Americas. These sources suggest that Paleolithic peoples traveled in foraging bands, mobile communities of perhaps thirty to sixty people connected by kinship. While large enough to provide their members with sustenance and protection, groups of this size, unencumbered by material possessions, were small enough to easily pack up camp and relocate to find new food sources and adjust to changing seasons or climates. As members of the same **kinship group**—an extended family comprising grandparents, parents, siblings, aunts, uncles, cousins, and other relatives—they were also bound together by familial obligations and affections.

Hominids live in family groups that raise children

Compared with many other large mammals, which grow to almost full maturity within a few months or years, human children remain physically immature, and thus dependent on older caregivers, for a dozen years or more. They therefore require a high level of protection, nurturing, and supervision, usually provided by their parents and other relatives, for an extended time. Furthermore, unlike many other animals, adult humans frequently form an enduring emotional bond with a specific sexual companion. These traits and conditions help to explain why human parents often stay together to care for their children, and why the central institution of most human societies has been the family.

Hominid families develop flexible gender roles

Family concerns may also help explain why our ancestors probably divided their work along gender lines. Evidence suggests that in foraging societies men usually did the hunting and fighting, while women were more likely to gather plant food, attend to the campsite, and care for the young. This division of labor was by no means rigid: women at times no doubt helped with the hunting or defense, while men at times assisted in tending the hearth and taking care of the children. Nor did the gender roles imply that women were valued less than men. On the contrary, since a group's survival depended on women to bear children, and since gathering plant food supplied a more reliable source of nutrition than hunting wild game, the functions of the women may well have been considered more important than those of the men. A community, after all, could endure the loss of several adult males, but women and children were essential to its long-term survival. Since the men were thus more expendable, under normal conditions it made sense for them to perform the dangerous duties of hunting wild animals and defending the camp against predators and outsiders, and for women to handle the safer yet more essential tasks of minding the campfire, foraging for plant food, preparing meals, and nurturing the young.

Since the foraging band was relatively small and its members were mostly related, its structure was probably quite simple. Although some members might have greater influence as a result of intellect, experience, or personality, there was no real need for government officials or class divisions such as those that would later arise in larger, more diverse societies.

The absence of rank in foraging bands did not mean that everyone was equal, but rather that the adults in the group could collaborate in making decisions, securing the campsite, procuring food, raising the young, and moving to new places. Societies in which the members cooperated—supporting one another, sharing both the burdens and the bounty, and passing on their knowledge to their young—tended to be stable and enduring. Some were also able, when the need arose, to migrate substantial distances to ensure their survival or improve their way of life.

Foraging societies have simple structures based on collaboration

Ice Age Migrations and *Homo Sapiens*

The Paleolithic period corresponded roughly with what geologists call the Pleistocene (*PLĪ-stuh-sēn*) epoch, also called the **Great Ice Age**, an immense stretch of time (roughly 2,000,000 B.C.E. to 8000 B.C.E.) marked by frigid glacial stages when enormous ice masses called glaciers spread across much of the globe (Map 1.1). These prolonged cold spells, or "ice ages," each lasting tens of thousands of years, alternated with somewhat shorter intervals of relative warmth. Although tropical regions did not experience glaciers, their climates fluctuated considerably, bringing major changes in vegetation and animal life.

Induced perhaps by growing populations or by environmental changes that threatened their food supply, many mammals migrated during the Pleistocene epoch to new habitats. Among these mammals were foraging hominid bands, some of which left Africa and traveled to Asia, possibly following herds of wild animals, by about 1.8 million years ago. Much later, by about 800,000 years ago, other groups of foraging hominids made their way to Europe. These hominid migrants used their cultural skills to adapt to their new surroundings, employing local materials such as wood, bamboo, and rock to make shelters, hatchets, and hunting axes.

Ice Age hominids migrate to Eurasia and adapt to new environments

Then, by about 150,000 to 200,000 years ago, as hominid development and migrations continued, there emerged a new species now called *Homo sapiens* (*HŌ-mō SĀ-pē-enz*). This term, which means "wise human," designates the species that includes all modern people, and distinguishes us from other types of hominids that no longer exist.

Some hominids evolve into Homo sapiens, *our human species*

The complex processes by which our species developed, and the reasons why it prevailed while other hominids died out, are far from being fully understood. Humans, it is clear, have larger skulls, housing larger brains, than earlier hominid species. But so did the people modern scholars call **Neanderthals**, an extinct group of large-brained hominids whose remains were first discovered in 1856 in Germany's Neander Valley, and who existed from roughly 200,000 to 30,000 years ago.

Other hominid groups eventually become extinct

FOUNDATION MAP 1.1 The Great Ice Age, 2,000,000–8000 B.C.E.

In the Great Ice Age, or Pleistocene epoch (2,000,000–8000 B.C.E.), ice covered much of the Earth's land surface during prolonged glacial stages, commonly called ice ages. Notice that the areas in green, which are now under water, were exposed as dry land as sea levels dropped during the last ice age. How might this development have aided human migrations, especially to the Americas?

ARCTIC OCEAN · SIBERIA · ALASKA · EUROPE · ASIA · NORTH AMERICA · ROCKY MTS. · Mediterranean Sea · ZAGROS MTS. · HIMALAYA MTS. · CHINA · JAPAN · ATLANTIC OCEAN · Red Sea · INDIA · AFRICA · PACIFIC OCEAN · Equator · ATLANTIC OCEAN · INDIAN OCEAN · NEW GUINEA · SOUTH AMERICA · AUSTRALIA · NEW ZEALAND · ANDES MTS. · ANTARCTICA

0 — 3000 km
0 — 3000 mi

Regions covered by ice 20,000 years ago
Land exposed by lower sea levels

Even the basic outlines of what happened have been subject to dispute. Some experts, for example, formerly asserted that distinct groups of *Homo sapiens* developed independently in separate parts of Africa and Eurasia, evolving from earlier hominids already living there. Most experts, however, now believe that *Homo sapiens* first appeared only in Africa, migrating later to Eurasia and thence to the rest of the world (Map 1.2).

Humans develop enhanced reasoning and communicating skills

In any case, *Homo sapiens* eventually developed greater intellectual and linguistic skills than other hominids and thus were able more effectively to reason, communicate, and cooperate, sharing information with each other and passing it on to future generations. Early humans thereby developed more effective tools and weapons, including needles and fishhooks carved from the antlers and tusks of wild animals and spears that could be hurled at large animals from a safe distance. Using sturdy plant fibers, people also began to fashion ropes and lines that could be tied to hooks and harpoons, used to make nets and traps, and eventually strung onto bows from which to shoot arrows at prey.

As hunting skills improve, human populations and migrations increase

These innovations helped some early humans to hunt more effectively, and thus to acquire warmer clothes and larger amounts of animal meat, which they could now supplement with fowl and fish. Modern scholars speculate that, with access to more and better food, people may have lived longer and been able to support more children. Increasing population no doubt led to growing competition for food, inducing some

Map 1.2 Humans Inhabit the Continents, 200,000–10,000 B.C.E.

Although prehuman hominids migrated from Africa to Asia over a million years ago, most scholars think that human beings (*Homo sapiens*) first emerged in Africa by about 150,000–200,000 years ago. Note that, about 100,000 years ago, humans began to migrate out of Africa, and that by about 12,000 years ago (10,000 B.C.E.), they inhabited all the continents except Antarctica. What factors prompted early humans to move to distant places?

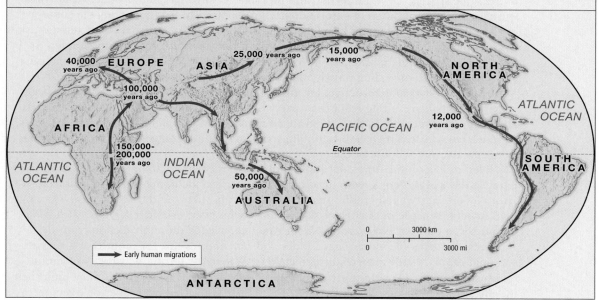

groups to migrate to new regions in quest of new food sources. Hence, as their hunting skills improved, human societies spread out across Africa and Eurasia. Eventually human hunters depleted the numbers of such mammals as bears, lions, deer, and gazelles, and destroyed the herds of fur-covered mammoths that once roamed across Eurasia.

In their ongoing search for sustenance, some human societies migrated even farther. By 50,000 B.C.E., according to evidence uncovered by archeologists, people had made their way from Southeast Asia to Australia, an impressive feat that entailed venturing out in boats on the open seas. Other humans apparently migrated from northeast Asia to the Americas by at least 12,000 B.C.E., during the last ice age, when the huge glaciers absorbed so much water that sea levels dropped by hundreds of feet, thus exposing a broad land bridge that connected Siberia with Alaska (Map 1.1). From Alaska the migrants spread throughout the Americas, where they found pristine lands that still teemed with mammoths, bears, and gazelles. By the end of the Paleolithic period, in almost every region of the globe that was fit for human habitation, there were human societies.

Human groups migrate to Australia and the Americas

Physical and Cultural Diversity

As humans moved to various lands and latitudes, their bodies adjusted to different climates and conditions. Over time, this biological adaptation apparently produced some modest physical differences. For example, some of the peoples who lived in northern regions eventually developed lighter skin coloration, which was better able to produce nutrients from the scarcer sunlight, and sometimes hairier bodies to protect them from the cold. Those who inhabited hotter regions typically had darker pigmentation, which was better able to protect them from the harmful rays produced by abundant sunshine.

Although skin colors differ, humans are all one species

Despite such differences in outward appearance, however, all human beings belong to the same species (*Homo sapiens*), and they can readily mate and produce healthy offspring with those of different coloration and other physical features. Thus the concept of **race**, which divides human beings into categories based on external characteristics, skin color in particular, relies on relatively insignificant distinctions. Indeed, in mapping the human genome, modern scientists have found that genetic variability among humans is remarkably small, providing no scientific basis for racial categorization.

From a historical perspective, far more important than physical diversity has been cultural diversity, resulting from the variety of ways in which separate human societies have adapted over time to their separate circumstances. In a number of ingenious ways, people have adjusted their habits and lifestyles to take advantage of the terrain, vegetation, climate, and wildlife of the regions they inhabit.

Even in Paleolithic times, substantial differences emerged among cultures in various parts of the world. People who lived on warm prairies, including the great grasslands of Africa, wore lightweight clothes made from skins and fibers and dwelt in easily assembled structures made of grasses or skins. Those who lived in colder regions, such as the northern parts of Eurasia and North America, needed more protection from the elements; these people wore rugged hides and furs and resided for months at a time in seasonal camps with warmer, sturdier shelters. Where the terrain was rocky or mountainous, people lived in stone structures and caves; where it was wooded they built their lodgings from branches, boughs, and bones. Those who lived near lakes or rivers teeming with fish had little need to travel for food; they thus built permanent, durable dwellings made of wood and stone.

Humans adapt to diverse conditions and develop diverse cultures

These early distinctions gradually developed into different ways of life, with societies diverging not only in clothing and shelter, but also in customs, institutions, languages, practices, and beliefs. Consequently, the great diversity among human beings has not been physical but cultural. The study of world history thus focuses mainly on the development of diverse cultures, their similarities and differences, and on the connections and conflicts that have arisen among them.

Paleolithic Cultural and Spiritual Perspectives

As Paleolithic peoples pondered the world around them, and thought about the meaning of life and death, they developed new forms of expression. Paintings, carvings, and burial sites surviving from the Stone Age attest to the various forms of art and ritual practiced by early peoples, seeking no doubt to understand and influence the forces shaping their lives.

Early humans develop symbols and artistic expression

In southern Africa, for example, researchers have found rocks adorned with geometric symbols, suggesting that more than 100,000 years ago humans may have been using symbols to express abstract ideas. Other discoveries, on the inner walls of caves in Australia, northern Africa, southern Europe, and southern South America, include impressive illustrations dating from between 35,000 and 10,000 years ago. Using charred sticks, brushes made of ferns, furs, or feathers, and natural pigments from the soil mixed with animal fats, prehistoric artists in these regions created life-sized paintings of large animals in motion (see page 1). Dramatic images of horses, reindeer, bulls, and buffaloes, many of them galloping or gamboling, leave little doubt that the artists who drew them were creative and contemplative human beings who could communicate and conceptualize as we do. Perhaps these artists were simply decorating their caves by portraying scenes from the world around them. Or perhaps, as some scholars have suggested, they were engaged in a magic or religious ritual by which they sought to capture or command the spirits and vitality of the beasts they portrayed, hoping to ensure the success of the hunt.

Venus figurine.

Other works of art from this era include sketches of humans adorned with paints and animal hides, discovered on cave walls in southern France, and little statues of women with enlarged breasts and reproductive organs, found throughout central Europe. The former may depict people engaged in a community ritual or celebration. The latter, which have been labeled Venus figurines, reflect a fascination with sexual reproduction, and they may have played a role in ancient fertility rites. These and other artifacts seem to suggest that early humans believed in spiritual forces and sought to influence them, employing arts and rituals in efforts to make hunting, gathering, and procreation more fruitful.

Burial practices provide further insights into Paleolithic outlooks. Archeological evidence suggests that people have been burying their dead for at least 100,000 years. At many prehistoric grave sites, found in central Asia, southwest Asia, and central Europe, human remains are often accompanied by tools, clothing, and other ornaments. The burial of such objects with the deceased might simply reflect a desire to show respect and honor for the dead. Or, more intriguingly, it might indicate that early humans believed in some form of life after death, and were equipping their departed loved ones with the essentials for an eternal journey.

Early humans engage in arts, rituals, and burials

Intercultural Connections and Conflicts

Although separate societies created distinctive cultures, they typically did not develop in isolation from each other. At various times and places, in the process of moving about or expanding their domains, some human groups inevitably came into contact with others. Scholars believe that most foraging groups developed contacts with neighboring societies, leading often to fairly extensive intercultural connections.

At times these connections were no doubt practical, based on agreements to divide up or share lands and other essential resources. At times the links may well have been familial, marked by intermarriage between members of separate communities, forming family ties and mutual interests that bound the communities together. At times connections involved exchanges of goods and information, sometimes over vast areas: in southwest Australia, for example, researchers have found prehistoric artifacts produced several thousand miles away, in that continent's northwest regions. These early connections helped pave the way for more elaborate arrangements, including formal trade agreements and diplomatic relations, that emerged later as societies grew larger.

Early societies form practical, familial, and commercial connections

Connections at times could also result in conflicts, especially when sharing or trading arrangements failed to meet the needs of all involved. If hunting depleted a region's wild game, for example, groups that had earlier shared the hunting grounds might clash,

Early societies engage in conflicts for resources and survival

compelling the losers to move elsewhere, where they might forge new connections or come into conflict with other groups. With resources scarce and survival at stake, human societies had to protect their habitats and hunting grounds against intrusions by others, or move to a new region if the outsiders proved stronger. People thus often feared outsiders as potentially dangerous foes.

Connections and conflicts have since been central to human societies

Because the Paleolithic period covered most of the duration of human existence, the behavior patterns that evolved in that era had a lasting effect on later societies. Hence throughout history humans have tended to identify closely with their own cultures, to connect with societies having similar interests, to unite with others in the face of common threats, and to engage in countless struggles for resources (such as land and food) against competing societies. Connections and conflicts among divergent cultures have thus been central components of the human experience.

The Origins and Impact of Agriculture

By the end of the last ice age, about 10,000 B.C.E., people in some regions, prompted perhaps by environmental changes, were beginning to turn from nomadic foraging toward a more settled way of life. In West Asia, in particular, as the warming climate expanded the area covered by grasses and grains, people developed new techniques to gather and process them for food. They made sickles out of flint stone, for example, to cut down the grain and grinding stones to husk and pulverize the kernels. Archeologists who first found evidence of such tools dating from this era designated it as the onset of a New Stone Age. But something far more important was happening than the use of new stone tools. People were beginning to grow their own food.

In Neolithic times people start raising their own food

In the New Stone Age, or **Neolithic** (*nē-ō-LITH-ik*) period, which lasted roughly from 10,000 to 3000 B.C.E., people not only developed better tools but also domesticated plants and animals, cultivated crops, herded livestock, and established permanent settlements. This transition from foraging to farming, one of history's most momentous developments, has been called the Neolithic or Agricultural Revolution. Although it took several thousand years, when compared to the many millennia of foraging that preceded it, and when measured by its immense long-range impact, agriculture's onset was revolutionary indeed.

The Origins of Farming and Herding

Farming and herding begin in West Asia by 8000 B.C.E.

Based on archeological evidence, including the remains of early farm settlements and tools, scholars have surmised that farming first began in West Asia, between 9000 and 8000 B.C.E., in a crescent-shaped region (sometimes called the "Fertile Crescent") that today encompasses Israel, Syria, and Iraq (Map 1.3). Although experts disagree about specific dates and events, they have provided a general outline of what probably took place.

As climate changes increase wild grains, some people settle in one place

Scholars believe that by 12,000 B.C.E., as the last ice age ended, a warming of the climate and melting of the glaciers had left much of this region—today mostly desert—covered with forests and grasslands. Over the next few millennia, some of the people who lived there began to subsist mainly by harvesting the wild wheat and barley grains that grew in abundance in the grasslands. Since they no longer had to move about in search of wild game and plant food, these people often settled in the same place for a number of years. Unlike nomads, whose need to move around precluded them from having too many children and possessions, the West Asian settlers had little need to limit their families or belongings. With less need to move, and more food to feed their offspring, these settlers could sustain larger families, build more permanent shelters, and accumulate a wider variety of tools, clothes, and other belongings. Their numbers thus began to grow as their mobility declined.

Eventually, however, as the region's population increased, and perhaps as drier weather reduced the abundance of wild wheat and barley that grew there, the supply of wild plant food was no longer sufficient to feed all the inhabitants. Some no doubt responded to this challenge by moving elsewhere to resume their nomadic ways. But others, encumbered by large families and numerous possessions, opted instead to stay put.

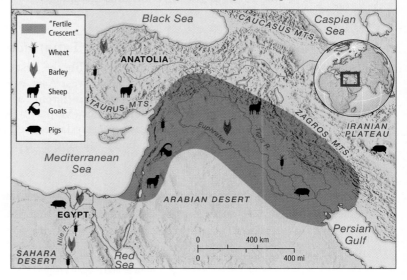

Map 1.3 Agriculture Emerges in West Asia, 9000–8000 B.C.E.

Scholars believe that humans first began to practice agriculture between 9000 and 8000 B.C.E. in a region of West Asia sometimes called the "Fertile Crescent." Observe that this region, extending from the Mediterranean Sea to the Zagros Mountains, included the valleys of the Tigris and Euphrates Rivers. What factors may have aided the rise of farming and herding in this region?

Settlements and food surplus foster population growth

Those who stayed put, in order to survive, gradually found new ways to produce more food. They learned that they could enhance the yield of the wild grains by pulling out the weeds that grew up among them. They also discovered that if they took the seeds from the most productive plants and sprinkled them in bare spots elsewhere, new plants would eventually grow there. In time some people found that they could save the seeds and sow them the next year, enabling them to plant and raise their own crops. These first farmers were most likely female, since women were the traditional gatherers of plant foods. Although they could scarcely have foreseen the immense long-term impact of their efforts, the resourceful people who first developed farming rank among the most influential innovators of all time.

As populations grow, settlers cultivate grain to enhance yield

Meanwhile, West Asian hunters were also developing another, equally momentous, food production process. They discovered that certain game animals, such as wild sheep and goats, could be captured and kept alive in captivity rather than killed in the hunt. At first this practice merely provided a useful standby food source: by keeping a few live animals, a family or community could kill the creatures and eat the meat from them when other edibles ran out. Eventually, however, people learned that sheep and goats—as well as cattle, pigs, and horses—would mate and reproduce in captivity. These animals thus

West Asians start raising, not just hunting, animals

were domesticable: they could be bred and adapted by people to meet the needs of human societies. People could raise their own herds and produce their own meat.

Domesticated animals furnish clothing, food, fertilizer, labor, and transport

Eventually many other uses were found for domesticable animals. Their fleeces and hides, for example, were used to make blankets and clothes. Their manure served as a fertilizer to replenish the soil and prolong its productivity. The milk provided by cows, mares, and ewes furnished an ongoing food source, readily available without killing the creature that supplied it. In time people also began to use large animals to pull plows and carts, providing enormous advantages for farming, transport, and travel.

Agricultural Innovation and Expansion

East Asians and Africans develop distinct forms of farming and herding

Although West Asians were probably the first inventors of agriculture, they were not the only ones. In places far from West Asia, adapting to their own environments and challenges, inhabitants developed different forms of farming and herding, using plants and animals native to their locales (Map 1.4). In the north central African region called the Sudan, for example, where grasslands then covered much of what is now the Sahara desert, people began herding cattle and cultivating sorghum (a starchy grain), perhaps

Map 1.4 Agriculture Develops and Spreads, 9000 B.C.E. – 1000 C.E.

Over thousands of years, through human ingenuity and contacts among cultures, agriculture developed and spread from its early areas of origin to other regions, as indicated by the arrows on this map. Note the large dots that indicate early areas of plant and animal domestication, with boxes indicating early food crops, domesticated animals, and estimated dates. What factors may have contributed to the development and spread of agriculture? Why did people domesticate different plants and animals in different parts of the world?

EUROPE
ASIA
China 7000 BCE rice, millet, pigs, chickens
NORTH AMERICA
PACIFIC OCEAN
ATLANTIC OCEAN
AFRICA
West Asia 9000 BCE wheat, barley, sheep, goats, pigs, cattle
Mexico 7000-4000 BCE pumpkins, chili peppers corn (maize), beans, squash
Sudan 8000 BCE sorghum, cattle
Equator
ATLANTIC OCEAN
INDIAN OCEAN
SOUTH AMERICA
New Guinea 7000 BCE taro
AUSTRALIA
Peru 8000-3500 BCE potatoes, sweet potatoes, llamas, alpacas

0   3000 km
0   3000 mi

● Early areas of farming and herding
→ The spread of farming and herding

ANTARCTICA

as early as 8000 B.C.E. In China, in the valleys of the great rivers, settlers started to grow crops of millet and rice, and to domesticate pigs, by about 7000 B.C.E. By this time also, on the island of New Guinea, early farmers were probably growing taro, a starchy root crop, on swamplands they had drained by digging ditches to channel away the water.

Farming and herding also spread through contacts among cultures. By around 7000 B.C.E., for example, agriculture had begun in ancient India's Indus Valley, and by 6000 B.C.E. it had started in Europe and Egypt's Nile Valley. The proximity of these regions to West Asia, and the fact that plants (such as wheat and barley) and animals (such as sheep and goats) domesticated in West Asia were raised in all these regions, suggests that agriculture probably spread there through intercultural connections. In exchanging goods and ideas, early societies also most likely exchanged knowledge about farming and herding.

Cultural connections spread farming and herding practices

Farmers and herders in these new areas, however, were by no means mere borrowers. They cultivated native food crops (such as oats in Europe and figs in Egypt), domesticated local animals (such as different types of cattle in the Nile and Indus Valleys), and eventually grew fibers (such as flax in Europe and cotton in Egypt and India) that could be woven into lightweight linens and clothes. But crops such as wheat and barley continued to predominate in these regions, especially as people learned to grind the grains into flour, to bake the flour into bread, and (especially in West Asia and Egypt) to brew the barley into a beverage similar to what we now call beer.

Egypt, India, and Europe develop new crops, foods, and drinks

In the Western Hemisphere, where people had no contact with farmers and herders in Africa and Eurasia, agriculture developed differently, with different crops predominating. In what is now southern Mexico, archeologists have found indications of farming as early as 7000 B.C.E., and evidence that, by 4000 B.C.E., farmers there were growing corn, beans, and squash, the cultivation of which would later spread throughout much of North America. By 3500 B.C.E., and perhaps much earlier, people in what is now Peru were planting potatoes and sweet potatoes (Map 1.4). In the Americas, however, since human hunters had earlier killed off most large domesticable animals, livestock herding was virtually unknown—except in Peru where people raised llamas and alpacas.

People in Mexico and Peru independently develop farming

The spread of farming was also interwoven with population growth. As farmers and herders produced more food, the size of their societies grew, leading them to cultivate additional lands and to clear away forests for farming. After all, only a small percentage of the plants that grew in the forest were edible, while almost everything that grew in a grain field could be used for human or animal consumption. An acre of crops could feed far more people than an acre of woods.

Spread of farming promotes population growth and deforestation

Therefore, to increase the land available for farming, people began to cut and burn down trees and bushes, diminishing bit by bit the forests themselves. In the process, they discovered that burned-over forests were extremely fertile, as the ashes from the burned vegetation served as a superb fertilizer. After several years of nourishing crops, however, the soil would be exhausted of its nutrients, and thus produce less food. So the Neolithic farmers simply moved to another region, cut and burned down more forests, and started the process anew. This "slash and burn" practice was in some ways quite destructive: it ravaged the habitats of wild plants and animals and undermined the subsistence of local hunters and gatherers. At the same time, however, it enabled farming societies to expand their food supplies, and helped to spread the practice of farming to additional places.

Foragers, Hunter-Farmers, and Pastoral Nomads

Not all groups of people, however, were quick to take up agriculture. Since raising crops and herds typically took more time and required harder work than hunting and gathering, societies were unlikely to turn to farming unless compelled to do so by some combination of population growth and diminished food supply. Even then, they could do so only where the climate and terrain made farming feasible, where some of the local plants and animals were suitable for domestication, and where people had developed the tools and techniques for planting, harvesting, breeding, pasturing, and storing. As a result, the transition from foraging to farming was a long, uneven process that lasted thousands of years. Clearly farming and herding were not the answers for everyone.

Foraging persists in regions too cold or too dry for farming

Some groups, indeed, never took up farming and continued to live as hunters and gatherers in small mobile foraging bands. In the far northern regions of Eurasia and North America, for example, where it was too cold to grow crops, people sustained themselves largely by hunting and fishing. In the arid plains and deserts of Australia, Africa, and central North America, where there was insufficient water for farming, foraging supported relatively sparse populations.

Societies without large domesticated animals combine farming and hunting

Other groups adopted farming but not herding, especially in the Americas, where there were few large domesticable animals. In eastern and southwestern North America, for instance, even after societies took up farming, hunting and fishing continued to play a key role, providing people with meat and fish to supplement crops of corn, beans, and squash. In many of these societies women did most of the farm work, since the men were often away hunting.

Pastoral nomads in semi-arid lands practice herding but not farming

Still other societies embraced herding but not farming, especially in Central Asia, where the arid climate and sparse vegetation were suitable for grazing animals but not for growing crops. Mobile herders such as these are known as **pastoral nomads**: people who raise livestock for subsistence and move occasionally with their herds in search of fresh grazing grounds.

Pastoral nomads connect and conflict with settled farming societies

Always looking for new pasturelands, without which they could not endure, pastoral nomads occasionally came into contact with settled agricultural societies. Sometimes the nomads clashed with the farming communities, fighting desperate battles for the use of lands that both groups saw as vital. Sometimes, however, the two groups traded, exchanging the herders' hides and fleeces for the farmers' grains and flour. Eventually, ranging across the open expanses between the settled societies, the nomads also served as conduits of commerce and information, conveying goods (such as carpets, cloth, and jewels) and techniques (such as horse breeding and metalworking) to distant and disparate cultures.

Thus, for many millennia, pastoral nomads coexisted uneasily with settled agricultural societies. Equipped by their harsh, itinerant existence with ruggedness and mobility, the nomads often managed to prevail in conflict. In the long run, however, since agriculture could support far more people than nomadic herding or foraging, settled societies eventually gained huge advantages in population, weapons, possessions, and power—enabling them to defeat, attract, or displace almost all nomadic peoples. The future belonged mainly to societies based on farming.

Agricultural Society: Village, Family, and Land

As time went on, the lives of farmers increasingly diverged from those of nomadic peoples. Although both farmers and pastoral nomads centered their societies on families and divided their duties by gender, many differences developed between them.

One key difference was permanence of place. Unlike nomads, who moved from place to place, farmers typically settled in one location. Almost everywhere they dwelt in **farming villages**, small settlements of homes in a compact cluster, surrounded by lands on which the villagers raised food. Village homes were mostly simple structures, fashioned from local materials such as earth, thatch, wood, or stone, and grouped together to facilitate socialization and defense. The lands around the village often included not only farm fields but also pasturelands for grazing livestock. A typical farming village was a permanent settlement: those who were born there usually lived and died there, and their descendants likely did the same for many generations.

Another key contrast was size. Agricultural communities frequently grew much larger than nomadic groups, whose numbers were limited by the need for mobility. A typical farming village, sustained by a steady food supply and stabilized by permanence of place, might include a few hundred people, and sometimes substantially more. Furthermore, as neighboring villages formed connections with each other, creating networks based on mutual protection and support, agricultural societies grew even larger.

The growing size of these societies, and the need to parcel out farmlands among families, required a higher degree of structure than was normally present among nomads. Possession of land, scarcely a concern for nomads, became an essential interest in agricultural societies, where people's livelihood depended largely on the land. As families grew larger, they often sought to maintain and expand their access to various lands and to pass this access on to their offspring. Thus, as village families intermarried with each other and with families from other villages, it became increasingly important to keep track of who was descended from whom, in order to determine who would control which lands.

Family relationships in farming communities therefore tended to be more structured than the informal kinship ties that existed in nomadic societies. Marriages between farming families were typically arranged by the parents of the bride and groom and often sealed by a transfer of assets, such as land or livestock, between the two families. Marriages between members of different agricultural societies, moreover, frequently took the form of an alliance, designed in part to create closer ties or to formalize arrangements for cooperation and support.

Farmers also diverged from nomads in terms of gender roles and status. In foraging bands, the role of women was crucial to the group's survival, since the women's work supplied the plant food on which the whole group relied and since women often had to manage the group while the men were off on a hunt. Among pastoral nomads, where women were often responsible for tending, breeding, birthing, and milking the livestock, their role was also essential to the society. In many farm communities, however, the men produced most of the food, laboring daily in the fields, while women for the most part stayed behind in the village. Their roles, which typically involved raising children, maintaining the household, and helping in the fields when needed, came to be seen as subordinate to the roles of men.

Most farmers live in villages and raise food on surrounding lands

Stability and food supply increase the size of farming societies

Larger size of farming societies requires greater organization

Farming societies develop structured families and gender roles

Women and men doing farm work in the Americas.

In farming societies women bear and raise many children

Family sizes further affected gender roles. In nomadic societies, where mobility was at a premium, large families could be a burden, so parents tended to keep their families small, freeing women to assume many duties outside of child-raising. In agricultural societies, however, where many hands were needed to help work the fields at sowing and harvest times, large families were considered desirable. Expected to bear, nurse, and raise many children, farming village women had limited ability to get much involved in affairs outside the household.

Farming societies are often patriarchal, dominated by men

Gender roles and gender status nonetheless varied among agricultural societies. In the Americas, for example, in farming villages where there was no livestock to provide meats and hides, the men often hunted wild game while women did most of the farming. In such societies, since women were the primary food producers and men were often absent on the hunt, women sometimes played a key role in managing village affairs. And even in Eurasia and Africa, capable women with strong personalities often played a prominent role in running their families and villages. For the most part, however, agricultural societies the world over tended to be **patriarchal** (*PĀ-trē-ARK-ul*), dominated by males who served as heads of household and as community leaders.

The Impact of Agriculture

Farming societies require hard labor and foster disease

Initially, agriculture's impact was not always advantageous. Early farmers and herders, for example, typically had to work much harder than gatherers and hunters. Farmers had to clear the land, till the soil, sow the seeds, tend the fields, pull the weeds, and do their best to shield their crops from insects, animals, and birds. They also had to harvest, process, and preserve the food that they grew, as well as to care for their livestock and protect it from predators. Furthermore, judging by remains found in excavations of early farming villages, Neolithic farmers appear to have been smaller, and probably less healthy, than nomadic foragers. From living in close contact with their pigs and cattle, farmers acquired new illnesses, the forerunners of deadly scourges such as influenza and smallpox. By settling continuously in the same place, they accumulated garbage and waste, which fouled their water and attracted disease-bearing insects and rodents. And, unlike small nomadic groups whose mobility and flexibility provided access to a variety of plant and animal foods, settled farming societies typically relied on a few basic crops to feed many people, leaving them vulnerable to disasters such as floods, droughts, crop failures, insect infestations, and famines.

Settled farming societies produce surplus food

In the long run, however, societies based on agriculture had a crucial advantage: they had the ability to produce surplus food. In good years the farmers could grow more food than they consumed, then store the surplus to meet future needs, initially in pits but later in bins and silos that were raised to protect against flooding.

Surplus food enables some to specialize in nonfarming pursuits

The production of surplus food in turn had enormous implications. It provided agricultural societies with a backup food supply, helping to ensure their survival, even during deadly droughts and famines. It enabled farming families to support more children, allowing their communities to grow into settlements of hundreds or thousands of people, and contributing to an overall increase in human population. And it freed some people in settlements based on farming from the need to provide their own food, allowing them to specialize in other pursuits—including arts, crafts, commerce, religion, warfare, and governance. Agriculture thereby supported and sustained the development of large, complex, regional societies, which would increasingly dominate human history.

The Emergence of Complex Societies

Toward the end of the Neolithic period, beginning in West Asia and North Africa, several factors combined to produce complex societies—large, organized, stable communities in which farm surpluses enabled many people to specialize in occupations other than farming. These societies included towns and cities, sizable permanent settlements supported by surplus food from surrounding farms. To manage their substantial populations, many of these societies formed governments, engaged in trade, organized religions, and extended control over surrounding territories, eventually creating very large and populous regional societies. The rest of this chapter discusses general features of early regional societies; the chapters that follow then examine the development of specific societies, as each was shaped by internal and external connections and conflicts.

Towns, Cities, Occupations, and Religion

By the seventh millennium B.C.E., as food supplies increased, the populations of some West Asian settlements were starting to grow quite large. Jericho (*JER-ih-kō*) in Palestine and Çatal Hüyük (*chah-TAHL hoo-YOOK*) in what is now Turkey, for example, developed into towns—large settlements, home to several thousand people, that served not only as residential centers but also as trading hubs (Map 1.5). Jericho, perhaps the world's oldest town, apparently started as a farming village, at some point before 8000 B.C.E., with huts constructed of mud-dried brick around a natural fresh-water spring. By 7000 B.C.E. it had many such homes, was surrounded by a stone defensive wall, and had become an active center of trade. Çatal Hüyük, an even more substantial population and trading center, had also emerged as a sizable town by around 7000 B.C.E. It included numerous houses made of mud brick, shrines to various gods and goddesses, and marketplaces for exchange of various foods and goods.

Over many centuries, the population of some settlements continued to grow. By the fourth millennium B.C.E., near the Tigris (*TĪ-gris*) and Euphrates (*yoo-FRĀ-tēz*) rivers in what is now Iraq, communities such as Ur (*OOR*), Uruk (*OO-rook*), and Lagash (*lah-GAHSH*) had developed into cities—

Surplus food makes possible the rise of towns and cities

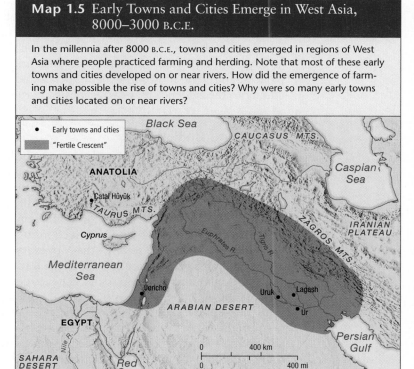

Map 1.5 Early Towns and Cities Emerge in West Asia, 8000–3000 B.C.E.

In the millennia after 8000 B.C.E., towns and cities emerged in regions of West Asia where people practiced farming and herding. Note that most of these early towns and cities developed on or near rivers. How did the emergence of farming make possible the rise of towns and cities? Why were so many early towns and cities located on or near rivers?

- Early towns and cities
- "Fertile Crescent"

very large, complex, densely populated settlements in which many people engaged in occupations other than farming. These early cities, which housed up to 30,000 people, also featured sizable buildings, bustling marketplaces, and extensive fortifications.

City-dwellers specialize in arts, crafts, production of goods, and commerce

Although towns and cities depended on farming, their most influential inhabitants were those who did not farm. With their food supplied by others, these people could specialize in various occupations. Some, for example, were artisans who specialized in tool making, basket weaving, pottery, and carpentry, as indicated by the remnants of their handiwork at archeological sites such as Çatal Hüyük and Uruk. Others no doubt were merchants, who exchanged goods in the urban marketplaces unearthed at these sites. Still others may have been artists and sculptors, as suggested by excavations of shrines and temples embellished with wall paintings and statues of goddesses and gods.

Early potters and pottery in West Asia.

These excavations also reflect the emergence of organized religion. Early peoples, as we have seen, probably engaged in rituals, summoning spirits to help secure food and ensure fertility. As societies grew more complex, these rituals grew more elaborate: people came to worship various gods and goddesses, divine beings believed to embody and control essential forces such as sun and rain, plants and animals, storms, rivers, forests, and fertility. Hoping to please or appease these divinities, priests and priestesses—people who specialized in the performance of religious rituals—conducted ceremonies and sacrifices in city shrines and temples. These religious structures also may have reinforced the authority of rulers, depicting them as divinities or as agents of the gods.

Organized religions and powerful rulers emerge in large complex societies

Other excavations add to the impression that rulers exercised great authority. Fortifications and weapons found at Ur, Uruk, and other early cities suggest that they must have had numerous laborers to build the walls and watchtowers, soldiers to defend against outsiders, and governing officials with the authority to organize and supervise large groups of workers and warriors. Also uncovered at these sites were remains of palaces, and royal tombs in which officials and servants were buried alongside the rulers, adding to the evidence that early cities were run by strong central governments.

States and Civilizations

Before complex societies emerged there was little need for strong central governments. Decisions could be made and conflicts resolved in foraging bands by the group as a whole, and in villages by the patriarchal leaders. If one villager injured another, for example, the heads of households could readily get together to determine punishment and compensation, usually in accord with community customs. Since everyone was acquainted, and frequently related, such informal mechanisms normally sufficed.

Large societies develop complex governance structures

As settlements grew so large that not everyone knew each other, however, residents could no longer rely on family and village leaders to settle disputes or decide issues for the whole community. Large societies hence developed governments, often starting with a single strong leader who, as the need arose, empowered others to assist him. Over time the result was an array of officials who carried out decisions, maintained order, organized food reserves, supervised construction projects, and resolved conflicts among strangers. If one city resident harmed another, the injured party could thus appeal, not to family and friends, but to a government official with the authority to impose punishment and compensation.

A government's main functions, however, were to secure the society's sustenance, ensure the survival of its ruling elite, and defend it against outsiders. Some cities, therefore, secured their food supply by exerting dominion over neighboring villages, using armed warriors to force village farmers to part with a portion of their produce. Some of this food was then used to feed the ruler and officials, as well as other urban residents, and some might be stored as a hedge against future shortages. The ruler and his warriors, in return, protected the villagers from conquest by rival outsiders.

By 3500 B.C.E. the rulers of several West Asian cities, including Ur and Uruk, were using this system, commonly called tribute, to maintain their food supplies and control the surrounding countryside. By thus establishing governance over a specific territory, these early West Asian rulers effectively formed **states**—territorial entities ruled by a central government. Several centuries later in North Africa, a legendary ruler called Menes (*MĀ-nāz*) extended his sway over numerous settlements in the Nile valley, creating an Egyptian state that stretched for hundreds of miles.

Historians have long noted that these early states, and others emerging somewhat later in northwest India and northern China (Map 1.6), all arose in river valleys in semi-arid regions. Many scholars have held that such environments prompted the formation of states, claiming that they were most likely created to organize vast numbers of people to build banks and dikes for flood control and to dig irrigation ditches for

To secure food supplies, cities exert control over neighboring farm villages

In governing sizable territories, early rulers form states

Early states arise along rivers

Map 1.6 Early States and Civilizations Emerge in River Valleys, 4000–2000 B.C.E.

In the fourth and third millennia B.C.E., early cities, states, and civilizations arose near rivers in Egypt, Mesopotamia, the Indus Valley, and China. Notice that these early complex societies also developed commercial and cultural connections with surrounding regions. What factors may have aided the emergence of early states and civilizations?

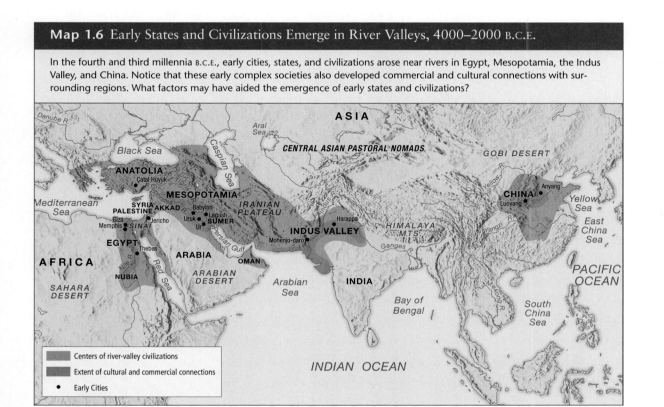

bringing river water to nearby farm fields. Other scholars, however, citing evidence that irrigation ditches existed before states in West Asia and China, have suggested instead that these societies formed states mainly to manage and control their growing populations. Whatever the case, it is clear that the rivers, by supplying plentiful water for people, crops, and livestock, and by enriching valley soils with periodic floods that left behind fertile silt, facilitated the formation and growth of permanent settled societies.

It is also clear that, by providing a convenient means of transportation, the rivers helped connect these societies up and down the river valleys. Thus, over many centuries, through trade, alliances, and conquests, cities and states along these waterways formed commercial, cultural, and political connections with each other. The result was the emergence of large, complex, regional societies in West Asia and Egypt by 3000 B.C.E., in India not long thereafter, and in China about a thousand years later.

River connections promote the rise of early regional civilizations

These large, complex regional societies are customarily characterized as history's first **civilizations**—a term applied to very large, complex societies, or regional groups of complex societies, with widely shared or similar customs, institutions, and beliefs. Historically, however, the word civilization has also been used to indicate an "advanced" level of social and cultural achievement, and hence by some peoples to claim they are superior to others. People in large, complex societies, for example, have frequently deemed themselves more "civilized" (that is, more culturally advanced) than outsiders, whom they have sometimes disparaged as savages and barbarians. To prevent ambiguity and avoid this kind of cultural bias, we will avoid the latter usage of the word, while noting nonetheless that the emergence of the early civilizations, discussed in the next four chapters, traditionally marks the beginning of the historical era.

Chapter Review

Putting It in Perspective

For tens of thousands of years, early humans lived in small, nomadic bands that were based on kinship and survived by hunting and gathering. Over time, as they adapted to a growing range of challenges and environments, our ancestors migrated to distant lands, eventually spreading throughout the entire world. They devised new tools and weapons, developed distinctive cultural expressions, divided their work along gender lines, formed marriage and family connections, exchanged information and goods, and occasionally engaged in conflicts with each other. Still, as long as they had to forage for food and move periodically from place to place, their societies remained simple and small.

Then came the advent of agriculture. People in some areas started to raise crops and animals and to form permanent settlements, some of which eventually grew into larger, more complex communities. In time some villages grew into towns, and some towns became cities, with large populations of people who specialized in nonfarming pursuits such as commerce, carpentry, tool making, warfare, religion, construction work, and governance. Some of these cities expanded their control over neighboring villages and towns, thereby creating states, which in turn would form the basis of large, complex, regional societies later called civilizations.

Henceforth, although nomadic cultures would long endure in areas unfit for farming, history would largely be dominated by complex, regional societies, and by the connections and conflicts that transpired among them. The first such regional societies, discussed in the next chapter, emerged in the fourth millennium B.C.E. along rivers in West Asia and North Africa.

Reviewing Key Material

KEY CONCEPTS

hominid, 2	Neanderthals, 5
Paleolithic, 3	race, 8
cultural adaptation, 3	Neolithic, 10
cultures, 4	pastoral nomads, 14
foragers, 4	farming villages, 15
kinship group, 4	patriarchal, 16
Great Ice Age, 5	states, 19
Homo sapiens, 5	civilizations, 19

ASK YOURSELF

1. How did hominid development differ from that of other animals? Why did hominids organize into nomadic kinship groups? Why did they divide their work along gender lines?
2. Why did early hominids, and later early humans, migrate to distant lands? Why did human societies develop a wide range of diverse cultures?
3. Why did humans begin to grow their own food? What were the advantages and disadvantages of farming and herding? Why did some societies remain nomadic?
4. How did agricultural societies differ from nomadic ones? What were the major long-range impacts of the emergence and expansion of agriculture?
5. Why did some Neolithic peoples organize cities and states? What were the major features and advantages of these complex societies?

GOING FURTHER

Bellwood, P. *First Farmers: The Origins of Agricultural Societies*. 2005.

Boaz, Noel T. *Eco Homo: How the Human Being Emerged from the Cataclysmic History of the World*. 1997.

Campbell, Bernard G. *Humankind Emerging*. 6th ed. 1992.

Christian, D. *Maps of Time: An Introduction to Big History.* 2004.

Cohen, Mark Nathan. *The Food Crisis in Prehistory: Overpopulation and the Origins of Agriculture.* 1977.

Coulson, D., and A. Campbell. *African Rock Art.* 2001.

Diamond, Jared. *Guns, Germs, and Steel: The Fates of Human Societies.* 1997.

Ehrenberg, Margaret. *Women in Prehistory.* 1989.

Fagan, B. *The Long Summer: How Climate Changed Civilization.* 2004.

Fagan, B. *People of the Earth: An Introduction to World Prehistory.* 11th ed. 2003.

Gamble, C. *Timewalkers: Prehistory of Global Civilization.* 1994.

Henry, D. O. *From Foraging to Agriculture.* 1989.

Johanson, Donald C., and Blake Edgar. *From Lucy to Language.* 1996.

Johnson Allen W., and Timothy Earle. *The Evolution of Human Societies: From Foraging Group to Agrarian State.* 1987.

Leakey, R. *The Making of Mankind.* 1981.

Manning, P. *Migration in World History.* 2005.

Megarry, Tim. *Society in Prehistory.* 1995.

Mellars, Paul, ed. *The Emergence of Modern Humans.* 1991.

Mithen, S. *After the Ice: A Global Human History.* 2004.

Stringer, Christopher, and Robin McKie. *African Exodus: The Origins of Modern Humanity.* 1997.

Sykes, B. *The Seven Daughters of Eve.* 2001.

Tattersall, I. *Becoming Human: Evolution and Human Uniqueness.* 1998.

Walker, Alan, and Pat Shipman. *The Wisdom of the Bones: In Search of Human Origins.* 1996.

Wenke, Robert J. *Patterns in Prehistory: Humankind's First Three Million Years.* 3rd ed. 1990.

Key Dates and Developments

Paleolithic Period/Pleistocene Epoch
2,000,000–10,000 years ago

by 2,000,000 years ago	Early hominids use stone tools
by 1,800,000 years ago	Early hominids migrate from Africa to Asia
by 800,000 years ago	Early hominids migrate to Europe
by 150,000–200,000 years ago	Modern humans (Homo sapiens) emerge in Africa
by 100,000 years ago	Humans in Africa fish, mine, and carve symbols
by 100,000 years ago	Humans begin to inhabit Eurasia
by 50,000 years ago	Humans migrate to Australia
by 35,000–10,000 years ago	Humans produce cave art in Australia, Africa, Europe, South America
by 12,000 years ago (10,000 B.C.E.)	Humans migrate to the Americas

Neolithic Period
10,000–3,000 b.c.e.

by 9000 B.C.E.	Farming begins in West Asia
by 8000 B.C.E.	Farming begins in the African Sudan
by 7000 B.C.E.	Farming begins in India, China, New Guinea, and Mexico
by 7000 B.C.E.	Towns emerge in West Asia
by 6000 B.C.E.	Farming begins in Egypt and Europe
by 3500 B.C.E.	Farming begins in Peru
by 3000 B.C.E.	Cities and states emerge in West Asia and Egypt

Early Societies of West Asia and North Africa, to 500 B.C.E.

- Early West Asian Societies

- Early Northeast African Societies

- West Asia and North Africa: The Phoenician Connection

- The Israelites and Their God

- Chapter Review

The Ziggurat Of Ur

Early West Asian and North African societies produced impressive monuments, such as this massive "ziggurat" temple in the ancient Sumerian city of Ur, amply attesting to the power of their rulers and religions (page 27).

According to legend, King Sargon of Akkad (*AH-kuhd*), regarded as history's first empire-builder, was a man of humble birth. Abandoned in infancy by his mother, who put him in a basket and set him adrift on a river, he was rescued and raised by a gardener. Having thus found favor with the fertility goddess Ishtar, the story continues, Sargon became a local ruler's cup bearer and grew into a great warrior. Assembling an empire in West Asia in the twenty-fourth century B.C.E., he conquered Sumer (*SOO-mehr*), a prosperous region northwest of the Persian Gulf. But rather than destroying its great cities he embraced their culture and later imposed it on other lands he conquered. He also expanded commerce, trading with lands as far away as India and Crete.

Early West Asian and North African Societies

Sargon's story exemplifies the challenge of studying ancient times. Fragmentary records surviving from that era often were compiled centuries after the events described. Many were based on oral traditions, passed on from one generation to the next and typically embellished by heroic legends and accounts of godly interventions. It is thus difficult for historians to determine precisely what occurred. The actual events of Sargon's early life, for example, as well as the boundaries of his realm and even the years of his reign, are open to question—as is the location of his capital city, which has yet to be found. Similar gaps exist in our knowledge of all ancient societies, which is based on fragmentary records and archeological evidence supplemented by the enlightened speculation of scholars. The accounts that emerge are incomplete and often differ in details, but the story they tell is fascinating nonetheless.

Sargon's story also shows how connections were created among cultures. Sometimes warriors conquered cosmopolitan societies and then adopted their culture, as Sargon did when he annexed and emulated the cities of Sumer. Sometimes conquerors imposed their values on the people they vanquished, as Sargon did by spreading his adopted culture to other lands he ruled. And sometimes cultures influenced each other through commerce, exchanging their ideas along with their commodities, a process encouraged by Sargon in his expansion of trade.

Such connections were central to the growth of the complex societies that emerged in West Asia and Northeast Africa more than 5,000 years ago. As we saw in Chapter 1, these societies arose along rivers (the Tigris, Euphrates, and Nile) where farming had long been practiced and where the resulting food supply supported sizable settlements. In each society people lived at the mercy of the rivers that, while sustaining their settlements, could also destroy them. In each society people worshiped many gods and goddesses, believing they could intervene in human lives and hoping to get their help. Through various connections and conflicts, over several millennia, these societies interacted with each other and with peoples in other regions, leaving striking legacies that endure to this day.

Early West Asian Societies

Agriculture, as we saw in the last chapter, first arose in West Asia around 9000 B.C.E. In the following millennia, it came to be practiced extensively in the plains around the Tigris and Euphrates rivers (now part of modern Iraq), where periodic floods deposited rich silt that kept the soil fertile.

By the fourth millennium B.C.E., as farming flourished in this region, its population seems to have grown considerably. Shielded from outsiders by mountains to the north and deserts to the south and fed by ample harvests from fertile farmlands, people there formed increasingly complex societies. Farming villages merged into towns, and some towns grew into cities, with central governments, organized religions, extensive commerce, and eventually even writing systems.

Thus emerged what is traditionally considered the world's first civilization, in a region that the Greeks would later call Mesopotamia (*MESS-uh-puh-TĀ-mē-uh*), a name that means "between the rivers." So impressive were its achievements that later conquerors, including Sargon of Akkad, adopted and imposed its ways throughout West Asia and beyond.

Towns and cities emerge in Mesopotamia, forming early civilization

Early Mesopotamia: The City-States of Sumer

The largest and most influential of the early Mesopotamian cities, such as Ur, Uruk, and Lagash, had emerged by 3500 B.C.E. in the region called Sumer, near where the Tigris and Euphrates rivers connect (Map 2.1). By 3000 B.C.E. some of these settlements, surrounded by protective walls, were more than a mile in diameter and home to more than 30,000 people. Most of the residents were farmers, living in huts made of sun-baked mud bricks, who went out by day to tend their crops in nearby fields. But other city-dwellers, supported by surplus food supplied by the farmers, specialized in a variety of occupations. Their numbers included artisans, merchants, laborers, priests and priestesses, soldiers, and government officials.

Conflict was common among Sumerian cities, many of which were actually **city-states,** independent urban political domains that controlled the surrounding countryside. Eager to enhance their security and wealth, the larger city-states sometimes sought to swallow up others, provoking periodic wars. Warriors who emerged as leaders in combat typically became the kings and officials of their city-states.

Early Sumerian city-states connect and conflict with each other

Over time the kings amassed great power to command armies, levy tribute and taxes, dispense justice, and organize the building of roads, canals, and dikes. In many places kingship became hereditary, as rulers succeeded in passing on their powers to their sons. Officials helped the kings govern, while priests and priestesses exalted the rulers as descendants of the gods. Royal authority was thus reinforced by religion.

SUMERIAN RELIGION AND WORLDVIEW. The most famous Sumerian ruler was King Gilgamesh (*GIL-guh-mesh*) of Uruk, hero of the *Epic of Gilgamesh*, a magnificent narrative poem from the third millennium B.C.E. In this epic the handsome young king, described as part god and part man, is confronted by Enkidu (*EN-kih-doo*), a former wild man who has been tamed by a prostitute. The two men battle ferociously, but emerge as friends. Together they embark on many adventures and overcome many challenges.

King Sargon and a High Official.

FOUNDATION MAP 2.1 Complex Societies Emerge in West Asia and Northeast Africa by 3000 B.C.E.

By the third millennium B.C.E., complex societies had emerged in Mesopotamia and Egypt and acquired extensive regional influence. Note that the lands on the eastern Mediterranean coast, later called Phoenicia and Palestine, connected Mesopotamia and Egypt, and were eventually influenced by both cultures. How did these connections develop, and how did each culture influence the other?

When fertility goddess Inanna (later called Ishtar) becomes infatuated with Gilgamesh, he brazenly spurns her advances, so in a rage she has her father the sky god send a wild bull to destroy him. Together, Gilgamesh and Enkidu manage to slay the beast. But the gods respond by taking the life of Enkidu, who describes to Gilgamesh the dismal underworld awaiting people after death. Hoping to avoid his friend's fate, Gilgamesh searches for immortality, only to learn that eternal life is beyond his grasp.

Gilgamesh epic illuminates Sumerian religion and worldview

The epic exhibits fundamental features of Mesopotamian religion. Like many ancient belief systems, it was **polytheistic** (*PAH-lē-thē-ISS-tik*), meaning that people worshiped more than one god. Gods and goddesses personified forces central to agricultural society, such as earth, sun, water, sky, fertility, and storms. Deities such as Ishtar and her father were temperamental figures, portrayed in human form and believed to affect every aspect of life. People who pleased the gods by rituals and sacrifices could hope for assistance and good fortune, but those who (like Gilgamesh and Enkidu) displeased the gods could expect retribution. The overall outlook was gloomy: humans had to serve unpredictable and often spiteful gods in this life, with little hope for a better fate in the next life.

Religion nonetheless played a central role in most ancient societies. It supplied an explanation for the forces of nature, and a means by which people could try to influence those forces. It provided a focus for festivals, such as new year holidays at the start of spring, celebrating life's natural cycles with rituals, dances, and songs. Religion also exalted the rulers as divine agents, thus enhancing their authority and helping them to maintain stability and order. Priests and priestesses, typically members of rulers' families or devoted followers, heralded the rulers as godlike beings descended from divinities and performed rituals intended to bring divine favor on the realm.

Religion was crucial to early cultures and rulers

To further enhance their status and the city's prestige, rulers built splendid temples to the gods and palaces for themselves. Beginning around 2200 B.C.E., some cities constructed **ziggurats** (*ZIG-uh-rahtz*), massive brick towers that ascended upward in a series of tiers, typically topped by shrines that could be used for religious ceremonies. Dominating urban landscapes, ziggurats also served as symbols of a city's power and as lookout towers for its defense (see page 23). Governance and religion were thus allied and intertwined, each supporting the other.

Early religion and governance are intertwined

COMMERCE, INNOVATION, AND CUNEIFORM WRITING. Secured by this alliance and sustained by surplus food, Sumerians made great strides in other endeavors. They promoted interregional commerce, pioneered the use of wheels, learned to fashion metals into tools and weapons, devised ways to keep track of time, performed architectural and engineering feats, and invented writing.

Although Sumer's farms produced abundant wheat and barley, and its herds of sheep supplied abundant wool, woods and metals were scarce in Sumer—so its cities traded with other lands to get them. As early as the fourth millennium B.C.E., Sumerians were exchanging their textiles and grains for cedar wood and copper from the eastern Mediterranean, gold from Egypt, and gems from what is now Iran. To carry these trade goods, Sumerians fashioned wooden boats for rivers, cargo ships for seas, and wheeled carts to be pulled over land by animals.

Sumerians connect commercially with neighboring cultures

Overland transport was vastly improved by the wheel, an innovation that, although often associated with Sumer, probably originated among nomads to its north. By 3000 B.C.E., Sumerian traders were transporting goods in carts with wooden wheels, and thus introducing wheels to other regions as they traveled. One of history's most useful inventions, wheels were later attached to chariots for warfare, thereby intensifying conflicts as well as contacts among cultures.

Development of wheeled carts improves overland connections

Sumerians also made advances in metalwork. In the late Neolithic period, hoping to improve on their wood and stone implements, some West Asians started fashioning tools out of copper ore. At first they simply pounded the copper into useful shapes; later they learned to heat it until it melted and pour it into clay molds to cool. However, although copper worked well for small tools and ornaments, it was too soft for larger tools and weapons. In the fourth millennium B.C.E., therefore, metalworkers began to mix the molten copper with tin, thereby producing a sturdier metal called bronze. By 3000 B.C.E., Sumerian artisans increasingly used bronze to make swords and shields for soldiers and sometimes knives and axes for farmers.

Development of writing aids governance, commerce, and spread of knowledge

Other innovations, involving calculation and record keeping, are credited to the Sumerians. They developed, for example, a calendar based on cycles of the moon. They devised a computation system, centered on segments of 12 and 60, which is still used for dividing time into hours, minutes, and seconds. And they used their architectural and engineering skills to construct palaces, temples, fortifications, and irrigation systems.

Furthermore, as trade and tribute grew extensive and society became more complex, Sumerians devised shapes and symbols to keep track of financial and administrative transactions. Later, as this system improved, they used it to record their rituals and laws, as well as the legends and exploits of rulers such as Gilgamesh. This momentous invention, which we now call writing, facilitated governance, enhanced commercial connections, and vastly aided the preservation and transmission of knowledge.

The Sumerians wrote by inscribing figures in wet clay, which then hardened into tablets, some of which are still preserved today. They etched their symbols from right to left, using wedge-like characters that scholars now call **cuneiform** (*KYOO-nē-ih-form*), which means "wedge-shaped." At first these characters were merely stylized pictures (pictographs) of people, animals, and objects such as carts, houses, baskets, and bowls. Eventually, however, as characters were added to express ideas (ideographs) and sounds (phonetics), writing became very complex, so schools were set up in palaces and temples to train writing specialists, or scribes. To enter this prestigious profession, relied on by rulers to help manage their realms, students in these early schools endured memorization, recitation, copy work, harsh discipline by teachers, and harassment by older classmates.

Cuneiform writing.

Few Sumerians actually learned to write, but those who did played a crucial role in spreading and preserving their culture. So useful, indeed, was their writing system that it was adopted not just by speakers of Sumer's various languages, but also by outside conquerors seeking to unite and rule the Sumer region.

Connections and conflicts help spread writing system

The Akkadian Conquest and Spread of Sumerian Culture

Conquest played a crucial role in spreading Sumerian culture. Beginning around 2350 B.C.E., the Sumerian city-states were conquered by King Sargon of Akkad, the ambitious ruler whose story is told at the start of this chapter. Sargon went on to conquer most of Mesopotamia, uniting the whole region under his rule and creating one of history's first empires (Map 2.2).

Akkadian conquerors adapt and spread Sumerian ideas

Sargon also established a pattern that repeated itself time and again throughout history: the conquerors learned from the people they conquered and helped to spread their culture. The Akkadians (*ah-KĀ-dē-inz*), for example, adopted the Sumerian calendar, writing system, and methods of computation, introducing them to other regions as Akkad's rule expanded westward. Hence, as a result of Akkadian conquests, Sumerian ideas spread across Mesopotamia and into the lands along the eastern Mediterranean Sea.

The Akkadian empire, which declined after Sargon's death, was overrun around 2230 B.C.E. by nomadic warriors from mountains to the northeast. The Sumerians later regained power, led by the city-state of Ur, which extended its rule over southern Mesopotamia until around 2000 B.C.E. After that the region came under the control of a people called the Amorites (*AM-uh-rītz*), who created their own extensive empire.

Map 2.2 Akkadian Empire Unites Mesopotamia in Twenty-fourth Century B.C.E.

King Sargon of Akkad created the Akkadian Empire in the twenty-fourth century B.C.E. and ruled it from his capital, known as Akkad (or Agade), whose ruins and precise location have yet to be found. Note that Sargon's empire embraced all of Mesopotamia and some of the surrounding regions. What steps did Sargon take to connect and unify his realm?

Babylonian Society and Hammurabi's Code

The Amorites, warlike pastoral nomads from Arabia, came to Mesopotamia shortly before 2000 B.C.E. through the region later called Syria, possibly in search of grazing lands for their herds. Through a series of conquests, they gradually extended their control over most of Mesopotamia, which they ruled until about 1600 B.C.E. Like the Akkadians before them, they embraced many aspects of Sumerian society, adapting the ruling and writing systems in order to meet their needs and even settling in cities supported by farming. Since their capital was a city called Babylon (*BAB-ul-ahn*) on the Euphrates River, their empire and culture are often called Babylonian (*bab-uh-LŌ-nē-in*).

Babylonians adapt and spread Sumerian ideas

The most notable Babylonian ruler was Hammurabi (*hah-moo-RAH-bē*), who reigned from 1792 to 1750 B.C.E. and issued the famous law code that now bears his name. **Hammurabi's code**, a compilation of earlier Mesopotamian laws, was carved on a black stone pillar and placed in a temple to promote public knowledge of the law (see "Excerpts from Hammurabi's Code"). The code sought to regulate matters such as trade and contracts, marriage and adultery, debts and estates, and relations among social classes. It assigned penalties based on retribution—the famous principle of "an eye for

Hammurabi's code seeks to regulate Mesopotamian society

Document 2.1 Excerpts from Hammurabi's Code

Hammurabi's Code had 282 articles, mostly assigning punishments for crimes or compensations for commercial and marital infractions. Today these articles provide fascinating insights into Mesopotamian society

6. If any one steal the property of a temple or of the court, he shall be put to death, and also the one who receives the stolen thing from him shall be put to death.

22. If any one is committing a robbery and is caught, then he shall be put to death.

104. If a merchant give an agent corn, wool, oil, or any other goods . . . , the agent shall give a receipt for the amount, and compensate the merchant . . . Then he shall obtain a receipt from the merchant for the money that he gives the merchant.

105. If the agent is careless, and does not take a receipt for the money . . . , he can not consider the . . . money as his own.

106. If the agent accept money from the merchant, but . . . quarrel with the merchant (denying the receipt), then shall the merchant swear before God and witnesses that he has given this money to the agent, and the agent shall pay him three times the sum.

108. If a tavern-keeper (feminine) does not accept corn . . . in payment of drink, but takes money, and the price of the drink is less than that of the corn, she shall be convicted and thrown into the water.

109. If conspirators meet in the house of a tavern-keeper, and these conspirators are not captured and delivered to the court, the tavern-keeper shall be put to death.

129. If a man's wife be [caught having intercourse] with another man, both shall be tied and thrown into the water, but the husband may pardon his wife and the king his slaves.

132. If the "finger is pointed" at a man's wife about another man, but she is not caught sleeping with the other man, she shall jump into the river for her husband.

142. If a woman quarrel with her husband, and say: "You are not congenial to me," the reasons for her prejudice must be presented. If she is guiltless . . . , but he leaves and neglects her, she shall take her dowry and go back to her father's house.

143. If she is not innocent, but leaves her husband, and ruins her house, neglecting her husband, this woman shall be cast into the water.

195. If a son strikes his father, his hand shall be hewn off.

196. If a man put out the eye of another man, his eye shall be put out.

199. If he put out the eye of a man's slave, or break the bone of a man's slave, he shall pay one-half of its value.

200. If a man knock out the teeth of his equal, his teeth shall be knocked out.

SOURCE: *Hammurabi's Code of Laws.* Translated by L. W. King. http://eawc.evansville.edu/anthology/hammurabi.htm

an eye"—in an effort not only to deter crimes but also to limit retaliation by ensuring that the punishment did not exceed the damage done.

Hammurabi's code provides many insights into Mesopotamian society. It reveals, for example, that society was divided into nobles, commoners, and slaves, as different penalties are assigned depending on social status. A noble who knocked out another noble's tooth, for example, was liable to have his own tooth knocked out ("a tooth for a tooth"), but a noble who knocked out a commoner's tooth would only have to pay a fine. A noble who hit a commoner would likewise have to pay a fine, but a commoner who hit a noble would be publicly whipped, and a slave who hit a noble would have an ear cut off.

Property rights, as reflected in the code, were valued very highly. Theft and robbery, for example, were punishable by death. Merchants and artisans could be penalized for providing shoddy goods, but the principle regulating commercial transactions was "let the buyer beware." Tenant farmers were expected to work the land diligently and give the landowner a portion of their crops. Slaves, who were most likely debtors, criminals, or prisoners of war, had limited rights, but they were allowed to own property, marry nonslaves, and even purchase their freedom.

Hammurabi's code also sheds light on marriage and gender roles. It shows, for example, that marriages were contractual, typically arranged by the parents. To seal the contract, the groom gave a gift to the bride's father, and her family supplied a **dowry**—a bridal endowment of money or property (preserved today in a custom whereby the bride's family pays for her wedding). The code gave greater rights and higher status to men than to women. A husband, for example, could legally have a mistress, or even take a second wife if his first one failed to bear children. But a woman who cheated or ran off on her husband could be cast into the water to drown.

Women did have some rights: they could buy and sell goods, and even own property, which they were allowed to inherit and pass on to their descendants. Records indicate that some women owned shops or taverns, worked as brewers or bakers, and even served as priestesses or scribes. But records also show that men sometimes sold their wives into slavery, and that women often died before age forty, victimized by infections associated with childbirth or worn out by ceaseless labor.

The law code was not Hammurabi's only achievement. He built fortifications, temples, irrigation channels, and dams that could cut off water to potential enemies downstream—a potent military tool in a region where survival depended on river water. He also centralized the state administration, appointing officials to control the regions of his realm and collect regular taxes from their residents. This practice was more efficient, and less disruptive to the economy, than the old Sumerian tribute system, in which armies were sent out from cities to the surrounding regions to collect tribute by force.

For all his accomplishments, however, Hammurabi failed to establish an enduring regime. Following his death in 1750 B.C.E. the Babylonian kingdom declined and was eventually overrun by warlike pastoral nomads using horse-drawn chariots.

Hammurabi's code regulates commercial and familial connections

Men had greater rights than women in Mesopotamia

Hammurabi centralizes administration and taxation

Indo-European Migrations

The warriors that challenged Babylon, beginning around 1600 B.C.E., spoke languages now classified as **Indo-European.** Since numerous languages in India, Iran, and Europe share many common features, modern linguists group them as a language family called Indo-European, divided into subfamilies such as Celtic, Greek, Italic, Slavic, Indo-Iranian, and Germanic (the branch to which English belongs). The ancient tongues from which this family evolved differed substantially from Sumerian languages, which form their own language group, and from those spoken by Akkadians and Babylonians, which scholars place in the **Semitic** language family along with Arabic and Hebrew.

The peoples who spoke ancient Indo-European tongues are also called Indo-Europeans. Although their origin is unclear, many scholars think they descended from pastoral nomads who had herded sheep, goats, and cattle since before 4000 B.C.E. on the grassy plains northeast of the Black Sea called steppes (*stepz*).

Indo-European nomads domesticate horses

Among the enduring influences of the early Indo-Europeans was the domestication of horses, which proved immensely useful for both transport and warfare. When hitched to carts, horses hauled tents and supplies, helping people to move about more easily and travel longer distances. When attached to war chariots, developed in Central Asia by 2000 B.C.E., horses enabled warriors to attack and maneuver with great speed, giving them a huge advantage over traditional foot soldiers. When harnessed to military supply wagons, horses conveyed the provisions needed to support an army on the move. Indeed, horses ultimately became the main form of military transport, and remained so until the Second World War in the twentieth century C.E. Long before that, however, horses had aided some of history's greatest migrations.

Indo-Europeans migrate to Anatolia, Europe, Iran, India

In the third millennium B.C.E., perhaps because population growth was outpacing the availability of good pastureland in the steppes, nomads apparently migrated great distances in search of fresh pastures for their herds. Aided and accompanied by their horses, some went southwest to Anatolia (*an-uh-TŌ-lē-uh*), the site of modern Turkey, while others moved south to the Iranian Plateau (Map 2.3). During the second millennium B.C.E., some went further west, dispersing throughout much of Europe, while others migrated east into northern India. Both the widespread use of horses and the wide distribution of Indo-European languages can be attributed to these nomadic migrations.

Map 2.3 Indo-European Migrations Connect Eurasian Societies, 3000–1000 B.C.E.

In the third and second millennia B.C.E., according to scholars, nomadic peoples who spoke Indo-European languages migrated from their original homelands to various other regions. Notice that their migrations, as indicated by the arrows, helped to create connections throughout Eurasia. What factors facilitated these migrations, and what key ideas and techniques did they spread?

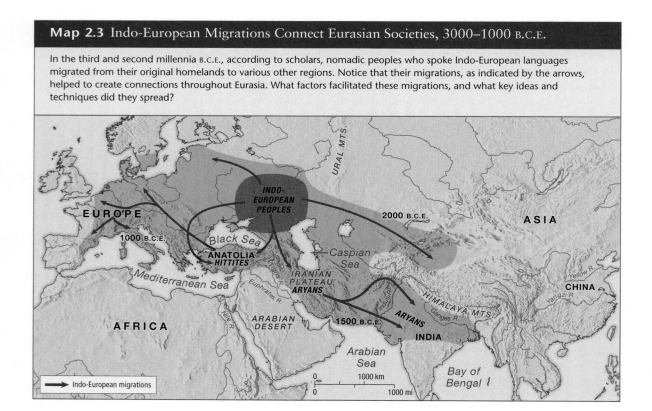

The Hittite Connection

Among the Indo-Europeans who settled in Anatolia were a people called Hittites (*HIT-tītz*). In the 1590s B.C.E., aided by horse-drawn war chariots and attracted by Babylonian wealth, Hittite armies swept into Mesopotamia, conquering the city of Babylon and ravaging the remnants of Hammurabi's realm. But unrest in their Anatolian homeland soon prompted Hittite armies to withdraw from Mesopotamia. After 1400 B.C.E., however, the Hittites again expanded into Syria and northern Mesopotamia, clashing eventually with Egyptians expanding from northeast Africa (Map 2.4). In these instances, as in so many others, conflict paved the way for cultural connections, as Hittites adopted various aspects of societies they encountered.

Indo-European Hittites settle in Anatolia

But the Hittites did not simply copy other cultures; instead they took features of the cultures they conquered and blended them into their own culture. The Hittites used cuneiform writing, for example, but modified it to fit their own Indo-European language.

Hittites blend Mesopotamian culture with their own

Map 2.4 Hittite Connections and Conflicts, 1600–1200 B.C.E.

Although the Hittite Empire was centered in Anatolia, its efforts at expansion brought connections and conflicts with Mesopotamian and Egyptian cultures. Note, for example, that Hittite influence extended into western Mesopotamia and the region now called Syria, where Hittites fought Egyptians in the thirteenth century B.C.E. at Kadesh, then formed a Hittite-Egyptian alliance that enhanced cultural and commercial ties. What factors facilitated Hittite expansion, and what key ideas and techniques did the Hittites develop?

They worshipped many Mesopotamian gods, but absorbed these gods into their own polytheistic religion, in which the God of Storms was the main divinity. They established law codes in the manner of Hammurabi, but based them on their own pastoral customs, prescribing fines for the killing or theft of livestock—and death for men who had sex with cows or pigs. They adopted farming, but adjusted it to their climate and soil, supplementing grain crops with grapes for making wines and olives from which they made oil.

Hittites develop ironwork, advancing agriculture and warfare

The Hittites also mastered the art of metalwork. At first they cast weapons and farm tools of bronze, as others in West Asia had done for centuries. But copper and tin, the components of bronze, were relatively scarce in Hittite lands. Artisans long had tried making items of iron, a metal abundant in Anatolia and elsewhere, by melting and molding it as they did with bronze, but resulting cast iron goods proved very brittle. By the thirteenth century B.C.E., however, Hittites learned to sear iron until it was red-hot, and then to shape it with hammer strokes before it cooled. Using this process, Hittites forged sturdy iron daggers, swords, spears, and shields, as well as farm hoes and other tools. Within several centuries, despite Hittite efforts to keep iron forging a military secret, it had spread to other lands in Europe, West Asia, and North Africa, and had been developed independently in East Africa. By vastly increasing the availability of inexpensive tools and weapons, the use of iron greatly advanced both agriculture and warfare, enabling far more people than ever before to engage in such pursuits.

Hittites form an agricultural, warlike, patriarchal kingdom

The Hittite kingdom, like most societies centered on agriculture and warfare, was hierarchical and patriarchal. Its various farming villages were united under a warrior king, who was assisted by an influential aristocracy in supervising the soldiers, merchants, artisans, and slaves who made up the rest of society. Women were generally subordinate to men, but they were not entirely subservient: a man could have only one wife, a woman could sometimes reject the husband chosen by her parents, and queens could play important roles as diplomats and priestesses.

Hittites connect and conflict with Mesopotamia and Egypt

Although their political unity was challenged at times by internal strife, by 1300 B.C.E. the Hittites had fashioned an empire that stretched across Anatolia from the Aegean (*ih-JĒ-in*) Sea to upper Mesopotamia, and south along the Mediterranean coast toward Egypt. During the next century, the Hittites clashed and connected with the Egyptians (above). But after 1200 B.C.E. the Hittites succumbed to new invaders, including the **Sea Peoples**, assorted marauders of uncertain origins who ravaged eastern Mediterranean lands, perhaps after being driven by famine from Aegean islands, western Anatolia, and the Black Sea region.

Later Mesopotamia: Assyrians and Chaldeans

Several centuries after the Hittite collapse, much of West Asia was reunited by Assyrians (*uh-SEER-ē-inz*), rugged warriors from the hill country near the northern Tigris River. From the ninth through seventh centuries B.C.E., mounting numerous military campaigns, they gained wealth and power by dominating the productive farmlands and profitable trade routes of West Asia. They created an empire stretching from the Persian Gulf to the Mediterranean Sea, and even into Anatolia and Egypt (Map 2.5). In expanding their domain, the Assyrians acquired a reputation for brutality, overwhelming their foes with well-organized horse-drawn chariot assaults; then torturing, slaughtering, and exiling conquered peoples to prevent rebellions.

But Assyrians also made important cultural contributions. Their magnificent city of Nineveh (*NIN-uh-vuh*), built near the northern Tigris, boasted gardens and zoos, a

An Assyrian warrior on horseback.

Map 2.5 The Assyrian and Chaldean (New Babylonian) Empires, Ninth Through Sixth Centuries B.C.E.

From the ninth through seventh centuries B.C.E., the Assyrians, a people from the hilly region north of the Tigris, conquered a vast empire that included Mesopotamia, Egypt, and surrounding regions. Notice that the Chaldeans, who helped destroy the Assyrian realm in 614–612 B.C.E., created a smaller "New Babylonian" empire. What were the key contributions of the Assyrians and Chaldeans? When and how did the Chaldean empire come to an end?

water supply system to conduct fresh water from outlying mountains, and works of art distinguished by brutal realism. Nineveh's royal palace, for example, was adorned with a sequence of sculptured reliefs depicting scenes from bloody battles and lion hunts, arranged so observers could follow the story of the conflict or hunt. And its royal library, unearthed by archeologists in the nineteenth century C.E., housed more than 20,000 clay cuneiform tablets, carried off from Babylon and elsewhere. It thus preserved many centuries of Mesopotamian writings, including the Epic of Gilgamesh.

The Assyrians were hated and feared as few other conquerors had been—and this hatred finally proved their undoing. In 614 B.C.E. the Chaldeans (*kal-DE-inz*) from southern Mesopotamia, smarting from Assyrian brutality, allied with the Medes, a people from east of Assyria, to stage a massive assault. The Assyrian empire, which had tyrannized West Asia for almost three centuries, was shattered, and in 612 B.C.E. much of Nineveh was destroyed.

Chaldeans and Medes conquer the Assyrians

The Chaldeans, also called New Babylonians, then became the new masters of Mesopotamia. Under King Nebuchadnezzar (*NEB-oo-kud-NEZ-ur*), who reigned from

604 to 562 B.C.E., the city of Babylon once again rose to greatness, surpassing even Nineveh's size and splendor. Babylon's magnificent city wall, including the splendid Ishtar gate (named for the fertility goddess), was adorned with paintings of yellow and white animals against a bright blue background. And Babylon's remarkable Hanging Gardens, a rising set of stone terraces covered with plants and trees, were counted among the great wonders of the ancient world.

But Babylon's new glory did not last. In 539 B.C.E. it was conquered from the east by the Persians, a people whose history and culture are discussed in Chapter 6. The Persians eventually overran all West Asia and moved into Northeast Africa. There, situated along a river that ran through a desert, they encountered wealthy, complex societies that had developed at the same time as West Asia's early societies.

The Hanging Gardens of Babylon.

Early Northeast African Societies

North Africa is dominated by the Sahara Desert, a hot, dry wasteland roughly the size of modern China or the United States. Only the Nile River, flowing north through the desert from sub-Saharan Africa (Africa south of the Sahara), interrupts the arid expanse. According to scientists, however, between 10,000 and 5000 B.C.E. much of what is now desert was covered by grasslands, with rivers, lakes, and enough rain to support herding and farming. During this era, as noted in Chapter 1, inhabitants of the grasslands started to herd cattle and grow sorghum, while Nile Valley residents learned to raise wheat, barley, sheep, and goats. By 5000 B.C.E., people practiced farming and herding across the northern half of Africa (Map 2.6).

As Sahara Desert expands, people move to moister regions

After 5000 B.C.E., however, the climate grew steadily drier. As rainfall became scarce, the grasslands receded and the desert expanded, so farmers and herders had to settle in places where they would have access to water.

Some settled along the Mediterranean coast, with its mild climate and seasonal rains, where they mainly herded cattle until after 1000 B.C.E., when many turned to commerce as coastal ports and colonies emerged with an expanding sea trade. Others settled in the grasslands that still existed south of the Sahara, especially in the regions around Lake Chad and the Niger River, where they grouped into villages and clans, herded cattle, raised sorghum and yams (a starchy root crop), and traveled the rivers in canoes. Eventually, after 2000 B.C.E., perhaps compelled by a shortage of farmland as the population grew, some of this region's people began migrating to the south and southeast, bringing their agricultural way of life to lands whose inhabitants had hitherto lived by foraging. The migrating peoples, who spoke a variety of related languages now collectively called Bantu (a word simply meaning "people"), may have helped to spread farming and herding across the southern half of Africa during the next three millennia (see Chapter 13).

Bantu migrations spread farming and herding throughout sub-Saharan Africa

Many farmers and herders settle in fertile Nile Valley

Most North Africans, however, settled near the Nile River, where they clustered in farming villages along its fertile floodplains. These villages in time would form the foundations of large, complex, dynamic societies later called Egypt and Nubia.

Egyptian Culture and Society

Nile settlements grow and unite into Kingdom of Egypt

After 4000 B.C.E., as the Nile Valley population grew, towns and villages along the river began uniting into small kingdoms. These kingdoms organized irrigation projects that

Map 2.6 African Environment and the Spread of Farming and Herding, Second Millennium B.C.E. Through First Millennium C.E.

Africa's widely varied environment supported the emergence of farming and herding in grasslands and river valleys, as noted by the labels on this map. Observe that people speaking Bantu languages, as indicated by the arrows, migrated throughout sub-Saharan Africa from the second millennium B.C.E. through the first millennium C.E. What factors facilitated the Bantu migrations, and what ideas and techniques did they help to spread?

brought river water to farm fields; they also traded with each other and sometimes fought one another. By 3100 B.C.E., through a series of conflicts and conquests, the northern kingdoms had combined into one large Kingdom of Egypt, destined to become one of the ancient world's most powerful and prosperous realms.

In some ways, developments in Egypt paralleled those in Mesopotamia. As in Mesopotamia, smaller states were combined by conquest into larger domains, with powerful rulers, polytheistic religions, writing systems, extensive commerce, and sophisticated technologies. As in Mesopotamia, trade and conquest created connections, with Egyptians adapting ideas and techniques from West Asians and from other Africans.

Egyptians develop connections with West Asians and other Africans

In other ways, however, Egypt differed markedly from Mesopotamia. Separated by seas and deserts from potential foes, and blessed by a river whose annual, soil-enriching floods enabled farmers to produce abundant crops year after year, ancient Egypt was bountiful, powerful, extensive, and predictable, much like the waterway that ran through its midst. Egyptian society seems to have been more stable, and its rhythms of life more regular, than those in West Asia. Egypt's worldview was less gloomy, and its religion more optimistic. And Egypt's women played more prominent roles than women in Mesopotamia.

RELIGION AND WORLDVIEW. Religion was as integral to life in Egypt as it was in Mesopotamia. Egyptians too worshiped many gods, among them the rulers of Egypt. An elaborate system of priests and priestesses perpetuated traditional beliefs, maintained numerous temples, performed sacred rituals, and sought to instill among the people respect for order and obedience to the rulers. In time, belief in the prospect of life after death prompted efforts to preserve and house the remains of rulers and other prominent people.

Central to Egypt's worldview was the concept of *ma'at* (*mah-AHT*), the universe's elemental order, which encompassed truth, justice, harmony, and balance. The rulers, eventually called pharaohs (*FARE-ōz*), were powerful, godlike figures whose main duty was to maintain *ma'at*, without which there would be chaos. They were regarded as descendants of Re (*RĀ*), also known as Amon (*AH-muhn*) or Amon-Re, the sun god and chief divinity, who ruled the heavens much as pharaohs ruled the earth. Religion and governance in Egypt were thus one and the same.

Despite Amon-Re's preeminence, the two most popular deities came to be Osiris (*ō-SĪ-ris*), god of vegetation and the Nile, and Isis (*Ī-sis*), goddess of the earth, who was both his sister and his wife. According to legend, Osiris, a divine early ruler who taught the Egyptians to farm, was slain and cut to pieces by his evil brother Seth, but Isis put Osiris back together and restored him to life. Isis and Osiris thus became symbols of fertility, devotion, and the victory of life over death, inspiring an outlook far more hopeful than that of early Mesopotamian religion.

Seeing life as cyclical, Egyptians come to believe in an afterlife

Sustained by such myths and the cycles of the Nile, whose annual soil-renewing floods were more regular and predictable than floods in Mesopotamia, Egyptians concluded that life itself was cyclical and renewable. They came to believe that death was not the end of life, that Osiris judged the dead by weighing their hearts, and that those whose hearts were light from honorable living would merit eternal life. Religion in Egypt thus reinforced morality, as the prospect of attaining life after death gave people an incentive for honorable behavior.

The prospect of life after death also promoted **mummification**, an elaborate process for preserving the bodies of prominent people after death. First the innards and brains were removed; then the bodies were thoroughly cleansed, packed in a special mineral for several months, tightly wrapped with strips of fine linen, coated with gum, and sealed in a wooden case. Anticipating immortality, those who could afford to do so often had splendid tombs constructed while they were alive, to house their remains and prized possessions after death. No other culture has lavished such care on the bodies of the dead.

HIEROGLYPHIC WRITING AND OTHER INNOVATIONS. Like the early Mesopotamians, ancient Egyptians made momentous contributions to culture, knowledge, and written communication. They produced impressive works of art, decorating their temples and tombs with splendid paintings and sculptures. They charted the constellations, created a sophisticated calendar, and practiced a form of medicine based on natural remedies. They even devised an accounting system and developed mathematics to advance their architectural and engineering skills.

Egyptians also originated a form of writing known as **hieroglyphics** (*HĪ-ruh-GLIF-ikz*). Like Sumer's cuneiform system, it started as a series of pictures and eventually added symbols for ideas and sounds. Like the Sumerians, Egyptians trained scribes to master and use their complex writing system. Unlike the Sumerians, however, Egyptian scribes wrote with ink-dipped reeds on papyrus (*puh-PĪ-russ*), a paperlike material made from plants that grew along the Nile, and then rolled it into scrolls for easy storage or transport. These scrolls, far less cumbersome than the clay tablets used in Mesopotamia, enabled the Egyptians to readily record their legends, rituals, laws, and exploits, providing portraits of their society and recording its history.

Later, however, after Egyptians abandoned early hieroglyphics for other writing systems, no one could read the early records. For many centuries, historians had to rely for knowledge of ancient Egypt on accounts that were written after 300 B.C.E. in Greek. But in 1799 C.E., archeologists with French armies in Egypt discovered the Rosetta Stone, a large black slab on which the deeds of a ruler from the second century B.C.E. were inscribed in early hieroglyphics, a later Egyptian writing system, and Greek. Working from the Greek, which they already knew, linguists learned to read the others and hence to decipher the records of ancient Egypt.

SOCIETY, FAMILY, GENDER ROLES, AND WORK. The records thus deciphered, combined with archeological evidence, reveal that Egypt had a high degree of political and social stratification. They also show that life focused mainly on family and farming, and on the cycles of the Nile.

Egypt's social structure tended to rank people according to status and wealth. Upper classes of priests and state officials lived in luxury; middle classes of merchants, scribes, and artisans enjoyed some prosperity; and lower classes of peasants and laborers worked hard to barely survive. The vast majority of Egyptians were peasants: humble farmers and herders who raised wheat, barley, cotton, cattle, and sheep.

Marriage and family were central to Egyptian society. Although some men practiced **polygyny**, which means they had more than one wife, marriages were mostly monogamous. As in West Asia, husbands provided the homestead while wives brought a dowry and furnishings into the marital union.

Gender roles were well defined but not totally rigid. In lower-class households men mostly worked the fields, but they might also be hunters, miners, craftsmen, or construction workers. Egyptian women mainly did household tasks, such as cooking and making clothes, much like women in West Asia.

Writing on papyrus aids communication and record keeping

Decorated wooden "mummy" case used for the remains of an ancient Egyptian woman.

Women often play key
roles in Egyptian society

But women in Egypt seem to have had higher status than women in other ancient cultures. Egyptian women could own and inherit property, seek and obtain a divorce, and engage in such trades as entertaining, nursing, and brewing beer. Furthermore, in contrast to West Asian households, Egyptian families often were matrilineal, with property descending through the female line, and wives in Egypt were recognized as dominant in the home. Egyptian women serving as priestesses played a key role in religion, and a few women even served as rulers. But governance and warfare were, as elsewhere, mainly the work of men.

Nile cycles govern
farming, irrigation, and
construction

The rhythm of work in Egypt followed the ebb and flow of the Nile, which typically overflowed its banks between July and September. In October, once the waters had receded, the growing season began. With the help of oxen and other farm animals, peasants plowed their fields and planted their crops, then tended them for the next several months, bringing in buckets of water from irrigation canals. The harvest usually started in February, with women and children helping the men to gather crops and thresh grain. Wheat and barley were the principal crops, but Egyptians also grew dates, grapes, and various other fruits and vegetables. In ordinary times, when food was abundant, the government took a portion of the grain to store for use in times of scarcity. Large projects requiring many workers, such as the construction and repair of palaces, temples, and irrigation systems, were normally undertaken after the harvest was over.

The Kingdoms of Egypt

For almost three millennia, with occasional interruptions, Egypt was ruled by a series of kings, who came to be called pharaohs in the fifteenth century C.E. These monarchs governed through a network of agents and officials who enforced royal edicts, collected taxes, dispensed justice, commanded soldiers, and supervised laborers in constructing buildings, monuments, and water-control projects.

The history of ancient Egypt is generally divided into a succession of major eras distinguished by three great "kingdoms" and the periods surrounding them. Although scholars disagree on the precise dates, the approximate durations of these eras are as follows:

The Archaic Period	3100–2700 B.C.E.
The Old Kingdom	2700–2200 B.C.E.
First Intermediate Period	2200–2050 B.C.E.
The Middle Kingdom	2050–1700 B.C.E.
Second Intermediate Period	1700–1570 B.C.E.
The New Kingdom (Empire)	1570–1075 B.C.E.
The Late (Post-Imperial) Period	1075–332 B.C.E.

Ancient Egyptian history can further be divided into dynasties—each a succession of rulers from the same royal family. From the Archaic through the Post-Imperial Periods, historians have identified 31 dynasties in all.

Lower and Upper Egypt
united in the Archaic
Period

EARLY KINGDOMS AND HYKSOS RULE. The Archaic Period, about which little is known, was the first time that Egypt was unified under a single ruler. Before that, it seems, there had been two separate realms: Lower Egypt, in the Nile River delta in the north, and Upper Egypt, which stretched along the river for hundreds of miles to the south (Map 2.7). Around 3100 B.C.E., the two were combined into one domain by a ruler from the south called Menes (*MĀ-nāz*), who began the first Egyptian dynasty.

Map 2.7 Egyptian Kingdoms and Imperial Expansion, 2700–1075 B.C.E.

During the Old Kingdom (2700–2200 B.C.E.) and Middle Kingdom (2050–1700 B.C.E.), ancient Egypt was a long, narrow country stretching along the Nile River. Notice, however, that during the New Kingdom (1570–1075 B.C.E.), Egyptians created an empire extending south along the Nile into Nubia and northeast into Palestine and Syria, where they clashed with the Hittites in the 1200s B.C.E. How did connections and conflicts with other cultures contribute to Egyptian wealth and power?

Legend:
- Old Kingdom and Middle Kingdom
- Hittite Empire
- Expansion of Egypt during New Kingdom
- Areas of contact during New Kingdom
- Major battle

Somewhat more is known about the Old Kingdom, which lasted roughly from 2700 to 2200 B.C.E. During this period Egypt's rulers presided over a mostly peaceful and stable society. Internally they focused on enhancing their power and grandeur, and on creating a centralized state with an effective bureaucracy and tax collection system. Externally they seem to have followed a cautious policy, conducting some trade with other societies, but avoiding aggression and warfare.

Pyramids are built as monumental tombs for Old Kingdom rulers

The most distinctive achievements of the Old Kingdom were the pyramids, monumental structures with triangular sides sloping upward toward a point. Used as burial chambers for departed rulers, the pyramids were built mostly between 2700 and 2500 B.C.E., centuries before the Mesopotamian ziggurats (which the pyramids may have inspired). The first pyramid, erected as a tomb for king Zoser (*ZŌ-sur*), was composed of steps ascending toward a 200-foot peak. Not to be outdone, Zoser's successors commissioned ever more grandiose tombs, the largest of which was the Great Pyramid built for the monarch Khufu (*KOO-foo*). Standing almost 500 feet high, it was assembled by tens of thousands of workers using millions of tons of limestone blocks, carefully raised and fitted into place with a series of temporary ramps. The Great Pyramid would later be considered the ancient world's foremost wonder.

The Great Pyramid.

The Old Kingdom ended around 2200 B.C.E. with a series of ruinous droughts, followed by an era of civil war and chaos known as the First Intermediate Period. As central authority weakened, individual nobles carved out their own domains and battled among themselves, while bandits and marauders ravaged the land.

Around 2050 B.C.E., however, unity was restored by a powerful ruler named Mentuhotep (*men-too-HŌ-tep*) from Thebes in southern Egypt, beginning the Middle Kingdom. This era brought an increase in trade with other regions, including Mesopotamia, and a growing belief in life after death. Rather than building great pyramids, the kings undertook vast irrigation and land reclamation projects to expand the amount of farmland and enhance the prosperity of their realm.

Middle Kingdom brings increased trade and connections with other cultures

The Middle Kingdom lasted until around 1700 B.C.E., when a warlike people called Hyksos (*HICK-sōs*), perhaps related to the Amorites who had earlier moved into Mesopotamia, invaded Egypt from West Asia. Using horse-drawn chariots and bronze weapons, which they brought with them from West Asia, the invaders at first proved unstoppable in combat. They conquered all of Egypt, beginning what was later called the Second Intermediate Period.

Horses and bronze weapons help Hyksos conquer the Middle Kingdom

The Egyptians resented the harsh rule of the Hyksos, whom they deemed culturally inferior. This disdain, however, did not stop Egyptians from adopting Hyksos techniques, including the use of bronze to make improved farm tools and eventually the use of horses in warfare. The Hyksos in turn embraced the complex customs and religion of the great civilization they had come to control. Egyptians nonetheless continued to despise the Hyksos, and ultimately united to expel them.

Egypt's New Kingdom adapts Hyksos ways to conquer large empire

THE EGYPTIAN EMPIRE. In the mid-1500s B.C.E. the Hyksos were driven out by Ahmose (*AH-mōs*), another great Egyptian unifier from the south, who established the New Kingdom. Unlike its predecessors, the New Kingdom, born of military insurrection, was warlike and expansionist. Within a century its rulers, employing an army equipped with weapons and techniques derived from the Hyksos, had established an Egyptian Empire stretching from Nubia in the south to Syria in the north. In the process emerged two new

Egyptian classes: one of professional soldiers who made up the standing army; another of slaves who had been captured as prisoners of war.

The New Kingdom produced some remarkable rulers. One was Hatshepsut (*hat-SHEP-soot*), who became regent for her six-year-old stepson, Thutmosis (*thoot-MŌ-sis*) III, around 1479 B.C.E., and later had the priests proclaim her king. Sidestepping Egypt's long tradition of male rule, Hatshepsut asserted that her father had made her his heir; she dressed in men's clothing, was portrayed on monuments wearing a beard, and often wore one in public. But above all she ruled with vigor and determination, providing Egypt with several decades of stability, commercial expansion, and peace.

Female ruler Hatshepsut fosters stability and trade

After Hatshepsut died around 1458 B.C.E., her stepson Thutmosis III, raised in the army during her rule, emerged as one of Egypt's greatest military leaders. He extended his dominion north to the upper Euphrates, vanquishing various West Asian realms, and south up the Nile, conquering the people known as Nubians. He was the first Egyptian monarch to use the title pharaoh ("great house"), which hitherto had meant the king's palace, and the first known ruler to recognize the potential of sea power, amassing a navy that made Egypt master of the eastern Mediterranean.

In the mid-1300s B.C.E., however, Egyptian power waned when a ruler named Amenhotep (*ah-mun-HŌ-tep*) IV, along with his wife Nefertiti (*nef-ur-TĒ-tē*), attempted a religious revolution. Promoting the worship of a universal deity called Aton (*AH-tun*), the pharaoh changed his own name from Amenhotep ("Amon rests") to Akhenaton (*AH-ken-AH-tun*), or "Aton is pleased." Akhenaton also expelled the temple priests and degraded the traditional gods, provoking a vast resistance among the priests and people. Obsessed with his religious reform, seen by some scholars as an early attempt at **monotheism** (belief in a single god), Akhenaton refused to dispatch soldiers to protect Egypt's Syrian provinces from the marauding Hittites, who were then expanding their West Asian empire. The results for Egypt were a loss of territory, a decline of income from tribute payments, and revolts in the provinces against the pharaoh.

Akhenaton and Nefertiti impose new religion and neglect empire

For most of his reign, Akhenaton seems to have ruled jointly with his wife Nefertiti, portrayed in the era's artwork as her husband's equal partner and a woman of great beauty. Late in his reign, however, she disappeared from public life; perhaps she died or fell from favor. Then, when the pharaoh himself died a few years later, the religious revolution ended. The old religion and traditional gods were restored under Tutankhamon (*toot-ahn-KAH-mun*), Akhenaton's youthful successor, today best known as the famed "King Tut" whose fabulous tomb was discovered intact by British archeologist Howard Carter in 1922 C.E.

Statues of Ramses II at Abu Simbel.

In the 1200s B.C.E., Egypt's most notable pharaoh was Ramses (*RAM-sēz*) II, the Great, who reigned for more than sixty years. Early in his reign, seeking to regain lands lost under Akhenaton, Ramses fought the Hittites in an epic battle at Kadesh (*KĀ-desh*) in Syria. Although Ramses later claimed victory, his armies neither destroyed the Hittites' power nor drove them out of Syria. So he turned to diplomacy, forming an alliance with his former foes and marrying a Hittite princess to seal the ties. To glorify his kingdom and himself, Ramses ordered the construction of colossal monuments and temples, using an abundance of slave labor.

Ramses II reinvigorates the empire and allies with the Hittites

Under Ramses' successors, however, Egypt was diminished by the attacks of the Sea Peoples, the same raiders who ravaged the Hittites around 1200 B.C.E. A century later, the high priests of Amon-Re seized control of southern Egypt, dividing the empire and making it vulnerable to new commercial and military challenges from abroad. In the eleventh century B.C.E., as Egypt's dominance waned, power in Northeast Africa shifted to the south.

Sea Peoples' raids and internal divisions undermine the Egyptian Empire

Nubian Culture and the Kingdoms of Kush

Nubians and Egyptians form commercial and cultural connections

South of Egypt was the region known as Nubia, a name said to mean either "gold" (its most precious product) or "black" (the color of its people). Since at least 7000 B.C.E. Nubians had raised cattle and grain along the upper Nile, forming a series of kingdoms after 4000 B.C.E. Rich in gold and copper, Nubia also provided a link through the desert with lands to the south that produced precious products such as ebony and ivory (Map 2.8). As Egypt grew wealthy and powerful, its rulers often sent caravans and armies to procure these valuable goods, trading and often clashing with the Nubian kingdoms. During the Old and Middle Kingdoms, Egypt dominated northern Nubia; in southern Nubia a kingdom called Kush endured until the fifteenth century B.C.E., when it was conquered and then ruled by Egypt for the next four centuries.

Nubians bearing gifts.

Nubia and Egypt were thus closely linked for over two millennia, during which Nubians combined various aspects of Egypt's culture and religion with their own. They adapted hieroglyphic writing to fit their various languages and blended Egyptian deities, such as Amon-Re and Isis, into the Nubian religion, which featured such divinities as Dedwen, the god of prosperity and incense, and Apedemak (*ah-PEH-deh-mak*), the lion-headed god of war. In some crafts, such as ceramics and metalwork, Nubians were even more skilled than their northern neighbors.

Nubians blend Egyptian culture with their own

With the decline of the Egyptian Empire in the eleventh century B.C.E., the Nubians regained their independence, and eventually formed a new Kingdom of Kush. Effectively imitating the Egyptian pharaohs, the rulers of Kush expanded their dominion commercially and militarily, and in the eighth century B.C.E. they brought all of Egypt under their control. But they came less as conquerors than as restorers, reunifying the realm and assuming all the titles and traditions of Egyptian pharaohs. The Kushites returned the Nile valley to peace and prosperity and helped revive art and architecture in Egypt. For a while it looked as if they might restore the stability and grandeur of days gone by. But in the seventh century B.C.E. they were driven back south by the expanding Assyrians, who briefly controlled the northern Nile. Egypt subsequently regained its independence, only to be swallowed up in the next century by the Persian Empire.

Kingdom of Kush conquers and reunifies Egypt

The Kingdom and Culture of Meroë

Nubians rule from Meroë and develop new cultural distinctions

Up the Nile, as Egypt's influence waned, Nubia continued to flourish, but its cultural and commercial focus gradually shifted southward. In the sixth century B.C.E., its rulers moved south to Meroë (*MER-ō-ē*), a city with ties to sub-Saharan Africa rather than the Mediterranean. Forsaking hieroglyphics, the Nubians devised their own writing system and began to emphasize new religious, cultural, and economic themes. These included increased worship of distinctive Nubian deities such as Apedemak and Dedwen; an enhanced political role for women, indicated by a growing number of female rulers; and increased reliance on camels for transport, rather than horses or donkeys. Iron smelting, invented independently in West Asia and East Africa, spread to Meroë and became a key feature of its economy.

Meroë links Mediterranean world with sub-Saharan Africa

Egyptian influence, although diminished, persisted in Meroë. Its people, for example, continued to entomb their departed rulers beneath sandstone pyramids and to conduct regular commerce with Egypt. Lasting from the sixth century B.C.E. to the fourth century C.E., the Kingdom of Meroë provided the main link between sub-Saharan Africa and the Mediterranean world.

Map 2.8 Egypt, Kush, and Meroë, Second Millennium B.C.E. Through First Millennium C.E.

The Nubian Kingdom of Kush, which flourished up the Nile south of Egypt, had numerous connections and conflicts with Egypt, which it conquered and ruled for a time in the eighth and seventh centuries B.C.E. Note, however, that Meroë, which later emerged farther south along the Nile, was located closer to the Ethiopian Highlands and sub-Saharan Africa, providing commercial and cultural links between these regions and the Mediterranean world. How did these connections influence the commerce and culture of Meroë?

West Asia and North Africa: The Phoenician Connection

Phoenicians form commercial empire linking Mediterranean lands

The Mediterranean world, meanwhile, had been connected into a commercial network with the help of the Phoenicians (*fih-NĒ-shinz*), Semitic-speaking people who lived in what is now Lebanon on the eastern Mediterranean coast. Dwelling by the sea, without large armies or extensive farmlands, Phoenicians turned to sea trade and established commercial cities and seaports. By the twelfth century B.C.E., following the attacks on Egypt conducted by the Sea Peoples, who may have been Phoenician allies, the Phoenicians gained sway over Mediterranean trade from the waning Egyptian Empire. Using hardy wood from the cedar trees of Lebanon, they built state-of-the-art ships with two decks of oarsmen to propel the vessel, a top deck of soldiers to protect cargo, and battering rams to smash enemy craft. Adept at both commerce and warfare, the Phoenicians formed a trading empire, founding city-states and colonies along the coast of North Africa, as well as in what are now Sicily, Sardinia, and Spain. The Phoenicians thus connected West Asia with North Africa and the western Mediterranean (Map 2.9).

Map 2.9 Phoenician and Carthaginian Colonies, Twelfth Through Second Centuries B.C.E.

The Phoenicians, a seafaring people from West Asia, conducted commerce and established colonies around the Mediterranean from the twelfth through eighth centuries B.C.E. Note that they had substantial connections in the western Mediterranean, where their largest colony, Carthage, founded around 800 B.C.E., would later become an independent commercial and naval power. How and why did the Phoenicians acquire such extensive influence?

A simplified writing system, developed by Phoenicians, further enhanced connections by easing communications. Employing only 22 symbols, or letters, each for a consonant sound, this system represented spoken words and phrases simply by combining these symbols. Far easier to learn and use than cuneiform or hieroglyphics, whose numerous symbols each represented a word, the Phoenician alphabet greatly aided the spread of writing and reading. As later modified by Greeks (who added vowels) and Romans, it provided a basis for phonetic alphabets eventually adopted throughout the western world—including the one used in writing English today (See Figure 2.1).

Phoenician alphabet advances written communication

Of the colonies founded by Phoenicia, the greatest was the city of Carthage on the North African coast, established around 800 B.C.E. In the following centuries, as Phoenician power waned, Carthage became independent. Building its own commercial empire in the western Mediterranean, Carthage grew into one of the world's largest cities, with a bustling harbor, a metropolitan population of perhaps 400,000, and a city wall more than 20 miles around. An urban republic ruled by its prominent merchants, Carthage dominated its region for centuries, and even sent its vessels into the Atlantic to explore the African and British coasts.

Carthage creates a commercial empire connecting western Mediterranean

HIEROGLYPHIC	REPRESENTS	PHOENICIAN	GREEK	ROMAN
⌐	Throw stick	⌐	Γ	G
𝍖	Man with raised arms	⪦	E	E
⌣	Basket with handle	↓	K	K
⋀⋀⋀	Water	⋀⋀	M	M
⌐	Snake	↘	N	N
◉	Eye	O	O	O
⬭	Mouth	?	Π	P
ℛ	Head	ϑ	P	R
⚊	Pool with lotus flowers	W	Σ	S
⊏⊐	House	ϑ	B	B
⊅	Ox-head	K	A	A

Figure 2.1
Table Comparing Egyptian, Phoenician, Greek, and Roman Characters

The Israelites and Their God

Of all the early West Asians, among the least in power and wealth were the Hebrews, a small group of tribes who spoke a Semitic tongue, herded sheep and goats, fought among themselves, and were often conquered and controlled by others. The Hebrews nonetheless had an enduring religious legacy. For in recording their exploits, customs, and creeds, first in oral and later in written form, some of them produced the Hebrew Bible, one of history's foremost religious and literary works. In the process, they developed a monotheistic faith that would serve as a basis for some of the world's most influential religions: Judaism, Christianity, and Islam.

The Children of Israel

Bible relates stories of Hebrews as Semitic pastoral nomads

The Hebrew Bible provides a striking story of the early Hebrews. According to its narrative, at the urging of his God, the patriarch Abraham left the realm of Ur in Mesopotamia to settle in the land of Canaan (*KĀ-nin*), later called Palestine. After several generations, the sons of his grandson Jacob, who was also called Israel, went to Egypt during a famine to find pastureland for their sheep. There these Hebrews, later called "Israelites" or "children of Israel," were eventually enslaved and spent years in bondage before being led by Moses, a prominent Egyptian born of Hebrew stock, in a flight to freedom called the Exodus (see "Excerpts from the Hebrew Bible"). On their way back to Canaan, the Bible asserts, the God of Israel embraced the children of Israel with his **covenant**, a binding agreement to protect them as his chosen people. He also instructed them to worship him alone, and to keep the Ten Commandments, religious and moral laws that he revealed to Moses. After wandering forty years in the desert, the story goes on, the children of Israel finally returned to Canaan.

A recreation of the ancient walled city of Jerusalem.

Like other ancient narratives, the Bible is based on oral traditions written down centuries after the events portrayed. It contains Hebrew versions of stories found in other narratives, as well as accounts that are not found anywhere else. The Bible tells of a great flood, for example, like one described in the *Epic of Gilgamesh*. And the Biblical account of infant Moses, placed by his mother in the river in a basket and later found by pharaoh's daughter, is similar to the Sargon story told at the start of this chapter. But the Bible's depiction of the Exodus, in which the pharaoh's army drowns in the Red Sea pursuing Israelites who had passed safely through it, is not found in existing Egyptian records. Scholars thus have difficulty determining exactly what took place, and there is much dispute about how much the Bible represents historical fact.

Israelite Hebrews settle in Palestine and create a kingdom

The first non-Biblical reports of the Israelites locate them around 1200 B.C.E. in Canaan, henceforth called Palestine, where they settled in tribes and fought sporadic wars against other local peoples. Among these foes were the Philistines (*FIL-ih-stēnz*), from whom the name Palestine derives, possibly one of the Sea Peoples that attacked the Hittites and the Egyptians. Within a few centuries, the challenge posed by the Philistines, whose military power made them a threat to all their neighbors, compelled the tribes of Israel to combine forces under a warrior king.

The Kingdoms of Israel

King David centralizes power in Jerusalem

The first such king, Saul, proved a better politician than a general: he united the Israelites under his rule but failed to defeat the Philistines decisively before his death

Document 2.2 Excerpts from the Hebrew Bible

The Hebrew Bible contains compelling stories of the Hebrews and their relations with their God, who reportedly delivered them from bondage in Egypt and then gave them commandments, or laws by which to live.

CROSSING OF THE RED SEA. When the king of Egypt was told that the people had fled . . . , Pharaoh . . . made ready his chariot and took his army with him . . . , and he pursued the people of Israel . . . When Pharaoh drew near, the people of Israel lifted up their eyes, and behold, the Egyptians were marching after them; and they were in great fear . . . And Moses said to the people, "Fear not, stand firm, and see the salvation of the LORD . . . " The LORD said to Moses, " . . . Lift up your rod, and stretch out your hand over the sea and divide it, that the people of Israel may go on dry ground through the sea." . . . Then Moses stretched out his hand over the sea; and the LORD drove the sea back by a strong east wind all night, and made the sea dry land, and the waters were divided. And the people of Israel went into the midst of the sea on dry ground, the waters being a wall to them on their right hand and on their left. The Egyptians pursued, and went in after them into the midst of the sea . . . Then the LORD said to Moses, "Stretch out your hand over the sea, that the water may come back upon the Egyptians, upon their chariots, and upon their horsemen." So Moses stretched forth his hand over the sea . . . The waters returned and covered the chariots and the horsemen and all the host of Pharaoh that had followed them into the sea; not so much as one of them remained. But the people of Israel walked on dry ground through the sea . . .

THE TEN COMMANDMENTS. And the LORD came down upon Mount Sinai . . . ; and the LORD called Moses to the top of the mountain, and Moses went up . . . And God spoke all these words, saying,

"I am the LORD your God, who brought you out of the land of Egypt . . . You shall have no other gods before me . . .

"You shall not make for yourself a graven image, or any likeness of anything that is in heaven above . . .

"You shall not take the name of the LORD your God in vain . . .

"Remember the sabbath day, to keep it holy. Six days you shall labor . . . , but the seventh day is a sabbath to the LORD your God; in it you shall not do any work . . .

"Honor your father and your mother . . .

"You shall not kill.

"You shall not commit adultery.

"You shall not steal.

"You shall not bear false witness against your neighbor.

"You shall not covet your neighbor's house; you shall not covet your neighbor's wife . . . , or anything that is your neighbor's."

SOURCE: New Revised Standard Version Bible, copyright 1989, Division of Christian Education of the National Council of the Churches of Christ in the United States of America. Used by permission. All rights reserved. Exodus 14: 5–6, 8, 13, 15–16, 21–23, 26–27, 28–29; 19: 20; 20: 1–3, 4, 7, 8–10, 12, 13–17.

---

around 1000 B.C.E. This task was left to his successor David, who won many battles, making his kingdom a prominent power in Palestine. King David also collected taxes, created a standing army, consolidated his realm, and established as its capital the city of Jerusalem. As a result, he is often revered as Israel's greatest ruler.

Israelite prominence nonetheless reached its height in the reign of David's son Solomon, lasting from about 960 to 920 B.C.E. Building on his father's foundation of military security, Solomon transformed Jerusalem into a cosmopolitan city. His lavish

Kingdom splits into Israel
and Judah after
Solomon's death

construction projects included a city wall, a royal palace, and an elaborate temple to Israel's God. He also forged connections with other realms, often through marital alliances: according to the Bible his 700 wives included women from Arabia, Phoenicia, and Anatolia, as well as an Egyptian princess.

Israel's people are
dispersed, then Judah's
are exiled to Babylon

But Solomon's splendor caused problems. His massive projects, financed by harsh taxes and built by forced labor, offended the proud people whose ancestors, according to the Bible, had fled such servitude in Egypt. The resulting dissent, after Solomon's death, helped split the realm into two kingdoms (Map 2.10). The northern one, called Israel, lasted until 721 B.C.E., when Assyrian conquerors dispersed and assimilated its people, who thereby vanished from history as Israel's "ten lost tribes." The southern kingdom, known as Judah (after one of Jacob's sons), had a more lasting impact: its people, later called Jews (a term derived from Judah), managed despite numerous hardships to preserve their unique religious heritage.

In the early sixth century B.C.E., Judah was conquered by Chaldeans (New Babylonians), who demolished the temple in Jerusalem and exiled the people to Babylonia. Later, following Persia's conquest of Babylon in 539 B.C.E., the Jews were allowed to return to Jerusalem and build a new temple. They remained, however, a part of the Persian Empire, free to practice their religion but lacking political autonomy. Eventually, along with the rest of West Asia, they were incorporated first into the world of the Greeks and then into the empire of the Romans.

Map 2.10 Israelites and Their Neighbors, Twelfth Through Eighth Centuries B.C.E.

After fleeing Egypt across the Sinai, as related in their Bible, the Israelites settled in Palestine, where they fought the Philistines and others, emerging as a united kingdom by the tenth century B.C.E. Notice, however, that their realm later split into two kingdoms: Israel, whose people were defeated and dispersed by the Assyrians in 721 B.C.E., and Judah, whose people, eventually called Jews, survived later conquest and exile. How and why did the Israelites, a relatively small group of people with little power or wealth, have such an extensive historical impact?

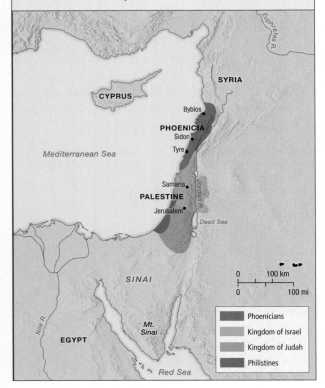

The God of Israel

Throughout their ordeals the Israelites developed what became the Jewish faith. Their deliverance from slavery in Egypt and their covenant with Israel's God laid the foundations of their identity as a chosen people. The unity imposed by their kings and the establishment of Jerusalem as their center of worship helped consolidate this identity. Through division, defeat, and Babylonian captivity they struggled to maintain this identity. During times of trouble prophets arose to speak for their God, whose name Yahweh ("I am") was considered sacred, and to remind them of the covenant and laws that bound them to him and to each other. All these experiences were passed on for ages by word of mouth and eventually recorded in the Bible.

At first the Israelites saw Yahweh as their tribal deity, fearsome and vengeful like other West Asian gods. Eventually, however, the Jews perceived Yahweh as unique. While other gods they knew of could be vengeful and fickle, Yahweh was seen as forgiving and faithful, true to his covenant even when his people turned their backs on him. While other gods were embodied in human forms or graven images, Yahweh was considered a spirit: immortal, invisible, all-powerful, and transcendent. While other gods could be unreasonable and unfair, Yahweh was perceived as just, proclaiming laws based on love of God and neighbor. Above all, Jews came to believe that Yahweh stood alone: he was the one and only God, and all other gods were false.

Jews come to believe in a single, all-powerful God

This concept of a single divinity had enormous potential significance, for it implied that Israel's God was really everyone's God. Centuries later, offshoot monotheistic religions such as Christianity and Islam extended this claim still further, proclaiming that the God of Israel was a universal God whose covenant and laws applied to all humanity. The Hebrew heritage has hence been central to many subsequent societies.

Jewish monotheism will give rise to Christianity and Islam

Chapter Review

Putting It in Perspective

After their emergence in fertile river valleys in the fourth millennium B.C.E., the early societies of Mesopotamia and Egypt developed their cultures and expanded their influence through a complex combination of connections and conflicts. Sometimes these civilizations conquered their neighbors, as in the expansion of Egypt's New Kingdom, imposing on the vanquished the culture of the victors. Sometimes these societies were themselves overrun, by warlike peoples, such as the Akkadians, Amorites, Hyksos, and Assyrians, who then went on to adopt and spread the cultures of those they had conquered. Sometimes other peoples, including the Hittites, Nubians, Phoenicians, and Carthaginians, created connections through both conquest and commerce.

By the first millennium B.C.E., both Mesopotamia and Egypt had lost their independence and come under foreign rule. But these misfortunes also enhanced their influence, which was dispersed far and wide by their successors and conquerors, including eventually the Persians, Greeks, and Romans (Chapters 6, 7, and 8).

Later cultures thereby learned much from ancient West Asia and North Africa. From the Mesopotamians and Egyptians they acquired extensive knowledge in the areas of astronomy, medicine, mathematics, art, sculpture, and architecture. From the Hyksos and Hittites they inherited the use of horses to pull carts and chariots, and the use of metals to make tools and weapons. From the Phoenicians they adopted the use of seafaring ships to maintain distant colonies, and the employment of an alphabet to express their ideas and sounds. From the Jews they eventually inherited monotheism, in the forms of Christianity and Islam. Extensive indeed were the enduring legacies of early West Asian and North African societies.

Reviewing Key Material
KEY CONCEPTS

city-state, 25	Semitic, 31
polytheistic, 26	Sea Peoples, 34
ziggurats, 27	mummification, 38
cuneiform, 28	hieroglyphics, 39
Hammurabi's code, 29	polygyny, 39
dowry, 31	monotheism, 43
Indo-European, 31	covenant, 48

KEY PEOPLE

King Sargon of Akkad, 24	Akhenaton, 43
Gilgamesh, 25	Nefertiti, 43
Enkidu, 25	Tutankhamon, 43
Hammurabi, 29	Ramses II, 43
Menes, 40	Abraham, 48
Zoser, 42	Jacob (Israel), 48
Khufu, 42	Moses, 48
Mentuhotep, 42	Saul, 48
Ahmose, 42	David, 49
Hatshepsut, 43	Solomon, 49
Thutmosis III, 43	

ASK YOURSELF

1. What were the main similarities and differences between Mesopotamian and Egyptian civilizations? What circumstances account for the similarities and differences?
2. What key roles did religions play in ancient societies? Why did rulers often portray themselves as descendants and agents of the gods?
3. How did the invention of writing contribute to governance, commerce, religion, law, and the recording of history?
4. How did the religious beliefs of the Hebrews differ from those of their neighbors? What were the main implications of these beliefs? How did these beliefs help the Jews to preserve their identity as a people?
5. How did conflicts and conquests help to spread the achievements of early civilizations? How did cultural and commercial connections contribute to the spread of these achievements?

GOING FURTHER

Aldred, Cyril. *The Egyptians*. Rev. ed. 1984.

Aubet, Maria Eugenia. *The Phoenicians and the West: Politics, Colonies, and Trade*. 1993.

Bahrani, Z. *Women of Babylon*. 2001.

Bertman, S. *Handbook to Life in Ancient Mesopotamia*. 2003.

Blackman, A. *Gods, Priests, and Men*. 1993.

Bottero, J. *Everyday Life in Ancient Mesopotamia*. 2001.

Bright, J. *A History of Israel*. 3rd ed. 1981.

Bryce, T. *The Kingdom of the Hittites*. 1997.

Bryce, T. *Life and Society in the Hittite World*. 2002.

Casson, Lionel. *Everyday Life in Ancient Egypt*. 2001.

Connah, G. *African Civilization: An Archeological Perspective*. 2004.

Crawford, H. *Sumer and the Sumerians*. 2004.

Dalley, Stephanie. *The Legacy of Mesopotamia*. 2006.

David, R. *Religion and Magic in Ancient Egypt*. 2002.

Ehret, Christopher. *The Civilizations of Africa*. 2001

Gil, Moshe. *A History of Palestine*. 1997.

Grant, Michael. *The History of Ancient Israel*. 1984.

Grimal, Nicolas. *A History of Ancient Egypt*. 1992.

Gurney, O. R. *The Hittites*. 2nd ed. 1980.

Ikram, S. *Death and Burial in Ancient Egypt*. 2003.

James, T. G. H. *Pharaoh's People: Scenes from Life in Imperial Egypt*. 1984.

Kemp, Barry J. *Ancient Egypt: Anatomy of a Civilization*. 1989.

Kramer, Samuel N. *History Begins at Sumer*. 1981.

Leick, G. *Mesopotamia: The Invention of the City*. 2002.

Malek, J. *Egypt: 4000 Years of Art*. 2003.

Markoe, G. E. *The Phoenicians*. 2000.

O'Connor, D. *Ancient Nubia*. 1994.

Oates, John. *Babylon*. 1979.

Oren, E. T., ed. *The Sea Peoples and Their World*. 2000.

Postgate, J. N. *Early Mesopotamia: Society and Economy at the Dawn of History*. 1992.

Ray, J. *Reflections of Osiris: Lives from Ancient Egypt*. 2002.

Rice, M. *Egypt's Making: Origins of Ancient Egypt*. 2003.

Saggs, H. W. F. *Babylonians*. 1995.

Shanks, H., ed. *The Rise of Ancient Israel*. 1991.

Shaw, Ian, ed. *The Oxford History of Ancient Egypt*. 2000.

Silverman, David P., ed. *Ancient Egypt*. 1997.

Stiebing, W. H. *Ancient Near Eastern History and Culture*. 2002.

Strouhal, E. *Life of the Ancient Egyptians*. 1992.

Taylor, John. *Egypt and Nubia*. 1991.

Torok, L. *The Kingdom of Kush*. 1997.

Van de Mieroop, Mare. *The Ancient Mesopotamian City*. 1997.

Van de Mieroop, Mare. *History of the Ancient Near East*. 2004.

Welsby, D. A. *The Kingdom of Kush*. 1996.

Key Dates and Developments

West Asia

3500–2350 B.C.E.	Sumerian city-states in lower Mesopotamia
3000–1000 B.C.E.	Indo-European Migrations
2350–2100 B.C.E.	Empire of Akkad in Mesopotamia
2100–1900 B.C.E.	Sumerians again rule lower Mesopotamia
1900–1600 B.C.E.	Babylonians (Amorites) rule in Mesopotamia (*Hammurabi's reign, 1792–1750: Law Code*)
17th–13th centuries B.C.E.	Hittites dominate Anatolia
11th–9th centuries B.C.E.	Phoenicians flourish in Eastern Mediterranean
11th–10th centuries B.C.E.	Kingdom of Israel flourishes in Palestine
10th–7th centuries B.C.E.	Assyrians dominate West Asia
7th–6th centuries B.C.E.	Chaldeans (New Babylonians) dominate West Asia
586–539 B.C.E.	Babylonian Captivity of the Hebrews
6th–4th centuries B.C.E.	Persians dominate West Asia

North Africa

3100–2700 B.C.E.	Archaic Period (*Egypt unified*)
2700–2200 B.C.E.	Egypt's Old Kingdom (*pyramids built*)
2200–2050 B.C.E.	Egypt's 1st Intermediate Period
2050–1700 B.C.E.	Egypt's Middle Kingdom
1700–1570 B.C.E.	Egypt's 2nd Intermediate Period (*Hyksos rule*)
1570–1075 B.C.E.	Egypt's New Kingdom (Egyptian Empire)
13th century B.C.E.	Hebrews leave Egypt (*Moses*)
10th–8th centuries B.C.E.	Egypt under Libyan rule
8th–7th centuries B.C.E.	Egypt under Nubian rule (Kingdom of Kush)
7th century B.C.E.	Assyrians invade Egypt
7th–3rd centuries B.C.E.	Carthage flourishes in eastern Mediterranean
6th–4th centuries B.C.E.	Persians dominate Egypt
6th century B.C.E.– 4th century C.E.	Kingdom of Meroë flourishes along Upper Nile

Societies and Beliefs of Early India, to 300 C.E.

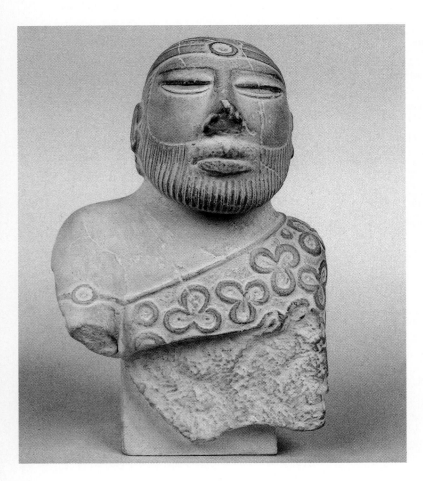

Early Indian Sculpture

India's earliest complex societies, which flourished in the Indus River valley over four thousand years ago (pages 56-59), left behind numerous cultural artifacts, including this sculpture of a bearded man. Based on his stately attire and serene expression, he may have been a ruler or priest.

The **Mahabharata** (*muh-hah-BAH-ruh-tuh*), the world's longest epic poem, tells of a legendary war between related families in ancient India. The epic's most famous segment, the "Song of the Lord" or Bhagavad Gita (*BAH-guh-vahd GĒ-tah*), recounts the reluctance of the warrior Arjuna to fight and kill his own relatives. His chariot driver, a god in human form, explains to Arjuna that, as a member of the warrior caste, it is his sacred duty to fight in battle and fight well. It is permissible to kill in war only if you resolve *not* to spare your kin, since even though the body is slain, the soul will be reborn:

> For certain is the death of the born,
>
> And certain is the birth of the dead;
>
> Therefore that which is inevitable
>
> Thou shouldst not regret.

— Early India

Thus emboldened by the wisdom of a god, and reassured of the inevitability of both death and rebirth, Arjuna and his kin engage in a lengthy battle that results in extensive slaughter.

In many ways ancient India, the society that produced the Mahabharata, was similar to Mesopotamia and Egypt. As in those two regions, in India cities emerged near a river where farming had long flourished. Like Mesopotamia and Egypt, India had powerful rulers and priests who served numerous gods and goddesses believed to interact with human beings. Like Mesopotamia and Egypt, India was overrun by outsiders who blended the cultures of the people they conquered with their own culture and spread the combined culture to surrounding regions. As in West Asia and North Africa, such connections and conflicts produced diverse societies that bickered and battled, engaged in commerce, and made major contributions to science, mathematics, literature, and the arts.

As reflected in Arjuna's story, however, India's society was unique in several ways. One was its widespread belief that, as Arjuna was assured, the spirits of those who die are reborn, or reincarnated, into new bodies. While other cultures believed in life after death, usually in another world or a different form of existence, people in India believed that the souls of the dead return to life in *this* world. Another distinction was India's segregation into hereditary occupational groups, such as Arjuna's warrior caste, which people had to stay in until they died and were reborn into another life. Other societies had social classes, but few were as rigid as India's. At the same time, despite the celebration of violence in such epics as the Mahabharata, India also produced belief systems embracing contemplation, passivity, and nonviolence. In a region noted for political fragmentation and almost constant conflict, Indians found hope in the prospect of a better incarnation, security in a rigid social structure, and peace through inner tranquility.

The Indian Subcontinent

India is a subcontinent, a huge land mass substantially separated from the rest of Asia by mountains and seas. To the north are the world's tallest mountains, the towering Himalaya (*HIM-uh-LĀ-uh*) and Hindu Kush (*HIN-doo KOOSH*) ranges. In the south, between the Bay of Bengal and Arabian Sea, is a vast subtropical peninsula that includes the Deccan, an extensive central plateau surrounded by low mountain ranges. Between these regions, stretching across northern India, are broad plains drained by two great rivers: the Ganges (*GAN-jēz*) and the Indus (Map 3.1).

India's geographic diversity promotes political disunity

India's great geographic diversity has fostered political fragmentation, long a dominant feature of Indian society. The challenges involved in vanquishing and ruling so vast and varied a land have deterred or defeated all but a handful of empire builders and leaders. Rare have been the rulers who have managed to unite all of India and keep it united for long.

The terrain and climate have also had other major impacts. The northern mountains have served as both a shield against invasion and a buffer against the icy winds that sweep across Central Asia. But this buffer, along with the subtropical location of much of the subcontinent, also helps to ensure that India has almost relentless heat. Rainfall is seasonal and uneven, with annual monsoon winds bringing heavy rains from surrounding seas in the summer and early fall, especially in the coastal areas and the Ganges valley. Other seasons and other regions, however, tend to be rather dry, and many areas experience recurrent drought.

Ganges and Indus Rivers dominate northern India

In the north, the two great rivers provide abundant water for humans, animals, and the irrigation of crops. The Ganges, rising in the Himalayas, flows south and east to the Bay of Bengal through fertile plains that are favorable for human settlement. Although heavy rains in the Ganges Valley sometimes cause serious flooding, the Ganges has traditionally been viewed as bounteous and benevolent. The Indus River, on the other hand, is far less predictable, prone to significant changes in its depth and course. But it was the Indus, not the Ganges, that gave the subcontinent its name. For it was along the Indus that India's earliest complex societies emerged.

Harappan India: Early Indus Valley Societies

Farming begins in Indus Valley by 7000 B.C.E.

From the majestic Hindu Kush and Himalaya mountains, through the arid plains of what is now Pakistan, the Indus River flows southwest to the warm Arabian Sea. The river usually floods twice a year: once in spring, when melting mountain snow swells the tributaries that feed the river, and once in summer, when the monsoon winds blowing in from the sea bring heavy rains. As in Egypt, the receding floodwaters deposit a rich layer of silt, enabling farmers in the river valley to plant and harvest two crops a year. Thanks partly to this fertility, and partly to farming's eastward spread from West Asia, agriculture came early to the Indus Valley. By 7000 B.C.E., the region was already home to a number of farming villages.

The Early Cities

Towns and cities emerge in Indus Valley by 3000 B.C.E.

As the population increased, the villages grew larger, and by 3000 B.C.E. towns and cities had begun to emerge. As in Mesopotamia and Egypt the growing population, combined perhaps with the need to control the river and irrigate the fields, led to the formation of larger, more complex, and better-organized communities, while farming advances supplied the food surplus needed to support them. Sustained by this surplus, from roughly 2800 to 1700 B.C.E., a cosmopolitan culture with large, thriving cities flourished in the Indus Valley.

The two main cities unearthed by archeologists in the Indus Valley are Mohenjo-Daro (*mō-HEN-jō-DAH-rō*), meaning "Mound of the Dead," and Harappa (*hah-RAP-puh*).

FOUNDATION MAP 3.1 India's Geography and Early Indus Cities, Third Millennium B.C.E.

The Indian subcontinent's main geographic features include the northern mountains that separate it from the rest of Asia, the great Indus and Ganges Rivers that flow from these mountains across northern India, and the vast southern Indian peninsula embracing the Deccan Plateau. Note that India's earliest cities emerged in the northwest, in the Indus River valley, by the third millennium B.C.E. What factors account for the early emergence of agriculture and the rise of cities and towns in this region? Why would this region have more contacts with other cultures than other parts of early India?

Excavations at
Mohenjo-Daro,
with citadel in
the background.

The entire culture, including these cities and others, is called the Indus Valley or Harappan civilization (Map 3.1).

With 40-foot-thick brick walls, more than three miles around, and populations of 30,000 or more, Harappa and Mohenjo-Daro were similar to cities in ancient Mesopotamia and Egypt. But the early Indus cities were also like many modern ones, with dwellings aligned along straight streets arranged in a grid-like pattern. Working-class districts, with rows of single-room barracks, bordered prosperous neighborhoods of multi-room brick houses with courtyards and bathrooms, served by an ingenious system of pipes that brought water from upriver and deposited waste downstream. Clearly there were disparities between the poor and the rich.

In each city there were temples, marketplaces, and a raised citadel with large buildings probably used by rulers and governing officials. Mohenjo-Daro had a beautiful public bath with a large brick-lined pool, while Harappa had a large grain storage facility, built with a raised floor to protect against floods. These features suggest that each city had a high degree of urban planning and a central authority with the power to carry out large public works projects.

Excavations shed light on early Indus civilization

Farming, Culture, and Commerce

At its height, between roughly 2500 and 2000 B.C.E., the Indus Valley civilization covered over a half million square miles and included hundreds of villages, towns, and cities. Its people raised abundant food, manufactured high-quality goods, devised an elaborate system of symbols, and traded with other societies.

Farming was the foundation of Harappan society. Although wheat was apparently their main food crop, Indus Valley residents also grew rice and barley and herded sheep, cattle, goats, and pigs. Key agricultural achievements included the domestication of chickens and the cultivation of cotton, used to make lightweight clothing suited to the hot climate.

Indus culture centers on farming, fertility, and family

Central to Indus peoples' outlooks were family, nature, and fertility. Numerous carvings and figurines found in their cities, including children's toys and depictions of animals, indicate great respect for family and nature. Religious artifacts, such as phallic symbols and images of large-breasted women, suggest that their worship involved fertility rites. And the sculpture of a stately bearded man, shown on page 54, hints that they may have had a priestly ruling class.

Excavations have also uncovered numerous pottery vessels, as well as farm tools and fine utensils made out of copper and bronze—products that display great metalworking skill. Yet few metal weapons have been found, suggesting perhaps that Harappan societies were less prone to warfare than those of Mesopotamia.

Also uncovered have been numerous square seals, made of soapstone or baked clay, carved with symbols that include depictions of humans, animals, and sacrificial rites. Many scholars have seen these symbols as features of an early writing system, and some speculate that Harappans spoke languages ancestral to those in the Dravidian (*druh-VID-ē-un*) language family that is now dominant in southern India. Other scholars, however, suggest that the symbols are religious, and claim that there is no clear evidence of any Dravidian connection.

One of many inscribed
square seals found in the
Indus Valley cities.

There is clear evidence, however, that Indus Valley peoples had connections with distant cultures. Harappan clay seals and other Indus artifacts, for example, have been found in the Tigris and Euphrates valleys, while various items made in Mesopotamia have been discovered in India. Especially intriguing are sculptures, excavated at Harappa, that appear to depict Sumerian epic heroes such as Gilgamesh and Enkidu, about whom the Indians must have learned through contact with West Asia.

Indus people connect commercially and culturally with Mesopotamia

The Decline of Harappan Society

In the centuries following 2000 B.C.E., the Indus Valley culture declined. Population seems to have fallen, perhaps on account of climate changes, diseases, or deforestation and soil exhaustion from centuries of intensive farming. There is evidence, too, that movements of the earth's tectonic plates may have unleashed floods and earthquakes that changed the course of the Indus and dried up other rivers in the region, fatally disrupting agricultural and urban patterns. Without surplus food to sustain them, large numbers of people—laborers, merchants, pottery makers, metalworkers, and government officials—apparently left the cities, moving most likely to farming villages so they could raise their own food. By 1700 B.C.E., although farming and herding in the Indus Valley continued, the Harappan cities, with their commerce, governments, and specialized occupations, had been largely abandoned.

Bronze statuette of a dancing girl, found at Mohenjo-Daro.

Vedic India: The Aryan Impact

As Harappan culture declined, according to many scholars, Indo-European pastoral nomads called Aryans (*AIR-ē-unz*) moved into the Indus Valley from the west and north (Map 3.2). Eventually they spread across northern India, interacting and often clashing with the people who already lived there. Over the next thousand years, from before 1500 B.C.E. until about 500 B.C.E., these connections and conflicts produced a blended culture, distinguished on one hand by political division and conflict, and on the other hand by social stability and control.

Indo-European Aryans migrate to north India by 1500 B.C.E.

Aryan Incursions and the Rise of Vedic Culture

The Aryan incursions most likely were part of the general Indo-European migrations described in Chapter 2. Like other early Indo-Europeans, the Aryans were pastoral nomads, herders of cattle and sheep, with metal-tipped weapons and horse-drawn chariots that made them effective warriors. Reputedly light-skinned and ruthless, the ancient Aryans were much later hailed as racial forebears by Nazis and other white supremacists. Scholars, however, reject such racial claims, and instead use terms such as Aryan and Dravidian to designate language groups.

Aryans arrive in India as herders and warriors

At some point before 1500 B.C.E., Aryan speakers started moving into northern India, bringing with them their horses and imposing weapons. There they encountered agricultural peoples, including perhaps Dravidian speakers, with farming villages and fortified towns that may have slowed but did not stop the Aryan advance.

Over several centuries the Aryans prevailed, eventually forming many small contentious kingdoms ruled by warrior kings called rajahs (*RAH-jahz*). As these realms fought one another for regional dominion, regularly raiding one another's herds and attacking each other's domains, conflict and political disunity emerged as central

Aryans prevail over farming peoples of northern India

Map 3.2 Aryans Migrate into India, Second Millennium B.C.E.

By 1500 B.C.E., Aryan-speaking peoples had begun moving into India from the northwest, creating historic connections and conflicts with the people who already lived there. Notice that the Aryans came first to the Indus River Valley, birthplace of Harappan civilization, and perhaps interacted with users of Dravidian languages, now spoken mainly in southern India. What were the major impacts on India of the Aryan migrations?

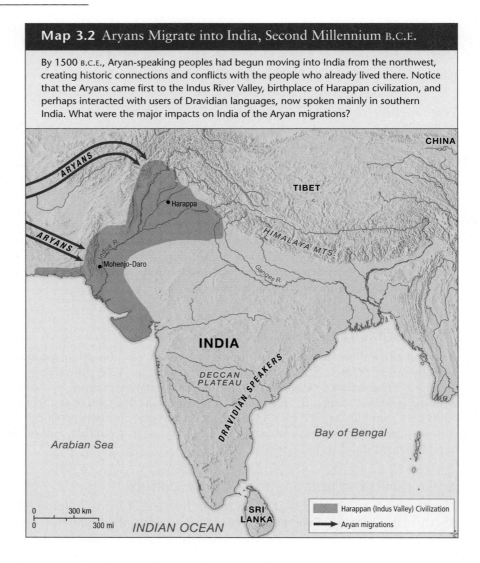

hallmarks of Indian society. But conflict and disunity did not prevent the development of Indian culture.

The culture that developed in Aryan India is often called **Vedic** (*VĀ-dik*), since much of what we know about it comes from Vedas (*VĀ-dahz*), sacred hymns composed by Aryan priests for use in religious rituals. Since the Aryans initially had no writing system, Vedas were composed in oral form, largely between 1500 and 1000 B.C.E., in meters and stanzas that made them easy to remember. Committed to memory, they were passed on by word of mouth for centuries. Only after 800 B.C.E., when a writing system emerged, were the Vedas actually written down.

Although religious in intent, the Vedas provide abundant information about Aryan culture (see "Excerpts from the Rig Veda"). They depict Aryans as people who loved

Document 3.1 Excerpts from the Rig Veda

The Vedas, composed as sacred hymns, provide many insights into ancient Aryan culture. The following excerpts from the Rig Veda reflect Aryan devotion to the war god Indra and Aryan fascination with warfare, competition, and gambling.

WHO IS INDRA?

The god who had insight the moment he was born, the first who protected the gods with his power of thought, before whose hot breath the two world-halves tremble at the greatness of his manly powers—he, my people, is Indra . . .

He . . . who drove the race of Dasas down into obscurity, who took away the flourishing wealth of the enemy as a winning gambler takes the stake—he, my people, is Indra . . .

He who encourages the weary and sick, . . . he who has lips for fine drinking—he, my people, is Indra . . .

He, the mighty bull . . . who with his thunderbolts in his hand hurled down [the enemy] as he was climbing up to the sky—he, my people, is Indra . . .

TO ARMS

His face is like a thundercloud, when the armored warrior goes into the lap of battles. Conquer with an unwounded body; let the power of armor keep you safe.

With the bow . . . let us win the contest and violent battles with the bow. The bow ruins the enemy's pleasure; with the bow let us conquer all the corners of the world . . .

Standing in the chariot, the skilful charioteer drives his prize-winning horses forward wherever he wishes to go. Praise the power of the reins: the guides follow the mind that is behind them . . .

Spare us, O weapon flying true to its mark; let our body be stone . . .

Whoever would harm us, . . . let all the gods ruin him. My inner armor is prayer.

THE GAMBLER'S LAMENT

The dice seem to me like a drink . . . keeping me awake at night . . .

When I swear, 'I will not play with them,' I am left behind by my friends as they depart. But when the brown dice raise their voice as they are thrown down, I run at once to rendezvous with them, like a woman to her lover.

The gambler goes to the meeting hall, asking himself "Will I win?" and trembling with hope. But the dice cross him and counter his desire, giving the winning throws to his opponent.

The dice goad like hooks and prick like whips; they enslave, deceive, and torment . . . They are coated with honey—an irresistible power over the gambler.

SOURCE: Wendy D. O'Flaherty, editor and translator, *The Rig Veda: An Anthology* (New York: Penguin Books, 1984) 160–161, 236–237, 240–241.

wine and music, lived in patriarchal families, worshiped numerous deities, sacrificed animals to the gods, and believed in life after death. As portrayed in the Vedas, Aryans also glorified bravery and warfare, often fighting among themselves as well as against other peoples. The Rig Veda, the oldest and most famous of the Vedas, exalts the Aryan war god Indra, wielder of thunderbolts and destroyer of towns, and asks him to help the nomadic Aryans destroy enemy settlements. The Vedas further suggest that Aryans were fond of competition and gambling, traits that may help explain why they are traditionally credited with inventing both dice and chess.

While thus acclaiming the Aryans, whose very name means "noble," the Vedas disparage the defeated peoples as Dasa (*DAH-suh*), a term meaning "subject" or "slave." This attitude reflects not only the conquerors' contempt for the conquered, but also the disdain of nomadic warriors for settled farming peoples, whom the nomads saw as enslaved to the land and shackled to their villages and towns.

Aryan ways blend with farming cultures to form a complex, diverse society

Eventually, however, as had happened after conquests in West Asia and North Africa, the conquerors adapted ideas and ways from the people they had conquered. In time, for example, Aryans built towns, took up settled farming, and even intermarried with Dravidian speakers and others. Aryan religion became infused with the spirituality of India's farmers, focusing on fertility, stressing nature's cycles of destruction and rebirth, and inferring from these cycles that people's spirits are reborn in a new body after death. As a result of such blending, by 500 B.C.E., India was home to a very complex and multi-faceted society.

The Emergence of Caste

Aryan society, as portrayed in the Vedas, was divided into classes called **varnas,** based on the functions fulfilled by their members in society. At the top were the priests, or Brahmins, who performed religious rituals and sustained sacred legends, and the warriors, or Kshatriya (*kuh-SHAH-trē-uh*), who protected society. At first the warriors apparently were preeminent, but over time the Brahmins, esteemed for their ability to gain favor with the gods, gained superior status. Below the priests and warriors were the commoners, or Vaishya (*VĪSH-yuh*), who performed basic services such as farming, herding, and trading. Below them were the servants, or Shudra (*SHOO-druh*), consisting initially of conquered peoples compelled to menial labor.

Indian society evolves into rigid class system

For centuries after the Aryan incursions, interclass mobility and marriage seems to have been fairly common, blurring class boundaries and diminishing distinctions between Aryans and non-Aryans. As time went on, however, the system became more rigid. Upper-class families, anxious to protect their status, increasingly refused to socialize or arrange marriages with those of lower rank. The classes thus hardened into **castes,** exclusive and restrictive hereditary occupational groupings, based on birth and ranked in hierarchical order. People were expected to fulfill their caste's occupational functions, to marry and share meals within their caste, and to observe its dress and behavioral codes.

Jatis emerge as social-economic subcaste communities

As society grew more complex, numerous regional subcastes, called **jatis** (*JAH-tēz*), emerged. As a rule each jati identified with a certain trade, a specific locale, and often a particular god or goddess. Each jati, embracing hundreds of families, functioned as a community: its members ate, worked, socialized, and intermarried mainly with each other, and cared for one another during times of need. Jatis often vied with each other for higher ranking in the social structure.

Castes also came to be connected with religious notions of purity and pollution. On one end of the spectrum were Brahmins, regarded as pure since they dealt with spiritual rather than bodily functions. On the other end were those who did work that was seen as impure—such as jobs involving contact with dead bodies and human or animal waste. Since touching people who did such work was considered a source of pollution, or spiritual contamination, they were widely shunned as "untouchables," ranking even below the Shudra at the bottom of Indian society.

Family, Status, and Stability

Although Indian society limited freedom and mobility, it provided considerable stability. Grouped by family, occupation, and heredity, people almost always knew their place and what was expected of them. Within the family, for example, women were clearly subordinate to men, and children were strictly subject to their parents. Within the larger society, occupations were determined by caste membership and duties were clearly prescribed. Each caste and subcaste supervised and protected its own members, providing them with security and employment. Deeply rooted in family and status, India's social structure was stratified, hierarchical, and stable.

Yet social interaction and upward mobility were not entirely impossible. Social interaction could occur when people of different castes worshiped together, for example, or when they participated jointly in village festivals and councils. Upward mobility could take place in several ways. One was available to subcastes: an entire jati that excelled in its work could hope to move up within the social hierarchy. Another was available to individuals: those who lived good lives and performed their duties well could hope for a higher standing in their next incarnation, according to India's distinctive religious beliefs.

Jatis and individuals can improve status through good work

The Religions of India

The religious beliefs that emerged in Vedic India, fostered largely by the Brahmin (priestly) caste, are often referred to as the Vedic religion or Brahmanism. Centered on a universal and eternal spiritual source called Brahman, and including a wide array of distinctive gods and rituals, this early religion set forth three basic concepts that have since been central to the Indian worldview: samsara (*sam-SAH-ruh*), dharma, and karma.

Samsara, sometimes called "reincarnation" or "transmigration of souls," was the basic belief that each being has a soul or eternal spiritual core called the Atman, identified with and encompassed in the Brahman, which is reborn into a new body after the old one dies. Each person thus has an ongoing series of lives. **Dharma** represented the faithful performance of the duties that pertained to one's caste or station in life. **Karma** referred to one's fate or destiny in the next incarnation, based on performance of one's dharma in the current life. Those who dutifully carried out their dharma would thereby have good karma and thus be reborn through samsara into a higher status. Those who did not fulfill their dharma would have bad karma and thus likely be reborn into a lower status. A servant who did her job well, for example, could improve her caste status in the next life, while a warrior who fought poorly could be reincarnated into a lower caste.

The Wheel of Dharma, an ancient symbol of Indian Buddhist values.

Dharma, karma, and samsara reinforce social stability

These three concepts reinforced the social structure. Fearful of acquiring bad karma, and thus undermining their chance for rebirth into a higher caste, lower caste members felt compelled to do their duties, accept their low status, and endure the dominance of priests and warriors. The privileged status of the upper castes was thus also preserved.

At the end of the Vedic era, however, around 500 B.C.E., several new religions began to challenge this social structure. Rejecting the concept of caste, Jainism (*JĪN-iz-um*) and Buddhism saw karma and samsara not as the means to a better life but as hardships trapping the soul in an endless cycle of lives. The ultimate goal of these new faiths was to free the soul from this cycle and provide salvation from suffering.

Jains and Buddhists seek salvation from endless cycle of lives

Jainism: Reverence for All Living Things

Jainism was based on the teachings of a wandering religious figure known as Mahavira (*mah-hah-VĒ-rah*), the "great hero," or Jina (*JĪ-nah*), the "conqueror," who lived from around 540 to 486 B.C.E. At the age of 30, according to tradition, he chose a life of **asceticism** (*uh-SET-ih-siz'm*), renouncing all possessions and practicing extreme self-denial, while also promoting pacifism and vegetarianism. His followers, called Jains, believed that all living things—including animals, insects, and plants—possess an eternal spirit and must be treated with reverence.

Jains therefore practiced **ahimsa** (*ah-HIM-sah*), or nonviolence toward all living things. Some Jains even swept the ground ahead of them to avoid stepping on insects and wore face masks to avoid inhaling tiny gnats and flies. By showing profound reverence for life in all its forms, Jains believed they could purify their spirits and eventually attain **moksha** (*MŌK-shah*), or liberation from the cycle of death and reincarnation.

Although Jains, who spurned the inequalities of caste, were widely admired by members of the lower castes, few actually practiced Jainism in its entirety. Most engaged in occupations, such as farming or herding, that at times involved the killing of plants or animals, practices that went against Jainist teachings. Only people such as merchants or scholars, whose trades did not involve such practices, or monks and nuns, who renounced worldly pleasures, could hope to lead a fully Jainist life. Jainist ideals were influential, but few could fully follow them. Jains thus remained throughout the centuries a small religious minority.

Jains stress ahimsa: nonviolence toward all living things

Buddhism: The Path to Inner Peace

Buddhism, on the other hand, became one of the world's most widely practiced religions. It grew out of the teachings of Siddhartha Gautama (*sih-DAHR-tah GOW-tah-mah*), a spiritual leader whose influence compares to that of Moses, Confucius, Jesus, and Muhammad. Born into a princely family in the Himalayan foothills of what is now Nepal, Gautama reportedly lived from 563 to 483 B.C.E. According to Buddhist traditions, he enjoyed great comfort in his early life, protected by his parents from all distress. At age 29, however, he ventured outside his palace, eventually encountering an old man, a sick man, and a dead man. Determined to discover the meaning of aging, illness, and death, he left his wife and family to lead an ascetic life. For six years he practiced extreme self-denial, eating sparsely and avoiding most other pleasures. But he found this life no more fulfilling than his earlier self-indulgence.

Finally, while meditating near the Ganges River underneath a tree, Gautama experienced enlightenment, a revelation enabling him to comprehend the secrets of salvation from human suffering. For the rest of his life he traveled throughout northeastern India, gathering disciples, preaching to all who would listen, and sharing the wisdom that had been imparted to him. He came to be known as the Buddha ("enlightened one"), and his followers eventually were called Buddhists.

Siddhartha Gautama gains enlightenment, becoming the Buddha

The Buddha's central teachings, known as the "Four Noble Truths," can be summarized briefly as follows: (1) Life consists of pain and suffering. (2) Pain and suffering are caused by desire. (3) To escape from suffering, one must curb desire. (4) Desire can be curbed by righteous living. To live righteously, one must follow the "Eightfold Path," which entails right thinking, right purpose, right conduct, right speech, right livelihood, right effort, right awareness, and right contemplation. Buddhists are expected to be kind, pure, truthful, and charitable, and to refrain from faultfinding, envy, hatred, and violence—although their adherence to ahimsa is typically less total than that of the Jains. If the faithful absorb these truths and follow this path they can eventually achieve enlightenment, like the Buddha himself, and ultimately escape the cycle of karma and samsara by attaining **nirvana** (*nir-VAH-nah*), a state of infinite tranquility.

These beliefs made Buddhism widely attractive. Like Jainism, Buddhism respected all beings and rejected caste inequalities, thus appealing to people of low social status, such as servants, merchants, and farmers. Unlike Jainism, however, Buddhism counseled moderation: it provided a simple and elegant formula for escape from suffering, not through extreme self-sacrifice or rigid adherence to ahimsa, but through self-awareness, meditation, avoidance of ambition, and pursuit of inner peace.

Buddhism's simple, attractive teachings gain it a wide following

Hinduism: Unity amid Diversity

Challenged by Jainism and Buddhism, which spread slowly throughout India in the centuries after 500 B.C.E., the Vedic religion adapted and endured in the form of Hinduism, an assortment of beliefs and practices that eventually evolved into India's main faith. Unlike Jainism, Buddhism, and other major religions, Hinduism was not based on the revelations of a famous founder or teacher; instead it developed organically in concert with Indian society. Rather than becoming an organized church with a fixed ritual and creed, Hinduism remained a flexible faith with a wide array of divinities, doctrines, and devotions. Supremely adaptable, it readily embraced new gods and new beliefs, including concepts adapted from the Jains and Buddhists.

Traditional Vedic beliefs evolve into Hindu religion

Hindu deities Vishnu and Lakshmi depicted in stone sculpture as sensuous lovers.

Like their Vedic ancestors, Hindus worshiped a multitude of deities, the most prominent of which was Brahma, seen as the supreme creator and universal being. Other gods and goddesses, however, came to be more widely revered. Shiva (*SHĒ-vah*), the mighty "destroyer" and "lord of the dance," was a god who embodied the eternal cycle of destruction and renewal. Vishnu (*VISH-noo*), the valiant "preserver" and protector of the world against demonic powers, was a god said to take on different incarnations as needed—including Rama (*RAH-muh*), the ideal man and a model of virtue and reason, and Krishna (*KRESH-nuh*), a benevolent god who involved himself directly in human affairs. Among the main goddesses were Lakshmi (*LUK-shmē*), a popular deity identified with wealth and good fortune; Kali, a fearsome divinity linked with violence and death; and Durga, a multi-armed warrior often pictured riding on a lion or tiger. All three were seen as manifestations of a supreme mother goddess, sometimes called Devi (*DĀ-vē*), a Hindu term for goddess.

Unlike Jains and Buddhists, Hindus accepted the caste system, including the notion that an honorable life meant fulfilling one's caste functions. Like Jains, however, Hindus came to believe that they could eventually achieve moksha, gaining an eternal peace akin to the Buddhist nirvana—except that for Hindus this peace involved a union of the personal soul or spiritual core (Atman) with the universal life force (Brahman). Hindus sought to secure this salvation by dedication to their caste duties, devotion to the gods, meditation, and reverence for life.

Hindus come to seek eventual salvation through devotion to caste duties

Although, like Jains and Buddhists, Hindus revered all forms of life, they developed a special veneration for certain places and beings. For example, they regarded the

Hindus revere shrines, pilgrimages, the Ganges River, and cows

Ganges, the source of life-giving waters, as a sacred river, bathing in it for spiritual purification. They treated cows, the source of nourishing milk, as sacred, allowing them to roam undisturbed through towns and villages as symbols of nature's benevolence. They prayed at numerous sacred sites and shrines, making regular pilgrimages to these places. Believing in a rich diversity of divinities, Hindus saw them all as manifold expressions of Brahman—the single, unifying, universal force.

Post-Vedic India: Connections and Divisions

Buddhism's spread and West Asian connections shape post-Vedic India

In the late sixth century B.C.E., several key developments marked the transition from India's Vedic era, traditionally dated as ending around 500 B.C.E., to the post-Vedic era. One was the emergence of Buddhism, a compelling new religion that gained widespread influence throughout India and beyond. Another was the invasion and conquest of northwestern India, between 518 and 513 B.C.E., by the Persians, whose rule of that region vastly increased India's connections with other cultures. In the centuries that followed, both the spread of Buddhism and contacts with outside cultures played key roles in shaping Indian society.

Magadha flourishes south of the Ganges, but India remains disunited

Political disunity continued in post-Vedic India. In the sixth century B.C.E. there were 16 major kingdoms and principalities in northern India alone, including the one where Siddhartha Gautama was born. The dominant kingdom in the north was Magadha (*MAH-guh-duh*), located mostly south of the lower Ganges, in a hilly area laden with visible iron ore deposits. For several centuries Magadha flourished, prospering from its iron mines, agriculture, and control of the Ganges regional trade. But its sporadic efforts to gain sway over its neighbors achieved only limited success.

Conflicts and Contacts with Persians and Greeks

Persian conquest of Indus Valley links India with West Asia

While Magadha flourished in northeast India, new intruders arrived in the northwest. Around 518 B.C.E., forces from the Persian Empire, a realm that had recently expanded across West Asia, began probing the Indus Valley, eventually subjecting it to Persian rule for most of the next two centuries (Map 3.3). Although only this part of India was actually ruled by Persia, most of the subcontinent was affected in some way by the Persian presence. It brought unprecedented trade and contact, not just with Persia but also with cultures in West Asia and North Africa that came under Persian rule. These contacts, for example, enabled Indians to export spices, perfumes, gems, and cotton textiles to the lands of the eastern Mediterranean and in return to receive such goods as wine, tin, and gold.

Alexander invades northwest India, but his forces refuse to go farther

These increased connections, by spreading awareness of India's vast resources and potential wealth, eventually brought new conflicts. In 326 B.C.E. the famed Macedonian warrior Alexander the Great, having overrun Persia with his Greek and Macedonian armies (Chapter 7), invaded India in hopes of bringing its lands and wealth under his control. One Indian rajah tried to halt the intruders with a force of 200 war elephants. But Alexander's soldiers fired flaming arrows, frightening the huge beasts, who then stampeded and trampled the rajah's infantry.

Alexander, however, was unable to follow up on his victory. His men, already far from home, refused to advance any farther, compelling him to turn back toward West

Map 3.3 Persian Empire Connects India with West Asia and North Africa After 518 B.C.E.

For almost two centuries, from about 518 until 326 B.C.E., the Persians ruled northwestern India, enhancing its commercial and cultural connections with West Asia and North Africa. Note, however, that the rest of India, also affected by these enhanced connections, was governed by various independent principalities and kingdoms, most notably the wealthy Magadha realm in the lower Ganges region. What were the major impacts on India of the Persian connection?

Legend:
➡ Goods traded to India from the west
⬅ Goods traded from India to the west
▨ Region of India ruled by Persian Empire
— Farthest advance of Alexander the Great

Asia. Although he left behind some officials and soldiers to administer northwest India, they could not perpetuate his control of the region. His unexpected death in 323 B.C.E. created widespread confusion, clearing the way for the formation of India's first full-fledged empire.

The Rise of the Mauryan Empire

In the muddled situation surrounding Alexander's death, Chandragupta Maurya (*chahn-druh-GOOP-tah MOW-rē-ah*), ruler of a minor Ganges Valley principality, saw a chance to expand his power. Having joined in the struggle against Alexander's forces, he adopted some of their military methods to defeat his Indian rivals. By 321 B.C.E. he had gained control of the Magadha kingdom and much of the Ganges basin. He then moved northwest into the Indus Valley, vacated by Alexander's departure, and added it to his domains. In 305 B.C.E. he turned back an effort by Seleucus Nikator (*sih-LOO-kus nih-KAH-tor*), Alexander's former lieutenant and founder of the Seleucid (*sih-LOO-sid*) kingdom in Persia, to retake the

Chandragupta Maurya forms Mauryan Empire in northern India

Map 3.4 Mauryan Empire Unites Much of India, 321–184 B.C.E.

The Mauryan Empire, founded by Chandragupta Maurya, united and connected most of northern India by 300 B.C.E. Notice that by 250 B.C.E., during the reign of his grandson Ashoka, the empire connected much of the subcontinent. How did the Mauryans learn and benefit from contacts with other cultures, and what were the major impacts on India of Mauryan rule?

HINDU KUSH MTS.

CHINA

TIBET

HIMALAYA MTS.

Indus R.

Ganges R.

MAURYAN EMPIRE

Pataliputra

MAGADHA

DECCAN PLATEAU **KALINGA**

Arabian Sea

Bay of Bengal

Mauryan Empire under Chandragupta, 300 B.C.E.

Areas added under Ashoka by 250 B.C.E.

SRI LANKA

0   300 km

0   300 mi

Mauryan Empire expands to control much of India

Indus region. In exchange for 500 war elephants, Seleucus agreed to withdraw his forces from northwestern India, leaving this entire region under Chandragupta's rule.

Chandragupta Maurya thus created the Mauryan (*MOW-rē-un*) Empire, uniting much of India in a prosperous and populous domain that lasted from 321 to 184 B.C.E. (Map 3.4). The empire exemplified the benefits of connections among cultures, combining Indian religion and social structure with Persian administrative methods and Macedonian military techniques, while expanding India's commerce with the Mediterranean world.

The Mauryan Empire developed an impressive system of roads and public works, a magnificent capital city at Pataliputra (*PAH-tah-lih-POO-trah*)—now called Patna (*PUTT-nah*)—on the Ganges, and an extensive bureaucracy of officials who administered the realm. The empire also had a huge standing army, reportedly consisting of more than a half million soldiers, and a vast network of spies and special agents to protect its ruler against rebellion or assassination. Imperial laws and decrees were rigidly enforced, and those who defied them were brutally punished. According to legend, however, in his final years Chandragupta embraced Jainism and practiced ahimsa, giving up his throne to become a simple monk.

By this time, around 300 B.C.E., Chandragupta's realm included most of northern India. His policies were continued and extended by his son, who conquered and annexed the vast central Indian plateau called the Deccan. But it was Chandragupta's grandson Ashoka (*ah-SHŌ-kah*), reigning from around 270 until 232 B.C.E., who proved the most memorable of all the Mauryan rulers.

Ashoka's Reign: Buddhism and Paternalism

Ashoka's reign began in violence when he defeated his older brothers in a bloody civil war. Then, like his predecessors, Ashoka embarked on a course of military expansion. In conquering the east coast region of Kalinga, his armies killed many thousands of people. The carnage is said to have so sickened Ashoka that he had a profound change of heart, renouncing violence and publicly expressing remorse for the misery he had caused. He converted to Buddhism, gave up hunting and eating meat, and embraced ahimsa.

Ashoka then used his imperial powers to propagate his new faith. He traveled about preaching Buddhist principles and urged his officials to do likewise. He built numerous Buddhist temples and shrines, patronized Buddhist scholarship and art, and established a number of Buddhist religious communities. He had huge polished stone pillars, carved with his edicts and Buddhist teachings, erected throughout his realm. He hosted Buddhism's Third Great Council, helping thereby to standardize doctrines and resolve religious disputes. According to tradition, he even sent his daughter and son as Buddhist missionaries to the island now called Sri Lanka off India's southern coast. Buddhism, formerly practiced only in parts of northern India, thus spread across the subcontinent and beyond.

Ashoka renounces violence and widely promotes Buddhism

Ashoka also practiced what he preached, creating a benevolent, paternalistic government devoted to the welfare of his subjects, whom he referred to as his children. He dispatched special agents throughout the realm to learn people's needs and ensure that local officials treated them with compassion and respect. To encourage commerce and religious pilgrimages he constructed numerous roads, with rest houses, shade trees, and watering spots along the way. To improve his people's lives, he established hospitals, had wells dug for water, and built irrigation systems. Despite his devotion to Buddhism, he respected and supported other faiths such as Hinduism and Jainism, helping to maintain their shrines and promote their worship. During his long and successful reign he personified the ideal Buddhist king, setting a standard of humanitarian rule that few other monarchs in history would match.

Ashoka's rule, however, was based not just on Buddhism and paternalism, but also on political control, sustained by the empire's large bureaucracy and army. His numerous officials and soldiers collected taxes, enforced his laws, and supervised his public works projects, effectively administering a huge kingdom with numerous people speaking many different languages. Ashoka's authorities used force sparingly, but the threat of its use helped hold his vast realm together. Indeed, Ashoka's promotion of Buddhism and nonviolence, while no doubt sincere, also served to dissuade his subjects from violently resisting his rule.

India After Ashoka: New Connections and Conflicts

Unfortunately for India, Ashoka's successors were neither as humane nor as capable as he. The Mauryan Empire under their rule was weakened by corruption and local revolts, and by financial problems that were worsened by the huge expenses of its bureaucracy and army. As its power steadily declined, so did the territory under its control. The empire finally ceased to exist in 184 B.C.E., when its last ruler was killed by one of his own commanders.

The collapse of the Mauryan Empire began five centuries of political disunity in India. In both the north and the south, a series of small kingdoms emerged. As in the Vedic era, India's great size and diversity once more stood in the way of centralization.

Mauryan collapse initiates five centuries of Indian disunity

Disunity, however, was by no means a disaster. During this era, in spite of their divisions, Indians greatly expanded their contacts with other cultures. Sea lanes linked the subcontinent with Egypt and Arabia across the Arabian Sea, and with southeast Asia across the Bay of Bengal, while land routes connected it through Persia with the West, and through central Asia to China (Map 3.5). Indian monks traveled to southeast and

Indian connections grow with other cultures east and west

Map 3.5 Trade Routes Link India with Other Lands by Late First Millennium B.C.E.

In the centuries of disunity following the Mauryan Empire's collapse in 184 B.C.E., Indians expanded their commercial and cultural connections, using land and sea routes that linked India with other parts of Asia. Notice that, because the Himalaya Mountains were virtually impassable, the main land routes from India to China went north from the Indus Valley, then east through Central Asia along the Silk Road (Chapter 4). Note also that sea routes connected India with diverse cultures to its east and west. What key impacts did these connections have on Indian culture and commerce?

central Asia, and from there to China, preaching the Buddha's message and translating Buddhist writings into different languages. Indian merchants traded extensively with other lands, exporting pepper and other spices, cottons, and precious gems, while importing horses, metal wares, silks, and wines.

Southern India, separate from north, develops regional connections

Meanwhile southern India, separated from the rest of the subcontinent by the Deccan plateau and its adjacent mountain ranges, remained largely indifferent toward the north. Buddhist missionaries often traveled from the north to the south, and merchants conducted trade between the two regions, but given the lengthy and dangerous land travel required, such commerce was not extensive during this period. The kingdoms in the south found it more rewarding to trade by sea, first with the Mediterranean world and later with Southeast Asia. They also warred incessantly with one another and showed no interest in unification.

NORTHERN KINGDOMS AND CONNECTIONS. In the north, around 180 B.C.E., descendants of the soldiers of Alexander the Great established a Greco-Bactrian kingdom in the Indus

Valley and neighboring Bactria (present-day Afghanistan). This regime, looking westward toward Greece, expanded northern India's connections with the Mediterranean world. Beginning around 100 B.C.E., however, the Greco-Bactrians were invaded by Scythians (*SIH-thē-unz*), pastoral nomads driven from their Central Asian homelands (Map 3.5). By 88 B.C.E. the Scythians were entering the Indus Valley, and in 50 B.C.E. they overran that region and destroyed the Greco-Bactrian kingdom.

Scythian rule lasted only a century. By 50 C.E. the Kushans (*koo-SHAHNZ*), the nomadic people who had originally pushed the Scythians out of Central Asia, now drove them from northwest India as well. Forced to move south, many Scythians eventually assimilated into Indian culture, settling in central India, adopting new names, and converting to Hinduism. The Kushans, meanwhile, established in the north a sizable kingdom centered in the upper Indus Valley.

Kushans displace Scythians, driving them south, around 50 C.E.

For almost two centuries, from around 50 to 240 C.E., the Kushans dominated Bactria and parts of northern India. Their kingdom sat astride the trade routes connecting India with China and West Asia, making it a crossroads of both commerce and ideas. From the West, for example, came products such as wines, jewelry, and horses, as well such ideas as the seven-day week, the 60-minute hour, and the solar calendar. From China came porcelain wares and especially silk, a cloth so prized that the main east-west trade route was known as the Silk Road (Chapter 4). From India came spices and cotton cloth, scholars, artists, and poets, and above all Buddhist ideals, which spread from India to Central and East Asia by way of the Kushan Kingdom.

Kushans dominate trade routes connecting India with much of Eurasia

BUDDHISM'S SPREAD AND DIVISION. The most influential Kushan king was Kanishka (*kah-NISH-kah*), whose reign of several decades began at some point between 78 and 144 C.E. A man of broad vision and territorial ambition, he expanded southward toward central India and north into central Asia, creating a large, multicultural kingdom. He is best known, however, for supporting Buddhism and helping to spread it throughout his kingdom and beyond (Map 3.6). Kanishka, who like Ashoka may have been a convert to Buddhism, sent Buddhist missionaries into Central Asia, where they preached the faith to merchants and others in towns along the trade routes. From there Buddhism eventually spread to East Asia, where it later flourished in China, Korea, and Japan. Like Ashoka, Kanishka promoted Buddhist architecture, sculpture, and art. Indeed, the famous popular depictions of the Buddha, seated in meditation with his legs crossed, originated in the Kushan era.

Kanishka expands Kushan Kingdom and widely promotes Buddhism

Kanishka was assisted in his efforts by Ashvaghosha (*ahsh-VUH-gō-shuh*), a gifted Indian dramatist and poet who seems to have been a spiritual advisor to the Kushan king. Raised as a devout Hindu of the Brahmin caste, Ashvaghosha was reportedly a staunch opponent of Buddhism until he was won over in a spirited debate with a noted Buddhist teacher. The author of elegant essays, plays, and poems, including a famous *Life of the Buddha* written in poetic verse, Ashvaghosha was influential at Buddhism's Fourth Great Council, hosted by King Kanishka, which confirmed the division of Buddhism into two major branches.

Aided by poet Ashvaghosha, Kanishka hosts great Buddhist council

In the centuries before the council, Buddhism as practiced in northwestern India had evolved into an elaborate religion, marked by devotions to numerous divinities and holy persons. Its followers there exalted the Buddha not just as a man who had attained enlightenment but also as a god who could help them gain salvation from suffering. They also venerated various other buddhas and bodhisattvas (*bō-di-SAHT-vuhz*), saintly

Map 3.6 The Kushan Kingdom (50–240 C.E.) and Buddhism's Spread

Over many centuries, Buddhism spread from its birthplace in northern India throughout much of Asia. Notice that the Kushan Kingdom (50–240 C.E.), where Mahayana Buddhism flourished, sat astride the trade routes (shown on Map 3.5) that connected India with Central Asia and China. How did the Kushans contribute to the development and spread of Mahayana Buddhism?

figures who, having gained enlightenment, were moved by compassion to postpone their own nirvana so they could help save others.

Mahayana dominates Kanishka's council, leading to Buddhist split

Devotees of this form of Buddhism called it Mahayana (*mah-hah-YAH-nah*), the "greater vehicle," claiming it saved more people than traditional forms, which shunned such devotions and stressed instead withdrawal from worldly pursuits. Merchants, artisans, officials, and others who were unwilling or unable to set aside their worldly pursuits thus tended to favor Mahayana, which enabled them to seek salvation through devotions and compassion. Mahayana supporters, including Ashvaghosha, dominated the Fourth Great Council, which affirmed their teachings. As the form of the faith embraced by the Kushans and spread by them to Central and East Asia, Mahayana was the main branch of Buddhism that later took hold in China, Korea, and Japan.

Mahayana Buddhism spreads throughout Central and East Asia

Traditional Buddhists, however, rejected the Fourth Council and its teachings. They promoted instead strict adherence to the Buddha's original principles, focusing on righteous living and enlightenment rather than devotions to divinities. Scorned by Mahayana supporters as Hinayana (*HĒ-nah-YAH-nah*), the "lesser vehicle," traditional Buddhism nonetheless endured in several forms. One, known as Theravada (*ter-ah-VAH-dah*), the "way of the elders," flourished in Sri Lanka and spread to Southeast Asia, where it remains the main belief system today.

HINDUISM'S EVOLUTION AND ENDURANCE. The reign of Kanishka marked a high point of Kushan power. His successors, less talented than he, failed to consolidate and maintain their hold on the regions he had conquered. By 240 C.E. the Kushan Kingdom had lost most of its lands and had ceased to be an important regional force.

Kanishka's reign also marked a high point of Buddhist influence in India. Divided into competing factions and deprived of its most powerful patron by the Kushan Kingdom's decline, Buddhism began its own slow decline in the Indian subcontinent, even as the faith was spreading to other Asian cultures.

Buddhism's gradual decline in India coincided with Hinduism's gradual evolution into a popular religion. Hinduism competed successfully with Buddhism partly by making the Buddha one of the various incarnations of the Hindu god Vishnu. Above all, however, Hinduism evolved in ways that widened its appeal, softening its asceticism and elitism, while helping it better meet the needs of the lower classes.

As practiced over time by the masses, popular Hinduism invited believers to fully enjoy life within the context of their caste. Although Hindus still had to fulfill their caste's occupational functions, within this framework they were encouraged to seek material success. Merchants or farmers, for example, could pursue prosperity by doing their caste duties honorably and well, thereby improving both their comfort in this life and their status in their next incarnation. Likewise, although Hindus were still expected to associate and intermarry with members of their own caste, within this context they were encouraged to experience the pleasures of social engagement, so central to the community, and the joys of sexuality, so central to the family. While Buddhism, even in its Mahayana form, urged its adherents to curb their worldly desires, popular Hinduism placed the common people under no such restraint.

In addition, as it evolved over the centuries, popular Hinduism also let its followers tailor their devotions to meet their individual needs. Rather than relying on rituals performed by Brahmins, for example, Hindus increasingly sought to develop a personal relationship with a particular god or goddess, typically an incarnation of Vishnu, Shiva, or Devi. By repeatedly invoking the name, singing the hymns, and visiting the shrines of their personal deity, Hindus could hope to create a bond that would help them eventually gain moksha. In the long run, then, Hinduism's ability to meet the daily needs of diverse peoples, combined with its multiplicity of divinities and devotional practices, helped it to adapt better than Buddhism to the needs of Indian society.

Traditional Theravada Buddhism endures in Southeast Asia

Hinduism, competing with Buddhism, evolves into popular faith

Hindus develop devotions to personal divinities

Indian Society and Culture

Except for a short period of peace and unity under Mauryan rule, most of India's early history was marked by conflict and political fragmentation. These conditions, however, did not prevent the emergence of a stable social structure and a flourishing culture. Like ancient Mesopotamia, India showed that society and culture could thrive amid regional diversity, political disunity, and religious discord.

Caste, Family, and Gender

Hindu society centers on
caste and family

Hindu society was dominated by the caste system, which influenced almost every aspect of life. Each caste had its own particular dharma, carrying with it rights, obligations, and restrictions. Beyond this was a generalized dharma applicable to all: deference to the Brahmins, devotion to the gods, and reverence for the Ganges and for sacred cattle. Procreation, too, was considered a sacred duty: large families were seen as blessings from the gods, and any attempt to limit family size was frowned upon. Since reproduction was essential to reincarnation, for most people marriage and parenthood were moral obligations. Some Jains and Buddhists might seek sanctity as celibate monks or nuns, but for Hindus the single life was socially unacceptable, and prolonging virginity was considered perverse.

Parents arrange
marriages, often when
children are quite young

Naturally, to fulfill their dharma, people had to marry within their caste. Unwilling to leave such a crucial concern to romance or personal choice, parents arranged proper unions for their children, sometimes at ages as young as eight or nine, before sexual attraction had a chance to complicate things. Marriages based on romantic love were possible but rare, and generally not regarded as respectable.

Indian society was patriarchal, centered on villages and extended families dominated by males. The villages, in which most people lived, were administered by men, who served on village councils typically composed of male heads of households. The households were largely supported by the labor of the men, who performed the occupational duties associated with their caste, which for most meant farming and herding. Families were governed by their senior males, who exercised ownership of family possessions and authority over the women and children.

In Vedic days the position of women was not entirely subordinate: they could participate equally with men in religious rituals and, within the framework of marriages arranged by their parents, they could have some say in the selection of their spouse. As a rule they could leave home on their own to shop, visit friends or family, and attend celebrations. If they were widowed, they were usually free to remarry, as long as their new husband was a member of the same caste.

Indian society restricts
women's rights and roles

During the post-Vedic era, however, the opportunities available to women declined. Women were increasingly barred from religious and social activities, forbidden to remarry after their husbands died, and confined to the home and family. Girls were often engaged before age ten, and then wed at the onset of puberty to men in their twenties, a practice promoting both bridal virginity and male domination. Within the family framework, as in other societies, women might gain substantial influence over household management. But their primary dharma was to serve their husbands; if they performed it with grace and devotion, they might expect a better status in their next incarnation.

The most extreme example of female subordination was **sati** (*suh-TĒ*), a practice whereby widows cremated themselves on their dead husbands' funeral pyre (a pile of wood used to burn a dead body rather than burying it). Although sati, which means "loyal wife," may have predated Vedic India, in Vedic times the widow was allowed to lie briefly on the pyre and then get off before it was set ablaze. By post-Vedic times, however, the practice had returned to its lethal form. Brahmins at first condemned it, but then accepted it as a testament to the eternal sanctity of marriage, and sometimes even promoted it as an exemplary display of a woman's marital fidelity. Although denounced by Buddhists and others, and never practiced extensively, sati survived among some segments of Indian society well into the twentieth century C.E.

The Visual Arts

Early Indian society, while focusing on stability and structure, produced a culture distinguished by its delicacy, intricacy, and subtlety. In areas such as sculpture, art, and architecture, India ranked among the ancient world's most creative and productive societies.

Early Indian sculptors, for instance, produced many superb statues and reliefs, portraying gods and goddesses, animals, and humans in exquisite detail. These sculptors often depicted female figures in alluring and sensuous poses, reflecting a deep fascination with beauty and grace, passion and pleasure, fertility and sexuality.

Later the spread of Buddhism shifted the focus of Indian sculpture and art from the sensual to the spiritual. At first the Buddha's followers, anxious to avoid idolatry, refused to depict him in any lifelike way. In time, however, contacts with Greek culture and the rise of Mahayana Buddhism overcame their concerns. By the second century C.E., sculptors were producing scores of statues of buddhas and bodhisattvas, some of which still adorn the landscapes of southern and Central Asia.

More impressive still was early Indian architecture. Before the coming of the Persians and Greeks, buildings in India were made mainly of wood, but thereafter stone construction became more and more common. During the Mauryan Empire, and especially under Ashoka, artisans erected thousands of shrines and prayer halls, some of them carved into mountainsides and hewn out of solid rock. Even more spectacular were the numerous **stupas**, massive domed edifices constructed of stone, initially built to house relics such as bones of the Buddha and later used as temples for pilgrimage and worship. The faithful flocked to these stupas, and typically prayed while walking around them on a circular path.

Buddhism's spread changes Indian art from sensual to spiritual

Persians, Greeks, and Buddhists influence Indian architecture

The Great Stupa at Sanchi in India, commissioned by the Emperor Ashoka.

Science and Mathematics

Early Indian thinkers, like those in West Asia and Egypt, made a number of crucial contributions to science and mathematics. Indian astronomers, for example, accurately plotted the paths of the planets and stars, and even determined that the Earth is a sphere revolving on its axis. And ancient Indian mathematicians devised an early form of algebra.

India's most valuable mathematical innovation, however, was its method of expressing numbers. As early as 250 B.C.E., Indians were using a place-value system of numerical notations, based on the number ten. A thousand years later, Arab scholars adopted this system and then spread it to the West, where the notations were thus called Arabic numerals. This system, far more functional than the cumbersome symbols (such as Roman numerals) used in other ancient cultures, so vastly facilitated numeric computation that it is used almost everywhere today.

Indians develop place-value number system, ancestor of 'Arabic' numerals

Philosophy and Literature: Upanishads and Epics

Like the Epic of Gilgamesh, the Hebrew Bible, and other ancient West Asian works, early Indian literature focused on connections and conflicts between physical and spiritual forces. Its main works were the **Upanishads** (*oo-PAH-ni-shahdz*), philosophical and religious texts composed by learned writers over many centuries beginning in late Vedic

Upanishads reflect
introspective and
intuitive philosophy

times, but it also included superb epic poems recorded in the post-Vedic era. Composed in Sanskrit, an Aryan language used for religious and literary purposes, these works serve as the basic scriptures of the Hindu faith.

Unlike the works of ancient West Asia, however, the Upanishads look inward rather than outward in their search for answers, valuing intuition and flashes of insight over intellectual speculation. They puzzle over such fundamental questions as where we came from, why we are here, how we should live, and where we are going. The answers, consistent with Hindu tradition, seek to connect mortal beings with the immortal and divine. One's spiritual core is Atman, the soul and depth of one's being; the core of the world is Brahman, the life force of all existence. Properly understood, however, Atman and Brahman are identical; thus each individual is one with the divine and cannot be alienated from any manifestation of the infinite. The Upanishads provide guidance for attaining internal peace, rather than an analysis of the external world. They thus exemplify the intuitive introspection often said to distinguish "eastern" thought from the more worldly and analytic "western" approach.

Epics describe the virtues
and ventures of gods
and legendary heroes

A worldly approach was nonetheless reflected in India's two great epic poems, the Mahabharata and the **Ramayana** (*RAH-mah-YAH-nah*), both written in the post-Vedic era based on Vedic oral traditions. The Mahabharata is a massive masterpiece that not only recounts an ancient war, full of legends and godly interventions, but also prescribes proper conduct and devotion to duty. As noted in this chapter's introduction, it includes the splendid Bhagavad Gita, regarded as one of India's most important ethical and spiritual works. The Ramayana describes the wanderings and adventures of Rama, heir to the throne of a northern Indian kingdom caught up in the great war. Later revered as a human manifestation of the god Vishnu, Rama was seen as a model of courage, fidelity, and devotion to family. These virtues were exemplified in the loving relationship between him and his wife Sita (*SĒ-tah*), whose hand he won by bending and breaking her father's great war bow, and who remained loyal to him through many tribulations (see "Ramayana Excerpts: Rama and Sita").

Upanishads and epics
entertain and inspire
Indians over the ages

For centuries these epics were recited from memory at family meals and at roadside inns, delighting and entertaining listeners. Their elegance and directness are enchanting, even to many people today who do not share India's religious traditions.

To Indians for thousands of years, however, these works have been sources of inspiration, not just entertainment. Often incorporated into religious rituals, they have served as guides to proper conduct, illustrated by valiant role models who enact the search for answers to life's most basic questions. Over the ages, millions of people have followed the precepts of the Upanishads and epics, hoping thereby to be cleansed of imperfections and eventually attain moksha.

Indian culture provides
harmony and beauty
amid diversity and
disunity

On the whole, then, early India's culture, developed through interactions among India's diverse peoples, was characterized by complexity and inner depth. It was also shaped by contacts with other cultures, and profoundly influenced by the teachings of Hinduism, Jainism, and Buddhism. It reflected a society that sought unity in the midst of diversity, order in the midst of instability, tranquility in the midst of turmoil, beauty in the midst of bedlam, and virtue in the midst of violence.

Document 3.2 Ramayana Excerpts: Rama and Sita

In these excerpts from the Ramayana, heroic Rama, son of King Dasa-ratha, wins the hand of the princess Sita by bending and breaking the great war bow of her father, King Janak of Videha. Rama and Sita then wed and exemplify the loving, faithful husband and wife.

Rich in royal worth and valour, rich in holy
Vedic lore,
Dasa-ratha ruled his empire in the happy days of
yore . . .

Janak, monarch of Videha, spake his message near
and far,
He shall win my peerless Sita who shall bend my
bow of war,

Suitors came from farthest regions, warlike princes
known to fame,
Vainly strove to wield the weapon, left Videha in
their shame . . .

Stalwart men of ample stature pulled the mighty
iron car
In which rested all-inviolate Janak's dreaded bow of
war, . . .

"This the weapon of Videha," proudly thus the
peers begun,
"Be it shown to royal Rama, Dasa-ratha's righteous
son" . . .

Rama lifted high the cover of the pond'rous
iron car,
Gazed with conscious pride and prowess on the
mighty bow of war.

"Let me," humbly spake the hero, "on this bow
my fingers place,
Let me lift and bend the weapon, help me with
your loving grace."

"Be it so," the rishi answered, "be it so," the
monarch said,
Rama lifted high the weapon on his stalwart arms
displayed,

Wond'ring gazed the kings assembled as the son
of Raghu's race

Proudly raised the bow of Rudra with a warrior's
stately grace,
Proudly strung the bow of Rudra which the kings
had tried in vain
Drew the cord with force resistless till the weapon
snapped in twain! . . .

And the chiefs and gathered monarchs fell and
fainted in their fear,
And the men of many nations shook the dreadful
sound to hear!

Pale and white the startled monarchs slowly from
their terror woke,
And with royal grace and greetings Janak to the
rishi spoke:

Now my ancient eyes have witnessed wond'rous
deed by Rama done,
Deed surpassing thought or fancy wrought by
Dasa-ratha's son,

And the proud and peerless princess, Sita glory of
my house,
Sheds on me an added lustre as she weds a godlike
spouse,

True shall be my plighted promise, Sita dearer than
my life,
Won by worth and wond'rous valour shall be
Rama's faithful wife . . .

With a woman's whole affection fond and trusting
Sita loved,
And within her faithful bosom loving Rama lived
and moved,

And he loved her, for their parents chose her as his
faithful wife,
Loved her for her peerless beauty, for her true and
trustful life,

Loved and dwelt within her bosom though he
wore a form apart,
Rama in a sweet communion lived in Sita's loving
heart!

SOURCE: R. C. Dutt, translator, *The Ramayana: The Great Hindu Epic,* Book I: *The Bridal of Sita.* http:/ /hinduism. about.com/ library/ weekly/ extra/ bl-ramayana1. htm

Chapter Review

Putting It in Perspective

By the third century C.E., all the basic elements of Indian civilization were in place. In many ways these elements were a study in contrasts. India's Aryan-inspired literature glorified violence and warfare, but its Jain and Buddhist traditions exalted nonviolence and compassion. India's religious structure accommodated numerous gods, but it also insisted that all beings are one with each other and with the divine in an infinite cycle of life. India's political climate was marked by disunity and conflict, but its social system emphasized stability and control.

These contrasts are hardly surprising, given India's vast size and its great geographical and cultural diversity. Ancient India was not in fact a single society but a wide assortment of societies that interacted through numerous connections and conflicts. These interactions were shaped not only by Harappan, Aryan, and Dravidian influences, but also by peoples who at times ruled parts of India, including especially the Persians, Greeks, Scythians, and Kushans.

Nor is it surprising that ancient India produced no long-enduring empire. In the ancient world, of all the great conquerors and leaders, only a few were able to create and maintain immense, diverse, and populous domains that lasted for centuries. The most successful of these realms, discussed in upcoming chapters, were the empires established by the Chinese, Persians, and Romans.

Reviewing Key Material

KEY CONCEPTS

Mahabharata, 56	asceticism, 65
Vedic, 61	ahimsa, 65
varnas, 63	moksha, 65
castes, 63	nirvana, 66
jatis, 63	sati, 75
samsara, 64	stupa, 76
dharma, 64	Upanishads, 76
karma, 64	Ramayana, 77

KEY PEOPLE

Arjuna, 56	Chandragupta Maurya, 68
Mahavira (Jina), 65	Ashoka, 69
Siddhartha Gautama (Buddha), 65	Kanishka, 72
	Ashvaghosha, 72
Alexander the Great, 67	Rama, 77
Seleucus Nikator, 56	Sita, 77

ASK YOURSELF

1. In what ways were the societies and cultures of India similar to those of West Asia and North Africa? In what ways were Indian cultures and belief systems unique?
2. How did the system of castes develop in ancient India? What were its advantages and disadvantages for the Indian people? How did dharma and samsara help to reinforce the system?
3. What were the basic features and beliefs of Hinduism, Jainism, and Buddhism? In what ways did they support, and in what ways did they challenge, the political and social structures?
4. How and why did Buddhism evolve and divide into separate branches? How and why did Hinduism evolve and endure as a popular religion?
5. What factors made it difficult to achieve and maintain political unity in India? What factors enabled India to flourish despite its political divisions?

GOING FURTHER

Akira, H. *A History of Indian Buddhism.* 1990.
Armstrong, Karen. *Buddha.* 2001.
Auboyer, Jeannine. *Daily Life in Ancient India.* 2002.
Basham, A. L., ed. *A Cultural History of India.* 1975.
Conze, Edward. *A Short History of Buddhism.* 1980.
Flood, Gavin. *An Introduction to Hinduism.* 1996.
Foltz, R. C. *Religions of the Silk Road.* 1999.
Huntington, S. L. *The Art of Ancient India: Buddhist, Hindu, Jain.* 1985.
Kenoyer, Jonathan Mark. *Ancient Cities of the Indus Valley Civilization.* 1998.
Kinsely, David R. *Hinduism: A Cultural Perspective.* 1982.

Klostermaier, K. K. *A Survey of Hinduism.* 1989.

Kulke, Helman, and D. Rothermund. *A History of India.* 3rd ed. 1998.

Masson-Oursel, Paul. *Ancient India and Indian Civilization.* 1998.

McIntosh, Jane. *A Peaceful Realm: Rise and Fall of the Indus Civilization.* 2002.

Pandian, Jacob. *The Making of India and Indian Tradition.* 1995.

Pearson, M. *The Indian Ocean.* 2003.

Possehl, Gregory. *The Indus Civilization: A Contemporary Perspective.* 2002.

Robinson, R. H., W. L. Johnson, and S. A. Wawrytko. *The Buddhist Religion: A Historical Introduction.* 4th ed. 1996.

Sharma, R. S. *India's Ancient Past.* 2005.

Thapar, Romila. *Asoka and the Decline of the Mauryas.* 1961.

Thapar, Romila. *Early India: From Origins to AD 1300.* 2002.

Trainor, Kevin, ed. *Buddhism.* 2001.

Williams, P. *Buddhist Thought.* 2000.

Wolpert, Stanley A. *A New History of India.* 7th ed. 2003.

Key Dates and Developments

by 7000 B.C.E.	Farming in Indus Valley
2800–1700 B.C.E.	Harappan (Indus Valley) civilization
by 1500 B.C.E.	Indo-European Aryans arrive in India
1500–500 B.C.E.	Vedic Age: Vedas, caste system, early Upanishads
563–483 B.C.E.	Siddhartha Gautama (Buddha): founder of Buddhism
540–486 B.C.E.	Mahavira (Jina): founder of Jainism
518–513 B.C.E.	Persian conquest of northwest India
500–300 B.C.E.	Initial compilation of Mahabharata and Ramayana
327–326 B.C.E.	Alexander the Great's invasion of northwest India
321–184 B.C.E.	Mauryan Empire
321–297 B.C.E.	Reign of Chandragupta Maurya
270–232 B.C.E.	Reign of Ashoka
180–50 B.C.E.	Greco-Bactrian kingdom in northern India
50–240 C.E.	Kushan Kingdom; Spread and division of Buddhism

The Origins of the Chinese Empire, to 220 C.E.

The First Emperor's Underground Army

The tomb of China's First Emperor, guarded by a huge underground clay army rediscovered in 1974, attests to the power and grandeur of ancient China. This sketch shows how scholars think the tomb was constructed in the third century C.E.

In 1974, workers drilling a well near the Chinese city of Xi'an (*shē-AHN*) made an extraordinary discovery. Much to their surprise, they found a huge underground chamber filled with thousands of elaborate statues: an army of life-sized clay horses and soldiers armed with real bronze weapons. Nearby chambers, seemingly guarded by this clay army, were later found to contain hundreds of additional artifacts, scores of human remains, and a magnificent bronze mausoleum. Scholars soon determined that this subterranean sepulcher, dating from the third century B.C.E., was the tomb of an ancient Chinese ruler known to history as the First Emperor.

The realm of the First Emperor centered on a culture that had arisen in northern China several thousand years before his time. Here, as in Mesopotamia, Egypt, and India, early societies emerged along a waterway, in this case the treacherous Yellow River that flows across North China. Farming villages grew into towns, some of which evolved into city-states that expanded into larger domains. Here, as in West Asia and India, moral and religious concepts developed that over the ages would influence millions of people. Here, too, as in other ancient empires, the land was united through the conquests of a mighty ruler, in this case the First Emperor.

Early Chinese Empire

Despite such similarities, however, the culture that arose in ancient China was in certain ways distinctive. The Chinese adopted an outlook on governance, for example, that held state officials accountable for public welfare and justified revolts against rulers who failed to maintain it—an outlook most uncommon in the ancient world. The Chinese developed a worldview that conceived reality as a balance of complementary forces, unlike other cultures that perceived life as a struggle between good and evil. The Chinese produced goods, such as paper and silk, found in no other early cultures. And Chinese leaders, building upon the centralized state created by the First Emperor, assembled a professional civil service system to administer one of history's most extensive, populous, and enduring empires.

China's Geographic Diversity

China's geography provides a study in contrasts. The west and southwest are mountainous and bleak. The north is arid and barren, dominated by the Gobi (*GŌ-bē*) desert and Mongolian plateau (Map 4.1). Desolate and forbidding, these regions have remained sparsely inhabited throughout Chinese history. They have also separated China from other societies. Although ancient China had contacts with other cultures, connections were sporadic and hard to maintain.

China's diverse geography impedes early intercultural connections

Eastern China is defined by its two great rivers. In the south is the Yangzi (*YAHNG-DZUH*) River, or Changjiang (*CHAHNG jē-AHNG*), sometimes called "China's

Yangzi and Yellow Rivers irrigate and connect eastern China

FOUNDATION MAP 4.1 China's Geography and Environment, Third Millennium B.C.E.

China's northern deserts and western mountains made connections with other cultures challenging. Note, however, that the great rivers flowing eastward from the mountains aided internal connections and facilitated farming, while seasonal monsoon winds from the South China Sea brought China regular rainfall. How could ease of internal connections and productive farmlands help to form the foundations for a strong Chinese state?

blessing." A broad, deep waterway that seldom floods, it is excellent for transport and reliable for irrigating nearby lands. The climate is warm, the growing season long, and rainfall abundant, as seasonal monsoon winds bring in moisture from seas to the south. The terrain is lush and green, sustaining a variety of fruits, vegetables, and grains. In the north, by contrast, is the Yellow River, or Huanghe (*HWAHNG-HUH*), also known as "China's sorrow." It is shallow, flows through flat plains, and has no regular river bed, so its frequent floods and occasional course changes devastate those who live nearby. In the north the climate is cold and dry, the growing season short, and nature harsh, with recurrent danger of drought, floods, and frost.

Early Chinese Societies

Despite its harsh environment, however, the north was where China's first settled societies emerged. Several factors help to explain this development. One was the profusion of brownish-yellow silt carried by the Yellow River, giving it both its appearance and its name. Deposited through the countryside by periodic floods, this silt was rich in nutrients, regularly restoring the soil's fertility. Farming thus came early to this area, helping to sustain the growing population needed to form cities and states. Another key factor may have been the Yellow River's unpredictability, compelling those who lived nearby to organize into communities large enough to build dikes and channels to control the current.

The Yellow River.

Responding to the benefits and challenges of their environment, from the seventh through second millennia B.C.E. the people of northern China developed a culture that served as the basis for later Chinese societies. They adopted farming and herding, settled with their families in villages, instituted religious rituals, and learned to produce silk. In time they also built towns and cities, fashioned bronze tools and weapons, established a social class structure, created a centralized state, and devised a writing system. As a result, by the second millennium B.C.E., many basic features of Chinese civilization already existed in the Yellow River valley.

Predynastic China

Aided by the silt-enriched soil, people started farming near the Yellow River as early as 7000 B.C.E. As in other agricultural societies, farmers resided in villages and raised food on the surrounding lands. To protect themselves from wind and cold, the villagers lived in pits dug in the ground and covered with thatch roofs. To feed themselves they grew millet, and eventually cabbage and wheat; they also produced fine pottery and domesticated cattle, sheep, goats, and pigs. Later some villagers additionally cultivated silkworms, little short-lived caterpillars that feed on mulberry leaves and spin cocoons of fine soft thread. After painstakingly unraveling these cocoons, Chinese peasants wove the thread into silk, eventually valued as the world's finest cloth.

Farming villages emerge near Yellow River by 7000 B.C.E.

According to legend, early China was blessed with heroic benefactors who began its development. Fuxi (*FOO-SHĒ*) supposedly established the family and taught the people how to domesticate animals. Shennong (*SHUN-NUNG*) is said to have invented farming and basic farming tools. Huangdi (*HWANG-DĒ*) is credited with the development of silk, the bow and arrow, boats, and a system of writing. Huangdi is also considered the first of China's predynastic rulers, a series of fabled monarchs who reigned before the rise of ruling dynasties.

Early Chinese pottery.

Legend also credits the last predynastic ruler, a former poor peasant named Shun, with selecting a man named Yu to harness the floods that disrupted life along the Yellow River. The ingenious Yu purportedly dug channels to divert the floodwaters, thereby creating northern China's other rivers. Shun was said to have been so impressed that he selected Yu to rule after him. Then, when Yu died, the Chinese installed Yu's son as their next ruler. Thus, according to tradition, began the pattern of familial rule, initiating a series of dynasties that would dominate China from then until modern times.

Legend says heroic predynastic rulers initiate Chinese society

Although they are legends, these accounts reveal the perceptions and priorities of the ancient Chinese. They show that the Chinese saw family, farming, writing, river control, and dynastic rule as central elements of their culture. Furthermore, when supplemented

Legends reflect Chinese focus on farming, family, rivers, and rulers by archeological evidence, these stories help historians discern the general features of early Chinese society, especially as it existed under China's first two dynasties.

Xia and Shang Societies

Yu and his son are traditionally regarded as the first two rulers of the Xia (*shē-AH*) dynasty, which reigned in the central Yellow River region from approximately 2200 to 1750 B.C.E. (Map 4.2). Once seen as a figment of folklore, the Xia is now considered China's first historical dynasty, as cities and towns unearthed near the Yellow River appear to have been part of a real Xia realm. One large city called Erlitou (*ER-lē-TŌ*), possibly the capital, had stately palaces and tombs, paved roads, and even a foundry for making bronze tools and weapons.

Map 4.2 China's Early Cities and Dynasties, Second Millennium B.C.E.

China's earliest cities were located in northeast China, around the Yellow River, in lands governed by the Xia Dynasty (2200–1750 B.C.E.) and Shang Dynasty (1750–1122 B.C.E.). Observe, as indicated on the inset map, that some Indo-European nomads apparently migrated to the region west of China by around 2000 B.C.E. What ideas and techniques might the Chinese have learned through contacts with these Central Asian nomads?

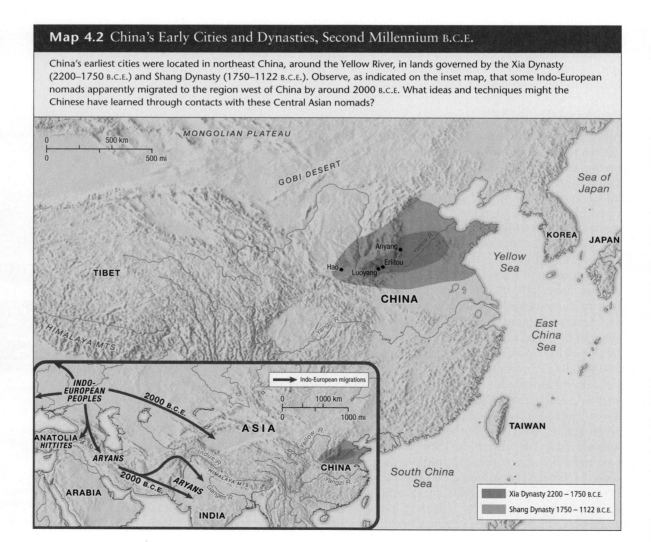

Bronze metallurgy probably came to China by way of the Indo-European migrations, discussed in Chapter 2, which provided early connections among Eurasian cultures. Much as the Hittites moved to Anatolia and the Aryans to India, other Indo-European pastoral nomads moved to what is now northwest China, during the Xia dynasty, with their horse-drawn chariots and bronze weapons (see Map 4.2 inset). The subsequent appearance of such devices in Yellow River societies, and similarities between old Chinese and Indo-European words for wheels and chariots, suggest that China learned of these devices through contacts and conflicts with the nomads.

Central Asian nomads introduce horses and bronze weapons to China

Some Chinese warriors made good use of these vehicles and weapons. In the eighteenth century B.C.E., according to both legend and archeological evidence, the Xia regime was defeated and displaced by a new dynasty known as the Shang (*SHAHNG*), whose warrior nobles were armed with bronze spears, protected by bronze armor, and skilled in the use of war chariots.

Shang dynasty replaces Xia by 1700 B.C.E.

Since the Shang dynasty, which reigned from roughly 1750 to 1122 B.C.E., produced some written records, historians know much more about it than they know about the Xia. Along with evidence from excavations of Shang settlements, especially the capital, Anyang (*AHN-YAHNG*), these records portray a complex, warlike, stratified society.

By Shang times, a number of city-states had emerged in northern China. Although each had its own local ruler, many of these rulers were tied by allegiance, and often also by kinship, to the Shang royal family. These ties brought some political unity to the Yellow River valley.

Shang rule unites and connects Yellow River region

Shang society was stratified into several classes. At the top were the king and his warrior aristocracy, who lived in the city centers in palatial homes, wore fine silk garments, and indulged in food and beverages served in splendid bronze vessels. Below the aristocrats were artisans, who lived elsewhere in the cities in homes made of earth and wood, and who produced bronze vessels and weapons, lacquered wood containers, and fine pottery for the upper classes. Less well off were the peasants, who lived in pit homes in rural villages and worked the fields to supply the society's food. At the bottom of the social structure were slaves, typically prisoners of war, who worked as servants in royal and noble households and as forced laborers in the construction of walls, roads, palaces, and dikes.

Although the leaders of Shang society believed in a supreme deity and numerous lesser gods, the most common form of religion appears to have been **ancestor** worship, veneration of a family's departed relatives and forebears. Based on the belief that the spirits of the dead can influence the gods to help relatives who are still living, this worship involved rituals performed at graves and shrines set up to honor dead kinfolk.

Remains of early Chinese chariot, with bones of horses and driver.

People in Shang times also took part in other religious rituals. On occasion, for example, they seem to have sacrificed domestic animals, and even human slaves, to win divine favor. The early Chinese also studied the sun, stars, and planets, presuming that by doing so they could come to know the will of the gods. In the process they devised a calendar, recorded eclipses of the sun, and invented a form of mathematics.

Chinese Writing

The writing system used in ancient China also evolved out of religious practices. For centuries Chinese oracles—spiritual leaders who sought to communicate with the gods—inscribed little pictures on a tortoise shell or cattle shoulder bone and then heated the

Chinese writing evolves from efforts to receive divine messages

Shang oracle bone.

shell or bone until cracks appeared in its surface. The oracles then followed the cracks to connect the pictures, each of which represented a word, in a sequence believed to convey a divine message. By inscribing pictures denoting the sun, clouds, rain, and upcoming days, for example, and then observing how they were connected by the heat cracks, oracles could theoretically foretell the weather. By using other pictures and symbols, oracles could similarly predict the results of battles, harvests, hunts, and other endeavors.

Shang rulers, anxious to foresee the outcome of their endeavors, made extensive use of these "oracle bones," thousands of which have been rediscovered in modern times. Scholars have been able to decipher the oracle bone symbols, and to determine that they are early versions of modern Chinese characters.

In Chinese writing, each character represents an entire word, not just a single sound as in Western alphabets derived from the Phoenician writing system (Chapter 2). Learning to read and write in China has hence meant mastering thousands of symbols. Because it was not closely tied to the sounds of spoken works, however, the system proved very useful in China, where people in one region often could not understand the dialects spoken in other regions. Since each written character conveyed the same concept no matter what the dialect, people could communicate in writing even if they could not understand each others' spoken words. The written character for horse, for example, conveyed the concept of a horse to people who spoke different dialects, even if the spoken words for horse did not sound the same. Chinese writing thus helped ruling centers communicate with outlying regions, thereby helping to unite a vast and disparate land. As it did elsewhere, writing in China also enabled people to record their history and convey their ideas.

Chinese writing helps to connect a vast and diverse realm

State and Society During the Zhou Dynasty

By the late twelfth century B.C.E., according to traditional accounts, the Shang kings had become oppressive and corrupt, provoking rebellions against them. The victor in these struggles was King Wu, the ruler of Zhou (*JŌ*), a small realm west of the Shang domain. In 1122 B.C.E. he defeated the Shang and started a new dynasty that reigned for more than 800 years in much of northern China (Map 4.3). The Zhou era is traditionally divided into two periods: the Western Zhou (1122–771 B.C.E.), when the kings resided at Hao (near modern Xi'an) in the west, and the Eastern Zhou (770–256 B.C.E.), when they lived further east at Luoyang (*LWŌ-YAHNG*).

The Mandate of Heaven and Dynastic Cycle

Zhou Dynasty replaces Shang regime, calling it corrupt

Composed by Zhou era writers, traditional accounts of the Shang's overthrow tend to discredit the old dynasty and exalt the early Zhou leaders—especially King Wu's brother, the legendary Duke of Zhou. Based on these accounts, after King Wu died in 1116 B.C.E., the duke served as regent for the new king, the late ruler's son, who was too young to rule on his own. The energetic duke reportedly went on to consolidate his family's control and destroy the vestiges of Shang rule, serving as a wise and loyal administrator. When King Wu's son came of age, the duke turned over power to the young king, thus affirming the succession of father to son and setting an example of loyal devotion for future public servants.

Map 4.3 The Zhou Dynasty, 1122–256 B.C.E.

The Zhou dynasty connected much of northern China for centuries, extending its rule throughout the Yellow River region and beyond. Note, however, that in the Warring States Era (403–221 B.C.E.), although the dynasty still existed in name, various nobles with their own large armies acted as independent warlords, fighting among themselves and eventually controlling a very large area. What commercial and cultural developments continued to connect Chinese society despite these divisions and conflicts?

The Duke of Zhou's most important contribution, however, may have been his success at laying the philosophical foundation for Chinese dynastic authority. To justify his family's ouster of one dynasty and creation of another, he is said to have developed the idea of the **Mandate of Heaven.** This concept asserts that, in order to rule China, a dynasty must have the authorization of "Heaven," perceived not as a place but as the main divinity, god of the skies and ancestor of Chinese rulers. This mandate empowered the ruler to reign as "Son of Heaven," but it also required that he govern justly and humanely. If a ruler grew corrupt and oppressive, and if the people were suffering, Heaven would withdraw the mandate and bestow it on someone else, who would then take power and rule with virtue and benevolence. This principle allegedly legitimized the Zhou overthrow of the Shang.

Mandate of Heaven legitimizes Chinese rulers only if just and humane

Rise and decline of
dynasties creates
dynastic cycles

In claiming this mandate, however, Zhou leaders unwittingly provided both a precedent and a pretext for future rebels to challenge the reigning power, establishing a pattern that would recur throughout Chinese history. This pattern, known as the **dynastic cycle**, had four basic phases. First, a strong leader would arise and conquer all of China, creating a powerful and effective regime. Then he would pass on the rule to his heirs, initiating a dynasty that would reign for some time in stability and prosperity. Eventually, however, the rulers would grow oppressive and corrupt. Taxes would increase, prosperity would decline, and a series of natural and military disasters would signal the loss of Heaven's Mandate. In the cycle's final phase, a new hero would arise to challenge the old dynasty, claiming the mandate for himself and his heirs. If he failed to gain power, he was seen as lacking Heaven's favor; if he succeeded he would found a new dynasty, starting the cycle anew.

Mandate of Heaven
implies right to rebel if a
dynasty grows corrupt

The rise and fall of ruling families was not unique to China; Egypt, for example, also had a long chain of dynasties. But the concept of Heaven's Mandate, combined with the persistence of the dynastic cycle, eventually set up expectations that were distinctively Chinese. In China, at least in theory, a dynasty's survival depended on its ability to provide security, stability, and prosperity. If it failed to do so, for whatever reason, it forfeited its mandate, giving the people a right to rebel and replace it.

Conflict, Chaos, and Commerce

Decentralized Zhou
regime provides land
and power to nobles

This implicit right of rebellion, combined with China's vast dimensions and cultural complexity, made governance a formidable challenge. Rather than trying to control their territories directly, early Zhou rulers developed a decentralized regime in which the regions were governed by subordinates, who received large landholdings in return for their service. These lands were then handed down from father to son, creating a hereditary nobility based on service to the king. But for the kings this system also had a potential drawback: the leading nobles, who had their own lands and armies, might acquire enough power to threaten the regime.

This drawback almost ended the Zhou dynasty in 771 B.C.E., when rebellious nobles joined with nomadic invaders to overthrow a king named You. According to legend, King You sometimes played an extravagant game to entertain a female consort. He lit beacon fires signaling his soldiers to prepare for enemy attack, and then had his consort watch in delight as armies assembled from all directions to meet the imaginary threat. But eventually the soldiers, tired of this game, failed to respond to the beacon fires when real attackers appeared. The capital was overrun, the palace was ransacked, King You was killed, and his lover was captured.

Whatever the truth of this tale—patriarchal societies often have legends blaming women for men's misfortunes—it did help King You's foes justify his removal. But his heir managed to maintain some power by fleeing east to the city of Luoyang, making it his capital and starting a new era now called the Eastern Zhou.

During the Eastern Zhou era (770–256 B.C.E.), many Chinese nobles, acquiring more wealth and power than the king himself, began to act as independent warlords in their own domains. Centuries of chaos and civil war resulted in the Era of Warring States (403–221 B.C.E.), during which all sense of unity and central authority ceased.

Commerce keeps China
connected in Warring
States era

As political conflict tore China apart, however, commerce was tying it together. The Eastern Zhou era saw the rise of many new cities, which served as centers of trade, with markets where farmers, artisans, and merchants from near and far exchanged their goods. Roads and canals connecting these cities, built by rulers to move troops and supplies, were traveled by traders transporting such items as metal tools and utensils, lacquered wood plates and boxes, silk, pottery, gems, salt, and lumber. A money economy emerged, using copper coins called cash, with holes in the center so they could be strung together for counting and carrying. China's towns and cities were likewise linked into a large economic system. Although trade between China and faraway lands was difficult and dangerous, by the end of the Zhou era Chinese merchants were trading by sea with Southeast Asia and by land routes crossing Central Asia.

A metal bell from the Zhou era.

The Central Asian Connection

Central Asia, the vast expanse to China's north and west where the climate was too dry for farming (Map 4.3), was inhabited mainly by pastoral nomads who grazed their herds on its plateaus and plains. Skilled on horseback, the nomads often attacked Chinese settlements to carry off goods and supplies, but they also spread commerce and useful knowledge. Some nomads, for example, exchanged their hides, wool, and horses for Chinese silk, pottery, metalware, and wood products, and then traded what they did not use with others across Central Asia. Direct connections with the nomads, and indirect connections through the nomads with other Eurasian societies, had major impacts on China over time.

Central Asian nomads connect China with other cultures

Interactions with the nomads, for example, transformed Chinese warfare in the Eastern Zhou era. Chinese armies adopted horseback riding from the nomads, replacing charioteers with mounted riders who could move and maneuver much more quickly. The nomads in turn began using the crossbow, a Chinese invention that could kill with precision from a distance.

Nomads and Chinese adopt horse riding and crossbows from each other

Even more momentous was ironworking, a West Asian innovation that spread across Central Asia to China during the Zhou dynasty. Since iron was far more abundant than the copper and tin employed in making bronze, ironworking could be used to produce vast numbers of shields and daggers, enabling rulers to field much larger forces. No longer limited to fairly small forces of bronze-armed noble warriors on horseback, Chinese armies in the Warring States era also fielded tens of thousands of peasant foot soldiers armed with iron weapons.

Iron tools and weapons spread to China from west

Ironworking also brought economic benefits to China. Crop cultivation was vastly enhanced by the use of iron-bladed plows, pulled by oxen hitched to a wooden harness, and by iron-bladed spades, used in tilling soil and digging irrigation ditches to expand the amount of farmland. Iron picks and shovels were used in building earthen dams and dikes to protect against floods, earthen walls to defend against nomad attacks, and roads and canals to aid the movement of both armies and goods. Central Asian connections thus helped to expand warfare, farming, and commerce in early China.

Iron tools and weapons enhance farming, warfare, and commerce

The Classical Age of Chinese Philosophy

The Eastern Zhou era, with its ongoing warfare, political turmoil, and economic growth, also produced ideas intended to promote harmony and stability. These ideas laid the basis for China's main belief systems, including especially Confucianism, Daoism, and Legalism.

Confucius and his disciples.

Historians have noted that this era, from the eighth through third centuries B.C.E., also produced Buddhism, Jainism, and the Upanishads in India, the Avesta (sacred book) of Persia, the major Hebrew prophets, and the foremost Greek philosophers. Although China's great thinkers had no direct contact with those in distant societies, increasing connections among these societies doubtless fed the intellectual ferment that helped inspire some of history's main belief systems.

Confucianism: Noble-Minded Conduct and Familial Respect

The central Chinese philosopher was Kongfuzi (*KONG-FOO-DZUH*) or Master Kong the Sage (551–479 B.C.E.). Later known in the West as Confucius, he laid the foundations for China's foremost ethical system. Like other famous moral teachers, including the Buddha and Jesus, Confucius left behind no writings, so it has been hard to separate his ideas from those added later by his followers. His impact nonetheless has been enormous.

Born into a minor noble family in east central China, and raised in humble circumstances after his father's early death, Confucius aspired to a political career. He dreamed of becoming a wise and loyal official who, following in the footsteps of the Duke of Zhou, would help some ruler create a just society based on the wisdom of the past. For years he sought such a post, and briefly held several government positions. Frustrated, however, by administrative indifference to his ideas, he became a wandering teacher, earnestly preaching his convictions to a growing group of disciples.

Confucius aspires to help form a just society

After Confucius was gone, his followers compiled his reflections to produce the *Analects*, a collection of sayings, each typically prefaced by the phrase "The Master said . . ." As a whole, they depict a man deeply troubled by the chaos and corruption of his day, and eager to bring social order and harmony to the violent Eastern Zhou era. The *Analects* envision a society regulated not by rigid enforcement of laws, but by the virtuous behavior of its leaders and citizens. They idealize especially the honorable, "noble-minded" public servant who inspires the people by example and treats them with wisdom, moderation, compassion, and respect. Over the next several centuries, these ideas were elaborated and organized into **Confucianism**, a system of thought that would dominate Chinese public life for more than 2,000 years.

Disciples of Confucius compile his sayings and ideals

Although Confucians recognized the divinity called Heaven, and later built many temples, Confucianism was not so much a religion as an ethical philosophy. Based on the *Analects* and the Five Classics, a set of Chinese literary works compiled over many centuries, Confucian philosophy focused on human behavior rather than divine worship. Its main virtues included:

- *ren* (*RUN*), or "humanity," involving compassion, humane conduct, and benevolence;
- *li* (*LĒ*), or "ritual," the courtesy, etiquette, and civility by which people should treat one another; and
- *xiao* (*shē-OW*), or "filial piety," the devotion that a son owed to his father (and, by extension, that all people owed to their parents, ancestors, and leaders).

In promoting these virtues, Confucianism envisioned a hierarchical society in which all people knew their place, based on mutual respect between rulers and subjects, parents and children, spouses, siblings, and friends (the "five relationships"). Its main premise was that people would irresistibly follow and emulate wise, benevolent leaders. Although

Document 4.1 Excerpts from the *Analects*

In the *Analects*, followers of Confucius recorded his wise sayings and thoughtful exchanges with disciples. Over the centuries, his insights and advice would serve as guides for providing noble-minded public service and leading honorable lives.

The Master said: "Worthy admonitions cannot fail to inspire us, but what matters is changing ourselves. Reverent advice cannot fail to encourage us, but what matters is acting on it . . ."

The Master said: "Above all, be loyal and stand by your words. Befriend only those who are kindred spirits. And when you're wrong, don't be afraid to change."

Adept Lu asked about governing, and the Master said: "Put the people first, and reward their efforts well . . ."

Adept Lu asked: "To be called a noble official, what must a person be like?" "Earnest and exacting, but also genial," replied the Master. ". . . Earnest and exacting with friends, genial with brothers."

The Master said: "The people should be broadly educated by a wise teacher for seven years—then they can take up the weapons of war."

The Master said: "Sending the people to war without educating them first: that is called *throwing the people away*."

The Master said: "The noble-minded seek within themselves. Little people seek elsewhere."

The Master said: "The noble-minded stand above the fray with dignity. And when they band together with others, they never lose track of themselves."

The Master said: "The noble-minded don't honor a person because of something he said, nor do they dismiss something said because of the person who said it."

The Master said: "We're all the same by nature. It's living that makes us different."

Adept Chang asked Confucius: "What makes a person fit to govern?" "Honoring the five graces and despising the four deformities," replied the Master . . . "What are the five graces?" asked Adept Chang. "The noble-minded are generous without expense, hard working without resentment, wishful without greed, stately without arrogance, stern without cruelty . . ." "And what are the four deformities?" asked Chang. "Killing instead of teaching, which is called terror. Expecting results without telling people what you want, which is called tyranny. Issuing vague orders and expecting prompt action, which is called plunder. Grudging and miserly when giving people what they deserve, which is called officialdom."

SOURCE: Confucius, *The Analects,* translated by David Hinton (New York: Counterpoint, 1998) 97, 139, 148, 176, 195, 230–231.

elitist in upholding an all-male ruling class of scholars and gentlemen, Confucianism favored noble-mindedness of spirit rather than nobility of birth. Although conservative in championing the virtues and values of the past, Confucianism was progressive in stressing the rulers' duty to provide good government (see "Excerpts from the *Analects*").

The Confucian ethic had momentous implications for the practice of governance. The Master was not a revolutionary in the modern sense, but he clearly detested political oppression, as recorded in this parable: One day the Master came upon an old woman sitting by the mouth of a cave, weeping. When he asked her what was troubling her, she replied, "First my father-in-law, then my husband, and now my son were all killed by a tiger at this place." When Confucius inquired as to why she insisted on living in so dangerous an area, the grieving woman replied, "There is no oppressive government here." Confucius then said to his students, "My children, remember this. It is better to live among tigers than to live under a bad government."[1]

---

[1] James Legge, *The Life and Teachings of Confucius* (London, 1895) 67.

Mencius justifies rebellion against repressive rulers

The Master himself may not have intended his message to be subversive, but many of his followers taught that unjust leaders should be held accountable for their actions. Foremost among them was Mengzi (*MUNG-DZUH*), or Mencius, an eminent Chinese sage who lived from roughly 370 to 290 B.C.E. Mencius held that all humans are equal and good, and that a ruler must both practice and promote the virtue of *ren*. If a ruler failed to do so, Mencius claimed, it was a sign that the ruler had lost Heaven's Mandate, and his subjects had the right to rebel.

Confucianism holds rulers and officials to high moral standards

By holding rulers and officials to high moral standards, the Confucian tradition, over the centuries, promoted good governance and served as a check against tyranny. Some oppressive regimes sought to suppress Confucianism, but their efforts had little lasting success.

Daoism: The Way That Cannot Be Spoken

Daoism urges harmony with nature and avoidance of ambition

Another prominent school of ideas arising in the Eastern Zhou era was **Daoism** (*DOW-iz-um*), a naturalistic philosophy that, unlike Confucianism, had little use for organized social and political institutions. Its main text was the *Daodejing* (*DOW-DUH-JING*), or "Classic of the Way and Its Power," supposedly written in the sixth century B.C.E. by a legendary figure called Laozi (*LAOW-DZUH*), the Old Sage, but probably compiled later from sayings ascribed to him. Centered on the notion of a mysterious, unchanging cosmic force called *Dao* ("The Way"), Daoism was naturalistic in calling on people to live in harmony with nature. It was also passive, and even escapist, urging people to "be bland like melting ice," let go of control, avoid worldly ambition, and accept whatever came their way (see "Excerpts from *Daodejing*"). It delighted in noting that if there were no property there would be no theft, if there were no law there would be no crime, and if there were no fame there would be no disgrace. Beginning as a simple, romantic worldview, Daoism developed into a religion with numerous sacred rituals and shrines.

Unlike Confucianism, Daoism values silence, contemplation, and passivity

Daoism in many ways contrasted with Confucianism. While Confucians relished intellectual and political discourse, Daoists tended to be anti-intellectual and anti-political, focusing instead on silence, contemplation, and passivity. These values were reflected in Daoist precepts, often expressed as paradoxical sayings, such as, "Those who talk do not understand; those who understand do not talk," and, "The way that can be spoken of is not the true Way."

Chinese see Confucianism and Daoism as mutual correctives

Although Confucianism and Daoism might seem contradictory, many Chinese people espoused both. They saw them not as opposites but as mutual correctives, both necessary, each complementing the other. One could, for example, be Confucian in one's public life and Daoist in one's private life. Confucianism produced scholars and politicians, while Daoism inspired artists and poets, but each was essential to the Chinese culture and character.

Yin and Yang: The Balance of Forces in Nature

The balancing and blending of dissimilar concepts, such as those of Confucianism and Daoism, was a crucial characteristic of Chinese culture. This characteristic was reflected especially in another key concept that emerged in ancient China, the notion of **yin and yang**, a principle emphasizing the balancing and blending of natural forces.

Document 4.2 Excerpts from *Daodejing*

Unlike Confucianism, which promoted an active life of public service to others, Daoism advocated simplicity, passivity, avoidance of ambition, and conformity with a silent, shapeless cosmic force called Dao ("The Way"). The following excerpts from Daodejing ("Classic of the Way and Its Power") provide a sampling of basic Daoist ideals.

When you never strive, you never go wrong . . .

Just do what you do and then leave: such is the Way of Heaven . . .

Way is perennially nameless, an uncarved simplicity. Though small, it's subject to nothing in all beneath heaven . . .

Heaven mingling with earth sends down sweet dew, and the people free of mandates share justice among themselves . . .

Way flowing through all beneath heaven: it's like valley streams flowing into rivers and seas . . .

Way is perennially doing nothing, so there's nothing it doesn't do . . .

Uncarved nameless simplicity is the perfect absence of desire, and the absence of desire means repose: all beneath heaven at rest of itself . . .

Bustling around may overcome cold, but tranquility overcomes heat. Master lucid tranquility, and you'll govern all beneath heaven.

When all beneath heaven abides in Way, fast horses are kept to work the fields. When all beneath heaven forgets Way, war horses are bred among the fertility altars.

What calamity is greater than no contentment, and what flaw greater than passion for gain? The contentment of fathoming contentment—there lies the contentment that endures.

You can know all beneath heaven though you never step out the door, and you can see the Way of heaven though you never look out the window.

The further you explore, the less you know. So it is that a sage knows by going nowhere, names by seeing nothing, perfects by doing nothing . . .

. . . To work at Way brings less each day, still less and less until you're doing nothing yourself. And when you're doing nothing yourself, there's nothing you don't do.

To grasp all beneath heaven, leave it alone. Leave it alone, that's all, and nothing in all beneath heaven will elude you . . .

. . . a tree you can barely reach around grows from the tiniest rootlet; a nine-tiered tower starts as a basket of dirt; a thousand-mile journey begins with a single step.

Work at things and you ruin them; cling to things and you lose them. That's why a sage does nothing, and so ruins nothing, clings to nothing, and so loses nothing.

SOURCE: Lao Tzu, *Tao te ching*, translated by David Hinton (New York: Counterpoint, 2000) 10, 11, 35, 40, 54–57, 73.

Rather than seeing life as a conflict between mutually exclusive forces, such as good versus evil and hatred versus love, yin and yang expressed cosmic harmony and unity, with alternating forces supporting and completing each other. Yang represented light, heat, daytime, dryness, and masculinity, while yin signified darkness, coolness, nighttime, moistness, and femininity. Yang was active, aggressive, logical, and rational; yin was passive, nurturing, intuitive, and emotional. Yang was dominant in spring and summer; yin prevailed in fall and winter. Yang was rock and yin was water; yang had strength and yin had stamina; yang was the sun and yin was the moon.

> Yin-yang concept stresses natural harmony and balance, not good versus evil

As complementary forces, yin and yang both blended and gave way to each other, just as sun yielded to moon, day yielded to night, and summer yielded to fall. Nature needed both sun and rain, heat and coolness, and, of course, male and female. Society required both reason and emotion, strength and stamina, logic and intuition, action and passivity. Yin and yang represented a natural order based not on conflict and competition but on harmony, symmetry, and balance (see Figure 4.1).

Figure 4.1

Yin-Yang Symbol

The traditional symbol of yin and yang, with the light (yang) side (representing light, heat, daytime, dryness, and masculinity) blending into the dark (yin) side (representing darkness, coolness, nighttime, moistness, and femininity), signifies cosmic harmony and unity, with alternating forces supporting and completing each other.

The notion of yin and yang furnished Chinese people with a framework not only for understanding nature, but also for bringing balance to their everyday lives. Farmers, for example, had to have both strength and stamina, parents needed to be both assertive and nurturing, and the same person might be both a Confucian scholar by day and a Daoist poet by night. Indeed, Confucianism seemed to be rooted in rationality and logic, coinciding with yang, while Daoism relied on intuition and inspiration, corresponding with yin.

Legalism: Regulation, Coercion, and Control

At the end of the Eastern Zhou era, another approach arose that, unlike Daoism, saw harmony and order not as existing naturally in society, but as needing to be imposed on people from above. This approach evolved from the insights of Xunzi (*SHOON-DZUH*), a Confucian scholar who lived from approximately 300 to 230 B.C.E. Witnessing the disorder and violence of the Warring States era, Xunzi concluded that humans are by nature brutal and selfish, and that their ambitions and passions must be curbed by rigorous laws, institutions, rewards, and punishments. Although Xunzi was a Confucian, his disciples Hanfeizi (*HAHN-FĀ-DZUH*) and Li Si (*LĒ-SUH*) expanded his ideas into **Legalism**, a philosophy advocating strict enforcement of stringent laws by a powerful authoritarian state.

Legalism favors strong ruler to impose law, order, and stability

Legalists believed above all in law and order, maintaining that only an authoritarian regime could instill the fear and discipline needed to impose unity and control. If the state was to be strong and prosperous, Legalists asserted, the ruler must possess both the power and the will to enforce strict laws, to punish those who disobeyed, and to suppress all disunity and dissent.

The Birth of the Empire Under the Qin Dynasty

With Legalist backing Shihuangdi creates a huge Chinese empire

In 247 B.C.E., anxious to implement his ideas, the Legalist Li Si became a key official in the state of Qin (*CHIN*), a rising power in northwest China that nine years earlier had overthrown the last Eastern Zhou king. Under Li Si's guidance, a talented, ambitious new Qin ruler set out to create a mighty empire. In one eventful decade, from 231 to 221 B.C.E., he conquered all the other northern states and much of southern China as well (Map 4.4). For the first time ever, almost all of China was united under one ruler. He came to be called Shihuangdi (*SHUR-HWAHNG-DĒ*), that is, the First Emperor, the man whose spectacular tomb was described at the start of this chapter.

Map 4.4 The Qin Empire, 221–206 B.C.E.

In a single decade, from 231 to 221 B.C.E., the state of Qin in west-central China conquered most of the rest of the country, creating China's first empire. Note that the First Emperor, who conquered and ruled all the area shaded on this map, also expanded China's northern fortifications against nomadic invasions, thus creating China's first "Great Wall." How did the Qin Empire, which disintegrated soon after the First Emperor's death in 210 B.C.E., help set the stage for even larger and much longer-lasting Chinese empires?

The First Emperor

Ably assisted by Li Si, the First Emperor ruled a regime remarkable for both its accomplishments and its brutality. He abolished the conquered states, disarming their forces and executing their rulers. He divided China into provinces and districts headed by officials selected for their talent and loyalty. Rather than appointing his relatives or members of the old nobility, he instead chose able civil servants who were wholly accountable to him. He made the local nobles move to his capital so he could both keep them under close watch and take away their rural lands, causing them also to deplete their wealth by building costly new city homes. Inspired by Legalism and his own

The First Emperor creates a centralized, repressive Qin regime

ambitions, he maintained a huge army, a pervasive surveillance system, and a brutal penal code—branding, burning, boiling, or burying alive those who defied his will.

Nothing, it seemed, could escape the First Emperor's determination to regulate Chinese society. To improve command, communication, and commerce, he standardized the written language and laws, coins and taxes, weights and measures, and even the width of roads and axle-width of carts. To intimidate his subjects he made periodic grand inspection tours of his realm. To suppress dissent he is said to have banned the study of philosophy and history, burned the books on those subjects, and buried several hundred scholars alive (ensuring his eventual vilification by later Chinese historians).

> *The First Emperor standardizes laws, writing, money, weights, and roads*

Using vast armies of forced laborers, at a huge cost in human lives, the First Emperor constructed massive projects that testified to his magnificence and megalomania. His extravagant palace, for example, measured over 120,000 square feet and could house up to 10,000 persons. Even more colossal was his tomb, whose chance discovery and fantastic features are described at the start of this chapter. His more practical projects included a complex irrigation system, a network of canals connecting China's rivers, and more than 4,000 miles of roads, fifty paces wide, which extended like spokes to link his capital with the regions of his realm. His most renowned achievement, however, was to connect all the fortifications built in the north to protect against nomadic invasions. The resulting structure, 1,400 miles long, later rebuilt and extended, came to be known as the Great Wall of China.

> *The First Emperor builds huge palace, canals, roads, and first Great Wall*

As time went on, and as his inhumane policies alienated his people, the First Emperor grew increasingly paranoid. After several assassination attempts by embittered subjects, he became obsessed with the fear of death. He had oracles and magicians try to find him a formula for everlasting life, and he even sent out a sea expedition to search for "islands of immortality." These efforts apparently failed: in 210 B.C.E., on one of his grand inspection tours, the First Emperor fell ill and died.

China's Great Wall, now built of brick, began as an earthen barrier under the First Emperor.

The End of the Qin Dynasty

The First Emperor had intended that his dynasty would last 10,000 generations. Instead it outlived him by only four years. His death was followed by provincial rebellions that plunged China into chaos, and by government intrigues that killed both Li Si and the Second Emperor, leading in 206 B.C.E. to the Qin dynasty's collapse. The rebel leaders then battled among themselves until one of them, a former peasant named Liu Bang (*L'YOO-BAHNG*), perceived as a man of the people, emerged victorious in 202 B.C.E. Building upon the centralized state created by the First Emperor, but ruling far more flexibly and humanely, Liu Bang assumed the Mandate of Heaven, starting a dynasty called the Han (*HAHN*) that endured for over 400 years.

> *The Qin regime is overthrown after the First Emperor dies*

The Growth of the Empire Under the Han Dynasty

The Han dynasty (202 B.C.E.–220 C.E.), started by Liu Bang, presided over one of the world's largest and wealthiest domains. In size and population, it matched the vast Roman Empire, then flourishing in the West. The Han Empire also produced a large, effective imperial administration, a sophisticated urban culture and intellectual life, and

> *The Han Dynasty rules huge powerful empire for centuries*

major advances in technology and commerce. The dynasty's impact was so enduring that, even today, the Chinese still call themselves the Han people.

The Early Han: Confucian Bureaucracy and Military Expansion

Liu Bang, later known as Emperor Gaozu[2] (*GOW-DZUH*), achieved considerable success by both extending the Qin state bureaucracy and reducing its severity. During his brief reign (202–195 B.C.E.) he lowered taxes, moderated punishments, and invited Confucian scholars, rigorously repressed by the Qin regime, to serve as state officials. Under his successors, in fact, these scholars came to dominate the bureaucracy, and Confucianism became the official ideology. The result was a ruling synthesis, combining the central authority of Legalism with the humane civility of Confucianism, that would endure for two thousand years—a shining example of China's ability to balance and blend dissimilar forces into a successful system.

Han rulers blend Legalist authority with Confucian civility

In the first few centuries of Han rule the bureaucracy became more formal. Initially, the emperors simply asked local officials to recommend talented young men for government posts. In 165 B.C.E., however, the emperor started examining these candidates to determine which ones were best qualified. Then, to improve the preparation of candidates, in 124 B.C.E. the dynasty established an imperial university at Chang'an (*CHAHNG-AHN*), the capital, not far from modern Xi'an. Later the regime would use written exams, based on mastery of Confucian thought, to decide whom to appoint. These developments laid the groundwork for what would become a key feature of Chinese governance—a professional civil service made up of educated scholars. Elsewhere officials were often warriors trained in military combat; in China they were scholars educated in Confucian civility and ethics.

Han Empire forms the first strong, effective civil service bureaucracy

But China did not lack warriors. After early Han emperors consolidated their realm, Han Wudi (*WOO-DĒ*), the Han Martial Emperor (141–87 B.C.E.), built the Chinese army into an expansive force. In a vigorous series of military campaigns, he extended his control to the south into northern Vietnam, to the north into southern Manchuria and northern Korea, and to the west into distant Central Asia (Map 4.5). He also attacked the Xiongnu (*shē-ONG-NOO*), warlike nomads who had menaced northern China for years, beginning a long struggle that continued under his successors. At its height the Han Empire ruled a vast territory extending more than 3,000 miles east to west and 2,000 miles north to south, embracing almost 60 million people.

The Han Martial Emperor builds a huge army and conquers neighboring lands

Rebellion, Reform, and Ruin

Wudi's many wars, however, and the massive recruitments and harsh new taxes required to support these conflicts, exhausted both China's resources and its people's patience. His successors, less capable than he, were further weakened by repeated Xiongnu raids and internal revolts. The imperial court was racked by intrigues between the emperor's in-laws and his **eunuchs**, castrated males who ran his palace and guarded his many **concubines**, women who served him sexually to ensure that he would have a male heir. As the only males besides the emperor allowed to have contact with his concubines, these men were rendered sexually impotent to ensure that potential heirs born to these

Han Wudi and companions, as pictured by a later artist.

---

[2] Chinese emperors often were awarded a historical name that differed from their given name. *Gaozu*, for example, means *High Progenitor*. The historical name is sometimes preceded by the dynasty name, for example, *Qin Shihuangdi, Han Gaozu*. The *first* name is the *family* name in China.

Map 4.5 The Han Empire, 202 B.C.E.–220 C.E.

China's longest enduring empire was that of the Han Dynasty, which reigned for over 400 years, extending its rule west into Central Asia, south into Southeast Asia, and northeast into Manchuria and Korea, forging cultural and commercial connections with these diverse regions. Observe that the Han also conflicted and connected with the Xiongnu, warlike nomads who threatened China from the north. How did the dynasty's territorial expansion, and its conflicts with the Xiongnu, impact developments in China?

women were really the ruler's sons. Nonetheless, with their management of the palace and regular access to the emperor, talented and ambitious eunuchs often acquired great influence. In the process, they tended to clash with the royal in-laws, who likewise sought to use their position to gain power and wealth.

In 22 B.C.E., as palace intrigues between eunuchs and in-laws continued to cripple the court, revolts erupted throughout the empire. It looked as if the dynasty was losing Heaven's Mandate. Then, in 9 C.E., a palace coup deposed a child emperor and replaced him with Wang Mang (*WAHNG-MAHNG*), a devoted Confucian who had been on the young ruler's regency council.

Idealistic and egalitarian, Wang Mang launched a series of reforms designed to improve the common people's welfare. He abolished slavery, for example, and tried to take land away from wealthy landlords for use by the poor peasants. He also declared himself emperor, intending to start his own dynasty. But a series of droughts and bad harvests interrupted his plans, and his land transfers sparked fierce opposition among the rich

Palace intrigues among eunuchs and royal in-laws undermine Han rule

landlords. Then, in 11 C.E., a catastrophic Yellow River flood drowned hundreds of thousands and left millions homeless. As China descended into chaos, various groups began to revolt, demanding the return of the Han dynasty. In 23 C.E., when victorious rebels beheaded Wang Mang and ate the rest of his body, it became clear that they did not think he possessed the Mandate of Heaven.

The Later Han: Revival and Decline

After a few more years of chaos, Han rule was restored under Guangwudi (*GWAHNG-WOO-DĒ*), the Shining Martial Emperor, who reigned from 25 to 57 C.E., initiating an era known as the Later Han (25–220 C.E.). Guangwudi moved the capital east to Luoyang, perhaps because it was near his power base and perhaps also to signify a fresh start. For the next few generations, he and his heirs maintained peace and prosperity, thanks partly to their energetic and conscientious rule, partly to a long stretch of disaster-free weather, and partly to internal strife among the Xiongnu nomads who threatened northern China. In 89 C.E., Chinese generals took advantage of this strife to inflict a crushing defeat upon the nomads, thus ending for a while the chronic Xiongnu threat. In the following decade the generals restored Chinese rule in Central Asia, and one of them even ventured as far west as the Caspian Sea. By 100 C.E. the Han realm had recovered much of its former size and wealth.

The Shining Martial Empire restores Han rule and stability

During the next century, however, dynastic decline resumed. A succession of youthful and short-lived emperors set off a new series of conflicts between their in-laws and court eunuchs. Dismayed by these intrigues, several groups of Confucian civil servants and students sought to rebel in the 160s, only to be tortured and butchered in a wholesale purge. Then came floods and droughts, locust infestations that destroyed the crops, and a deadly epidemic (perhaps smallpox or plague), apparently brought to China by Central Asian nomads, that took millions of lives. The result was massive suffering and population decline, adding to the impression that the Han rulers were losing Heaven's Mandate.

Landlords impose serfdom, sparking mass rebellions

Taking advantage of the anarchy, powerful landlords seized the occasion to subject the villagers to serfdom, a status that bound them to perpetual service on the land. This action in turn triggered peasant revolts, led by a rebel group called the Yellow Turbans, whose head cloths signified solidarity with the earth, traditionally associated in China with the color yellow. Han armies ultimately crushed these revolts, but the generals then took the land for themselves and emerged as regional warlords. After the year 190 C.E., when one of these generals seized Luoyang, deposed the reigning ruler, and slaughtered hundreds of his relatives and eunuchs, all semblance of centralized authority ceased. In 220 C.E., after several more disastrous decades of chaos and civil war, another general forced the last Han emperor to abdicate, officially ending one of China's longest, strongest, and most illustrious dynasties.

Revolts and civil war end Han rule in 220 C.E.

Society, Technology, and the Silk Road

Nonetheless, while the Han dynasty lasted, China boasted one of the world's most stable and productive societies, and many of the world's most useful technologies. As it extended its reach into Central Asia, China also increased its commerce with other cultures along a network of trade routes that came to be called the Silk Road.

Han Society

Han society, like that of other ancient civilizations, was based mainly on village farming and herding. In northern China, where the climate was cool and dry, farmers grew wheat and millet. In the south, where it was warmer and wetter, they mainly raised rice in fields that were flooded to provide continuous moisture. Many peasants also raised chickens and pigs, and some had oxen or water buffalo to help plow the fields. Most agrarian labor, however, was accomplished by human effort.

Patriarchal Chinese families include all living relatives and dead ancestors

Chinese peasants' lives were centered on their families, including not just their parents and children but also the rest of their living relatives and even their departed ancestors, widely believed to be actively concerned with the fortunes of their descendants. Families were ruled by their patriarchs, elder males who made the major decisions, and these men consulted with the spirits of family forebears and conducted ceremonies to venerate both their ancestors and the gods. All family members were expected to obey their elders and superiors.

Women seen as subservient to men in traditional Chinese society

Chinese women, as a rule, were subordinate to men. A bride's father arranged her marriage, typically providing a dowry, and she then became part of her new husband's family. Due to such customs, daughters were often seen by their parents as a burden, to be raised and fed as children only to join and benefit another family as adults. Girls were thus treated as inferior to boys, and young women were trained chiefly to serve as wives and mothers. Wives were required to cook, make clothes, and clean—in Chinese script the character for wife was a woman using a broom. They were also expected to help in the fields when needed and, above all, to bear and raise sons. Women's lives were said to be governed by the "three submissions:" first to their fathers when they were young, second to their husbands when they were married, and third to their sons when they were ultimately widowed.

Chinese women, despite subordinate status, often run their households

Despite their duties and submissions, Chinese women were to some extent protected by Confucian doctrine, which said that fathers, husbands, and sons should treat them with respect and dignity. In addition, Chinese custom made women the household managers, giving those with strong characters an opportunity for influence within the home and family.

Chinese peasants endure poverty and harsh labor

The lives of most peasants were likewise confined. In theory, farmers were highly valued, since the food they grew was vital to survival. Indeed, the Confucian social order ranked farmers higher than merchants, since the former were producers while the latter were viewed as mere traffickers and traders. In reality, however, this ranking meant little. Most peasants lived in poverty, dwelling in villages of wood and bamboo huts, often toiling in service to a wealthy landlord. They worked the fields, tilling, hoeing, and harvesting, with little or no protection from the heat, wind, rain, or cold. Peasants were also expected to pay taxes, to provide the state with periodic labor for building public works projects, and often to serve in the army. Rural life was dreary, with few diversions to break the daily routine.

Urban life provides comforts, entertainments, and diversions

Urban life was far more diverse and sophisticated. Metropolitan areas such as Chang'an and Luoyang, the two great Han capitals, had overall populations of up to a quarter million people, with some 100,000 of them living within the city walls. Wealthy officials and merchants resided in two- or three-story homes made of stucco or wood, with gardens and terraces, plentiful food, and servants to tend their needs. Poorer residents, mostly artisans and laborers, lived in much humbler circumstances, but unlike peasants they had access to urban recreations and diversions. Major cities had palaces, parks, marketplaces, and temples; Chang'an even had a zoo. Entertainment ranged from music, art, and poetry to magic shows, juggling acts, and puppet performances.

Urban life in Han China also had a seamy side. As in modern cities there were gambling houses, brothels, and gangs of youths who roamed the streets. Public executions, designed to deter both crime and disloyalty, typically attracted large crowds. Still, officials posted in small provincial towns, deploring their humdrum existence, often dreamed of reassignment to one of the large, vibrant cities.

Technical and Commercial Creativity

Han cities were also centers of creativity, commerce, and craftsmanship. Here scholars, officials, doctors, inventors, and artisans, freed from the need to farm, developed ideas and techniques that would distinguish Chinese culture as enterprising and ingenious.

Scholars and bureaucrats, for example, exchanged ideas and kept records by writing with small brushes on paper—a product invented in Han China. Astronomers charted the paths of planets and recorded sunspots; other scientists studied acoustics and measured earthquakes. Doctors diagnosed diseases, prescribed herbal remedies and drugs, and discovered the circulation of blood. Physicians also used acupuncture, the insertion of thin needles at various points in the body, to relieve pain and cure ailments, theoretically by restoring the body's yin and yang balance. Farmers benefited from innovations such as wheelbarrows to help carry their loads, water mills to help grind their grain, iron plows to help turn their soil, and harnesses to enhance the labor of their oxen and buffalo.

Commerce and craftsmanship also reflected Chinese ingenuity. Metropolitan markets had a wide array of shops and stalls run by manufacturers and merchants. Their wares were produced by skilled artisans, who worked with bronze, pottery, lacquer, jade, and silk to make tools, utensils, plates, vessels, jewelry, and clothing. These goods might then be purchased directly by people of means or sold to merchants who took the products elsewhere and resold them at a profit. Their travels were aided by a network of canals and roads, complete with suspension bridges. Carts and wagons traversed the roads, while boats plied the rivers and canals, carrying commodities all across China— and, increasingly, beyond (Map 4.6).

Model of a Han era house

Scholarship, science, medicine, and farming flourish in Han China

Networks of roads and canals aid commerce and crafts

The Silk Road and the Sea Trade

As conquest and commerce increased contacts with other cultures, Chinese products came to be highly prized in other lands. Indeed, by the second century B.C.E., several land and sea routes linking the Han Empire with southern and western Asia were already in operation. But long distance trade was risky, due to bandits, storms, and treacherous terrain.

Then, in 126 B.C.E., a Chinese general named Zhang Qian (*JAHNG chē-AN*), after spending many years in Central Asia in the service of the Martial Emperor (Wudi), returned to China with reports of peoples, plants, and products hitherto unknown in the Han Empire. He told of lands far beyond the western wastelands, such as Bactria, Ferghana (*fur-GAH-nuh*), and Persia, with bountiful vineyards whose grapes produced fine wines, as well as splendid horses superior to any in China. He also said that in markets of these regions he had sometimes seen Chinese products, including bamboo canes and silk cloth, no doubt conveyed there along early trade routes.

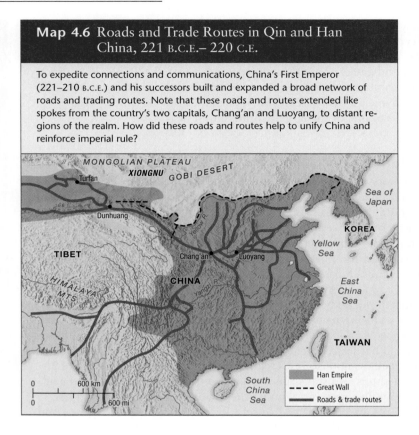

Map 4.6 Roads and Trade Routes in Qin and Han China, 221 B.C.E.– 220 C.E.

To expedite connections and communications, China's First Emperor (221–210 B.C.E.) and his successors built and expanded a broad network of roads and trading routes. Note that these roads and routes extended like spokes from the country's two capitals, Chang'an and Luoyang, to distant regions of the realm. How did these roads and routes help to unify China and reinforce imperial rule?

Chinese conquest of Central Asia boosts commerce with other cultures

Eager to expand his power and wealth, Wudi sent armies into Central Asia, adding cities and realms to his domains and making them tributaries of China. For many of these new subjects this arrangement had advantages, as Chinese soldiers provided protection from bandits, while Han officials sent valuable silk to retain the tributaries' allegiance. The Chinese presence also helped to establish and sustain the long-distance trading network later called the Silk Road.

Silk Road provides commercial connections across Eurasia

The **Silk Road**, named for the precious Chinese fabric often conveyed along its route, was actually a series of trails that connected trading towns across the heart of Asia. The route extended from China westward for thousands of miles across central Asia, with links from there through Bactria into India and through Persia into Mesopotamia and the eastern Mediterranean (Map 4.7). The Silk Road thus provided a commercial connection, though rather tenuous and treacherous, among the various societies of Eurasia and North Africa.

Merchants typically did not travel the whole length of the road; instead they made their way back and forth between certain trading cities, where they could exchange the goods they had brought for goods coming from the other direction. Merchandise was thus transported in a series of stages, passing through many hands along the way. Since

Map 4.7 The Silk Road and Sea Trade, by First Century B.C.E.

The Silk Road, opened by about 100 B.C.E., was a complex series of trade routes linking towns across Asia, providing connections among regions such as China, India, Persia, and West Asia. Note that overland links connected the Silk Road to several sea ports, from which goods were shipped by sea lanes connecting East and Southeast Asia, Indonesia, India, Persia, Arabia, and Africa. What key products were shipped along the Silk Road, and how were they transported? Along with goods, what else did the Silk Road and sea trade convey?

all who handled these items wished to make a profit, and since numerous local princes often imposed tolls and fees, items might well cost many times more at their final destination than they did at their point of origin.

Nonetheless the Silk Road flourished for more than a thousand years, as did the bustling cities and towns that grew up along its route. Located at key passes and junctures, cities such as Dunhuang (*DUN-WAHNG*), Kashgar (*KAHSH-gar*), Samarkand (*SAH-mur-KAHND*) and Bukhara (*boo-KAH-ruh*) bustled with traders, money-changers, camel breeders, and guides, and teemed with markets full of exotic goods. Less celebrated, but no less important, were many smaller settlements along the way, where travelers found rest and recreation as well as food and water for their horses and camels. Some of the cities were independent, with their own ruling princes and dynasties, but many in time came under the protection of larger domains such as China and Persia.

Trading towns flourish along the Silk Road for centuries

Goods from India, China, Europe, and West Asia are exchanged along Silk Road

Traffic on the trade routes typically consisted of items not produced in the country of destination. From the west came fine horses, highly treasured in China, as well as grapes and wines, olives and oils, precious stones and metals, jewelry, and arts and crafts. From the south came Indian cottons, along with cinnamon, ginger, and other Asian spices that were highly valued for flavoring food and for making medications, perfumes, and magic potions. From the east came Chinese pottery, bronze ware, and lacquerware, prized throughout Eurasia. But of all the choice items that made their way westward, perhaps the most treasured were the fine fabrics for which the Silk Road was named. By the first century B.C.E., Chinese silk clothing, with its brilliant colors and exquisite texture, was in fashion among the wealthy as far west as Rome.

Camel caravans transport goods along Silk Road

Cargoes were conveyed along the Silk Road sometimes by horses and wagons, but often by caravans of camels, especially the dual-humped Bactrian variety, whose shaggy hair helped them endure the harsh, windy Central Asian winters. In time camel keepers crossbred these creatures with single-humped Arabian dromedaries, producing a larger and stronger camel that still had a warm shaggy coat. Saddled with bulging sacks, draped on both sides to equalize the weight, and skillfully led by trained guides across mountains and deserts, these ill-tempered but invaluable animals carried loads weighing hundreds of pounds for dozens of miles a day.

Bactrian camel.

Some Chinese merchants, especially those near the southern coast and far from the Central Asian land routes, conducted their trade by sea. But as with the land routes, so along the sea lanes (Map 4.7), merchants and vessels rarely made the entire trip from one end of the line to the other. Instead, Chinese vessels typically traveled the South China Sea to trade with Southeast Asia and the lands later known as Malaya and Indonesia. From there some goods were transshipped, in Malayan or Indian vessels, to India and Sri Lanka, and thence in Persian or Arab crafts to Persia, Arabia, and Egypt. From Egypt some items were resold into the Mediterranean network, eventually ending up in places such as Greece or Rome.

Sea lanes link China with India, Persia, Arabia, Egypt, and Europe

Along with goods, diseases and beliefs were at times conveyed on the Silk Road. Epidemics of smallpox and plague, for example, including deadly outbreaks that ravaged both China and Rome in the second century C.E., spread through Central Asia along the trade routes. In that same century, as we saw in Chapter 3, Buddhist beliefs spread from India to Central Asia, and from there eventually to China along the Silk Road.

Silk Road connections also spread diseases and beliefs.

Despite the importance of the Silk Road and sea lanes, however, the contacts they provided between China and other lands were tenuous and indirect. The Chinese became acquainted with the goods of other regions, for example, but learned little about their people. And the Western societies that valued Chinese goods had little real knowledge of the eastern culture that produced such marvelous merchandise.

Chapter Review

Putting It in Perspective

In many ways, early China was similar to other ancient societies. Like the others, Chinese society began along a river, was based on agriculture, and developed extensive trade networks and large cities. Like the others, it came to be ruled by monarchs who had semi-divine status and governed by means of officials and armies. Like the others, its social structure was stratified, with an aristocratic elite, urban classes of merchants and artisans, and a rural peasantry that made up most of the population.

In other respects, however, Chinese society was distinctive. The Mandate of Heaven, for example, could justify rebellion against rulers who failed to furnish stability and security, a concept unknown in most other early cultures. The Confucian ethic, which held state officials accountable for public welfare, conveyed the relatively rare idea that government should serve society. The notion of yin and yang, with its focus on balance and harmony, provided a perspective that differed from the view of reality as a struggle between good and evil. And the Chinese civil service, with its stress on education and ethics, gave China a government whose officials were trained as scholars rather than as military leaders.

As China's contacts with other cultures grew, it was increasingly influenced by these connections. From Central Asian nomads, the Chinese learned to use chariots and cast bronze, and later to ride horses and forge iron. From the Silk Road and sea trade, the Chinese became acquainted with goods from India, Persia, and West Asia, while Chinese products likewise became available in these places. China nonetheless retained its distinctive character, a land whose products were prized, but whose ways were largely unknown, in expansive societies far to China's west, such as Persia, Greece, and Rome.

Reviewing Key Material

KEY CONCEPTS

ancestor worship, 85
Mandate of Heaven, 87
dynastic cycle, 88
Confucianism, 90
Daoism, 92

yin and yang, 92
Legalism, 94
eunuchs, 97
concubines, 97
Silk Road, 102

KEY PEOPLE

King Wu, 86
Duke of Zhou, 87
King You, 88
Confucius (Kongfuzi), 90
Laozi, 92
Mencius (Mengzi), 92
Xunzi, 94
Hanfeizi, 94
Li Si, 94

Shihuangdi (First
   Emperor), 94
Liu Bang (Emperor
   Gaozu), 96
Wudi (Martial Emperor), 97
Wang Mang, 98
Guangwudi (Shining
   Martial Emperor), 99
Zhang Qian, 101

ASK YOURSELF

1. In what ways was Chinese civilization similar to other ancient civilizations, and in what ways was it distinct? How do you account for these distinctions?

2. What were the advantages and disadvantages of the Chinese writing system? How did it benefit an empire that was vast and linguistically diverse?

3. What were the advantages and disadvantages of the Mandate of Heaven concept and the pattern of dynastic cycle? How did these concepts affect the development of the Chinese empire?

4. How did the concept of yin and yang differ from notions of good versus evil? How did the concept help the Chinese to embrace disparate belief systems such as Confucianism and Daoism?

5. Why did Legalist principles prove effective in creating a vast empire, but ineffective in maintaining it for long? Why did the Han ruling synthesis, combining elements of Legalism and Confucianism, prove so successful and enduring?

GOING FURTHER

Adshead, S. A. M. *China in World History*. 3rd ed. 2000.

Chang, Kwang-chih. *The Archaeology of Ancient China*. 4th ed. 1986.

Clements, J. *Confucius: A Biography*. 2005.

De Bary, T., ed. *Sources of Chinese Tradition*. 2000.

De Grazia, S., ed. *Masters of Chinese Political Thought*. 1973.

Di Cosmo, Nicola. *Ancient China and Its Enemies*. 2002.

Ebrey, Patricia B., et al. *Pre-Modern East Asia*. 2006.

Fairbank, J. K. *China: A New History*. 1992.

Fong, W. *Great Bronze Age of China*. 1980.

Franck, Irene, and D. Brownstone. *The Silk Road: A History*. 1986.

Grotenhuis, E. T., ed. *Along the Silk Road*. 2002.

Hansen, Valerie. *The Open Empire*. 2000.

Hinsch, Bret. *Women in Early Imperial China*. 2002.

Holcombe, Charles. *The Genesis of East Asia*. 2001.

Hsu, Cho-yun, and J. M. Linduff. *Western Zhou Civilization*. 1988.

Keightley, D. *The Origins of Chinese Civilization*. 1983.

Knapp, Ronald. *China's Walled Cities*. 2000.

Li Xueqin. *Eastern Zhou and Qin Civilizations*. 1985.

Loewe, Michael. *Everyday Life in Early Imperial China*. 1988.

Loewe, Michael. *The Pride That Was China*. 1990.

Mote, F. W. *Intellectual Foundations of China*. 2nd ed. 1989.

Needham, J. *Science in Traditional China*. 1981.

Shaughnessy, E. L., ed. *China: Empire and Civilization*. 2005.

Shwartz, Benjamin I. *The World of Thought in Ancient China*. 1985.

Temple, Robert. *The Genius of China*. 1986.

Van Norden, V. W., ed. *Confucius and the Analects*. 2002.

Waley, Arthur. *Three Ways of Thought in Ancient China*. 1983.

Wang, Zhongshu. *Han Civilization*. 1982.

Whitfield, Susan. *Life Along the Silk Road*. 2001.

Whitfield, Susan, ed. *The Silk Roads*. 2004.

Wood, Francis. *The Silk Road*. 2002.

Key Dates and Developments

by 7000 B.C.E.	Farming in Yellow River valley
2200–1750 B.C.E.	Xia dynasty
1750–1122 B.C.E.	Shang dynasty
1122–770 B.C.E.	Western Zhou dynasty
770–256 B.C.E.	Eastern Zhou dynasty
551–479 B.C.E.	Confucius
by 500 B.C.E.	Laozi and origins of Daoism
403–221 B.C.E.	Warring States Era (Mencius, Xunzi)
231–221 B.C.E.	China united by Qin Shihuangdi
221–210 B.C.E.	Reign of Qin Shihuangdi (First Emperor)
202 B.C.E.–6 C.E.	Early Han dynasty
202–195 B.C.E.	Reign of Han Gaozu (Liu Bang)
147–87 B.C.E.	Reign of Han Wudi (Martial Emperor)
by 100 B.C.E.	Origins of the Silk Road
9–23 C.E.	Reign of Wang Mang
25–220 C.E.	Later Han dynasty

Early American Societies: Connection and Isolation, 20,000 B.C.E.–1500 C.E.

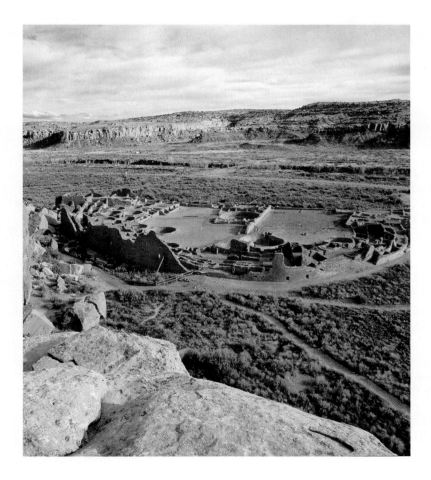

Pueblo Bonito, Chaco Canyone, New Mexico

Early Americans settled in many different parts of the western hemisphere. Their settlements conformed architecturally to their differing locations, as the ruins of this site in New Mexico are appropriate to a desert canyon setting (page 114).

Early in May 1945, as Soviet troops captured Berlin and ended World War II in Europe, a young Soviet soldier saw that the German National Library was on fire. He was able to save one book from the flames: an exceedingly rare collection of three manuscripts written by the Maya, an American Indian society that had flourished in present-day Guatemala and Mexico before the tenth century C.E. Fascinated by the symbols in the manuscript, the soldier—Yuri Knosorov—returned to the Soviet Union, left the army, and earned a degree in linguistics at Moscow State University.

In 1952 Knosorov quietly published an article entitled "Ancient Writing of Central America." Scholars had been unable to decipher Mayan writing, but his study of it convinced him that the symbols, called glyphs, represented ideas rather than sounds, as experts had previously thought. If true, this would make Mayan writing similar to the hieroglyphic writing of ancient Egypt, and would suggest ways to decipher it. In 1953 his article caught the attention of Tania Proskouriakoff, who had fled the Russian Revolution as an 8-year-old girl in 1917 and had earned a degree in architecture at Penn State. Proskouriakoff had studied Mayan architecture for two decades. She concluded that the figures depicted in Mayan pictorial writing were not gods but ordinary people. This insight, combined with that of Knosorov, led to one of the great intellectual breakthroughs of modern times: the decipherment of Mayan writing. Finally, three decades later, scholars were confidently translating Mayan glyphs and reaching a deeper understandings of Mayan society, one of the most complex of those formed by the peoples known as American Indians. Without the work of Knosorov and Proskouriakoff, much of what this chapter will say about the Maya would have remained unknown.

Areas of Amerind Settlement

Origins and Arrival of the Amerinds

Human life originated in eastern Africa and spread outward to other continents through migration. North and South America, remote from eastern Africa, were the last continents to be populated by humans. When groups of hunting-gathering peoples entered North America through Alaska and pushed southward in search of food and a milder climate, they found abundant wildlife that had never been hunted by humans and therefore did not fear them. Some of these people remained hunter-gatherers, pursuing many mammal species to extinction; others, thousands of years later, turned to agriculture in regions with fertile soils and abundant rainfall.

In most of the Western Hemisphere, human communities remained small and relatively isolated from one another. Some developed towns and even long-range trade networks, and some attempted to combine their societies into larger confederations, but their small populations did not generally require or give rise to complex political and social systems. In two regions, however, complex societies did develop: **Mesoamerica**, which comprises Mexico and northern Central America, and that portion of the Andean mountain range that stretches from Ecuador through Peru to Bolivia and northern Chile. Peoples in these regions were also the only ones able to offer organized resistance against the Europeans who invaded in the sixteenth century of the Common Era.

The Europeans mistakenly thought that the islands of the Caribbean where they first landed were part of the Spice Islands, or eastern "Indies," and so they called the people they encountered *Indians*. This term is still used. In recent years the term *Native Americans* gained popularity with some Indian and non-Indian groups, but it is technically inaccurate, since no human life was "native" to the Western Hemisphere. In this book, we follow anthropological practice in designating these people as **Amerinds** (*AM-uh-rinds*), or American Indians, to distinguish them from the Indians of Asia.

The first humans to reach the Western Hemisphere either walked or traveled in boats from Asia to Alaska. Anthropological evidence clearly points to their Asiatic heritage. Amerind languages are similar in syntax to those of northeastern Asia; Amerinds physically resemble the Mongolian peoples of central Asia, an ethnic group that at one time populated most of northeastern Asia; and, in overwhelming numbers, Amerinds have Type O blood carrying a specific antigen found only in Mongolian peoples.

Most Amerinds, however, do not accept these anthropological conclusions regarding their ancestry, preferring native religious accounts that tell of their origins in the Western Hemisphere. Navajo accounts of the Creation, for example, assert that the first American Indians ascended through three subterranean worlds before finally settling in this one, the fourth world. Snohomish lore states that the Creator and Changer began making the world and its peoples in the East, after which he slowly moved westward, creating as he came. The Amerinds, according to the Snohomish, were created in the West, in what came to be called the Americas.

Presuming that the linguistic and biological evidence is correct raises another question: how did the Amerinds cross from Asia to America? At least twice during the Ice Ages of the Pleistocene period, first between 50,000 and 40,000 B.C.E. and again between 26,000 and 8000 B.C.E., tremendous quantities of water were trapped in immense ice caps and glaciers, thus lowering ocean levels by several hundred feet. The Bering Strait, separating Siberia from Alaska, is only 120 feet deep; during the Ice Ages it stood hundreds of feet above sea level, forming a land bridge between Siberia and Alaska. At one point around 18,000 B.C.E. the land bridge was approximately 1,000 miles wide from north to south.

The Bering land bridge was used by caribou, reindeer, wooly mammoth, camels, and giant sloths. Some of these species survived in the Western Hemisphere, while others were hunted to extinction by the Amerinds. Since there is archeological proof of human occupation of the Americas beginning between 12,000 and 10,000 B.C.E., most scholars assume that Amerinds crossed around that time, that is, during the second long era in which the land bridge was exposed. There are no cultural artifacts or human bones datable to the earlier era of the land bridge, more than 40,000 years ago. Moreover, the absence of evidence of fur clothing and subterranean (or pit) houses, either in America or in northeastern Asia earlier than 15,000 years ago, supports the more recent dating, as protective clothing and underground dwellings would have been essential to the survival of nomadic groups in the frigid Siberian-Alaskan climate.

Amerinds move from the Eastern to the Western Hemisphere

Alternative accounts of Amerind origins

Clovis arrowheads found at sites in New Mexico, Arizona, and Colorado.

Arrows indicate the probable arrival and dispersal routes of the Amerinds. Note the enormous ice sheets that covered much of present-day Canada, and the southward flow of peoples from present-day Alaska through an ice-free corridor. This arrival pattern is the most widely accepted hypothesis, but not the only one: some archeologists suggest that Amerinds may have arrived before the North American glacier began melting and then traveled down the coast in boats rather than moving overland. If the most widely accepted hypothesis is true, why would many Amerinds have continued moving southward, rather than all stopping in the present-day United States?

Extent of glaciation c. 10,000 B.C.E.

Bering land Bridge c. 10,000 B.C.E.

Route of colonization

Early Amerind settlement

Complicating this theory is evidence of an extensive, impassable barrier of ice separating the area now called Alaska from northwestern Canada between 21,000 and 11,000 B.C.E. Only after that time did the climate warm sufficiently to create ice-free corridors along the continental divide (Map 5.1). Humans could pass through these corridors southward to Mesoamerica and from there to South America. Simultaneously the land bridge flooded and future human migration would have been possible only by boat. Many scholars therefore conclude that people crossed from Siberia to Alaska around 14,000 years ago, remained there for about a millennium, and moved south sometime after 11,200 B.C.E.

Most of the artifacts and skeletal remains found in the Americas are consistent with this explanation. However, DNA evidence from living South American Indians analyzed in 1994 indicates a probable human arrival date between 27,000 and 20,000 B.C.E. Further study in 1997 yielded a date between 41,000 and 31,000 B.C.E., before the peak of the last Ice Age, when the Canadian ice sheets merged. Coast-hopping in boats could have taken Amerinds down the entire Pacific coast of the Americas in fewer than twenty years. Since coastal settlements, if they existed, would have eventually been flooded by melting glaciers, archeological evidence would be unobtainable.

Historians dispute the timing of the Amerind arrival

As these analyses were being published in the late 1990s, dramatic archeological findings at Monte Verde in southern Chile appeared to confirm the existence there of an Amerind village dating to between 14,000 and 10,500 B.C.E. That would place Amerinds at the southern tip of South America before the ice sheets had melted sufficiently to permit human passage. But if the DNA evidence is true, why have no human remains from 20,000–40,000 B.C.E. been found in the Western Hemisphere? Is it because no such remains exist? Or have archeologists not been digging in the right places, or not yet dug deeply enough?

All such speculations are plausible, yet none is supported by convincing evidence. There are other intriguing findings from archeological digs. The Meadowcroft Rockshelter site in southwestern Pennsylvania contains artifacts that may have been fabricated as early as 14,000 B.C.E. Skulls found in Kennewick, Washington, and Spirit Cave, Nevada, suggest that not all Amerinds were of Central Asian origin. Faces reconstructed from these skulls resemble people from the South Pacific islands rather than Mongolia. In the first decade of the twenty-first century, we know that the Amerinds arrived in the Americas from somewhere in Asia. But that is all we know for certain.

The Amerinds of North America

The first people to set foot in North America were nomadic hunter-gatherers. Agriculture appeared about four thousand years later, apparently beginning before 3000 B.C.E. in southern Mexico. The first domesticated plants were probably pumpkins and chili peppers, grown perhaps as early as 7000 B.C.E. Maize (or corn) appeared in central Mexico around 5000 B.C.E. and in southern Mexico 2500 years after that. Between 2000 and 1000 B.C.E., farming villages emerged in central Mexico. Available evidence suggests that the idea of domesticating plants spread northward and southward from Mesoamerica. In North America, farming reached what is now the southwestern United States between 3500 and 2500 B.C.E., the "Eastern Woodlands" of the United States by 1000 B.C.E., and

American agriculture begins in southern Mexico

southern Canada sometime around 500 B.C.E. Agriculture therefore spread north from Mesoamerica over most of North America thousands of years after its appearance in the river civilizations of Asia, delaying the development of North American settled societies for an equivalent period.

Since few North American Amerinds had written languages, what we know of their early societies is based largely on archeological evidence and oral tradition. Scholars have categorized their societies (before the European invasion) into four principal types: hunter-gatherer bands, limited-scale tribal societies, full-scale tribal societies, and complex mound-building and trading societies.

Two Hunter-Gatherer Bands

Hunter-gatherers adapt to environmental conditions

Two North American societal groups, the Arctic and the Great Basin, lacked any genuine political organization. The environments these groups lived in hindered organizational development. In the *Arctic*, where the Eskimo (or Inuit) people lived, frozen, snow-covered ground and brief or nonexistent growing seasons made organized agriculture impossible. Their shelters, made of ice, often melted during the summer, further discouraging permanent settlement. The preinvasion Eskimo lived in small nomadic bands under the informal leadership of whoever happened to be the most proficient hunter. The *Great Basin* societies of Utah and Nevada, such as the Paiute (*PĪ-oot*) and Shoshone (*shō-SHŌ-nē*) peoples, were similarly nomadic, moving about the desert in family units during the lengthy summers and coming together in villages during the winters. Each family had its own leader.

Five Limited-Scale Tribal Societies

Nomadic peoples unite into tribes

More complex political organization emerged in five regions, where societies sometimes coalesced into **tribes**—large associations of villages, bands, or clans that share a common language and often a common leader. But tribes functioned only occasionally—during wartime, for example. Most of the time, these Amerinds associated in individual villages, bands, or clans. Authority was therefore mixed: family elders decided some issues, clan leaders others, and tribal leaders yet others.

In the eastern Canadian *Sub-Arctic* (Map 5.2), the Algonquian (*al-GON-kwē-un*) peoples banded together for the purpose of hunting caribou, a staple of their diet and an animal that, since it traveled in large herds, was best hunted by groups of at least a few dozen people. Hunting thus required that hunting bands combine into tribes, although the affiliation was loose and the tribes had little other impact on everyday life.

Along the *Northwest Coast*, from present-day Oregon north to Alaska, lived diverse maritime peoples whose access to rich food sources encouraged the formation of densely populated fishing villages. These people lived largely by hunting and by fishing the rivers and coastal waters for salmon and seafood, which they preserved by smoking so it would sustain them year round. From the region's great evergreen forests they built splendid wooden homes and carved large dugout canoes and elaborate totem poles that traced their genealogies. Some of their villages combined to form tribes, while others remained fiercely independent. In the neighboring *Plateau* region,

Totem poles from western Canada, carved from Western Red Cedar and depicting real or mythical events.

Map 5.2 North American Amerind Culture Areas, ca. 1500 C.E.

Many Amerind peoples moved through Canada and settled in what is now the United States. The more temperate climate there made agriculture possible, and the Great Plains were filled with buffalo and other large mammals that could be hunted for food and hides. Observe the distribution of peoples across this temperate climate zone: no region was free from settlement. What distinctions in lifestyle might be expected across such a wide area?

INUITS

KUTCHINS

INUITS

TLINGITS

INUITS

ARCTIC

Hudson Bay

INUITS

SUB-ARCTIC

BEAVERS

CREES

CREES

BELLA COOLAS

KWAKIUTLS

BLACKFEET

MANDANS

CHIPPEWAS

ALGONQUINS

HURONS

NORTHWEST COAST

PLATEAU

NEZ PERCÉS

CROWS

LAKOTAS

EASTERN WOODLANDS

IROQUOIS (HAUDENOSAUNEE)

COOS

SHOSHONES

CHEYENNES

POMOS

GREAT BASIN

GREAT PLAINS

MIAMIS

LENI-LENAPES

SHAWNEES

POWHATAN

CALIFORNIA

HOPIS

ARAPAHOS

OSAGES

APACHES

CHEROKEE

NAVAJOS

PUEBLOS

HOHOKAMS

COMANCHES

SOUTHEAST

ATLANTIC OCEAN

APACHES

NATCHEZ

SOUTHWEST

Gulf of Mexico

PACIFIC OCEAN

MESO-AMERICA

Caribbean Sea

0   500 km

0   500 mi

Anasazi cliff dwelling in the Canyon de Chelly, Arizona territory, photographed in 1873.

encompassing the inland areas of Washington, Oregon, and Idaho, people were originally grouped into individual villages, but eventually learned tribal organization from others to their southeast.

In the *Southwest* there emerged a wide variety of societies, ranging from Navajo and Apache (*NAH-vuh-hō, uh-PATCH-ē*) nomadic bands to the town-dwelling Pueblo (*PWĀ-blō*) Indians, who built walled settlements with central plazas and residences made of adobe (*ah-DŌ-bē*) brick or masonry (see page 107). Flourishing from the second through fourteenth centuries C.E., the early Pueblo peoples, also called Anasazi (*ah-nuh-SAH-zē*), grew maize, squash, and beans using complex irrigation techniques, and produced fine pottery, woven baskets, and cotton cloth. At one point, perhaps for protection, they built cliff dwellings and multistory terraced apartment houses, guarded by watchtowers. Many such cliff houses still survive in Arizona and New Mexico. After 1300, however, Anasazi society declined, probably as a result of drought and invasions by warlike outsiders. In *California*, the Amerinds lived in extended families organized as small tribes.

Four Full-Scale Tribal Societies

Four groups developed full-scale tribal organization, with the tribes functioning continuously. Each tribe was composed of thousands of people ruled by a variety of political chiefs, war chiefs, and religious leaders.

The Cheyenne develop a structured society

The *Plains* Indians included a large number of semi-nomadic tribes that cultivated maize along the region's rivers and hunted the great buffalo herds with bows and arrows. Perhaps the most highly organized among them were the Cheyenne, ruled by a council of 44 chiefs selected on merit. These chiefs oversaw the frequent moves from one camp to another and the tribal buffalo hunt, the success of which depended on teamwork and skill. Men hunted the animals while women repaired bows, made arrows, and sewed garments from the hides. Cheyenne chiefs also exercised day-to-day authority over all matters affecting the tribe. The peoples of the *Prairies*, such as the Sioux, were predominantly agricultural until the availability of horses imported by Europeans revolutionized the art of hunting buffalo. Prairie Indian tribal organization remained centered on village life.

In the *Southeast*, Amerinds formed powerful tribes such as the Cherokee and the Natchez, in which chiefs exercised total authority over their subjects. Some, such as the Natchez, had rigid hereditary castes ranging from "Suns" down to "Stinkards." Others, such as the Choctaws and Creeks, constantly waged war against one another. Southeastern Amerinds blended agriculture with hunting and gathering.

The Haudenosaunee create the Great League of Peace and Power

Finally, in the *Eastern Woodlands*, a variety of farming peoples grew squash, beans, and maize, fished the rivers and streams, and hunted deer in the forests. They typically lived in villages, surrounded by log walls for protection. The Haudenosaunee (*hō-d'nō-SAW-nē*) of what is now New York State lived communally in wooden dwellings called longhouses. Their clans were led by clan mothers, who appointed tribal chiefs. Eventually the Haudenosaunee formed a five-nation alliance called the Great League of Peace and Power, which in turn created a political organization known as the Iroquois Confederacy. This organization made war on other Indian tribes and made alliances with European settlers, but never achieved complete political unity.

Three Complex Societies

Three North American Indian groups developed urban economies and complex governance structures similar in some respects to the early river civilizations of Asia and Northeast Africa. These complex Amerind societies, emerging in the valleys of the Ohio and Mississippi Rivers, were eventually centered in large cities with specialized occupations and extensive trading networks.

ADENA AND HOPEWELL. One of these societies was that of the Adena people of the Ohio River valley, which flourished between 1000 and 300 B.C.E. The Adena constructed small villages near the Ohio River and enhanced them with immense earthworks and mounds. These impressive sites, the most famous of which is the 700-foot-long Great Serpent Mound in present-day Kentucky, were apparently used for ceremonial purposes such as burials. Construction of these mounds would have been impossible without large agricultural surpluses to support the laborers who built them. It seems likely, therefore, that the Adena had specialized occupations, one of the key features of complex societies.

After 300 B.C.E., the Adena were absorbed into what archeologists call the Hopewell culture, centered in Ohio but managing a network of trade contacts with dependent tribes throughout a vast region bounded on the north by Ontario, on the east by New York, on the south by Florida, and on the west by Wisconsin. Hopewell consisted of a series of towns, ranging in size from a few hundred people to a few thousand, each ruled by a chief. Its commercial networks were extensive: graves at Hopewell sites in Ohio contain copper from Minnesota; shells and sharks' teeth from the Gulf of Mexico; obsidian (*ob-SID-ē-un*, a sharp, black stone made of volcanic glass) from Arizona; and grizzly bear teeth from west of the continental divide.

> Complex societies emerge in North America

Although agriculture is typically the economic foundation of complex societies, Hopewell was an exception. The natural environment was so rich in fish, game, and plant life that even large towns could prosper through foraging for food. But this subsistence strategy meant that everyone did similar work, and occupational specialties never developed in the way that they did in the river civilizations in Mesopotamia, Egypt, India, and China. The reasons for Hopewell's disappearance around 400 C.E. remain unclear, but the culture's commercial networks survived: seashells from Florida, obsidian from the Rockies, and mica from Tennessee all ended up in Hopewell territory.

A modern photograph of Monk's Mound in Cahokia, where ancient Amerind temples once stood.

MISSISSIPPIAN SOCIETY. Of all the North American Amerind societies, the one most comparable to the Asian and North African river civilizations was that of the people now called Mississippians. Flourishing along and just east of the Mississippi River between 700 and 1500 C.E., their agriculturally-based society benefited from the river's rich deposits of silt, which kept their soil fertile. Their trading networks connected settlements within and beyond their region. The most noteworthy Mississippian center was Cahokia (*kah-HŌ-kē-ah*), the ruins of which lie near the city of East Saint Louis in southwestern Illinois. With between 10,000 and 30,000 inhabitants, Cahokia had a population comparable in size to that of many Eurasian cities, and surpassing that of any other Amerind settlement north of Mexico. Indeed, more people may have lived in Cahokia than in the entire Iroquois Confederacy.

The Mississippian people, like the Adena and the Hopewell, were mound builders. One of Cahokia's many mounds was the largest such structure in all of North America, a colossal earthwork 100 feet high and 1,037 by 790 feet at its base. Cahokia was a

> Mississippians develop a river civilization

ceremonial and administrative center, surrounded by residential areas and shops and supported by the cultivation of adjacent fields. In this way it resembled the cities of Mesoamerica. Mississippians, like the Haudenosaunee of the Eastern Woodlands, grew corn, beans, and squash—the "Three Sisters" whose cultivation originated in Mexico—suggesting some level of contact between these regional cultures.

Such a connection is also suggested by archeological evidence. In the only mound that has thus far been excavated at Cahokia, archeologists discovered the carefully positioned bodies of a nobleman and 260 other adults. The number 260 is also characteristic of sacrificial burials found in Mesoamerica, where a 260-day ritual calendar was widely used, dating from centuries before Cahokia. In addition, some of the skeletons found at Cahokia had their front teeth filed. Virtually unknown elsewhere in North America, this practice was widespread in Mesoamerica. It is possible that the skeletons at Cahokia are remains of visitors or traders from Mesoamerica.

The possibility of contact between Cahokia and Mesoamerica cannot, however, be conclusively substantiated, since Cahokia left no written records. The city was devastated by an earthquake around 1250 C.E., and no subsequent Amerind culture built on its foundations. Some evidence suggests that by this time Cahokia was beginning to evolve into a complex society with a variety of occupational roles, including soldiers, officials, artisans, and priests. But its collapse leaves more questions than answers.

Excavation of the Great Mound at Cahokia suggests connections to Mesoamerica

The Amerinds of Mesoamerica

Farther south, in what are now southern Mexico and northern Central America, civilizations developed to levels of social and political complexity unknown in North America. In this region, which scholars today call Mesoamerica, ample rainfall and rich soils supported a series of highly complex civilizations based on agriculture. Archeologists often divide the early history of this region into three periods: Preclassic (1800 B.C.E.–150 C.E.), comprising the Olmec and early Maya societies; Classic (150–900 C.E.), the era of the full-fledged Mayan society; and Postclassic (900–1500 C.E.), consisting first of the Toltec, and later the Aztec society.

The Olmec of the Preclassic Period (1800 B.C.E.–150 C.E.)

The Olmec construct a river civilization

Mesoamerica's earliest complex society was discovered by accident. In the 1930s, British archeologists Matthew and Marion Stirling were excavating ruins presumed to be from the Classic Mayan era (150–900 C.E.), when they realized that the huge carved stone heads they kept finding in swampy, tropical river plains along the Gulf Coast came from an earlier culture. This husband-and-wife team named the newly discovered culture Olmec and excavated three major sites, demonstrating that Mayan civilization was constructed on an Olmec foundation. The center of Olmec culture lay south of the Gulf of Mexico and west of the Yucatan peninsula. Rainfall there averages nearly 120 inches per year, causing the rivers to flood regularly, depositing rich silt in floodplains that extend for miles from the riverbanks. Well suited to tropical agriculture, the Olmec heartland resembled in many ways the areas where the river civilizations of Asia and Northeast Africa began.

OLMEC CITIES. Olmec society apparently emerged about 1800 B.C.E. and lasted until 150 C.E., encompassing the Preclassic Period. The city now called San Lorenzo, founded around 1200 B.C.E., was the most important of a cluster of Olmec cities near the Coatza-coalcos (*kō-AHT-za-kō-AL-kōs*) River (Map 5.3). There the Olmec created immense stone heads and monuments out of basalt mined fifty miles away. The massive stones must have been dragged to the river, floated downstream on rafts, and dragged up from the riverbank to the plateau on which the city is located. In the absence of large domesticable mammals, carts with wheels were unknown.

Enormous stone structures characterize Olmec culture

The human labor involved in the transportation of these stones must have been enormous, since some of the heads of San Lorenzo are more than nine feet high and weigh up to 25 tons. Equally impressive was the carving of the stones—done entirely with obsidian, not metal, tools. Obsidian implements were imported from other parts of Mexico and from Guatemala, indicating that the Olmec state's networks of commerce and trade covered large distances. The jade carvings, cave paintings, and relief sculptures found in this region testify further to the skills of Olmec artisans.

Olmec society creates long-distance trading networks

San Lorenzo was destroyed around 900 B.C.E. by some sort of revolution or invasion, but the Olmec culture survived, relocating its focus northeast to a new city at

Map 5.3 Mesoamerica: Olmec and Maya Homelands and Centers, ca. 2500 B.C.E.–900 C.E.

Olmec settlement was localized, while Maya city-states were concentrated in the Yucatan Peninsula of Mexico and modern-day Guatemala. Notice the relatively small areas of settlement: the entire Olmec homeland covers less than 200 miles from east to west. A good comparison can be made between Maya city-state development and that of the Greeks (Chapter 7): both societies evolved in confined geographic areas; both developed written languages; both formed intricate trade networks. What sort of connections would need to be forged with other peoples in order to permit complex societies to develop in such restricted regions?

Olmec head carved from basalt and found at La Venta.

La Venta, about 18 miles south of the Gulf of Mexico. There the Olmec built a mammoth clay ceremonial pyramid in the shape of a volcano, standing 110 feet high. At the Olmec city of Tres Zapotes (*TRĀZ zah-PŌ-tāz*), about one hundred miles northwest of La Venta, archeologists unearthed Stela C, one of the oldest dated monuments in the Western Hemisphere. This tall, stone column bears the date of September 3, 32 B.C.E., or (7).16.6.16.18 in the Long Count calendar used by the Mesoamericans.

THE LONG COUNT CALENDAR. Before the Stirlings' excavations, it was universally believed that the Maya had created the Long Count Calendar, but Stela C suggests its Olmec origin. The Long Count enabled Mesoamericans to date events from a starting point that corresponds to August 13, 3114 B.C.E., in our modern (Gregorian) calendar. Used by both Olmec and Maya, the **Long Count calendar** served a number of purposes, including astronomy, astrology, agriculture, genealogy, and even prophecy, as Mesoamericans believed that the world is repetitively created, destroyed, and re-created at precisely measured intervals. The calendar employed two huge cogwheels, one with 365 notches for the days of the solar year, the other with 260 notches for the days of the "sacred almanac," which embodied the sequence of Olmec and Mayan ritual and ceremonial life. When the wheels were turned, each intersection of two dates would recur only once every 52 years. The world came to an end (and was re-created in fire) approximately every 5,125 solar years. This was called the "great cycle," and since the current cycle began in 3114 B.C.E., the present world is scheduled to end on 21 December 2012 in the Gregorian calendar.

The Long Count Calendar demonstrates Olmec mathematical skills

The Long Count calendar testifies to Mesoamericans' convictions concerning the eternity of the world, the endless cycle of life, and the continuity of the traditions on which they organized their societies. Inscriptions on several Olmec objects appear to be early versions of Maya glyphs, but no Olmec writing has been discovered.

THE SPREAD AND COLLAPSE OF OLMEC CIVILIZATION. Some scholars theorize that the Olmec spread their religion and way of life over a wide area of southern Mexico by force of arms. Apparently they were not a peace-loving people. They depicted themselves in sculpture as ferocious warriors, clubbing their enemies to death and torturing their captives. Whether or not this theory is true, the Olmec clearly spread their commerce, art, and ideas through trade.

Eventually, however, the Olmec civilization collapsed. By 300 B.C.E. La Venta had been abandoned, and the population of Tres Zapotes had declined steeply. Well before the Preclassic period ended around 150 C.E., Olmec culture had been absorbed by Amerinds who would evolve into one of Mesoamerica's most complex civilizations: the Maya.

The Maya of the Classic Period (150–900 C.E.)

Time and again in world history, civilizations developed and prospered, only to be conquered by peoples from less complex societies, who then adopted elements of the conquered civilization that they found useful or appealing. Examples include the Akkadian and Babylonian conquests of Sumer, the Hittite conquest of Babylon, the Hyksos conquest of Egypt, and the Aryan conquest of the Indus Valley. But this pattern did not occur in Mexico, as the Preclassic period gradually flowed into the Classic. The Maya, a Mesoamerican people of Guatemala and Mexico's Yucatan Peninsula, did not conquer the Olmec civilization: they emerged in Mesoamerica after the Olmec collapse. They did, however, build on Olmec foundations and eventually transcended Olmec achievements.

AGRICULTURE, TRADE, AND CULTURAL CONTACTS. During the Preclassic period, the Maya developed village-based agriculture. Earlier Mesoamericans had domesticated maize by 2500 B.C.E. and other plants shortly thereafter. Between 7000 and 1500 B.C.E. the world was considerably warmer than it is today, and in much of North America and Mesoamerica the hot, dry weather, combined with excessive hunting by Amerinds, wiped out the giant bison, camels, horses, and mammoths that had once been abundant. Hunting therefore gradually became less important than agriculture, which served as the foundation of Mayan civilization.

The Maya use the Olmec heritage to structure a new society

Mayan agriculture provided a nutritious diet of corn, beans, squash, chili peppers (rich in several vitamins), and tropical fruits. Protein came from wild birds, deer, peccaries, armadillo, and a breed of barkless dog. Sea salt was widely marketed to preserve meat. The Maya, particularly the nobles, also consumed chocolate, drinking beverages made from the cacao bean, the source of chocolate, or snacking on the cacao bean itself.

The cacao bean was traded, as were obsidian, jade, and colorful feathers from a large bird called the quetzal (*ket-ZAL*). Such products were exchanged not only among the Maya themselves, but also with other civilizations in Mexico and Central America. In the process, the Maya established commercial and cultural connections with cultures both more and less socially complex than their own.

The Maya connect Mexico and Central America

Like most other civilizations, the Maya did not evolve in isolation. They were profoundly affected by the Olmec civilization that had existed to their west. From it they learned astronomy and mathematics, developed social and political structures, and adapted a belief system that sought to explain the meaning of human life. And they also had contacts with smaller and weaker groups of people, many of whom they dominated or absorbed.

SOCIETY AND RELIGION. As the Preclassic period became the Classic, Mayan society took shape. It was hierarchical, with a privileged hereditary elite exercising political power. Priests, high-ranking warriors, and wealthy merchants were all nobles. Commoners were free peasants and soldiers, while the lands of the nobles were worked by a group resembling serfs. Below them were slaves, typically commoners captured in battle; although slavery was hereditary, freedom could be purchased by relatives. Politically, the Maya organized themselves as autonomous city-states rather than in a strong central government.

At the top of the hierarchy in each city-state was a sacred king who was both a political and spiritual leader. Kings were brave warriors and shrewd political negotiators who defended the interests of their people. But they also served those interests as spiritual intermediaries between this world and the next. In the Mayan world, political leadership, success in warfare, and religious power were closely linked.

Mayans choose sacred kings as their leaders

The Maya pictured the earth as flat, with 13 layers of heaven above it and nine levels of underworld. An enormous number of gods populated the heavens, while the lower regions were the domain of the nine Lords of Death (see "Excerpt from the Council Book of the Quiché Maya, or *Popol Vuh*"). The Maya were terrified of death, believing that most ordinary people went to the underworld rather than to the heavens, where

Document 5.1 Excerpt from the Council Book of the Quiché Maya, or *Popol Vuh*

The *Popol Vuh*, or "Council Book" of the Maya living in the city of Quiché in southwestern Guatemala, told of the origins and development of Maya civilization. Along with all but four of the thousands of books written by the Maya, it was burned by the Spaniards in the 1520s. Thirty years later, several anonymous members of the Quiché Maya nobility attempted to reconstruct the *Popol Vuh*, using the Latin alphabet rather than the original Maya glyphic writing. Their manuscript was seen in Quiché between 1701 and 1703 by a Spanish friar, Francisco Ximénez, who copied it by hand and added his own Spanish translation. The original manuscript has been lost, and the reproduction and translation prepared by Fr. Ximénez has been in the Newberry Library in Chicago since 1911.

Historians must use such a document with caution. Maya glyphs represented concepts rather than words, and were intended to be used in combination with pictures. Both the glyphs and the pictures were burned in the sixteenth century. How well did the Maya authors remember the precise details of the *Popol Vuh* thirty years after they had last seen it? How accurate was their effort to change glyphs and pictures into words? Was their reconstruction influenced by events connected with the Spanish conquest? When Fr. Ximénez copied their manuscript, did he change it in any way? These questions cannot be answered. Finally, what we have is not the *Popol Vuh* itself, but a document written in the 1550s, decades after the last events described in this chapter. Yet what we have suggests to us how the Maya saw their world, and this excerpt is presented for that purpose.

The excerpt relates the conclusion of the story of the "hero twins," Hunahpú (*hoo-nah-POO*) and Xbalanqué (*zhbahl-ahn-KĀ*), who made too much noise while playing a Maya ritual ball game and were summoned to Xibalbá (*zhih-bahl-BAH*), the Underworld, by the Lords of Death. There they endured many torments and trials, all of which they overcame. But the twins knew that they could not defeat the Lords of Death by force, but could only escape from Xibalbá by trickery. This is the story of their deception.

[The twins disguised themselves as poor orphans and performed amazing dances for the people of Xibalbá.] . . . they worked many miracles. They burned houses

only kings and heroes could live. Special rituals to appease the gods were believed to be capable of holding death back, at least for a while, and also of ensuring the community's prosperity. Rulers and priests led these ceremonies, but ordinary people practiced them too, using their kings as role models.

These rituals involved bloodletting, a practice that connected the temporal and spiritual worlds and allowed departed spirits to materialize in the body of the bloodletter. That person, usually male, pierced some part of his body—often the ear lobe, lip, or penis—with a sharp thorn. Then he drew a knotted cord through the wound to force the blood to run. This type of sacrificial offering was believed to please the gods and bring good harvests, adequate rainfall, victory in warfare, personal happiness, cures for diseases, and many other benefits. Bridging the chasm between worlds brought creation into proper balance, harmonizing the relationship between spirits and mortals.

Maya bloodletting connects two worlds

When the king himself was the bloodletter, he became the portal between the two worlds. The spirits would enter the realm of the living through the wounds he inflicted upon his body. Simultaneously, his own spirit would pass through the wounds into the domain of the dead, where it could influence the gods on behalf of the king's people. The

Document 5.1 *Continued*

as though they were really burning and instantly they were as they had been before . . . they cut themselves into bits; they killed each other; the first one killed stretched out as though he were dead, and instantly the other brought him back to life. Those of Xibalbá looked on in amazement at all they did . . .

Presently word of their dances came to the ears of the Lords of Death, Hun-Camé (*HUHN-kah-MÁ*), or One Death, and Vucub-Camé (*voo-COOB-kah-MÁ*), or Seven Death. Upon hearing it they exclaimed, "Who are these two orphans? Do they really give you so much pleasure?"

"Surely their dances are very beautiful, and all that they do," answered he who had brought the news to the lords.

Happy to hear this, the [lords said], "Tell them to come here, tell them to come so that . . . we may admire them and regard them with wonder."

[So the boys appeared before the Lords of Death, who ordered them,] "Dance! And do the first part in which you kill yourselves; burn my house, do all that you know how to do. We shall give you pay . . ."

Instantly they put fire to the lord's house, and although the lords were within the house, they were not burned. Quickly it was whole again . . . the lords were astounded. "Sacrifice yourselves now, let us see it! We really like your dances!" said the lords . . . And [the twins] proceeded to sacrifice each other. Hunahpú was sacrificed by Xbalanqué, and instantly he returned to life . . .

Then One Death and Seven Death gave their commands. "Do the same with us! Sacrifice us!" they said. "Cut us into pieces, one by one!"

And so it happened that they first sacrificed the one, who was the chief lord of Xibalbá, the one called One Death, king of Xibalbá.

And when One Death was dead, they sacrificed Seven Death, and they did not bring either of them back to life.

The people of Xibalbá fled as soon as they saw that their lords were dead and sacrificed . . . In this way the Lords of Xibalbá were overcome. Only by a miracle and by their [own] transformation could [the boys] have done it.

SOURCE: *Popul Vuh: The Sacred Book of the Ancient Quiché Maya.* English version by Delia Goetz and Sylvanus G. Morley, from the Spanish translation by Adrián Recinos (Norman: University of Oklahoma Press, 1950) 156–160.

sacrifice and pain involved in bloodletting would earn the king the respect of the gods and spirits; in return, they would grant favors to him and to his subjects. In a few cases, women became kings, a status that also required them to serve as bloodletters, drawing the knotted cord through their ear lobes, lips, breasts, or genitals.

MAYA CULTURE. The Maya developed a complex and intellectually sophisticated culture. Using an intricate pictographic system of writing, they carved inscriptions on stone pillars and compiled libraries of thousands of books written on long strips of tree-bark paper (see "Excerpt from the Council Book of the Quiché Maya, or *Popol Vuh*"). (The invading Spaniards burned all but four of these books in the sixteenth century.) The Maya also created a numerical system using zero as a number rather than a placeholder, an idea unknown to their contemporaries in the Roman Empire. Their adoption of the Long Count calendar from the Olmec testifies to their belief in recurrent historical cycles, a conviction similar to those held by people in ancient Egypt and China.

The Long Count calendar, the sophisticated numerical system, the intricate glyphic writing system, and the intense interest of the Maya in astronomy led most historians to conclude that they were a contemplative, scientific, and essentially peace-loving people.

Mayans write and store thousands of books

A Mayan calendar showing the phases of the planet Venus.

The Pyramid of the Moon in the city of Teotihuacán.

But that was before Mayan writing was fully deciphered. Following on the work of Knosorov and Proskouriakoff described at the start of this chapter, scholars began to translate Mayan texts in 1988, and what they read overturned that assumption. Writings on bark-paper and in stone indicate that the Maya were warlike and territorial, like many other cultures, both in America and elsewhere. Warfare was a full-fledged institution, with not only sacrifice and the taking of captives to serve as slaves, but also with complex rites of purification and fasting in preparation for battle. Perhaps this Mayan love of combat was ultimately responsible for bringing down one of the great civilizations of the ancient world in the mid-ninth century, at approximately the same time that another notable Mesoamerican culture was collapsing, that of the city of Teotihuacán.

Teotihuacán: Rise and Fall of a Great City-State

The Maya were not the only complex society in Mexico during the Classic period. As early as 300 B.C.E. the city-state of Teotihuacán (*tā-ō-tē-wah-KAHN*) in the Valley of Mexico, just north of modern-day Mexico City, held a population of 10,000. That number grew to 40,000 by 100 B.C.E. and at least 120,000 by 500 C.E. At the height of the Classic period this city may have contained 200,000 people, making it one of the largest cities of its time.

Located near a rich source of obsidian, necessary for making weapons, and trading actively with other cities of central Mexico, Teotihuacán grew into a politically and commercially significant city (Map 5.4). With 600 pyramids, it was central Mexico's preeminent religious and ceremonial center. Along with its pyramids, two thousand apartment complexes and an immense market compound made Teotihuacán the largest and most significant Mesoamerican city-state of the Classic period, and one of the principal cities of the world. It was clearly the focal point of a powerful empire.

Teotihuacán creates a centralized empire

Teotihuacanos, unlike the Maya, did not seem to revere kings as supreme political authorities and intermediaries between two worlds. Indeed, since artistic depictions of the rulers are lacking and no written records have survived, it is not possible to determine precisely how Teotihuacán was governed. It did, however, maintain an army, probably to protect its commercial relationships with other Mesoamerican cultures, including the Maya. The army may also have forced peasants from the surrounding countryside to supply the city's political and religious elites with food.

Teotihuacán maintained commercial connections with Mayan, Zapotec (*za-PŌ-tek*), Mixtec (*MISH-tek*), and other Mexican civilizations. More than 400 workshops unearthed in its ruins indicate that its artisans fabricated exotic ornaments from seashells, onyx, and jade. In exchange, the Maya sent quetzal feathers and the Zapotec sent fragrant incense made from copal gum.

Mesoamerican societies collapse as the Classic period ends

In the late Classic period, however, all of these societies crumbled. Teotihuacán was deserted and burned, possibly as early as 650 C.E., certainly no later than 850. Several Zapotec cities and Mayan states were destroyed around the same time. Epidemic diseases, volcanic eruptions, earthquakes, and invasion by other Amerind tribes have all been proposed as causes. A great war lasting more than 150 years, from 526 to 682 C.E., between two powerful Mayan city-states centered at Tikal and Calakmul, weakened the Maya heartland the way the Peloponnesian War between Athens and Sparta from 431 to 404 B.C.E. (Chapter 7) weakened Greece.

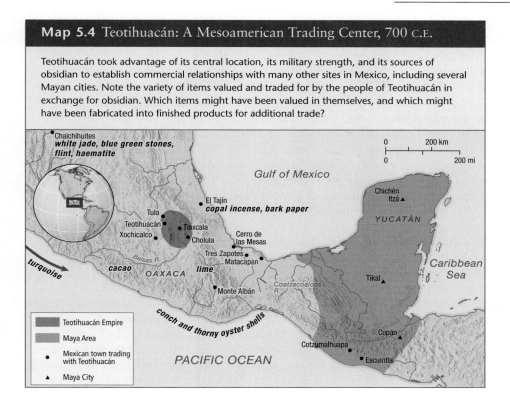

Map 5.4 Teotihuacán: A Mesoamerican Trading Center, 700 C.E.

Teotihuacán took advantage of its central location, its military strength, and its sources of obsidian to establish commercial relationships with many other sites in Mexico, including several Mayan cities. Note the variety of items valued and traded for by the people of Teotihuacán in exchange for obsidian. Which items might have been valued in themselves, and which might have been fabricated into finished products for additional trade?

These highly urbanized societies may also have collapsed from internal stresses. An expanding population, coupled with increasing demands by the warrior and ceremonial elites for food and goods, may have overstrained the food supply and embittered the peasantry whose labor supported the entire structure. In this theory, a rebellion of the peasants against the urban center destroyed the great cities, and their inhabitants scattered into small village communities of the kind the Spaniards found in the sixteenth century. Today this theory seems to be the most plausible explanation for the catastrophic end of the great civilizations of Mexico.

The Toltec: Conflict Between Warriors and Priests

This collapse created a power vacuum throughout the Mesoamerican world, which warrior tribes shortly filled. The most successful of these was the Toltec (975 C.E.–1200 C.E.), a people originating in northern Mexico. The Toltec established their capital at Tula, about thirty miles northwest of Teotihuacán, around 960 to 970 C.E. The Toltec ruling elite appears to have been divided between priests and warriors, with each faction struggling to dominate the other. According to legend, an early Toltec priest-king encouraged devotion to the god Quetzalcóatl (*kwet-zahl-KŌ-ah-tul*), or "Feathered Serpent," while the warriors opposed him in the name of a rival deity, Tezcatlipoca (*tetz-cat-lē-PŌ-kah*), or "Smoking Mirror." The two factions quarreled, and the worshipers of Quetzalcóatl were defeated and forced to leave Tula for the east, apparently in 987 C.E.

The Quetzalcóatl legend is created in Mesoamerica

According to legend, Quetzalcóatl vowed revenge, claiming that he and his followers would return one day on boats across the Gulf of Mexico. Appearing as white-skinned men, oddities which no Mesoamerican had ever seen, they would reclaim their rightful heritage and redeem their people from bondage. Interestingly, Mayan sources describe the arrival in 987 on the Yucatán peninsula of a man from the west named Kukulcán (*koo-kul-KHAN*), which means "Feathered Serpent" in Mayan; he apparently conquered the Yucatán peninsula and built the city of Chichén Itzá (*chi-CHAIN ēt-ZAH*) for his capital. Was Kukulcán a Toltec worshiper of Quetzalcóatl forced to leave Tula? Murals at Chichén Itzá depict a Toltec army defeating Maya warriors around that time. And when Spanish invaders led by Hernán Cortés landed in ships and marched into central Mexico in 1519, those Maya who remembered the Toltec legend were convinced that the prophecy had been fulfilled and Quetzalcóatl had returned.

The Toltec connect the Pacific and the Gulf of Mexico

In the year 1000 C.E. the Toltec capital of Tula served as the hub of a militaristic empire stretching across Mexico from the Pacific to the Gulf. Its warriors dressed themselves as jaguars, coyotes, and eagles; they proudly carried Toltec rule to peoples who would soon learn to hate and fear them. Human sacrifice, an occasional practice in Mayan lands, became more frequent under the Toltec.

Although the brutality and efficiency of its warriors permeated all aspects of Toltec society, the Toltec did not lack appreciation for beauty and grace. In Chichén Itzá, Toltec and Mayan architectural forms merged to create magnificent stepped temples and light, airy hallways bordered by colonnades. The Mayan ritual pastime of the ball game, in which teams competed in an effort to propel a small rubber ball through a stone ring 25 feet above the ground using only elbows, hips, or knees, was adopted enthusiastically by the Toltec. Their ball court at Chichén Itzá was the largest in Mesoamerica, 490 feet long with walls 27 feet high. The game was played for very high stakes, since the captain of the losing team (and sometimes of the winning one as well) was often sacrificed.

Massive stone statues of Toltec warriors stand atop the pyramid at the ruins of Tula de Allende, Mexico.

The Toltec maintained the commercial connections forged by Teotihuacán and the Maya city-states, expanding them by exporting exquisite metalcrafts, mosaics composed of quetzal feathers, and statuettes and jewelry made from precious gems. Toltec artisans skillfully blended their own methods with techniques learned from Mayan craftsmen. They used turquoise from modern-day New Mexico, gold from Central America, and obsidian and jade from their own realm to create stylized artifacts stunning in their simplicity. Their artistry was so breathtaking that, five hundred years later, the artisans of the Aztec Empire were called *tolteca*.

Toltec craftsmanship continues earlier commercial connections

No doubt the Toltec believed that their militancy would ensure their dominance, but in the 1160s Tula was torn apart and sacked. Its destruction may have been the result of irreconcilable animosity between warriors and priests or of some sort of internal uprising. In the Yucatán, Chichén Itzá gradually decayed, and in 1224 it was abandoned. No one knows why the Toltec empire collapsed, and no empire replaced it until the coming of the Aztecs in 1325.

South America: Societies of the Andes

The civilizations of Mesoamerica were built by only a small fraction of the Amerinds. Many Amerinds never penetrated that far south, remaining in North America, north of the Rio Grande. Many others passed through the region and continued into South

America. Forbidding in terms of topography and climate, South America remains the least explored of the earth's inhabited continents. The migrating peoples who first entered it confronted sweltering rain forests, snow-capped mountain ranges, and waterless deserts. There they created civilizations carefully adapted to such challenging environments.

South American societies must adapt to challenging environments

Hunter-Gatherers and the Chavín Society

At first glance, South America's southeastern corner would seem ideal for human exploitation. The rich grasslands and fertile soils of modern Argentina and Uruguay are ideal for raising cattle, horses, and sheep, and cultivating grains and fruits. But very few Amerinds settled there: they had not yet mastered agriculture, and this area of South America lacked any four-footed mammal larger than a tapir (a pig with a hooked snout). Additionally, these grasslands were covered by vegetation so thick that the land could not be broken without steel plows. Hunter-gatherers were more likely to settle in the immense rain forests of northern Brazil, where wild fruits and vegetables grew in abundance, and tapirs and capybaras (large, short-legged rodents) could be hunted. There the Tapajos (*tah-PAH-hōs*) people eventually developed a hierarchically structured, warlike culture in the central Amazon valley. Archeological exploration of the Tapajos sites is just beginning, and the arrival of humans in that area can only be estimated at between 8000 and 4000 B.C.E. They made the transition to agriculture after that time and were still dominating the region in the sixteenth century.

To the west, the entire Pacific side of South America, the environment is shaped by the Andes Mountains, part of a geologic formation running from Cape Horn, north through Peru, 11,000 miles to the north slope of Alaska. With peaks more than 14,000 feet high, the Andes stand as a barrier to cultural connections across the South American continent. Chile and Argentina would probably have evolved as a single cultural region had not the Andes stood between them. Part of the "Ring of Fire" surrounding the Pacific Ocean, these mountains include many active volcanoes. Earthquakes and mudslides, some of them extremely damaging, are common.

Unlike the rest of the continent, however, the Andean highlands are home to three large, closely related four-footed mammals, the llama, alpaca, and vicuña. Useful for carrying burdens and as a food source, these animals never spread farther north than present-day Colombia because they could not thrive in the heat of lower-lying regions. Hunter-gatherers arrived in the Andean region at some time around 10,000 B.C.E. Four thousand years later, a significant population increase along the seacoast suggests the evolving importance of fishing. Lima beans were domesticated around this time, although the rockiness and aridity of Andean soils delayed the full development of agriculture until irrigation was employed. Sometime after 4000 B.C.E., irrigated fields stimulated the growth of the first Andean society in the Norte Chico region of Peru.

The first Andean society develops in Peru's Norte Chico

Little is known of Norte Chico society, but its principal city, Huaricanga, built around 3200 B.C.E., is the oldest known city in the Americas. Large-scale public buildings were erected there at about the time the Sumerian civilization flourished in West Asia. There must have been some form of centralized government in the Norte Chico, as specialized occupations would have been necessary for the construction of large public monuments. Whatever government did develop was unique, not copied from another society or imported by conquerors.

Map 5.5 Pre-Inca Andean Empires and Culture Areas, ca. 800 B.C.E.–1400 C.E.

Several complex early cultures emerged in what is now Peru. Observe that these South American Amerind societies were intensively concentrated along the spine of the Andes Mountains. South America's challenging topography limited contact between peoples; the Tupi of the Amazon, for example, never learned of the existence of Andean societies, while the Mapuche of southern Chile were cut off from other groups by the Andes and the Atacama Desert. But groups living in this portion of the Andes knew of each other, and their societies developed using knowledge gained from contacts and connections between them. In what ways might life in such a challenging environment have encouraged people to learn from one another?

This early society vanished, and an Andean successor state, the Chavín, emerged during what archeologists call the Early Horizon Period (1200–200 B.C.E.). Centered on the ceremonial site of Chavín de Huantar (*cha-VĒN dā WAHN-tar*) in central Peru, it was organized around a polytheistic belief system whose gods were worshiped throughout the central Andes for centuries after Chavín's collapse (Map 5.5). Almost nothing is known of Chavín political structures, but this civilization produced durable textiles, pottery, and metalwork, whose uses reflected Chavín religious convictions.

Isolation was the most significant handicap facing the Chavín empire. Cut off from contact with other South American Indian societies by the Andes and separated from the Olmec civilization of Mexico by 1,600 miles of ocean and 2,000 miles of rugged terrain (Map 5.6), the Chavín people did not have the opportunity to adopt new technologies

The Chavín Empire remains isolated

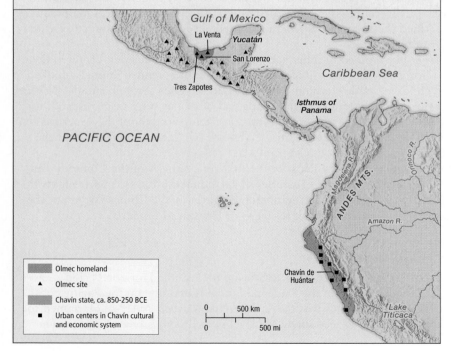

Map 5.6 Geographic Proximity of Olmec and Chavín Homelands, ca. 800 B.C.E.

All pre-Inca Andean societies were profoundly isolated from non-Andean cultures. Notice that the distances between the Chavín empire and the Olmec society of Mexico were simply too great to be traversed readily with available means of transportation. Early American societies knew of the wheel but used it only for children's toys, not for transportation. Even in the twenty-first century C.E., the trip from Olmec lands to Chavín lands cannot be completed by wheeled vehicles because of the absence of roads connecting southeastern Panama with northwestern Colombia. How might such isolation have been a disadvantage to Amerind societies once they were confronted by peoples from less isolated regions?

and ideas. All the Andean societies succeeding the Chavín were similarly isolated. Even today, there is no road connecting Mesoamerica to the Andes because the border between Panama and Colombia remains impassable.

Nazca and Moche Societies

During the Early Intermediate Period (200 B.C.E.–500 C.E.), two post-Chavín societies developed, the Nazca and the Moche. Archeological evidence indicates that they fought each other, but not that they developed commercial or other peaceful connections.

Little is known of Nazca political organization, but its artistic accomplishments continue to impress modern-day observers. Based in southern Peru, the Nazca traced immense patterns on the desert by removing surface debris to expose the underlying strata of rock. These designs, visible only from the air, depict birds, spiders, monkeys, fish, and cats. Some scholars believe that the designs were offerings or signals to the gods; others contend that they were ritualized pathways connecting local shrines. Delicately painted polychrome ceramics and elaborate mummification of the dead also characterized Nazca civilization (as they did the Chavín).

The Moche (*MŌ-chā*) society of northern Peru dominated that region without creating a formal imperial structure. Complex irrigation channels transported water from up to 75 miles away, allowing the Moche to develop a diversified agricultural base that they supplemented with meat from their herds of alpacas and llamas. An elaborate religious hierarchy presided over worship services performed in structures like the Pyramid of the Sun, an adobe building 1,140 feet long and 130 feet high. The first Andean culture to develop accurately representational art, the Moche created ceramic portrait vases and objects of silver and gold. They also took a dim view of medical malpractice: physicians who killed their patients through incompetence were staked out to be eaten alive by birds of prey.

Moche women, like women in other early American Indian societies, centered their lives around the home. There they raised fruits and vegetables, tended animals, cooked meals, nurtured children, made clothing, and appeased the gods through rituals. Political life, military service, hunting, and labor on roads and buildings were tasks reserved for men. This gender-based division of labor was so consistent throughout the Americas that scholars have been tempted to speculate, in the absence of concrete evidence, that the Amerinds brought it with them from Central Asia.

The Moche thrived in northern Peru for the first six centuries of the Common Era, finally collapsing under the pressure of a series of earthquakes, floods, and droughts that deprived the ruling elite of its political legitimacy. Apparently the Chinese were not the only people to monitor the environment for signs of Heaven's Mandate.

The Moche use irrigation to make agriculture possible

Amerinds use gender as a basis for assigning tasks

Tiahuanaco, Huari, and Chimor

The Moche were succeeded by three societies during the Middle Horizon Period (500–1000 C.E.). Two developed in the Andean highlands and one on the Pacific coast.

First of the mountain societies was the Tiahuanaco (*tē-wah-NAH-koo*), named for its impressive capital at 13,000 feet above sea level near Bolivia's Lake Titicaca. The city's population ranged between 30,000 and 40,000, making it the highest large city of the Andes but small in comparison to Teotihuacán. Tiahuanaco's agriculture centered on fields reclaimed from lakeside swamps by means of an immense drainage system. Commercial relationships over long distances were maintained by caravans of sure-footed llamas. Ceremonial buildings were constructed of stones joined together with such artistry and precision that no mortar was necessary; even the blade of a knife could not pass between them. The city of Tiahuanaco featured running water and a closed sewer system.

The second highland civilization of this period was the Huari (*WAH-rē*), located in the mountains of southeastern Peru. This culture developed later than Tiahuanaco and was similar to it technologically and tied to it commercially. In building their commercial enterprises, the two civilizations competed for the copper, lapis lazuli (*LAP-is LAZ-yoo-lē*, a deep blue mineral valued as a gem), obsidian, and turquoise deposits of local valleys. But the Huari culture differed in some ways from that of Tiahuanaco. Huari public buildings were much smaller than those of Tiahuanaco and were built from adobe rather than cut stone. Its capital was larger in area than Tiahuanaco but much less densely populated.

Neither of these highland cultures developed elaborate administrative structures, and like all early Andean civilizations, their lack of a system of writing makes it difficult to learn much about them. The Huari collapsed around the year 800 C.E., bringing to an end two thousand years of urban settlements in southern Peru. Tiahuanaco lingered for several centuries, declining slowly well before the arrival of the Europeans. No reasons for the weakening of either culture can be stated with certainty.

On the Pacific coast, the Moche were succeeded by Chimor (*chē-MOR*), a major imperial power that dominated coastal Peru until the emergence of the Inca in the fifteenth century C.E. Chan Chan, constructed in the heart of Moche territory on a huge site directly on the coast, became Chimor's capital and cultural center. The city was notable for its massive ceremonial structures, large warehouses, and extensive one-story living compounds, built without roofs, since rain occurred infrequently along the Peruvian coast. Chimor arose as a successor state to the Moche around 700 C.E., but does not appear to have developed into an expansionistic state before 1300. Once it did, it created the first Andean empire.

Chimor's social structure was hierarchical, topped by a warrior aristocracy supported by priests. Beneath these classes, artisans developed distinctive techniques of pottery-making, textile manufacture, and metalcraft. Close in status to the artisans, merchants organized and carried on commerce with the remotest regions of the empire as well as with other Andean cultures. Peasants, at the bottom of the social hierarchy, supported Chimor's social and economic structure with agriculture, fishing, and livestock raising. This social structure, especially the warrior class and the widespread commercial contacts, indicates that Chimor was intent on spreading its culture and control as far as the imposing mountainous topography of the region would allow.

Indeed, the people of Chimor, known as Chimú, conquered a number of less formidable neighbors, but they do not seem to have oppressed them or treated them as captives. Instead, unlike the Moche and Huari, they deliberately incorporated them into their empire, giving them a stake in the power and prosperity of Chimor. Imperial

Building Civilizations in the Andean Highlands

A woven polychrome textile panel depicting warriors from Chimor.

Chimor creates a warrior society

Chimor assimilates the peoples it conquers

administration was aided by a far-flung system of roads and bridges that encouraged communication, commerce, and coercion. Given their cultural achievements, the Chimú might well have been far better known today had they not been conquered between 1462 and 1470 by the Inca, who adopted many Chimú practices and policies on their way to becoming South America's most powerful civilization.

Chapter Review

Putting It in Perspective

The first groups of Central Asian nomads who crossed the Bering land bridge and entered the Western Hemisphere were probably very similar to one another in genetic composition, hunting techniques, weaponry, customs, and social life. Their descendants, however, who spread through North and South America through countless generations, diverged from one another in many ways as they adapted to widely varying environments.

In the Arctic and Sub-Arctic regions of North America, brief growing seasons and frozen, snow-covered ground made organized agriculture impossible. The peoples who remained in these regions maintained their hunter-gatherer lifestyles. In the southwestern corner of the present-day United States, arid soils and the absence of huge rivers for irrigation projects similarly limited agriculture. At the same time, agriculture seemed unnecessary in the Pacific Northwest, the Prairies, and the Great Plains, which teemed with abundant fish and game. In the Eastern Woodlands, the Iroquois founded an innovative confederacy based on agriculture, but its small population base prevented the sort of large-scale, complex development found in Mesoamerica. The Mississippi people seemed to be modeling their society on Mesoamerica when they built Cahokia, but its unexplained abandonment ended this experiment.

In Mesoamerica, organizationally complex societies arose, including the Olmec, the Maya, the Teotihuacanos, and the Toltec. In lands with plentiful rainfall, rich soils, a lengthy growing season, and a wide variety of possible crops, these peoples turned from hunting and gathering to agriculture, and agricultural surpluses made possible the development of complex political and social organizations. Mesoamerican civilizations developed elaborate belief systems, advanced mathematical and astronomical knowledge, considerable architectural and engineering skills, and impressive military establishments.

Farther south, the civilizations of the Andes met the challenges of their natural environment. Irrigating the dry soils and carefully shepherding livestock, they constructed a firm agricultural base in an arid environment. With each successive civilization building on the achievements of its predecessors, the Norte Chico, Chavín, Nazca, Moche, Tiahuanaco, Huari, and Chimú societies built temples and public halls, created goods of fabric and metal, threw bridges across raging rivers at dizzying heights, and gradually evolved toward imperial conquest. The later Inca civilization appreciated the accomplishments of the Chimú and adopted many of their practices.

Beginning their development much later than the civilizations that originated in Asia, Africa, and Europe, some Amerind societies had evolved to complex levels of social organization by 1500 C.E. Others, restricted by their environments, continued the ways of their ancestors. Some evolved in isolation from one another, but most had connections and conflicts. Over many centuries, they fought each other, traded with each other, and learned from each other. All did, however, develop in isolation from the cultures and civilizations of the Eastern Hemisphere until 1500 C.E.

Reviewing Key Material

KEY CONCEPTS

Mesoamerica, 109   tribes, 112
Amerinds, 109   Long Count Calendar, 118

KEY PEOPLES

Haudenosaunee, 114   Norte Chico, 125
Adena, 115   Chavín, 127
Hopewell, 115   Nazca, 128
Mississippian, 115   Moche, 128
Olmec, 116   Tiahuanaco, 128
Maya, 118   Huari, 129
Teotihuacán, 122   Chimor, 129
Toltec, 123   Chimú, 129

ASK YOURSELF

1. How did North American Amerinds react to their differing environments?
2. How did Olmec society influence the subsequent development of Maya civilization?
3. How did leadership in Maya civilization reflect the political, spiritual, and military aspects of society?
4. How did the Toltec build on the accomplishments of previous civilizations?
5. How did early South American societies influence one another?

GOING FURTHER

Bruhns, Karen. *Ancient South America*. 1994.
Burger, Richard. *Chavín and the Origins of Andean Civilization*. 1992.
Coe, Michael. *The Maya*. 1999.
Coe, Michael. *The Olmec World*. 1996.
Dickason, Olive. *Canada's First Nations*. 1992.
Fagan, Brian. *Ancient North America*. 2001.
Fiedel, Stuart. *Prehistory of the Americas*. 1992.
Friedel, David, Linda Schele, and Joy Parker. *Maya Cosmos*. 1993.
Keatinge, Richard, ed. *Peruvian Prehistory*. 1988.
Kehoe, Alice. *America Before the European Invasions*. 2003.
Kolata, Alan. *Tiwanaku*. 1993.
Mann, Charles. *1491: New Revelations of the Americas Before Columbus*. 2005.
Moseley, Michael. *The Incas and Their Ancestors*. 2001.
Pasztori, Esther. *Teotihuacán*. 1997.
Pauketat, Timothy, and Thomas Emerson, eds. *Cahokia: Domination and Ideology in the Mississippian World*. 1997.
Sabloff, Jeremy. *The Cities of Ancient Mexico*. 1989.
Schaffer, Lynda. *Native Americans Before 1492: The Moundbuilding Centers of the Eastern Woodlands*. 1992.
Schele, Linda, and David Friedel. *A Forest of Kings: The Untold Story of the Ancient Maya*. 1990.
Sharer, R. *Daily Life in Maya Civilization*. 1996.
Stuart, David. *Anasazi America*. 2000.
Weaver, Muriel. *The Aztecs, Maya, and Their Predecessors*. 1993.
Webster, D. *The Fall of the Ancient Maya: Solving the Mystery of the Maya Collapse*. 2002.

Key Dates and Developments

North American Chronology:

ca. 1000 B.C.E.	Adena society emerges in Ohio River Valley
ca. 100 C.E.	Adena merges with Hopewell society
400	Adena-Hopewell society disappears
700–1200	Anasazi society in southwestern United States
700–1500	Mississippian society along and east of the Mississippi River
1050–1250	Zenith of Cahokian society

Mesoamerican Chronology:

1800 B.C.E.– 150 C.E.	Olmec society: The Preclassic Period
1700 B.C.E.	Foundation of San Lorenzo
1200 B.C.E.	Foundation of Tres Zapotes
100 C.E.	Foundation of Teotihuacán
150–900 C.E.	Maya society: The Classic Period
ca. 750	Destruction of Teotihuacán
800–900	Abandonment of Mayan urban centers
ca. 970	Foundation of Tula by the Toltec
ca. 990	Foundation of Chichén Itzá
1156	Destruction of Tula
1224	Abandonment of Chichén Itzá

South American Chronology:

3200–2500 B.C.E.	Norte Chico society in Peru
1200–200 B.C.E.	Early Horizon Period: Chavín society in Peru
200 B.C.E.– 500 C.E.	Early Intermediate Period: Nazca and Moche societies in Peru
500–1000	Middle Horizon Period: Tiahuanaco, Huari, and Chimú societies in Bolivia and Peru
1300–1465	Chimú military expansion culminating in rivalry with Inca Empire

The Persian Connection: Its Impact and Influences, 2000 B.C.E.–637 C.E.

A Persian Soldier

The sculpted figure of a Persian policeman guards the entrance to one of Persia's royal palaces. This stylized image shows the braided hair and beard worn by Persian men, the long pike considerably taller than a man, and the attitude of vigilance and resolution that Persian emperors expected from their soldiers (page 142).

In 529 B.C.E., a solemn procession filed from northwest India across Afghanistan and onto the plateau of Iran. Its members were carrying the mutilated remains of one of the most powerful rulers of the ancient world. As his body was placed in the sturdy tomb that had been built for him years earlier, priests chanted hymns and recited prayers. Sacrifices were made on his behalf to the fundamental forces of fire and water. Then the tomb was sealed and guards were placed around it to safeguard his royal dignity even in death. Cyrus the Great of Persia had come home.

The Persian Empire

Cyrus, like other kings of his day, was a fearsome warrior. But a list of his military conquests would tell only part of his story. The Persian Empire he founded left a legacy that included an efficient system of government, a tolerant society, a model for fostering commerce and cooperation among many cultures, and a conception of a universal god who rewards those who lead good lives and work for justice. Though often portrayed as foreign and therefore barbaric by the Greeks, Persian civilization was rich in its own right. The empire might well have dominated southwest Asia for centuries had Alexander the Great not arisen in Macedonia and decided to destroy it. Even after its fall, the Persian Empire's legacy profoundly influenced Islamic culture and present-day Iran. The king whom the Persians buried in 529 B.C.E. was an extraordinary ruler who set in motion a series of events and influences that long outlived him.

The Persian Empire

Mesopotamia, Egypt, India, and China all originated in fertile river valleys. Persian society, in contrast, developed on the arid Iranian plateau in southwestern Asia. In that challenging environment, the Persians constructed an empire that at its height would encompass most of southwestern Asia.

Geographic Challenges Confront the First Persians

The Iranian plateau's topography makes it easy to defend

The Iranian plateau, comprising nearly one million square miles, is relatively inhospitable. It contains two immense salt deserts, and the small rivers that cross it are difficult to navigate and offer little water for agriculture. Even entering the plateau can be difficult. It is guarded on the west by the Zagros (*ZAH-grus*) mountains; on the northwest by the Caspian Sea, Caucasus (*KAW-cuh-suhs*) mountains, and Elburz (*el-BURZ*) mountains; on the east by the mountain ranges and arid depressions of Afghanistan; on the southeast by the Baluchi (*buh-LOO-key*) desert; and on the south by the Persian Gulf (Map 6.1). The easiest way to ascend the plateau is from the northeast, where broad corridors through the mountains link Iran to Central Asia.

FOUNDATION MAP 6.1 The Physical Geography of the Iranian Plateau

The geography of the region provides natural defenses for Indo-European peoples settling on the Iranian plateau. Notice that the Zagros and Elburz mountain ranges, the Persian Gulf, the Caspian Sea, and the Baluchi Desert make access to the region difficult for invaders. Sparse rainfall makes the population dependent on irrigation systems that channel runoff from mountain snows that melt in spring. Why might such an easily defensible region have appeared undesirable to earlier settlers?

Archeological evidence suggests that people domesticated sheep and goats, and cultivated wheat and barley, in the foothills of the Zagros mountains at least 10,000 years ago. Little is known of these early Iranians, but artifacts made of obsidian, a mineral not native to the region, indicate the existence of early trading networks. Pastoral nomadism dominated the Iranian plateau, where wide variations in water supply made regular farming impossible. Central Asian nomads arrived on the plateau, through the northwest corridors, about 5,000 years ago.

The Central Asian steppes were no more inviting than Iran, but they were much more difficult to defend against invaders. For thousands of years, hostile tribes had fought each other for control of the region, often contending at the same time with formidable empires such as China. Winners expelled losers and were then, in turn, driven out. Some of these tribes went to Iran, undismayed by its uncertain water supply, and grazed their herds on the plateau.

Central Asians migrate to the Iranian plateau

The first migrants were influenced by the Sumerian culture they found among peoples living on the plateau (see photo, page 139), but they blended it with their own customs and preferences. Archeological remains indicate that these early immigrants were skilled artists, particularly in ceramics. Then around 1000 B.C.E. an Indo-European tribe from Central Asia migrated down the eastern shore of the Caspian Sea into western Iran. This group was a branch of the Aryans who had earlier moved into India (Chapter 3), and they gave their own name to the plateau they occupied: Iran means "land of the Aryans" (Map 6.2).

The two principal subgroups of Aryan migrants were the Medes (*MĒDZ*), who took up residence in the Zagros Mountains, and the Persians, taking their name from Farsia, the central region of the Iranian plateau. Both spoke the same language, which today is known as Farsi (*FAHR-sē*). They had different accents, but the Greeks, who encountered them during the Greco-Persian Wars, were unable to distinguish between the two and called all of them Persians.

Map 6.2 Indo-Europeans Migrate from Central Asia, 3000–1000 B.C.E.

Between 3000 and 1000 B.C.E., many Indo-European peoples left their homeland in what today is southwestern Russia, relocating in many different directions. One such people, the Aryans, entered the Iranian plateau from the northwest and settled among indigenous peoples already living there. Observe that eventually some Aryans would continue to migrate eastward and settle in India (Chapter 3). How might the knowledge and customs shared by these peoples have forged connections between the widely scattered societies that they created?

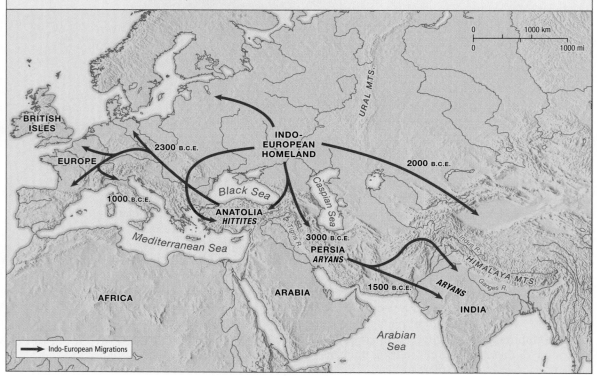

Although they periodically fought against invaders from the Assyrian Empire, the Medes were relatively well protected by the Zagros and established a thriving economy and culture. They mined minerals such as gold, silver, precious gems, marble, iron, copper, and lead, which they used in their artistic endeavors and traded with neighboring cultures.

The melting mountain snows provided the only reliable source of water for agriculture in a land that averages fewer than 12 inches of precipitation per year, so the Medes developed a sophisticated irrigation system. They trapped the waters of the melting snows and diverted them to fields. In one of the many valleys of the Zagros they built Ecbatana (*eck-BAH-tuh-nuh*), the seat of their government and center of their economy. Eventually, however, the Assyrian Empire conquered both the Medes and the Persians, forcing them to pay tribute but never completely subjugating them.

When Babylonia and Assyria erupted into civil war, the Medes and Persians took advantage of the conflict to free themselves from the invaders. First the Median king Cyaxares (*sī-AX-ar-ēs*) strengthened his army, reducing the Persians to the status of vassals. Cyaxares (640–584 B.C.E.) then allied with the Chaldeans against Assyria. But his plans were delayed by the arrival of Scythians (*SIH-thē-ahns*), nomadic warriors from Central Asia, who invaded Iran through the passage between the Caspian Sea and the Caucasus Mountains. Forced to pay tribute to the Scythians, Cyaxares decided to give a banquet for their leaders—at which he got them drunk and killed them. This enabled him to return to his original plan, and by 612 B.C.E. the Medes and Chaldeans had destroyed the Assyrian capital of Nineveh. Cyaxares ruled northern Mesopotamia until his death in 584, while the Chaldeans (or "New Babylonians") ruled in southern Mesopotamia (or "Babylonia"). The Assyrian Empire was shattered, making way for the creation of the Persian Empire.

Cyaxares defeats the Assyrian Empire

Cyrus the Great

The Median kingdom lasted for only a few decades before its Persian vassals started intriguing against it. The Persian ruling family, called the Achaemenids (*ah-KĒ-muh-nids*), married into the ruling house of Media. Cyrus, a child of this union, managed to unify the Persian tribes and wage war against the Median king, who was also his father-in-law. In 550 B.C.E. he captured the king and united the Medes and Persians under the Achaemenid house.

Following his defeat of the Medes, which extended his control from the Persian Gulf to central Anatolia, Cyrus next waged war against King Croesus (*CRĒ-suss*), ruler of a region called Lydia (*LIH-dē-uh*) in western Anatolia. Although Croesus, whose great wealth was legendary, struck first in an effort to expand Lydia eastward, his armies were no match for the Persians. In 547 B.C.E., the Lydian cavalry was poised to strike the Persian infantry when other Persian troops, mounted on camels, counterattacked. The Lydian horses, which had never before seen such animals, panicked and threw their riders into the dust. Cyrus's victory gave the Persian Empire access to the Mediterranean Sea and control of several Greek city-states on the shores of Anatolia, from which it could threaten Greece itself. Although Cyrus made no move against the Greek mainland, the Greeks were unnerved by the proximity of an empire with a large, well-equipped army that enjoyed a reputation for winning. During the following decades they watched the Persians carefully.

Cyrus expands the Persian Empire to west and east

Cyrus next moved east, conquering the lands of Parthia and Bactria (modern-day Afghanistan) and extending his dominion from the Aegean (*ih-JĒ-uhn*) Sea in the west to the Hindu Kush mountains in the east. In 539 B.C.E., he invaded southern Mesopotamia, then controlled by the Chaldeans' New Babylonian Empire. By allying himself with various tribes that had struggled against the Chaldeans and portraying himself as their liberator, Cyrus was able to enter the city of Babylon without a fight. The rich Babylonian domains, from Mesopotamia to Palestine, were now under his control. By the time of his death in 530 B.C.E., he had clearly earned the title of Cyrus the Great, one of history's most successful empire builders.

ASSIMILATION AFTER CONQUEST. The importance of Cyrus lay not just in his conquests. For its time, Cyrus's rule was remarkably sophisticated in its approach to subjugated peoples. Conquerors of that era normally pillaged defeated cities and enslaved their populations. Cyrus, by contrast, had a shrewd instinct for governing that allowed him to win the trust of those he defeated. An examination of some of his principles of government illustrates this instinct.

Cyrus the Great leads through persuasion and compromise

First, Cyrus demonstrated early in his reign that he would rule through persuasion and compromise rather than force and humiliation. When he conquered the Medes, he granted their leader honors and respect, and he united the Medes with his own people rather than subjugating them. He retained not only Median administrative and military structures but also the Medes who directed them. In this way he won the trust of the Medes and reduced the possibility of rebellion against his rule.

Second, Cyrus treated conquered peoples benevolently, allowing deported peoples to return to their homelands rather than enslaving them. He won the gratitude of the Jews when he freed them from captivity in Babylonia and allowed them to return to Jerusalem. He even encouraged them to rebuild their temple, which the Babylonians had destroyed.

Finally, Cyrus permitted the peoples he defeated to retain their own religions and cultures while simultaneously offering them partnership in the Persian Empire. This two-pronged approach persuaded various ethnic groups to accept his rule; in doing so, they understood that they would not be humiliated and would retain their self-respect. Cyrus also realized that his own people could learn from many of the societies he conquered. At his command, Persians sought out and copied the most useful practices of their new subjects. He also standardized taxes and measurements, codified laws, and fostered commercial and cultural connections within his vast domains.

Cyrus's policies of tolerance were based not so much on benevolence as on pragmatism. He acted in ways he knew would work. He understood that people treated humanely were not likely to rebel. But he also understood the nature of nomadic societies that occupied the Iranian plateau. These groups, often called tribes, usually resisted joining settled societies. They tended to pursue their own interests, migrating at will to various parts of the plateau and following their own traditions and governing methods. Tribal fighters were bound to their chiefs by ties of loyalty cemented by blood relationships and patronage, the voluntary submission of a family or clan to a powerful leader (or patron). Thus chiefs commanded considerable leverage that could be used to support a central leadership, as long as that leadership did not monopolize power or impose its culture on others. In such circumstances, Cyrus acted prudently, accepting conditions he could not change and turning necessity to his advantage by granting autonomy magnanimously.

That magnanimity was not, however, unlimited. Tribal leaders were expected to place their own interests within the context of the empire's larger interests, recognizing that cooperation would benefit everyone. Defense and trade were empire-wide priorities. Permitting the Jews to return to Palestine helped Cyrus assimilate the Phoenician and Palestinian remnants of the Babylonian Empire, and the rebuilding of the temple at Jerusalem was followed by the construction of fortifications designed to protect the western regions of the empire against invasion from Egypt. The Jews were expected to cooperate in this task, and evidence suggests that they did. So did the Babylonians, whose merchants welcomed membership in an empire that offered them secure trade routes to markets in Egypt and Syria. Cyrus's ability to transform conflict into connection thus created an extensive commercial network in Southwest Asia.

Cyrus transforms conflict into connection and cooperation

Persian Governance and Society: Links with Mesopotamia

The Persian Empire, ruled by ambitious, creative leaders, dominated both Iran and Mesopotamia by the middle of the sixth century B.C.E. Then its rulers proceeded to consolidate their hold over their subjects and project Persian influence westward, toward an eventual confrontation with Greece.

From Cyrus to Darius

After the conquest of Babylon, Cyrus presided over the largest empire on earth. He had won the loyalty of most of his subject peoples by treating them humanely. Only one corner of his realm resisted his rule, and the Great King finally overreached himself. The Massagetae (*mahs-ah-JET-ē*), a nomadic people of Scythian origin in northwestern India, were contemptuous of Persian ideals and indifferent to Persian control. In 530 B.C.E., Cyrus, now in his sixties, led his army into the region to subdue these difficult people. The battle went badly for the Persians, and Cyrus himself was knocked from his horse by Tomyris (*tum-Ē-riss*), queen of the Massagetae. She severed his head with a single blow of her sword and returned his mutilated corpse to the Persians, who retreated westward and buried him in the tomb described at the beginning of this chapter.

Cambyses (*kam-BĒ-sēz*), Cyrus's son, succeeded him and wisely decided to leave the Massagetae alone. Instead he invaded Egypt, bringing the Nile Valley under Persian control. But the campaign there took three years and Persians at home, unnerved by Cyrus's defeat and tired of war, revolted in 522 B.C.E. Cambyses (r. 530–521 B.C.E.) rushed back from Egypt to suppress the uprising, but he died along the way. The Persian Empire had never established a routine order of succession, and with three different heirs of the Achaemenid dynasty contending for power, the empire fell into disarray.

The eventual winner was Darius (*duh-RĪ-us*), a 28-year-old soldier who married both Cambyses' grieving widow and a daughter of Cyrus the Great (Persian rulers sometimes married more than one woman for political gain). But he was widely viewed as a

The "Cyrus Cylinder", a damaged clay cylinder completely inscribed with cuneiform writing that shows the influence of Sumerian culture on Persia.

Map 6.3 The Persian Empire Expands, 549–490 B.C.E.

The Persian Empire stretched across portions of three continents on a broad east-west axis. Note that Persia recentered power in southwest Asia eastward away from Mesopotamia, controlling territory from Libya and Macedonia in the west to the Indus valley in the east. The Royal Road facilitated communication and connections across this geographically challenging region, while local governors known as satraps enforced the Persian King's will in areas the monarch himself never visited. What effects would Cyrus the Great's policies of assimilation have had on the peoples of such a vast and diverse region?

	Persian homeland
	Expansion by Cyrus the Great, 529 B.C.E.
	Expansion by Cambyses II and Darius I, 500 B.C.E.
	Royal Road

Darius claims the Persian throne

usurper, and rebellions broke out throughout the empire. Claiming divine support, Darius (r. 521–486 B.C.E.) put down the uprisings by force. It was a bloody beginning for a ruler who would one day be known as Darius the Great.

Prudently, Darius waited a few years before resuming Persia's imperial expansion, using the time to reorganize his army. But he did not wait too long, for he understood that the arrogance he had shown in claiming divine support would have to be justified by victories. In 517 B.C.E., he struck eastward, driving into southwestern India and putting its gold mines to the service of the empire (Map 6.3). His victories in the Indus Valley completed Persia's conquest of three of the four great river civilizations. Only China remained outside his grasp, and it is unlikely that he ever thought of going there. Instead he moved westward, securing Egypt and Libya, and then struck north into southeastern Europe, pressing on as far as the Danube River by 512 B.C.E. With future conquests in mind, he settled down for the time being to solidify his rule.

Administration of the Empire

Cyrus, Cambyses, and Darius had built an enormous empire, many times larger than the Assyrian Empire that Cyrus had overthrown (Map 6.4). Ruling that realm—a vast expanse of many different peoples and cultures—would require a carefully structured bureaucracy. Central control had to be ensured, even as local autonomy was preserved, in order to avoid inefficiency, rebellion, or both.

Darius chose strong central rule. Whereas Cyrus had governed through cooperation backed by the ever-present threat of superior force, Darius emphasized authority. Cyrus had acted benevolently toward defeated rulers and turned them, where possible, into allies. Darius, in contrast, called his enemies "Kings of The Lie" and singled them out for special punishment. More distant from his people than Cyrus and less willing to permit autonomy, Darius grounded his government on the unswerving loyalty of political appointees.

Map 6.4 The Assyrian and Persian Empires Compared, 625–500 B.C.E.

The sprawling Assyrian Empire had dominated southwest Asia, but observe how the conquests of Cyrus, Cambyses, and Darius I dwarf it. Ruling an empire as enormous as Persia was an unprecedented task, requiring administrative innovations such as satrapies. It also required a willingness to grant substantial autonomy to local rulers and leaders, a feature that had characterized Persian governance even before Cyrus. What other policies or institutions might have been devised to permit efficient rule of such an enormous realm?

Darius centralizes Persian administration

These concerns led Darius to divide the Persian Empire into twenty provinces, each known in Farsi as a **satrapy** (*SĀ-trap-ē*) and ruled by a governor called a satrap. Most satraps were not Persians but members of the ethnic group they were expected to rule. In this way, Darius strengthened central control while perpetuating the local autonomy characteristic of nomadic society. Linked to the Achaemenids through marriage or birth, satraps were referred to as "the eyes and ears of the Great King."

Selected for their loyalty and their familiarity with local conditions, satraps exercised considerable authority, reinforced by rapid communication. A carefully maintained highway system, dominated by the Royal Road running from Sardis, near the Aegean Sea to Susa (*SOO-suh*), near the Persian Gulf, guaranteed that information would travel quickly. Persia's superb mounted postal service could, under the best conditions, carry a message more than a thousand miles in the course of a week. Foot soldiers, however (see page 133), even if marching at the breakneck pace of 19 miles a day, would take three months to travel the Royal Road. Beyond Susa, the roads eastward to India were less satisfactory, and the terrain rougher.

Darius knew, however, that the swift delivery of a royal message did not necessarily guarantee compliance. The emperor might be master of all he surveyed from his capital, but beyond that horizon he depended on the willing cooperation of subordinates. He needed men, particularly in remote areas, who would carry out his commands without question and who would act in his own best interests. Satraps were the men he chose.

Satraps play a vital role in Persian governance

The satraps were crucial to the prosperity and peace of the empire they served. They conducted diplomacy with border states and warrior peoples. Both inside and outside the empire, they blended persuasion and force as Cyrus and Darius had done. The stability they ensured allowed trade and commerce to thrive. In addition, they were entrusted with the collection of royal taxes. If the satraps failed at this task, the empire would fail. That its fall came with defeat by a military genius, rather than as a consequence of poor administration, is a tribute to the diligence and skill of the satraps as well as to the design of the administrative system developed by Darius the Great.

Mesopotamian Influences: Law, Administration, and Commerce

As Persia expanded and as its bureaucracy grew, its connections with other cultures multiplied. The emperors were particularly attracted by Mesopotamia, birthplace of the Sumerian, Babylonian, and Assyrian cultures and worthy of imitation in several respects.

Hammurabi's Code influences Persian law

Law was one area in which Persians could learn from Mesopotamia. Darius needed a legal system applicable throughout the empire in order to support his administrative structures. Adhering to Cyrus's principle of tolerance for subject peoples, Darius permitted local customs and regulations to remain in place. But he established a system of royal judges to ensure that local laws would be enforced in a manner consistent with the interests of the empire. Deliberately seeking to be known as a lawgiver like the Babylonian king Hammurabi, Darius authorized the compilation and codification of Persian laws. But while Hammurabi's Code survived in numerous cuneiform tablets, Darius's *Ordinance of Good Regulations*, written on parchment (treated sheepskins or goatskins), completely disappeared. In fact, until recent archeological discoveries, some scholars did not believe it once existed. The few indirect references to it found in contemporary Babylonian commercial documents suggest that it was modeled on Hammurabi's Code but altered to apply Persian ethics to both civil and criminal matters.

Persian government was also influenced by Mesopotamia. The Aryans who entered Iran brought with them a simple social structure adapted to life on the steppes of Central Asia. But Cyrus's invasion of Mesopotamia brought Persia into contact with a very complex civilization. Ruling it required levels of organization beyond those present in a nomadic society. The Babylonian Empire had developed a system of provincial governors, many of whose duties were now taken over by Persian satraps and their subordinates, such as tax collectors, police officials, and record keepers. These officials constituted an administrative class of their own, developing codes of conduct specific to their roles in Persian life. In addition, the military occupation of Mesopotamia and its assimilation into the Persian Empire forced the satraps to share power with local warriors, who resented the Persians for their literacy and their knowledge of diplomacy. Soldiers did not generally have these skills, and Persian administrators, responding to their antagonism, gradually became more militaristic.

The conquest of Mesopotamia also brought Persia into contact with western Asia and northwestern Africa. International trade expanded, fostered by the empire's political stability, its control of sea routes, and its well-maintained roads. Persia traded extensively with Syria, Egypt, Greece, and Ethiopia, connecting those regions with Central Asia through Afghanistan. Far more cosmopolitan than its Mesopotamian, Egyptian, and Indian predecessors, the Persian Empire forged connections between cultures separated by thousands of miles.

Persepolis: the east stairway to the great audience hall of Darius I, showing visiting dignitaries bringing tribute.

Possession of Mesopotamia helps Persia create connections

Persian Society and Culture

Contact with Mesopotamia also affected Persian society. To meet the needs of an expanding empire, social classes began to develop in Persian cities. Artisans now needed to fabricate more than saddles and weapons: they created items of metal, fiber, and leather required by an urbanizing society in the process of forsaking its nomadic past. Merchants carried on trade, both locally and over long distances, making use of the Royal Road and Silk Road. Nomads had no need for elaborate systems of irrigation, but settled societies based on arid plateaus did, and the skilled and unskilled workers who built and maintained them were highly valued.

In addition, Persian society included a slave class. Persia had a history of slave-owning—in Central Asia the Aryans had owned slaves—and when invading Persians occupied Mesopotamia, they saw the Babylonians using slaves on large construction projects. Most Persian slaves were prisoners taken in battle, but others were ordinary individuals who, on account of debts, were forced to sell themselves or even their families into slavery to repay their creditors. Slaves were the property of their owners in every sense and could make no decisions (including marriage) without permission. Although some slaves became highly skilled at their tasks and were rewarded with increasing levels of responsibility and respect, most led short lives of hard labor and deprivation.

Persian society develops a class structure

What little is known of Persian family structure suggests a self-reliant society. A Persian man could have more than one wife, provided that he could afford to maintain each of them above the poverty level, a restriction that limited polygamy to the upper classes.

Elite Persian women exercise considerable authority

The fact that men were frequently away from home on business or at war meant that elite Persian women normally enjoyed substantial independence. They administered their family estates, organized celebrations, and traveled freely throughout the empire with or without their husbands. Most men and women, of course, lived from one meal to the next and never acquired wealth. These families, on whose labor the empire depended, had little time to contemplate anything other than survival.

Everyone, however—elites, ordinary people, and slaves—benefited from the Persian love of celebration. Festivals were common throughout the empire, particularly once Zoroastrianism took root. That religion, described below, obligates people to seek happiness and considers fasting and penance to belong to the realm of demons. Accordingly, Persians enjoyed feasts filled with music, dancing, and fun. The staple food was barley bread, supplemented by fruits, vegetables, and date or grape wine. Merrymakers on holy days were required to give to the poor and invite even the most destitute to join the revelry. The spring festival of Nō Rōz (*NO ROSE*), commemorating the creation of fire, was celebrated with special foods, the exchange of gifts, and the wearing of new clothes and ornaments. In addition to seven "high feasts," there were many local fairs and frolics. The love of celebrations gave the Persians a spirit of joy that counterbalanced the empire's military might and administrative control.

Persians loved objects made of gold or silver, like this silver figurine of an antelope.

Persians also enjoyed fine jewelry and clothing. Like their Median and Scythian ancestors, they wore a wide variety of bracelets, necklaces, chains, and earrings, often made of gold or silver. Contemporary non-Persian accounts often refer to Iranians as taking great pride in their appearance, and it is likely that their clothing was durable and attractive. Bowls, goblets, and ceremonial vessels were made of brass, gold, and silver, and appear to have been widely used not only by the elite but by many ordinary households.

Much of the empire's cultural inheritance came from the Medes and Persians. The Persians spoke Farsi, which featured a 36-character alphabet, an intricate grammatical structure, and a rich, expressive vocabulary. This language was written not on clay in the Sumerian style, but with pen and ink on parchment.

Another original aspect of Persian culture was architecture. Once the formerly nomadic Persians became sedentary, they made effective use of the column and constructed huge monuments depicting bulls and lions with wings. Persian art that has survived the centuries generally takes the form of sculpture and reliefs carved into the walls of buildings. These monuments reveal a culture sensitive to beauty and aware of its political uses. For example, the emperor, his generals, and courtiers are portrayed as regal, powerful persons of great dignity. Often they are depicted as stylized, mythical heroes, adorned with wings or engaged in single-handed combat with lions or bulls. Delegations from subject kingdoms like Babylonia and Lydia are shown bearing tribute and paying homage to Cyrus or Darius, particularly on the walls of the city of Persepolis (*per-SEH-puh-lis*), the most visually striking of Persia's cities (see photo, page 143).

Persian architecture celebrates the emperor's power

The emperor maintained official residences in the cities of Ecbatana, Babylon, and Susa, enabling him to rule the empire from whichever city he happened to be living in at the time. During the winter this was usually Susa, centrally located in Mesopotamia; Ecbatana or Babylon served as the capital in the summer. Shortly after his accession to the throne, Darius began building a ceremonial capital at Persepolis, intending to demonstrate his greatness through its massive buildings and sculptures. He died before the work was completed, and his son Xerxes (*ZURK-zēz*) finished the task. Festivals, celebrations, and major imperial functions were held there in an atmosphere that suggested the largest empire of its day would last for thousands of years.

Persepolis survives today only as ruins, but even those fragments are impressive. It contained a series of massive public buildings, including the royal treasury and several superbly designed reception halls. These structures and colossal monuments portrayed the power and ferocity of the Persian Emperor. Anyone witnessing such grandeur would conclude that Persia in 500 B.C.E. was truly the center of the world. But just as Cyrus the Great had been unexpectedly brought down in battle by a small tribe of nomadic Scythians far to the east, his successors would inadvertently lead the empire to destruction in wars with seemingly unimportant people along its western frontier.

A photograph of the ruins of the entrance to the Palace of Darius in Persepolis.

Zoroastrianism

Those assimilated into the Persian Empire participated in a dynamic, expanding state and a flourishing economy. Many also practiced a religion that gave divine sanction to the ambitions of the Persian emperors: **Zoroastrianism** (*zohr-ō-ASS-trē-ahn-iz'm*).

At first the Medes and Persians were polytheistic, worshipping a variety of deities including two powerful gods, Ahura and Mazda (*uh-HOOR-uh* and *MAHZ-duh*). Like other polytheistic peoples, the Medes and Persians incorporated religion into their daily lives, believing that various gods represented natural forces such as wind, rain, and sunlight and praying to the one whose benefits they sought. This belief system changed significantly in the sixth century B.C.E. with the empire's adoption of the ideas of a holy man who had lived centuries earlier on the Iranian plateau.

A Religion of Good and Evil

Zoroastrianism was based on the ideas of the prophet Zoroaster—or Zarathustra (*zah-rah-THOO-strah*), as he is more commonly known today—who apparently lived in Persia sometime between 1300 and 1000 B.C.E. Zoroaster sensed that two powerful Persian gods, Ahura and Mazda, were in fact a single god, whom he called Ahura Mazda. He perceived Ahura Mazda as the universal god of light who had created human beings and given them free will to choose between right and wrong. To explain the existence of evil, Zoroaster maintained that Ahura Mazda had a malignant twin, Ahriman (*AHR-ē-mun*), whom Ahura Mazda had defeated and banished from paradise but who still sought to influence human behavior as lord of the forces of darkness.

Zoroaster's promotion of monontheism—belief in one god—won few converts until he blended it with an ancient cult emphasizing fire worship. Zoroastrians built fire temples to enshrine the light of Ahura Mazda. They conceded that lesser gods existed but characterized some as attributes of Ahura Mazda, while others were manifestations of The Lie, a set of false doctrines propagated by Ahriman to lead people astray.

Once the Persian emperors adopted Zoroastrianism, they gave control of it to the Magi (*MĀ-jī*), the scholar-priests of the Persian world who guarded the temples and compiled Zoroaster's ideas in a sacred text called the *Avesta* (see "Excerpt from the *Avesta*"). The Magi, who later played a role in the Christian story of the birth of Jesus

Zoroaster preaches a monotheistic religion

Document 6.1 Excerpt from The *Avesta*.

The *Avesta*, the Holy Scripture of Zoroastrianism, is a collection of prayers to Ahura Mazda and to lesser spirits and beings.

Purity is the best good. Happiness, happiness is to him: Namely, to the best pure in purity.

Broken, broken be Satan Ahriman, whose deeds and works are accursed. May his works and deeds not attain to us. May Ahura Mazda be victorious and pure.

Let Ahura Mazda be king, and let Ahriman, the wicked holder-aloof, be smitten and broken.

All the evil thoughts, evil words, evil deeds, which I have thought, spoken, done, committed in the world, which are become my nature—all these sins, thoughts, words, and deeds, bodily, spiritual, earthly, heavenly, O Lord, pardon; I repent of them.

In the name of God, the Lord, the Increaser. May he increase in great majesty. I praise and exalt Ahura Mazda, the Brilliant, Majestic, Omniscient, the Perfecter of deeds, the Lord of Lords, the Prince over all princes, the Protector, the Creator of the created, the Giver of daily food, the Powerful, Good, Strong, Old, Forgiving, Granter of forgiveness, Rich in Love, Mighty and Wise, the pure Supporter. May thy right rule be without ceasing.

SOURCE: *The Avesta*, translated by Arthur Henry Bleeck (New York: Gordon Press, 1974) 3–6.

of Nazareth, came to see all creation as a cosmic struggle between the forces of good, led by Ahura Mazda, and the forces of evil, led by Ahriman. At the end of life, each individual would be judged by Ahura Mazda: those who had led lives of goodness and truth would be rewarded with eternal bliss; those who had practiced wickedness and deceit would be doomed to everlasting pain. At the Last Judgment, righteousness would overcome The Lie.

Zoroastrianism influences later monotheistic religions

Many beliefs later important to Judaism, Christianity, and Islam first appeared in Zoroastrianism: the existence of one God of justice and benevolence, the conflict between God and the Devil, the divine judgment of individuals based on their moral behavior, and the notions of heaven and hell. Zoroastrianism was also the source of the cult of Mithras (*MITH-rahs*), a divine-human "god of day" revered as Ahura Mazda's main deputy, which later spread widely in the Greek and Roman worlds. Zoroastrianism survived for more than a thousand years, until, in the seventh and eighth centuries C.E., it was displaced by Islam. Refugees fled to the area surrounding Bombay in India, where Zoroastrianism survives today, practiced by Parsees, the descendants of these refugees.

Social and Political Content

Zoroastrianism delivers a social message

Zoroastrianism was more than theology: it also carried a strong social and political message about how people should conduct themselves. Zoroastrians believe that the entire purpose of the struggle between good and evil is the improvement of life on earth before the Last Judgment, and that individuals will be judged not only by what they have believed but also by what they have done. Thus Zoroastrians feel compelled to engage in government, political affairs, and issues of social justice.

From 521 B.C.E. onward, the Zoroastrian faith was strongly supported by the Persian kings, who liked to portray themselves as Ahura Mazda's earthly agents. Darius the Great had the magnificent Behistun relief carved to depict his triumphs over his enemies through the divine assistance of Ahura Mazda, who appears in the relief as a winged god blessing the proceedings. Zoroastrianism's sociopolitical ethic proved very useful to the

Persian kings: it established a moral order in Persia and designated the Great King as God's vice-regent on earth. To disobey his commands was equivalent to sinning against God and humanity.

Neither Darius nor his successors imposed Zoroastrianism on Persia's subject peoples; to do so would have violated the cultural autonomy that formed the basis of Persian rule. But Darius seems to have believed that Ahura Mazda had bestowed upon him the awesome yet appropriate duty of unifying the known world into a single empire based on justice and peace. In pursuit of that sacred goal, the emperor believed he had to respect the various cultures of the peoples entrusted to his care. He also had to draw them away from The Lie by giving them positions of responsibility (such as satrap) and demonstrating that obedience to the empire carried with it not slavery but opportunity. In this way Zoroastrianism reinforced attitudes that Darius had already learned to value. Or perhaps, given his enormous influence, it was the other way round.

Confrontation with Greece

The Persian Empire first came into contact with Greece when Cyrus completed the conquest of Lydia in 546 B.C.E. Several Greek city-states in the region of Ionia along the western coast of Anatolia thereby fell under Persian domination, since Lydia had previously protected them. The Greeks knew little about Persian culture prior to Lydia's defeat and liked little of what they learned thereafter. Zoroastrian monotheism and musings about social justice baffled polytheistic people who believed that justice for humans was not a high priority for the gods. To the fiercely independent Greeks, Persia's tolerance for its subject peoples seemed only a strategy for making bondage less offensive. For their part, the Persians regarded the Greeks as no more sophisticated or dangerous than the other peoples the empire had subdued. The conquerors of Assyria and Babylon were not intimidated by a land divided into many competing city-states that seemed to lack military potential. For several decades after the defeat of Lydia, the west Anatolian city-states reluctantly accommodated themselves to Persian rule. Then, in 499, the Ionian Revolt began.

The Ionian Revolt and the Persian Response

The uprising in Ionia took Persia by surprise. The Persians had followed their standard policy of working with local leaders, but the Ionian officials with whom they worked discredited themselves with their own people by their collaboration with Persia. The rebellious cities were far away from Susa, and the Greeks, who never understood Persians, apparently thought that this distance would discourage the emperor from retaliating. Almost as an afterthought, the rebels appealed for aid to the Greek city-states across the Aegean Sea. Athens, one of the leading city-states, responded by sending a fleet, which was defeated in 494 B.C.E. The revolt disintegrated and Darius sought to consolidate his victory by directing the city-states of the Greek mainland to submit to Persian domination of Aegean commerce. He was astounded when Athens and Sparta, another important city-state, promptly killed his messengers, an act of sacrilege from the Persian perspective and an insult to the emperor. Deeply offended, Darius prepared for war.

The Ionian revolt brings
Persia into conflict with
Greece

In 492 B.C.E., a powerful Persian fleet heading for Greece was wrecked near Mount Athos. A second force was dispatched two years later and landed in the Bay of Marathon (Map 6.5). The Persians expected to defeat their enemy easily—an expectation the Athenians in fact shared. Persia's army of 20,000 soldiers outnumbered the Greeks two to one, but in the Battle of Marathon more than six thousand Persians perished, while the Greeks lost only 192 men.

Darius's defeat at
Marathon causes Persia
to rethink its strategy

The Greeks believed that their victory at Marathon had frustrated Persia's intention to conquer the entire Greek mainland. But to the Persians, Marathon was only a small setback that did nothing to change Darius's strategy of ensuring Persian domination of the Aegean Sea. He had intended merely to punish the Greeks for their revolt, not conquer them; but his loss at Marathon convinced him that conquest was necessary. Darius intended to return with a much larger army but died in 486 B.C.E., before his forces were ready. It was a foregone conclusion, however, that his son and successor, Xerxes, (r. 486–465 B.C.E.) would renew the struggle.

Map 6.5 Conflict Between Persia and Greece, 492–479 B.C.E.

Persia's suppression of the revolts of the Ionian city-states in western Anatolia provoked Greek intervention. Persia responded with two separate invasions of the Greek peninsula. Note that Persia, a land-based empire, was forced by geography to construct a powerful navy in order to fight the Greeks. Persia's inability to conquer Greece meant that Greek civilization would continue to evolve apart from eastern influences, and would eventually form part of the foundation of what came to be known as Western civilization. Had Persia been victorious, what might have happened to Greek society and culture?

Xerxes and the Invasion of Greece

Xerxes invaded Greece with the explicit intention of subduing its mainland. Although he was confident of victory, he had learned from Marathon not to underestimate his opponents, and in 481 B.C.E. he left Susa at the head of a massive army. The Greek historian Herodotus (*hair-AH-duh-tuss*), who chronicled the Persian Wars, reported that an invading host of 2,641,000 men drank entire rivers dry when camping for the night. This was a wild exaggeration—there probably weren't two million men of military age in all of Persia—but Xerxes could have brought about 250,000 soldiers, enough to frighten the usually quarrelsome Greeks into creating an anti-Persian alliance. Sparta provided leadership on land, while Athens mobilized a formidable navy. At stake in the struggle was the future leadership of Greece, western Anatolia, and the entire Aegean basin.

Greeks put aside their quarrels to unite against Persia

The Persians struck simultaneously by land and sea. At a narrow mountain pass near the town of Thermopylae (*thur-MAH-puh-lē*), 360 Spartans held out for days against more than 10,000 Persians. The Spartans died to the last man, delaying the Persian advance long enough to permit their comrades to mount a successful defense on the plains beyond. Today a plaque at the entry to the pass commemorates the Spartan ideal that inspired such sacrifice: "Go tell the Spartans, stranger passing by/ That here, obedient to their laws, we lie." Shortly thereafter, further dramatic Greek victories forced the Persians to withdraw.

In retrospect it is clear why the Persians lost. First, they faced massive logistical problems in trying to sustain such huge military forces so far from home. Second, their lightly armed soldiers, equipped for mobile fighting on the plains of Asia, were surprised to find the Greek infantry better equipped to fight in the narrow passes and rocky hills of Greece. Finally, the Greeks were more highly motivated than their enemy, because they had more to lose. The Persians could withdraw to fight again, but if the Greeks lost they would lose their independence.

A variety of factors prevent Persia from conquering Greece

Stalemate

Their defeat in Greece astounded the Persians and convinced Xerxes to return home. He had been absent too long for a monarch with such extensive ambitions and responsibilities. Moreover, he faced a rebellion in Babylonia, probably provoked by news of his difficulties in Greece. If he failed to put it down his throne stood in jeopardy.

But the Greco-Persian conflict was far from over. Misinterpreting Xerxes' withdrawal as evidence that the Persians had given up, Athens and its allies landed troops in western Anatolia to pursue the Persians and secure Ionian independence. After nearly three more decades of intermittent warfare, the two sides signed the Peace of Callias (*KAHL-ē-us*) in 448 B.C.E.: Athens agreed to leave Anatolia to the Persians, who in turn promised to stay out of Ionia and the Aegean Sea.

What had begun as the small-scale Ionian Revolt had turned into an unanticipated stalemate, and Persian ambitions were frustrated. Darius and Xerxes had discovered their reach exceeded their grasp: Persia could land forces on the Greek mainland and devastate the countryside, but it could neither conquer Greece nor hold Ionia. The Greeks had seen the benefits of cooperation in the face of a powerful enemy, but they learned little from the experience. Athens and several of its allies, after driving Persia from Ionia, soon took up arms against Sparta.

Greek resistance blocks further Persian expansion

Xerxes returned home in 479 B.C.E., and though he had intended to return to Greece, he never rallied himself for war again. After suppressing the Babylonian rebellion, he was content to live in luxury, gradually withdrawing from affairs of state. Then, in 465 B.C.E., he was assassinated. Thereafter Persia endured a succession of weak rulers who were unable to deal effectively with rebellion in Egypt and rising discontent at home. But in 431 B.C.E., when the Greek city-states went to war with one another, the Persians found themselves with a new opportunity for conquest.

Persian Resurgence

The Peloponnesian War gives Persia a new opportunity

From 431 to 404 B.C.E., Greece was racked by the Peloponnesian (*pell-luh-puhn-Ē-zhē-un*) War. Rival alliances led by Athens and Sparta clawed at one another and left the Greek mainland open to intervention or invasion. At first Persia alternated between supporting one alliance or the other, but eventually it funded the expansion of the Spartan fleet. That fleet enabled Sparta to challenge Athens's longstanding control of the sea and eventually defeat the Athenian alliance, which had been Persia's most persistent antagonist. Artaxerxes (*AR-tuh-zurk-zēz*) II, Persian emperor from 404 to 358 B.C.E., then took advantage of Greek exhaustion and moved to reclaim the Ionian city-states.

Had the Greeks united, it is likely that they could have defeated the Persians, whose army, consisting largely of draftees, was weakened by low morale. But Persian diplomacy and bribery combined with centuries of Greek rivalry to keep the Greeks divided. Finally, in 387 B.C.E., Artaxerxes gained enough leverage to impose a treaty called the King's Peace, withdrawing his forces from Greece in exchange for recognition of his control of Ionia. After 16 years of struggle, Persia had emerged as the real winner of the Peloponnesian War. The Persian city of Susa was now the capital of the Aegean world.

The Macedonian Conquest and Its Successor States

The days of the Achaemenids, however, were numbered. The satraps, sensing the weakening of royal authority, enriched themselves in the provinces at the emperor's expense. Plots, intrigues, and assassinations grew more frequent. Emperor Artaxerxes III (358–338 B.C.E.) proved too distracted by these troubles to pay attention to Macedonia, a new threat to Persian power arising north of Greece (Map 6.5).

The End of the Persian Empire

Persia's failure to fight Macedon leads to the defeat of the Persian Empire

In 341 B.C.E., Persia refused to assist Athens in its war against Philip II of Macedon (*MASS-uh-dun*), preferring to negotiate with the Macedonian leader. It was a shortsighted policy. By 339 B.C.E., Persian troops had been drawn into the war, and in the following year Philip (r. 359–336 B.C.E.) had united all Greece under his leadership. Artaxerxes was poisoned by satraps seeking to weaken the emperor's position, and his eventual successor, Emperor Darius III (336–330 B.C.E.), was not an effective leader. Suddenly vulnerable, Persia stood alone against the new Macedonian power in the west.

Philip would have been a formidable enough adversary even for Cyrus the Great, but his murder at his daughter's wedding in 336 B.C.E. brought to the Macedonian throne his son Alexander III, later known as Alexander the Great, a military genius whose talents have never been surpassed. Alexander, whose story is told in Chapter 7, defeated the Persian army in a series of battles in 334–333 B.C.E. Yet Darius III and his counselors underestimated the abilities of this 22-year-old novice. The Persian Empire had lost many battles but had always won the wars, provided that its leadership had the sense to play for time.

The problem was that the impetuous Alexander had no intention of letting the Achaemenids stall. He sacked Persepolis in 330 and stood over the corpse of Darius III, murdered that summer by his own troops while fleeing from Alexander's advance. The Achaemenid dynasty died with Darius III, but by officiating at his funeral ceremony, Alexander designated himself as that dynasty's rightful heir. The former Persian Empire, which had conquered so many peoples itself, was subjugated under the Macedonian empire of Alexander the Great.

Part of a mosaic illustrating the Battle of Issus, in which Darius III (in chariot) led the Persians to defeat against Alexander the Great.

Persia Under Macedonian Rule

Persian government, always tolerant of subject peoples, was now forced to accept Greek political institutions and culture. Alexander wisely retained most of the local Achaemenid administrative structure, but he encouraged the mixing of Greeks and Persians, taking several Persian wives himself, and significant numbers of Macedonian and Greek soldiers settled permanently in Persia. Alexander's policies appear to have worked well, since no noticeable unrest marred his rule and no rebellions followed his unexpected death in 323 B.C.E. at the age of 33.

Alexander attempts to combine Greek and Persian institutions

Soon thereafter, one of Alexander's generals, Seleucus Nikator (*sell-LOO-kus ni-KĀ-tur*), assumed control over most of the old Persian Empire; the new state was called the Seleucid (*sell-LOO-sid*) kingdom. But in an effort to secure his position with the Macedonian leadership, Seleucus (r. 305–280 B.C.E.) promoted Macedonian officials over Persians and displayed no sympathy for or connection to the Persian culture or language. Soon he lost the support of the Persian nobility on the old empire's eastern fringes. Rebellions broke out there, and by 304 B.C.E. Seleucus was forced to turn control of western India over to Chandragupta Maurya, founder of the Mauryan Empire. Thus the disintegration of the Persian Empire helped create a new empire in India. By 129 B.C.E., the Seleucid kingdom had fallen apart, with two principal successor states emerging: the Greco-Bactrian kingdom, comprising northern Afghanistan and part of northwestern India, and the Parthian empire, extending from Armenia southeastward to the Arabian Sea.

The crumbling of Alexander's empire creates successor states

The Parthian Empire

The collapse of the Seleucid kingdom opened the way for the Parthians, a Central Asian tribe that had moved onto the Iranian plateau during the Achaemenid dynasty. The Parthians ruled formerly Seleucid lands using Persian-style satrapies and administrative flexibility—both essential for governing a region composed of so many different ethnic groups. The Romans, whose empire arose to the west of Persia in the second and first centuries C.E. (Chapter 8), considered the Parthians worthy heirs of the Persians. After Roman armies were routed by the Parthians in 53 B.C.E., Roman Emperor Caesar

Augustus (31 B.C.E.–14 C.E.) refrained from provoking them. Subsequent Roman emperors launched repeated attacks on the westernmost portions of the Parthian empire but never succeeded in conquering Parthian Persia.

Parthian Persia facilitates commerce across Asia

Parthian Persia was a critical crossroad of Asian trade because of its strategic location along the Silk Road (Map 6.6). The Parthians eagerly participated in trans-Asiatic commerce, serving as middlemen between China and Southwest Asia while maintaining safe roads and centers of hospitality for passing merchant caravans from many different cultures. Parthian merchants filled Chinese orders for alfalfa plants, grape vines, and Persia's magnificent Ferghana horses. Their contact with China also promoted the transmission of Indian goods and Buddhist doctrines eastward during the third century C.E. Like the Persians, the Parthians connected East and West. But the Parthians lacked the forceful leadership necessary to win back the westernmost provinces of the old Persian Empire. Following their collapse as a result of internal intrigue in 224 C.E., the imperial throne passed to a people known as the Sasanians (*suh-SAY-nee-uns*).

The Sasanian Empire

Sasanians defeat Rome and rebuild Persia

For the first time in recorded history the Iranian plateau was ruled by a people who were not invaders. The Sasanians had arrived in Fars, just north of the Persian Gulf, even before the Medes and Persians. Now they seized an opportune moment, first to help the Parthians fight the Romans, and then to replace the Parthians and construct their own empire. They fought the Roman Empire for several decades, taking Mesopotamia in 256 under the leadership of King Shapur (*shah-POOR*) I (r. 240–271 C.E.). Four years later, the Roman Emperor Valerian (r. 253–259) personally commanded the Roman legions in a campaign to expel the Sasanians from the Roman province of Syria. Shapur's forces defeated the Romans, however, captured Valerian, and brought him back to Persia as a prisoner. The Sasanians then drove through Syria into central Anatolia.

Shapur stood firmly in the tradition of the Achaemenians, Macedonians, Seleucids, and Parthians, ruling diverse ethnic groups simultaneously through the time-honored recognition of local autonomy. He tolerated the practice of Judaism, Christianity, and Buddhism, but he institutionalized Zoroastrianism as Persia's state religion and made it a powerful ally of the Sasanian monarchy. Shapur's successors were strict Zoroastrians who ended toleration and persecuted those who followed other faiths.

Sasanian Persia builds on the Zoroastrian concern with justice

Zoroastrianism reinforced the Sasanian ruling concept of the circle of equity: there could be no monarch without an army, no army without prosperity, and no prosperity without justice. Zoroastrianism's emphasis on social justice and ethical conduct made it the ideal faith for Sasanian rulers. They insisted that the emperor, who was believed to have been chosen by God, must be obeyed, but he in turn had to ensure prosperity and a just and equitable society. They proclaimed that the circle of equity limited the emperor's authority because that authority depended on his own righteous conduct. But, coupled with traditional Persian respect for local autonomy, it also enabled the Sasanians to claim divine sanction and to compel popular support.

Persia's struggle with Rome continued throughout the Sasanian period, intensifying after Emperor Diocletian's division of the Roman Empire in 284 C.E. (Chapter 9). The eastern portion of the Roman Empire, later called the Byzantine Empire (Chapter 10), fought the Persians for control of Anatolia and eastern Mediterranean trade routes.

Map 6.6 The Parthian and Sasanian Empires, 247 B.C.E.–637 C.E.

The Parthians and Sasanians occupied pivotal positions in turn. Notice that Persia's location on the Silk Road made it important in trans-Asiatic commerce, while its location at the eastern edge of first the Roman and then the Byzantine Empire connected it to those regimes, making it sometimes a natural partner and sometimes an antagonist. Neither Parthians nor Sasanians were as economically or militarily powerful as Rome or Byzantium, but they were nevertheless significant forces in southwest Asia. Why might Rome and Byzantium have chosen to coexist with these empires rather than trying to conquer them?

Parthian Persia, 247 B.C.E. – 224 C.E.

- Parthian homeland, 247 – 176 B.C.E.
- Territory gained by Parthians, 53 B.C.E. – 224 C.E.
- Vassal or allied kingdoms
- Roman Empire, 138 C.E.
- Maximum extent of Parthian influence
- Silk Road

Sasanian Persia, 224 – 637 C.E.

- Sasanian heartland before 224 C.E.
- Territory governed by Sasanian Empire, 225 – c. 360 C.E.
- Byzantine Empire, c. 600 C.E.
- Maximum extent of Sasanian empire, 6th century C.E.
- Silk Road

Under King Khusrau I (531–579), the Sasanians fought with the Byzantines over Arabia. Both sides cultivated client tribes in southern Arabia, hoping to dominate trade routes between the Red Sea and the Arabian Sea.

Persia's conflict with Byzantium gives the Arabs an opportunity

But one of Khusrau's successors, King Khusrau II (590–628), pushed the quarrel with the Byzantines too far. Taking advantage of a power struggle in Byzantium, between 604 and 619 Khusrau II defeated Byzantine armies in Mesopotamia, Syria, Palestine, Anatolia, and Egypt. At that point the Byzantine Emperor Heraclius reorganized his armies, counterattacked against the overextended Sasanian forces, and, by 628, had pushed them out of all the territories they had conquered. This disaster threw the Sasanian monarchy into disarray and left it open for conquest by Islamic Arab armies between 637 and 651 (Chapter 11). In 651 the last great pre-Islamic Persian dynasty ceased to exist, and Persia became part of a new Arab empire.

Chapter Review

Putting It in Perspective

Starting from an inhospitable plateau in Southwest Asia, the Achaemenid dynasty of Persia created the largest empire the world had yet known. The Persians ruled by a combination of force and flexibility. Though they could be brutal, they were also tolerant and practical, allowing various degrees of local autonomy among the many cultures and ethnic groups that they conquered. By permitting those they subdued to retain their cultural identities while enjoying the benefits of Persian order and prosperity, the Persians won their loyalty. Persia's excellent road system and centralized governmental organization enabled its emperors to govern this huge region effectively. In Zoroastrianism, those emperors had a belief system whose clearly developed social ethic enabled them to cast themselves and their officials as warriors for truth and light against evil and The Lie.

In its efforts to centralize its control and its methods of governing, Persia stood in the company of the great river civilizations. In its attempts to expand rapidly over vast expanses of territory, it outperformed them. But Darius and Xerxes overreached themselves in attempting to subdue the mainland of Greece, and their persistence carried with it repercussions that eventually doomed the Achaemenians.

Alexander the Great's Macedonian Empire conquered Persia, but its founder's early death split his realm into three parts. The former Persian Empire was then ruled by three successor states: the Seleucids, Parthians, and Sasanians. Persia's strategic location across Asian trade routes such as the Silk Road assured its continued economic viability, and Khusrau II's dramatic victories over the Byzantine Empire seemed to signal the reestablishment of the western boundaries of the Achaemenian Empire. But the Byzantines struck back, leaving the Sasanians open to the unanticipated invasion of Arab armies that ended the Persian Empire. Persia's administrative efficiency and social tolerance, both well in advance of similar developments elsewhere in the world, continue to mark its place in world history.

Reviewing Key Material
KEY CONCEPTS

satrapy, 142	Zoroastrianism, 145

KEY PEOPLE

Cyrus the Great, 137	Herodotus, 149
Cyaxares, 137	Artaxerxes, 150
Cambyses, 139	Philip of Macedon, 150
Darius the Great, 139	Alexander the Great, 151
Zoroaster (or	Seleucus Nikator, 151
Zarathustra), 145	Shapur I, 152
Xerxes, 145	Khusrau II, 154

ASK YOURSELF

1. Do Cyrus and Darius merit the appellation "Great"? In what ways were they different from rulers who preceded and followed them?
2. What was distinctive about Zoroastrianism? In what ways did it differ from Hinduism and Buddhism?
3. Why were Persia and Greece frequently at war? Why did the Persians eventually fail to defeat the Greeks?
4. In what ways did the Persian Empire create connections with other peoples and cultures?
5. Why were the Seleucids, Parthians, and Sasanians never able to fully reconstruct the Persian Empire after the death of Alexander the Great?

GOING FURTHER

Allen, Lindsay. *The Persian Empire*. 2005.

Balcer, Jack. *Sparta by the Bitter Sea: Imperial Interaction in Western Anatolia*. 1984.

Boyce, Mary. *Zoroastrians: Their Religious Beliefs and Practices*. 1979.

Briant, Pierre. *From Cyrus to Alexander: A History of the Persian Empire*. 2002.

Brosius, Maria. *Women in Ancient Persia*. 1996.

Cawkwell, George. *The Greek Wars: The Failure of Persia*. 2005.

Curtis, John. *Ancient Persia*. 2000.

Dandamaev, Muhammad. *A Political History of the Achaemenid Empire*. 1989.

Dandamaev, Muhammad, and Vladimir Lukonin. *The Culture and Social Institutions of Ancient Iran*. 1989.

De Souza, Philip. *The Greek and Persian Wars, 499–386 BC*. 2003.

Frye, Richard. *The History of Ancient Iran*. 1984.

Garthwaite, Gene. *The Persians*. 2005.

Herzfeld, E. *Iran in the Ancient East*. 1987.

Holland, Tom. *Persian Fire*. 2005.

Miller, M. *Athens and Persia in the Fifth Century B.C.* 1997.

Sekunda, N., and S. Chew. *The Persian Army, 560–330 BC*. 1992.

Sherwin-White, Susan, and Amelie Khurt. *From Samarkand to Sardis: A New Approach to the Seleucid Empire*. 1993.

Wiesehofer, Josef. *Ancient Persia: From 550 B.C. to 650 A.D.* 1996.

Zaehner, Robert. *The Dawn and Twilight of Zoroastrianism*. 1994.

Key Dates and Developments

Date	Development
ca. 1000 B.C.E.	Medes and Persians settle on Iranian plateau
ca. 1300–1000 B.C.E.	The Prophet Zoroaster preaches that there is one god, Ahura Mazda
612 B.C.E.	Destruction of Nineveh by Median King Cyaxares
550 B.C.E.	Persian King Cyrus unites Medes and Persians under the Achaemenid dynasty
550–530 B.C.E.	Reign of Cyrus the Great
546 B.C.E.	Persia conquers Lydia
539 B.C.E.	Persia conquers Babylonia
530–522 B.C.E.	Reign of Cambyses
525 B.C.E.	Persia conquers Egypt
521–486 B.C.E.	Reign of Darius the Great
	Construction of Persepolis and the Royal Road
	The *Ordinance of Good Regulations*
517 B.C.E.	Persia conquers the Indus Valley
512 B.C.E.	Persian forces reach the Danube River (Europe)
499 B.C.E.	Ionia revolts against Persian rule
490 B.C.E.	Athens defeats Persia at Marathon
486–465 B.C.E.	Reign of Xerxes
480–479 B.C.E.	Xerxes invades Greece and is defeated
448 B.C.E.	Peace of Callias: stalemate with Greece
334–330 B.C.E.	Alexander the Great defeats Persia
323 B.C.E.	Death of Alexander; creation of the Seleucid Kingdom
240 B.C.E.–224 C.E.	The Parthian Empire
227–642 C.E.	The Sasanian Empire

Classical Greece and Its Conflict with Asia, 2000–30 B.C.E.

Greek Athletes

Runners in ancient Greece sprint in a race depicted on a glazed Athenian vase. Athletic events, such as the Olympic Games (page 172), were extremely important in Greek culture and were often portrayed on ceramic pieces.

Late in the year 334 B.C.E., an army of Greeks and Macedonians entered Gordium in Anatolia (modern Turkey), capital city of the fabled King Midas whose touch turned all things to gold. Led by an energetic young Macedonian who sought to become a legend in his own right, the army paused at a bridge that symbolically linked Europe with Asia. At the entry to the bridge stood a large wagon designed to be pulled by yoked oxen. The wagon was fastened to the bridge abutment by an immense knot—three feet in diameter—tied around both the yoke and the wagon pole. Popular belief held that the man who could untie this Gordian Knot would conquer Asia.

The young commander, who indeed sought to conquer Asia, tried for nearly two hours to untie the knot. Eyewitness accounts disagree over what happened next. Some say that in a rage, he severed the knot with a single stroke of his sword. Others claim that after staring silently at the knot for several minutes, he simply removed the pin connecting the yoke to the pole and slipped the knot off. The first version calls attention to the commander's strength and ruthlessness, the second to his practicality. In either case, the commander—known to history as Alexander the Great—possessed all these traits in abundance. He went on to conquer much of southern Asia.

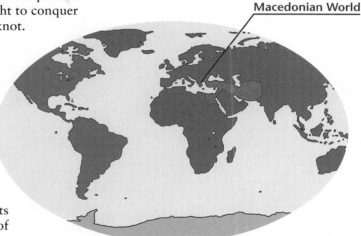

The Greco-Macedonian World

Centuries before Alexander, numerous small city-states had emerged in the mountains and islands of Greece. Fiercely independent, these city-states had often clashed but occasionally also cooperated. In the fifth century B.C.E., many banded together to fight off Persian invaders, but later they returned to warring among themselves. In the fourth century B.C.E., weakened by wars, they were conquered by the northern armies of Macedonia. United under the leadership of Alexander, the Greeks built a vast empire that included Egypt, Palestine, Mesopotamia, Persia, and northwest India. Although Alexander's empire proved short-lived, it spread Greek culture to all these regions, connecting far-flung realms to what would evolve into Western civilization.

Early Greece

Mesopotamia, Egypt, India, and China emerged in the valleys of great rivers, while Persia developed on the Iranian plateau. In the final millennium before the Common Era, a new society took shape on both the Greek mainland in southeastern Europe and on nearby islands in the Aegean Sea.

Greek civilization developed on a rocky land. An extension of the Balkan Peninsula, Greece has neither fertile plains nor irrigating rivers, and its mountains cut the peninsula into isolated areas. River travel made communication rapid in the civilizations of

Indo-Europeans occupy the Greek Peninsula

FOUNDATION MAP 7.1 Greece and Western Anatolia

The Greek Peninsula has a rugged topography. Greece's mountains impeded communication between settlements only a few miles apart, while its numerous islands and peninsulas further made travel difficult. Note that Greek city-states are separated from each other not only by mountains, but also by the Aegean Sea. What impact did this isolation have upon Greek economic and political development?

Mesopotamia, Egypt, India, and China; in Persia, the relative flatness of the Iranian plateau made land travel much easier than in Greece. Despite these drawbacks, however, Greece attracted a wave of Indo-European settlers who at some time prior to 1650 B.C.E. migrated there and called it Hellas.

Those early inhabitants proved to be hardy and resilient, able to survive on the sides of rugged mountain ranges (Map 7.1). From their hardships, they created a rich body of heroic legends and epics, which would serve as a basis for Greek religion and culture. As the mountainous terrain proved a barrier to political unification, they organized into many independent city-states with distinctive forms of governance.

Because it lacked a single centralized kingdom, Greek civilization appeared less complex than the other early societies. Eventually, however, it spread through much of the ancient world. During its expansion it changed significantly, as it absorbed elements from the cultures it encountered.

Fresco from the Palace of Knossos, Crete, showing the Minoan sport of bull dancing.

Mycenae and Crete

The early centuries of Greek history are enveloped in myth, but historians and archeologists have gradually uncovered the reality behind the fables. The Indo-European migrants, speaking a language that evolved into ancient Greek, settled on the Greek peninsula before 1650 B.C.E. No records of a previous population exist. The first well-organized Greek civilization on the peninsula is called Mycenaean (*mī-SĒ-nē-an*), after a site named Mycenae, mentioned in ancient Greek legend and excavated in the late nineteenth century C.E. by a German entrepreneur and amateur archeologist, Heinrich Schliemann (*SHLĒ-mahn*). Other early sites were unearthed in subsequent years.

Mycenaean culture seems to have been influenced by a civilization that flourished on the island of Crete, about 60 miles southeast of the Greek peninsula. This culture, called *Minoan* after a mythical Cretan ruler named Minos (*MĪ-nus*), built impressive monuments and government complexes. Minoans possessed a system of writing, now called "Linear A," which scholars have never deciphered. Mycenaeans appear to have borrowed from the Minoans a variety of artistic and architectural techniques, the principles of centralized bureaucracy, and the idea of using a palace as the seat of government. They also appear to have conquered Crete around 1450 B.C.E.

Mycenae developed a diversified civilization. By 1450 it was a thriving center of trade, with satellite cities at Athens and Thebes. Mycenaean metalwork was traded as far west as Sardinia and as far south as the upper Nile. The Mycenaeans used a system of writing similar to the Minoan script; known as "Linear B," it has been translated successfully. Mycenaeans used writing not to describe heroic feats or to create poetry or drama, as the Greeks later did, but to compile inventories of nearly everything made in the kingdom. From these massive lists emerges a picture of a highly centralized government intensely interested in every aspect of the economic life of its people. Its rulers, however, like those of Crete, remain unknown: no representations of them have been uncovered. Only through the *Iliad* do we know the name of the most famous Mycenaean, Agamemnon.

Mycenaeans develop a centralized government

The *Iliad* and the *Odyssey*, two epic poems allegedly written in the eighth century B.C.E. by a Greek poet named Homer, may actually have been composed by several writers using earlier traditions. The *Iliad* tells the dramatic stories of the Mycenaean siege of Troy (a city in what is today western Turkey), the quarrel between Mycenae's King Agamemnon and the warrior hero Achilles (*ah-KILL-ēz*), the interaction between gods and men during the battle, and the eventual fall of Troy. The *Odyssey* depicts the adventurous journey home of Odysseus (*ō-DISS-ē-us*), one of the Greek heroes of the Trojan War.

Gold mask of Agamemnon.

The people depicted in Homeric poetry were long believed to be entirely mythical. Then in 1876 C.E. Heinrich Schliemann, who believed the poems had a historical basis, discovered evidence of a complex culture at Mycenae. Six years later Schliemann unearthed the ruins of Troy, which indicated that the story told in the *Iliad* might be based in fact. Archeological evidence suggests that Troy was destroyed around 1200 B.C.E.,

Schliemann uncovers the history behind Homer

perhaps following the Greek siege described in the Homeric poems. Whatever the proportion of myth and reality in these epics, they encouraged the Greeks to perceive themselves as a warlike, heroic, and resourceful people.

The Polis

Homer's writings were composed during the so-called Dark Age of Greece (1150–700 B.C.E.), a chaotic era during which the Greeks evolved from Mycenaean monarchy to a political form more suited to the regional isolation imposed by terrain. The English word "political" is derived from the Greek word **polis** (*PŌ-liss*), meaning "city-state," referring to a city, its people, and the surrounding countryside that they controlled.

Early Greek city-states were small. The largest, Thebes, contained about 40,000 adult males, who alone were citizens exercising full civil rights. Women, children, slaves, and resident aliens had no such rights. Over the centuries, some city-states extended their domination over large rural areas, which provided them with the population required for economic expansion and military power.

Greek isolation leads to the development of multiple forms of government

The Greeks developed several methods for governing a polis, all of which entered the political vocabulary of the western world. One-man rule was known by Greeks as **monarchy**; rule by a select few, as **oligarchy**; rule by a class of well-born families, as **aristocracy**; and rule by the entire body of citizens, as **democracy**. These four methods were all considered legitimate, differing from **tyranny**, the illegal seizure of power (usually in a time of emergency) by someone who had no right to it and who thereby became a "tyrant" for the duration of the crisis.

Of all these systems, many Greeks thought democracy the least efficient. Since *all* citizens had the right to participate in *every* decision, democracy was cumbersome. It was also impractical: in Athens, for example, votes were cast and counted at a meeting place in the center of the city, so some citizens who lived at a distance were unable to participate. Both then and in subsequent centuries, democracy was considered inappropriate for city-states or countries with large, dispersed populations. These almost always chose one of the other methods of rule.

In the Greek city-states, individualism flourished, voters knew the leaders they elected, and large bureaucracies were unknown. This political arrangement was very different from centralized empires such as Egypt and China, where governments were remote from their subjects. The polis became both a significant force in Greek history and culture and a model for future civilizations to adapt or imitate.

Archaic Greece, 700–500 B.C.E.

Greek techniques of government matured during the era later called the **Archaic Period**. During this time, overpopulation and a shortage of land suitable for farming prompted many Greeks to colonize Sicily, Italy, France, Spain, and North Africa. In this way, Greek culture came to dominate and define the Mediterranean world. At the same time, those remaining in Greece responded to overpopulation through other changes in society and government.

Greek Colonization and the Spread of Greek Culture

Rocky terrain limited the size of Greek farms, and although some crops, such as olives, could be grown on hillsides, the available soil could not support significant population expansion. Midway through the eighth century B.C.E., many city-states began to look to overseas colonization as a safety valve by which to reduce population pressures. In the course of a few decades, Greek settlements were established on the shores of the Black Sea (Map 7.2), on the coast of North Africa in present-day Libya, in southern Italy and Sicily, and in southern Gaul (today France).

The farmlands that the Greeks carved out of these new settlements were not necessarily larger or more fertile than those they left behind, but these new holdings expanded significantly the total amount of land available for cultivation. Since the climate and topography of much of the Mediterranean and Black Sea basins were essentially similar to that of Greece itself, the transfer of Greek agricultural techniques was relatively simple. As in any migration of populations, some settlers went willingly, even eagerly, while others would much rather have remained at home. The city-states gave every willing person the opportunity to go and forced others to leave.

Map 7.2 The Greek Colonies, 750–550 B.C.E.

Faced with an expanding population and limited arable land, Greek city-states exported their surplus people to colonies throughout the Mediterranean basin. Notice that these colonies, which cover a distance of 2,300 miles from east to west, are all located on the shores of the Mediterranean, Aegean, and Black Seas. Colonial expansion by water came naturally to the Greeks, a maritime people who looked at the sea as a highway rather than an obstacle. How might this extensive colonization forge connections between Greeks and other peoples?

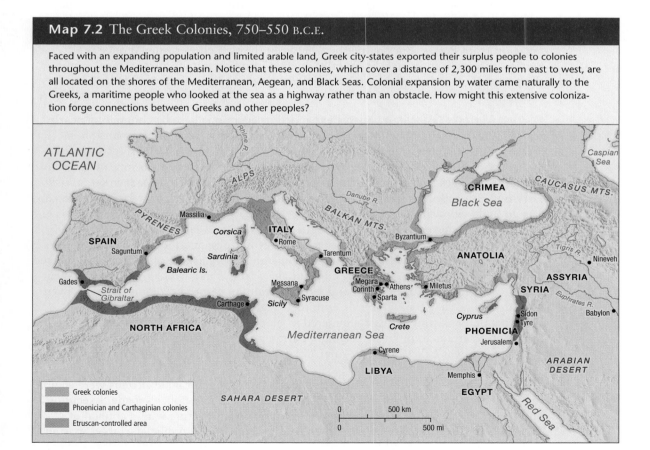

Greeks connect much of
the Mediterranean world

As Greeks spread throughout the region, they carried their culture with them. Greek words, coins, and religious practices were transmitted to areas hundreds of miles away. As the colonists encountered other peoples, they began to build trading networks with merchants in cities on the Greek peninsula itself, linking Greece not only to its new colonies but also to previously unfamiliar cultures. From these peoples, such as the Phoenicians in North Africa, the Greeks learned new methods of plowing fields, new ways to lay out cities, and new ideas about the nature of existence. Colonization proved a two-way street, connecting Greece to parts of Europe, Africa, and Asia in ways that enriched peoples and cultures in all these places. The Mediterranean basin became active and vibrant with the exchange of commerce and culture.

Rivalry Between Sparta and Athens

Most Greeks, of course, remained on their peninsula, dealing with overpopulation and land scarcity in ways other than colonization. Two of these ways are illustrated by two city-states that developed on the peninsula, becoming bitter rivals for influence and power. The first of these, Sparta, created a society organized along militaristic lines and entrusted power to an oligarchy. The second, Athens, chose a limited democracy in which all adult male citizens enjoyed the right to cast votes that counted equally. Later, cooperation between these two states would enable Greece to beat back a dangerous invasion from Persia. But competition between the two cities resumed once the Persian threat disappeared. Eventually divided into two antagonistic armed camps, the peninsula was vulnerable to an equally dangerous invasion from Macedonia, in the north.

SPARTAN MILITARY OLIGARCHY. Sparta expanded its economic base by conquering nearby regions, creating a highly militarized society in the process. Territorial expansion increased the available farmland and food supply, which in turn kept Spartans satisfied and enhanced prospects for peace among its people. Sparta's very name, meaning "The Scattered," suggests its origin as five small villages on the plain of Lacedaemon (*lah-sih-DĀ-mun*), a location so well protected by mountain ranges that Sparta found it unnecessary to build city walls for defense.

Spartans believed that under Lycurgus (*lī-SUR-juss*), a legendary lawgiver who may have lived in the seventh century B.C.E., they had rejected their individuality in favor of the collective mentality of a garrison state. Every aspect of society was directed toward military strength. Boys left home at age 7 to live in barracks, where they spent twelve years in rigorous physical and military training before becoming soldiers. Even after marriage, they took all meals with their regiments. The basic food served was black broth, consisting of pork simmered in blood and seasoned with vinegar and salt; most non-Spartans found it disgusting. Spartan girls were also raised under a strict discipline, for it was believed that regular physical exercise would help them produce strong children.

Sparta creates a
regimented oligarchy

Sparta was not, however, a military dictatorship. All adult male citizens were eligible to attend the public assembly, at which laws were passed and policies made. Execution of the laws was entrusted to Sparta's two hereditary kings, acting with a council of 28 members. The councilors were chosen for life terms by the public assembly. Spartan government was an oligarchy, responsive to the wishes of this assembly.

The regimented organization of Spartan society was not imposed on a reluctant people, but sprang from the needs of daily Spartan life. Spartans had to coax a living from rocky soil and suppress local peoples resentful of Spartan domination. The oligarchs perceived these needs, but the citizens recognized them too. Indeed, the basis of Sparta's rivalry with Athens was neither economic nor militaristic, but political. The Spartans were convinced that regimentation and oligarchy offered the best guarantee of social peace, while Athenians found them offensive.

Spartan oligarchy grows out of a shared conviction

During this period the Greek city-states frequently fought among themselves. After 550 B.C.E., however, Sparta attempted to minimize conflict by persuading neighboring states to join with it in the Peloponnesian (*pel-uh-puh-NĒ-zhun*) League, so called since most of its members lived on the large peninsula known as the Peloponnesus (*pel-uh-puh-NĒ-suss*). By 510 that alliance had enough power outside the Peloponnesus to force Athens into a form of dependency, thus ensuring its cooperation against possible external enemies, particularly Persia.

ATHENIAN DEMOCRACY. Although the Spartan military oligarchy was unappealing to Athens, its involvement of all adult male citizens in the responsibilities of government was not. During the Archaic Period the Athenian aristocrat Draco (*DRĀ-kō*) developed a legal code, the first of its kind in Greece, to regulate a similar political participation among Athenians. Published in 621 B.C.E., this code was harsh and in parts brutal (hence our adjective *draconian*, meaning "severe"), but it held that the law belonged to all citizens and must exist in written form so that all might consult and understand it. At this time Athens was an aristocracy, although its evolution in the direction of democratic forms had already begun.

Spartan warrior.

Building on this foundation, the chief magistrate Solon (*SŌ-lun*) reformed the Athenian state in the 590s, banning enslavement for debt and guaranteeing basic rights to even the poorest citizens. Solon was a skilled political operator, undermining aristocratic privileges and allowing all citizens to participate in government, while positioning himself as a mediator between aristocrats and commoners. Finally, beginning in 508 B.C.E., the Athenian aristocracy transformed itself into a democracy. An assembly of all male citizens over the age of 18 accepted or rejected proposed laws; a council of five hundred proposed those laws and supervised major governmental committees; and a board of ten officials called *archons* administered the polis, handling all military and legal issues. This type of participatory governance was not radically different from Spartan practice, except for the absence in Athens of hereditary kings.

Athens evolves from aristocracy to democracy

Excluded from voting, and all other political rights, were women, slaves, and males under the age of 18. Athenian democracy therefore differed significantly from present-day conceptions of democracy, which are based on political equality and on the participation of every citizen above a certain age, regardless of gender or social class. Most important positions in Athens were still held by aristocrats, since ordinary men had neither the leisure nor the money to devote themselves to state service full-time. But however exclusive Athenian democracy was, it offered a clear alternative to the Spartan model. In Athenian democracy, the state existed for the citizen rather than the citizen for the state. The citizen therefore served the state as a matter of self-interest, a principle that has inspired and challenged democracies from Athenian times to the present.

Classical Greece, 500–338 B.C.E.

The Peloponnesian League provided an initial framework for defending Greece against outside invasion. That defense, however, was sorely tested during the **Classical Period** (500–338 B.C.E.), an era in which classical Greek philosophy, art, and drama were flourishing. Early in that period, the Greeks combined to repel the attacks of the powerful Persian Empire. Later, however, the city-states resumed fighting among themselves, weakening each other and opening the way for the conquest of Greece by Macedonians from the north.

The Persian Wars

As we saw in Chapter 6, the revolt of the Ionian city-states in western Anatolia provoked war between Persia and Greece. Darius I and Xerxes invaded Greece between 492 and 479 B.C.E., but Persian forces were unable to overcome a Greek alliance that included Athens, Sparta, and their respective allies. By 479 B.C.E. Persia had abandoned the struggle and retreated to Anatolia.

Greece gains self-confidence by defeating the Persian invasion

The Persian Wars influenced Greece significantly. Victory boosted its self-confidence and strengthened its identification with accountable government rather than what Greeks saw as arbitrary Persian rule. Yet the image of heroic Greeks resisting Persian invaders ignores the fact that most Greeks failed to fight at all: hundreds of city-states collaborated with the Persians, remained neutral, or tried to ignore the threat. Not all Greeks were convinced of the value of cooperation.

Athenian Dominance and the Spartan Response

Pericles.

The dramatic demonstration during the Persian Wars of the strength to be found in co-operation might have impelled the Greeks toward unity. Instead, however, it promoted division and eventual disaster. With hindsight, the Greeks probably should have left the Persians alone. But in 477 B.C.E. Athens formed the Delian (*DĒ-lē-un*) League, an alliance that embarked upon a thirty-year naval campaign aiming to drive the Persians out of the Aegean, secure the independence of the Ionian city-states, and ensure Athenian domination of the region. Indeed, Athens soon dominated the League, forcing its allies to pay tribute and threatening Spartan influence. Spartan skepticism at the prospect of chasing the Persians into Asia, coupled with its fear of Athenian power, ended the fragile collaboration between the two dominant Greek states. The Spartans used their own Peloponnesian League to counter the Delian League. Now Athens and Sparta, without the common danger of Persia to unify them, faced off against each other as heads of rival alliance systems (Map 7.3).

It was not the Spartan militaristic oligarchy but the proud Athenian democracy that created this predicament. The confrontation began during a period considered the pinnacle of Athenian greatness, often termed the Age of Pericles (*PAIR-ih-clēz*). It was named for an Athenian aristocrat who was repeatedly elected to the highest positions in government between 467 and 429 B.C.E. Under his leadership the Acropolis, a hilltop citadel in the midst of the city, was transformed into a magnificent architectural display of Athenian power. Building on its extensive agricultural base, its population of over 300,000, and its large merchant fleet, Athens under Pericles'

Map 7.3 The Delian and Peloponnesian Leagues, 431 B.C.E.

Cooperation between the most powerful Greek city-states prevented the Persian Empire from conquering the Greek Peninsula. But that cooperation did not survive the withdrawal of the Persian threat. Observe that Athens and its allies in the Delian League controlled the area surrounding the Aegean Sea, while Sparta and its Peloponnesian League partners, like Thebes and Corinth, tended to be land-based. Eventually these two alliance systems fought the Peloponnesian War against each other between 431 and 404 B.C.E. How did this conflict make the eventual conquest of Greece by Philip of Macedon possible?

leadership became an economic and commercial power unlike anything previously imagined in Greece.

That sort of domination generated envy and fear in Sparta. Athenians defended their political and economic dominance on the grounds that their city needed to protect its commerce. But Pericles exerted Athenian power throughout the region, putting down uprisings in several smaller cities that resented paying tribute. The city-state that revered liberty and democracy at home had become an agent of expansion abroad. Sparta regarded the Athenian policy of establishing democracies in its satellites as a threat to the continued existence of oligarchic and aristocratic governments and called on its Peloponnesian League.

Pericles builds Athens into a powerful city-state

The Peloponnesian War

In confronting the Peloponnesians, Pericles had to choose between Athenian expansion and retreat. He preferred war, and he was not alone. As Thucydides (*thoo-SID-uh-dēz*), the first major historian to report events accurately and analytically, wrote in his

History of the Peloponnesian War, "The Peloponnesus and Athens were both full of young men whose inexperience made them eager to take up arms." In 431 B.C.E. a commercial dispute led Sparta to demand that Athens give all Greek cities independence. In essence, such a policy would have dismantled the Athenian empire. Athens refused, and the competing alliances went to war. Thucydides concluded, "The thing that made war inevitable was the growth of Athenian power and the fear this caused in Sparta." It was the first thesis statement written by a genuine historian, and the conflict it spoke of is often called "the suicide of Greece."

The Peloponnesian War weakens Greece

The Peloponnesian War (431–404 B.C.E.) devastated Greece, bringing destruction of property, famine, disease, and death. It lasted more than two decades due to a central paradox: because Sparta had a powerful army but no navy, while Athens had a superb navy but a small army, neither found it easy to engage the other. Although Sparta eventually defeated Athens, the duration and severity of the conflict ensured that there would be no real winner—at least not in Greece itself.

Philip of Macedon conquers Greece

Exhausted, the warring city-states fell to an outsider: Philip II of Macedon, who between 359 and 336 B.C.E. turned his primitive realm on Greece's northern frontier into a formidable political and military power. Modifying the phalanx (a closely arrayed formation of troops difficult for infantry to penetrate) by lining it with men wielding pikes 18 feet long, Philip swept down from the north in 338 B.C.E. to defeat the Athenians and Thebans. Greek independence was thus extinguished by foreigners, who took command of the temples and palaces of Athens. These catastrophes might have been avoided had Sparta and Athens not weakened each other in the Peloponnesian War.

The Arts and Philosophy in Classical Greece

Greece in the Age of Pericles was not focused exclusively on politics and war. This was also a golden age of Greek culture. In Greece, the division of the peninsula into separate city-states seems to have fostered an appreciation of the virtues, capabilities, and rights of individual people. Although often inspired by belief in the gods, Greek artistic forms also demonstrate a profound fascination with the human person.

Architecture, Sculpture, and Pottery

The Parthenon.

Ancient Greek gods and goddesses inspired the magnificent temples of the Acropolis, a hilltop complex of public buildings in Athens. The Acropolis was dominated by the Parthenon, a temple of Athena, goddess of wisdom, for whom the city was named. Avoiding thick walls, Greek architects used a variety of handsome columns, on the Acropolis and elsewhere, to support the roofs of public buildings in a graceful yet functional style.

Greeks develop increasingly realistic art forms

Inside the Parthenon, a variety of lifelike sculptures paid tribute to Athena. Since Greeks believed their gods and goddesses looked and acted like humans, Greek sculpture portrayed them in human form. They were also shown in action rather than in frozen, artificial poses. Greek sculpture was therefore qualitatively different from the comparatively static, stylized depictions of humans in the art of Egypt, Persia, and China. The Greeks also portrayed the human form on their pottery, which combined artistic beauty with utilitarian value. Potters created an extensive array of jars, bowls, urns, vases, cups, and other vessels, glazed in vivid colors and fired in kilns. Decorating these pieces were depictions of men and women in realistic, active poses, some of them heroic (such as in combat against soldiers or wild beasts), some of them ordinary (for example, weaving, cooking, or farming). Greek pottery was prized not only in the peninsula but also throughout the Mediterranean world and in much of Asia. Greek art and architecture mark the beginning of a lengthy transition to styles today's observers would recognize as modern.

Galloping horses pull a chariot across the face of a ceramic Greek vase.

Greek Drama

In Greek literary life, the Classical Period produced four Athenian dramatists whose works remain influential in the present. The earliest of these playwrights was Aeschylus (*ES-kuh-luhs*), who lived from 525–456 B.C.E. He wrote complex plays dealing with people caught in conflict between their personal wishes and the claims of justice and reason. A generation later, Sophocles (*SAH-fuh-klēz*) wrote carefully crafted dramas such as *Antigone* and the *Oedipus* (*an-TIH-guh-nē, ED-ih-pus*) cycle. The works of Sophocles (496–406 B.C.E.) draw a precise line between the divine and the human; when pride causes men and women to think that they can cross that line, the consequences for themselves and their families are tragic.

Oedipus, whose career is described in Sophocles' trilogy of plays, was a fictional ruler fated by the gods to inadvertently kill his father and unknowingly marry his mother. Terrible results flowed from these actions, and Oedipus stood as a warning to those who would doubt the awesome power of destiny (see "Excerpt from Sophocles' *Oedipus the King*"). People may not understand divine law, but they must obey it for the sake of order and rationality in the world.

Greek drama concentrates on human personalities

The third dramatist was Sophocles' contemporary Euripedes (*yoo-RIP-ih-dēz*). Euripedes (ca. 480–406 B.C.E.) focused not so much on the divine, but on the tragic flaw of human beings: the tendency to subordinate reason to emotion. The three eminent tragedians were complemented by Aristophanes (*air-ih-STAH-fuh-nēz,* ca. 445–386 B.C.E.), a comic writer who poked fun at the famous and powerful. In their examination of human personality as well as divine law, of the demands of reason and justice as well as the necessity of action and heroism, these dramatists served as a bridge between the more limited horizons of ancient literature and the psychologically complex plays of later Western culture.

Philosophy

Greek philosophy has been even more foundational than drama to Western culture and thought. Following the "pre-Socratic" thinkers, who inquired into the nature of the universe, philosophers in the early Classical Period, called Sophists, taught rhetoric, mathematics, science, and philosophy to young men throughout Greece.

The Sophists' most influential critic was the great Athenian philosopher Socrates (*SOCK-rah-tēz,* ca. 470–399 B.C.E.), who taught that fulfillment meant attaining the good, the beautiful, and the true through the pursuit of excellence in learning. "The unexamined life is not worth living," Socrates asserted, and he taught his pupils by means of **Socratic dialogue**—rigorous questioning and analysis of ethical issues.

Document 7.1 Excerpt from Sophocles' *Oedipus the King*

Oedipus, King of Thebes, attempts to find his father's murderer by consulting the blind prophet Teiresias. The tragedy of the play is that Oedipus, who never knew his father, is himself the murderer. Teiresias tries to show him the truth, but Oedipus is proud and contemptuous of those beneath him and will not listen.

TEIRESIAS

Alas, how terrible is wisdom when
it brings no profit to the man that's wise!
This I knew well, but had forgotten it,
else I would not have come here . . .
I say you are the murderer of the king
whose murderer you seek . . .

OEDIPUS

Do you imagine you can always talk
like this, and live to talk of it hereafter?

TEIRESIAS

Yes, if the truth has anything of strength.

OEDIPUS

It has, but not for you; it has no strength
for you because you are blind in mind and ears
as well as in your eyes.

TEIRESIAS

You are a poor wretch
to taunt me with the very insults which
every one soon will heap upon yourself . . .

Eventually Oedipus learns the truth, and, in despair over having inadvertently killed his father and then married his own mother, blinds himself. The *Chorus* of the play deplores the pride which led him to his fate:

CHORUS

If a man walks with haughtiness
of hand or word and gives no heed
to Justice and the shrines of Gods
despises—may an evil doom
smite him for his ill-starred pride of heart!—
if he reaps gains without justice
and will not hold from impiety
and his fingers itch for untouchable things.
When such things are done, what man shall contrive
to shield his soul from the shafts of the God?

The Socratic dialogue was meant to draw students out by pressing them to answer a series of leading questions, such as "Is democracy the most reasonable form of government?"

Socrates' rigorous questioning leads to his execution

Eventually Socrates ran into difficulties with Athenian authorities, who convicted him on charges of undermining the gods and teaching young people to question their elders. At his trial, Socrates refused to apologize for his conduct, claiming that his actions were proper behavior for an educated and inquisitive person. Sentenced to death, he met his fate with dignity and grace, drinking a cup of hemlock (a potent poison) and continuing to converse with his followers until a cold numbness overcame him. But Socrates' teachings guaranteed him immortality. Although he had written nothing himself, his student Plato (427–346 B.C.E.) recorded the master's reasoning and founded his own school of thought.

Born early during the Peloponnesian War and shaped by its social and political turbulence, Plato saw civil society as deeply flawed. Many of his dialogues, including

The Republic, aimed to nudge the Athenian elite toward a more effective form of government for the polis. He contended that the state exists to serve its people, and that only a philosopher-king, a statesman whose education equips him to know the truth, is genuinely qualified to lead. For Plato, democracy was absurd: it gave power not to the most knowledgeable individual but to the most popular. Government should be led by the most competent, he argued, and only an aristocracy that honors learning and the quest for truth can produce competent leaders.

Plato's broad inquiry went beyond considerations of governance to contemplate the nature of reality itself. He argued that the world we experience with our senses is not truly real. Things such as horses, trees, and human beings are but copies of ideal forms of horses, trees, and human beings; copies are all that the human mind is able to perceive. A divide therefore exists between our physical world (an imperfect reflection of reality) and the ideal (or "real") world, composed of unchanging absolutes called Forms. In a famous allegory, or story with a symbolic meaning, he illustrated the two perceptions by asking his readers to imagine a prisoner sitting in a cave with his back to the light (see "Excerpt from Plato's 'Allegory of the Cave' "). All the prisoner can see on the cave walls are the shadows of objects moving and actions taking place behind him. The prisoner thinks that the things he sees are reality, because he knows no better. But they are copies of reality. The task of the educated person is to see with the mind the true

Greek philosophy seeks to understand the world

Document 7.2 Excerpt from Plato's "Allegory of the Cave"

This is part of a dialogue between two philosophers who are considering the reality or unreality of the world we perceive with our senses.

First Speaker: And now, let me show in a figure how far our nature is enlightened or unenlightened: Behold! Human beings living in an underground den . . . here they have been from their childhood, and have their legs and necks chained so that they cannot move, and can only see before them . . . Above and behind them a fire is blazing at a distance, and between the fire and the prisoners there is a raised way; and you will see, if you look, a low wall built along the way, like the screen which marionette players have in front of them, over which they show the puppets.

Second Speaker: I see.

First Speaker: And do you see men passing along the wall carrying all sorts of . . . statues and figures of animals made of wood and stone and various materials, which appear over the wall? Some of them are talking, others silent.

Second Speaker: You have shown me a strange image, and they are strange prisoners.

First Speaker: Like ourselves; and they see only their own shadows, or the shadows of one another, which the fire throws on the opposite wall of the cave?

Second Speaker: True; how could they see anything but the shadows if they were never allowed to move their heads? . . .

First Speaker: And if they were able to converse with one another, would they not suppose that they were naming what was actually before them?

Second Speaker: Very true . . .

First Speaker: To them, the truth would be literally nothing but the shadows of the images.

Second Speaker: That is certain.

reality of the world that our senses perceive, and thus to understand the ideal essence of physical things. This understanding is truth.

Plato's most brilliant student, Aristotle (*AIR-ih-STAH-tul*), revised his mentor's teaching. Aristotle (384–322 B.C.E.) asserted that both the nature and the substance of an object are part of that object and not part of some ideal world. This realism led him to surpass Plato's breadth of inquiry and to become one of the most influential thinkers of all time.

Philosopher, scientist, poet, and student of politics, Aristotle took the entire universe as his field of study. He wrote on physics, chemistry, biology, geography, and cosmology. The classification of political systems discussed earlier in this chapter is Aristotelian, based on his rigorous analysis of 158 Greek city-states. Aristotle proposed that the universe is composed of five elements: earth, air, fire, water, and ether, this last being an invisible medium through which stars and planets supposedly move around the earth. Those celestial bodies, he argued, were impelled by a "prime mover," a force that initiates all motion but that cannot itself be moved.

In his later years Aristotle became tutor to Alexander the Great, molding that Macedonian conqueror into an enthusiast for, and transmitter of, Greek culture. Aristotelian ideas and principles, preserved and transmitted by Muslims and Byzantine Christians, shaped the thought of the medieval Islamic and Christian European worlds.

Classical Greek Society and Religion

Most Greeks, of course, never had the opportunity to learn from Socrates, Plato, or Aristotle. The vast majority were artisans, farmers, slaves, and women whose labors allowed little time for philosophy, and who believed that their destinies were not in their own hands, but were controlled by an assortment of unpredictable gods.

Free Labor and Slavery

Greek civilization relies on agriculture

As with the societies in other ancient civilizations, labor in the Greek economy was organized around both rural and urban activities. Daily life in the countryside was simple and primarily agricultural. Greeks ate grains and fruits, enjoying vegetables and fish on occasion. The goats and sheep they raised provided milk and cheese, while pigs provided the modest amount of meat that Spartans ate every day. In the cities, men earned their living as artisans or skilled laborers. The unskilled worked alongside slaves in manual jobs such as garbage removal and street-sweeping, with the same daily wage going to both the enslaved and the free.

Slavery was common in Greece, as in most of the ancient world. Greek slaves generally shared the material standard of living of their owners, who were not necessarily wealthy. They were paid modest wages for their work, and might eventually save enough to purchase their freedom. Most slaves were foreigners captured in warfare or in slave raids. Well-born prisoners of war were usually ransomed by their families, so slaves tended to come from the ranks of the poor. Criminals, debtors, and orphans were also sometimes forced into slavery, but because most Greeks considered all non-Greeks to be inferior, foreigners were more likely to be enslaved than native Greeks.

Slavery differed in various parts of Greece. In Athens, slaves constituted nearly one-third of the total population. Since male prisoners of war were routinely imprisoned or killed, nearly all Athenian slaves were women. They helped the master with his farm or business, or the mistress of the house with her domestic chores. Legally they were human property. They could be beaten, usually for disobedience or laziness, but not killed. They were clearly inferior to citizens in civil rights and considered inferior also in natural abilities.

Greek culture rests on a slave foundation

In Sparta, slaves were bound to the land that they worked on their masters' behalf, but otherwise enjoyed considerable freedom of action. Although many Spartan slaves were foreigners, others were *helots* (*HĒ-lots or HELL-uts*), named after the nearby town of Helus, which Sparta had conquered. Most Spartan slaves were male, in contrast to the situation in Athens, and the Spartan oligarchy lived in permanent fear of helot revolts. This fear helps explain the intense militarization of Spartan society.

The Status of Women

Greek women enjoyed a status above that of slaves but below that of free men. In Sparta, women were highly valued for their ability to bear and rear healthy young warriors who would defend the city-state and make possible its expansion. In recognition of this status, Spartan women were permitted to voice their opinions on all state issues. Girls there were raised in much the same way as boys, with an emphasis on physical training and horsemanship. Some evidence suggests that Spartan girls as well as boys competed naked in athletic events, and that girls performed ritual dances in the nude before mixed audiences.

Greek women.

Spartan women usually married at 18, later than women in other Greek city-states, while men married in their mid-twenties. Since men remained in the barracks until age 30, young husbands visited their wives secretly at night, and they might father children before ever seeing their wives by daylight. As a consequence, the mother was the dominant figure in Spartan family life. Women could own property and transact business without the consent of their husbands, who spent most of their time in the barracks or away on military campaigns. Women were also guaranteed full civil rights under the law, except for the right to vote, a right no Greek polis ever granted them.

Athenian women, in contrast, were confined to the home, except for infrequent occasions such as celebrations or funerals. As full citizens of a state that relied on substantial male political participation, Athenian husbands possessed nearly total authority over their households and everyone living in them. A woman was protected by her father or male guardian until she married; if divorced or widowed, she returned to him. Virginity before marriage was highly prized for both men and women. After marriage, wives were expected to remain faithful, but a husband's casual adultery, particularly when away from home, was not considered immoral. Wives ran their households, supervised slaves, and wove clothing for family members. Once menopause occurred, Athenian women enjoyed greater freedom, working as midwives, nurses, and seamstresses.

The subordination of women to men was written into Greek law. Protections for women actually protected the rights and interests of their husbands. In Sparta, women were honored as mothers of the next generation of warriors; in Athens, women were

Female status differs in Athens and Sparta

Asklepios, the Greek god of medicine.

prized for conveying economic and political rights to their male children. Authority in Greece was a male monopoly.

Greek Religion

What is now called Greek mythology was originally a belief system reflecting ancient Greek culture. The twelve major Greek gods were said to live on Mount Olympus, the highest mountain in the northwest Peloponnesus. Unlike the divinities in other early civilizations, the Greek gods were not believed to have created the universe; both the universe and the earth were assumed to be eternal. The major Greek gods were believed to have created men and women, but not out of dust and a rib (as in Jewish and Christian tradition), nor out of a clot of blood (as in Islamic belief). Instead they engaged in sexual intercourse with mortals to produce heroic humans whose own offspring then became the human race.

Among themselves, the gods had love affairs that produced additional gods. Zeus, figuratively and literally the "Father of the Gods," sired Ares (*AIR-ēz*), the god of war, by his wife Hera, and six other gods by a variety of women. The children of Zeus also included Apollo, Athena, and Aphrodite (*aff-rō-DĪ-tē*), gods and goddesses of exceptional beauty and varying sexual appetites. Poseidon (*puh-SĪ-dun*), god of the sea, was Zeus's brother, and Demeter (*dih-MĒ-ter*), goddess of grain, their sister. All played significant roles in Homer's *Iliad*, as they intervened on one side or the other during the Trojan War.

Greek religion depicts the gods as similar to human beings

Greek deities were clearly more powerful than humans, but they had human traits. They could be greedy, generous, lusty, chaste, envious, kind, angry, and affectionate. Generally the gods on Mount Olympus took little direct interest in humans, but from time to time, out of boredom, they sought pleasure in manipulating human affairs, playing with people on earth as children play with dolls and toys. Other deities, who did not reside on Olympus, lived closer to mortals, affecting their lives each day by rewarding or punishing them. All gods and goddesses were believed to crave worship, adoration, and sacrifices of food and drink, which fearful humans provided to win divine favor.

Greeks honor the gods in the Olympic Games

For example, every fourth year men and women competed in a great festival of athletic events (see page 156) in honor of the deities they worshiped. These Olympic Games, named for the mountain on which the main gods lived, consisted of nine events, including a chariot race. The Olympic Games attracted participants and spectators from throughout Greece, and all warfare between city-states stopped whenever the games were held. Presumably the gods' enjoyment of these sports made them more kindly disposed toward humans. The ancient games were last held in 395 C.E., but were revived by Europeans in 1896.

The Greek gods live today in Western literature and drama, but in ancient times they were believed to be never far away from their people. That humans served as their puppets did nothing to diminish this closeness. The gods could feel pain (when a god was wounded in battle, his blood ran black), and what kept them immortal was their diet of ambrosia and nectar. They quarreled with each other and took delight in frustrating each other's plans. For Greeks, the gods were not remote beings but a part of everyday life.

The Empire of Alexander the Great

When Philip of Macedon conquered Greece in 338 B.C.E., it is unlikely that the Greeks felt the gods had deserted them. Greeks simply believed that Philip, for all his power and glory, was just one more tool in the hands of the Olympians. When he was assassinated in 336, only two years after his dramatic triumph, his new subjects nodded knowingly to one another: the gods had grown tired of him. The chief murder suspect was his first wife, Olympias, who had been cast aside by Philip in favor of a younger woman, also killed, along with her young daughter, soon after the king's murder. Since these events left Olympias and her 20-year-old son Alexander in control of the kingdom, many Macedonians suspected that Alexander had been part of the plot, though there is no evidence of his involvement. These sorts of intrigue, of course, would have been typical among the gods, and therefore familiar to both Greeks and Macedonians.

Alexander's Conquests

Alexander III of Macedon (336–323 B.C.E.), who quickly succeeded Philip, was a young man of unusual political and military talents. Having been tutored in his youth by Aristotle, he had developed a profound admiration for Greek culture, especially as his native Macedonia was looked upon by the Greeks as a backward frontier area, good only at fighting. Alexander, whose mother claimed descent from Achilles, immersed himself in Homeric poetry and by his late teens had become, in the words of one scholar, "self-confident, endlessly curious, and reckless," much like Achilles himself. After his father's murder, Alexander moved swiftly to ensure the loyalty of the army and to kill anyone questioning his claim to rule. Then he descended upon Greece, destroying the powerful city of Thebes and forcing the Greeks to recognize him as Philip's legitimate successor.

Alexander consolidates Macedon's hold on Greece

After subduing Greece, Alexander resumed the invasion of Persia that Philip had planned. That invasion appeared wildly risky. Persia was not the power it had been under Darius I and Xerxes, but it had a strong army, and its immense size placed any invader at a disadvantage. In addition, Alexander's position at home, resting (unlike his father's) on no domestic achievements whatsoever, was not yet secure. But he was eager for conquest and moved quickly against Persia with a mixed army of Macedonians and Greeks. In 334 B.C.E., at the Granicus (*grun-Ī-kus*) River in northwestern Anatolia, he won his first major victory. After that, as he entered Asia by way of the bridge at Gordium, he cut the Gordian Knot.

Alexander the Great.

Alexander justified his attack on Persia by claiming to be the champion of Greek culture against barbarian values and the instrument of Greek revenge for Xerxes' invasion in 480. Despite all justifications, Alexander's principal objective was heroic conquest, and he was talented enough to achieve it. In battle, Alexander was able not only to plan a sequence of moves but also to anticipate his enemy's likely responses and to be ready with countermeasures. He was also able to change his course of action in the midst of the confusion of battle. Complementing these impressive abilities was Alexander's religious faith. The incident of the Gordian Knot convinced him that the gods had willed that he rule Asia, which he defined as the Persian Empire. Seeing himself as a second Achilles, he had no doubt he would succeed.

Alexander claims to be promoting Greek culture in southwest Asia

Map 7.4 The Empire of Alexander the Great, 336–323 B.C.E.

The armies of Alexander the Great created Greek-based connections across southwest Asia. Note that his enormous empire, constructed in only 13 years, duplicates almost exactly the Persian Empire of Cyrus, Cambyses, and Darius I (Map 6.3). Alexander's conquests placed a permanent Greek imprint on millions of people, while eastern concepts like despotism flowed westward into Greece. What kinds of changes would have occurred during this blending of such varied cultures?

Macedonia, 336 B.C.E.

Alexander's empire at its height, 323 B.C.E.

Route of Alexander, 334 BCE–323 B.C.E.

▲ Towns founded by Alexander and his followers

Alexander invades the Persian Empire

Alexander met the Persians in battle at Issus, in southwestern Anatolia, in 333 B.C.E. The Persian Emperor Darius III was an experienced military leader, and his army was more than twice as large as Alexander's. The outcome was in doubt at first, but Alexander personally led a headlong cavalry charge that broke through Darius's bodyguard, forcing the Persian emperor to flee the field. Next Alexander moved south through Syria and Palestine into Egypt, adding to his dominions the rich former realm of the pharaohs, and founding there the city of Alexandria, destined to become one of the world's great cultural centers. This conquest of Egypt secured the Mediterranean coastline so that Persia could not use it as a springboard for invading Greece.

No longer underestimating Alexander, Darius offered to surrender to him all of the Persian Empire west of the Euphrates. To the dismay of his commanders, Alexander rejected the offer. He marched northeast to Mesopotamia, where he again vanquished the Persians, paving the way for his conquest of their entire empire. Storming across Persia, he crossed into Afghanistan and through the Khyber Pass (Map 7.4) into India. By 326

B.C.E. he was east of the Indus River and dreamed of pressing on to the "eastern sea" (which may have been either the Ganges River or the Bay of Bengal), but his men, having been away from home for eight years, refused to continue. Compelled to turn back, Alexander returned to Persia but never saw Greece again.

The Fate and Impact of Alexander's Empire

Ruling the former Persian Empire turned out to be more difficult than defeating it. But Alexander was insightful about how an empire should be run and wise in his decision to retain satrapies and other features of Persian government. Like previous outsiders who had overrun complex civilizations, the Macedonian leadership quickly adopted useful techniques from its new subjects.

Alexander tried to fuse Persian and Greek cultures, taking several Persian wives, encouraging his commanders and officials to do the same, and placing both Greeks and Persians in important political and administrative positions. These moves won him more praise in Persia than in Greece. In Persia, Alexander sought to have his rule recognized as a continuation of the imperial tradition by retaining the satrapies and by officiating at the burial services of Emperor Darius III. In Greece, however, he was still resented as an outsider. Most Greek cities feared Macedon more than Persia, and during Alexander's long absences they frequently rebelled. Accustomed to independence, they resented centralized rule under Macedonian governors and charged (without evidence) that Greeks were being denied privileges that Alexander was granting to Persians.

Alexander adopted Persian governing practices, but he had little use for Persian culture. According to his Greek biographer Plutarch, he considered himself "a governor from God and a reconciler of the world." He hoped that Greek language, literature, philosophy, and art would, through his actions, permeate all of Asia, inspiring its peoples to pursue virtue, excellence, wisdom, and truth. This heroic idealism blended with practicality in his plan to develop the Tigris, Euphrates, and Indus Rivers as commercial waterways linking all of Asia.

Alexander spreads Greek culture eastward

These undertakings promised to be long and arduous, however, and Alexander was an impatient man. His soldiers' unwillingness to proceed eastward from the Indus was a great disappointment to him, for which he compensated by exalting his own greatness and indulging in festivals and celebrations. At one in 323 B.C.E. he reportedly consumed more than a gallon of wine in half an hour. He quickly developed a fever, grew weaker, and died several days later from symptoms consistent with tropical malaria. He was only 33 years old.

Alexander's sudden death threw his empire into confusion. Each of his most important generals seized a portion for himself: Ptolemy (*TAHL-em-ē*) took Egypt, Antigonus (*an-TIH-guh-nuss*) held Greece and Macedonia, and Seleucus Nikator controlled all the rest, from western Anatolia to the border of India. The Seleucid Empire, as we saw in Chapter 6, was the first of a series of successor states to the Asian portions of Alexander's empire. It was followed by the Greco-Bactrians, Parthians, and Sasanians, none of whom were able to reconstitute the Persian Empire that Alexander had conquered.

Alexander's early death dissolves his empire

Although Alexander's empire was no longer unified, the importance of his accomplishments remained. He had defeated the immense Persian Empire, spread Greek culture throughout southwest Asia, and connected Europe, Asia, and Africa in ways that would later benefit the Roman Empire. These connections are delineated later in this chapter.

Alexander leaves a
mixed legacy

At the same time, Alexander's legacy should not be romanticized. Although he championed Greek civilization, he developed no appreciation for the achievements of the Persian Empire he opposed. He demolished one of the great powers of the ancient world without replacing it with a culture that demonstrably improved the lives of its people. In addition, his model of kingship, which exalted an aloof, militaristic, divinely inspired monarch, blended West with East but benefited neither. Finally, Alexander's conquests, for all their brilliance, were personally motivated. Despite his love for Greek culture and his oft-stated desire to fuse the Greek and Persian worlds, he never thought seriously about establishing political and economic institutions that could have helped unify a realm stretching from Macedonia to Egypt and from Greece to India.

Connections and Conflicts in the Hellenistic World

Alexander's diffusion of Greek values and practices eastward was accompanied by the westward spread of values and practices from the civilizations of the East. His penetration of southwest Asia and Egypt created a set of new societies and political entities that were not simply Greek, Persian, Egyptian, or Indian but a blend of them in varying combinations. To distinguish it from the earlier **Hellenic** culture developed by the Greeks, this new culture is traditionally called **Hellenistic**.

Commercial and Cultural Connections

Hellenistic kingdoms
promote commerce
and trade

Nowhere was this convergence of cultures more obvious than in economics. The post-Alexander monarchies of southwest Asia (Map 7.5) used confiscated Persian wealth to construct roads and harbors for the promotion of trade. These improvements kept Mediterranean goods flowing eastward and Asian luxuries moving westward. Foodstuffs were shipped by sea, while luxury goods traveled overland by camel caravans, protected by the Seleucid and Ptolemaic states. Spices from India and silks from China became widely prized in Greece, while exquisite examples of Greek sculpture and pottery were prized in India and China. Greek law and custom became the foundation on which business was transacted. Greece benefited immensely from this commerce, particularly in agricultural commodities: the grain produced in surplus in the eastern Hellenistic monarchies improved the nutrition of people throughout the rocky peninsula who had always lived on the edge of malnutrition. Greek fish, wine, and olive oil were exported to the East in return.

Cultural contact in the Hellenistic world extended beyond trade and commerce. In astronomy, physics, mathematics, and medicine, Greek thinkers profited from the knowledge and techniques of the East. In Egypt, Alexandria grew into a renowned center of learning and inquiry. Most of its population spoke Greek, which rapidly became the tongue of educated people throughout the Hellenistic world. Alexandria remained a predominantly Greek city through the early years of the Roman Empire.

Map 7.5 The Hellenistic Kingdoms, 323–146 B.C.E.

No one knows whether Alexander the Great could have held together the enormous territories he conquered. We do know that after his death at age 33, none of his successors could do so. The division of Alexander's empire into a variety of kingdoms ended the temporary political unity of southwest Asia and created a region in which the only unifying factor was Hellenistic culture. Notice the unequal distribution of lands between Alexander's three successors and their dynasties. Which do you think would prove the most powerful and influential? Why?

Alexandria's library was justly famous, and in 245 B.C.E. its chief librarian, Eratosthenes (*air-uh-TAHS-thuh-nēz*), calculated the circumference of the earth at 24,675 miles—an error of only seven-tenths of one percent. More than 17 centuries before Columbus, he also predicted that a ship leaving Spain could reach India either by sailing around the southern tip of Africa or by sailing west. Educated people throughout the ancient world knew that the earth is round and had a good sense of its size.

Another Hellenistic astronomer, Aristarchus of Samos (*air-ih-STAR-kuss, SĀ-mus*), constructed his ideas on Babylonian foundations. More advanced in his thinking than Aristotle, Aristarchus (310–230 B.C.E.) proposed that the earth revolves around the sun and that the far-off stars orbit neither the earth nor the sun. But Aristarchus's view, though correct, did not prevail. The astronomer Claudius Ptolemy (85–165 C.E.), working in Egypt, endorsed Aristotle's concept of heavenly bodies moving around the earth, and Ptolemy's writings proved so influential that the idea of a heliocentric (sun-centered) system was not taken seriously until the publication of the work of Copernicus nearly 14 centuries later.

Hellenistic science makes significant advances

More influential than Aristarchus was Archimedes (*ark-ih-MĒ-dēz*) of Syracuse (285–204 B.C.E.), a master of mathematics, physics, and mechanical engineering. The creator of the science of hydrostatics (fluid pressure), Archimedes determined that when an object is immersed in a container of liquid, it displaces from the container the precise equivalent of its own volume in liquid. According to legend, he solved this problem while stepping into his bathtub and became so excited that he ran through the streets naked, shouting, "Eureka!" (Greek for "I have found it!"). Less dramatic but equally significant were his discoveries of a compound pulley to raise heavy weights and a screw system to lift water to higher levels.

Alexander the Great's dynamic conquests also affected the pursuit of philosophy in Greece. In response to the changes wrought by Alexander, Hellenistic thinkers sought permanence and stability. Epicurus (*EP-ih-KYOOR-us*) (341–270 B.C.E.), for example, advised that nothing is to be gained by trying to appease the gods, who are indifferent to human problems. As all matter, including the gods, is composed of atoms, he argued, the soul dies with the body. Pleasure is simply the absence of pain. Epicureans therefore held that one should not be troubled by change, resent fate, or try to alter destiny. Zeno (*ZĒ-nō*) refuted this position with a complex philosophy called Stoicism. Release from pain is not an end in itself, he charged, and Epicurean withdrawal into private life is wrong. Stoics must show courage, cultivate wisdom, and do their duty, remaining steadfast in time of crisis even in the face of overwhelming odds. It is not success that matters, but the virtuous pursuit of duty. Neither Epicureanism nor Stoicism became the dominant philosophy of the day. Most people were attracted by one and then by the other, depending on the circumstances.

Eastern mystery religions spread westward

In religion, the two-way flow of ideas benefited the West more than the East. The cults of Greek deities like Apollo and Athena were transported eastward with the spread of Greek culture, but they had little theological content and enjoyed limited appeal among eastern peoples interested in problems involving sin and salvation. Even Greeks who emigrated eastward eventually found Greek religious views sterile. The westward flow, on the other hand, brought eastern mystery religions (also called "salvation religions") to the Greek world, with profound historical consequences.

Mystery religions addressed directly the problems of human weakness, divine redemption, and eternal life. In each of them, a god or goddess either became human or became deeply involved with human beings, teaching his or her followers certain divine secrets or mysteries. Through initiation into these mysteries, new converts, or novices, were believed to become one with the deity, whose sacrifices redeemed the sins of the novices and promised them immortality. Once the initiation was complete, the novice felt "born again" into a new life.

Two of the most important Hellenistic mystery cults centered on the god Dionysus (*dī-uh-NĪ-suss*) and the goddess Demeter. Dionysus was the god of fruitfulness and wine. His festivals, preceded by solemn performance of the mystery rituals he allegedly taught his followers, included choral singing, pantomime, free-spirited sexual activity, and great quantities of wine. Worshippers believed they were linked with deceased ancestors, fellow revelers, and generations of believers yet to be born.

Rituals devoted to Demeter, the goddess of grain, were called the Eleusinian (*el-yoo-SIN-ē-un*) Mysteries because they were celebrated only at Eleusis, a city-state near Athens. Demeter's followers memorialized the cycle of life as represented in the sowing, sprouting, and harvesting of grain. The grain that is scattered on fertile soil germinates, sprouts, and is reaped for bread and future seeding. Similarly, a girl is taken from her parents, is "seeded" through sexual intercourse, and produces offspring. When men and women die, they are buried in the earth and remain part of the cycle of life. New life springs forth from every grave, and those devoted to Demeter look forward to eternal life.

Mithras slaying the sacred bull.

Mystery religions became extremely popular in the Hellenistic world. The cult of Mithras, a Persian god who created the universe by catching and sacrificing a sacred bull, eventually reappeared in Western culture. Devotions to the Egyptian deities Isis and Osiris, involving a god who is slain but then restored to become the judge of humankind (Chapter 2), also became highly influential in Greco-Roman civilization. But in the long run, the main beneficiary of eastern religious influences was Christianity. In the first century C.E., the Apostle Paul preached the message of this eastern-inspired religion to a Greek population already familiar with many of its basic conceptions.

Politics and Governance

Politically, too, the impact of Hellenization was two-sided. Alexander's conquests removed the Persian Empire from world history and spread the Greek language and Greco-Macedonian military techniques into southern Asia. But distinctively Greek forms of government were not transmitted in the same way. Athenian democracy and Spartan oligarchy may have been suitable forms of governance for small, internally cohesive city-states, but they were not suited to sprawling, multiethnic empires. For leaders wishing to rule such diverse states, monarchy seemed to work best, as it permitted the creation of royal dynasties in which the authority of the king was believed to derive from the gods. The royal family thus became the symbol of political unity within the empire, transcending tribal loyalties and language differences.

Hellenistic kingdoms reject democracy and oligarchy

Although monarchy was nothing new to the Greeks—the word itself is Greek—it had belonged to the legendary past. Homer's *Iliad* sang of kings like Agamemnon and Priam, but the Greeks of the fourth century B.C.E. thought that monarchy had been replaced by better forms. Then the eastern empires that Alexander conquered made them appreciate the power of a central authority. Emperors disposed of their subjects like Athenians disposed of used clothing, and they cared little for the opinions of the people. To an ordinary Greek this was tyranny, not monarchy, but to Ptolemy, Seleucus, and their successors it was convenient.

Hellenistic Kingdoms revitalize monarchy

Yet the post-Alexandrian empires were ruled entirely by Greeks, even if the form of government they adopted was eastern. Greeks held every influential political, diplomatic, military, and administrative post. The Hellenistic rulers were anxious to recruit Greeks and Macedonians for their armies and navies, as they believed that relying on local warriors would be politically dangerous. Cities laid out in the Greek style, designed and constructed by Greek architects and engineers, were built throughout the new empires, and Greek immigration into these empires was encouraged.

The political structures of Hellenistic expansion proved strikingly fragile. Although there were too many Greeks for their rocky homeland, there were not nearly enough to staff every important position in southwestern Asia. The Hellenistic kingdoms could not sustain the vigor, curiosity, and enthusiasm of Alexander the Great. They declined slowly for a hundred years and eventually collapsed when challenged by a dynamic new dominion arising in the west, centered on the city of Rome.

Chapter Review

Putting It in Perspective

The Greeks developed sophisticated forms of government, created magnificent works of poetry and drama, formulated enduring answers to fundamental questions about the nature of reality, and made striking advances in scientific inquiry. But their refusal to cooperate with one another ultimately delivered them into the hands of conquerors. Their short-lived alliance against the Persians ran aground on the rocks of Athenian ambitions, and the ensuing Peloponnesian War so weakened them that they fell to Macedonia.

Nevertheless, the accomplishments of Greek culture spread throughout the Mediterranean basin with Greek colonies, and Alexander's soldiers carried them into Egypt and across southern Asia to the Indus valley. Greek learning enriched the lives of hundreds of millions and altered the course of history. Europeans were particularly fascinated by Greek culture. They adapted its methods for governing the polis to their own states. Words such as tyranny, aristocracy, oligarchy, and democracy continue to be used to describe governmental systems throughout the world. Europeans produced their own philosophies, dramas, and architectural forms on foundations laid by Greece. Alexander spread Greek culture eastward, but its long-range influence lay to the northwest, in its appeal to a Europe that did not yet exist in the era of great confrontations and connections between Greece and Persia.

Reviewing Key Material

KEY CONCEPTS

polis, 160
monarchy, 160
oligarchy, 160
aristocracy, 160
democracy, 160
tyranny, 160

Archaic Period, 162
Classical Period, 164
Socratic dialogue, 167
Hellenic, 176
Hellenistic, 176
mystery religions, 178

KEY PEOPLE

Alexander the Great, 157, 173
Homer, 159
Lycurgus, 162
Draco, 163
Solon, 163
Pericles, 164
Thucydides, 165
Philip of Macedon, 166
Aeschylus, 167
Sophocles, 167

Euripedes, 167
Aristophanes, 167
Socrates, 167
Plato, 168
Aristotle, 170
Eratosthenes, 177
Aristarchus of Samos, 177
Archimedes, 178
Epicurus, 178
Zeno, 178

ASK YOURSELF

1. Why were the Greek city-states unable to create a permanently unified state?
2. How did the Persian Wars affect the Greeks, both for good and for ill?
3. How did Greek religion differ from eastern "mystery religions"? What does Greek religion tell us about the Greeks themselves?
4. Describe the connections forged between ancient Greece and other civilizations.

GOING FURTHER

Blundell, Sue. *Women in Ancient Greece.* 1995.

Burkert, Walter. *Greek Religion.* 1985.

Cartledge, P. *Spartan Reflections.* 2001.

Cohen, G. *The Hellenistic Settlements in Europe, the Island, and Asia Minor.* 1996.

Cook, R. *Greek Art: Its Development, Character and Influence.* 1991.

Davies, J. *Democracy and Classical Greece.* 1993.

Demand, Nancy. *A History of Ancient Greece.* 1996.

Donlan, W., S. Pomeroy, J. Roberts, and S. Burnstein. *Ancient Greece: A Political, Social, and Cultural History.* 1998.

Freeman, Charles. *Egypt, Greece and Rome: Civilizations of the Ancient Mediterranean.* 1996.

Hammond, N. *The Genius of Alexander the Great.* 1997.

Hanson, Victor. *The Other Greeks: The Family Farm and the Agrarian Roots of Western Civilization.* 1995.

Kagan, Donald. *The Peloponnesian War.* 2003.

Lawrence, A. *Greek Architecture.* 1996.

McDonald, William, and Carl Thomas. *Progress into the Past: The Rediscovery of Mycenaean Civilization.* 1990.

Miller, S. G. *Ancient Greek Athletics.* 2004.

Murray, Oswyn. *Early Greece.* 1993.

Osborne, Robin. *Greece in the Making, 1200–479 B.C.* 1996.

Patterson, Cynthia. *The Family in Greek History.* 1998.

Shipley, G. *The Greek World After Alexander, 323–30 BC.* 2000.

Walbank, F. *The Hellenistic World.* 1993.

Key Dates and Developments

Date	Event
1100–750 B.C.E.	The "Dark Age"; Homer's writings are composed
750–500 B.C.E.	The Archaic Period
750–550 B.C.E.	Greece colonizes the Mediterranean basin
621 B.C.E.	Draco's legal code in Athens
594 B.C.E.	Solon's reforms in Athens
ca. 560 B.C.E.	Formation of the Peloponnesian League
500–338 B.C.E.	The Classical Period
499 B.C.E.	Beginning of the Ionian revolt against Persia
490 B.C.E.	Athenians defeat Persians at Marathon
480 B.C.E.	Sparta's sacrifice at Thermopylae
	Athenian victory over Persians at Salamis
478 B.C.E.	Formation of the Delian League
461–429 B.C.E.	Age of Pericles at Athens
431–404 B.C.E.	The Peloponnesian War
399 B.C.E.	Trial and execution of Socrates
338 B.C.E.	Philip of Macedon conquers Greece
336–323 B.C.E.	Conquests of Alexander the Great
323–30 B.C.E.	Era of the Hellenistic Kingdoms

The Romans Connect the Mediterranean World, 753 B.C.E.–284 C.E.

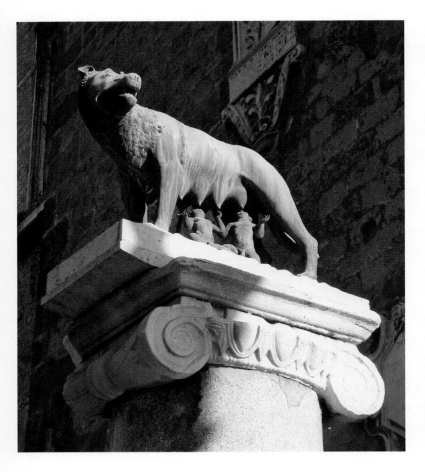

Romulus And Remus

A statue of Romulus and Remus being suckled by a she-wolf. This legend encouraged Romans to consider themselves tough, resilient people accustomed to overcoming hardships (page 183).

According to Roman legend, in the early eighth century B.C.E. the daughter of a local king in central Italy was impregnated by Mars, the god of war. Then she was killed by her uncle for having disgraced the family by surrendering her virginity. Just before she died, she gave birth to twin sons, who were left on a roadside to die. But a she-wolf came upon them, and rather than devouring the helpless infants, she nursed them. Eventually the twins were discovered by passing shepherds, who adopted them and raised them as their own.

The twins of this legend were named Romulus and Remus. Their upbringing was unconventional, and their adolescence was tempestuous: Romulus killed his brother and fled from the shepherd family that had raised him. Then in 753 B.C.E., on the banks of the River Tiber in the fertile plain of Latium (*LĀ-shē-um*) in west-central Italy, he founded a village that, according to the story, became the city of Rome.

Although legendary, this account of Rome's origin reflects the Romans' image of themselves as offspring of the god of war, toughened by the milk of a she-wolf. (see page 182). Proud of their origins, the Romans created influential institutions and helped spread the cultural contributions of ancient Greece and Christianity as they conquered and then managed one of history's most adaptable, effective, and enduring empires.

The Roman Empire

The Roman Republic to 133 B.C.E.

The true story of Rome's founding is somewhat less dramatic than its legendary one. Archeological evidence dates the initial habitation of Latium, in west-central Italy, to around 1000 B.C.E. Three tribes from central Italy appear to have clustered there, possibly on account of the location's advantages. Built on seven hills surrounding a place on the Tiber River that could be bridged, the developing city enjoyed formidable natural defenses against land-based attacks. At the same time, the 14 miles that separated it from the Mediterranean Sea provided defense against both pirates and naval landings. As the city's later inhabitants also learned, their central location in the Mediterranean basin was close to major trade routes and a good place from which to rule the entire region. Potential competitors, such as Sicily's Syracuse and North Africa's Carthage, were also well located, but, being seaport cities, they were more vulnerable to naval assaults (Map 8.1).

Rivalry with Etruria

At first the Romans were ruled by the kings of Etruria (*ih-TRUR-ē-uh*), a plain northwest of Latium (Map 8.2). The people of Etruria, known as Etruscans, had adapted the Greek writing system to fit their local language, thereby creating what came to be known as the

Etruria creates a trading network in the Mediterranean basin

FOUNDATION MAP 8.1 Rome, Carthage, and the Central Mediterranean

Italy's topography is as rugged as that of Greece, but while Greece remained divided, Rome managed to unite the entire Italian peninsula. The mountains of Greece encouraged the development of independent city-states with different forms of governance. In Italy, Rome's domination of the peninsula, based in large measure on its central location astride principal north-south communication routes, made unification possible. Note that only 350 nautical miles separated Carthage from Rome. Why would Carthage's location, at the southwestern end of the neck of water between Sicily and North Africa, eventually lead to rivalry with Rome?

Latin alphabet. They also brought Rome into a Mediterranean commercial network.

What little we know about the Etruscans comes primarily from their cemeteries. Their durable tombs, cut out of solid rock, were filled with exquisite goods made of iron, bronze, and gold. Etruscan pottery and copper and tin metalwork found in these tombs have also been uncovered in North Africa, the eastern Mediterranean, and along the Rhine and Danube Rivers in Europe. Clearly Etruria had a broad trading network that used central Italy's rich tin and copper deposits to advantage. Rome's resistance to Etruscan rule probably was due not only to political and ethnic differences but also to Rome's desire to capture and expand Etruscan trade routes.

In addition to archeological knowledge, we have very few written accounts of Etruria. We do, however, have this suggestive description from the Greek historian Theopompos of Chiops: "Sharing wives is an established Etruscan custom. Etruscan women take particular care of their bodies and exercise often. It is not a disgrace for them to be seen naked. Further, they dine not with their own husbands, but with any men who happen to be present. They are expert drinkers and are very good looking."

Roman legend assigns the early city seven kings, the last of whom was an Etruscan tyrant whose misdeeds provoked the ambitious Romans to revolt in 509 B.C.E. According to Roman tradition, the uprising succeeded, although archeological evidence indicates that the Etruscans did not withdraw from Latium until after their defeat at the hands of a Greek naval force in 474 B.C.E. Nevertheless, the expulsion of the Etruscans was commemorated by Romans for centuries as the end of tyranny and the beginning of rule by a *res publica* (*RĀZ POOB-lick-ah*, or "public possession"). Thus began the Roman **Republic**, a flexible form of government by elected representatives that proved capable of military conquest and administrative efficiency.

Map 8.2 Italy in 600 B.C.E.

Italy in 600 B.C.E. was heavily influenced by non-Italian peoples. Observe that Carthaginians controlled Corsica, Sardinia, and western Sicily, while Greeks dominated the remainder of Sicily and the southwestern tip of the Italian Peninsula. Etruscans controlled most of Italy north of Rome. Rome's victory over Etruria guaranteed the Romans domination over Italy and laid the foundation for their rivalry with Carthage for control of the Mediterranean. Why would the Greek colonies, as outposts not of a centralized Greek state but of individual city-states, be unable to intervene decisively in the Roman-Carthaginian rivalry?

Rome dominates Italy by defeating Etruria

The Republic and Its Foundation in Law

The government of the Roman Republic was grounded in principles and practices unlike those developed earlier in Greece. Athenian democracy was based on the right of all adult male citizens to debate, deliberate, and vote. This type of government—a direct democracy—was possible in a city-state with a limited population, but Rome was larger than Athens, and it tended to keep growing. The Romans therefore governed themselves through a republic—a system in which all adult male citizens voted not on the issues of the day but for representatives elected to a variety of assemblies that drafted, debated, and passed laws. If the citizens did not approve of the laws, they could vote the representatives out of office in the next election.

The Roman representative assemblies, however, did not have full authority over public affairs. The Republic's principal political institution was the senate, which was an advisory body composed of the most prestigious statesmen of Rome. The senate was dominated by patricians, wealthy landowners who led Rome's military units and who constituted the majority of the educated class. Senators selected new members of the senate, often nominating their own sons or relatives. The senate elected Rome's two consuls, officials who administered the state for one-year terms.

Rome establishes a Republic based on law

The governments of Mesopotamia, Egypt, China, and Persia were based largely on the power and personalities of individual rulers, but Rome's government was based on laws. Rulers in those other civilizations made the laws; in Rome, rulers were subject to the laws. Roman law distinguished between civil and criminal procedures. It aimed at developing solutions that would be fair to all parties in a dispute. In this pursuit it proved remarkably flexible, sometimes relying on precedent, sometimes on concepts of both common and individual good, and sometimes on common sense. As Rome expanded beyond its traditional boundaries, it amplified its civil law into "law of peoples," which applied to Romans and foreigners alike. The "law of peoples," in turn, evolved into **natural law**, a Roman vision of legal principles applicable to all societies regardless of time or circumstance. The necessity of ruling many non-Roman peoples encouraged Roman jurists to develop universally valid legal standards, and these influenced subsequent legal systems and laid the foundations of international law.

This legal system helped regulate a bitterly divisive social contest between patricians and plebeians known as the **Struggle of the Orders**. Common people, or plebeians (*plih-BĒ-uns*), frustrated in their attempts to attain a meaningful voice in state affairs, went on strike in 494 B.C.E. and withdrew from the city, creating their own assembly apart from the senate. This new assembly elected tribunes, or spokesmen who were charged with protecting the plebeians' rights and presenting their concerns to the senate. Even more alarming to the patricians, however, was the plebeians' refusal to serve in the army. Since commoners were the foot soldiers, without whom there would be no army, the patricians were forced to give in. Over the next two centuries they yielded their privileged legal and political positions bit by bit.

The Struggle of the Orders strengthens the Roman Republic

By 471 B.C.E. the patricians accepted the assembly, although its decisions did not enjoy the status of law until 287 B.C.E. In 450 B.C.E., plebeian agitation forced patricians to publish the famous Law of the Twelve Tables (see "Excerpt from the Twelve Tables"), a series of laws displayed on twelve tablets along with regulations governing legal procedure. Published and public laws thus opened the legal system to full use by all free men, breaking the patricians' monopoly. By 342 B.C.E. the patricians yielded further, agreeing to the plebeian demand that one of the two consuls be a plebeian. Gradually, wealthier plebeians moved into the patrician class, which grudgingly allowed them a role in the governing of the Republic. But when the Struggle of the Orders ended in 287 B.C.E., all Roman citizens were equal before the law. Roman practicality and flexibility prevailed,

Document 8.1 Excerpt from the Twelve Tables

The Roman Republic encapsulated its most important laws in the book of Twelve Tables, which the great orator Cicero praised as follows: "Though all the world exclaim against me, I will say what I think: that single little book of the Twelve Tables, if anyone look to the fountains and sources of laws, seems to me, assuredly, to surpass the libraries of all the philosophers, both in weight of authority, and in plenitude of utility." (Cicero, *De Oratore*, I, 44.)

TABLE I

1. If anyone summons a man before the magistrate, he must go. If the man summoned does not go, let the one summoning him call the bystanders to witness and then take him by force.

3. If illness or old age is the hindrance, let the summoner provide a team. He need not provide a covered carriage with a pallet unless he chooses.

TABLE II

2. He whose witness has failed to appear may summon him by loud calls before his house every third day.

TABLE IV

1. A dreadfully deformed child shall be quickly killed.

2. If a father sell his son three times, the son shall be free from his father.

5. A child born after ten months since the father's death will not be admitted into a legal inheritance.

TABLE V

1. Females should remain in guardianship even when they have attained their majority.

TABLE VIII

3. If one is slain while committing theft by night, he is rightly slain.

4. If a patron shall have devised any deceit against his client, let him be accursed.

13. It is unlawful for a thief to be killed by day . . . unless he defends himself with a weapon; even though he has come with a weapon, unless he shall use the weapon and fight back, you shall not kill him. And even if he resists, first call out so that someone may hear and come up.

TABLE IX

4. The penalty shall be capital for a judge or arbiter legally appointed who has been found guilty of receiving a bribe for giving a decision.

TABLE XI

1. Marriages should not take place between plebeians and patricians.

SOURCE: Oliver J. Thatcher, ed., *The Library of Original Sources*, Volume III: *The Roman World* (Milwaukee: University Research Extension Co., 1901) 9–11.

and rather than being plunged into civil war, the Republic evolved into a healthier, stronger system of government.

The equality of all citizens before the law naturally exalted citizenship, a privilege conferred upon all adult males who, by birth or adoption, belonged to one of the three tribes that had founded the city. Roman citizenship entitled the holder to a number of rights, including the right to appeal any official decision to the highest authorities. Citizens of Rome were also safe from unjust imprisonment, and the authorities were required to treat them with respect. The highest positions in the Republic were open to any citizen, regardless of ancestry or wealth.

Like the Persians, Rome tried to assimilate the peoples it conquered, and eventually the benefits of citizenship were employed in this process. The most talented and useful males in tribes or ethnic groups subdued by Rome were offered full citizenship and the opportunity to advance their careers in the service of a great and powerful state.

This practice made Roman citizenship one of the most highly prized distinctions of its day. The proud boast, *"Civis Romanus sum"* (*CHIH-vis rō-MAHN-us SOOM*, "I am a Roman citizen"), commanded immediate respect throughout the Roman Empire. Some foreigners even sold themselves into slavery to Rome, hoping someday to be freed and become citizens. But Rome's decision to grant citizenship to some foreigners while withholding it from others transformed citizenship from a right into a privilege. The legacy for some modern European nations has been to use citizenship as a reward that can be revoked if a citizen's conduct proves offensive to the state.

Romans were proud of their government and laws. Representative government, the Twelve Tables, equality before the law, and citizenship as privilege combined to make it possible for Rome to rule the Mediterranean basin.

Rome uses citizenship as a benefit

The Punic Wars and Rome's Mediterranean Domination

Rome's domination of the Mediterranean basin was first achieved, however, by its powerful army. The Roman army was divided into legions of approximately 5,000 men each, subdivided into centuries of 100 men, each of which was commanded by a centurion. Every adult male was required to serve in the army for as long as he was needed, and no man was permitted to run for public office unless he had served at least 10 years, thus making military service a springboard for influence in politics. In ordinary times, between 10 and 15 percent of men served in the legions; in emergencies, this figure rose to 25 percent. No society matched this degree of militarization before World War I, and Rome managed it for centuries.

Rome's legions enable it to project its power beyond the Italian peninsula

Rome's army was superbly trained and equipped. Infantry legions were accustomed to 20-mile forced marches, the distance being measured by counting the soldiers' steps: each double (left-right) step was about 5 feet, and 1,000 such steps took them a "mile" (derived from *mille*, the Latin word for "thousand"). Food consisted of bread and vegetables, a diet so ingrained that on one occasion soldiers objected when they had to eat meat instead. Courage was richly rewarded through promotions and honors, while cowards were stoned or flogged to death. If a century broke and ran in the face of the enemy, the penalty was *decimation*: every tenth soldier in the entire legion would be executed.

This combination of harsh discipline and constant training, together with skilled, experienced commanders, gave the legions a degree of self-assurance bordering on arrogance. Like tightrope walkers who remain unafraid because they *know* they will not fall, the armies of the Roman Republic moved steadily from conquest to conquest, losing an occasional battle but never a war. They reacted to defeat with bemusement and returned until they finally won. Magnanimous in victory, they aimed not merely to conquer but also to rule diverse peoples and integrate them into the Roman state.

Rome and Carthage struggle for Mediterranean domination

Rome's principal rival for control of the Mediterranean was the city of Carthage, the former Phoenician colony (Chapter 2) that had become a great naval power on the central North African coast (Map 8.3). Carthage tried for decades to conquer the large island of Sicily, off the tip of southern Italy, which it intended to use as a staging area

Map 8.3 The Mediterranean World at the Time of the Roman Republic, 264–44 B.C.E.

Rome grew from a centrally located city on the Italian Peninsula (Map 8.1) to the dominant power in the Mediterranean basin. Success in the Punic Wars against Carthage removed Rome's military and commercial rival in North Africa and facilitated its conquest of Gaul, Anatolia, and Syria, thereby connecting the entire Mediterranean world. Notice that Rome's conquests and dependencies spanned a distance of nearly 3,000 miles. What impact did the vastness of Rome's holdings by 133 B.C.E. have on its republican institutions?

from which to expand into continental Europe. From the Romans' perspective, however, Carthaginian control of Sicily would threaten their control of Italy. From 264 to 146 B.C.E. the two cities fought what would later be called the three Punic (*PYOO-nik*) Wars. In the First Punic War (264–241 B.C.E.), Romans gained control of Sicily by applying land-based military techniques to war at sea. They developed powerful ships with iron-tipped bows designed to ram opposing vessels. In the tumult following a ramming, a gangplank would slide from the bow of the Roman ship onto the deck of its enemy. Foot soldiers would run down the gangplank, board the crippled vessel, and fight what amounted to a land battle on a ship. Given the power of its infantry, Rome usually won such engagements.

Now Rome owned territory outside Italy and would have to defend, tax, and govern it. Within three years, Rome also took control of the Mediterranean islands of Sardinia and Corsica. Sicily, Sardinia, and Corsica were designated as provinces, subordinate regional units, each of which had its own governor and local administration and were not directly subject to the authority of the senate, an arrangement that later contributed to the fragmentation of the Republic.

Hannibal's tactical innovations frustrate but do not defeat the Romans

Carthage fought back, led by Hannibal, a brilliant military tactician outraged by Rome's seizure of Sardinia and Corsica. Hannibal began the Second Punic War (218–201 B.C.E.) by crossing the Mediterranean to southern France, then invading Italy from the north, crossing the Alps with troops and war elephants. It turned out that the elephants' huge feet could grip the narrow, slippery Alpine paths more securely than the hooves of horses. Hannibal's innovative tactics enabled him to surround and crush the Roman legions, but he never marched on Rome itself, probably realizing that subjugating and occupying the city would be beyond the strength of Carthage. From his viewpoint, the most desirable outcome would be Rome's surrender of its provinces, so that its domains would be limited to the Italian peninsula. But Hannibal was eventually forced to return to Carthage when Roman forces conquered coastal Spain, and there he lost the Second Punic War.

Over the next 53 years, the Mediterranean balance of power was firmly reoriented in favor of Rome. During this period, the Republic acquired an extensive empire. The senate authorized the pacification of Spain and the subjugation of Macedon and Greece, placing each of these areas under a Roman governor and, as with the three Mediterranean islands, designating them as provinces. In the Third and final Punic War (149–146 B.C.E.), Rome completely destroyed the city of Carthage, sold the survivors into slavery, and claimed Carthage's empire. North Africa's grain surpluses henceforth fed the masses of Rome.

Rome's triumph preserves its political values

The Punic Wars constituted a major turning point in the history of the Mediterranean basin. Carthage neither shared nor appreciated Rome's devotion to the rule of law, representative government, and equality of all citizens. A Carthaginian victory would have relegated Rome to the status of a historical oddity, a high-minded political experiment that was unable to compete effectively with less sophisticated states. Rome's triumph, on the other hand, helped to preserve these political values, as well as to ensure Rome's domination of the Mediterranean. By 133 B.C.E., the Roman Republic had established nine non-Italian provinces, making it an empire in all but name. Its new status changed it considerably.

Changes in Society and Culture

Victory over Carthage alters Roman society

Rome's domination of the Mediterranean led to changes in social stratification, gender relations, and the institution of slavery. The first change altered Rome's social divisions from political to economic. The wealth that came with conquest obscured the old patrician-plebeian distinction and replaced it with a gap between those who profited economically from expansion and those who did not. The newly rich as likely came from plebeian background as patrician. Now talent, ambition, and good fortune, rather than birth alone, were the means to success. The new gap that developed between the rich and the poor proved more difficult to bridge than the old distinction between patrician and plebeian.

Changes in Roman society also gave women a more elevated status than that found in other societies of the time. Persia and Greece had relegated women to the private life of the family, but in Rome, women routinely appeared in public and presided at meals where both sexes were present. Within the family the patriarch ruled, but clearly women were active participants in decision-making, consulted by their husbands in all matters pertaining to the family's welfare. They enjoyed their own religious rituals, cults, and festivals from which men were excluded.

Outside the home, Roman women enjoyed a significant measure of independence—able to own property, conduct monetary transactions, and even manage businesses. A few women became physicians, practicing gynecology, and many plebeian women became midwives. Even at the highest levels of male-dominated society, women's influence was felt: Roman senators spoke freely of being lobbied by their wives, and under the Empire women, such as the Empress Livia, second wife of Caesar Augustus, exercised considerable indirect power over political affairs. From time to time the Roman assemblies passed laws restricting the rights or mobility of women. These laws sparked formal protests, most notably in 195 B.C.E., when numerous women picketed the senate and forced the repeal of a law forbidding women to ride alone in carriages. Men retained ultimate authority in private and public life, but few of them underestimated or ignored female influence.

Roman women resist male attempts to limit their independence

A third change altered the Roman institution of slavery. Like many other ancient civilizations, Rome enslaved people to labor on behalf of others. In Rome's early days many citizens owned a few slaves, who worked as domestic servants or agricultural laborers. These slaves were almost always from the Italian peninsula, usually captured through warfare with non-Roman tribes. Chronic debt, alcoholism, or mental incompetence could cause even native Romans to become slaves, and in some cases, parents who could not afford to raise their own children sold them into slavery.

A contemporary mosaic shows female Roman students wearing togas.

This situation changed after the Third Punic War. Rome's succession of military conquests brought tens of thousands of captive foreigners to Italy as slaves. It then became a mark of status for a Roman to own many slaves and to employ them not only for manual labor but also as skilled workers, musicians, and tutors.

Slaves, of course, resented their condition. They lacked freedom and were forced to labor for someone else's prosperity or pleasure. While some worked for owners who were decent and compassionate, many others endured brutal punishments. Those who worked in mines or as part of agricultural work gangs experienced particularly harsh forms of servitude. At times slaves rebelled. While slave revolts were not frequent, they terrified the Romans and were suppressed with deadly force, much as the Spartans suppressed the helots. The most famous such revolt, led by a gladiator named Spartacus in 73 B.C.E., involved more than 70,000 slaves and lasted two years. Rome sent a succession of legions to crush the uprising, but Spartacus and his forces defeated all of them but the last. In 71 B.C.E. Spartacus was killed, and thousands of his followers were crucified.

Rome suppresses slave revolts

Slavery in Rome declined after the string of Roman conquests ended, but it never disappeared as long as Rome lasted. The use of forced labor and the fear of slave revolts remained ingrained in Roman life until the empire collapsed.

Dissatisfaction with the Republic

The Roman ability to adapt and synthesize was put to the test once the Punic Wars ended. The governing system of multiple assemblies advised by a senate had to be restructured to serve the needs of an increasingly complex and extensive empire. A tax system was required to fund a permanent standing army and to pay administrators to govern distant provinces. Otherwise, the senate feared, military leaders might rule those lands and use them as a base for challenging senatorial authority. The senate also hoped to organize the entire Mediterranean basin into a vital center of commerce and manufacturing. Yet this wealth encouraged an opulent lifestyle among the Roman elite and growing resentment among the Roman lower classes.

Social Discontent and Decline in Popular Rule

The expanding Roman state faced serious social problems. The Punic Wars had laid waste much of the Italian countryside, and since most of Rome's citizen-soldiers were farmers in civilian life, their frequent absences on military campaigns left their families unable to sow and harvest crops. Upon returning home, many veterans sold their devastated or run-down farms to wealthy buyers, who pieced the lands together to form immense private estates. The veterans then worked for inadequate wages in cities, where they competed with slave labor. Their discontent threatened Rome's stability as their plight threatened its defense: only landowners could serve in the army, and given the harm done to the land and the declining number of landowners, Rome's ability to field its famous armies was threatened.

The Roman Republic faces serious social problems

The senate tried to address the problem by dividing some public lands among the poor, but this practice affected only a small number of families. Ominously, generals began accepting propertyless men into the legions, promising them farms upon their retirement. These men were, quite naturally, more loyal to their commanders than to the senate, and many Romans began to think that the senate had lost touch with the needs of the people.

As Rome's domain expanded, the Republic lost control of events. The more territory it occupied, the more borders it had to defend. The greater the burdens of defense became, the more power was delegated to military commanders. The more powerful military commanders became, the less willing they were to take orders from the senate. As this sequence spiraled out of control, the advocates of republican rule found themselves isolated.

Sulla's dictatorship ends the Roman Republic

In 91 B.C.E. the senate defeated a bill to extend citizenship to all Rome's allies in the Italian peninsula. Many of the disappointed allies revolted, and civil war was waged sporadically until 79 B.C.E., when the Roman general Sulla (*SOO-la*) put down the strife and emerged as **dictator**—a tyrant ruling for the duration of the crisis. His seizure of power effectively ended the Roman Republic, although he tried unsuccessfully to restore it and many of his successors claimed to be loyal to it. But the Republic's usefulness was over: it could no longer control its own generals, as the rise of Sulla indicated, and it had failed to evolve to meet the changing needs of an expanding state. Generals such as Sulla and Pompey, who served in Spain, pretended to bow to the senate's will while effectively ignoring it and making their own policy at the far-flung extremities of empire.

Julius Caesar

With the Republic approaching its end, ambitious generals maneuvered to follow Sulla's lead. After Pompey subdued and colonized Spain, he used that province as a base for advancing his power. Elected consul in 59 B.C.E., he formed a political alliance, the First Triumvirate, with two other prominent generals, Caius Crassus and Julius Caesar. Caesar enjoyed military success in Spain and also in Gaul (today France), which he used as a power base for splitting the Triumvirate. In 48 B.C.E. he defeated Pompey at the battle of Pharsalus. Pompey fled to Egypt and was murdered there. Three years later, Julius Caesar proclaimed himself dictator of Rome.

Julius Caesar ruled Rome for only one year, but he left an enduring mark on world history. Descended from Rome's original aristocracy, he was educated by tutors and studied oratory and rhetoric in Greece. He blended political ambition with military genius in pursuit of his overriding goal: to restore order to the Greco-Roman world. Caesar accomplished a great deal in his one year as dictator: he revised the Roman calendar, made the senate more representative of the citizenry, and gave discharged soldiers and even the urban poor the opportunity to own a bit of land. A masterful literary stylist whose works are still enjoyed two millennia after his death, Caesar spread Roman culture into the lands he helped conquer, such as Spain and Gaul, where he founded colonies. Popular in many quarters for his willingness to implement reforms, he was resented in others for his shrewdness and his betrayal of Pompey. He rewarded his non-Italian supporters with Roman citizenship, ensuring their loyalty but angering many citizens of Rome.

As dictator, Caesar was remarkably magnanimous, granting pardons to many of his opponents and enemies. Within a short time this generosity destroyed him. On March 15, 44 B.C.E. (the famous "Ides of March"), he was stabbed to death in the Roman Forum by several conspirators, two of whom (Gaius Cassius and Marcus Brutus) were among the opponents he had pardoned. Caesar's assassination terminated the brief stability he had created, plunging Rome into renewed civil strife.

Julius Caesar's dictatorship moves Rome closer to empire

Tombstone of a Roman soldier.

The Birth of the Roman Empire

Caesar's assassination was followed by a struggle for power in which his grandnephew and adopted son Octavian (*ock-TĀ-vē-un*) emerged triumphant. Octavian then reshaped the governing institutions of Rome, molding them into a structure that would support his military dictatorship while seeming to remain republican in nature. As Caesar Augustus, Octavian served as a towering transitional figure between the Roman Republic and the Roman Empire.

The Rise of Octavian

Caesar's killers were swiftly defeated by his followers, led by the Second Triumvirate: Caesar's eloquent defender Marcus Antonius, immortalized as Marc Antony in Shakespeare's *Julius Caesar*; the skillful and subtle politician M. Amelius Lepidus; and Octavian, then only 18 years of age. Rome, however, was not large enough for two dynamic leaders such as Octavian and Antony. Lepidus was pushed aside, and Octavian took Rome's western possessions while Antony took Greece, Egypt, and the east. Caesar had dreamed of uniting Rome and Egypt, hoping to transfer his capital eastward. He had courted the Queen of Egypt, the clever Cleopatra VII, last of the Ptolemaic dynasty that had ruled that land since the death of Alexander the Great. Caesar had acknowledged to friends his paternity of her son Caesarion (*seh-ZAIR-ē-un*), born in 47 B.C.E. Now Antony seemed to have taken Caesar's place, spending the winter of 41–40 B.C.E. with Cleopatra in Alexandria and, in 32 B.C.E., marrying her.

Octavian outmaneuvers the Triumvirate and becomes Caesar Augustus

Octavian resolved to destroy Antony, fearing that if Antony became sole leader of Rome, he and Cleopatra would probably subordinate Italy to Egypt. Cleverly Octavian declared war against Cleopatra rather than Antony, mobilizing Rome's forces in a patriotic struggle to preserve Italian supremacy. Antony and Cleopatra responded by urging eastern princes to fight for their liberation from the tyranny of Rome.

In September 31 B.C.E. Octavian's forces defeated Antony and Cleopatra at the battle of Actium (*ACK-tē-um*). The following year Octavian's armies attacked Egypt itself. Antony, hearing a rumor that Cleopatra had been killed, took his own life by falling on his sword; the Queen of Egypt, after her lover's suicide and her empire's defeat, put an asp to her breast and died from its poisonous venom. Octavian had overcome all his rivals. Returning to Rome in triumph, he was hailed as the man who had ended decades of civil war. In 27 B.C.E. the senate voted him the title **Augustus**, meaning "one who rules with majesty and grandeur." Octavian now called himself Caesar Augustus.

Rome's defeat of Egypt orients its empire eastward

Octavian's victory at Actium shifted Rome's focus toward the east. As Caesar Augustus, Octavian claimed the Egyptian throne and began Egypt's gradual absorption into Roman civilization. Alexandria, which for nearly three centuries had been the world's center of Hellenistic learning and culture, now became subject to Rome. The cultures of the eastern provinces, including Egypt and Syria, were attractive to the Romans. And now with northern Africa and Palestine, Rome's Mediterranean empire was a "Greco-Roman world" and the Mediterranean Sea Rome's *Mare Nostrum* (*MAH-rā NAHS-trum*, "our sea").

From Republic to Empire

At the time, however, Rome seemed the center of the world, and its governance, following fifteen years of turmoil, was a matter of some concern. Ironically Caesar Augustus, the first Roman Emperor (27 B.C.E.–14 C.E.), hated dictatorial rule and wanted to restore the Republic. Although he tried to reinvigorate republican institutions, especially the senate, most of his political innovations enhanced his own authority.

Augustus consolidates an empire while ruling a republic

As commander of Rome's army, Augustus was called *Imperator*, which after his death evolved into "Emperor." But the term *Imperator* was a military title that said nothing about Augustus's position in civil government. In that sphere he ruled not as king or emperor but as one man holding a broad variety of republican offices. He served a succession of one-year terms as consul, giving him influence over those who served one year only. The senate appointed him to several magistracies and conferred on him powers normally reserved to tribunes. Thus, as consul, he spoke to the people on behalf of the government, while as tribune he spoke to the government on behalf of the people. All these positions were republican, but they were not designed to be held by one man. Augustus made himself emperor in everything but name, and in so doing he transformed Rome into an empire while claiming loyalty to the Republic.

The Roman Empire was a work in progress. Spain, Germany, the Balkan Peninsula, and much of southeastern Europe fell to Augustus's legions. Virtually the entire coastline of the Mediterranean was Rome's, giving substance to the claim of *Mare Nostrum*. Rome's control of the waves eased communication between the empire's remotest regions, overcoming the administrative problems that distance might have created. Augustus also constructed fortified camps and connected them to one another with well-built Roman roads. These camps extended Roman rule and brought Rome's culture to many parts of continental Europe.

The distant regions were inhabited mainly by tribal peoples who spoke Germanic languages and whom the Romans labeled "barbarians." As Rome defeated one tribe after another, Augustus and his successors consolidated their control by offering command positions in Roman armies to the highest-ranking Germanic chieftains and Roman citizenship to some of their most important followers. This systematic use of privilege and citizenship to win over the most powerful Germans helped Rome lay the foundations of a truly multiethnic empire while reducing foreign pressure on its extended borders. The result was the **Pax Romana** (*POCKS rō-MAHN-ah*), or "Roman peace." Until his death in 14 C.E., Augustus presided over a stable and prosperous society.

Rome's skillful use of citizenship helps create the Pax Romana

Caesar Augustus, Emperor of Rome.

Greco-Roman Culture

The *Pax Romana* was founded on a number of interlocking factors: military superiority, Augustus's political skills, the integration of foreigners into the empire, and material prosperity. In addition, **Greco-Roman culture**, rich and attractive, helped keep Roman society stable. Rome's familiarity with Greek culture began through contacts with Greek colonies on the Italian peninsula and on Sicily and continued when Rome conquered Greece. For centuries Rome had envied and attempted to imitate Greek arts and letters, in the process preserving Greek literary and philosophical masterpieces and making them known throughout the immense, multiethnic Roman Empire. This cultural transmission was enhanced by the incorporation into the empire of Egypt, especially Alexandria, where a fabulous library contained many Greek manuscripts. Some Greek philosophical schools, such as the Stoics, appealed to the Romans, who appreciated the Stoic insistence on living in harmony with natural forces. Now the "Augustan Age," or age of Augustus, brought forth a dazzling display of poetry that rivaled anything produced by the Greeks. Much of it sang the praises of the *Pax Romana* and of the ruler who created it.

Virgil, one of Rome's most noteworthy poets, lived from 70 to 19 B.C.E., long enough to enjoy the early years of the age of Augustus. Using a Greek literary form, the epic poem, Virgil in the *Aeneid* (*ih-NĒ-id*) narrates the legend of Aeneas (*ih-NĒ-us*), a Trojan warrior who fled from Troy as the Greeks sacked it. In the legend, Aeneas makes his way to Italy, where he acquaints early Romans with the ancient splendor of Greece. The *Aeneid* provides an alternative creation story for the origins of Rome, shifting the Roman self-image away from the tough and ruthless descendants of Mars who were nursed by a she-wolf and toward the refined and enlightened bearers of Greco-Roman culture. Virgil portrayed Rome as the benefactor of the known world, enlightening barbarian peoples and staunchly upholding Greek ideals of the good, the beautiful, and the true. The *Aeneid* remains, with the *Iliad* and the *Odyssey*, one of the world's great epics.

Greco-Roman culture helps build the empire

Ovid (*AH-vid*) (43 B.C.E.–ca. 17 C.E.), a generation younger than Virgil, wrote for a less learned audience. He immortalized Rome's most popular religious and seasonal festivals in verses that nearly everyone who could read could enjoy. But Ovid was surpassed in popular appeal by Virgil's contemporary Horace (65–8 B.C.E.), whose eloquent, soaring odes praised the accomplishments of Caesar Augustus. All educated Romans, and many learned people since that time, memorized Horace's stirring lines celebrating Greco-Roman virtues and exalting the heroic victories of the noble Romans over the so-called barbarians. In Virgil, Ovid, and Horace, Rome had a trio of poets whose work, by incorporating Greek themes and styles, immortalized Roman civilization.

<p style="margin-left:2em">

Latin becomes the dominant language of the Roman Empire and of most of Europe

The language in which Roman literature was written and in which Roman ideas were spoken was Latin, the language of Latium. Rome's newly acquired subject peoples continued to speak their own languages, but any who wished to take advantage of Roman contacts had to learn Latin. Gradually, Latin became the common language, first of the educated classes and then of the ordinary people of the Roman Empire. Over centuries, it evolved into many of Europe's languages, including French, Italian, Portuguese, Romanian, and Spanish; these are called "romance languages" because of their Roman origins. The dominance of Latin demonstrated that Rome's conquests were linguistic and cultural as well as military and economic.

The Romans also made permanent contributions to architecture, and Roman building can still be seen not only in Italy, but also in southern France, Spain, and North Africa. Rome went beyond the graceful pillars of Greek architecture to create enormous domed interior spaces, vaulted ceilings, and arches. Central to these innovations was Rome's invention of concrete, a combination of water, sand, and powdered limestone that provides impressive strength and durability when set. Concrete enabled Romans to create not only buildings of great beauty, but also large sports arenas and utilitarian projects such as bridges and aqueducts. An aqueduct was a long conduit supported by arches that brought fresh water from mountain lakes to lower-lying urban centers, using nothing more than gravity. Many Roman aqueducts still exist two thousand years after their construction, and a few remain in service, a convincing testament to both the durability and the usefulness of Roman architecture.

Roman aqueduct, Segovia, Spain.

Challenges to Augustus's Work

When Augustus died in 14 C.E., Rome was undisputed master of Europe, the Mediterranean, and much of Southwest Asia (Map 8.4). To Romans, those were the only useful portions of the known world. No other state of the day could challenge Rome's control of its empire. There were, however, three factors threatening the stability of Augustus's imperial domain.

Augustus's personal authority cannot be passed on to his successors

First, Augustus himself had never formalized his position within the empire. Insisting that the Republic would one day be restored, he called himself *princeps civitatis* (*PRIN-cheps chi-vē-TAH-tis*), "first citizen of the state," a modest title that died with him. His other title, *Imperator*, was purely military in nature, but his control over the army was personal rather than institutional. His generals were loyal to him because of his personal attributes. If future emperors lacked such qualities, the army would not hesitate to destroy them and replace them with more suitable candidates—possibly with one of the generals themselves. In short, Augustan rule was personal rather than institutional.

Map 8.4 The Roman Empire, 138 C.E.

The Roman Empire, using the conquests of the Republic as a foundation (Map 8.3), expanded into Britain, Dacia, Cappadocia, Thrace, Judaea, and Mauretania. Note that the extent of the Empire from northwest to southeast was greater than its extent from east to west. Why would this impressive expansion actually weaken Rome's security and place the continued existence of the Roman Empire in jeopardy?

Legend:
- Roman Empire under Augustus, 27 B.C.E.-14 C.E.
- Territory added by the time of Hadrian, 117-138 C.E.

Second, the empire itself had grown too large. Sea travel on the Mediterranean made possible rapid communication between distant points, and Rome's willingness to purchase loyalty with citizenship and privilege helped it hold the borders for many years, even expanding them northward into Britain. But even though the Roman legions constituted an unparalleled fighting force, those borders were too extensive to be held forever by armies of the ancient world. Sooner or later, invaders would press on enough points simultaneously to uncover a weak spot and break through. Skilled leadership could delay but not prevent eventual collapse.

Rome confronts challenges to imperial rule

Finally, Rome's expansion and multiethnic diversity brought it into contact with monotheism, or belief in a single god, which differed substantively from the traditional Roman polytheistic religion. As the new religious beliefs spread throughout the empire, they presented significant challenges to the core values of the Roman world.

Roman Religion and the Rise of Christianity

Polytheism and monotheism embrace conflicting values

Rome's original belief system reflected what it regarded as the civic virtues of tolerance and cultural pluralism, in which various conquered societies were permitted to retain their own cultures. Roman polytheism also permitted the gods of the conquered to be incorporated into the larger pantheon of Roman deities. Monotheism, however, is by its very nature intolerant of what it considers "false gods." The monotheistic religions of Judaism and Christianity, at first merely irritating to the cosmopolitan Romans, actually represented serious challenges to a belief system that had served the Romans well.

Rome's Polytheistic Religion

The religion of Rome, like that of most other ancient cultures, was polytheistic. Its principal gods, such as Jupiter, Juno, Mars, Neptune, and Bacchus, presided over a great many lesser deities, each identified with some natural or human-made force: Mars was the god of war, Neptune of the sea, and Bacchus of wine. Each god had his or her personal cult of devotions and rituals. If the proper ceremonies and sacrifices were offered, the god was appeased and would bless and protect the worshipper. Those who ignored the gods earned their wrath, expressed in the form of natural disasters and personal tragedies. Roman religion was another manifestation of fundamental Roman practicality, based not so much on morality as on a contractual relationship with the gods. Those who fulfilled the contract would be rewarded with good fortune on earth.

Tellus, the Earth, sits with infants and animals, surrounded by personifications of the Four Winds in this relief from the Altar of Peace in Rome.

Today this sort of religion is often termed "pagan," but actually it served Rome's complex, sophisticated society well, constituting yet another example of the adaptability of Roman culture. In particular, polytheism's tolerance for previously unfamiliar gods enabled the empire to assimilate conquered peoples without forcing them to abandon their beliefs. It was easy for Rome to integrate the religious beliefs and practices of the people it conquered. Foreign gods, such as Mithras of Persia and Osiris of Egypt, were simply added to the Roman array of deities after their native lands were conquered. All that was expected was that conquered peoples would be courteous enough to respect the festivals of the principal Roman gods, such as Jupiter, thereby appeasing those gods and deflecting their wrath from Rome.

Jewish Resistance and Eastern Cults

When Rome overran Judaea in the eastern Mediterranean region, however, it discovered that the Jews, who believed in a single, all-powerful God, were intolerant of all other belief systems and unwilling to participate in Rome's rituals. Perplexed by this conduct, the Romans isolated the Jews, a policy that worked fairly well, since the Jews considered themselves the **Chosen People** and prized their separateness. They had no interest in converting Romans to their own faith and simply wanted to be left alone; the more militant among them hoped that Rome would someday be overthrown or simply go away.

The intolerance of the Jews irritated the Romans, and Roman rule embittered the Jews, who revolted on the death in 4 B.C.E. of Herod, a puppet king whom Rome had elevated from among the Jewish people. Augustus sent his legions to put down the insurrection and replaced Herod with an official who reported directly to the *Imperator*. After suppressing the revolt, Rome attempted to make peace with the Jews by assigning responsibility for Jewish religious matters and local affairs to the Sanhedrin (*san-HED-rin*), the highest Jewish judicial body.

Jews and Romans mistrust one another

Nevertheless, Jews continued to resist Roman domination, and especially the taxes that Augustus imposed in order to pay for the Roman legions permanently stationed in Judaea. Some Jewish sects, advocating direct action, not only refused to pay taxes but also engaged in serious though futile efforts to dislodge the Romans. Best known among these groups were the Zealots (*ZELL-uts*), who practiced terrorism and assassination not only against Romans but also against Jews who collaborated with the occupying legions. Other sects revived the traditional Jewish prophecies of the coming of a Messiah who would liberate God's Chosen People from earthly oppression—in this case, from the Roman Empire. John the Baptist, a desert preacher, prophesied that the arrival of the Messiah was near. In contrast to these groups, Jewish apocalyptic sects such as the Essenes (*ESS-ēnz*) concluded that the world would end soon and that pious people should withdraw from public life and prepare for the end.

Simultaneously, interest in eastern mystery religions was spreading across the Roman Empire, affecting not only Jews but polytheists as well. Alexander's conquests had acquainted Greeks with eastern cults that promised personal immortality through the sacrifice of a god who had died and risen from the dead. Mystery cults became widely popular in Greece and the eastern Mediterranean region. Rome's absorption of Hellenism spread familiarity with those cults to all parts of the empire, including Judaea. It was in Judaea that Jesus of Nazareth preached.

Eastern mystery cults spread throughout the Roman Empire

JESUS OF NAZARETH. Born around 4 B.C.E. in Jerusalem, Jesus was raised in the town of Nazareth in the Zealot stronghold of Galilee and was thoroughly familiar with the apocalyptic predictions of the Essenes. But as a man of peace, he disagreed with the Zealots, and his teachings regarding how to live in this world, rather than only preparing for the next, also distinguished him from the Essenes. Jesus, who declared that he did not intend to change Jewish law, was permitted to preach in the synagogue. Like the great Jewish rabbi Hillel (30 B.C.E.–9 C.E.), with whose teachings he was undoubtedly familiar, Jesus taught in texts such as the Sermon on the Mount (see "Excerpt from the Sermon on the Mount") that Jews must love one another as they loved God and treat others as they themselves wished to be treated. A small group of his followers thought he was the Messiah, and Jesus reportedly revealed himself to them as exactly that. But he did not intend to destroy the Roman Empire; he sought to establish a spiritual kingdom, not a political one.

Excavations at Qumran, northwest of the Dead Sea, reveal how the Essenes lived around 150 B.C.E.

Jesus's emphasis on the spirituality of his rule disappointed those Jews who hoped that the Messiah would deliver them by force from Roman bondage. Other aspects of Jesus's teachings alarmed more traditional Jews, particularly those closely connected with the Sanhedrin. To them, Jesus appeared as a radical reformer threatening their established place within the Jewish hierarchy or as a troublemaker who might provoke their Roman rulers.

Document 8.2 Excerpt from the Sermon on the Mount

Soon after the beginning of his public ministry in 26 C.E., Jesus of Nazareth spoke from a mountain to a large crowd. His address, as recounted in the Gospel of St. Matthew, has become known as the Sermon on the Mount. It contains many of his most fundamental teachings.

And seeing the multitudes, He went up on a mountain, and when He was seated His disciples came to Him.

Then He opened His mouth and taught them, saying,

"Blessed are the poor in spirit, for theirs is the kingdom of heaven.

"Blessed are they who mourn, for they shall be comforted.

"Blessed are the meek, for they shall inherit the earth.

"Blessed are those who hunger and thirst for righteousness, for they shall be filled.

"Blessed are the merciful, for they shall obtain mercy.

"Blessed are the pure in heart, for they shall see God.

"Blessed are the peacemakers, for they shall be called sons of God.

"Blessed are those who are persecuted for righteousness' sake, for theirs is the kingdom of heaven.

"Blessed are you when they revile and persecute you, and say all kinds of evil against you falsely for My sake.

"Rejoice and be exceedingly glad, for great is your reward in heaven, for so they persecuted the prophets who were before you . . .

"You have heard that it was said, 'An eye for an eye and a tooth for a tooth.'

"But I tell you not to resist an evil person. But whoever slaps you on your right cheek, turn the other to him also.

"If anyone wants to sue you and take away your tunic, let him have your cloak also.

"And whoever compels you to go one mile, go with him two.

"Give to him who asks you, and from him who wants to borrow from you do not turn away.

"You have heard that it was said, 'You shall love your neighbor and hate your enemy.'

"But I say to you, love your enemies, bless those who curse you, do good to those who hate you, and pray for those who spitefully use you and persecute you,

"that you may be sons of your Father in heaven; for He makes His sun rise on the evil and on the good, and sends rain on the just and on the unjust . . .

And so it was, when Jesus had ended these sayings, that the people were astonished at His teaching . . .

SOURCE: *The Holy Bible,* The New King James Version (1983), Matthew 5: 1–12 and 38–45, 7:28.

Jesus of Nazareth challenges orthodox Judaism

There was nothing politically revolutionary in Jesus's thought, but he was clearly an unsettling figure within Judaism. Pontius Pilate (*PUNCH-us PI-lut*), Roman procurator of Judea from 26 to 36 C.E., a tough former legionary turned political official, was indifferent to Jewish religious quarrels and concerned solely with the maintenance of peace and order. The crowds acclaiming Jesus in Jerusalem during the Jewish Passover festival in 29 C.E. alarmed him. To avert civil unrest and possible riot and bloodshed, Pilate condemned Jesus to death by crucifixion.

Paul of Tarsus and the Spread of Christianity

After Jesus' death, the unrest subsided in Jerusalem, where his disciples continued to live. Pilate did not attempt to suppress them, assuming they were just another of the many different Jewish cults. As rumors began to circulate that Jesus had risen from the dead, however, his followers grew increasingly outspoken. They came to be known as Christians, or those who believe that Jesus was the Christ (a Greek word meaning Messiah).

The head of the Christian sect was Peter, a Galilean follower of Jesus and a man of traditional Jewish beliefs who felt that Jesus' teachings were meant exclusively for Jews. The new sect therefore continued to observe Jewish laws and customs, accepting only circumcised males and people who obeyed Jewish dietary regulations. To these it added new practices such as baptism (in which new members were sprinkled with or immersed in water as a symbol of new spiritual birth) and communion (at which believers consumed bread and wine in commemoration of Jesus' Last Supper with his disciples). Without Paul of Tarsus, Peter's sect might have remained a purely Jewish offshoot, ignored by mainstream Jews.

Paul of Tarsus (a town in what is today Turkey) was a Jewish Roman citizen fluent in Hebrew, Latin, and Greek. He helped persecute Christians until, while traveling from Tarsus to Damascus in Syria around 31 or 32 C.E., he experienced a vision that convinced him of the truth of Christian belief. Paul promptly converted to Christianity and, noting that the sect was largely ignored by mainstream Jews, decided to proclaim it to non-Jews, whom the Jews called Gentiles. He taught that Judaism was essentially preparation for the arrival of the Messiah, who by his coming had fulfilled the ancient prophecies and inaugurated a new age. Paul proclaimed that Jesus was not only the Messiah but also the Son of God, and that his teachings were meant for all people on earth.

Traveling and preaching throughout Greece, Turkey, Syria, and Palestine, Paul spread Christianity among the Gentiles. Many, familiar with eastern mystery religions, embraced the new religion. They were drawn to its forgiveness of sinners who repented, its promise of personal immortality, its emphasis on community, its inclusiveness (for example, treating women and slaves as the spiritual equivalents of free men), and its message that each individual had a part to play in the completion of God's work on earth. A small, physically unimpressive man, Paul was a compelling preacher whose devotion and intensity inspired many conversions.

Paul preaches Christianity to the Gentiles

Paul's decision to preach to the Gentiles transformed Christianity from a minor Jewish sect into a distinct and dynamic new religion. Insisting that male converts should not have to endure the Jewish rite of circumcision (the Greeks considered circumcision a form of mutilation), he made it possible for people to become Christians without first becoming Jews. Soon Gentile communities of Christians were larger than the original community of Christians in Jerusalem, which persisted in vainly attempting to convince other Jews that the Messiah had come. When Judaea revolted against Rome in 66 C.E., the Christianized Jews were accused of collaborating with the Romans, and by the close of the first century it was apparent that Christianity's future lay solely with the Gentiles.

Paul's vision of Christianity as a religion speaking to all humanity distinguished the new faith not only from Judaism but also from the other mystery religions. It gave Jesus's message a universal character rather than limiting it to one ethnic group selected by God. The only initiation required was baptism. Within the Roman Empire, Christianity began to challenge polytheism, offering converts a sense of mission and a place in God's plan for the redemption of the world. It also, of course, offered a powerful reward that

Paul's teachings give the message of Jesus a universal appeal

polytheists considered absurd: eternal life. In time, Christianity's strong appeal and consequent spread transformed the Roman Empire, and the teachings of a Galilean preacher became the foundation of one of the principal religions of the world.

ROME'S VIEW OF CHRISTIANITY. Traditional Roman religion, with its intricate rituals and great range of deities, continued to serve most of the empire's citizens. But Rome's integration of the eastern Mediterranean made it relatively easy for Christianity to spread throughout the region. Paul traveled along well-established trading routes to Greece and Anatolia, while other missionaries carried the new faith to Syria and Egypt. In the northern and western reaches of the empire, however, Christianity encountered indifference bordering on hostility. By 250 C.E. fewer than 10 percent of Romans were Christian.

Rome becomes suspicious of Christianity

Nevertheless, imperial authorities were suspicious of Christianity. Its practitioners owed their allegiance to a king who, although his kingdom was spiritual, seemed to rival the emperor. In addition, unlike the public Roman rituals, Christian ceremonies were conducted privately, appearing to be secret and thus potentially subversive. Finally, Christians' intolerance of all other gods and refusal to offer sacrifices to the official Roman pantheon—including deceased emperors, whom Romans openly worshiped—threatened the stability of the state.

By the reign of the Emperor Nero (54–68 C.E.), Christianity had become enough of an annoyance within Rome itself to provoke this unstable and incompetent ruler to atrocities and persecutions. Between 64 and 312 C.E. several imperial persecutions consigned Christians to martyrdom by fire, beheading, crucifixion, or mauling by wild beasts. Sometimes Christians were slaughtered in front of tens of thousands of spectators in the Colosseum, a large stadium in Rome. Those who died during persecutions were considered by Christians to be holy martyrs. Their memories were honored and their heroism used to spread the new religion even further. But as long as the force and power of the state remained arrayed against it, Christianity could never attract more than a small minority of Romans.

St. Mamai of Georgia, a Christian martyred by the Romans, is shown with a cross in one hand while riding a lion, symbolizing his triumph over death and ignorance.

From Golden Age to Disarray

Nero's relentless pursuit of Christians did not obscure his inadequacies as a ruler. He was so ineffectual that the army ousted him in 68, and two years of political turmoil were finally ended by the triumph of Vespasian (*vess-PĀ-zē-un*), a general who abandoned all pretenses of ruling a republic and openly established his own imperial dynasty, the Flavians (*FLĀ-vē-uns*).

The next century was the golden age of Rome. By 180 the emperor had come to be recognized as a guarantor of peace, stability, and prosperity. An enormous commercial network integrated the entire Mediterranean basin and attracted trading partners from Asia and Africa. After 180, however, a combination of epidemic disease, political incapacity, and external pressures weakened the empire and left its continued existence in doubt.

Commercial Connections

Rome's golden age brings prosperity to the Mediterranean and connects the Mediterranean to the wider world

Economic prosperity made it grand to be a Roman citizen during the golden age. The city of Rome itself was exciting. Noisy and cosmopolitan, with a multiethnic population exceeding 600,000, it was the most impressive European city of its time. All citizens received free grain, wine, and oil; those who were not citizens were fed at low, government-subsidized prices. Chariot races, gladiatorial combats, and other athletic contests provided entertainment.

Roman economic productivity increased and Roman commerce dominated the Mediterranean world (Map 8.5). The Roman Empire after Augustus developed a productive agricultural system. The number of small farms increased, many of them worked by retired military veterans who settled in the regions where they had been stationed. The result was the cultivation of large expanses of rich farmland in Gaul, Britain, and central and eastern Europe, ensuring Romans an abundant supply of food.

The Romans also built an enormous interconnected area of free trade and transport. They developed a system of paved, well-maintained roads connecting Rome to all parts

Map 8.5 Rome's Economic Organization of the Mediterranean World, 180 C.E.

The economic linkages forged by Rome united the Mediterranean world into an enormously powerful economic engine. Roman roads, most of them paved with stone, linked cities throughout the empire and connected Rome to caravan routes serving Asia and Africa. Notice that the shipping times indicate how rapidly Roman galleys could cross the Mediterranean. Observe also the large number of products listed in the legend, which demonstrates the complexity of trade within the Roman world. But what does the clustering of legionary headquarters in northern Europe and the eastern Mediterranean suggest about the negative aspects of the extent of the Roman Empire?

The Roman Colosseum
(see page 202).

A modern photo of the
Appian Way, part of the
network of Roman roads
that facilitated travel and
commerce throughout the
Empire.

"Barracks Emperors"
weaken the Roman
Empire

of its vast empire. These ensured the regular flow of goods into and out of the city, and of soldiers to frontiers and trouble spots.

Rome's provinces were encouraged to trade not only with the capital but also among themselves. Wine from Gaul and Italy, wool from Britain, olive oil from Syria, and grain from Egypt traveled in Roman ships across the Mediterranean, transshipped at ports connected by land routes to the far-flung reaches of the empire. Prosperity and security stimulated the growth of manufacturing, particularly in northern Europe, which grew to rival Italy itself in the production of glass, pottery, brass, and bronze.

Rome's commercial expansion affected the eastern Mediterranean profoundly. Roman ships cleared the sea of pirates and incorporated it into the empire's commercial network. In addition, Rome used its eastern lands to launch further contact with the Parthian and Sasanian Empires, which had consolidated the remnants of the Persian and Alexandrian empires. This easterly orientation that began after Actium brought Rome into contact not only with Persian and Macedonian successor states but also with India and China.

In the second century C.E., Roman mariners sailed regularly from ports in Egypt through the Indian Ocean to the Indus River, trading goods of Roman manufacture for the varied wares of the Indian subcontinent, especially fragrant and flavorful spices. Earlier, in the first century B.C.E., Han Wudi, China's Martial Emperor, had opened the Silk Road between China and the Parthian Empire; in the course of this commerce, Chinese merchants often met their Roman counterparts. Chinese silk and porcelain sold well in Roman markets, and in 96 C.E. China dispatched an ambassador to Roman Syria, where he observed the Greeks and Romans and filed a report of his impressions. But neither Chinese nor Roman rulers concluded that the other civilization had much of interest to offer, and this intriguing set of contacts resulted in nothing that would alter either's view of the world or of itself.

The Empire in Disarray

Toward the end of the second century C.E., the golden age of the Roman Empire came to an end. The Flavians and their successors, known as the "five good emperors," had ruled efficiently and effectively. They kept the army under control, defended the borders of the empire, reformed and revitalized the bureaucracy, and consolidated their own authority. But during the reign of Marcus Aurelius (165–180 C.E.), the last of the "five good emperors," a deadly epidemic of smallpox drastically reduced the empire's population, eventually even killing the ruler himself. To make matters worse, the incompetence of his son Commodus soon plunged the empire into civil war.

In 235 the empire fell under the rule of the so-called barracks emperors, a succession of generals who typically gained power by force and quickly lost it the same way. Between 235 and 284 more than twenty different emperors tried to rule. The administrative structure that Augustus had established degenerated into military despotism.

Such developments would have been dreaded even under normal circumstances, but it was Rome's misfortune that they coincided with intense pressure on its frontiers caused by the migration of the Germanic peoples, whom the Romans called barbarians. In the second and third centuries C.E., some of these Germanic tribes, originating in northern and eastern Europe, began to force their way across the borders of the Roman Empire, attracted by Rome's prosperity and the fertility of the lands it controlled.

Chapter Review

Putting It in Perspective

Rome, which began in the eighth century B.C.E. as a tiny city in the midst of the Italian peninsula, eventually assembled an empire that surpassed the Persian Empire in size and wealth. Victory over Carthage gave the Romans dominance over the Mediterranean basin, enabling them to build an extensive trading network that would spread their goods and influence. However, Rome's republican form of government, which was admirably suited to the proper functioning of a small city-state, could not satisfy the demands of a far-flung seaborne empire. Roman generals contended for the right to exercise political power, and in 27 B.C.E. Octavian eliminated his opponents and became "the first citizen of the state."

As Caesar Augustus, Octavian managed the transition from republic to empire by perpetuating the institutions of the former while employing the broad powers of the latter. But Octavian's successors never created a coherent philosophy of government with which to supplant the Republic, and Rome's golden age eventually degenerated into misrule as military dictators sought unsuccessfully to defend lengthy frontiers.

Rome's genius lay in winning conflicts and forging the cooperative connections that often grew out of them. Its legions stormed across the Mediterranean world, conquering all rivals and dominating the region for centuries. Its rulers brought the lands and peoples they defeated into a multiethnic realm that rewarded ability with citizenship. Romans rarely rejected a good idea, taking the achievements and even the gods of their subject peoples and making them their own. The very extent of the empire ultimately doomed it, but it lasted for centuries.

Benefiting from Roman cultural connections, Christianity spread across the Roman world and eventually grew into one of the most influential of the world's religions. Paul of Tarsus transformed the message of Jesus of Nazareth from the belief system of a small Jewish sect into a compelling faith that promised salvation and resurrection to all people. Paul's travels and preaching would probably not have been possible had not Rome united the eastern Mediterranean region and had not Paul himself possessed Roman citizenship.

Eventually, however, the Roman Empire's control of the Mediterranean world weakened. The strong leadership of the "five good emperors" gave way after 180 to the military rule of the barracks emperors, which was marked by constant power struggles and assassinations. The Chinese principle of the dynastic cycle explained the inevitability of good rulers being succeeded by bad ones and prescribed a change of dynasties as the proper cure for such troubles. But China was not pressed on all sides by the ambitious invaders who now sensed Rome's weakness and sought to take advantage of it.

Reviewing Key Material

KEY CONCEPTS

Republic, 185	Augustus, 194
Struggle of the Orders, 186	Pax Romana, 195
Natural law 186	Greco-Roman culture, 195
Dictator 192	Chosen People, 198

KEY PEOPLE

Hannibal, 190	Virgil, 195
Livia, 191	Ovid, 196
Spartacus, 191	Horace, 196
Sulla, 192	John the Baptist, 199
Pompey, 192	Jesus of Nazareth, 199
Julius Caesar, 193	Pontius Pilate, 200
Caesar Augustus	Peter, 201
(Octavian), 193	Paul of Tarsus, 201
Marcus Brutus, 193	Nero, 202
Marc Antony, 193	Vespasian, 202
Cleopatra, 194	Marcus Aurelius, 203

ASK YOURSELF

1. How did the Roman Republic differ from Athenian democracy? In what ways did the Roman Republic's governing framework respond to the political needs of Romans?

2. How did Rome use citizenship as a tool of governing its pluralistic empire?

3. How was the Roman Republic transformed into the Roman Empire?

4. How did the Roman Empire's organizational structure facilitate the spread of Christianity? What challenges did this new religion present to Rome?

5. Reflect on this statement: "Rome's genius resided in its superb talents for winning conflicts and forging connections."

GOING FURTHER

Beard, W., and M. Crawford. *Rome in the Late Republic.* 1984.

Boren, Henry. *Roman Society.* 1992.

Cameron, Averil. *The Later Roman Empire.* 1993.

Cornell, T. *The Beginnings of Rome.* 1995.

Crawford, M. *The Roman Republic.* 1993.

David, J.-M. *The Roman Conquest of Italy.* 1996.

Dickson, Suzanne. *The Roman Family.* 1992.

Drinkwater, J., and A. Drummond. *The World of the Romans.* 1993.

Dupont, Florence. *Daily Life in Ancient Rome.* 1992.

Eck, W. *The Age of Augustus.* 2003.

Garnsey, P., and R. Saller. *The Roman Empire: Economy, Society, and Culture.* 1987.

Goldsworthy, A. *The Punic Wars.* 2001.

Hildinger, E. *Swords Against the Senate: The Rise of the Roman Army and the Fall of the Republic.* 2002.

Kallet-Marx, R. *Hegemony to Empire.* 1995.

Kamm, A. *The Romans.* 1995.

MacMullen, Ramsay. *Christianizing the Roman Empire.* 1984.

Scullard, H. *A History of the Roman World, 753–146 B.C.* 1993.

Shotter, D. *The Fall of the Roman Republic.* 1994.

Turcan, Robert. *The Gods of Ancient Rome: Religion in Everyday Life from Archaic to Imperial Times.* 2000.

Wheeler, Mortimer. *Roman Art and Architecture.* 1985.

Key Dates and Developments

The Roman Republic

753 B.C.E.	Traditional date for the founding of Rome
509 B.C.E.	Establishment of the Roman Republic
494–287 B.C.E.	Struggle of the Orders
450 B.C.E.	Law of the Twelve Tables
264–241 B.C.E.	First Punic War
218–201 B.C.E.	Second Punic War; Hannibal crosses the Alps
149–146 B.C.E.	Third Punic War; destruction of Carthage
200–133 B.C.E.	Rome's conquest of the eastern Mediterranean
91–88 B.C.E.	Conflict between Rome and its allies
45–44 B.C.E.	Julius Caesar's dictatorship
March 15, 44 B.C.E.	Assassination of Caesar
44–42 B.C.E.	The Second Triumvirate defeats Caesar's murderers
41–30 B.C.E.	Antony and Cleopatra

The Roman Empire to 284 C.E.

27 B.C.E.–14 C.E.	Caesar Augustus's rule as *Imperator* Conquest of Spain, Germany, southeastern Europe
ca. 4 B.C.E.	Birth of Jesus of Nazareth
29 C.E.	Crucifixion of Jesus in Jerusalem
45–58 C.E.	Paul of Tarsus: preaching Christianity in the eastern Mediterranean
54–68 C.E.	Misrule of Emperor Nero
69–180 C.E.	Rome's Golden Age
235–284 C.E.	Rule of the "barracks emperors" Onset of the Germanic migrations

Germanic Societies and the Emergence of the Christian West, 100–1100 C.E.

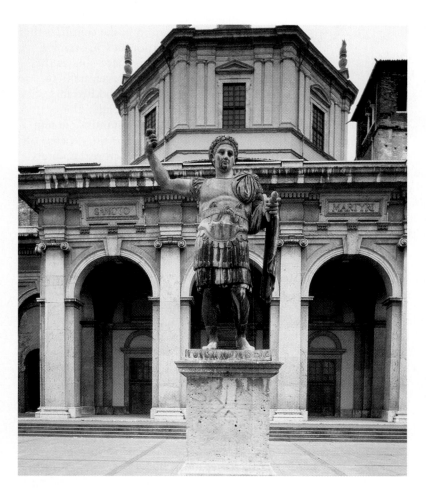

- The Germanic Peoples
- The Decline of the Western Roman Empire
- Early Medieval Europe: Germanic and Christian Connections
- The Decline and Revival of the Western Church
- Chapter Review

Emperor Constantine I

Roman Emperor Constantine I, depicted by this statue, legalized Christianity and moved the empire's capital east from Rome to Constantinople. The western part of the empire, including Rome, was then overrun by Germanic peoples who in time developed a new culture, blending Roman, Christian, and Germanic ways to create the Christian West.

In 312 C.E. Constantine (*KON-stun-tēn*), son of a Roman emperor who had died in 306, advanced with an army on the city of Rome to secure his own claim to the throne. His main rival, with a much larger army, was blocking access to Rome at the Milvian Bridge. According to legend, as Constantine prepared for battle, he saw in the sky a symbol of Christ and a phrase proclaiming "In this sign you will conquer." He adopted the symbol as his battle standard and the next day won a great victory.

The Christian West

Constantine went on to become one of the most pivotal Roman emperors. Interpreting his vision and his victory as signs from the Christian God, he legalized Christianity, which had been banned and periodically persecuted since 64 C.E. He moved the empire's capital eastward from Rome to Byzantium, a city he rebuilt as a grandiose New Rome, soon known in his honor as Constantinople. And he defended the realm against Germanic peoples who threatened it from the north.

Constantine's endeavors set the stage for Europe's transformation in the centuries that followed. His legalization of Christianity, and its designation by his successors as the Roman state religion, helped eventually to make it Europe's main faith, embodied in a wealthy and powerful institution called the Church. And his new capital at Constantinople reinforced the empire's eastward orientation at the expense of the west. The prosperous eastern half of the Roman realm, later called the Byzantine Empire, was ruled from Constantinople for another millennium (Chapter 10). But the western half was conquered in the fifth century by Germanic peoples, whose connections and conflicts with the Romans and their heritage eventually produced a new civilization, often called the Christian West, combining Germanic and Roman elements with Christian religious beliefs.

The Germanic Peoples

To the north and northeast of the Roman world lived an assortment of tribal societies, now collectively called Germanic peoples, since most spoke languages belonging to the Germanic branch of the Indo-European language family. These peoples included, among others, the Franks, Angles, Saxons, Lombards, Alemanni (*AH-luh-MAH-nē*), Vandals, and Goths (Map 9.1). Their tribal warrior societies, disparaged by Romans as "barbarian," in time would overwhelm Rome itself, Germanicize the Christian West, and help to shape what came to be known as Western Civilization.

Germanic Society: Kinship and Combat

Early German pastoral nomads live by herding, hunting, and fighting

Initially the Germans were mainly pastoral nomads who lived in northern Europe by herding, hunting, and fighting. They herded cattle to get meat, milk, and cheese for food and hides for making clothes. They hunted deer and other wild game for additional meat

FOUNDATION MAP 9.1 Germans, Celts, and Romans, by the First Century C.E.

In the first several centuries C.E., Germanic-speaking peoples engaged in connections and conflicts with the Roman Empire. Note that Celtic-speaking peoples, displaced from central and western Europe by Germanic migrations, resettled in what are now Scotland, Wales, Ireland, and Brittany. What advantages did Germanic peoples have in their clashes and contacts with the Romans? Why did Germanic invasions and infiltration pose a serious threat to the Roman Empire?

and hides. They made swords and spears from iron, an ore abundant in northern and central Europe, and used these weapons to stage raids and attacks on neighboring peoples. The Germans were not much interested in commerce, preferring instead to get their goods from raids and the spoils of war.

Like many tribal peoples, the Germans based their societies on kinship ties, involving loyalty and patriarchy, rather than on territory or formal institutions. The members of each tribe, linked by family connections, saw themselves as an extended clan with a common ancestry and heritage. These kinship loyalties frequently led to blood feuds: if an outsider killed a member of the tribe, the victim's kinsfolk felt bound to avenge this crime by killing either the murderer or someone from the

Germanic tribal societies feature kinship ties and blood feuds

murderer's clan, an act of vengeance that often triggered battles between tribes. These tribal ties foreshadowed the notion of **nation**, a political community united by its people's sense of common heritage and culture, which later played a prominent role in European history.

The tribes were often organized as chiefdoms, ruled by a chief who was typically elected by an assembly of warriors. Attached to the chief by bonds of mutual loyalty, these warriors were expected to protect him with their lives or die with him in battle. In future centuries some of the chiefdoms matured into monarchies, with the chief becoming a king and his men of war nobles who served on his royal council. Germanic tribal structure thus helped to shape later Europe's stratified societies, dominated by warrior kings and nobles.

Much as male warriors ran Germanic societies, senior males dominated Germanic families. In these patriarchal households, women were valued mainly for their reproductive roles and service to the male warriors. Men of means and status could have more than one wife, and fathers were free to sell their daughters in marriage to whoever made the best offer. The main role of women was to support the men, who fought the wars that protected the society and secured the food that sustained it—a function and relationship that would prevail throughout much of European history.

Like most other early societies, including the pre-Christian Greeks and Romans, Germans were polytheistic, worshiping numerous gods and goddesses who personified various aspects of the world around them. The main divinities included Woden (*WŌ-dun*), creator of the earth and sky; Tiu (*TĒ-oo*), the god of war; Thor, the god of thunder; and Friia (*FRĒ-uh*), the goddess of fertility and love. Although the Germans later adopted Christianity and abandoned these deities, their names would survive in Anglo-Saxon week days such as Tuesday (Tiu's day), Wednesday (Woden's day), Thursday (Thor's day), and Friday (Friia's day).

Sometimes the Germans called on the divinities to decide legal issues brought before the chief and his assembly. Believing that the gods would protect a guiltless person from harm, the chief might order a trial by ordeal, in which the defendant was put to a test to determine innocence or guilt. An accused woman, for example, might undergo ordeal by fire: if she could walk through flames without being burned, she would be considered innocent. Or, when faced with conflicting testimony, the chief might order an accused man to face his accuser in battle, typically in face-to-face combat with swords. This practice endured into the Christian era, when it took the form of a duel, in which the combatants appealed to "God's judgment" to bring victory for the side that embodied justice and truth.

Patriarchal males dominate society, with women in supportive roles

Germanic jewelry.

Germanic Migrations and Their Threat to Rome

Germanic peoples migrate toward Roman frontiers

During the last several centuries B.C.E., while Rome was extending its control over the Mediterranean basin, many Germans began moving south into central and western Europe, driven perhaps by a scarcity of food resulting from population growth. By the first century C.E. they had largely displaced these regions' tribal peoples, who spoke Celtic (*KELL-tik*) languages (another branch of the Indo-European family) and lived mainly by farming. As Celtic tribes resettled in the regions now called Scotland, Wales, Ireland, and Brittany (in western France), the Germans moved toward the Roman frontiers, where they increasingly took up farming and interacted with the Roman world (Map 9.1).

The Germans thus became more settled and agricultural but no less warlike. They came to reside in villages, where they lived in wooden huts and grew grains such as wheat, oats, and barley on the surrounding lands. Women did much of the field work and most household chores, boiling grains to make thick gruel, grinding them into flour for flat baked bread, and fermenting them into lush, hearty beer that has since been a favorite German beverage. The men helped with planting and harvesting but still hunted and herded, made war against other German tribes, staged raids on Roman towns and farmlands, and even fought the famed Roman legions.

The Romans responded to the growing German threat not only by waging numerous battles against the Germanic "barbarians" but also by seeking to assimilate them. Roman leaders recruited many Germans as soldiers, awarded German leaders with command positions, and sometimes even made them Roman citizens. By employing Germanic warriors, the empire secured the services of its most dangerous adversaries. It also, however, brought growing numbers of Germans into the Roman armies. As Germans became a large portion of these armies and bore much of the empire's defensive burden, they began to think that they should enjoy a substantial share of its riches. The pressure on the empire from Germans in its armies was further compounded by war among German tribes. The losers, forced off their lands, typically moved toward the fertile soils and ample wealth of the Roman world.

Romans combat Germans but also recruit them into Roman armies

Beset with internal power struggles throughout much of the third century, the Romans proved unable to control or pacify the Germans, who invaded and raided at will. By the late third century, the Roman Empire was in serious danger.

Germans increasingly invade and raid Roman lands

The Decline of the Western Roman Empire

Beginning in the late third century, to deal with the growing crisis, Roman rulers divided the empire into eastern and western sectors, hoping to make it easier to manage and defend. This division, however, combined with the eastward relocation of the capital from Rome to Constantinople in the early fourth century, mainly strengthened the eastern sector at the west's expense. In the fourth and fifth centuries, while Christianity replaced polytheism as the empire's dominant religion, the western half of the realm was wracked by continued Germanic invasions, culminating in the fall of Rome and the end of the Western Roman Empire.

The Divided Empire and Its Eastern Orientation

In the third century C.E., as noted in the last chapter, a prolonged crisis shook the Roman Empire. Increasing Germanic attacks coincided with a series of military revolts that proclaimed as emperor more than twenty different generals within fifty years (235–284), bringing to power "barracks emperors" more focused on fighting for power than defending the frontiers. Germans repeatedly raided and infiltrated the western parts of the realm, disrupting commerce and provoking social chaos. In the east, taking advantage of the tumult, the Sasanian Persians drove the Romans out of Mesopotamia. The Roman world seemed to be in disarray.

Diocletian divides empire to improve its administration

But desperate times brought forth an exceptional leader in 284, when Diocletian (*dī-uh-KLĒ-shun*), a common soldier who had risen through the ranks, seized power as Roman Emperor. Faced with continual revolts and invasions, he quickly concluded that the empire was too vast for one man to rule alone. So he divided it into two parts, along a line running north and south between Italy and Greece (Map 9.2), keeping himself in charge of the east and naming a co-emperor to administer the west. Later he added a junior ruler to assist each emperor, creating a four-ruler system called a tetrarchy (*TET-rar-kē*). For a while this imaginative reform seemed to work, enabling the leaders to restore order and fight invasions more effectively.

Diocletian's retirement in 305, however, led to a new power struggle, eventually won by Emperor Constantine I (312–337), whose victory in 312 at the Milvian Bridge is

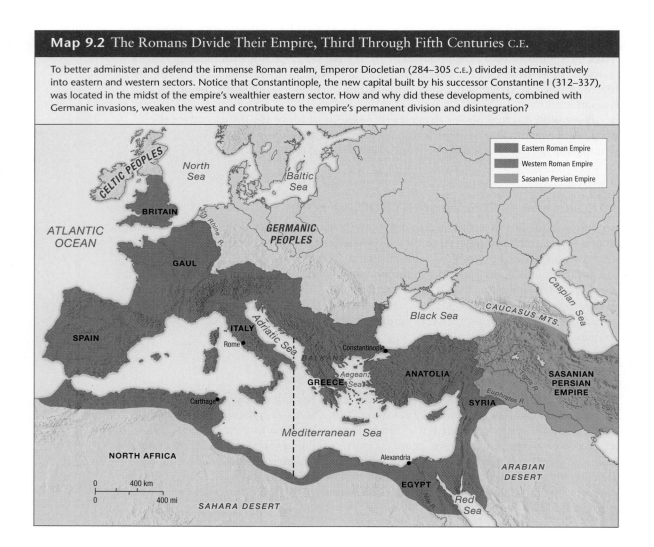

Map 9.2 The Romans Divide Their Empire, Third Through Fifth Centuries C.E.

To better administer and defend the immense Roman realm, Emperor Diocletian (284–305 C.E.) divided it administratively into eastern and western sectors. Notice that Constantinople, the new capital built by his successor Constantine I (312–337), was located in the midst of the empire's wealthier eastern sector. How and why did these developments, combined with Germanic invasions, weaken the west and contribute to the empire's permanent division and disintegration?

noted at the start of this chapter. He restored the empire's unity, defeating all his rivals and emerging as sole ruler by 324. He also shored up its defenses, enlarging the army and bureaucracy and stationing more forces along the frontiers. Furthermore, as noted above, he moved the capital east from Rome to Byzantium, where he built a splendid New Rome that came to be called Constantinople.

Constantine restores unity and moves capital east to Constantinople

In many respects, the new capital's site was superb. Surrounded by water on three sides, the New Rome would prove much easier to defend than the old Rome in the west. Situated astride the trade routes connecting Europe with Asia, Constantinople flourished for centuries, not only as the seat of imperial authority, but also as one of the world's leading commercial and cultural centers. The new capital's location strengthened the realm's wealthy eastern sector politically and militarily. In reinforcing the empire's eastward orientation, however, the change of capitals further relegated the less prosperous west to a secondary status, setting the stage for its continuing decline under ongoing Germanic onslaughts.

Moving capital strengthens eastern empire but weakens west

The Triumph and Transformation of Christianity

Constantine's reign also heralded the triumph of Christianity, an eastern salvation religion that, in spite of Roman persecutions, had by then attracted a sizable following (Chapter 8). Following his vision and victory in 312 at the Battle of Milvian Bridge, Constantine became an avid supporter of the Christian faith. He did not at once become a baptized Christian, in part because his position as emperor made him the high priest of the polytheistic Roman state religion. But he legalized the Christian faith in 313, took an active interest in its internal affairs, and finally was baptized in 337 on his deathbed, preparing the way for Christianity's later adoption as the empire's official religion.

Constantine legalizes Christianity and plays active role in Church

The Arch of Constantine in Rome.

Constantine's delay in converting to Christianity reflected an abiding Roman ambivalence toward the new religion. Like its parent Judaism, Christianity was monotheistic and intolerant of all other gods and forms of worship. Roman authorities did not demand that Christians adopt polytheism, only that they pay homage to the Roman gods and then worship in their own way as other cults and creeds did. But Christians refused to participate at all in the Roman state religion, in effect defying imperial authority. To many Romans, Christians thus seemed not only narrow-minded and intolerant but also disloyal to the empire.

Still, by the time of Constantine, many Romans were losing faith in the traditional gods, who were supposed to protect the empire in return for Roman performance of the proper rituals. As German invasions continued, it became increasingly obvious that these rituals were not working, and Roman devotion to the old gods steadily declined.

Meanwhile Christianity was gaining influence. Its promise of potential salvation for all, whatever their social status, attracted numerous converts, especially among women and the urban poor. Constantine's military success, achieved in the name of the Christian faith, showed loyal Romans that this new religion could protect imperial interests, perhaps more effectively than the old gods did. His legalization of Christianity hence met little opposition, even among prominent polytheists, whom Christians categorized as pagans ("country-dwellers") since many lived on rural estates. It also helped to advance the Christian faith, to such an extent that in 380 one of his successors, Emperor Theodosius (*thē-uh-DŌ-shus*) the Great, declared Christianity the official religion of the Roman Empire (see "Decree Making Christianity the Official Roman Religion").

Christianity becomes the official Roman state religion

Document 9.1 Decree Making Christianity the Official Roman Religion

In 313 C.E., Roman Emperor Constantine the Great legalized the Christian faith, which his predecessor Diocletian had recently persecuted. In 380 C.E., Emperor Theodosius the Great issued the following decree, making Christianity the Roman state religion and promising to punish those who disagreed with Christian teachings. In less than a century, the empire thus went from persecuting to enforcing Christianity and punishing as heretics those who dared to dissent.

It is our desire that all the various nations which are subject to our Clemency and Moderation, should continue in the profession of that religion which was delivered to the Romans by the divine Apostle Peter, as it hath been preserved by faithful tradition; and which is now professed by Pontiff Damasus and by Peter,

Bishop of Alexandria, a man of apostolic holiness. According to the apostolic teaching and the doctrine of the Gospel, let us believe in the one deity of the Father, the Son and the Holy Spirit, in equal majesty and in a holy Trinity. We authorize the followers of this law to assume the title of Catholic Christians; but as for the others, since, in our judgment, they are foolish madmen, we decree that they shall be branded with the ignominious name of heretics, and shall not presume to give to their conventicles the name of churches. They will suffer in the first place the chastisement of the divine condemnation, and in the second the punishment which our authority, in accordance with the will of Heaven, shall decide to inflict.

SOURCE: Henry Bettenson, ed. Documents of the Christian Church, 2nd ed. (London: Oxford University Press, 1963) 22.

Christianity's triumph helped to transform it, in the course of the fourth century, from a persecuted popular movement with little power and wealth into a powerful and wealthy institution widely known as the Church. Theodosius and his successors supported Christian efforts to destroy paganism by banning pagan worship, closing temples to Roman and Greek gods, and even ending the Olympic games, which had been staged to honor Greek gods for more than a thousand years. In return, the Church became a pillar of the Roman state, calling on Christians to fully support the imperial leaders.

By this time the Church had also organized itself along Roman imperial lines, with numerous priests who served as its local agents and above them officials called **bishops** who presided over districts known as dioceses (*DĪ-uh-sis-iz*). At the head of this hierarchy was the bishop of Rome, also known as the **pope** (from the Latin word for "father"), a religious leader who headed the Church much as Roman rulers headed the empire and who claimed to be the vicar (or agent) of Christ on earth. Pope Celestine (*suh-LES-tēn*) I (422–432) even asserted that whoever held this office also possessed the "keys of the kingdom of heaven," which Christ had entrusted to his disciple Peter (see "Bible Passage on 'The Keys of the Kingdom' "). The popes saw themselves as successors to Peter, the leader of Christ's disciples, whom Christians considered the first head of the Church.

Thus developed the concept of **papal primacy** (supremacy of the pope), later to become Church doctrine, which held that the pope had authority over the whole Christian Church. Claiming to be vicars of Christ, a poor preacher who said his kingdom was "not of this world," the popes paradoxically headed a Church with great wealth and power in this world. Their claims of papal primacy helped to fuel discord with eastern Church leaders—a discord deepened by the empire's east-west division and by growing German dominance in the west.

Christian Church is structured on imperial lines, under pope in Rome

Document 9.2 Bible Passage on "The Keys of the Kingdom"

In this passage from the Christian scriptures, Jesus promises to build his Church upon his disciple Peter (whose name means "rock") and to give Peter "the keys of the kingdom of heaven." The popes who later headed the Christian Church, seeing themselves as Peter's successors, would use this passage to assert that they too held the keys to eternal salvation.

Now when Jesus came into the district of Caesarea Philippi, he asked his disciples, "Who do men say that the Son of man is?"

And they said, "Some say John the Baptist, others say Elijah, and others Jeremiah or one of the prophets."

He said to them, "But who do you say that I am?"

Simon Peter replied, "You are the Christ, the Son of the living God."

And Jesus answered him, "Blessed are you, Simon Bar-Jona! For flesh and blood has not revealed this to you, but my Father who is in heaven.

And I tell you, you are Peter, and on this rock I will build my church, and the powers of death shall not prevail against it.

I will give you the keys of the kingdom of heaven, and whatever you bind on earth shall be bound in heaven, and whatever you loose on earth shall be loosed in heaven."

SOURCE: *The Bible*, Revised Standard Version, Matthew 16: 13–19 (New Revised Standard Version Bible, copyright 1989, Division of Christian Education of the National Council of the Churches of Christ in the United States of America. Used by permission. All rights reserved.)

Crisis and Chaos in the West

Christianity's triumph coincided with the empire's disintegration, as Constantine's successors proved unable to preserve its unity or to protect it from Germanic invasions. After Constantine's death in 337, his sons divided the empire anew and fought among themselves, initiating decades of sporadic civil wars and succession struggles. On several occasions the realm was reunified but never for very long. By the century's end, in many respects, it had become two distinct states: an Eastern and a Western Roman Empire, each with its own separate ruler.

Eastern and Western Empires diverge under Constantine's successors

The empire's vast size, moreover, continued to compromise its defenses. The Roman army was capable of defeating either the Germans in the west or Sasanian Persians in the east, but not both at the same time. Since a normal day's march covered only twenty miles, and since two thousand miles separated the western and eastern frontiers, Roman forces could not be moved quickly back and forth. Sooner or later, the empire's enemies were bound to wear it down on one frontier or the other.

The threat in the west proved more serious. Persia in the east, though a formidable foe, was a single state with specific lands and borders to defend; Roman forces there could thus focus their efforts against a well-defined adversary. In the west, however, there were many German tribes, often with ill-defined homelands, who frequently struck the Roman realm in several places at once. Furthermore, with their nomadic roots, the Germans proved highly flexible and mobile: when defeated in battle, they often simply moved elsewhere to attack.

German mobility and flexibility frustrates Roman defenses

Faced with this danger, Constantine's successors sought valiantly to stabilize the west. Some took a forceful approach: Emperor Valentinian I, who ruled the western half of the realm from 364 to 375, ruthlessly imposed and collected heavy taxes for imperial defense, then led large armies north into France (then called Gaul) and Germany to crush Germanic forces. Other emperors pursued the time-tested practice of assimilation, trying to pacify warlike tribes by giving them farmlands on the Roman frontiers while employing their best warriors and generals in the Roman legions.

Such efforts might have staved off disaster had not a new threat emerged in the east in the late fourth century. Around 370 the Huns, aggressive nomads probably related to the warlike Xiongnu who long had tormented China, swept in from Central Asia and attacked the Goths, Germanic peoples living north of the Black Sea (Map 9.3). The eastern Goths, or Ostrogoths (*OST-ruh-goths*), who lived in what is now Ukraine, fell to the Huns and were ruled by them for the next eight decades. The western Goths, or Visigoths (*VIZ-uh-goths*), who lived in what is now Romania, were driven south into the Balkan peninsula, where they defeated the Roman armies in 378. Theodosius the Great (379–395), the Roman ruler who made Christianity the official religion, bought them off for a time by giving

Attacks from east by Huns drive Germans deeper into Roman lands

Map 9.3 Hunnic and Germanic Invasions, 370–500 C.E.

Beginning around 370 C.E., invading Huns from Central Asia drove Germanic peoples to the west and south, leading to further invasion and infiltration of Roman lands. Note that Visigoths invaded Italy and sacked Rome in 410, that Huns invaded the western Roman realm before turning back in the 450s, and that Vandals attacked Rome by sea in 455, setting the stage for the fall of the Western Roman Empire in 476. Why was the Western Roman Empire unable to withstand these onslaughts?

them Roman lands in the eastern Balkans, where they settled and soon converted to the Christian faith.

After Theodosius died, however, the situation changed. His sons, who split the empire (briefly reunified by their father) between them, angered the Visigoths by failing to award a Roman command post to Alaric (*AL-uh-rik*), their brilliant young leader. The Visigoths promptly rebelled, moved south into Greece, and later invaded Italy. For years the Western Roman Empire fought them off, its forces led by Stilicho (*STILL-ih-kō*) the Vandal, a Germanic general who emerged in those days as the empire's best military leader.

Alaric and the Goths strike deep into Roman lands

Alaric and Stilicho, each with Germanic heritage, embodied both the potentials and perils of Roman assimilation efforts. Alaric the Goth, like Stilicho the Vandal, valued the empire and had no desire to destroy it; what Alaric sought was a high Roman post for himself and a secure homeland for his people. Stilicho, who instinctively understood these motives, hoped eventually to ally with Alaric against other Germanic tribes. But the Western Roman Empire's leaders, seeing Stilicho's willingness to work with the Visigoths as a sign of treason, convicted and beheaded him in 408, depriving the realm of its finest commander at an hour of maximum danger.

Angered by news of Stilicho's alleged treason, Romans massacred hundreds of Germans living in the Western Empire, including Germans who served as Roman soldiers and members of their families. Many German soldiers who escaped swore vengeance and joined Alaric, whose army grew to exceed 30,000 men, while the Western Empire found itself without an effective commander. Alaric asked for a permanent Visigothic homeland in return for his army's commitment to defend the empire. The Romans, distrusting the Germans, refused this offer, so in August 410 the Visigoths attacked Rome itself—and for the first time in eight centuries the city fell to foreigners. After sacking the city, Alaric's forces moved south in search of further plunder, but their leader died of an illness later that same year.

Alaric and the Goths sack Rome in 410 C.E.

The pope characterized Alaric's death as divine punishment for the sack of Rome; the Goths attributed it to his having eaten some spoiled meat. Either way, the resulting respite for the Western Roman Empire proved relatively brief. In 434 a warrior named Attila (*uh-TILL-uh*) became leader of the Huns, and in 441 he began to threaten the Eastern Roman Empire. Constantinople bought him off with tribute, and so in 451 he turned against the west.

Alaric dies, but Rome is soon threatened by Attila and the Huns

Attila the Hun, called the "scourge of God," was a brutal man—but then so were most warriors of his day. Unlike Alaric, however, Attila was neither a Christian nor an admirer of the Roman Empire. As the Huns devastated northern Italy, fear spread that they would move south and lay waste to Rome itself. This fate was avoided in 452 when Pope Leo the Great, having ventured north from Rome to the Huns' encampment, met with Attila and apparently persuaded him to withdraw. Possibly Attila learned from his scouts that Constantinople had sent an army to attack the Huns; probably Attila's forces had been weakened by a recent famine and plague. For whatever reasons, the king of the Huns turned away—and died in his sleep the very next year from a severe nosebleed, reportedly after getting drunk to celebrate his own wedding.

Pope Leo dissuades Attila from marching on Rome

The Fall of Rome and End of the Western Roman Empire

Rome had been saved from the Huns, but the position of the Western Roman Empire continued to deteriorate. Germanic tribes continued to invade, often meeting little resistance, driving into Britain, Gaul (France), Spain, northwest Africa, and Italy itself (Map 9.3).

Chaos in the west ruins commerce and regional connections

Interregional commerce, hampered by constant warfare, virtually disappeared in the west, as did collection of imperial revenues. People subsisted in self-contained local economies, with little access to goods or information from other parts of the empire. Commerce continued to thrive in the east, but in the west the connections that knit the empire together increasingly unraveled.

Germans force last western emperor to abdicate in 476 C.E.

The western emperors could no longer control what happened in the provinces or even defend Rome itself. The Vandals sacked the city in 455, marking the beginning of the end. Twenty-one years later a Germanic general called Odoacer (*Ō-dō-Ā-sur*) forced the abdication of a boy named Romulus Augustulus (*ROM-yoo-lus ah-GUS-tyoo-lus*), the last Roman emperor in the west. This action completed the process, begun by Diocletian and Constantine, of reorienting the Roman Empire to the east. In the west, with Rome itself in the hands of the Germans, the empire simply ceased to exist in 476 C.E.

Technically, the Roman Empire did not end in 476: since it continued to function in the east, all that had fallen was its ancient capital and its western provinces. Emperors reigned in Constantinople for almost another millennium, claiming all the while to rule the Roman Empire. Indeed, when Constantinople finally fell to the Turks in 1453, the victorious Turkish sultan promptly assumed the title of "Roman emperor."

Empire continues in the east while popes dominate in the west

Yet two things changed dramatically in 476, and history changed with them. First, by deposing the last western emperor, Odoacer removed from Rome its traditional symbol of imperial authority. This authority soon would be claimed by the popes, who, as bishops of Rome, held the most prestigious position remaining in the west. In succeeding centuries, by asserting secular as well as spiritual authority, the popes would place the Christian Church at the center of Europe's politics as well as its religion. Second, with the Germans in control of Rome, the rulers in Constantinople, later called Byzantine emperors, could no longer assert their authority in the west. Although it would take centuries for Europeans to recognize this reality, the Western Roman Empire was gone, and the future of the west would hence be shaped by its Germanic conquerors.

Early Medieval Europe: Germanic and Christian Connections

In Europe the period from the fall of Rome through the fourteenth century, since it came between ancient and modern times, is known as the Middle Ages, or **medieval** (*mē-dē-Ē-vul*) era. In the early part of this era, dominated by Germanic tribes that had overrun the Western Roman Empire, European society was characterized by tribalism and localism. In central and western Europe, with the end of Roman rule, Roman cities, roads, trade, and money fell into disuse. Learning and literacy declined, interregional commerce dwindled, and central administration virtually disappeared.

The end of Western Empire gives rise to Medieval Western culture

In the long run, however, conflict and fragmentation in the west helped foster creative new connections. Europeans gradually developed a new culture, blending Germanic and Celtic customs with Christian beliefs and the remnants of the Roman heritage. For a time in the early 800s, a Germanic empire reunited much of the Christian West. That realm, however, soon disintegrated, and Europe was devastated by new nomadic invasions and raids from the north, east, and south. Nonetheless, by the eleventh century, led by a landed warrior nobility and an energized Christian Church, Europe experienced a political and cultural revival.

The Emergence of Germanic Kingdoms

At the start of the Middle Ages the Germans were still grouped in tribes, united by kinship and custom, and ruled by chieftains typically elected from among the strongest warriors. Although hunting and fighting remained central to their heritage, most tribes by this time had settled into an agricultural life, dwelling in villages while tending their crops and herds. Families remained patriarchal, dominated by male heads of household, with women in supportive roles. Men typically tended cattle and raised grains such as wheat and barley, while women ground the grain, baked bread, and helped work the land. Wealth was measured in cattle and land, often acquired by the warriors, who thus came to form an early kind of rural nobility.

As cultivation increased food supplies that supported population growth, some Germanic groups—including the Ostrogoths and later the Lombards in Italy, the Visigoths in Spain, the Franks in what is now France, and the Angles and Saxons in England—set up kingdoms (Map 9.4). Unlike tribes, which were groups of people,

Germanic peoples set up kingdoms, ruled by dynastic monarchies

Map 9.4 Germanic Peoples Divide the West into Kingdoms, Fifth and Sixth Centuries C.E.

In the fifth and sixth centuries C.E., as they overran the Western Roman Empire, Germanic peoples divided its lands into separate kingdoms. Notice, however, that the east remained united under the Eastern Roman Empire, later called the Byzantine Empire. How did Germanic conquest and division affect the culture and religion of the former Roman West?

kingdoms were large units of territory ruled by monarchs often chosen from the same royal family, or dynasty. The national monarchies that later grew out of these kingdoms eventually became Europe's foremost form of governance.

The Early Medieval Church: Expansion and Adaptation

The central institution of the early Middle Ages, however, was not the Germanic kingdoms but the Christian Church. Led by the popes in Rome, the Church managed to win the allegiance of the Germans and Celts, to preserve elements of Christian learning from the Roman era, to care for the poor and the sick, and to provide religious unity in the midst of political fragmentation. By maintaining its Roman heritage, while adapting the Christian faith to Germanic and Celtic cultures, the Church also helped to shape a new European society.

Church converts Celts and Germans to Christianity

The Church strove to Christianize the Germans and Celts, usually by working through tribal chiefs or kings. In the mid-fifth century, for example, a bishop from Britain named Patrick, who as a youth had spent time as a slave in Ireland, used this approach to convert that island's Celtic tribes. Around 496 King Clovis of the Franks adopted Christianity, supposedly after his prayers to the God of his Christian wife Clotilda had helped him win a great battle. In 597 a Roman monk named Augustine (*AW-gus-tēn* or *ah-GUS-tin*), heading a mission sent by the pope to convert the Anglo-Saxons in England, began by baptizing one of their kings and several thousand of his people. Later, after Ireland and England had become Christian strongholds, Irish and English missionaries promoted Christianity elsewhere in Europe.

Baptism of Clovis as depicted in a later engraving.

In adopting Christianity, however, Celts and Germans did not abandon their traditional ways. Instead, with Church approval, they converted their old shrines into Christian churches and modified their festivals into Christian holy days. Rather than praying for good fortune to their traditional gods, the people now asked Christian saints to help them gain God's blessings. Rather than conducting trials and ordeals based on tribal ritual, priests and bishops now presided at them in the name of Christ. The Christian faith was thus adapted to fit Celtic and Germanic cultures.

Germanic Western Christianity diverges from Eastern Christianity

In adjusting to these rural, tribal cultures, western Christianity increasingly diverged from the more urbane and cosmopolitan Christian culture of the Byzantine east. Aware of the growing gap, the Church in the west sought to preserve some semblance of Christian learning and Roman culture, especially in Christian monasteries.

Monasteries help preserve faith and learning in west

Medieval Europe thus was shaped by **monasticism** (*muh-NASS-tih-siz-um*), a movement in which especially devout men (called monks) and women (called nuns) withdrew from secular society to live in religious communities (monasteries for monks and convents for nuns), where life was characterized by prayer and self-denial. During the Middle Ages, Christian monasteries played a prominent role in western scholarship, education, agriculture, hospitality, charity, and health care. They worked effectively to spread the Christian faith, and later to reform the Christian Church.

Although Christian monasticism originally emerged in third-century Egypt, its most influential western expression was developed by Saint Benedict (480–543). An earnest and devout young man from a wealthy family, Benedict withdrew from the affluence of urban Rome to live a life of poverty and meditation in the wilderness, in time attracting

Document 9.3 Excerpts from the *Rule* of Saint Benedict

In founding his monastic movement, Saint Benedict (480–543) wrote a Rule, or set of regulations for monks, which his sister Scholastica later adapted for nuns. As reflected in the following excerpts, the Rule prescribed a life of austere humility, based on renunciation of personal possessions (poverty), repression of "desires of the flesh" (chastity), and total submission to superiors such as the abbot who headed the monastery (obedience).

Holy Scripture, brethren, cries out to us, saying, "Everyone who exalts himself shall be humbled, and he who humbles himself shall be exalted" (Luke 14:11) . . .

The first degree of humility, then, is that a person keep the fear of God before his eyes and beware of ever forgetting it. Let him be ever mindful of all that God has commanded; let his thoughts constantly recur to the hell-fire which will burn for their sins those who despise God, and to the life everlasting which is prepared for those who fear Him. Let him keep himself at every moment from sins and vices, whether of the mind, the tongue, the hands, the feet, or the self-will, and check also the desires of the flesh . . .

As for self-will, we are forbidden to do our own will by the Scripture, which says to us, "Turn away from your own will" (Eccles. 18:30), and likewise by the prayer in which we ask God that His will be done in us . . .

And as for the desires of the flesh, let us believe with the Prophet that God is ever present to us, when he says to the Lord, "Every desire of mine is before You" (Ps. 37:10). We must be on our guard, therefore, against evil desires, for death lies close by the gate of pleasure . . .

The second degree of humility is that a person love not his own will nor take pleasure in satisfying his desires, but model his actions on the saying of the Lord, "I have come not to do My own will, but the will of Him who sent Me" (John 6:38) . . .

The third degree of humility is that a person for love of God submit himself to his Superior in all obedience, imitating the Lord, of whom the Apostle says, "He became obedient even unto death."

. . . Let no one presume to give or receive anything without the Abbot's leave, or to have anything as his own—anything whatever, whether book or tablets or pen or whatever it may be—since they are not permitted to have even their bodies or wills at their own disposal; but for all their necessities let them look to the Father of the monastery. And let it be unlawful to have anything which the Abbot has not given or allowed. Let all things be common to all, as it is written (Acts 4:32), and let no one say or assume that anything is his own.

SOURCE: The Order of Saint Benedict, *The Rule of Benedict*. Chapter 7: On Humility (http://www.osb. org/rb/text/rbejms3.html#7), Chapter 33: Whether Monks Ought to Have Anything of Their Own (http://www.osb.org/rb/text/rbejms3.html#7).

similar young men to join him as monks. He eventually founded a monastery on a hill called Monte Cassino and wrote for the monks a *Rule*, or set of regulations for monastic life, which his sister Scholastica (*skuh-LASS-tih-kuh*) later adapted for women. Throughout the Middle Ages, the *Rule* of Saint Benedict would set the standards not only for his followers, known as Benedictines, but also for most other western monastic communities (see "Excerpts from the *Rule* of Saint Benedict").

In keeping with Benedict's *Rule*, monks and nuns took vows of poverty, chastity, and obedience, pledging thereby to forsake personal possessions, abstain from sex, and fully submit to their monastic superior. They lived in communities based on equality and hard work: whether sons of nobles or slaves, monks were expected to labor in the fields and

Abbey of Monte Cassino, on the site of Saint Benedict's first monastery.

Monasteries provide
havens for prayer,
learning, farming,
and charity

live a life of self-denial. They promoted learning by setting up local schools, maintaining libraries, writing books, and copying religious manuscripts. They advanced agriculture by clearing swamps and woodlands and by implementing new farming methods. They provided charity for people in need, hospitality for travelers, and sometimes even health care for the sick. In a fragmented and dangerous world, monasteries provided a safe haven for prayer, learning, farming, and charity. They also promoted Christian beliefs throughout Europe, with significant assistance from the rulers of the Franks.

The Franks and Their Effort to Reunite the West

Frankish rulers expand
their realm and help
spread Christianity

The realm of the Franks was the most expansive of all the Germanic kingdoms. King Clovis (481–511) not only accepted Christianity but also expanded his domain to include most of what is now France and western Germany (Map 9.4). His heirs, however, proved less capable than he, and by the early eighth century they were largely relying on an official called the mayor of the palace to run their affairs. One such mayor was Charles Martel, who defended the Frankish kingdom against the Muslims, recent conquerors of Spain, by defeating their forces near Tours (*TOOR*) in central France in 732 (Chapter 11). As a result, he gained fame in the west as Europe's savior from Islamic conquest. He also supported Benedictine monks from England, led by Saint Boniface (*BAH-nih-fiss*), in their efforts to Christianize central Europe. In return, Boniface anointed Martel's son Pepin (*PEP-in*) as King of the Franks in 751, helping him take the throne from an ineffective ruler. Charles Martel's descendants, later known as the Carolingian (*kar-uh-LIN-jun*) dynasty (from *Carolus*, Latin for Charles), thus came to rule the Frankish realm.

Charlemagne's conquests
reunite much of western
and central Europe

These events set the stage for the remarkable reign of Pepin's son Charles (768–814), known to history as "Charles the Great," or Charlemagne (*SHAR-luh-MĀN*). Standing well over six feet tall in an age when most men were much shorter, Charlemagne, who had boundless energy, was the most commanding of all the early medieval warrior-kings. In a pivotal series of conflicts he conquered the Saxons in north Germany, the Lombards in north Italy, and various other Germanic peoples; he also took land from the Muslims in northeast Spain and the Byzantines in east central Europe (Map 9.5). He thereby reunited most of western and central Europe for the first time since the fall of Rome.

The symbolic climax of Charlemagne's career was provided by the pope. In 799, attacked by his enemies in Rome, Pope Leo III (795–816) escaped and found refuge in northwest Germany with Charlemagne, who then restored the fugitive pope to the papacy (office of the pope). Leo soon found a dramatic way to show his appreciation, as well as to assert the Church's secular political power. On Christmas Day 800, as Charlemagne knelt in solemn worship during a visit to Rome, the pope suddenly crowned him "Charles Augustus, . . . Emperor of the Romans." It looked as if the Roman Empire had been revived in the west.

Charlemagne's chapel at
Aachen.

But Charlemagne's realm, vast as it was, was still in many ways a Germanic kingdom. Its capital was not in Rome but at Aachen (*AH-ken*) in northwest Germany; its center was not the Mediterranean Sea but the Rhine River; its rulers were not Romans but Franks; and its emperor, for all his talent, was still a semi-literate warrior king. Indeed, Charlemagne's coronation horrified the Byzantine rulers at Constantinople, who regarded their realm as the real Roman Empire and resented the new Germanic imitation of it in the west.

Map 9.5 Charlemagne's Empire Reunites the West, 768–814 C.E.

In his long and eventful reign, Charlemagne, ruler of the Franks, created an empire that reunited much of Western and Central Europe. Notice that he not only conquered the Saxons and Lombards but also subjected some Slavic states to tribute. Note also, however, that his realm was a Frankish, not a Roman, Empire, with its capital in the north at Aachen rather than in Rome. How did Charlemagne differ from the former Roman rulers, and how did his empire differ from the former Roman realm?

Undeterred, Charlemagne strove to consolidate and educate his empire. He compelled the Saxons and other polytheists in his realm to adopt Christianity. At Aachen, under the guidance of a learned English Benedictine monk named Alcuin (*AL-koo-in*), he assembled scholars who copied manuscripts, founded libraries, and set up schools at monasteries and cathedrals throughout Europe. Alcuin's curriculum, divided into a *trivium* (*TRIV-ē-um*) made up of grammar, rhetoric and logic, and a *quadrivium* (*kwah-DRIV-ē-um*) of arithmetic, astronomy, geometry, and music, became the standard for medieval European education.

Charlemagne promotes Christianity and learning

Charlemagne's efforts, however, had only a limited impact. Very few people, for example, actually received an education. By this time most people in the west spoke Germanic dialects, which later evolved into languages such as German and English, or regional offshoots of Latin, which developed into languages such as French, Italian, and Spanish. Only the literate elite, mostly monks and Church officials, could read and write formal Latin, which remained the language of learning throughout the Middle Ages.

Regional languages develop, but the Church and the learned use Latin

Furthermore, after Charlemagne died in 814, his Carolingian Frankish Empire did not long endure. In 843 his three grandsons, after fighting among themselves, divided the

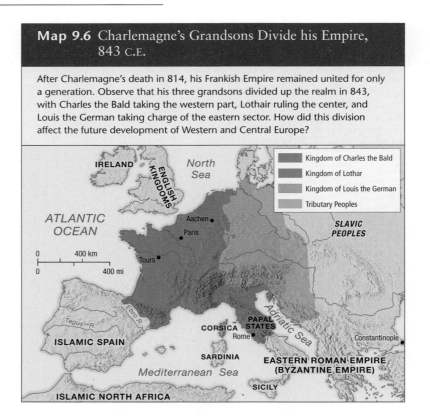

Map 9.6 Charlemagne's Grandsons Divide his Empire, 843 C.E.

After Charlemagne's death in 814, his Frankish Empire remained united for only a generation. Observe that his three grandsons divided up the realm in 843, with Charles the Bald taking the western part, Lothair ruling the center, and Louis the German taking charge of the eastern sector. How did this division affect the future development of Western and Central Europe?

realm into three separate kingdoms (Map 9.6). The middle kingdom soon fragmented still further, while the western one went on to form the basis for medieval France, and the eastern one the basis for medieval Germany.

Vikings, Muslims, and Magyars: Invasions and Connections

Christian Europe after Charlemagne also experienced a series of new invasions. In the ninth and tenth centuries, it was assaulted by outsiders, coming first by sea from the north and the south and later by land from the east. Although these invaders pillaged towns and ravaged the countryside, they also helped to create new connections between Europe and other cultures.

By sea from the north came Norsemen, or Vikings, seafaring warriors who exploded out of Scandinavia in the ninth and tenth centuries, propelled perhaps by a growing population and a scarcity of food. With superior seamanship and shallow-draft ships, using both sails and oars, they dominated the coasts and rivers of Europe, plundering numerous towns for slaves and booty, and even robbing churches and monasteries of their precious vessels and vestments. But the northern invaders were not always destructive. Many settled along the European coasts, trading with Muslims and Byzantines and eventually adopting Christianity. Some Norsemen, known as Normans, took control of the region now called Normandy in northwestern France, from which their successors in 1066 conquered England

Viking ship.

Vikings ravage Europe but create new kingdoms and commerce

Map 9.7 Viking, Muslim, and Magyar Invasions, Ninth and Tenth Centuries C.E.

In the ninth and tenth centuries, Christian Europe was beset by sea and land attacks from all directions. Note that Vikings invaded from the north, ravaging coastlines and plying the rivers from Western Europe to Russia, while the Magyars came by land from the east and the Muslims by sea from the south. How did these incursions, which brought widespread loss and destruction, also help expand commercial and cultural connections between the Europeans and their neighbors?

and became its kings and nobles. Other Norsemen, called Varangians (*vuh-RAN-junz*), reportedly served as early rulers of Kievan Rus (*KĒ-ev-un ROOS*), the first Russian state, which forged commercial and religious links with the Byzantine Empire (Chapter 10). Still other Norsemen explored the north Atlantic, founding settlements in Ireland, Iceland, Greenland, and even for a time on the coast of North America (Map 9.7).

Muslim "Saracens" plunder southern Europe but also forge commercial ties

By sea from the south in the meantime came Muslims, also known in Europe as Saracens (*SAIR-uh-senz*). In the mid-ninth century, seaborne marauders from Islamic North Africa staged periodic raids along Europe's Mediterranean coast. Unlike the eighth-century Muslim warriors defeated by Charles Martel, who came to conquer lands and spread their faith, the skillful Saracen sailors came mainly to plunder. Indeed, in 846, they pillaged the city of Rome. Still, these Muslim raiders, by plying the sea routes between Europe and North Africa, helped create a basis for later commercial connections between the Islamic and western Christian worlds.

Magyars invade Central Europe and then settle in Hungary

By land from the east a bit later came the Magyars (*MAH-jarz*), warlike tribes that had migrated westward from their Ural mountain homeland. Starting in the late ninth century they struck deep into central Europe. Like the Vikings before them, the Magyars pillaged towns and plundered the land. In 955 they were finally defeated in a decisive battle at Lechfeld (*LEK-feld*) by the forces of King Otto I (936–973), ruler of the eastern Frankish domains in Germany. Eventually the Magyars, later called Hungarians, settled in what is now Hungary, adopted Christianity, and combined their eastern culture with western Christian ideals. Their conqueror, who emerged as a heroic figure known as Otto the Great, was crowned by the pope as emperor in 962. Claiming connections with the Christian Church of Rome and the imperial Roman heritage, Otto and his successors were called Holy Roman Emperors—although they were really Germanic warriors whose realm was mostly German, not Roman.

German rulers in Central Europe form the Holy Roman Empire

Germanic warriors in fact proved vital to Europe's recovery from the disasters of the ninth and tenth centuries, but this recovery relied on regional warlords rather than on powerful monarchs who ruled large domains. Their security shattered by outside raiders and invaders, and their hopes for unity dashed by the dissolution of Charlemagne's empire, Europeans increasingly looked to warrior nobles to protect their society.

Europe's Warrior Nobility: Protection, Land, and Power

Responding to the invasions and political fragmentation of the ninth and tenth centuries, Europeans developed a new set of arrangements to restore the security and stability needed for a farming economy. Rather than submitting to a strong central state, as in the days of the Roman and Frankish Empires, they came to depend for their defense on autonomous regional warlords. Connected by complex allegiances and sustained by landed estates, these warlords developed into a hereditary landed nobility.

As central power wanes, hereditary regional warlords emerge

Although rooted in the warrior assemblies that long had served Germanic chieftains, the landed nobility arose directly from the ruins of the Frankish realm. To administer their vast domain, the Franks had divided it into counties, each managed by a count, and later also created large duchies, regions directed by dukes. As central authority waned in the decades after Charlemagne's death, these counts and dukes eventually became autonomous warlords. Treating their positions as hereditary, they amassed landed wealth and assembled powerful armies.

Lords grant lands to warrior vassals, creating a landed nobility

With the onslaught of outside invaders in the 800s and 900s, lesser lords and landowners were forced to accept the protection of these great warlords and become their **vassals**, subordinate warlords who swore allegiance and pledged military service to a higher lord, their overlord. In return for such allegiance and service, the overlords often gave their vassals grants of land called fiefs (*FĒFZ*). In the absence of strong central government, these warlords exercised political and military power on the local and regional level. Strengthened by their warrior status and sustained by their possession of land, they evolved into hereditary nobles. Typically less than 5 percent of the population, they exercised enormous influence based on their family's rank and status, the extent of their land holdings, the size of their armies, and the number of their vassals.

Warfare was central to the status and family life of the medieval nobility. The lords (noblemen) fought wars, training for combat and hunting between conflicts to sustain their military skills, while the ladies (noblewomen) managed the households, caring for children and supervising servants so the lords could go off to hunt, train, and fight. Noblemen served on horseback as **knights**, armed mounted warriors whose code of conduct entailed strict devotion to their overlords and to the Christian Church. As early as age 7, looking forward to future knighthood, boys in noble families were taught by their fathers to ride horses, to hunt, and to use bows and arrows, swords, shields, lances, and armor. Girls in noble families often also learned to ride and hunt, but they were trained mainly for marriage, motherhood, and household management, duties that typically precluded most women from engaging in combat.

Although later observers characterized the arrangements between lords and vassals as a comprehensive system called feudalism, there was really no set system or consistent feudal order. Instead there were numerous individual agreements, often quite different from each other, creating an extremely complex web of relationships. Many vassals, for example, served several lords, based on separate agreements with oaths of service to each. Most lords in turn served as vassals to higher lords. A count, for example, might be a powerful lord with vast landholdings and numerous vassals of his own, but he might also be the vassal of a duke, who might in turn be the vassal of a king. Thus, during wartime, a count and his vassals could be called into service of a duke who had been called into service of a king. Yet the medieval king, despite his lofty status, was not an absolute ruler: he depended on the support of his vassals, the great lords of his realm, some of whom might have stronger armies than he did.

Economy and Society: Manors, Lords, and Serfs

The nobles, occupied with military duties, did not raise their own food. Instead their **manors**, or landed estates, were worked by peasant farmers. Typically, each noble owned at least one manor. Some were huge, with a massive castle and vast stretches of forest and field; others were much smaller. But even the lowest noble was the lord of his manor and master of all who dwelt there. The peasants, who lived on the manor in a village and cultivated the surrounding fields, were typically required to give the lord a portion of their crop, and perhaps to labor several days a week on land set aside to feed the lord and his family. The peasants thus supported the lord so he could fight, providing some protection and security in a dangerous world.

The peasants, who made up 80 to 90 percent of the population, varied widely in status. Some remained free, and a few even prospered. Most, however, became **serfs**, bound to the manor and under the control of its lord. Without the lord's permission, serfs as a rule could not own or inherit property, leave the manor, or even get married. Unlike slaves, serfs supposedly had rights—they did not have to serve in the army, they were not

Role of nobles centers on combat and knighthood

Medieval peasant women helping with the harvest and grinding grain into flour.

Nobles own manors, landed estates, worked by peasant farmers

Peasant serfs, bound to the manor, provide food and labor for landlords

Figure 9.1

Diagram of a Typical Medieval Manor. On a typical medieval manor, the lord who owned it and his family lived in a large manor house, while peasants lived in a village elsewhere on his manor. Each peasant family had a hut in the village and a few strips of land in each surrounding field to farm, as shown by the hut and strips of one family shaded here in red. Each year crops were rotated according to a 3-field system, with one field planted for spring-summer crops, another for autumn-winter crops, and a third left fallow (uncultivated) to regenerate its soil.

supposed to be bought and sold apart from the land, and the lord was expected to provide them with plots of land to farm. In practice, however, there were few restraints on the lord, who could punish his serfs for perceived transgressions by flogging and beating them, sometimes even to death.

Peasant life was monotonous and routine, centered on fields, family, and Church. Men were mainly responsible for working the land and tending the herds, the mainstays of economic life. But women typically played numerous crucial roles, grinding grain, baking bread, brewing beer and ale, curing cheese, cooking meals, making clothes, raising children, and often also helping to care for animals, cultivate fields, and harvest crops. Peasants ate mostly dark bread, supplemented by cabbage and carrots, peas and beans, and perhaps eggs and cheese, washed down with wine, beer, or ale. Some peasant families had wood or brick homes that, while modest, had two or more rooms; others lived in one-room windowless huts with dirt floors, thatch roofs, and walls of mud or clay. Peasants received no formal education, rarely traveled beyond the safety of the manor, and had few diversions aside from celebrating baptisms, weddings, and holy days at the village church—their main link to the larger Church and hence to the outside world.

Harsh peasant life centers on farming, family, and faith

The Decline and Revival of the Western Church

Despite its exalted status in medieval Europe, by the tenth century the Church in the west was in trouble. In some respects, its problems were symptoms of success, since its great wealth and power attracted unscrupulous men to its service, fostering corruption and intrigue. In other respects the decline of the Church was connected with the rise of the regional warlords, who often managed to gain control over local Church offices. The lords used their influence to fill Church positions with their relatives and supporters, at times even selling these positions to the highest bidder. Chosen thus for their loyalty rather than their ability, and provided with little education, local priests were often illiterate and incompetent, while bishops were frequently dishonest and corrupt. In Rome the papacy itself was controlled by powerful local clans, who secured the selection of their family members and agents. A series of scandalous popes led lives of open debauchery, commanding neither influence nor respect.

From Scandal to Reform

In 963 Pope John XII (955–964), an unprincipled young man who had become pope through the influence of his powerful father, was deposed by a council of bishops for crimes including adultery, incest, and murder. Declaring the council illegal, he violently reclaimed his throne, only to die soon thereafter—reportedly either from a stroke that he suffered during an adulterous affair or from a beating inflicted by his lover's furious husband.

Scandals compromise Christian Church in the West

Eighty years later Pope Benedict IX, another immoral young man who became pope through his father's influence, was run out of town by the people of Rome, who replaced him with their own choice as pope. The next five years (1044–1049) saw a rapid succession of popes, as Benedict regained the papacy, sold it to another man, and then later claimed it back. In the meantime, Holy Roman Emperor Henry III placed several of his hand-picked German bishops on the papal throne.

This sorry spectacle actually marked the onset of the Church's revival. The Germans installed by Henry III were the first of a number of reforming popes, many of whom had close connections with Cluny, Europe's most influential monastery. Founded in the tenth century, this French Benedictine monastic institution had been made subject directly and only to the pope in order to keep it free from the control of local rulers and nobles. Its monks over the years had become known for their piety and rigor, and by 1050 they had founded more than sixty daughter houses, all ruled by the mother house at Cluny. Its leaders pushed openly for Church reform, calling for strict priestly **celibacy** (*SELL-ih-buh-sē*), or abstinence from marriage and sex, and an end to **simony** (*SIM-uh-nē*), the sale of Church offices. The Cluniac monks who became pope resolutely attacked Church abuses, restoring the papacy as Europe's preeminent institution. Their efforts were fated to have far-reaching consequences.

Reforming popes enforce priestly celibacy and attack Church abuses

The Great Schism of 1054

Among the most crucial consequences of this papal revival was a reinforcement of a growing rift between eastern and western Church leaders. Ever since Rome had fallen to Germanic tribes, the cosmopolitan Christians of the Eastern Roman Empire had found it hard to accept the supremacy of the Church in the west, increasingly run by Germanic leaders the easterners saw as "barbarians." The four main centers of the eastern Church—Constantinople, Antioch, Jerusalem, and Alexandria—were each led by a patriarch who saw himself as equal to the pope. Although patriarchs might grant the pope senior status as the bishop of Rome, they saw him as "first among equals," regarding him as a senior leader but not as supreme ruler. Over the centuries, in the interests of unity, the eastern patriarchs had usually gone along with the papacy, but they nonetheless resented its claims to overall supremacy.

The papacy's growing strength deepens conflict with Eastern Church

By the eleventh century, however, centuries of friction had worn away any willingness to compromise, and the recent papal scandals had intensified eastern disdain for the papacy and the western Church. Now the new reforming popes, in an effort to attack abuses, were asserting even greater powers and claiming unlimited primacy over the whole Church. The eastern patriarchs found these papal assertions offensive and threatening.

A climax came in 1054, when the patriarch of Constantinople issued an insulting letter to a western bishop that found its way to the dying Pope Leo IX (1049–1054), who then sent envoys to Constantinople to press the patriarch for an apology. Although Leo died several weeks after they arrived, the envoys had several tense meetings with the patriarch and then issued an edict of "excommunication," formally excluding him from Christian worship and from the Christian community. The patriarch responded with a similar edict against the papal envoys.

Conflict in Church brings enduring east-west schism

This episode produced an enduring split between eastern and western Christendom, often called the Great Schism of 1054. Although deepened by longstanding disputes about the wording of the official creed (profession of beliefs) approved during Constantine's reign, the rift was actually rooted in the conflict concerning whether the pope should have total supremacy over the entire Church. The division was not really caused by a single event, but rather by a series of political, cultural, and theological developments occurring over many centuries. The result was the emergence of two separate branches of Christianity: an Eastern Orthodox religion over which the patriarchs presided, and a Western, or Roman Catholic, Church, ruled by the pope in Rome.

The Power of the Popes

Schism frees the popes to focus on reform in West

As divisive as it was, the schism freed the papacy from its involvement in affairs of the eastern Church, thereby allowing subsequent popes to focus on reform in the west and to assert their authority over all other western religious and political leaders. The stage was thus set for conflict between the Roman popes and Europe's secular rulers.

Popes claim supremacy over all secular rulers

In 1059, to ensure that future popes would not be chosen by powerful families or emperors, Pope Nicholas II decreed that new popes must henceforth be elected by a group of specially designated bishops called cardinals. In 1073, the cardinals elected a radical reformer named Hildebrand who had spent time at Cluny. As Pope Gregory VII (1073–1085), he extended the concept of papal supremacy into secular affairs, holding that all lords and princes were his subjects and that he could depose or punish them if he judged their conduct immoral. To free the clerics who served the Church from family attachments and distractions, he made celibacy the rule for all priests and bishops throughout the western Church. He also insisted that only the pope could appoint Church officials.

This attack on corruption and insistence on papal appointment directly threatened Europe's kings and lords, who were used to selecting loyal supporters as bishops in their realms. When Gregory banned lay investiture, a practice in which secular ("lay") rulers conferred on new bishops the symbols of spiritual authority, the German emperor Henry IV openly defied him, refusing to forsake this practice. The pope responded in 1076 by excommunicating and deposing Henry, giving German nobles a convenient pretext to rebel against him. Alarmed but inventive, in January 1077 the deposed emperor went to Canossa in Italy and reportedly stood barefoot in the snow to beg forgiveness of Gregory, who was compelled as a priest to pardon the penitent prince. Henry thus regained his title and later even drove Gregory into exile. But the specter of an emperor humbling himself before the pope nonetheless reinforced the notion of papal authority over secular rulers, paving the way for an even more sensational exercise of papal power.

Pope and emperor clash over right to "invest" bishops

In 1095 Pope Urban II, a former Cluniac monk and disciple of Gregory VII, dramatically proclaimed a great crusade, or holy war, calling on Europe's lords and princes to restore Christian control over the "holy lands" in Palestine where Christ had lived and died. Urban's call touched off a chain of crusades that, although they failed in the long run to achieve their original goal, created further connections and conflicts between the Germanic West and the Byzantine and Muslim worlds (Chapter 16).

Pope Urban II preaches crusade against Muslim rule of 'holy lands'

Chapter Review

Putting It in Perspective

The Germanic migrations, and the resulting division of the Roman Empire, ultimately transformed the west. The German tribes attacked, infiltrated, and eventually triumphed over the Western Roman Empire, replacing it with their own tribal institutions, developing over time into territorial kingdoms. Despite sporadic efforts to restore the empire in the west, central authority waned and Roman institutions fell into disuse. Political, social, and economic life became largely regional and rural, dominated by warlords who also controlled the land. The peasant farmers who tilled the soil eventually sank into serfdom, effectively forsaking freedom in return for security and protection.

The main exception to this decentralization was the Christian Church, which maintained its headquarters in Rome despite the disappearance of the Western Roman Empire. The Church's administrative structure, modeled on that of the old empire, helped to preserve some measure of central authority in the west, while the Church's monasteries helped to sustain some semblance of Latin learning. Indeed, in the absence of other strong central institutions, the Church became Europe's predominant religious and cultural organization, with the popes who led it exercising vast religious and political powers. In converting and incorporating the Germans, however, the Church in the west was altered by their conventions and customs. Eastern Christians hence found it hard to accept the leadership of the Germanicized West, which they considered culturally inferior. Eventually Christianity split into Western and Eastern churches.

In the west, as the warrior nobles and manorial economy helped to restore stability following the Viking, Muslim, and Magyar invasions, a reformed and re-energized papacy asserted its authority over secular rulers. In the east, although the Eastern Roman Empire survived, it too developed new institutions and ideals, forming the basis of what would later be called the Byzantine World.

Reviewing Key Material
KEY CONCEPTS

nation, 210	vassals, 226
bishops, 214	knights, 227
pope, 214	manors, 227
papal primacy, 214	serfs, 227
medieval, 218	celibacy, 229
monasticism, 220	simony, 229

KEY PEOPLE

ASK YOURSELF

1. What were the basic characteristics of the Germanic societies? How and why did these societies connect and conflict with the Roman Empire?

2. Why were the Roman emperors unsuccessful in their efforts to protect the western part of the empire from the Germanic invaders? How did the division of the empire contribute to the fall of the western part?

3. How and why did Christianity become the Roman Empire's main religion? How did this change in status transform the Christian Church?

4. Why did the western Church emerge as the dominant institution in medieval Europe? How did the Church adapt to the Germanic cultures? What factors contributed to divergence and discord between the Western and Eastern churches?

5. Why did Europe's warrior nobility become so powerful in the ninth and tenth centuries? What were the main roles of lords, vassals, manors, and serfs?

GOING FURTHER

Barbero, A. *Charlemagne: Father of a Continent*. 2004.

Brown, Peter. *The Rise of Western Christendom: Triumph and Adversity, A.D. 200–1000*. 2003.

Collins, R. *Early Medieval Europe, 300–1000*. 1991.

Constable, Olivia R. *Housing the Stranger in the Mediterranean World: Lodging, Trade, and Travel in Late Antiquity and the Middle Ages*. 2004.

Coulton, George G. *The Medieval Village*. 1991.

Cruz, Jo Ann, et al. *Medieval Worlds*. 2004.

Duby, Georges. *Rural Economy and Country Life in the Medieval West*. 1990.

Dunn, M. *The Emergence of Monasticism*. 2000.

Edwards, M., trans. *Constantine and Christendom*. 2003.

Fletcher, R. *The Barbarian Conversion: From Paganism to Christianity*. 1997.

Gies, F. and J. *Marriage and Family in the Middle Ages*. 1987.

Hanawalt, Barbara. *The Middle Ages*. 1998.

Haywood, John. *Encyclopedia of the Viking Age*. 2000.

Herrin, J. *The Formation of Christendom*. 1987.

James, Edward. *The Franks*. 1988.

Lawrence, C. H. *Medieval Monasticism: Forms of Religious Life in Western Europe in the Middle Ages*. 1984.

Le Goff, Jacques. *Medieval Civilization, 400–1500*. 1989.

Logan, F. Donald. *The Vikings in History*. 3rd ed. 2005.

Lopez, Robert, et al. *Medieval Trade in the Mediterranean World*. 2001.

Lot, F. *The End of the Ancient World and the Beginning of the Middle Ages*. 2000.

McCormick, Michael. *Origins of the European Economy*. 2001.

McKitterick, R., ed. *Early Middle Ages: Europe, 400–1000*. 2001.

McKitterick, R. *The Frankish Kingdoms Under the Carolingians, 751–987*. 1983.

Pelikan, Jaroslav. *The Excellent Empire: The Fall of Rome and the Triumph of the Church*. 1987.

Power, Eileen. *Medieval People*. 1993.

Reynolds, Susan. *Fiefs and Vassals*. 1994.

Reynolds, Susan. *Kingdoms and Communities in Western Europe, 900–1300*. 2nd ed. 1997.

Riche, P. *The Carolingians: A Family Who Forged Europe*. 1993.

Rosenwein, B. *A Short History of the Middle Ages*. 2002.

Southern, Richard W. *The Making of the Middle Ages*. 1992.

Ward-Perkins, B. *The Fall of Rome and End of Civilization*. 2005.

Wolfram, H. *History of the Goths*. 1988.

Key Dates and Developments

100s–200s	Early Germanic attacks on Roman territory
284–305	Reign of Diocletian (division of the Roman Empire)
312–337	Reign of Constantine (building of Constantinople)
380	Proclamation of Christianity as the Roman state religion
410	Sack of Rome by Alaric and the Visigoths
432	Beginning of Patrick's efforts to Christianize Ireland
451–453	Invasion of Italy by Attila and the Huns
476	Abdication of the last Western Roman Emperor
496	Adoption of Christianity by Clovis and the Franks
529	The *Rule* of Saint Benedict
597–605	Augustine's efforts to Christianize England
732	Defeat of Muslim forces by Charles Martel at Tours
768–814	Reign of Charlemagne, formation of Frankish Empire
843	Division of Frankish Empire by Charlemagne's grandsons
800s–900s	Viking, Magyar, and Saracen invasions
1054	Schism of 1054 (Eastern Orthodox vs. Roman Catholic)
1073–1085	Reign of reforming Pope Gregory VII (Hildebrand)
1095	First Crusade proclaimed by Pope Urban II

The Byzantine World, 284–1240

- The Foundations of Byzantine Governance

- Early Byzantium: Challenges and Survival

- Foreign Conflicts and Byzantium's Decline

- Pre-Christian Russia

- Kievan Rus Connects to the Byzantine World

- Chapter Review

The Basilica Of Saint Sophia, Constantinople

Interior of the former Basilica of Saint Sophia in Constantinople, a Byzantine church converted to a mosque in 1453. Notice the domed Romanesque architecture (page 244), and imagine the impression such a magnificent building would have made on citizens of Constantinople during the Byzantine Empire.

Justinian, the ailing Roman emperor's nephew and recently appointed co-ruler, prepared to enter a magnificent church on April 4, 527. It was the day of his formal coronation. At his side was his wife Theodora, who would be crowned as empress. The imperial couple was greeted by black-robed priests who prepared them for the ceremony by covering them in clouds of fragrant incense. Once inside the church, Justinian and Theodora proceeded slowly through an immense throng of guests down a long aisle leading to the main altar. Waiting there was another group of priests, robed in cloth-of-gold and wearing jeweled crosses and rings. These priests stood in front of a glittering screen made of gold and silver; on it paintings of holy men and women of early Christianity were displayed. Choirs chanted hymns and prayers as Justinian and Theodora knelt before the priests, beginning the six-hour ceremony.

Byzantine claims in Europe

Kievan Rus

The Byzantine Empire

Justinian was crowned Roman emperor, but his coronation took place hundreds of miles east of the city of Rome. The religious ceremony took place in Constantinople, the "New Rome" founded in the fourth century by Emperor Constantine I. Rome itself was conquered by Germanic invaders in 476, and only the eastern portion of the empire survived. There a new society evolved, preserving Rome's heritage but grounded in its own variant of Christianity and its own conception of the relationship between political and spiritual authority. The realm would be known as the Eastern Roman Empire and later as the Byzantine Empire, after the old city of Byzantium on which the new Constantinople had been built. Situated where Europe and Asia meet, the Byzantine world, often called simply Byzantium, blended elements of East and West but was truly part of neither.

Still, the empire's eastern rulers, however distinct their civilization was becoming, had no intention of writing off the western half. For centuries they would claim it and occasionally succeed in retaking portions of it, though only temporarily. The Byzantine Empire endured without the west for a thousand years. And even after it declined, through centuries of internal and external conflict, its legacy lived on in Russia, which in the tenth century adopted eastern Christianity and joined the Byzantine world.

The Foundations of Byzantine Governance

When Constantine legalized Christianity (Chapter 9), he did not know that he would soon be compelled to resolve its internal disputes and thereby assume leadership in the Christian Church. And when moving his capital east to Constantinople, he scarcely envisioned that the empire's western section would eventually fragment into separate Germanic kingdoms, leaving only the eastern portion intact. But these events set in motion trends that allowed the Eastern Roman Empire to develop separately, with governing structures substantively different from those in the west.

FOUNDATION MAP 10.1 The Early Byzantine Empire, 481 C.E.

After Constantine reoriented the Roman Empire eastward, Germanic tribes gradually overran the western portion of the realm. Following the abdication of the last Western Roman Emperor in 476, only the Eastern Roman Empire, known as the Byzantine Empire, remained. Notice that the Eastern Roman Empire controlled the prosperous commercial region of the eastern Mediterranean. How might this location have assisted the Byzantines in defending the legacy of Rome?

Constantine and the Christian Church

No sooner had Constantine become sole emperor in 324 than he became involved in a serious dispute among Christians. For a decade or so, an Egyptian Christian priest named Arius (*AIR-ē-us*) had been preaching that since God had created Christ, God the Father was older than and superior to God the Son. This perspective differed from the prevailing Christian belief that the Father, Son, and Holy Spirit were three co-equal persons of the Blessed Trinity. Arius's teaching, which his opponents branded a **heresy**—a religious opinion contrary to accepted Church doctrine—left the Christian Church sharply divided. In fact, the Arian Heresy, as it was called, threatened to produce a **schism**, or division of the church into separate, competing churches.

Constantine was perplexed: why should anyone want to quarrel about something that was irrelevant to everyday life and could never be proven or disproven? He instructed the opposing parties to settle the issue amicably. But this advice enraged both sides, provoking Constantine into calling an ecumenical (*eck-ū-MEN-ih-kull*), or worldwide, council of Christian bishops and theologians. It convened in 325 in the Byzantine town of Nicaea (*nī-søĒ-uh*), near Constantinople (Map 10.1), with the emperor himself presiding.

Constantine intervenes in Christian affairs

Assuming the role of practical counselor in matters of religion, Constantine intended to enforce uniformity within the Church to which he did not formally belong but with which he sympathized. His presence at Nicaea demonstrated that he was in charge, and he shaped the council's findings in a manner that satisfied the great majority of bishops. The Nicene Creed, a statement of belief drafted by the council that is still recited today in many Christian churches, declared that Christ was "of the same being" as God the Father. A few delegates, including Arius, refused to sign this creed; they were expelled from the council and exiled by the emperor.

The Union of Church and State

Constantine's forceful intervention in the Council of Nicaea illuminates how governance would develop in the Eastern Roman Empire. While western institutions evolved under the influence of Germanic concepts of kingship, the Byzantines held to and amplified the authoritarian legacy of the caesars. Their political institutions were also derived in large measure from the monarchist principles of Alexander the Great and his successors, in which the ruler was exalted above all. For example, the eastern Roman emperor was referred to as "lord of the world." After the Emperor Theodosius the Great proclaimed Christianity the official religion of the empire in 380, he and future rulers were also called "equal of the Apostles." The interchangeable use of these two titles reflected the combination of secular and spiritual authority in one man.

In Constantinople, the rulers embraced Christianity fervently. The emperor was viewed as God's vice-regent on earth, a sacred person who headed the Church as well as the state and who acted with the fullness of divine as well as human authority. This was the Byzantine concept of **caesaropapism** (*sē-zar-ō-PĀ-pizm*), the vesting of all spiritual and political authority in a single person—a man who served as both caesar and pope. It contrasted profoundly with the position taken by the bishop of Rome, who claimed no political supremacy, but called himself head of the Christian Church (or pope) and used his spiritual authority to curb the ambitions of kings and princes after the Western Roman Empire collapsed in 476.

Caesaropapism unifies spiritual and political authority

In the east, however, a patriarch exercised spiritual leadership over a Christian community equivalent to that exercised by a bishop in the west. Each of the four eastern patriarchs—of Constantinople, Antioch, Jerusalem, and Alexandria—considered himself equal to the bishop of Rome and subject solely to the emperor in Constantinople. They did not recognize the bishop of Rome's claim to lead the entire Christian Church, maintaining instead that overall leadership was vested solely in the emperor.

In the emerging Byzantine world, then, Church and state were united in the person of the ruler. In relocating the capital of the empire, Constantine infused it with the spirit of a new, dynamic faith that half a century later would be proclaimed the empire's official religion. These actions revolutionized both government and society in the Eastern Roman Empire, accelerating the decline of paganism and embedding Christianity in the popular culture. This all-embracing, vigorous Christianity made caesaropapism work and laid the foundations of Byzantine governance.

Early Byzantium: Challenges and Survival

In the two centuries following Constantine's death in 337, the Roman Empire's western section gradually gave way to Germanic pressure, its own internal weaknesses, and the neglect it suffered after the transfer of the capital to Constantinople. But the stability of the eastern part was by no means ensured. First, religious problems continued to distract the empire. In 361 Emperor Julian (361–363) tried to revive paganism and reverse the trend toward Christianization. For his actions he was called "the Apostate"—a person who abandons a religion and returns to a previous belief system. Julian's return to paganism might have led to civil war had he not been killed fighting the Persians in 363. Sasanian Persia constituted a second threat to the empire's stability. Fortunately for the Byzantines, the Sasanian Empire was large and cumbersome, and if it sent too many soldiers against Constantinople, it risked uprisings among the non-Persian peoples along its own eastern frontiers.

Sasanian Persia challenges the Byzantine Empire

For the next century, as Germans overran the western empire, Constantinople survived, for it was too strategically situated and too well defended to be attacked directly. When the Western Roman Empire collapsed in 476, the eastern empire was holding off the Ostrogoths in southeastern Europe. Constantinople could not have dispatched a powerful army to save Rome without endangering itself. Now only the eastern empire remained. Although future emperors would long refuse to acknowledge the loss of the west, their efforts to regain it proved futile.

Justinian and Theodora

Gradually the eastern character of the empire intensified. The Emperor Justinian, who ruled from 527 to 565, exercised power even more forcefully than Constantine had. He was determined to make the most of the awesome powers of caesaropapism.

Justinian resolves to reunify both Church and Empire

Born in Macedonia in 482, Justinian became in his mid-thirties the power behind the throne of his uncle, the Emperor Justin. Through Justin he negotiated a reunification of the Christian Church, which had been divided since the Roman pope and patriarch of Constantinople had excommunicated one another in 484. Justinian stood firm in his belief in unity, both religious and imperial: just as there was one God, so must there be one Church and one Roman Empire. When he came to the throne in 527, he was determined to restore and maintain those unities under God, of whose will he considered himself, as a caesaropapist, the chief executive on earth.

Justinian was a disciplined autocrat—a ruler whose authority was unlimited. He was also a shrewd judge of men and a gifted administrator. In addition, he married a woman whose skills complemented and enhanced his own. Theodora, a comic actress and strip-tease dancer whose parents were circus people, had enthralled Justinian when she performed at his court. He promptly overcame the horrified protests of his counselors and made her his wife. When he was crowned Emperor in 527, he insisted that she be crowned

Empress—a formal designation as co-ruler. With an iron will and outstanding political judgment, Theodora worked tirelessly in the service of her husband and the empire.

In 532, when a violent uprising against his rule threatened his life, Justinian consulted his advisors and decided to flee Constantinople. But Theodora disagreed, arguing that in an hour of peril a ruler must not abandon his responsibilities. Neither emperor nor advisors would ordinarily have taken that sort of rebuke from a woman, but Theodora was Empress, a regular participant in imperial deliberations and a superb politician. Shamed by her courage and logic, Justinian and his advisors remained in Constantinople and put down the rebellion.

Theodora overcomes Justinian's caution

CODIFICATION OF ROMAN LAW. Justinian and Theodora were autocrats, but they ruled by Roman law and not by whim. With Roman order overturned by Germanic control of the West, Justinian decided to codify and streamline the law. He appointed prominent jurists to compile all the laws of Rome that were still in force; they were published in 529 as the Code of Justinian. This pathbreaking collection of statutes made Roman law the most influential legal system in history. The Byzantine Empire preserved it for centuries, eventually returning it to Western Europe.

Byzantium codifies Roman law

The Code not only preserved Roman law, however, but also inadvertently froze it. Exalted by the Byzantines as a perfect system, Roman law was closed to the possibility of further change. It remains the foundation of the modern legal systems of many Western nations but never displayed the flexibility to adapt and change that would later characterize Anglo-American law (see "Excerpt from the Code of Justinian").

Empress Theodora and attendants.

ATTEMPTS TO REUNITE THE EMPIRE. Justinian's Code was the foundation of his honest and efficient administration. But his government was in constant financial distress, largely because of its extensive and expensive military commitments. Throughout his reign, Justinian waged war to reunify the Roman Empire.

Reunification was unlikely, however, given the circumstances of the day. By the time of Justinian, two distinct cultures had evolved, the one Byzantine, the other a blend of Roman and Germanic. Their political and religious institutions were so different that permanent reunification could have been achieved only by occupation, and a standing occupation force large enough to secure Rome was too large for the Byzantines to afford. The Germanic tribes that had conquered the western empire were powerful forces in their own right, and in any case Byzantine troops were needed to defend the eastern empire against the Persians on its eastern border.

Nevertheless, Justinian's political and economic realism was overridden by his religious faith. Not only did a Roman Empire without Rome seem absurd, but he was also disturbed by the heretical Germanic kingdom that ruled Rome. Those Germans were Arian Christians, believing that Christ was a divine creature made by God. The Arian Heresy had been condemned at the Council of Nicaea more than a century earlier, and Justinian would not tolerate its presence in Rome.

So for the next three decades the Byzantine Empire waged war, despite lacking forces to fight on its eastern and western frontiers simultaneously. Whenever Byzantium advanced in Italy and reoccupied Rome, the Persians attacked in the east. When Byzantine troops were shifted to the east, the Germans took back the territory they had lost in Italy. The arrival of the bubonic plague in 541—its first recorded appearance in the eastern Mediterranean region—further weakened the Byzantine forces.

Justinian's religious convictions drive him to attack Rome

Document 10.1 Excerpt from the Code of Justinian

"The compilation of Roman law which was enacted under the Byzantine emperor, Justinian I . . . has been without doubt the most important and influential collection of secular legal materials that the world has ever known. The compilation preserved Roman law for succeeding generations and nations. All later Western systems borrowed extensively from it." (Allen Watson, page xxiii)

BOOK ONE, PART I

10. Justice is a steady and enduring will to render unto everyone his right. The basic principles of right are: to live honorably, not to harm any other person, to render to each his own. Practical wisdom in matters of right is an awareness of God's and men's affairs, knowledge of justice and injustice.

11. The term "law" is used in several senses: in one sense, when law is used as meaning what is always fair and good, it is natural law; in the other, as meaning what is in the interest of everyone . . . it is civil law.

BOOK ONE, PART III

31. The emperor is not bound by statutes.

BOOK ONE, PART IV

1. A decision given by the emperor has the force of a statute. This is because the populace commits to him and into him its own entire authority and power . . .

BOOK ONE, PART V

1. All our law concerns [either] persons or things or actions.

3. Certainly, the great divide in the law of persons is this: all men are either free men or slaves.

4. Freedom is one's natural power of doing what one pleases, save insofar as it is ruled out either by coercion or by law. Slavery is an institution . . . whereby someone is against nature made subject to the ownership of another. Slaves are so-called, because generals have a custom of selling their prisoners and thereby preserving rather than killing them.

9. There are many points in our law in which the condition of females is inferior to that of males.

BOOK TWENTY-FOUR, PART II

3. A true divorce does not take place unless an intention to remain apart permanently is present. So things said or done in anger are not effective unless the parties show by their persistence that they are an indication of their considered opinion. So where repudiation takes place in anger and the wife returns shortly afterward, she is not held to have divorced her husband.

BOOK TWENTY-FOUR, PART III

1. An action for the dowry takes precedence at all times and in all circumstances; for it is in the public interest for women to keep their dowries, since it is absolutely essential for women to have dowries so that they can produce offspring and replenish the state with their children.

SOURCE: Allen Watson, trans. and ed. *The Digest of Justinian,* Volume I (Philadelphia: University of Pennsylvania, 1985).

The Byzantine Empire becomes culturally Greek rather than Latin

As the Byzantine Empire became increasingly eastern and less Roman, it became increasingly Greek. Constantine's creation of a new capital had at first expanded knowledge of Latin in the east, since much of the empire's administration was transferred to Constantinople. But Greek remained the spoken language of the Eastern Roman Empire, and gradually it replaced Latin in official transactions. Greek was also more prestigious than Latin: public speeches in Constantinople were normally given in Greek, and it was

Map 10.2 The Byzantine Empire During Justinian's Reign, 527–565

Justinian, the last of the Latin-speaking emperors, never accepted the loss of the Western Roman Empire. In comparing this map with Map 10.1, note that Justinian's armies reconquered sizable segments of the West. Pressure from other areas, however, made it impossible for Justinian to hold his gains and prevented his successors from undertaking further westward initiatives. Where might this pressure have come from?

the language of instruction in all Byzantine schools except those teaching law. Justinian was the last native Latin-speaking Byzantine emperor.

Justinian's death in 565 was a significant event in the ongoing turning of the empire away from Rome. His successors, lacking his commitment to reunification, did little to realize it. As Rome receded in significance, Byzantine efforts were concentrated against pressures from the Persians in the east (Map 10.2). Then, from the seventh century onward, the Arabs in the south and southeast proved an even more dangerous foe. Eventually, Constantinople had little choice but to let go of the west.

Byzantine Society

During the two centuries from Constantine to Justinian, Byzantine society was prosperous and even wealthy. The Roman emperors brought from the west a privileged imperial court; a large, generally efficient and well-compensated bureaucracy; legions of ambitious entrepreneurs; clever con men on the lookout for every angle; and assorted hangers-on hopeful that some of the glory of the New Rome would rub off on their cloaks.

This transplanted society's showplace was Constantinople, whose population approached 400,000 in the early sixth century C.E. Ships docked in the Golden Horn, the city's inner harbor, bringing treasured goods from Asia and Africa. The city's artisans created splendid wares and textiles. The imperial court glistened with jewels, while visitors admitted to the emperor's presence passed by artificial trees filled with mechanical songbirds crafted in gold.

Constantinople becomes a major trading center

Constantinople's superb location gave it control of the trade routes of the eastern Mediterranean, and its vibrant economy amply justified Constantine's decision to build his new capital there. Grain and cotton from Egypt, spices from India, and silks from China were traded on the docks not only of Constantinople but also of other cities throughout the realm. Transporting goods by sea instead of land made trade in bulk profitable and lowered prices on imported goods enough so that they could be purchased not only by the aristocracy but also by a developing middle class.

Constantinople.

As the Byzantine Empire's urban economy expanded, it was run by an increasingly wealthy and confident commercial class. City women enjoyed substantial mobility and freedom of action. Many owned shops, kept the books for merchant houses, and bartered with traders from three continents. But this prosperity rested not only on trade but also on the labors of masses of peasants who worked the land and supplied food and soldiers for the empire. Rural people remained largely impoverished, tied to the land, the production of food, and the reproduction of enough children to keep the ranks of farmers and soldiers filled. Social mobility between farm and city was virtually unknown, and rural and urban people seemed to inhabit two different worlds.

Byzantines hold celebrations and sporting events in hippodromes

Social life for peasants centered on weekly religious services, religious holidays, and celebrations of family events such as baptisms and weddings. Activities in cities were more varied; many were centered around the Church, but secular attractions were also available. Crowds gathered in large outdoor arenas, known as hippodromes, to watch chariot races, combats between men and wild animals, and athletic competitions. Young male spectators cheered for their favorite teams—the "Blues" or the "Greens"—wearing the team colors, cutting their hair in outlandish styles, and often fighting in the stands against supporters of the opposing side.

By the seventh century C.E., however, Byzantine prosperity had begun to fade. The hippodromes were half empty and the religious pageants lost much of their luster. The decline was due primarily to two invasions—Muslim soldiers from Arabia and microbes carrying bubonic plague. The bacterial threat proved even more deadly than the military one.

Crises of the Seventh Century

The bubonic plague, which repeatedly ravaged the empire, took a dreadful toll. Plague germs are ingested by fleas that suck the blood of infected black rats. The fleas then move from rats to humans and pass on the microbes by biting their new hosts. Before the development of broad-spectrum antibiotics in the twentieth century, mortality rates from the three varieties of plague were very high. Pneumonic plague, spread by a victim coughing directly into the face of an uninfected person, killed 50 percent of its victims; septicemic plague, occurring when a flea transmits the germs directly into a blood vessel, killed 100 percent. But the most common form of the disease was bubonic plague, occurring when a flea bites soft tissue anywhere on the human body. Mortality was about 35 percent fifteen centuries ago and is approximately 20 percent today.

Bubonic plague, which Europeans later called "the Black Death," appeared in the Byzantine Empire in 541 when ships from North Africa inadvertently carrying infected rats docked in Byzantine ports. Victims died horribly, their bodies covered with "buboes," or large nodules filled with blood that turned black. The high fevers, delirium, and intense pain that accompanied the plague terrified the uninfected population; frightened citizens left the sick untended and bodies unburied in the streets. Epidemics hit the urban centers particularly hard, disrupting commerce and culture and causing millions to perish. The empire's population declined drastically, from 17 million in 610 to 7 million in 780, owing not only to the plague but also to incessant wars.

Bubonic plague devastates Byzantium

These wars constituted the second of the Byzantine Empire's crises. Between 613 and 628 the emperor Heraclius (610–641), a devout Christian and tenacious warrior, fought a series of devastating conflicts against the Persians, the age-old eastern enemies of the Byzantine realm. Led in combat by their courageous emperor, who personally slew a number of enemy generals, the Byzantines emerged victorious. Worn down, however, by the recurrent plague and the draining wars against Persia, they soon found themselves hard pressed to resist an even more dangerous foe.

Out of Arabia in the 630s swept formidable desert warriors who spread the world's third major monotheistic religion—Islam—by conquest. The military forces of this vigorous new faith, whose rise is described in the next chapter, quickly overran Syria, Mesopotamia, Palestine, Egypt, and much of North Africa, depriving the Byzantine Empire of many of its richest lands. The Muslims, as practitioners of Islam are known, also subjugated Persia, which had been weakened by its wars against the Byzantines. Constantinople did not fall to Islamic forces until the fifteenth century, but in the seventh century the loss of so many of its most cherished lands impoverished the Byzantine Empire not only materially but also psychologically.

The material losses were especially significant. Commerce withered as Byzantine trade routes with Mesopotamia and Syria passed into Islamic hands. This trade reduction weakened the wealthy, self-confident Byzantine commercial class and coincided with an alteration in the status of women. Theodora had been the first in a series of important Byzantine empresses: seven governed as regents for their young sons, two ruled the empire themselves, and others were quietly yet effectively influential. But in spite of the prominence of such powerful women, the situation for women in general deteriorated after the onset of the plague. As in Persia and Arabia, women were now required to veil themselves in public and to remain at home for most of their lives, their social contacts with men restricted to members of their own families. As Byzantine society became more agrarian and less commercial, women's lives became increasingly confined and their roles increasingly subordinate to those of men.

Islamic expansion weakens Byzantium

The crises of the seventh century did not prove fatal to the Byzantine Empire, however. Recovering from their extensive initial losses, the Byzantines eventually managed to hold back the armies of Islam, establishing the empire as a bulwark against Islamic expansion into southeastern Europe. But Byzantium by this time was considerably weaker, both from the effects of disease and the ravages of foreign wars, than it had been a century earlier. These circumstances amplified the divisions and weaknesses within the Christian Church, making them dangerous to the continued stability of the empire.

Eastern Christianity's Culture and Conflicts

Christianity and Byzantine daily life reinforce one another

The Christian Church dominated the empire's spiritual and cultural life. Spiritually that domination was penetrating and vibrant. As one historian has observed, for the Byzantines, "Christ, his Mother, and the Saints were as real as members of their own families." To be Byzantine was to be deeply Christian and to express that faith in elaborate rituals and observances. Byzantine church services were usually between four and six hours long. The emperor took part in all major worship services held in Constantinople, often marching to church at the end of a procession that could include as many as 50,000 gloriously robed officials. During services, the churches resounded with chants and hymns; clouds of incense perfumed the air. Christianity was the connective tissue of Byzantine life and the worldview that gave life meaning.

The former Basilica of Saint Sophia in Constantinople, with its massive dome surrounded by four graceful Islamic minarets following its conversion into a mosque.

Culturally, Christianity inspired architectural works of exquisite beauty. Beginning around 450, the Church built basilicas, shrines, and monasteries from one end of the empire to the other. Byzantine architecture was noted for its elegant domes, and the emperors ordered the construction of massive ones. For example, the Basilica of Saint Sophia in Constantinople commissioned by Justinian featured an immense dome held up by several smaller ones (see page 234). The ceilings were adorned with elaborate ornamental mosaics depicting scenes from the life of Christ, the lives of the saints, and the principal events of the Jewish and Christian Scriptures. Angels and holy men and women were portrayed in the colorful, stylized paintings, called icons, that hung on the walls. As the exteriors of these domed structures were frequently rather plain, those entering them were often awed by the grandeur inside.

Doctrinal quarrels divide eastern Christendom

Yet despite the devotion of its faithful and the grandeur of its culture, eastern Christendom suffered from serious shortcomings. First, the Church engaged in recurring doctrinal quarrels over the precise nature of Jesus Christ. The Monophysites (*mahn-AH-fizz-ītz*) contended that Christ was purely divine, while the Nestorians asserted that he was actually two persons, one human and the other divine. In 681, at an ecumenical council in Constantinople, representatives of all Christian churches agreed on an official definition: Jesus was one person with two distinct natures, one divine and one human, each the equal of the other. This statement should have settled the issue, and over time it did. But in the short term Monophysitism (*mah-NAH-fizz-ih-tizm*) remained strong in the empire's eastern provinces, such as Armenia and Anatolia, which were crucial to Byzantium as the source of much of its food and most of its soldiers. Not until the eleventh century did the issue of Monophysitism vanish, and then not by agreement among Christians, but rather because these provinces were conquered by Islamic forces.

Iconoclasm creates a passionate controversy

While struggling with the insoluble issue of Jesus's true nature, the empire was also divided by a controversy over icons, the religious paintings of Jesus, Mary, and the saints that were distinctive to Byzantine art. Popular belief held that divine graces flowed through these images to anyone who looked at them with reverence. One of the consequences of this belief was the worship of icons, a form of idolatry and arguably a violation of the Second of the Ten Commandments, which decreed that "Thou shalt not make any graven images." In 726 Byzantine Emperor Leo III banned icons, calling their worship perverse and superstitious. His prohibition provoked a wave of **iconoclasm** (*ī-KAHN-ah-klah-zum*, or image breaking) throughout the empire, resulting in the destruction of many priceless works of art and triggering a bitter dispute that tore the empire apart. A revolt against iconoclasm then broke out in Greece, and in Rome the pope, supporting the use of icons, denounced

Leo. The destruction of icons was prohibited at a Church council in 787, restored by another in 815, and banned again in 843. For two more centuries iconoclasm remained a divisive force in Byzantine life, although it was gradually overshadowed by the growing division between the eastern and western Church.

As explained in the preceding chapter, the Christian Church's most divisive problem was the prospect of a rupture between eastern and western Christendom. Ever since the empire's capital had moved to Constantinople, the two branches of the Christian Church had developed radically different organizational structures. At various times between 476 and 1054, the western papacy attempted to assert its authority over Constantinople; at other times, Byzantine patriarchs and sometimes emperors adopted initiatives designed to enhance their privileges.

Icon of St. Michael the Archangel.

From a Byzantine perspective, the struggle was doctrinal as well as political. The Byzantines, in designating the emperor as an equal of the apostles, could not then subordinate him to the pope in theological matters. Church tradition held that questions of doctrine could only be solved by an ecumenical council, at which the Holy Spirit would make its wishes known. Although the pope asserted authority over both the emperor and an ecumenical council, Byzantines could not accept what to them would have amounted to a redefinition of Christianity and of the emperor's role within it. At the same time, from a western perspective, the eastern Church's tendency to debate obscure theological issues was dangerous to Christian unity.

So many issues separated the two branches of Christianity that, when the formal schism finally came in 1054 (Chapter 9), it merely ratified a reality that had existed for centuries. Henceforth, despite occasional short-lived efforts at reconciliation, the Eastern Orthodox Churches, functioning under their own patriarchs and caesaropapist rulers, remained independent of the pope in Rome and the Roman Catholic West.

The Great Schism divides Christendom

Foreign Conflicts and Byzantium's Decline

Religious issues disturbed the middle years of the Byzantine Empire, but conflicts with foreign powers determined its ultimate fate. These, too, possessed a religious dimension, as Islam's compelling spiritual vision, combined with its relentless armies, posed a persistent challenge to the Christian world.

Muslims fail to conquer the Byzantine Empire

The Arab Conflict

After subjugating Persia by 642, the Arab armies, eager to spread Islam westward, continued their assault on Byzantium. In 655 they destroyed the Byzantine navy, enabling them to besiege Constantinople from 673 to 678. But the Byzantines were able to break the siege with the help of a secret weapon called Greek Fire. A flaming liquid whose precise composition remains unknown, Greek Fire was sprayed on the hulls and sails of enemy ships. Since it was oil-based, any of the substance that missed its target floated on the water, where it spread to other ships and incinerated anyone who fell or jumped overboard. In 678 the perplexed Muslims raised the siege and withdrew, turning their energies in the next decades to completing the conquest of North Africa. Then, moving across the Straits of Gibraltar and through Spain into Europe, they were finally stopped in 732 near Tours, by Franks led by Charles Martel (Chapter 9).

Ruins of the fifth-century walls of Constantinople in present-day Istanbul.

Byzantines fighting the
Bulgars.

Although the Byzantine Empire survived the initial Arab onslaught, its territorial holdings were greatly diminished (Map 10.3). Beginning in the mid-800s, however, Byzantine power gradually revived. The Arab threat waned, and in the tenth century, rejuvenated Byzantine armies invaded Syria, destroying the bases from which the Arabs had launched their raids. Later the Byzantines conquered much of Bulgaria and established a strong imperial position in the Balkans. From 843 until 1025 the Byzantine Empire prospered under a series of forceful, farsighted leaders. Its position was stronger than at any time since the age of Justinian.

The Turkish Conquests

Then, between 1025 and 1070, a series of incompetent leaders undermined the strength that the Byzantine Empire had won with such difficulty in the preceding two centuries. This weakness opened the way to a challenge from a nomadic central Asian tribe called the Seljuk (*SELL-yook*) Turks.

During the eleventh century, the Seljuks had gradually been conquering Persia and Mesopotamia. In the process they had become Muslims, and, as part of an overall plan to unify Islamic lands, they intended to strike next at Egypt and destroy the regime there. To do so they would have to move from Mesopotamia to the east and south of the Byzantine Empire, whose eastern Anatolian provinces they coveted but whose existence as the region's major power they had no intention of challenging.

The Seljuk Turks threaten the Byzantine Empire

Adjacent to the Turks' new Mesopotamian territories was Armenia, populated by Monophysite Christians who had been antagonized by Byzantine policies of religious discrimination and crushing taxation. The Turks decided to take advantage of Armenia's dissatisfaction with Byzantine rule, hoping to secure their borders before attacking Egypt. In 1064, led by Sultan Alp Arslan, Turkish forces destroyed the capital of Armenia and penetrated deep into Byzantine Anatolia, where they met only sporadic resistance. Six years later, hoping to prevent further Turkish advances, the Byzantine emperor Romanus IV Diogenes (*rō-MAH-nus dī-AH-juh-nēz*) concluded a truce with the Sultan.

The truce was almost immediately broken by Turkoman raiding parties composed of southwest Asians who spoke a language related to Turkish but who refused to accept Seljuk control. Romanus, erroneously concluding that Sultan Alp Arslan was behind these raids, moved eastward to punish him in 1071. At the same time the Sultan, considering the truce still in force, moved southward against Egypt. When he learned that the Byzantines had broken the truce, however, he turned north to intercept Romanus.

The two armies met on August 26, 1071, at Manzikert in Armenia, where the Byzantines were soundly defeated. The battle proved disastrous for the Byzantine Empire. Romanus was captured, and the new Byzantine emperor, Michael VII Ducas, soon broke the generous treaty that Alp Arslan had granted the Byzantines after Manzikert. Exasperated, the Sultan gave up his plan to attack Egypt and moved forcefully against the empire. By 1080 the Seljuk Turks controlled nearly all of eastern Anatolia.

Defeat at Manzikert severely weakens the Byzantine Empire

The Byzantine Empire still held the coasts of the Mediterranean and Black seas and western Anatolia (Map 10.3). But eastern Anatolia and Armenia had been the empire's source of food and soldiers, and, once lost, these valuable territories could neither be retaken nor replaced. The Turks, who had had designs on eastern Anatolia but had never thought of conquering Byzantium itself, now held the strategic initiative and possessed

Map 10.3 The Gradual Retraction of the Byzantine Empire, 628–1328

By 1200, the Byzantine Empire was considerably smaller than it had been in 481 (Map 10.1). Arabian invasions from the south in the seventh century surprised the Empire's leaders and forced them to divide their forces between Persian and Arab threats. Observe that the Empire was gradually pushed westward, and that it lost all its North African territories to the Arabs. At the start of the thirteenth century, Byzantium's collapse was not assured, but its long-term survival was clearly questionable. How might the loss of these regions have handicapped the Byzantine emperors?

Map A

Map B

Map C

the resources necessary for eventual victory. It came in 1453, when the Ottoman Turks, successors to the Seljuks, completed the Islamic conquest of West Asia and defeated the Byzantine Empire.

Pre-Christian Russia

The Byzantine Empire was largely shattered after Manzikert, but Byzantine influence lived on in the north. There, in 988, the Grand Prince of an area called Kiev had converted to eastern Christianity. His decision meant that even after Byzantium's collapse, its culture and religion would continue in his realm. This area of Byzantine influence eventually grew into an enormous country known as Russia.

Russia's Difficult Climate and Terrain

Russian territory stretches from eastern Europe across northern Asia. Endless forests blanket its northern expanses, while its south is covered with vast treeless plains known as steppes (Map 10.4). Although Russia today possesses thousands of miles of seacoast, throughout most of history it was in effect landlocked. Its long northern coastline borders the Arctic Ocean, ice-bound for much of the year, while access to its Baltic and Black Sea ports, acquired in recent centuries, is controlled by countries that have often been hostile. This landlocked condition inhibited trade routes and frustrated Russia's development for centuries.

Geography impedes Russian development

Russia is not only landlocked but cold, the most heavily populated frigid land in the world. Even its southernmost portions lie no farther south than North Dakota. The Gulf Stream, which moderates the climate of continental Europe, touches only a tiny portion of Russia. Siberia, in Asian Russia, is known for its brutally cold conditions, and in the northern part of European Russia the soil remains frozen for more than half the year. This cold severely restricts both the quantity of arable land and the length of the growing season. Central Asian Russia suffers from both severe cold and inadequate moisture, making agriculture impossible there without irrigation. Finally, as nearly all the region's principal rivers flow north or south, rather than east or west, travel across Russia has always been difficult, hindering commerce and the use of its natural resources.

Early Cultures and Conflicts

Sarmatians use the stirrup to conquer and rule southern Russia

Societies appear to have developed earliest in southern Russia, where the cold was less severe. The Cimmerians (*sih-MARE-ē-uns*), linguistically related to the Greeks, ruled the lands north and east of the Black Sea between 1000 and 700 B.C.E. They were conquered by the Scythians, a Central Asian nomadic people who also invaded Persia. Between 700 and 200 B.C.E. the Scythians dominated southern Russia, but their formidable military state collapsed under pressure from another group of nomads called Sarmatians (*sahr-MĀ-shuns*), who then ruled the region until about 200 C.E. Fighting from horseback with heavy armor and long swords, the Sarmatians made good use of stirrups, a Central Asian innovation that secured the feet of a mounted warrior, allowing him to charge and thrust without being knocked from his horse.

The Scythians and Sarmatians were related to the Persians. Their occupation of southern Russia brought them into contact with Greek colonies on the northern shore of the Black Sea. They were accomplished metalworkers and outstanding fighters whose kings

Map 10.4 The Topography of Russia

Russia's formidable topography impeded its settlement and development for centuries. Its great rivers flow north-south rather than east-west, dead-ending travelers from its southern regions in the frigid Arctic rather than linking its Baltic and Pacific coasts. Notice that between taiga and desert lie vast expanses of forest and grassy steppes, areas in which large-scale farming has always been difficult. Battling these geographic challenges, the Grand Princes of Kiev laid the foundations of the Russian Empire. How might Russia's location across extreme northern latitudes restrict its development?

ruled by divine right; the Greeks were skilled fishers and tireless traders who elected their leaders. Neither group made any systematic attempt to conquer the other. Both preferred to reap the benefits of commercial contact and frequent intermarriage, practices that resulted in a blending of their cultures. But both found themselves displaced by the nomadic invasions that were having such a disastrous impact on the Western Roman Empire.

First among the invading nomads were the Germanic Ostrogoths, discussed in Chapter 9, who established a powerful kingdom between the Baltic and Black seas from 200 to 370 C.E. Then the Huns, a fearsome collection of Turkic-speakers, arrived on their way to Central Europe and an eventual confrontation with Pope Leo the Great (Chapter 9). The Avars were next, extending their control over a wide band of southern and western Russia beginning in 558. They threatened both Europe and Byzantium before collapsing in the mid-seventh century. Clearly the southern Russian plain was well-traveled by nomadic peoples heading for the more moderate climes of southwest Asia and Europe.

Nomadic invasions cross Russia

When the Khazars (*KAH-zars*) moved into the lower Volga region of southwestern Russia in the seventh century, they appeared at first to be simply another invading culture that would dominate the region for a while and then be replaced. But their influence surpassed that of their short-lived predecessors. They abandoned their nomadic heritage and built large towns along the trade routes connecting Asia and Europe. Thus they served as a commercial and cultural crossroads. As one of the first peoples in the world to create a professional, paid army, they developed military skills that helped hold back Islamic armies. But they tolerated Islam, as well as paganism, Judaism, and Christianity, within their borders. In the eighth century they adopted Judaism, an unprecedented conversion based not on conquest but conviction. The legacy of the Khazars to the development of a Russian state was rich and surprising.

But the people who were destined to organize that state and dominate its successors lived well to the north and west of the Khazar realm. These people were the eastern Slavs, members of a linguistic group that today includes the speakers of Russian, Belarussian, and Ukrainian languages. The Slavs were skilled ironworkers and woodworkers, with well-established agricultural patterns that were exceptional in northern lands. One of their tribes, in fact, may have been the "Rus" (*ROOS*) who gave the land its name: Russia.

Kievan Rus Connects to the Byzantine World

The origin of the people who called themselves "Rus" is disputed. Some scholars argue that they were Norsemen from Scandinavia, also known as "Varangians," who allegedly arrived in northwestern Russia around 862 and imposed order on the Slavs who lived there. Other historians contend that the Rus lived in the south and were known to both Arab and Byzantine observers before 862. But one point is not in dispute: late in the ninth or early in the tenth century, the Rus, wherever they originated from, founded the state known as Kievan Rus. By 988 this state had become part of the Byzantine world.

The First Period: Early Rulers and Campaigns

Kievan Russia's history is customarily divided into three periods. The first, lasting from approximately 882 until 972, was the era in which the state was established and consolidated. Its first ruler was Oleg, a prince who gradually extended control over several neighboring East Slavic tribes. They were forced to pay tribute to him in Kiev, his capital, a town on the lower Dnieper (*nē-YEH-pur*) River in southern Russia (Map 10.5). In 907 Oleg went to war against the Byzantine Empire in what seems to have been an inconclusive series of skirmishes. Constantinople did, however, buy off the Rus with a highly generous commercial treaty.

Oleg's successor, Prince Igor (913–945), conducted a series of campaigns designed to maintain Kiev's domination over its tributary peoples. He also fought a large-scale war against the Byzantines from 941 to 943, during which his forces plundered the suburbs of Constantinople. But Greek Fire kept him from conquering the city, and in 945 he was killed while collecting tribute (always a dangerous undertaking) from one of the East Slavic tribes. His widow Olga assumed his powers, ruling Kiev as regent for their young son Sviatoslav (*svē-AH-tuh-slav*) from 945 to 962.

Olga became the first prominent female leader in Kievan Russia, in part by relentlessly enforcing her control over the tributary groups, in part by coming to terms with

Map 10.5 Kievan Rus, ca. 900

While the Orthodox Christian Byzantine Empire contended for supremacy in southwest Asia with the Muslims (Chapter 11), a new Orthodox Christian monarchy was emerging farther north. Grand Prince Vladimir's conversion to Orthodoxy in 988 oriented Kievan Rus to the south and west, turning it away from Asia and toward Europe. Note that Kievan Russia's location, on the western edge of Asia and the eastern fringe of Europe, would have supported a turn in either direction. This made Vladimir's adoption of Orthodox Christianity decisive for future Russian development. Could Kievan Russia have offered any support to the Byzantine Empire in its ongoing struggle with the Muslims?

the Byzantine Empire. She converted to eastern Christianity and traveled to Constantinople, where she met the emperor himself. The two appear to have concluded a cautious alliance, providing Sviatoslav with a degree of security on his southern frontier when he became Grand Prince (or ruler) of Kiev in 962. Although her son did not convert to Christianity, ultimately Olga's efforts on behalf of her new faith were recognized by the Orthodox Church, which canonized her as a saint.

Sviatoslav ruled for only ten years, but they were a pivotal decade for Kievan Rus. In 965 he boldly attacked the Khazars, sacking their capital and fatally weakening their state. But this action was shortsighted, since the Khazars had been useful as a buffer against nomadic Central Asian tribes, particularly the ferocious Pechenegs (*PEH-chen-egs*). Three years later Sviatoslav, as the ally of Byzantium, conquered Bulgaria. The Pechenegs seized upon his absence to besiege Kiev, and in 969 Constantinople suddenly awoke

Sviatoslav's defeat of the Khazars leaves Kiev open to attack

to the dangers of instability on its northern border. The Byzantine Emperor broke his alliance with Kiev, and in 971, after two years of bitter warfare, Sviatoslav withdrew from the Balkans. On his way home in 972 he was killed by the Pechenegs, who boiled the flesh off his skull, then made it into a cup from which they drank in the hope of imbibing his courage. The first period of Kievan Russia's history had come to a discouraging end.

The Second Period: Connections to Christendom

Eight years later, following civil war among Sviatoslav's three sons, Vladimir (*VLAD-i-mēr* or *vlad-Ē-mēr*), the youngest, emerged victorious. His accession as Grand Prince in 980 ushered in Kiev's second and most glorious era, which lasted until 1054. Vladimir did much to unite and consolidate his realm, secure its borders, and enhance both its culture and its commerce. But his most momentous step was conversion to the Christian faith and his insistence that it be adopted throughout his realm. Vladimir's historic conversion took place in 988–989, when Christianity was spreading swiftly into Scandinavia, Poland, and Hungary. As part of a complex set of arrangements with Constantinople, he not only was baptized a Christian but also married the Byzantine emperor's sister.

Vladimir Christianizes Kiev

Russian legend offers an explanation for the conversion. According to popular accounts, Vladimir had summoned to Kiev representatives of the three great monotheistic religions, requiring each delegation to present arguments in support of its beliefs. After the presentations, he and his advisors decided against Judaism because its principles had not prevented the conquest of Judea by the Romans or the more recent defeat of the Jewish Khazars by Kiev itself. Islam was attractive as a dynamic, expanding movement, but its expansion had slowed considerably since the eighth century. A more practical problem was that the Islamic faith forbade the use of alcohol, and Russians could not imagine getting through the harsh winter months without it. Impressed with the majesty and beauty of Byzantine ritual, Vladimir chose Christianity. In so doing, he connected his realm with the Christian world.

It is significant that Russia adopted eastern rather than western Christianity. By 988 those two branches had diverged dramatically from one another, and in 1054, as already noted, the Great Schism formally divided them into two distinctly regional religions. Vladimir's preference for the Byzantine branch, known after 1054 as the Orthodox Church, carried with it three monumental consequences for Russia.

Russia inherits caesaropapism through Orthodox Christianity

First, Russia attached itself to a Christian church that remained firmly anchored in the rituals, practices, and doctrines of early Christianity. Western Christendom, by contrast, had gradually revised many of these traditions, exalting one bishop (the pope) above all others, altering the liturgy of divine worship, forbidding the marriage of priests, and later fragmenting with the rise of Protestantism in the sixteenth century. The rigorous internal questioning and self-criticism characteristic of western Christendom remained alien to Russia, as did the notion of a spiritual authority that was separate from and superior to that of the secular state. The Russians instead inherited the eastern caesaropapist tradition, which closely connected the church and state and placed both under the authority of the ruler of the realm.

Second, the slow weakening and eventual collapse of the Byzantine Empire eventually made Russia, by default, the leader of the Orthodox world. Outside of Russia, the Orthodox Church was increasingly marginalized and reduced to the status of a weak minority faith. Russia thus became the flagship of eastern Christianity.

Finally, Vladimir's choice made his country the beneficiary of the Byzantine cultural heritage. Orthodox Christianity linked Kiev to a rich, dynamic collection of rituals and traditions that enriched its rather spartan Slavic culture. Byzantine art, with its extensive use of gold and vivid depictions of Christian saints and events, left an indelible stamp on Russian symbolism. Orthodox worship services, chanted and sung in a liturgical language developed for Slavic peoples (rather than in Hebrew, Arabic, or Latin, as would have been required had Russia converted to Judaism, Islam, or Western Christianity) played a key role in the development of the Russian language. So did the Cyrillic alphabet, adapted from the Greek with extra letters added to represent Slavic sounds. Over the centuries, these and other influences, flowing from the Byzantine connection, contributed to the formation of a distinctive, energetic, and inspirational Russian culture.

Byzantine culture enriches Kievan society

Vladimir was later canonized a saint in the Orthodox Church. His actions provided a platform for the accomplishments of his successor, Iaroslav (*YAHR-ah-slahv*) the Wise (1019–1054), who governed at the height of Kievan power. Iaroslav's military campaigns against Pechenegs and Poles consolidated a state ranging from the Black Sea to the Baltic. He authorized the preparation of Russia's first legal code, built churches and monasteries throughout the land, and transformed the city of Kiev into a vibrant center of commerce and culture. He also appointed a wise Russian churchman as metropolitan of Kiev, Russia's leading church official, thus giving Russia its first native-born church leader. But his decision to divide his lands upon his death among his five sons condemned Kievan Rus to political turmoil and civil war, starting in 1054. Taking advantage of this instability, a new wave of Turkic-speaking invaders from the steppes, the Polovtsy (*pah-LAHV-tsē* or *pah-lahv-TSĒ*), appeared in the southeast and harassed the Kievan state for decades.

The Third Period: Chaos and Conflict

With this civil war and the subsequent Polovtsy invasion, the third era of Kievan Rus began, a lengthy period of chaos and conflict (1054–1240) during which its very survival was often in doubt. Iaroslav's grandson Vladimir Monomakh (*MAH-nō-MAHK*), who served as Grand Prince from 1113 to 1125, fought constantly to defend the state, primarily against the Polovtsy but also against other invaders from the west and south. Monomakh managed to preserve his realm but was unable to guarantee its long-term survival. His successors quarreled among themselves, sacked Kiev itself, and eventually transferred the capital northeast to the city of Vladimir. Repeatedly raided by the persistent Polovtsy and increasingly detached culturally and commercially from the declining Byzantine Empire, the Kievan realm fragmented into feuding principalities. By the time Kiev fell to the Mongols in 1240, the center of Russia had shifted to the northern forests, affording its people a more defensible position against the seemingly unending stream of invaders moving across the southern steppes.

The Polovtsy invade and weaken Kiev

Economy and Society

Agriculture was the source of Kievan prosperity. Because of Russian geography, the growing season was relatively brief, but the black soil of the region was rich and plentiful. Northern areas produced barley, oats, and rye, while wheat was the principal crop farther south. Farmers divided their lands into two parts, leaving each one fallow, or uncultivated, in alternate years. Eventually this alternation evolved into a three-field system, in which a parcel of land would be sown in one year with a spring crop, in the second year with a winter crop, and in the third with no crop at all. This system enhanced the fertility of the soil and increased food production.

Grain cultivation was supplemented by cattle raising and beekeeping, which supplied candle wax to light homes and honey to sweeten food and drink. Fishing and hunting were also important. Russia was a snowy land, but its vast forests and numerous lakes and rivers contained enough game and fish to feed a population much larger than the one that lived there. The majority of that population, of course, was rural; in Kievan Rus there were many towns but few cities. Most townspeople, including artisans who practiced skills in tanning, metalworking, and woodworking, also worked on the land.

Kiev connects southwestern Russia commercially

Townspeople were also merchants. Kiev's location on the Dnieper River north of the Black Sea gave it control of, or easy access to, the principal trade routes of southwestern Russia. The Grand Prince was in some ways the chief merchant as well as the chief executive. Collecting tribute from subject peoples in the form of honey, beeswax, furs, hides, and slaves, he presided over an active and complex trade with Byzantium, Bulgaria, and Baghdad. Relations with Constantinople were commercial as well as cultural and religious.

In addition to directing trade, waging war, and regulating affairs of state, the Grand Prince presided over a social and governing elite centered on his siblings and cousins. His courtiers intermarried with local Kievan nobles to form the **boyar class**, an aristocracy that played a significant role throughout much of Russian history. Most Kievan peasants were free, although some fell into debt so burdensome that they were scarcely better off than the slaves who formed the base of the social structure.

Byzantine Christianity influences Kiev

From bottom to top, Kievan society was interlaced with Byzantine Christianity. The Orthodox Church offered much more than services on Sundays and holy days. It provided a colorful, enriching series of rituals designed to guide the believer from birth through life to death. It owned and administered early forms of charitable institutions, hospitals, and schools. It dominated Russian art, architecture, and literature, giving each a distinctively Byzantine flavor. In addition, its married clergy sent their children not only back into the Church but into all other walks of life, spiritualizing Kievan society to a degree unmatched in Western Christendom.

The End of Early Russian Civilization

The spiritual richness of Kiev, impressive though it was, could not prevent the state's collapse. A number of factors converged to make that outcome possible. Economically, in the eleventh century, Kiev began to lose its privileged commercial position, as Polovtsy occupation of the south disrupted Kievan connections with both the Byzantine Empire and Islamic southern Asia. Socially, a gradual reduction in peasant status led to serious unrest in the twelfth century. Politically, Kievan Russia failed to develop as a fully centralized state. It was instead a loose federation of principalities, which only unusually talented rulers such as Vladimir and Iaroslav could hold together.

Nomads besiege Kievan Rus

Recurrent civil strife in turn left Kiev vulnerable to unending attacks by Turkic-speaking nomads such as the Khazars, Pechenegs, and Polovtsy. Although Russia defeated them time and again, they continued to undermine its vitality. In 1240, the Mongols sacked Kiev, ending the third period of early Russian civilization.

Chapter Review

Putting It in Perspective

In the fourth century C.E., when Emperor Constantine legalized Christianity, took a leading role in Church affairs, and moved the Roman Empire's capital eastward to Constantinople, he laid the foundations of the Byzantine realm. After 476, when Germanic forces conquered Rome and ended the empire in the west, the Eastern Roman Empire continued to develop a distinctive society, blending Roman traditions with Greek culture and a vibrant version of the Christian faith that united Church and state authority in the person of the emperor.

Byzantine emperors continued to claim all the western territory they had lost, but their efforts to retake it achieved no lasting success. Far more significant were the achievements of Byzantium itself. Among these were Justinian's Code, which systematized Roman law and guaranteed its survival into modern times. In the area of religion, Byzantine Christianity developed a rich set of rituals that preserved early Christian practices to the present day. And, beginning in the tenth century, Byzantine religion and culture took root in Russia, where they were destined to outlast the Byzantine Empire itself.

Byzantium's culture was splendid, its commercial connections were extensive, and many of its emperors were effective, capable leaders. Some, however, proved to be incompetent or corrupt. A political system that restrained executive power could have survived the mistakes of these emperors, but the Byzantine Empire's caesaropapist heritage exalted the ruler's authority, even if he or she was disastrously ineffective. Although the emperors worked to unify their people religiously, Byzantium's chronic quarrels over doctrinal differences that could not be resolved frustrated their efforts and weakened the empire in the face of its enemies.

In the end the empire's enemies proved its undoing. Drastically diminished by Arab conquests during the seventh century, the realm regrouped and regained a measure of power and prosperity, only to be battered by the Turks beginning in the eleventh century. Both the Arabs and Turks were driven by a compelling, militant new faith that arose in Arabia in the early 600s. That dynamic force, to which we now turn, was known as Islam.

Reviewing Key Material

KEY CONCEPTS

heresy, 236	iconoclasm, 244
schism, 237	boyar class, 254
caesaropapism, 237	

KEY PEOPLE

Justinian, 235, 238	Romanus IV Diogenes, 246
Theodora, 238	Oleg, 250
Constantine, 236	Igor, 250
Arius, 236	Olga, 250
Theodosius, 237	Sviatoslav, 250
Julian "the Apostate", 238	Vladimir, 252
Heraclius, 243	Iaroslav the Wise, 253
Leo III, 244	Vladimir Monomakh, 253
Alp Arslan, 246	

ASK YOURSELF

1. Why was caesaropapism important in the administration of the Byzantine Empire? How did Justinian and Theodora utilize it?
2. Why was Byzantium unable to reconquer and hold Rome?
3. Could the Great Schism of 1054 have been avoided? Why or why not?
4. How and why did Kievan Rus emerge as a powerful state in Russia? How was Kievan Rus affected by Byzantium?
5. Which features were distinctive about Byzantine civilization? Which of these features were passed on to later cultures?

GOING FURTHER

Agold, Michael. *The Byzantine Empire, 1025–1204.* 1985.

Barnes, T. *The New Empire of Diocletian and Constantine.* 1982.

Grant, Michael. *Constantine the Great.* 1993.

Harvey, A. *Economic Expansion in the Byzantine Empire, 900–1200.* 1989.

Hussey, Joan. *The Byzantine World.* 1982.

Hussey, Joan. *The Orthodox Church in the Byzantine Empire.* 1986.

Kazhdan, A., and Ann Wharton Epstein. *Change in Byzantine Culture in the Eleventh and Twelfth Centuries.* 1985.

Magoulias, Harry. *Byzantine Christianity: Emperor, Church, and the West.* 1982.

Mango, Cyril. *Byzantium: The Empire of New Rome.* 1980.

Martin, Janet. *Medieval Russia, 980–1584.* 1995.

Obolensky, Dmitri. *The Byzantine Commonwealth: Eastern Europe, 500–1453.* 1971.

Pohlsander, H. *The Emperor Constantine.* 1997.

Treadgold, Warren. *A History of the Byzantine State and Society.* 1997.

Vernadsky, George. *Kievan Russia.* 1973.

Ware, Timothy. *The Orthodox Church.* 1993.

Key Dates and Developments

The Byzantine Empire

284 C.E.	Diocletian's division of the Roman Empire
325	Constantine's intervention at the Council of Nicaea
527–565	Rule of Justinian and (until 548) Theodora
529	Code of Justinian
541	Bubonic Plague appeared in Constantinople
681	Council of Constantinople defined the nature of Jesus
726	Leo III's ban on icons and images; Iconoclasm
1054	The Great Schism
1071	Battle of Manzikert Kievan Rus
700–200 B.C.E.	Scythians controlled southern Russia

200 B.C.E. – 200 C.E.	Sarmatians controlled southern Russia
200–650 C.E.	Germanic invasions
7th century C.E.	Arrival of the Khazars
ca. 862	Varangians arrived in northwestern Russia
882–972	Foundation and First Period of Kievan Rus
945–962	Regency and Conversion of Olga
962–972	Rule of Sviatoslav
980–1054	Second Period of Kievan Rus; Vladimir as Grand Prince (980–1019)
988	Conversion of Russia to Byzantine Christianity
1054–1240	Third Period of Kievan Rus
1240	Mongol conquest of Kiev

The Origins and Expansion of Islam, 100–750

The Great Mosque At Mecca

The Great Mosque at Mecca during pilgrimage season. The large black structure at the center is the Ka'ba (page 262).

- Pre-Islamic Arabia

- The Rise of Islam

- Islam Expands, 632–661

- The Umayyad Caliphate, 661–750

- Society and Culture in Early Islam

- Chapter Review

Night was approaching in the Arabian desert. Moving eastward from the Red Sea, a caravan of camels laden with goods hastened to reach the gate of the city before darkness fell. Safely inside, the handlers fed and watered the camels while the merchants shook the dust from their clothing and bought food at a bazaar. Before retiring for the night, they visited the center of the city, an open square filled with shrines and statues. There they performed a series of rituals, thanking their gods for protecting them in the desert and leading them to safety.

The Expansion of Islam, 632-732 C.E.

This was the city of Mecca, a haven for travelers in an unforgiving wasteland. For centuries Mecca had provided food, water, rest, and sanctuary for anyone passing through its gate. Its food sellers, craftsmen, and peddlers prided themselves on making everyone welcome, regardless of the traveler's station in life or religious beliefs. The city's shrines offered every passerby a chance to worship his favorite god. But in the early seventh century, Mecca was changing. In 630, a man who had been born there six decades earlier returned to his home. He brought with him a new, monotheistic faith, preaching belief in one god, Allah, and rededicating Mecca to the worship of that god. In the following centuries that new faith, known as Islam, spread throughout the world. Neither Mecca nor the Arabian peninsula would ever be the same.

Pre-Islamic Arabia

In the sixth century of the Common Era, the world of the eastern Mediterranean had long been a commercial crossroads attracting all sorts of believers, including those who believed in no gods at all. It was a place where not only goods but cultures, languages, values, and customs intermingled. On the fringe of this world lay the Arabian Peninsula, a land of searing heat at the southwestern tip of Asia. Arabia was not a centralized state but home to a collection of tribes and clans. The region was noted for fragmentation and rivalry rather than unity. Yet out of Arabia came Islam, a vigorous, zealous form of monotheism that aspired to unify not only its home peninsula, but the entire world, under a banner of allegiance to one God. Islam excited the entire region, spreading its beliefs, its values, and the Arabic language over much of southern Asia and northern Africa within the next century. Lands once devoted to Greek, Roman, or Persian gods, to Judaism and Christianity, were united as a new Islamic world.

Camels and Commerce

Arabia in the centuries before Islam was an isolated area, even though it lay just south of the eastern Mediterranean basin, one of the busiest places in the world. An immense peninsula bordered by five seas should constitute an ideal location for oceangoing commerce, but Arabia had just two decent harbors. It has no rivers at all, so internal transportation was difficult, and fresh water was almost completely unavailable. Only the southwest receives ample rainfall. The rest of the peninsula consists of imposing mountains and arid, scorching deserts, culminating in the Empty Quarter of the southeast, the largest expanse of uninterrupted sand anywhere on the planet. Much of Arabia was unsettled, traversed only by Bedouin (*BED-oo-win*) peoples, nomads who moved from one oasis to another on camels.

Aptly nicknamed "the ships of the desert," camels were indispensable to what commerce there was in Arabia. Able to carry 500-pound loads for distances up to 25 miles per day, camels can work for as much as three weeks without drinking, taking advantage of their huge stomachs and their ability to retain water until needed. Defiant and ill-tempered, camels were nevertheless crucial to travel, even though a sizable portion of each beast's load had to be reserved for food and no less than a gallon of water per day for the man who guided it. Despite this limitation, camels made trade possible across the forbidding interior of Arabia, and caravans of camels traveled up and down the Red Sea coast.

Camel transport sustained the economic life of both the nomads of the north and the more settled peoples of the fertile, rain-fed southwest. But given the importance of water in a desert land, it is not surprising that southern Arabia grew to dominate the peninsula. City-states developed in that area after 1000 B.C.E., led by kings and fed by slaves. The region also produced luxury goods such as frankincense and myrrh, aromatic substances that appear in Christian accounts of the birth of Jesus. Compensating for lack of harbors, southern Arabians built ships that traveled the waters of the Arabian Sea and Indian Ocean in search of products and profits. By 400 B.C.E. the southerners had created a commercial network that operated in two directions. Southward, their ships of the sea carried imports and exports to and from eastern Africa, Persia, and India. Northward, their "ships of the desert" carried these goods across oceans of sand, linking southern Arabia to Mesopotamia and the eastern Mediterranean. These trade routes connected with one created by the Phoenicians in the Mediterranean to form the longest commercial highway in history. Southern Arabians were primarily responsible for introducing Indian spices to the Mediterranean world, initiating a spice trade whose importance lasted more than a thousand years. In this commercial network northern Arabia was subordinate to the southern city-states, which, protected by the same deserts and mountains that made their existence so precarious, did not fear their northern neighbors.

Camels make commerce possible in Arabia

A camel caravan.

The Collapse of Southern Arabia and the Rise of Mecca

Eventually, however, in spite of the early commercial advantages of southern Arabia, its prosperity collapsed. The Ptolemaic (*tahl-ih-MĀ-ick*) Empire of Egypt, one of the successor states of the vast empire of Alexander the Great, had by 100 B.C.E. established its own commercial route linking Egypt to India by way of the Red Sea. Simultaneously, the Ethiopian kingdom of Axum on the western bank of the Red Sea, which actually owned territory on the Arabian Peninsula, threatened the commerce of the declining Arabian city-states. Finally, the northern Arabians took this opportunity to interfere with overland

FOUNDATION MAP 11.1 Physical Geography of the Arabian Peninsula

Mesopotamians, Assyrians, Babylonians, Egyptians, Persians, Greeks, and Romans all knew of the existence of Arabia, but none of them considered it important. Its forbidding geography explains this lack of interest. Observe the lack of rivers to channel the small amount of moisture that falls as rain. An enormous limestone plateau jutting into the Arabian Sea, the Arabian Peninsula bakes under intense heat and lacks subsurface supplies of fresh water. How might Arabia have forged connections with other societies if its topography had been less discouraging?

Map 11.2 Arabia and Adjacent Regions, 500 C.E.

Isolated and arid, the Arabian Peninsula in 500 C.E. was divided into states and subdivided into feuding clans. Nearby states like Axum traded with Arabian states but otherwise left them alone. Note that the eastern shore of the Red Sea could serve as a highway for camel caravans linking the Kingdom of Saba to the ports of the eastern Mediterranean. What role could cities like Medina and Mecca play in the development of such commerce?

trade routes, eroding southern control over the peninsula's interior (Map 11.1). By 300 C.E. the southern city-states had lost much of their power and wealth (Map 11.2).

As the city-states weakened, regional powers engaged in a military, commercial, and religious contest for Arabia. At this time the capital of the Roman Empire was being transferred from Rome to Constantinople, while the Sasanians, energized by Zoroastrianism, were revitalizing Persia six centuries after the Greco-Macedonian conquest. Byzantium, inspired by Christianity, also considered the Arabian Peninsula open for commercial exploitation and religious conversion.

Monotheistic beliefs had entered Arabia as early as 70 C.E., when the Roman destruction of the second Temple in Jerusalem initiated a dispersal of Jews throughout

Competing forces contend for Arabia

Southwest Asia. Southern Arabian kings, observing that two of their most dangerous enemies, Byzantium and Ethiopia, were Christian, adopted Judaism in the early 400s. But in 520 an Ethiopian invasion destroyed the southern city-states and established a Christian protectorate. Judaism was weakened through forcible conversion to Christianity, but Ethiopian military domination was never secure, and in the 570s the Ethiopians were replaced by the Persians. Under Persian rule, Judaism, Christianity, and Zoroastrianism were all tolerated in southern Arabia.

The destruction of the southern Arabian states proved to be highly significant, because it ended the southern domination of the peninsula and created a politico-economic vacuum that neither Ethiopia nor Sasanian Persia could fill. The Bedouin nomads of the interior now gravitated toward the less highly developed towns of the north, linking them with the city of Mecca on the western edge of the Arabian desert.

Mecca emerges as a principal Arabian sanctuary

For several centuries Mecca had been a place of sanctuary where both travelers and the bandits pursuing them could rest and refresh themselves undisturbed. It was also a religious center, housing tribal idols from much of the peninsula and offering numerous pilgrims an opportunity to view the Ka'ba (*KAH-bah*), a shrine containing large stone idols (see page 257). As southern Arabia's commercial power vanished following the Ethiopian and Persian invasions, Mecca took on added importance as a resting place for camel caravans traveling up and down the Red Sea coast and across the desert. Making the most of this opportunity, the Quraysh (*kurr-ISH*) tribe, which rose to dominate the city around 500 C.E., became custodians of the Ka'ba, protectors of pilgrims, and traders determined to establish an international commercial dynasty.

The Rise of Islam

As the sixth century drew to a close, the Arabian Peninsula was changing rapidly. The powerful southern city-states were gone, and no central authority had taken their place. Traditional trade routes had been disrupted and new ones were being formed. Monotheistic religions had been introduced but none had succeeded in converting very many. Mecca, now flourishing as a religious and commercial center, seemed to offer a promising new focus for regional control.

Then a boy, born into a minor clan of the Quraysh tribe in Mecca, transformed the changing Arabian Peninsula. He was Muhammad ibn Abd'Allah (*muh-HAHM-ahd ibn abd-AHL-lah*), and he would become one of the most influential figures in history.

The Prophet Muhammad

Muhammad was born in 570, shortly after his father had died. The boy was raised by a grandfather and later by an uncle. He worked on caravans up and down the Red Sea coastline, first as a camel tender and then as a merchant, and at age 25 he married his employer, a wealthy widow named Khadija (*kah-DĒ-jah*). In Mecca he earned a reputation as a responsible businessman and camel merchant, despite his inability to read or write, and as a spiritual person committed to living an ethical life. Often he went to the mountains near the city to pray and meditate. While doing so, in 610 he experienced the first of a series of revelations. He described these revelations as transmitted to his unconscious mind by the Archangel Gabriel, a figure in both Jewish and Christian scriptures. But Muhammad claimed to have felt the words rather than to have heard them, and said that they came directly from Allah, the one and only God.

Allah's name was known to Arabians. He was one of a number of gods whom they worshiped, but no cult was devoted solely to him and his nature was not well defined. He was not the one God worshiped by the few Arabs who had come to believe in monotheism. But Muhammad said that his revelations identified Allah as the only God, and they clarified his nature.

At first the disclosures Muhammad reported concerned God's nature and his relations with humanity. Allah is omnipotent and merciful, Muhammad claimed; he created everything, and it is the duty of everyone to acknowledge his greatness and worship him. He expects the rich to assist the poor and requires that all people live honest, faithful, and upright lives in compliance with specific rituals and regulations. On the Last Day, according to Muhammad, Allah will bring all souls before him and will judge them according to their actions on earth, consigning some to heaven and others to hell.

Muhammad's definition of God and of people's relations with him clearly paralleled those of other religions with which Meccans were familiar. Jews were uncompromising monotheists who accepted the Mosaic code of ethical conduct and followed clearly defined religious practices. Christians believed in the Day of Judgment and described it in words and images similar to those transmitted to Muhammad. Zoroastrians believed in the eternal struggle between good and evil and in the eventual triumph of Ahura Mazda over the forces of The Lie. But Judaism, Christianity, and Zoroastrianism had failed to win significant numbers of followers in Arabia, possibly because in a land fragmented into tribes and clans, polytheism seemed more reflective of the realities of daily life. Now Muhammad believed that Gabriel had instructed him to do much more than simply believe in a single god. He was to prophesy in the tradition of Moses and Jesus, to speak to men and women on behalf of Allah, to turn them away from the errors of polytheism and lead them to the worship of the one true God.

Muhammad's revelations provided a religious explanation for why other monotheistic religions had failed to win the hearts and minds of Arabs. According to Muhammad's account, Gabriel had said that Jews and Christians possessed their own scriptural texts and were recognized by Allah as **People of the Book**. Their books—the Jewish and Christian scriptures—were valid but incomplete and only partially accurate. They had been copied, translated, and revised over the centuries until they no longer contained the fullness and purity of divine revelation. Muhammad's mission was to communicate the totality of God's teaching in its pure and final form. He was to be the last and greatest of the prophets, the Messenger of God.

This charge was a daunting prospect for an illiterate merchant, but Muhammad believed he knew how to proceed with his mission. He recited his revelations over and over to secretaries who recorded his words carefully in Arabic, and many of his followers memorized them. These recitations became the **Qur'an** (*kuh-RAN*, also spelled *Koran*), the sacred scripture of the religion that would soon become known as Islam (*IZ-lahm* or *is-LAHM*), Arabic for "submission" to the will of God. Organized neither topically nor chronologically but roughly by length of recitation (from the longest to the shortest), the Qur'an is a difficult text. But individual believers felt compelled to read it, and it became a powerful force in their lives (see "Excerpts from the Qur'an"). It was also a force in

Muhammad's visions introduce a new religion

The Shahadah (see page 266): "There is no God but Allah, and Muhammad is His messenger."

Muhammad sees his mission as the completion of God's revelation

A hand-copied page from a nineteenth-century edition of the Qur'an.

Document 11.1 Excerpts from the Qur'an

The Prophet Muhammad stated that the Qur'an was the authentic word of God, and was dictated to him by the Archangel Gabriel. It is the Holy Scripture of Islam.

Q 1: 1–7.

In the name of Allah, the beneficent, the merciful.
All praise is due to Allah, Lord of the worlds—
The beneficent, the merciful,
Sovereign of the Day of Judgment.
You alone do we worship; You alone we ask for help.
Guide us to the straight path,
The path of those upon whom You have bestowed favor,
Not of those who have evoked Your anger,
Nor of those who are astray.

Q 2: 190.

Fight in the way of Allah those who fight you
But do not commit aggression.
Indeed, Allah does not like aggressors.

Q 80: 33–42.

But when there comes the Deafening Blast
On the Day of Judgment a man will flee from his brother
And his mother and his father
And his wife and his children,

For every man, that Day will be a matter to occupy him.
Some faces, that Day, will be bright—
Laughing, rejoicing at good news.
And other faces, that Day, will have upon them dust,
Blackness will cover them.
Those are the disbelievers, the wicked ones.

Q 3: 104.

Let there be arising from you one community (*umma*),
Inviting to good, enjoining what is right
And forbidding what is wrong,
And those will be the successful.

Q 29: 46.

And do not argue with the People of the Scripture
Except in a way that is best,
Except for those who commit injustice among them,
And say, "We believe in that which has been revealed to us
And revealed to you.
And our God and your God is one,
And we are in submission to Him."

SOURCE: *The Qur'an.* Saheeh International. (Abul-Qasim Publishing House: Jeddah, Saudi Arabia, 1997).

Muhammad's recitations become the Qur'an

Arab history, as its compilation and eventual publication standardized classical Arabic, and the Qur'an and the Arabic language became the two principal unifying forces within the Arab world.

In 613 Muhammad began to preach publicly outside the circle of his own family and friends. He quickly encountered opposition from the merchant elite of the Quraysh, who probably viewed the Qur'an as a challenge to their own tribal values. They certainly realized that the new teachings would disrupt the polytheistic traditions and genial tolerance of the sanctuary at Mecca, which would rapidly lose its attractiveness as a haven for commercial travelers. The tribal chiefs, moreover, felt that Muhammad's claim to be God's messenger challenged their political authority. The elite tried to buy Muhammad off with an offer of membership in their inner circle. When he refused their bribes, they tried intimidation and then a boycott of his family and associates that prevented them from buying food in local markets. But nothing persuaded Muhammad to give up his religious mission.

From Mecca to Medina

By 619 Muhammad had some one hundred followers in Mecca, a small return on his investment of six years of preaching and teaching. At the same time, the oasis town of Medina (*meh-DĪ-nuh* or *meh-DĒ-nuh*), two hundred miles north, took an interest in his message. Medina was jealous of Mecca's economic domination, and the town was friendly to monotheism, since many of its residents were monotheistic Jews. In 622, after sporadic negotiations, 75 men from Medina invited Muhammad to move there to mediate some internal disputes. Late that summer he, his closest relatives, and their families undertook a nine-day journey known as the *Hijra* (*HĒJ-rah*, sometimes rendered as "flight" or "severing of relationships"). They reached Medina on September 24, 622, making that year the beginning of the Islamic lunar calendar. It was the pivotal event of Islamic history, symbolizing a flight from polytheism to monotheism.

Medina had been divided by religious quarrels among various tribes, some of them polytheistic and some Jewish. Muhammad offered them a monotheistic creed with scriptures in Arabic and a rigorous moral code that he himself would apply as a neutral judge. The polytheistic tribes accepted his arrival and soon converted to Islam, but the Jewish clans resisted despite Muhammad's willingness to incorporate some obviously Jewish practices into his evolving faith. The Jews rejected his claim to stand in the tradition of their great prophets Moses, Elijah, and Isaiah (*ē-LĪ-jah*, *ī-ZĀ-uh*).

Muhammad establishes an Islamic community at Medina

Faced with Jewish resistance, Muhammad reported receiving a new series of revelations that became part of the Qur'an. These recitations disclosed that the Hebrew patriarch Abraham was a greater prophet even than Moses and that, at God's command, he had built the Ka'ba shrine in Mecca. Muhammad now claimed that Abraham was the father of the Arab people, a pure monotheist whose beliefs had been corrupted by subsequent generations of Jews, just as subsequent generations of polytheists had placed idols in the Ka'ba. Now, Muhammad claimed, Allah had directed him to make Islam a completely independent religion, replacing both Judaism and Christianity because it represented the ultimate revelation of God.

Over the next several years Muhammad carried out this charge, building an **umma** (*OOM-mah*), a purely Islamic community under his leadership. Believers called themselves Muslims, or "those who submit" to the will of God. The foundation of the *umma* was five basic religious tenets; a Muslim is anyone who follows them, and following them, Muslims believe, will guarantee life in paradise with Allah after death.

The **five pillars**, as these tenets are called, were adapted from existing Christian, Jewish, and Arabian practices (see "The Five Pillars of Islam"). Together they constituted a foundation for the *umma*, giving it a religious charter and shared identity. In turn, the *umma* provided a means for social unity in a fragmented Arabia, demonstrating that the belief in a single god carried with it serious political implications. If polytheism had proven attractive to Arabians because its fundamental disunity reflected their daily realities, then monotheism's insistence on obedience to one god had the potential to end social and political disunity.

The umma is founded on the Five Pillars of Islam

Muhammad's construction of an *umma* at Medina gave him a base from which to attempt to convert Mecca. His followers plagued Meccan trading caravans, provoking the

Muhammad strives to convert Mecca

Document 11.2 The Five Pillars of Islam

1. **Shahadah,** or *bearing witness* (by proclaiming that "There is no God but Allah and Muhammad is His Messenger")
2. **Salat,** or *saying prayers* five times daily while facing in the direction of the Ka'ba in Mecca
3. **Zakat,** or *giving alms* to the poor
4. **Sawm,** or *abstaining from food and sex during daylight hours in the holy month of Ramadan* (*RAHM-ah-dahn*)
5. **Hajj,** or *making a pilgrimage* to Mecca during one's lifetime

---

Meccan commercial establishment into open hostility. In three battles between 624 and 627, Meccans failed to destroy Islam, and Muhammad's survival was widely interpreted as evidence of divine approval of his mission. Then in 628 Muhammad led a large band of Muslims from Medina on a pilgrimage to the Ka'ba. This gesture of reconciliation, designed to show that Islam was an intrinsically Arabian belief system rooted in tradition, persuaded many Arabian tribes to support Muhammad. In 630 he returned to Mecca, bearing gifts and pardons for his former enemies.

With Mecca now supporting him, Muhammad was able to extend his influence over even the most polytheistic Arab tribes. The simplicity of Islam's five pillars made it highly attractive. Compared to Judaism and Christianity, with their complex doctrines, regulations, and rituals, Islam was easy to understand. By the time of his death in 632, Muhammad, now known as the Prophet, had unified most of the peninsula around his inspired leadership and religious vision. He had also provided a spiritual framework within which to resolve the blood feuds that had long devastated the region. These successes in Arabia are best explained by Muhammad's claim to authority not on the basis of tribal ascendancy—unconvincing in such a fractured land—but on the basis of his status as the final messenger of God.

Islam Expands, 632–661

Islam's second generation demonstrated that this new religion would not remain confined to the Arabian Peninsula. Once certain internal leadership questions were settled, Arab warriors burst forth into southwest Asia and the eastern Mediterranean basin. Their advance startled the rulers of the long-established empires of Persia and Byzantium, who had not anticipated either a military or a political challenge from desolate Arabia. Barely three decades after the death of the Prophet, Islamic forces were masters of an extensive empire of their own, held together by contacts and connections that were forged in conflict.

An Agreement Between Leader and Followers

Muhammad's death provoked a crisis in Mecca. But this was not a crisis of spiritual leadership. Obviously no one could succeed him as Prophet, since the Qur'an indicated that Allah would send no more such messengers. Besides, Islam was individualistic, based on a personal relationship between Allah and each believer. There was no self-evident need for continuing spiritual directorship such as that provided in Christianity by popes and patriarchs.

Political leadership was a different issue entirely. To leave the *umma* leaderless would be to undermine all of Muhammad's work in unifying the peninsula. Muslims from Medina, still suspicious of Meccans, decided to select their own head, a move that if implemented would fragment Islam. This threat was averted in a highly contentious all-night meeting that selected the Prophet's father-in-law, the Meccan Abu Bakr, as **caliph** (*KĀ-liff*), meaning "successor of the Messenger of God." As Muhammad's successor, he would lead the *umma*.

Muslims wrestle with the question of leadership

Abu Bakr, like his son-in-law, was a member of the Quraysh clan. His selection established the principle that future leaders must also belong to the Prophet's tribe. Abu Bakr lived only two more years, but that was long enough to convince nearly everyone that the position of caliph should continue. The caliphate, or the territory governed by a caliph, developed into an institution that existed only in the Islamic world. Grounded in the idea that Islam must become more than an individualized, person-to-God relationship, it evolved into a compact binding all Muslims to one another within the *umma*. The caliph's appointment constituted a sort of agreement between leader and followers, imposing a set of obligations on both. Any violation of these obligations was both a political breach of contract and a sin against God.

The Ka'ba in Mecca.

This combination of political and spiritual authority carried with it awesome responsibility. Abu Bakr did not hesitate to exercise the former and live up to the latter. He and his successors believed that, since Muhammad's revelations were true, Islam, as the only true faith, must be spread by the faithful throughout the entire world. The contractual understanding implicit in Abu Bakr's concept of the caliphate helped transform Islam from a purely Arabian version of monotheism into a dynamic faith committed to spiritual and political expansion. Abu Bakr and the other companions of the Prophet thus embarked on a series of small-scale military expeditions that quickly developed into full-fledged campaigns. Islamic expansion, which took place between 632 and 732 mostly through armed conquest, was justified by Islam's claim to be a superior religion and achieved by the superiority of Arabian military tactics. It transformed the futures of Asia, Africa, and Europe.

The first caliph transforms Islam into a faith designed to connect all peoples

JIHAD AND THE TWO HOUSES. Islam's expansion conformed to the Qur'an's commandment to pursue **jihad** (*JĒ-hahd*). Often translated into English as "holy war," jihad is literally translated as "striving" or "struggle." In the Qur'an and in the sayings of the Prophet, it is used in the military context of waging war against unbelievers. Some theologians in Islam's early centuries, and some Muslim reformers in the nineteenth and twentieth centuries, suggested that jihad also should be interpreted as an injunction to wage an inner, spiritual struggle against sin and weak faith rather than solely military conquest for the purpose of spreading the faith. But most Islamic jurists and theologians interpret its original intent as military, as did the Muslim soldiers who conquered lands for Islam under the leadership of the caliphs.

The obligation to wage jihad, whether militarily or peacefully, is grounded in Islam's claim to be a universal religion. For Muslims, Allah's revelations apply not simply to Muhammad and his fellow Arabs but to all humanity. Those who have accepted these revelations are required to work diligently to convert those who remain in error. This obligation remains in force until all peoples have either embraced Islam or come under the rule of Islamic governments. While this struggle lasts, the world is divided into two houses, the House of Faith and the House of Disbelief. Conflict exists between these two

Jihad reflects Islam's claim to universality

houses and will continue until the final triumph of Islam throughout the world. A military interpretation of the commandment of jihad draws a clear, uncrossable line between Muslims and unbelievers and is consistent with the military expansion of Islam's first century. Interpretations that emphasize self-defense, or the individual's spiritual struggle to become holy, have become more prevalent in recent times.

THE CALIPHATE AS EMPIRE. In pursuit of jihad, Abu Bakr began to build an Islamic empire, sending forces in 632 against the Byzantine Empire's frontier posts in Syria and Sasanian Persia's installations in southwestern Mesopotamia. Commanded by Khalid ibn al-Walid (*KAHL-ēd ibn ahl wah-LĒD*), whom the Prophet himself had dubbed "The Sword of Allah," these remarkable fighters, emerging by surprise from the desert wastes on horses and camels, quickly established Islamic rule on non-Arabian soil for the first time. This force, though only a few thousand strong, used the desert to its advantage, withdrawing into it when danger threatened and returning only when it chose.

Islam expands beyond Arabia

In the midst of these military expeditions, Abu Bakr died and was succeeded by his kinsman Umar (634–644), a huge man who was feared and respected rather than loved. Under Umar, Islam's expansion continued (Map 11.3). Two years later, when Khalid's army took the Syrian city of Damascus, the Byzantines in Constantinople realized that this was no typical Arabian raiding party but a serious invasion. Jerusalem fell in 638, and only an outbreak of plague and the formidable mountains of northern Lebanon prevented the Muslims from expanding further. In the same year, another Muslim force attacked Sasanian Persia, conquering it completely by 642 in exploits unmatched since the days of Alexander the Great.

Umar turned next against the Byzantine province of Egypt. Byzantine forces there were defeated in a series of engagements, and the patriarch of Alexandria surrendered the entire province in 642. The Arabians took Tripoli, in Lebanon, the following year. But then geographic challenges—the mountains of northern Lebanon, the unfamiliar deserts of northern Africa (where native Berber warriors held the advantage), and the Iranian plateau—slowed them down. Meanwhile the Byzantine Empire reconquered Alexandria with a naval expedition in 645. Arabs, accustomed to fighting on ships of the desert, now had to learn to fight on ships of the waves. They made the transition, but future conquests took longer than their first ones.

Umar creates a multi-ethnic caliphate

Under Umar the caliphate became an empire composed of many different ethnic groups. In Syria, Persia, and Egypt, he ruled through local officials wherever possible and left agricultural lands in the hands of their owners. Unoccupied lands were awarded to his soldiers, who cultivated them with slaves taken from the conquered peoples. Arabs thus became an elite warrior caste rather than immigrants who assimilated into the peoples and cultures they conquered.

This Islamic empire differed in several ways from the great empires of China, Persia, and Rome. It was significantly larger than any of those realms and too extensive to be governed by one man ruling from one capital. Unable to centralize authority in the caliph, Muslims delegated considerable power to his representatives, or *emirs*, who did not always follow his wishes. Eventually distant lands, such as Egypt and Spain, broke away to form their own caliphates. Most important, the Islamic empire was held together by religious faith, not by centralized authority, as in Persia, or by military superiority, as in Rome.

Map 11.3 Islamic Expansion in Southwest Asia, 632–661

In the century following the death of the Prophet Muhammad, Islamic soldiers poured out of the Arabian Peninsula to conquer lands spanning three continents. Notice that they started with southwest Asia before being blocked in their northwestward expansion by the Byzantine Empire. Spreading the Islamic faith and the Arabic language into the eastern Mediterranean, Mesopotamia, Persia, and the Indus Valley, they forged commercial and cultural connections that endure today. What similarities and differences can you see between the Persian Empire and this new Islamic Empire, which Muslims called a caliphate?

Map legend:
- Under Muhammad, 622–632
- Islamic Expansion, 632–661
- Byzantine Empire
- Territory gained from Byzantine Empire
- → Expansion

The Arabs were set apart not only by their status as conquerors but by their practice of Islam. Their aim was to take the pure truth of Islam to the world, but in the seventh century they did not force conversion on those they conquered. In fact, Christians and Jews in Arabia were permitted freedom of worship, as long as they submitted to Islamic rule. In Persia, Zoroastrians were initially extended these same rights. Umar considered Islam an Arab religion to be practiced by an ethnic elite, the people to whom Muhammad revealed the Qur'an. Those conversions that did occur were immediately suspect, since Muslims were exempt from tribute. There were, of course, entirely legitimate spiritual reasons for conversion. The appeal of Islam's doctrines and rituals was not confined to the Arabian Peninsula. Many of those who converted considered this new faith a distinct improvement over those it displaced.

Islam serves a conquering Arab elite

The Challenge to a Unified Islam

In 644 Umar was assassinated by a Persian slave. The new caliph, Uthman (*UHTH-mahn*), was chosen over his rival Ali by a committee of six Quraysh electors. Both men were sons-in-law of the Prophet. This election was closely contested, and Uthman's victory left a legacy of difficulties. A member of the Umayyad (*oo-MĪ-yahd*) family of Mecca, Uthman openly appointed his relatives to high positions, thereby alienating many high-ranking Muslims. Ali's defeat drove his followers underground and placed the unity of Islam in doubt.

For the time being, warfare held the empire together. In response to the Byzantine reconquest of Alexandria, the Arab governor of Egypt built an Islamic fleet that captured Cyprus in 649, pillaged Sicily three years later, and in 655 moved against Constantinople. But these successes could not save Uthman from the consequences of his favoritism. Exasperated by his relatives, Arab garrisons in Mesopotamia and Egypt intrigued against him, and in 656 Uthman was stabbed to death while reading the Qur'an.

The murder of Uthman provokes a split within Islam

Uthman's murder scandalized the Islamic world. Umar had been killed by a foreign slave bearing a grudge, but the assassins of Uthman were Muslims, including in their ranks a son of Abu Bakr. They were also kinsmen and associates of Ali, who was promptly elected caliph in his own right. Civil war broke out because Uthman's family was now compelled to avenge him, a duty required by Arabian custom. After massacres perpetrated by both sides, Ali was stabbed to death in 661 by one of his former followers. Muawiya (*moo-AH-wē-ah*), a kinsman of Uthman, was elected caliph after persuading Ali's eldest son to renounce his own claim.

Islam divides into Sunnis and Shi'ites

Two major consequences flowed from this sequence of events. First, Muawiya's selection created the Umayyad Caliphate, a succession of caliphs from the same family that presided over nine decades of Islamic expansion. Second, and far more significant in the long term, the *umma* split permanently into two antagonistic groups. The Umayyads and their followers constituted the majority, calling themselves **Sunni** (*SOO-nē*, from the *Sunna* [*SOO-nah*], or traditional practices of the Prophet) and claiming to be the true heirs of Muhammad and the doctrinally pure practitioners of orthodox Islam. The followers of Ali and his line made up the minority, or *Shi'at Ali* (*SHĒ-at ah-LĒ*, "Party of Ali"), calling themselves **Shi'ites** (*SHĒ-īts*).

Doctrinal differences between the two groups were inconsequential in the beginning, but significant differences in practice emerged. For example, Shi'ite Muslims developed a religious hierarchy, while Sunnis did not. In addition, after Hussein (*hoo-SĀN*), second son of Ali and a grandson of Muhammad, led an uprising against the Umayyads in 680 in Iraq and was slain with nearly all his family, Shi'ites developed a sense of persecution and martyrdom that divided them emotionally from the majority.

The Umayyad Caliphate, 661–750

The split between Sunnis and Shi'ites changed the political nature of the Islamic empire. The Party of Ali never gave up asserting that they were the true heirs of the Prophet and that the Sunnis were usurpers. They constituted a minority within the caliphate, but they spread throughout it, preaching opposition to Sunni Islam in North Africa, Egypt, Syria, Mesopotamia, and Iran.

Muawiya was forced to deal with Shi'ite factionalism in his efforts to rebuild the moral authority of the caliphate. To limit fragmentation, he transformed the caliphate into a centralized authority, convincing its leaders to recognize his son Yazid as his successor before his own death. The elective system thereby died out and was replaced by the dynastic principle. Muawiya hoped that this transformation would settle the issue of succession and block the Shi'ites from power. In practice claimants to the title continued to emerge, particularly when the new caliph was very young. Nonetheless, the centralization of authority kept the Umayyads in power until 750 and helped their eventual successors, the Abbasids (*ah-BAH-sids*)—descended from Abbas, one of the Prophet's uncles—rule for a full five centuries.

The Umayyads centralize political authority in Islam

Umayyad Expansion

Factionalism within Islam slowed but did not stop the empire's dynamic expansionism. Its centralized authority continued the drive for conquest. Muawiya had been proclaimed caliph in Jerusalem, but he promptly moved his government to Damascus, from which he could more readily threaten Byzantine power. His forces moved against Constantinople again in 669, blockading it between 673 and 678 but eventually failing, primarily because of the Byzantines' lethal incendiary weapon, Greek Fire. Events farther east were more encouraging: Muslim armies overran eastern Afghanistan in 664 and penetrated western India as far as the lower Indus valley. In North Africa, they reached the eastern border of Algeria by 670. However, in 680, Muawiya's passing led to a Shi'ite rebellion. When the Shi'ite leader Hussein was defeated and killed, Shi'ite hatred for Umayyad rule intensified.

Islam continues to expand

For a time internal difficulties slowed the Islamic advance. In 682 rebellious Muslim forces besieged Mecca and burned the structure housing the Ka'ba. Yazid died that same year, and his son and heir perished several months later. Another branch of the Umayyad family now assumed power, and a new caliph returned to the centralizing policies of Muawiya. All administration and tax collection throughout the empire were now conducted in Arabic, replacing the Greek and Persian languages for administrative purposes. Local officials were replaced by Arabians loyal to the caliphate, and a professional administrative elite replaced tribal chiefs. By 705, the caliphate rested on firmer foundations and was ready to return to conquest.

The wars that began in 705 differed substantively from earlier Islamic campaigns. With the nearby lands of Syria, Mesopotamia, Iran, and Egypt already in the caliphate, campaigns were undertaken in distant places that involved the cooperation of non-Arabian armies. Islamic forces penetrated deep into western India and stormed across northern Africa while preparing for a mammoth, although ultimately unsuccessful, siege of Constantinople. This new expansionist wave not only spread the faith farther from Mecca but also laid the foundation for Islamic commercial dominance throughout the region, linking the trade routes of the Mediterranean Sea, the Red Sea, the Arabian Sea, and the Indian Ocean.

In 711 a mixed expedition of Arabs and Berbers crossed the strait of Gibraltar and invaded Spain. Within four years this army had pushed organized Christian resistance to the northern mountains of Iberia. For the first time Islam was entrenched on the continent of Europe, and the Muslim advance appeared unstoppable. It appeared to be

Islam moves into southwestern Europe

Map 11.4 Islamic Expansion, 661–732

After expanding throughout southwest Asia (Map 11.3), Islamic forces were blocked from entering southeast Europe by the Byzantine Empire. They thereupon swept across North Africa, crossed the strait of Gibraltar, and landed on the Iberian Peninsula in 711. Note that in present-day France, they were defeated at the battle of Tours by a Frankish army headed by Charles Martel. What sort of problems might such a far-flung empire pose for those trying to administer it?

only a matter of time before all of the European kingdoms would fall, after which the Byzantine Empire could be assaulted from Europe as well as Asia.

Collapse of the Umayyad Caliphate

The Franks halt Islam's expansion into Europe

The Islamic impulse had, however, reached its westward limits. Continued Shi'ite claims to the caliphate distracted the empire. Eventually they found support from another branch of the Quraysh, the Abbasids. Although Sunni Muslims, the Abbasid clan advocated the overthrow of the Umayyads and reconciliation between Sunni and Shi'ite. At the same time, a joint Arab-Berber invasion of France was defeated in 732 at the battle of Tours (Map 11.4) by a Frankish army commanded by Charles Martel. Unable to sustain a prolonged campaign so far north of their base in Spain, the invaders retreated south of the Pyrenees, ending a tumultuous century of Muslim expansion.

During that century the Umayyad Caliphate had come to rule immense stretches of territory—from the straits of Gibraltar to the Indus River valley. This political empire had also been unified economically into a Muslim zone of trade and commerce. Culturally, the spiritual principles of Islam and the widespread adoption of the Arabic language glued the far-flung empire together and gave it a sense of religious purpose. Ultimately, the economic and cultural connections forged by a century of Islamic conquest endured long after political unity had crumbled.

Meanwhile the Abbasids were waiting for Umayyad power to decline. By 747 their patience was rewarded. In a ten-year period the Muslims had been defeated by the Khazars (730), the Franks (732), the Turks (738), and the Greeks (740). In addition, the Syrian base of Umayyad rule was running out of soldiers, and the Arabian armies were exhausted. Revolts broke out in Afghanistan, Iran, and Mesopotamia, culminating in the seizure of the caliphate by Abbasid forces in 750. Umayyad rule was over, as was the heroic period of Islamic expansion. The Abbasids would emphasize consolidation over conquest.

Society and Culture in Early Islam

By 750 Islam was the principal belief system of the rulers of a vast empire stretching from Spain in the west, through North Africa to Egypt, including Lebanon, Syria, and the Arabian Peninsula, and east through Mesopotamia, Iran, and Afghanistan into India. Unlike the other two major monotheistic religions, Islam combined a personal relationship with God, a dynamic military impulse, and a political succession based on a family relationship to a divinely inspired prophet. Preaching total submission to the will of God, Islam changed all the societies and cultures it conquered, blending with them to produce an entirely new Islamic society and culture.

Islam connects various peoples into a far-flung empire

Religious Observance: The Mosque

Among the distinctive creations of Islamic culture was the **mosque**, or Islamic house of worship, which architecturally blended the influences of many different societies. Immediately after conquering an area, Muslims marked it as their own by building mosques. Muhammad apparently did not intend to build any sort of temples, emphasizing personal prayer five times a day rather than prayer in communities. But his own home in Medina quickly became sacred space, and the Prophet himself had decided that each such space should orient prayer in the direction of the Ka'ba in Mecca.

Muslims develop a unique house of worship

Mosques include no statues, portraits, or any other depictions of God, angels, or any person living or dead. The interior spaces are simply furnished. There are no chairs or benches for worshipers, and although some mosques contain a pulpit, this feature is not mandated. Walls are covered with artistic geometric designs and with verses from the Qur'an inscribed in Arabic; the rugs that cover the floors are similarly patterned. Minarets, or ornamental towers, are often attached to the sides of mosques so that an Islamic cleric can ascend to call the faithful to prayer at the appointed times of day.

In some cases, Muslims took existing churches in Christian lands they conquered and converted them to mosques. Usually, however, they built new structures, using them to demonstrate the supremacy of Islam over the "old" monotheistic faiths of Judaism

The Dome of the Rock.

The Dome of the Rock connects Islam to Judaism and Christianity

and Christianity. The magnificent Dome of the Rock in Jerusalem, built by an early caliph, served that purpose by establishing an Islamic house of prayer on a site sacred to all three faiths. That place is the traditional site of King David's altar and King Solomon's temple, making it significant to both Jews and Christians. In Islamic tradition, it is the spot on which Abraham was told by God to sacrifice his son Isaac and from which Muhammad rode his horse into heaven during one holy night. Construction of a mosque on such a site carried the obvious implication that Islam had come to replace what it considered ancient and inadequate forms of worship.

Byzantine and Persian motifs were often incorporated into Islamic architecture, not only in mosques but also in other public buildings and private residences. Arabian culture, being primarily desert based, had few architectural styles of its own and readily adopted those from other lands that it found beautiful. Frescoes and mosaics decorated many such buildings. The overall impression of grace, beauty, and harmony is intended to replicate the ideal qualities of the universe as Muslims believe God designed it. Islamic architecture reflected the God-centered nature of Muslim society.

Legal Uniformity: The Shari`ah

The God-centric nature of Muslim society was probably most completely expressed in Islamic law, considered more important than theology to a practicing Muslim. Although pre-Islamic Arabia had no formal legal structure, the roots of the **Shari`ah** (*SHAH-rē-ah*), the Islamic legal code, are to be found there, and Muhammad himself was more an arbitrator, lawgiver, and judge than a theologian or politician. He endorsed many customs common to the pre-Islamic social order and enshrined them in the Shari`ah, a compilation of religiously sanctioned obligations and duties intended to regulate daily life so that men and women might more easily carry out the will of God in the *umma*. Consequently the Shari`ah differs from secular legal systems, which use punishment to achieve social control. Shari`ah, in contrast, prescribes the pathway to paradise.

Islamic law provides a foundation for daily life

Islamic law, in other words, is essentially moral and spiritual, the product of a new religion's concerted effort to turn a nomadic, tribal society away from the things of this world and toward the wishes of God. The Shari`ah accordingly prohibits gambling, intoxication, and the lending of money at interest. It restricts personal revenge and outlaws the blood feud that turned so much of Arabian tribal life into never-ending cycles of murder between rival families. It attempts to strengthen sexual morality and affirm the sanctity of marriage. It provides legal recourse for women, orphans, the disabled, the mentally infirm, the poor, and anyone else who might be termed defenseless within the social structure. In a culture that valued strength, the Shari`ah protected the weak.

Large sections of the Shari`ah are concerned with family life and gender relations. The wife is integrated into her husband's family and guaranteed a portion of his inheritance. Men are required to treat women with honor and respect. The insistence that women be veiled in public and spend much of their lives sequestered in their homes comes not from the Shari`ah but from Byzantine and Persian customs, which are designed in part to promote honor and respect for women. A man may marry as many as four wives, but if he does so, he must treat them equally in terms of financial support, sexual intercourse, household duties, and respect. Women are permitted to practice contraception, initiate divorce proceedings, remarry after divorce, and own property in their own names. Harsh penalties are provided for physical abuse of wives, adultery, and other such crimes.

The Shari`ah was compiled in the eighth, ninth, and tenth centuries C.E. and still forms the basis of civil and criminal law in some Islamic states. It provided legal uniformity throughout the early Islamic world and survived the subsequent deterioration of Islamic caliphates. But altering the Shari`ah in any meaningful way is considered impossible in Islamic society, as Muslims believe it represents the will of God as transmitted by the last and greatest of the prophets.

Thus the same rigidity that helped perpetuate Islamic law's influence also made it increasingly obsolete as Islamic societies modernized and certain traditional practices and beliefs came into question. The status of women under the Shari`ah provides a valid example. While it offered protections for women not available in eighth-century Arabia, it now places women in a position unequal to men. Women may sue for divorce only if they can show cause; a man needs no cause. Women can testify in court, but a man's testimony is weighted more heavily. Women are to be honored and respected but may have only one husband, while a man may have four wives. Penalties for adultery are much more severe for women than for men.

Islamic law treats men and women differently

Tolerance of Other Faiths

Islamic law applied, of course, to all Muslims, and it formed the basis of civil law in all early Islamic states. But not all citizens of such states were Muslims. The dramatic expansion of Islam aimed to convert those unbelievers who were willing to accept Allah's message as delivered by Muhammad, and to subjugate those who would not convert. While conquered peoples were invited and encouraged to embrace Islam, forced conversions were rare and are in fact prohibited by the Qur'an. Non-Muslims were free to practice their religions under conditions imposed by Islamic law, and were required to pay a heavy tax each year. This tax, which was not paid by Muslims, helped underwrite the expenses of the state. Obviously, if everyone converted to Islam, the financial impact on the government would have been negative. That fact made forced conversions both religiously forbidden and fiscally unwise. Tolerance for other creeds was characteristic of most Islamic societies, and Jews in particular often found it more congenial to live under Islamic rule than under Christian governments.

Salat, or ritual worship, mandates a sequence of prayers to be performed five times each day (see page 266).

This level of tolerance, while impressive by the standards of the day, did not mean that people of other faiths accepted Islamic conquest. Christians in particular were horrified at the prospect of domination by rulers practicing a faith they considered heretical. The Byzantine Empire fought desperately to prevent the triumph of Islam, and Charles Martel's victory over the Muslims at Tours caused rejoicing throughout Europe. Although Muslims were required to tolerate other monotheists and treat them decently, they often treated those they conquered with thinly concealed contempt and sometimes with overt hostility. Polytheists and atheists, on the other hand, were barely tolerated, and many converted to Islam in order to improve their condition.

Chapter Review

Putting It in Perspective

As the Umayyad Caliphate passed into history, Islam was only 140 years old. From a set of revelations claimed by an obscure merchant living on a desert peninsula, Islam had evolved into a powerfully attractive monotheistic belief system with many more followers than Judaism or Zoroastrianism and only slightly fewer than Christianity. The Prophet Muhammad had provided a series of ideas that unified the previously fragmented Arabian Peninsula, setting aside tribal rivalries in the name of faith in Allah.

In addition to establishing Arab unity, Islam inspired warriors to spread their faith across thousands of miles of Europe, Africa, and Asia. The new religion offered Spaniards, Berbers, Egyptians, Syrians, Mesopotamians, Persians, Afghans, and many others a set of easily comprehensible beliefs as well as a centralized governing structure that gave Muslims throughout the world a sense of community. The Shari`ah, a complex yet readily accessible religious law, helped ensure legal uniformity throughout the Islamic empire.

In the Golden Age of Islam, just ahead, this dynamic new culture would attain unprecedented heights as a dominant force in much of Africa and most of south Asia.

Reviewing Key Material

KEY CONCEPTS

People of the Book, 263	jihad, 267
Qur'an, 263	Sunni, 270
umma, 265	Shi'ites, 270
five pillars, 265	mosque, 273
caliph, 267	Shar`iah, 274

KEY PEOPLE

Muhammad, 262	Uthman, 270
Khadija, 262	Ali, 270
Abu Bakr, 267	Muawiya, 270
Khalid ibn al-Walid, 268	Hussein, 270
Umar, 268	Charles Martel, 272

ASK YOURSELF

1. How did Islam transcend Arabian tribalism?
2. To what extent were Muhammad's beliefs original? In what ways were they derived from other belief systems familiar to Arabia?
3. Explain Islam's appeal to Arabs and to those they conquered.
4. What was the significance of the office of caliph in Islam's expansion between 632 and 732?
5. How and why do Sunni and Shi'ite Muslims differ?

GOING FURTHER

Armstrong, Karen. *Muhammad: A Biography of the Prophet.* 1992.

Bloom, Jonathan. *Paper Before Print: The History and Impact of Paper in the Islamic World.* 2001.

Bonney, Richard. *Jihad from Qur'an to bin Laden.* 2004.

Denny, Frederick. *An Introduction to Islam.* 1996.

Donner, F. *The Early Islamic Conquests.* 1986.

Esposito, John. *Islam: The Straight Path.* 1998.

al-Hassan, Ahmad, and Donald Hill. *Islamic Technology: An Illustrated History.* 1986.

Hawting, G. *The First Dynasty of Islam.* 1986.

Hitti, Philip. *The Arabs: A Short History.* 1996.

Hourani, Albert. *A History of the Arab Peoples.* 1991.

Ibrahim, Mahmood. *Merchant Capital and Islam.* 1990.

Kennedy, Hugh. *The Prophet and the Age of the Caliphates.* 1986.

Lapidus, Ira. *A History of Islamic Societies.* 2002.

Lewis, Bernard. *The Political Language of Islam.* 1991.

Lombard, M. *The Golden Age of Islam.* 1975.

Ochsenwald, W. *The Middle East: A History.* 2004.

Perry, G. *The Middle East: Fourteen Islamic Centuries.* 1992.

Peters, F. *Muhammad and the Origins of Islam.* 1994.

Renard, John. *Islam and the Heroic Image.* 1994.

Richard, Y. *Shi'ite Islam.* 1994.

Rodinson, Maxime. *Mohammed.* 1971.

Rogerson, B. *The Prophet Muhammad: A Biography.* 2003.

Spellberg, Denise. *Politics, Gender, and the Islamic Past.* 1994.

Watson, Andrew. *Agricultural Innovation in the Early Islamic World.* 1983.

Key Dates and Developments

520 C.E.	Ethiopian incursion into southern Arabia
570	Persian occupation of southern Arabia begins Birth of Muhammad ibn Abd'Allah
610	Muhammad's revelations and the beginning of his preaching
622	The *Hijra*, or emigration from Mecca to Medina of Muhammad and his followers
630	Return of Muhammad to Mecca
632	Death of Muhammad; Caliphate of Abu Bakr (632–634)
634–644	Caliphate of Umar; Muslims take Damascus, Jerusalem, Persia, and Egypt
644–656	Caliphate of Uthman; Muslim naval victories
651	First compilation of the Qur'an
656–661	Caliphate of Ali, marked by blood feuds following Uthman's assassination
661–750	The Umayyad Caliphate, initiated by the murder of Ali; division between Sunni and Shi'ite Muslims
664	Muslim seizure of eastern Afghanistan
670	Muslims' arrival in eastern Algeria
673–678	Blockade of Constantinople
705–715	Islamic conquest of Algeria, Morocco, and Spain
713	Islam in India
732	Umayyad expansion halted by Charles Martel's victory at Battle of Tours
750–1258	The Abbasid Caliphate

Religion and Diversity in the Transformation of Southern Asia, 711–1400

- Islam Expands Eastward
- Islamic Persia and the Abbasid Caliphate
- Cosmopolitan Islam
- The Decline of the Abbasid Caliphate
- The Gupta Empire in India
- The Islamic Impact on India
- India's Influence on Southeast Asia
- Chapter Review

Angkor Wat

The temples of Angkor Wat are reflected in the moat surrounding the temple complex in Siem Reap, Cambodia. Angkor Wat testifies to the influence of Hinduism in portions of Southeast Asia (page 296).

In 711 an Arab ship passed the mouth of India's Indus River, sailing northwest from the island of Ceylon. Laden with spices, silks, and exquisite objects made from metal and jewels, it was bound for a Persian Gulf port at the mouth of the Tigris and Euphrates Rivers. But the ship never arrived at its destination. From an inlet near the Indus, a pirate ship moved swiftly to intercept the Arab craft. The pirates captured the ship, killed the crew, and sailed off to tally the value of their plunder.

Hearing the news, the Umayyad governor awaiting the cargo was furious. How dare these pirates steal from Muslims? The governor probably realized that he could not locate the pirates or recover the cargo, but he could punish the entire region, as a warning that Arab ships were not to be disturbed. He promptly sent 12,000 mounted warriors against the rajahs (kings) of the western Indian region of Sind. Conquest proved easy, and suddenly the Muslims stood on the banks of the Indus, considering how attractive it might be to seize all of India for Islam.

This sequence of events, initiating direct contact between Muslims and Hindus, launched 13 centuries of conflict and connection between practitioners of the two religions.

Buddhism, Hinduism, and Islam Affect South Asia

Islam Expands Eastward

Islam's swift conquests in North Africa and southwestern Asia encouraged its further expansion into Persia, Afghanistan, and India, where its impact was dramatic. The Abbasid Caliphate, which assumed leadership of Islam by overthrowing the Umayyad dynasty in 750, relocated its capital eastward to Baghdad. It then extended its domination over the Iranian plateau and the remains of the Persian Empire. The Abbasids presided over Islam's Golden Age, a flourishing of learning and culture across the Muslim world that, at the time, stretched from west and South Asia across North Africa to Spain. But this vast region was unified only by religion. In the long run, the Abbasids proved no more capable than the Umayyads of imposing centralized governance on such a diverse set of realms and peoples. They themselves fell victim to a series of revolts in outlying provinces, and in 945 a group of Iranian warlords reduced them to the status of a puppet government.

The Abbasids are unable to unify the caliphate politically

Islam was also beginning to penetrate the vast expanses of the Indian subcontinent, which since the collapse of Mauryan rule in 184 B.C.E. had been unified just once, under two centuries of Gupta rule (320–550). The arrival of Islam did not cause disunity but perpetuated it, as Hindus and Muslims persistently fought one another, creating hostility that endures today.

Neither religion was able to prevail over the other, and as India divided between Hindus and Muslims, Hindu priests, Buddhist monks, and energetic merchants carried Indian culture into the mainland societies and islands of Southeast Asia. There a

FOUNDATION MAP 12.1 The Abbasid Caliphate in 800 C.E.

Islam spread so rapidly that its practitioners were unable to develop political institutions that could govern its extensive acquisitions adequately. The Abbasid Caliphate sprawled from Syria to the Indus Valley, but the caliphs never exerted central control over their realm. Notice that their decision to relocate their capital from Damascus eastward to Baghdad testifies both to the importance of the eastern portion of the caliphate and to the difficulty of controlling the western portion. In the absence of political centralization, what techniques could the caliphs use to control their empire?

fascinating set of hybrid cultures emerged, influenced by India yet clearly distinct from the customs and traditions of the subcontinent.

Islamic Persia and the Abbasid Caliphate

The caliphate profits from the Persian-Byzantine wars

The Islamic conquest of Iran was made possible by the decline of Sasanian Persia, which had been weakened by its numerous inconclusive campaigns against the Byzantine Empire. Early in the seventh century the Sasanian King Chosroes (*KAHS-ress*) II attacked the Empire, taking Antioch, Damascus, Jerusalem, and Egypt (Map 12.1). But the Byzantines reconstructed their armies and in 622 launched a devastating drive into the Sasanian lands, burning a magnificent Zoroastrian fire temple in 624 and penetrating Mesopotamia three years later. By 633 both Sasanians and Byzantines were exhausted, and at this precise moment Muslim warriors burst forth from Arabia. The Muslims' timing could not have been less convenient for the Sasanians, who were unable to mount an effective defense. Their armies were defeated by Islamic forces in 636, and their empire collapsed in 642.

Persia's conquest by the Muslims marked a dramatic break with its Zoroastrian religious heritage. Although the new rulers tolerated Zoroastrianism, its followers were subject to discrimination and taxation. Many converted to Islam; others moved to western India near Bombay, where their descendants (called Parsees) remain to this day. A few persevered in remote corners of the Iranian plateau. Politically, the once-glorious Persian Empire was now absorbed into the Islamic empire. Muslim conquest marked the end of historic Persia as a powerful, independent political force.

Persian Influences on Islamic Governance and Culture

Although the Persian Empire had ended, its culture survived in an altered form under the alien Islamic regime. Persian culture blended with Islamic ideas of government to form a distinctive new culture exhibiting both Iranian and Arabian elements.

The Muslims proved just as susceptible as the Greeks to the attractions of eastern forms of governance. Persian kings had exercised centralized powers far beyond those held by local Arabian tribal leaders, and the caliphs promptly adopted as much of that authority as they dared. In particular, the caliphs admired the Persian policy of subordinating the religious authority of Zoroastrian priests to the political will of the emperor. Soon interpreters of Islamic law found themselves overruled by political officials who had subordinated themselves to religious authority during the time of the Prophet but intended to do so no longer. The power of the caliphate grew dramatically in the years following the conquest of Persia. This enhancement of the caliph's authority, coupled with the growing importance of Arabic as a common language, provided a degree of unity in this region of the developing Islamic empire.

Persian influences modify Islam

Arabic, of course, had always been the language of Islam. The *Qur'an* required that Arabic be used for all prayers. Thus all converts had to learn Arabic, and many who did not convert realized that knowledge of that language was essential for dealing with their new masters. But the Persian language did not disappear, as Arabs were enchanted by its richness and beauty. Poets and scholars who wrote in Arabic began to adopt Persian expressions, imagery, and syntax; Persian plot lines found their way into Arabic folktales; Persian vocabulary supplemented and enriched spoken Arabic. The result was an Arabic language that grew beyond its roots in the Arabian Peninsula to become a cosmopolitan tongue that Islamic conquerors could use to enhance their influence in Southwest Asia.

The Impact of Shi'ite Opposition

The conquest of Persia took place within the context of the great Sunni-Shi'ite split, which divided the Islamic world after 661. Refusing to accept the Sunni leadership of the Umayyad caliphs, who set up their government in Damascus, Persian Shi'ites had made great progress preaching their beliefs on the Iranian Plateau. This made it impossible for the Umayyads to impose an Islamic Peace on their vast holdings. This failure annoyed merchants, who depended on political stability for their commerce to prosper.

Shi'ites undermine
the caliphate

The people of Persia suffered from additional grievances. Non-Muslims in Iran were required to pay a special tax as the price of religious toleration. Upon conversion, this tax was supposed to disappear, but the Umayyad government, unable to balance its accounts, was reluctant to lift this burden from Persian converts. Moreover, the caliphate inexplicably refused to reinvest any of the income it derived from taxes in Persia itself, where arid conditions required constant, expensive irrigation. These grievances fueled a revolution in 747, led by a man who called himself Abu Muslim. His real name and ancestry are unknown, but his rhetorical and political skills energized Persian malcontents and attracted Shi'ite Arab dissenters.

Abbasids use Persian
connections to
overthrow the
Umayyads

The resulting turmoil squeezed the Umayyads between two angry groups, a situation that worked to the Abbasids' advantage when they overthrew the Umayyads in 750. The Abbasid revolt, which had begun in a northeastern Persian province in 747, was led by Muslims loyal to the family of a man named Abbas, an uncle of the Prophet Muhammad. Its success aided by uprisings in Persia, the Abbasid Caliphate took care to look after the needs of this province. Persia suddenly benefited from tax revenues, and Persian influence rose at the Abbasid court. Although they were themselves Sunni Muslims, the Abbasids strove to placate Persian Shi'ites, hoping perhaps to heal the century-old schism within the Islamic world or at least to ensure their continued domination of that world.

The Rise of Baghdad

The Abbasids reorient
the caliphate eastward

The Abbasids also shifted the focus of the Islamic world eastward. The gateways to Europe through Constantinople and southern Africa through Ethiopia were barred by Christian states hostile to Islam. Northern Asia was mountainous and cold, filled with wolves and unfriendly Turkic tribes. Opportunity for Islamic expansion clearly lay in the east. In 763 the caliphate moved its capital east to a new city, which it built on the site of a tiny village known as Baghdad. Located in eastern Mesopotamia near the site of ancient Babylon, Baghdad's founding embodied the Abbasid transfer of emphasis from western to eastern Islam.

The caliphate's decision to relocate was considered carefully. In addition to being close to the eastern Islamic lands, Baghdad was strategically located at the juncture of the trade routes connecting Syria, Mesopotamia, and Persia. It had easy access to the Tigris and Euphrates rivers in one of the most fertile areas of Mesopotamia. Favored by its location, Baghdad quickly became the largest urban area in the history of western Asia, populated in the early 800s by somewhere between 300,000 and 500,000 people. By comparison, Constantinople at that point contained about 200,000 people. Baghdad proved to be central to the development not only of the Abbasid Caliphate but of Islamic civilization.

Cosmopolitan Islam

Islam now developed a prosperous, cosmopolitan civilization. The Islamic faith had originated in the Arabian Peninsula, grounded in local Arab customs and culture. Its explosive century of expansion, however, had exposed it to a broad variety of ethnic and linguistic groups across southern Asia. For the leadership of Islam, a religion that claimed universality, the next step was both obvious and challenging: it must grow beyond its Arabian origins. To do so, it would have to reach out to people of diverse ancestries, offering them a path to salvation and combining their backgrounds and cultures into a new civilization that would be greater than the sum of its parts. To do otherwise would limit Islam's appeal, restricting it to an ethnic Arabian elite, denying its claim to worship the one true God of all humanity, and perpetuating it as a conquering rather than a constructing faith.

Baghdad enabled the Abbasids to take that next step. They made Islam a universal religion and inspired a golden age of Islamic civilization. Cosmopolitan and diverse, Baghdad welcomed Arabians, Mesopotamians, Syrians, Persians, Indians, Egyptians, Central Asians, Christians, Zoroastrians, Jews, and many others. In this new, vibrant city these people were assimilated into a new, vibrant civilization built on a self-confident, dynamic faith that offered spiritual equality to all who embraced it. Growing into a major industrial and commercial center, Baghdad provided jobs for all who sought them and ample revenues to sustain Abbasid ambitions.

Islam becomes a universal faith

Abbasid Governance

Chief among Abbasid ambitions was correcting the errors of the Umayyads. While the Umayyads had reserved influential positions for Arabs, the Abbasids sought to advance talented people, regardless of ethnicity, to positions of responsibility. The government at Baghdad recruited personnel from throughout the empire with the promise of equality of opportunity in a large empire serving a universal faith. The privileges and elite status long enjoyed by Arabs were abolished. Jews served the caliphate as bankers and financial advisors; Persians as bureaucrats and scribes; Mesopotamian Christians as engineers and diplomats.

Abbasids utilize all conquered peoples

Although Arabs supervised all these groups, they were Arabs completely devoted to the Abbasid regime. Loyalty to the caliph was more important than ethnic ancestry. The exclusively Arab armies were replaced by a skilled force of paid professional soldiers of mixed ethnic background. No longer needed for conquest, they were assigned to maintain internal order, patrol the frontiers, and keep watch on the Byzantine Empire. Their leadership was still Arabian, but their most important characteristic was loyalty.

The inner city of Baghdad c.800

A sketch of the inner city of Baghdad around the year 800 C.E.

The Abbasids built on governmental foundations laid by the Umayyads, particularly their centralization of authority. Control was maintained by the Caliph and his advisors. Government bureaus collected taxes, kept records, handled correspondence, and disbursed tax revenues. Judges were charged with applying the Shari`ah, or Islamic law (Chapter 11), to everyday life in every corner of the realm. A *wazir* (*WAH-zēr*) supervised and coordinated the entire politico-legal system in Baghdad. Governors closely tied to the caliph's family ruled outlying provinces with degrees of loyalty proportionate to their distance from the capital. As messages had to be transmitted slowly across the caliphate by either camel or ship, the caliph's operational authority dwindled significantly on the remote fringes of the empire. Although fully centralized political control eluded the Abbasids, the overall extent of centralization in the caliphate was impressive.

Commerce and Culture in the Abbasid Caliphate

The administrative stability of the Abbasid era also promoted significant commercial and cultural achievements. Abbasid caliphs nurtured trade routes that crossed both Asia and Africa, while in the caliphate itself they fostered literature and the arts.

Muslims promote
commerce and trade

Perhaps because Muhammad himself had been a merchant, commercial activity was generally held in higher esteem in Islamic lands than it was in either Christian Europe or Confucian China. The Abbasid caliphs, eager to increase both their own immense wealth and the prosperity of the lands they ruled, lowered trade barriers, promoted the work of artisans and merchants, and encouraged long-distance commerce. A vast network of trade routes stretched by land across both Central Asia and the Sahara Desert, and by water across the Mediterranean and the Red and Arabian seas. Products widely traded included Chinese silks and Indian spices; gold, salt, slaves, and ivory from Africa; steel and leather from Spain; and magnificent hand-woven carpets and textiles from southern and western Asia. Banking and credit helped to finance expensive commercial enterprises. The widespread use of the Arabic language eased business transactions, and Arabic numerals simplified and standardized bookkeeping.

Islamic culture prospers
under the Abbasids

Eager to imitate the Indo-Persian civilizations, which they considered superior to that of the Arabian Peninsula, the Abbasids led their empire into a spectacular cultural renaissance. The Caliph Harun al-Rashid (*hah-ROON al rah-SHĒD*), who ruled from 786 to 809, built a magnificent palace that reflected both his astonishing wealth and his reputation as a generous patron of the arts. He brought to Baghdad authors, artists, architects, and entertainers from as far away as Morocco in North Africa and Delhi in India, and they made the city a radiant cultural center. Harun's son established in Baghdad an academy called the House of Wisdom. There some scholars translated ancient Greek, Latin, and Sanskrit writings into Arabic, while others laid the foundation for the devotion to keen observation and objective thinking that became characteristic of Arab scientific and intellectual life.

From the eighth through the twelfth centuries, Islamic learning blossomed. In philosophy, Muslims such as Ibn Sina (*ib-un SĒ-nah*), later known in Europe as Avicenna, translated and wrote commentaries on the works of the ancient Greek philosopher Aristotle, which at this time were unknown in the West. Ibn Sina was also inspired by the discovery of Indian and Greek writings on medicine, which he and other Muslims translated, compiled, explained, and amplified. The Persian scholar al-Khwarizmi (*al kwa-RIZ-mē*) analyzed the findings of various classical thinkers, including Claudius Ptolemy, whose detailed conception of an earth-centered universe was later revised by other Muslims, including Ibn al-Haytham (*ib-un al-hī-THAHM*) and Nasir al-Din al-Tusi (*nah-SEER al-dēn al-TOO-si*). Ptolemy's view of the universe, as modified by Muslim scholars, prevailed until the seventeenth century both in the Islamic world and in the West.

A page from a twelfth-century Islamic manuscript dealing with alchemy.

Muslims develop
navigational and
scientific instruments

Inspired by their contacts with India and China, Muslims under the caliphate also proved to be talented innovators. For example, they developed the quadrant, the astrolabe, the celestial globe, and other instruments of navigation. Most of these had been invented by other peoples, but Muslims refined and used them to great advantage. Muslims also excelled at physics and optics, and they developed windmills, watermills, water-clocks, new methods of irrigation, and instruments used in meteorology. Applying Persian and Indian mathematics, al-Khwarizmi devised both algebra and the Arabic numerals that are universally used today.

Muslims use durable
paper to record and
preserve knowledge

The production of paper provides an excellent example of Islamic development of an earlier invention. Paper had been invented in China sometime between 200 and 50 B.C.E. When the Muslims encountered this product, they found that it was made of wood-based

Document 12.1 Quatrains from *The Rubaiyat*

Omar Khayyam's collection of quatrains, or four-line poetic stanzas, was translated from Omar's elegant Persian into English by Edward FitzGerald in 1859. This translation made the work accessible to Western readers, and it has since been translated into more than one hundred languages. Omar was a master of astronomy, history, jurisprudence, mathematics, medicine, and philosophy as well as poetry. *The Rubaiyat* reveals his fatalistic fascination with questions of eternal interest: Who are we? Why are we here? Where are we going? What is the nature of our relationship to God?

The moving finger writes; and, having writ,
Moves on; nor all your piety nor wit
Shall lure it back to cancel half a line,
Nor all your tears wash out a word of it.

Oh, threats of hell and hopes of paradise!
One thing at least is certain: **this** life flies.
One thing is certain and the rest is lies:
The flower that once has blown forever dies.

fibers derived from tropical plants like bamboo, hemp, and jute. Papers made from these fibers were not particularly durable, and since these plants did not grow in Islamic lands, Muslims looked for new sources of fiber. They began to use rags made from linen or from cotton cloth, which produce paper that is extremely durable. In 794, the first Islamic paper mill was built in Baghdad. Soon the availability of this paper throughout Muslim lands encouraged scholarly writing in virtually every area of knowledge. Paper made it possible for Muslims to preserve, and eventually transmit, Greek and Byzantine knowledge and culture. When Europe first came into contact with this Islamic knowledge base in the twelfth century, its scholars were both impressed and intimidated.

Works of fiction and folklore also flourished in this era. The most famous of these was probably *The 1,001 Nights*, also known in the West as *The Arabian Nights*. Embellished over the centuries, this assortment of fanciful and fantastic fables eventually came to include such well-known adventure stories as "Sinbad the Sailor" and "Aladdin and His Magic Lamp." Of the many marvelous works of poetry produced in this period, among the best known is *The Rubaiyat*, a collection of verses originally composed around 1100 by a famous scientist and mathematician named Omar Khayyam (see "Quatrains from *The Rubaiyat*").

A Muslim astronomer's depiction of the constellation Sagittarius, copied from the original manuscript in 1730.

Sufis and Fundamentalists

Not everyone in the caliphate participated in the economic and cultural achievements of Islam's Golden Age. Many devout Muslims worried that the Age's emphasis on material prosperity, its encouragement of artistic expression, and its wide-ranging intellectual efforts were undermining the simplicity and spirituality of their faith. As various groups sought different ways to revitalize Islam and return it to its roots, several distinct responses emerged.

One was **Sufism** (*SOO-fizm*). Deriving from Persian influence on Shi'ism, Sufism was a mystic strain of Islam that advocated direct union with God through prayer, contemplation, and religious ecstasy. Sufism developed gradually during the first three centuries of Islamic history. In its early stages, it was characterized by rejection of the

Islamic mysticism seeks direct connection with God

luxury and wealth that Islam had come to emphasize under the influences of Persia and Byzantium. Sufism favored a simple lifestyle, recalling the devout Muslim to the origins of the faith on the austere deserts of the Arabian peninsula. In Arabic, *suf* (*SOOF*) means "wool," and Sufis (*SOO-fēz*) wore rough woolen clothing, obviously uncomfortable in the Middle Eastern heat, to symbolize their renunciation of worldly pleasures, a renunciation also practiced by Buddhist and Christian mystics and monks. Later Sufism also came to involve the pursuit of a mystical union with God through elaborate dances and ceremonies. Sufi doctrines varied widely as different brotherhoods of Sufis developed. One principal tradition was centered in Mecca and another in northeastern Persia, although Sufi brotherhoods also became common in India.

Sufism and fundamentalism offer alternatives to Abbasid materialism

Another response to the materialism of the Abbasid Caliphate was the growth of militant Islamic fundamentalism. Unlike the Sufis, who strove mainly to withdraw from the secular world, the fundamentalists sought to combat and repress it. In general, fundamentalists believed that Islam itself had become corrupted by secular influences, and that purification of the Muslim community, or *umma*, was necessary to restore fidelity to the original revelations of Allah transmitted through Muhammad. Like Sufism, Islamic fundamentalism took a wide variety of forms, including Wahhabism, which eventually became the dominant form of Islam on the Arabian Peninsula.

Fundamentalists oppose modern developments

Inspired by a deep suspicion of intellectual pursuits, the fundamentalists who led eleventh-century Spain exiled both the great Muslim scholar-physician Ibn Rushd (*ib-un ROOSHD*), known in the West as Averröes, and the Jewish philosopher Moses Maimonides (*mī-MAH-nih-dēz*), charging them with polluting the Qur'an by trying to reconcile it with modern philosophy. Later Islamic governments in Spain appointed religious courts, instructing them to enforce the Shari`ah against any attempts at secularization.

Fundamentalist resistance to secularization fostered a climate of intellectual repression. As Islamic scientific and technological curiosity was submerged in a rising tide of fundamentalist religious fervor, Islam was poorly prepared to face the cultural and military challenges soon to be posed by the West.

The Decline of the Abbasid Caliphate

Like all the large empires before them, the Abbasids found their vast territory difficult to rule. Communication over the thousands of miles separating Spain from Baghdad was challenging enough under the best of circumstances. Quarrels between rival leaders, disputes between Sunni and Shi'ite Muslims, and tensions between various ethnic groups also interfered with the ability of the Abbasids to govern effectively and frustrated their dream of conquering the world for Islam.

Forces of Disintegration

The glory of Islamic learning could not obscure the disintegration of the caliphate, which set in even before its consolidation was complete. First, Harun al-Rashid (786–809), the most powerful of the caliphs, unintentionally weakened his own system. In attempting to ensure that his older son would succeed him as caliph, he gave his younger son, al-Mamun, a governorship in northeastern Persia. But Al-Mamun used this position to challenge his older brother, initiating four years of civil strife. Al-Mamun won, but the conflict alienated Mesopotamia and the Abbasid armies, both of which had supported the older son. Legitimate succession, a vexing problem in Islamic states since the death of Muhammad's son-in-law Ali, proved to be the first problem to erode the strength of the Abbasids.

Second, al-Mamun gained the crucial backing of the Persian prince Tahir (*TAH-hēr*) only by making Tahir hereditary governor of northeastern Persia. This grant of authority undermined the Abbasid drive for centralization. It also helped create a warlord nobility that rivaled and eventually replaced the caliph and provided a focus for Persian Shi'ite opposition to the Sunni regime in Baghdad.

Third, to increase their power the Abbasids established armies of Turkish slaves from central Asia called Mamluks (*MAM-lukes*). These male slaves, purchased before they turned 13, were converted to Islam and segregated in military barracks. There they studied military tactics, developed loyalty and comradeship, and after several years, became soldiers in the caliph's armies. In theory, every Mamluk was a disciplined servant of the state, without ties to family or region; his loyalty was to the caliph and the army. In practice, Mamluks fought for the caliph only so long as he paid them well and proved a competent leader. Failure in either respect could easily lead to his overthrow, as Mamluks quickly became the state's most efficient warriors. They antagonized the people of Baghdad, most of whom considered them uncivilized foreigners, so the caliphs built a new capital at Samarra (*sah-MAR-rah*) in Mesopotamia in 836 and took the Mamluks with them. The move solved one problem but created another by eroding the caliphate's authority.

The Abbasid Caliphate decays

Finally, a growing disloyalty in the Abbasid bureaucracy accelerated the caliphate's decline. Dominated by factions based on family ties and cronyism, the bureaucrats began to peddle their services and influence to the highest bidders. As the caliphs became less able to maintain control of the central government, discontented factions in outlying areas took advantage of the situation and revolted. In the ninth century, unrest broke out in Egypt, Mesopotamia, and Iran. Occasionally the caliphs were able to restore order, but only through the use of the unpopular Mamluks. As the authority of the central administration disintegrated, the empire itself collapsed.

The Mosque of Ibn Tulun, Cairo.

Although the last caliph did not leave the throne until his murder by the Mongols in 1258, the tenth century marked the end of effective Abbasid rule. One by one, provinces of the empire had broken away. Egypt was taken over by a Mamluk family in 868 and then by the Shi'ite Fatimid dynasty in 969. The governor of Islamic Spain created his own independent caliphate in 929, confirming a separation that had actually begun much earlier. A mass revolt of frontier troops that could not be repressed resulted in the loss of Persia in the ninth century. By 935 the Abbasid caliph had lost control of every province outside the immediate vicinity of Baghdad. After a power struggle lasting nearly a decade, the Buyid (*BOO-yid*) dynasty of Shi'ite Persian warlords seized control of Baghdad in 945. The caliphs were allowed to remain as puppet rulers, but they exercised no authority. The glorious era of Abbasid rule was over.

Abbasid power ends in the tenth century c.e.

Continuity of Islamic Unity and Expansion

Political fragmentation did not, however, destroy the unity of Islam. Despite its multitude of rulers and cultures, the Muslim community was still held together by Shari'ah and the Qur'an. Islamic law provided a code of conduct that differentiated Muslims from all other

Muslims preserve unity through scripture, language, and law

peoples, giving them a common identity. Stipulations that the Qur'an must be read only in Arabic helped to make that language a common means of communication—and a unifying force—across different Muslim cultures. Finally, the pilgrimage to Mecca, a common practice in pre-Islamic Arabia that Muhammad eventually required of all believers, also helped to create cohesion.

The pilgrimage symbolized the equality of all Muslims in the context of their complete submission to Allah. Pilgrims were greeted at the outskirts of Mecca, where they exchanged their clothing for simple white robes in which they entered the holy city. During the entire seven days of the pilgrimage, no distinctions of birth, race, wealth, or position separated one Muslim from another. All wore the same white robes, performed the same rituals, and professed the same unworthiness in the sight of Allah. The pilgrimage also promoted contacts and common values among Muslim pilgrims from diverse cultures, inspiring them to foster these values in their native lands.

Nor did political division put an end to Islamic expansion. Indeed, even as the caliphate declined and the various Muslim factions fought against each other, Islamic faith and Islamic armies were penetrating into India, clashing with the ancient cultures of that immense subcontinent.

An Islamic schematic world map, dating from the Abbasid caliphate and showing the Ka'ba at the center of the world.

The Gupta Empire in India

After the end of the Mauryan Empire in 184 C.E., India remained divided among several states, a subcontinent whose cultural pluralism seemed both the reflection and the principal cause of its political disunity. Then the unexpected happened: a relatively unknown Indian family reunified the north and created the Gupta Empire (320–550), the first centralized Hindu state.

Gupta Rule and Achievements

The Gupta family came from northeastern India, where they controlled the Barabar (*bah-RAH-bur*) Hills, rich in high-quality iron ore. This guaranteed them an ample resource for swords and shields and a favorable cash flow. The dynasty's founder, Chandra Gupta I (320–335), was not related to the man of the same name who established the Mauryan Empire, and little is known about him. The actual architect of the Gupta Empire was Chandra's son, Samudra (*sah-MOO-drah*) Gupta, whose 40-year rule (335–375) gave northern India its first centralized monarchy since the Mauryans five centuries earlier.

Samudra Gupta was encouraged by his father to rule the entire known world. He fell short of that lofty goal but did manage to overthrow no fewer than 20 regional Indian kings, and in the process he gained control of both the Indus and Ganges river valleys. He also conquered several states on the central Deccan Plateau, but chose to rule those kingdoms through vassals. In turn his son, Chandra Gupta II (375–415), extended the empire's power by expelling the Scythians from west central India (Map 12.2). The new empire then exercised direct authority over port cities on the Arabian Sea, enabling it to profit handsomely from trade with western and southeastern Asia. Neither Samudra Gupta nor Chandra Gupta II had any success in subduing the independent Tamil states of south

The Gupta dynasty unifies northern India

India. The size of the subcontinent, as always, posed a formidable obstacle to any would-be unifiers.

Chandra Gupta II is known more for the stability of his reign than for his military success. Accounts by both Hindus and Buddhists describe a period of religious tolerance and peace across northern India, signs of a rare social stability. The Guptas, although Hindus themselves, not only tolerated Buddhists and Jains but also subsidized their religious temples and monasteries. During this time spiritual, artistic, and philosophical culture flowered. Magnificent Hindu temples were constructed throughout the subcontinent, setting the tone for Indian architecture for centuries to come, and a number of schools of classical Hindu philosophy were established. Of these schools, **yoga**, which emphasizes meditation and self-knowledge, is the most widely known and practiced in the West.

The Guptas' preference for Hinduism affected more than philosophy and architecture in northern India. It also affected gender relations. From the Persians, Hindus had adopted **purdah** (*PURR-dah*), the seclusion of married women through their confinement to certain rooms of the house. Under this custom a respectable woman could show her face only within the family, and she had to wear a thick veil when going out in public. In northern India the custom became so vigorous that to ask after the health of a man's wife might be considered impolite. Purdah was not, however, imposed upon Buddhists or Jains, and even Hindus were free to modify it according to local custom.

Map 12.2 The Gupta Empire in 413 C.E.

India's size and topography (Map 3.1) deterred centralization, so unified governments were often confined to particular geographic subdivisions of the subcontinent. Note that early in the fourth century C.E., the Gupta Empire unified much of northern India from its base on the Gangetic Plain. Although not as large as the Mauryan Empire (Map 3.4), the Gupta Empire received tribute from areas like the Indus Valley and Nepal, bringing a degree of stability to most of India north of the Deccan Plateau. Why would governments in northern India find it difficult to expand their control southward?

The spiritual and artistic development characteristic of Gupta India was rooted in material prosperity and wealth. Trade with the West flourished, particularly with Byzantium and Rome. Indian perfumes, spices, ivory, and wood were prized in Europe. When Alaric the Goth besieged Rome in 408, part of his ransom for withdrawing his forces included 3,000 pounds of Indian pepper. But commerce with the East was even more extensive and profitable. China coveted Indian ivory, brass, cotton cloth, and unusual animals like mongooses and elephants; in return the Indians received Chinese amber, silk, and oils. Some of the trade went by sea, but ocean routes were vulnerable to weather and pirates; camel caravans traveling the Silk Road through Central Asia were far more likely to arrive intact. In the late Gupta era, however, the opening of trade with resource-rich Southeast Asia made the sea passage worth the risk.

Guptas connect far-flung regions commercially

At home, Gupta prosperity was based on agriculture, which was productive enough to enable peasants to pay significant taxes-in-kind (a portion of their harvest). The subcontinent's climate and soil supported good harvests of wheat, rice, citrus and noncitrus fruits, and sugarcane. Because of Hindu religious prohibitions, Indians rarely ate meat, but dairy products were widely available, and fish constituted a staple in the south. The main obstacle to agriculture was weather, especially the periodic flooding in the Bay of Bengal and long periods of intense heat requiring irrigation. But famine was rare in Gupta India. The government supplemented tax revenues through ownership of all metal and salt mines, which provided a steady, substantial income.

Conflict and Collapse

Chandra Gupta II was followed by Kumara (*kuh-MAH-rah*) Gupta, whose 40-year reign (415–455) witnessed the first signs of trouble. The Central Asian migrations continued, and this time it was not the Scythians but the Huns who came calling. They were a particularly dangerous breed of Central Asian nomads: violent, ruthless fighters who killed frequently and indifferently. Kumara Gupta blocked them at the Khyber (*KĪ-burr*) Pass in the mountains between northern India and Central Asia, through which nomadic tribes seeking the more fertile lands of South Asia had long traveled. This success enabled him to hand the empire intact to his son Skanda Gupta but not to preserve it. Throughout Skanda Gupta's reign (455–467) the Huns were a constant menace, and the treasury could scarcely bear the strain of holding them back.

The Gupta Empire collapses under pressure from the Huns

Once the Huns penetrated northern India, other nomadic tribes followed, disrupting Gupta trade with Central Asia and severely reducing the empire's income. Economic setbacks combined with Hun aggression caused north Indian political unity to crumble. The Huns took the Punjab in 499, conquering Kashmir and most of the plain of the Ganges River shortly thereafter. The Gupta Empire collapsed by 550.

The Huns were not interested in replacing the Gupta Empire with one of their own. They were restless warriors, not empire builders. As the north Indian empire shattered into a series of independent kingdoms, the Huns were content to collect tribute. Some kingdoms paid, while others ignored the Huns and were ignored by them, as was the case in eastern Europe.

Centralized control existed nowhere in the subcontinent. In south India, the Tamil states disappeared, and authority was divided between forest-based tribes and valley-based villagers, both of which were ruled by warrior aristocracies. India drifted in this way for nearly two centuries, with most of its people oblivious to issues of state control and foreign threats. Then came Islam.

The Islamic Impact on India

Islam's initial venture into India occurred almost by accident. The piracy of an Umayyad ship in 711, described at the beginning of this chapter, led directly to Muslim invasion and occupation of the Sind in western India. Those actions established a contact between Muslims and Hindus that altered the economic and cultural frameworks of the Indian subcontinent. Eventually India became part of a sprawling Indian Ocean Islamic trading network, while conflict between Hindu polytheists and Muslim monotheists divided the region for centuries.

Islamic Invasions from Persia

After 711, Muslim raids from the Sind devastated the northern Indian region of Gujarat (*guh-jah-RAHT*), temporarily provoking a unified defense. Northern India successfully resisted further Islamic invasions until 998 when a new threat emerged, this time from Persia.

By this time Persia was divided among three groups of Muslim warlords. The Buyids, who had conquered Baghdad and subordinated the Abbasid caliphs in 945, ruled Mesopotamia and western Persia from then until 1055; the Samanids (*sah-MAH-nids*) controlled eastern Persia from 819 to 999; and the Ghaznavids (*gaz-NAH-vids*) dominated northeastern Persia and Afghanistan from 962 until 1040 (Map 12.3). Baghdad's fall in 945 had opened the frontiers between the Middle East and Central Asia to nomadic Turkish tribes that crossed between these regions at will. In the eleventh century, one of these tribes, the Seljuk (*SELL-jook*) Turks, took both Persia and Anatolia from the weakened Abbasids, adding Turkish customs and genes to an already simmering stew of ethnicities.

The Buyids of western Persia legitimized themselves by propping up the caliphs and then governed like the warlords they were. In eastern Persia, the Samanids tried to replicate the early Abbasid bureaucracy. They presided over a cultural renaissance centered on the city of Bukhara (*boo-KAH-rah*), in which Arabic literary and legal forms blended

Muslims invade India from the west

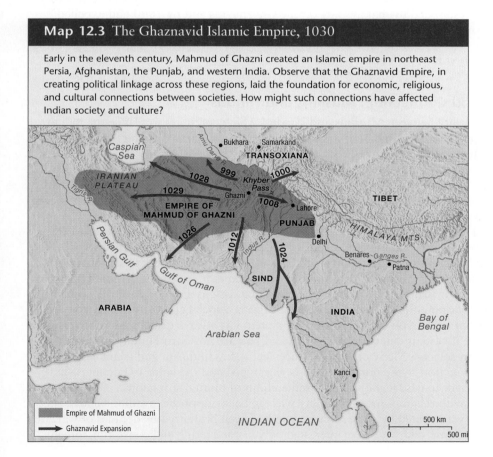

Map 12.3 The Ghaznavid Islamic Empire, 1030

Early in the eleventh century, Mahmud of Ghazni created an Islamic empire in northeast Persia, Afghanistan, the Punjab, and western India. Observe that the Ghaznavid Empire, in creating political linkage across these regions, laid the foundation for economic, religious, and cultural connections between societies. How might such connections have affected Indian society and culture?

with Persian, and Farsi joined Arabic as a language of transmission for Islamic culture. Finally, in northeastern Persia and Afghanistan, the Ghaznavid government of Mamluks took control of both state and bureaucracy, creating a hybrid Persian-Islamic culture while attacking every non-Islamic area within reach. The most attractive area was India.

Mahmud of Ghazni connects Persia, Afghanistan, and India

The Ghaznavids took their name from the Afghan city of Ghazni, just west of the Khyber Pass. From that stronghold they could plunder the trade routes between India and southwestern Asia. Between 998 and 1030 Mahmud of Ghazni (*MAH-mood of GAZ-nē*), known as the "Sword of Islam," led 17 raids on the northwestern Indian region of Punjab. He pillaged its cities remorselessly, destroying magnificent Hindu temples (whose idols, from his Islamic viewpoint, were abominations) and confiscating every jewel, coin, and woman he could find. This plunder enriched Ghazni, which quickly became a major cultural center of the Islamic world. Its glittering mosques and palaces were heavily influenced by Persian architectural concepts. But the empire was founded on bloodshed, rape, and destruction, all carried out in the name of God and in the interest of profit.

An extensive cave/temple complex near present-day Mumbai.

Shortly before his death in 1030, Mahmud annexed the Punjab. The Ghaznavid dynasty now controlled all of northwestern India, including the Indus Valley. But in Ghazni the political situation was deteriorating. Ignoring the advice of his Persian counselors, Mahmud had permitted the Seljuk Turks to use grazing pastures in Ghaznavid territory. The Seljuks responded by making war on the Ghaznavids and by 1040 had expelled them from northeastern Persia. Leaving that region to their enemies, the Ghaznavids relocated to northwestern India, which they plundered relentlessly while generating hatred and bitterness within the Hindu population.

Conflict and Connection: Muslims and Hindus

The deep hostility between Muslims and Hindus, which continues to plague the Indian subcontinent today, is rooted both in the behavior of the Ghaznavids and in religion itself. There was little compatibility between these two belief systems. Islam's rigorous, uncompromising monotheism holds that there is only one God and that all human beings must subordinate themselves to his will in every act of daily life. To Muslims, Hinduism, with its vast number of gods and goddesses, is simply polytheistic idolatry. To Hindus, however, the Muslims' monotheistic conviction is both presumptuous and preposterous.

Muslims and Hindus confront one another in India

Beyond this fundamental fissure, Islam asserts the essential equality and unworthiness of all people who stand before Allah. This view, grounded in ancient Arab tribal customs, gives any Muslim the right to address even the most exalted leader as an equal. Hinduism, in contrast, is based on a rigid caste system that reinforces inequality between different levels of society. To Muslims, a system that assigns a majority of the population to lifelong discrimination is offensive. Since a caste is a social class into which you are born and from which you cannot move, this system has always discouraged conversion to Hinduism: if caste is determined by birth and you are not born Hindu, how can you fit into Indian society? Many other differences between Hinduism and Islam exist, but these two distinctions—the number of gods worshiped and the value of equality—have proved sufficient to ensure more than a millennium of mutual suspicion.

Ghaznavids persecute Hindus in India

Coupled with religious incompatibility was the behavior of the invading Ghaznavids. Their regime was created by slave soldiers who had been brutalized by decades of warfare with Central Asians and who were interested only in conquering and converting foreign peoples, not in assimilating them. Considering Hindus' polytheism, they placed little value on Indian culture, customs, art, or architecture, much of which they destroyed. The Hindus understandably judged all Muslims by the conduct of the Ghaznavids and fought back, often, for example, setting fire to Islamic mosques and burning the worshipers alive.

Consequently, the basic incompatibility between Islam and Hinduism was intensified by atrocities and persecutions on both sides. Yet despite this hostility, from the tenth century onward, Hindus and Muslims shared the subcontinent. Eyeing each other warily, they maneuvered for position. The Ghaznavids retained the advantage until 1186, when they were ejected by another Islamic Turkish tribe, the Ghurids (*GUR-ids*). Hindus put up fierce resistance against the Ghurids, having learned in the eleventh century exactly what Islamic occupation meant for their families and their culture. Buddhists suffered even more than Hindus, in part because their faith's rejection of violence made them reluctant to resist aggression, in part because, like Islam, their faith sought converts and Muslims viewed it as competitive. The Ghurids destroyed Buddhist monasteries throughout India, driving the faith from its native soil. While flourishing in exile in Tibet, Japan, China, and Southeast Asia, Buddhism did not return to India with any significant presence until the 1950s, when India was unified under a secular democracy that granted toleration to all faiths (Chapter 35).

Despite Hindu resistance, the Ghurids eventually triumphed, establishing what came to be known as the Delhi Sultanate. From 1206 to 1526, a succession of sultans tackled the challenge of consolidating an Islamic regime in a region dominated by Hindu culture and beliefs. The result was a society combining both Indian and Islamic characteristics. Although at first the Delhi Sultanate leveled Hindu temples and sought conversions, it soon changed course, staking its stability on values that Hindus and Muslims could share, including loyalty to kings, strong relationships between patrons and clients, and virtues such as service and honor. Delhi's ruling elite was primarily Islamic, but meritorious or wealthy Hindus were permitted to enter it while retaining their faith and customs. No more than a quarter of the northern Indian population converted to Islam, and for three centuries the Delhi Sultanate ruled a predominantly Hindu population through collaboration rather than confrontation.

> The Delhi Sultanate attempts to unify India

Delhi brought stability to northern India and at one point was able to expand its holdings into the southern part of the subcontinent. But it could not hold all of India together: the subcontinent was simply too large and too diverse, linguistically and culturally. India continued to be buffeted and battered by internal conflicts and external attacks, and eventually it was conquered by invaders from the north.

The Quwwat-ul-Islam mosque in Delhi, featuring Hindu motifs such as tasselled ropes and bells.

India's Influence on Southeast Asia

Islam was not the only religion to transform southern Asia. As Muslim rule migrated across southwest Asia and India, Hinduism and Buddhism spread into Southeast Asia, bringing India's influence to a vast region already affected by China.

Funan: The First Southeast Asian State

Geographically, Southeast Asia is divided into three subregions: the Southeast Asian mainland (sometimes called Indochina), the Malay (*MĀ-lā*) peninsula, and the Indonesian archipelago (*ahr-kih-PEL-ah-gō*), or group of islands. Southeast Asia is a seismically active area,

> Geographic and climatic challenges confront Southeast Asia

Map 12.4 Southeast Asia, 800–1400

In Southeast Asia, Islam, Buddhism, and Hinduism coexisted at the crossroads of the Indian and Pacific Oceans. All three religions entered the region on ships carrying goods between India and China. Notice the strategic location of the Indonesian islands, perfectly placed as connectors between these two great oceans. In what ways did the convergence of these three religions, combined with the intense commercial activity typical of Southeast Asia, create unique societies?

part of the "Ring of Fire" surrounding the Pacific Ocean, and most of the islands are volcanic in origin (Map 12.4). Its tropical climate, abundant rainfall, and highly fertile soils give it great agricultural potential. But this promise has been difficult to realize. As much of the area is covered by teeming rain forests, farmland must be cleared again and again but without removing so much cover that the soil itself washes away. As a result, the large populations of Southeast Asia walk a fine line between survival and catastrophe.

Little is known of the origins of the first inhabitants of Southeast Asia. They had lived there for many centuries before the sustained immigrations from southern China that began around 3000 B.C.E. Many of these original inhabitants remained in the region, becoming the peoples now referred to as Malays. Others moved eastward across the Pacific Ocean or westward across the Indian Ocean, sailing in sturdy double-outrigger canoes built to compensate for strong oceanic swells. They populated many of the islands that dot those seas.

Southeast Asia lay across a trade route widely used in the first centuries of the Common Era to transport goods from China to India and from there to the Mediterranean

Commercial traffic creates Southeast Asian states

basin. Eventually Malay merchants, who controlled oceangoing traffic, added spices from Southeast Asia to their shipments of Chinese silk. As a connection point for traders from both India and China, Southeast Asia eventually absorbed cultural elements from both of its wealthy and powerful neighbors.

In what is today southern Vietnam, the first Southeast Asian state emerged in the first century C.E. Chinese traders referred to it as Funan (*foo-NAHN*). Its point of origin was the Mekong (*MĒ-kong*) River delta, but quickly it expanded southward into the Malay peninsula, enabling it to control trade across the strategically located Isthmus of Kra (*KRAH*). This was a narrow neck of land between the South China Sea and the Bay of Bengal. Merchants preferred to carry their cargoes across it rather than risk the lengthy ocean voyage around the Malay peninsula. Funan's control of this transfer point increased its prosperity as well as its exposure to foreign peoples and cultures.

With the traders came their ways of life. Most of the actual transporting, buying, and selling was done by Indians. Accordingly, Buddhist monks and Hindu priests from India arrived in Funan shortly after the merchants. The learning of these religious men, as well as their familiarity with events outside the region, quickly made them sought-after counselors to local princes, and their religious beliefs and artistic tastes spread readily through the population. As intermarriage increased, a cultural synthesis occurred, featuring the adoption of Sanskrit as a written language and considerable mixing of cuisine and customs. Literary works native to India were also sometimes adopted by Southeast Asians, who added their own villains and heroes to the ancient Vedic sagas. For many years Indian influence was so pervasive that all of Southeast Asia was known as "farther India." The Chinese remained aloof from most of Southeast Asia, but they took a close commercial interest in Vietnam, and Chinese expansionism affected both Vietnam and Thailand.

Indian traders and religious leaders influence Funan

Following Funan's lead, other Southeast Asian states began to consolidate after 600 C.E. In what today is Thailand, for example, the local tribes, fearful of Chinese territorial expansion, unified into a loose confederacy heavily influenced by Buddhism. They maintained a tense, uneasy relationship with the Chinese until both were overrun by the Mongols in 1253. Farther east, another state developed in Vietnam, partly in response to periodic Chinese invasions, some of which were followed by occupation but usually by reduction to tributary status. The country finally expelled the Chinese in the tenth century, but memories of its long, bitter subjugation linger to this day, as does a powerful Chinese influence upon Vietnamese culture. In particular, Confucian social doctrine and the prevalence of a highly educated bureaucracy recruited through merit endured in Vietnam until the middle of the twentieth century, as have many elements of Chinese cuisine.

The Cambodian Empire

Dominating the southern portion of the Southeast Asian mainland was the Cambodian empire. Funan enjoyed well-developed links to the Khmer (*k'MARE*) people, the main ethnic group of modern Cambodia, who originated north of that state along the Mekong river valley in what is today Laos. Around 600 C.E. the developing Khmer state of Chenla absorbed Funan, and over the next two centuries the framework for a Cambodian empire emerged, locating its capital near the inland town of Angkor (*ANG-kor*).

Funan connects to the Khmer people of Cambodia

Cambodia was heavily influenced by Hinduism, although Buddhism was welcomed and amiably tolerated. Strong Hindu influence was seen particularly in the construction

Hinduism influences Cambodia

of religious buildings. Over two centuries an extensive Hindu temple complex was constructed near the Khmer capital at Angkor Wat (see page 278). Dedicated to the Hindu god Vishnu, the elaborate buildings and ceremonial rooms in this temple complex entranced visitors long after the collapse of the state that had built it. Following that collapse, the complex at Angkor Wat was abandoned and forgotten. Only in the nineteenth century was it rediscovered by French explorers.

Hindu influence was also apparent in Cambodian government. The king was assisted, and to some extent restricted, by an intricate Hindu bureaucracy dominated by military leaders and Hindu priests. But the Hindu caste system was never replicated in Cambodia, which retained an unusually egalitarian social structure.

The Cambodian empire slowly expanded south to the Gulf of Siam. It endured until the early 1200s, when it was overthrown and replaced by a Thai tribal regime.

Srivijaya: Coalition and Cultural Blend

The most complex of the early Southeast Asian states was centered not on the mainland, where Funan and the Khmer state were located, but on the Indonesian island of Sumatra (*soo-MAH-trah*). This was the Malay kingdom of Srivijaya (*srē-vē-JĪ-yah*), first described to the outside world by a Chinese Buddhist pilgrim in 671.

Srivijaya is a Sanskrit word meaning "Great Conquest." It appears to have been created as a maritime trading empire, catering to oceangoing traffic between China and India that was bypassing the overland portage across the Isthmus of Kra. As sailors became more familiar with the dangerous passage through the straits between Sumatra and the Malay Peninsula, the time saved outweighed the risks incurred, and the new kingdom prospered while Funan's power declined.

Relief sculpture at the temple complex of Borobodur in central Java, depicting scenes from the life of the Buddha.

Srivijaya becomes a Buddhist commercial empire

The capital of Srivijaya was the Malay port city of Palembang (*pah-lum-BANG*) on the coast of Sumatra. Its rulers, usually called by the Indian term *maharajah,* were accomplished diplomats, stitching together a coalition of Malay maritime principalities through a careful balance of Hindu spiritual leadership, bribery, and intimidation. Although known to history as an empire, Srivijaya was politically decentralized. It never expanded its territorial control even to the neighboring island of Java, preferring to influence principalities there through the same combination of tactics that worked so well on Sumatra.

While the Cambodian empire was grounded in Hinduism, Srivijaya was overwhelmingly Buddhist. The spectacular Buddhist temple complex called Borobodur (*bō-rō-bō-DUHR*), built in central Java between 770 and 825, was constructed with more than two million cubic feet of stone. At the time it was the largest integrated network of buildings south of the equator. A ten-tiered megaplex, it represents the ten levels of increasing enlightenment passed through by the pilgrim on his or her spiritual journey to nirvana. Borobodur testifies to the pervasiveness of Buddhist cultural influence in Southeast Asia, as Cambodia's Angkor Wat testifies to Hindu influence.

Srivijaya blends Indian and Southeast Asian cultures

But whether they adopted Hindu or Buddhist architecture, whether they adopted Sanskrit as a written language or translated Vedic epics into their own tongues, the Southeast Asian states did much more than *adopt* Indian culture. They *adapted* it to their own tastes and purposes, integrating it, for example, with their own customs of spirit worship and tribal rule. Ancient Indonesian deities were transformed into Hindu gods and goddesses, while traditional Indonesian dances and songs were blended with

Indian rhythms and played on Indian instruments. These processes created a series of hybrid, blended cultures unlike any others.

Srivijaya flourished for several centuries, until in 1025 it was weakened by a devastating raid launched by one of its commercial competitors, the southeastern Indian state of Chola (*CHŌ-lah*). After that Srivijaya's fortunes declined sharply, and by the thirteenth century it had disintegrated into smaller maritime principalities. The Javanese king Kertanagara (*kur-tan-ah-GAH-rah*) constructed a short-lived successor state in the late 1200s, but after that no comparable system arose in the Indonesian archipelago until the Dutch East India Company arrived at the beginning of the seventeenth century.

Chapter Review

Putting It in Perspective

Islam's Abbasid Caliphate looked eastward rather than westward, and its willingness to accept a synthesis of Arabic and Persian cultures on the Iranian plateau added greatly to the richness of Islamic civilization. The Abbasids presided over an Islamic golden age in commerce, culture, poetry, and power. But they were unable to unify the Islamic world, owing to the immensity and ethnic diversity of their conquests.

In the eleventh century, the caliphate was superseded by the rule of Central Asian warlords who carried Islam into India. They were no better at unification than the Abbasids. The Indian subcontinent's vastness, diversity of geographic features and cultures, and attachment to Hinduism consistently frustrated both external and internal efforts to impose unification. The Mauryas and the Guptas succeeded for a time, each by creating a centralized empire, but ultimately failed, as did early Muslim endeavors. Between 1206 and 1526, the Delhi Sultanate attempted to create a hybrid Indian-Islamic system, with more success culturally than politically.

The peoples of Southeast Asia were influenced by commercial contacts with China and by the Indian religions of Hinduism and Buddhism. Funan, Cambodia, and Srivijaya developed states that tried to manage the trade flowing between China and India. They succeeded for a time, but eventually dissolved in the face of external invasion or internal ethnic rivalry. Hinduism and Buddhism offered many insights into the nature of human life and the destiny of human souls but few into administrative organization and political power. Eventually, Islam and European imperialism would contend for dominance in Southeast Asia.

Reviewing Key Material

KEY CONCEPTS

Sufism, 285
yoga, 289

purdah, 289

KEY PEOPLE

Abu Muslim, 282
Abbas, 282
Harun al-Rashid, 284
Ibn Sina, 284
al-Khwarizmi, 284
Omar Khayyam, 285
Ibn Rushd, 286

Moses Maimonides, 286
al-Mamun, 286
Chandra Gupta I, 288
Samudra Gupta, 00
Chandra Gupta II, 288
Kumara Gupta, 288
Mahmud of Ghazni, 292

ASK YOURSELF

1. How did Persia and Arabia influence one another in the seventh century C.E.? What were the consequences of this mutual influence?
2. Why was the Abbasid Caliphate at first so successful in ruling its vast territories? What accounts for its eventual failure and collapse?
3. How did Islam affect India?
4. How did Hindus and Muslims view one another? What impact did their rivalry have on India?

GOING FURTHER

Adshead, S. *Central Asia in World History.* 1993.

Ahsan, Muhammad. *Social Life Under the Abbasids.* 1979.

Bloom, Jonathan M. *Paper Before Print: The History and Impact of Paper in the Islamic World.* 2001.

Bosworth, C. *The Later Ghaznavids.* 1977.

Cady, J. *Southeast Asia: Its Historical Development.* 1964.

Chauduri, K. *Trade and Civilization in the Indian Ocean.* 1985.

Frye, Richard. *Islamic Iran and Central Asia.* 1979.

Hall, K. *Maritime Trade and State Development in Early Southeast Asia.* 1985.

Higham, Charles. *The Civilization of Angkor.* 2001.

Ikram, S. *Muslim Civilization in India.* 1964.

Kwanten, Luc. *Imperial Nomads: A History of Central Asia, 500–1500.* 1979.

Lombard, M. *The Golden Age of Islam.* 2004.

Morgan, David. *Medieval Persia, 1040–1797.* 1988.

Osborne, Milton. *Southeast Asia: An Introductory History.* 1995.

Risso, Patricia. *Merchants and Faith: Muslim Commerce and Culture in the Indian Ocean.* 1995.

Sandhu, Kernial. *Early Malaysia.* 1973.

SarDeSai, D. *Southeast Asia: Past and Present.* 1994.

Schimmel, A. *Islam in the Indian Subcontinent.* 1980.

Sharon, Moshe. *Black Banners from the East: The Establishment of the Abbasid State.* 1983.

Wolpert, Stanley. *India: A New History.* 1997.

Key Dates and Developments

184 B.C.E.	Collapse of the Mauryan Empire in India
50 B.C.E.–50 C.E.	Scythian rule in northwestern India
50–250 C.E.	Kushan rule in northwestern India
78 C.E.	Fourth Great Council of Buddhism, in Kashmir
ca. 100 C.E.	Funan, the first Southeast Asian state
320–550	The Gupta Empire
455–550	Invasion of India by the Huns
ca. 600s	Establishment of the Kingdom of Srivijaya
636	Muslim defeat of the Sasanian Empire
711	Arab rule in the Sind in western India
750	Establishment of the Abbasid Caliphate
770–825	Construction of Borobodur
786–809	Rule of Harun al-Rashid as caliph in Baghdad
ca. 800	Establishment of the Cambodian Empire
800–1000	Construction of Angkor Wat
945	Buyid warlords' seizure of Baghdad
962–1040	Ghaznavid rule in Khurasan and Afghanistan
969	Establishment of the Fatimid Caliphate in Egypt
998–1030	Mahmud of Ghazni's invasion of India
1040	Seljuk Turks' seizure of northeastern Iran
ca. 1100	*The Rubaiyat* of Omar Khayyam
1206	Establishment of the Delhi Sultanate by the Ghurids

African Societies and the Impact of Islam, 1500 B.C.E.–1500 C.E.

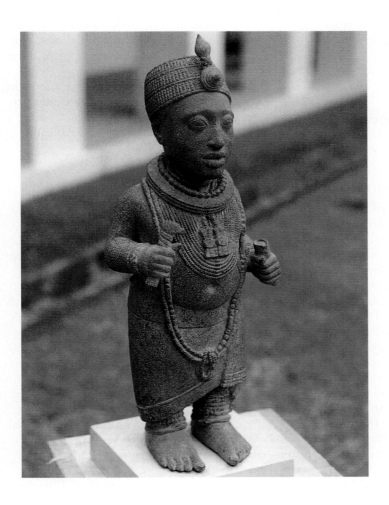

Figure Of A Sacred King

This bronze sculpture of a sacred king was created in the Ife region of southwestern Nigeria between the 12th and 15th centuries C.E. Many African kings were sacred personages who served as intermediaries between the tangible world of human beings and the unseen world of the gods (page 304).

It was just past midday on a humid summer's day in West Africa in 685 C.E. In a small village on the border between grassy plains and the desert, in what would later be the kingdom of Ghana, the men were resting in whatever shade was available. They had spent the morning weeding their root crops of sorghum and yams. The women were inside their huts, preparing the midday meal. Children were tending a flock of goats and a few scrawny cattle. Then, from the north, they sighted an animal unlike anything they had ever seen before.

The children spotted it first and ran whooping to fetch their parents. Everyone rushed out to catch a glimpse of this amazing beast, awkward and ungainly, as it slouched across the sands toward the grassland. By the time the village assembled, there was not just one camel in view, but several dozen. They were loaded with cargo and led by men wearing loose-fitting white robes and turbans on their heads. The leader approached one of the men of the village and asked for water. But he spoke a strange tongue, and no one could understand his words.

Muslims had come to West Africa, bringing goods from the eastern Mediterranean, a written language, a monotheistic religion, and many other things. The region was about to change dramatically.

Trans-Saharan trade area

East African city-states

Bantu homeland

Africa Before Islam

Human life first evolved in Africa, but not written history. Although Egypt, Nubia, and the northern coast have recorded histories that date back thousands of years, most of Africa has no form of writing, and thus no written records, before the arrival of Islam. Consequently, most of what we know about early African history is known through legend and folklore, transmitted from one generation to the next by word of mouth, and through the work of modern archeologists and anthropologists.

Absence of written records restricts knowledge of early African history

Compounding the difficulty of knowing early African history is the means by which writing came to most of the continent. As it was introduced primarily by Islamic and Christian traders, invaders, and missionaries, Africa was often seen and interpreted by foreigners, and early African voices were ignored. Foreigners usually judged Africa by the standards and institutions of their own worlds, rather than evaluating the continent within its own frame of reference. These facts make the study of early African history particularly challenging.

Yet this study is also rewarding. African societies were as varied as the continent's geography and climate (Map 13.1). They ranged from the Mediterranean and desert societies of the north to the forest and grassland societies of central and southern Africa and from the wealthy farming and trading empires of West Africa to the commercial city-states of Africa's east coast. In some regions, especially those that came under Islamic influence, sophisticated systems of governance and commerce emerged. Elsewhere

FOUNDATION MAP 13.1 Early Africa, Including Bantu Migrations and Trade Routes, 1500 B.C.E.–1500 C.E.

The African continent, bisected by the Equator, runs north-south through 70 degrees of latitude. This provides it with widely differing climates to accompany its diverse topography. Notice that Africa hosts a lengthy and varied coastline, tropical grasslands, equatorial rain forests, and enormous deserts. How did the Bantu migrations help Africans overcome the isolation this topography would encourage?

people lived largely in stateless societies, based mainly on clans and villages, without strong regional governments or rulers.

The Bantu Migrations: Cohesion in Diversity

Despite the geographic breadth and social diversity of African societies, there were connections among them. Between 500 B.C.E. and 1000 C.E., tribes of Africans known as **Bantu** (from their word for "people"), who spoke closely related languages also known by that name, migrated gradually from their homeland in West Africa, near the boundary between what are now Nigeria and Cameroon. Research into the Bantu migrations is made difficult by the absence of written sources mentioned earlier, but many historians believe that over the centuries Bantu peoples moved into eastern, central, and southern Africa, spreading their knowledge of farming and ironworking and a common set of Bantu languages and customs.

Bantu migrations connect African regions

Although no written accounts of this migration exist, many scholars presume that it resulted from pressures on available land and food resources exerted by an expanding population. Bantu peoples had mastered agriculture before the migrations began, and by 500 B.C.E. they had acquired technology sufficient to smelt iron for tools, equipment, and weapons. Thus they were able to clear forests rapidly and cultivate crops efficiently. They dominated and in some cases displaced the foraging societies they encountered as they spread across eastern, central, and southern Africa.

Bantu peoples organized themselves into families and clans. Bantu villages, towns, and cities were governed by ruling councils composed of male heads of families. One of these men, elected chief, spoke for the community in dealings with other Bantu and non-Bantu societies. This decentralized method of rule served the Bantu well until population growth put pressure on resources of land and food. By the fourteenth century C.E., a centralized Bantu kingdom known as Kongo had emerged in Central Africa. The king of Kongo ruled through a multilevel administration to manage resources equitably, dispense justice, and defend the kingdom against external threats.

Muslim travelers connect West and East Africa to the Islamic empire

As the Bantu migrations were ending, Islamic connections were beginning. Muslim merchants from Arabia and North Africa crossed the Sahara with caravans of camels, establishing commercial and cultural contacts with West African empires such as Ghana and Mali. At the same time, Muslim mariners sailed down the eastern coast of Africa, bringing their religion and the Arabic language to local city-states. These Islamic travelers forged links between West and East Africa, connecting both regions to the growing Islamic empire stretching from Spain to south Asia. The connections created by Muslims and Bantu continue to affect Africa today.

Regional Cultural Adaptations

The development of these varied trade, travel, and cultural connections across Africa testifies to the creativity and adaptability of Africans, not to the hospitality of the African environment itself. This immense continent, home to the first human beings, presented significant challenges to the growth and prosperity of their societies.

Covering 20 percent of the land surface of the globe, Africa is the second largest continent (after Asia), a landmass of remarkable diversity in climate and topography. But in all its diversity, Africa, located almost entirely in the tropics and subject to extremes of heat, rainfall, and dryness, has never been an easy place in which to live. Most of its precipitation is seasonal rather than consistent, and in its vast desert regions—the Sahara (the world's largest desert), the Kalahari (*kah-lah-HARR-ē*), and the Namib (*NAH-mib*)—there is virtually no rain at all. Here agriculture is impossible and pasturage for livestock scarce. On both sides of the equator, however, lie dense rain forests with far too much moisture for raising grain crops and herds. Only the valleys of the Nile and Niger rivers, and the grassy regions that stretch across the continent both north and south of the tropical rain forests, offer opportunity for settled societies. Fortunately these grassy areas, known as savanna, constitute more than half of Africa's land surface; without them the continent would be largely empty of people and domesticable animals.

Africans adapted their cultures and societies to these topographical and climatic variations in several ways. In the north, where the weather is relatively mild, the Berbers, Caucasian peoples who had earlier adopted Phoenician culture and language, lived along the Mediterranean coast. They fished, farmed, and engaged in maritime commerce with the Egyptians and Phoenicians and later with the Greeks and Romans. Eventually they also developed a series of trade routes by camel caravan across the scorching Sahara to the south. Even after being conquered by the Arabs, they managed to maintain their way of life and distinct ethnic heritage.

South of the Sahara, but still north of the rain forest, across the region known as the Sudan, stretch endless expanses of savanna. Since perhaps as early as the fifth millennium B.C.E., people in this area have herded cattle and raised crops such as sorghum, millet, and yams. As in most agricultural societies, these people lived in villages, grouping themselves into families and clans and organizing their lives around the care of their crops and herds.

Cattle were prized as symbols of status and wealth and were often offered as part of the bargain in commercial and political agreements. A man's family also offered them to the family of his bride as part of their marital agreement, though upon divorce the bride's family would be obligated to return the cattle. Cow's blood was also prized as a highly desirable beverage. The central position of these animals in the lives of their owners, even in modern times, is attested to by the decision of a small village in Kenya to send 14 cattle to the United States in 2002 as a gesture of condolence for the September 11, 2001, terrorist attacks on the World Trade Center and the Pentagon.

The most influential early residents of the Sudan were the Bantu-speakers. Beginning around 500 B.C.E., perhaps in search of more ample food and water to support their growing population, Bantu peoples gradually moved out of the Sudan into Africa's equatorial savannas and forests, where they raised livestock and cleared the land so they could practice agriculture. Their knowledge of ironworking enabled them to fashion weapons and farming tools that gave them an advantage over the foraging societies they encountered, and they incorporated many of these foragers into Bantu culture. By the time they finally reached southeastern Africa, around 1000 C.E., the Bantu had created a large set of societies, related by language and culture, throughout the continent.

Wide climatic variations challenge African societies

The San people of the Kalahari.

Bantu knowledge spreads over much of Africa

Clans and Kingdoms

Despite cultural and linguistic similarities, the Bantu developed differing social organizations. In the sub-Saharan savanna, kingdoms often emerged as large groups of villages combined under a regional ruler who exercised both spiritual and temporal authority. Farther south, however, although small groups of villages sometimes formed coalitions, societies tended to remain stateless, ruled autonomously by local chiefs and councils. Along the eastern coast a series of city-states emerged, each with an independent ruler. Finally, in the central rain forests and eastern plains, some foraging societies managed to survive as small, nomadic clans.

Clans provide foundation for African life

Africans relied primarily for their protection and survival on their families and clans, which formed the foundation of their social, cultural, and religious life. Although some African societies were matrilineal (in which children trace their ancestry through their mother's lineage), the dominant figure in most families was the male head of household. This patriarchal figure was typically responsible for performing religious rituals, maintaining contact with the spirits of departed ancestors, and serving on the council of the village chief.

African clans unite groups of families

Men who had sufficient means often practiced polygamy, thereby establishing links with a number of families and creating an intricate network of kinship ties and loyalties that bound the community together. For example, a man marrying women from two different families could expect support—such as food in time of drought or assistance during illness or injury—from both. Moreover, the marriages also bound these families in relations of mutual support and hospitality. Polygamy therefore connected families in beneficial ways.

African Traditional Religion

Local rituals that have survived into modern times suggest that most African societies were polytheistic, like their contemporaries in Mesopotamia, India, Southeast Asia, Greece, early America, and elsewhere. Each god represented a different natural force and was believed to perform a different function, bringing, for example, rain, wind, or sun to local people. Many such societies practiced **animism**, the belief that spirits existed that could either help or harm human beings. Many other African societies also appear to have believed in a single god that created the earth and the first human beings. This god, whether endowed with human characteristics, as in Ghana, or considered to be a supreme creative force, as in many Bantu-speaking lands, was extremely powerful and could help or injure humans at will. Africans therefore believed it wise to behave properly and to worship this and all other gods through carefully prescribed rituals.

In some African societies, a caste of priests or prophets performed the rituals. These people were believed to be able to communicate with the gods if the community desired rain, good harvests, or good health. In other African societies, the privilege of contacting the single creator was reserved for the king alone (see page 299). This personal relationship between king and creator was a principal element of royal power as well as a foundation for the eventual development of large empires. Indeed, many African peoples believed that after death the king was rewarded by becoming a lesser god.

An Akuba wooden doll from Ghana, a classic African fertility symbol.

African religion reinforces royal authority

As in China, ancestor worship was widely practiced in early Africa. The spirits of deceased clan or family members were thought to exercise considerable influence over the day-to-day lives of their descendants. Bad luck or accidents were assumed to be reminders that living people must continue to perform ceremonies in honor of the dead. To stop such devotions would be to condemn ancestral spirits to extinction; they survived as spirits only as long as the living remembered them.

When the Muslims arrived in Africa, they found a variety of creeds practiced by the peoples they encountered. Some elements of those beliefs, such as faith in a supreme creator, were similar to Islam and might ease conversion to the creed of the Prophet. Others, such as the king's role in contacting the creator god, would discourage rulers from embracing the new Islamic faith, in which all people were equal before Allah. Still others, such as the Christianity practiced in Ethiopia, held that Jesus of Nazareth was the Son of God and were clearly incompatible with Islam.

Early African Culture

In early Africa, religious beliefs and practices often affected artistic expression, which played many roles in daily life. Literature and poetry, set to music in the form of chants or songs, often performed a religious function. Music and chanting not only accompanied but formed a crucial component of every stage in the lives of Africans: birth, coming-of-age rituals, weddings, political ceremonies, and funerals. Dancing served not only as a pastime but also as a method of communicating with ancestral spirits. Religious incantations and folk legends were transmitted from one generation to the next through music and song.

Architecture, too, fulfilled religious requirements. In most of Africa, ordinary people lived in huts constructed of mud or thatch, the materials most readily available, but religious buildings were constructed of more durable stone. In northeastern Africa, Egyptians, Nubians, and Ethiopians built pyramids and religious monuments out of stone. In southern Africa stone structures seem to have served practical as well as ceremonial purposes. When Muslims arrived in West Africa, they introduced techniques of brickmaking that Africans then used to build palaces and mosques.

African architecture, art, and music reinforce religion

Finally, woodcarving served explicitly ceremonial needs throughout Africa. Elaborate wooden headpieces and masks were carved to depict spirits and gods, and to communicate with them. Often these masks were used in rituals featuring dancing and chanting. The masks helped the clan elders teach lessons to the young and transmit the collective folk wisdom of the people from one generation to the next. With their great beauty and vivid expression, African masks testify to both the artistic talents and the deeply held beliefs of those who created them.

Grass-skirted masks represent the spirits of ancestors among the Kuba people of the Congo.

Islamic Africa and Spain: Commercial and Cultural Networks

Even before Islam created strong commercial and cultural links that tied Africa to the larger world, North Africa was in touch with that world. It had been influenced by the Egyptian and Phoenician civilizations, with their links to the Persians and Macedonians, and was eventually absorbed into the Roman and Byzantine empires. The Romans, however, did little for the region, since their attention was directed largely toward Europe and West Asia. Diocletian's division of the empire in 284 C.E. partitioned North Africa as well: modern-day Morocco, Algeria, and Tunisia remained with the western empire until its collapse in 476 while Libya and Egypt passed under Byzantine rule.

Map 13.2 Islamic North Africa and Iberia, 910

The Sahara Desert cuts North Africa off from the rest of the continent and orients it toward the Mediterranean. When Muslims moved from east to west across the top of Africa, they eventually turned north toward Iberia rather than south toward the desert. Note that by 910, the Iberian Peninsula was divided into an Islamic Caliphate, independent Christian kingdoms, and independent Muslim states. What do these subdivisions suggest about Muslim prospects for conquering Europe from a base in Iberia?

During all this time, however, North Africa remained on the margins of Mediterranean commerce, and its political connections with Rome and Constantinople were fragile. But when North Africa became part of Islamic civilization early in the eighth century, its entire orientation changed.

Islamic North Africa

Between 476 and 639 North Africa was isolated, not greatly influenced by either Germanic Europe or the Byzantine Empire. It was populated largely by Berbers, who pursued their own heritage and scorned outsiders. In the northeast, the Egyptians had a long and rich cultural heritage, but their civilization had been in eclipse for more than a thousand years. Although an outside influence, Christianity flourished in North Africa as a distinctively Egyptian faith—Coptic Christianity—whose Monophysite view of Jesus as a purely divine being was viewed as heresy by both Rome and Constantinople. Byzantine efforts to replace Monophysitism created hostility that Arab armies, bringing Islam, were able to use to their advantage.

When it came, the Arab onslaught was swift, taking North Africans by surprise. Between 639 and 642 the Arabs used a combination of force and generosity to conquer Egypt, whose fertile Nile valley attracted and enriched the Islamic caliphate. More than one million Arabs had moved to Egypt by 750. Most Egyptians converted to Islam, not only for spiritual but for economic and practical reasons, as Muslims were

North African cultures become isolated after the Roman Empire's collapse

Islam connects North Africa and Southwest Asia

exempt from taxation and free from intimidation or coercion. Within a century fewer than a third of the Egyptians remained Christian.

Initial Arab plans to move south into Nubia were frustrated by the skills of Nubian archers and a Christian government that had long experience fighting Egyptian attacks. But prosperity and population growth made Egypt an ideal base for expansion to the west. In the next few decades the Arabs moved across North Africa, taking advantage of the fact that the region's various inhabitants feared one another as much as they despised the Muslims. Refusing to cooperate, North African groups fell one by one. By 711, little more than 70 years after the Muslim invasion of North Africa began, the Islamic empire stretched across that entire region, and its soldiers were crossing the Strait of Gibraltar into Spain.

Cosmopolitan Umayyad Spain

The Muslims first arrived in Spain as invited guests. The Germanic king of Spain had died in 709, and in the contest over his succession one contender for the throne appealed to the Islamic *amir* (*AH-mēr*, or governor) of North Africa for help. The *amir* responded by sending an Arab-Berber expeditionary force under General Tariq ibn Ziyad (*tah-RĒK ibn zē-YAHD*), which landed in 711, defeated the other contender, and prepared to go home. But Tariq heard rumors that the legendary treasure of the ancient Jewish King Solomon was hidden in a cellar in Toledo (Map 13.2). He took the city and found nothing but rats in its cellars, but saw to his astonishment that many of the residents welcomed his forces and converted to Islam. The next year the *amir* himself conquered Spain with an army of 20,000 men. About four-fifths of the Iberian peninsula (modern Spain and Portugal) came under Muslim control, while the Christians were pushed into a few surviving kingdoms in the Spanish north. The Muslims called their newly acquired territory *al-Andalus* (*al-AHN-dah-loose*); Spaniards called it Andalusia. For the next five centuries, Spain was closely linked with North Africa and was the westernmost part of Islam's growing commercial and cultural network.

Islam is invited into Spain

The Court of the Lions at the Alhambra in Granada, Spain.

From 711 to 756 Islamic Spain was ruled by the *amir*, who for most of that time reported to the Umayyad caliphate in Damascus. From Spain, the Muslims tried to advance into France, but they were defeated by the Franks at Tours in 732. When the Umayyads were overthrown by the Abbasids in 750, one of the Umayyad family's princes escaped from Damascus and governed Spain from Córdoba (*CŌR-duh-buh*). Al-Andalus thereupon became the last bastion of Umayyad rule during the Abbasid caliphate. This unusual situation lasted for nearly two centuries: Iberia was a long way from Baghdad, the new capital of the Abbasids, and as long as Spain remained loyal to the Sunni brand of Islam, the Abbasids, Sunnis themselves, were willing to leave the Spanish Umayyads in peace.

Umayyad Spain fused Arabic culture and language onto a Spanish and Berber population base. The result was a civilization of distinctive cultural achievements. The Arab occupiers created exquisite irrigated gardens, splendid mosques and palaces like the Alhambra in Granada (*gra-NAH-dah*), elegant fountains and courtyards, and important works of science, poetry, and philosophy. They also married into Spanish families, converted large numbers of people to Islam, and assimilated the local population to a degree unheard of in other Islamic lands. In so doing, they joined with the Spaniards to create a uniquely Hispano-Arab culture, vestiges of which endured for centuries after the collapse of Spanish Islam in 1492.

Islam shapes a distinctive Spanish culture

This cosmopolitan culture emerged gradually from Islamic Spain's flourishing urban centers of Seville (*suh-VIL*), Córdoba, and Granada. Poetry praising warrior virtues and romantic conquests was written either in Arabic or in a Spanish language thick with Arabic words and expressions; the rhyme schemes and meters were Roman. Scholars from throughout the Islamic empire came to Spain, building libraries, studying medicine and mathematics, and translating Aristotle's philosophy and the medical works of the Greek physician Galen from Arabic into Latin, all under the patronage of the state.

Economic prosperity and cultural connections made such achievements possible. Accustomed to sunny, dry climates, Arabs brought to arid Spain methods of irrigation perfected in Yemen and Syria, some based on timed water flow. Soon the Iberian Peninsula was abundant with figs, dates, cherries, pears, pomegranates, and dozens of other crops whose cultivation was imported from the southern and eastern Mediterranean. As Byzantine naval power declined in the western Mediterranean, Islamic Spain established seaborne trading routes with Africa, non-Spanish Europe, and western Asia. This flourishing commerce made the Spanish Umayyads financially independent of Damascus, free to promote not only cultural magnificence but political autonomy. A series of capable governors consolidated the new Hispano-Arab state on a model congenial to the Abbasids, who in turn did not interfere in Spain's affairs.

Spain loosens its ties with the Caliphate

In 909, a political development in Islamic Egypt accelerated Spain's distinctive cultural development. The **Fatimid** (*FA-ti-mid*) family, a Shi'ite dynasty in Egypt, began a six-decade struggle to break away from Abbasid rule and establish a caliphate of their own along the Nile. The Umayyad governor of Spain seized the opportunity provided by this distraction to claim the title of caliph for himself in 929. The unity of the *umma* was now shattered, with three different men claiming to be its true leader. The Islamic state of Spain, now known as the Caliphate of Córdoba, was a separate Sunni Muslim government presiding over a luxuriant hybrid culture unlike any other in the Islamic world.

The Caliphate of Córdoba deepens the connection between Spain and Islam

Although the Caliphate of Córdoba lasted little more than a century, Hispano-Arab culture continued to prosper there. Córdoba's population grew to 500,000, and by the twelfth century the caliphate was noted for its immense paper mills. Its intellectual life blossomed with scholars such as Ibn Rushd (*Ib-un ROOSHD*), known in Latin Europe as Averröes (*uh-VAIR-ō-ēz*), a philosopher and physician who argued that the Qur'an was an allegory requiring rational interpretation and who reintroduced the work of Aristotle and Plato to European readers. Jews and Christians were not only tolerated in Córdoba but also encouraged to contribute their talents to Islamic civilization.

Nevertheless, internal dissent undermined the caliphate: Arabs fought with Berbers, Arab clans intrigued against each other, and by the late tenth century Umayyad control was crumbling. In northern Spain, the surviving Christian kingdoms sensed weakness and began to pressure the Muslims.

Fatimid Egypt

As the Umayyads had managed to survive for centuries in Spain, remote from the Abbasid world, so in Egypt the Shi'ite Fatimids found refuge. Abbasid rule was always stronger in Asia and Arabia than in North Africa, particularly after the capital of their caliphate moved eastward from Damascus to Baghdad in 763. The Abbasids appointed Mamluks, Turkish slaves from Central Asia, to rule Egypt on their behalf, but the resulting Mamluk dynasties proved short-lived. Then between 909 and 969 the Fatimids set forth their claim, not only to the province of Egypt but to spiritual and political authority throughout the Islamic world.

Shi'ism finds a foothold in Egypt

The Fatimids were **Isma'ilis** (*iss-mah-ILL-ēs*), a branch of Shi'ite Islam. Isma'ilis claimed to be the true imams (or direct descendants of Muhammad's son-in-law Ali), and they denied the legitimacy of both the orthodox Shi'ites and the Sunnis. Orthodox Shi'ites believed that the last imam had hidden himself in a cave after 874 and would return one day as the Messiah. Isma'ilis disputed this belief and claimed direct descent from Isma'il, the last publicly seen imam, who died in 760. These doctrinal disputes, like those in Christian Byzantium, plagued the Islamic empire. In Baghdad, the Abbasid Caliphate was in decline, its power eroded by the size and complexity of its empire. Ultimately, it could not hold Egypt.

Having established their own caliphate, the Fatimids moved their capital from Alexandria to Cairo, a new city they founded in 969. For worship of their cult dedicated to the family of Ali, they built magnificent mosques rivaling those at Mecca and Medina, such as the exquisite Al-Azhar Mosque in Cairo. But they left the Egyptian population undisturbed in its Sunni Muslim faith, a political necessity but a spiritual contradiction: if they were indeed the true imams, how could they fail to oppose Sunni doctrine and practice? This tolerance undermined their claim to universal legitimacy and eventually destroyed their caliphate. Lacking adequate support, the Fatimids were defeated first by European crusaders who took Jerusalem in 1099 and ultimately by the Muslim general Salah al-Din (*sah-LAH al-DĒN*), also called Saladin (*SAH-lah-dēn*), who brought together several Muslim states to fight the crusaders. By 1173 Fatimid rule in Egypt was over.

Far from the seats of Islamic power in Damascus, Baghdad, and Mecca, North Africa developed as a series of distant states out of touch with mainstream Muslim spiritual and political evolution. Islam's impact on the continent of Africa was, however, profound. Through commerce as well as conquest, Islam spread from North Africa to the west and south, with consequences that shaped the course of African history for centuries to come.

The Fatimids break away from the Abbasids

Al-Azhar Mosque, Cairo.

Fatimid Egypt is defeated by Sunni Muslims

Trade Across the Sahara

The Sahara resembled an ocean of sand, which the Arabs could navigate on camels, their ships of the desert. Muslim caravan trade brought Islam and other changes to West Africa, and Africans, in turn, reached out to the Islamic world.

Early Saharan Trade

In the first millennium B.C.E., long before the arrival of caravans from North Africa, kingdoms had been established in the western part of Africa's vast savanna region known as the Sudan. These early kingdoms were based on villages, each containing families and clans linked by kinship ties. Councils of elders advised the chief in governing each village; the chief represented the village in dealings with regional and provincial leaders, who in turn answered to a king.

West African kingdoms seem to have protected their peoples effectively and saw no compelling reason to expand until the development of north-south trade across the Sahara. The trade was made possible by the arrival of camels from Central Asia some time before 200 C.E. Without them the Sahara would have remained unexplored and uncharted; with them merchant caravans crossed the desert in search of profit.

Once the camel came, Berber tribes such as the Tuareg (*TWAH-reg*), accustomed to an arid environment, set out to cross the Sahara, exploring its vastness and mapping safe, direct trade routes. Financed by Jewish merchants operating out of oases in North Africa, Berber caravans carried salt, dates, and manufactured goods to the Sudan, exchanging these commodities for slaves, gold, ivory, and gum. By the seventh century, commerce by camel across the Sahara was regular and profitable.

Camels make the trans-Saharan trade possible

Islam's Interaction with West Africa

Following the Islamic conquest of North Africa, the trans-Saharan trade became part of a huge commercial and cultural network extending from Persia to Spain. Eager to expand both their faith and their fortune, Muslim merchants replaced the Jewish financiers, and many traders and camel drivers converted to Islam. By the eighth century, trade across the Sahara was generating great wealth, and some caravans included thousands of camels, braving sandstorms, bandits, and withering heat on difficult journeys lasting for months.

Islam influences West Africa profoundly

The effects of the trans-Saharan trade on West Africa were highly significant. First and foremost, it introduced Islam into the region. Berber and Arabian Muslims brought with them not only their faith but their complex cultures. West African rulers and councils became literate in Arabic and began to keep written records. Islamic laws, institutions, and administrative forms also took shape. Muslims brought new goods to trade and taught Africans how to make bricks, enhancing the durability of buildings in societies that had previously used dried mud for walls. Beyond these advantages, West Africa became part of an extensive community of Islamic peoples.

Second, the trade created a tremendous potential market for African gold. Mines established in the areas that are now Ghana, Senegal, and Nigeria, all in West Africa, provided work that raised standards of living across the area. The ready availability of African gold stimulated the economy of the entire Mediterranean basin, and gold became the medium of exchange for the silks and spices of India. Legends of African riches, many of them exaggerated, fascinated both Europe and Asia. Africa seemed to be an exotic realm of cities overflowing with gold, ruled by fabulously wealthy kings. The lure of gold linked Africa, Asia, and Europe.

Trade connects West Africa to Southwest Asia

Third, the camel caravans carried cargoes of slaves, and in this trade Islamic influence was decisive. Upper-class Muslims wanted African slaves for their households; Muslim military commanders purchased them for their armies; local operators of salt and gold mines in West Africa used them for labor. Muslims purchased, transported, and sold the slaves at huge profits. This trade involved moving the captives across the desert to the Middle East, a crossing that was stressful even for well-fed camel merchants but agonizing, and sometimes fatal, for slaves.

African slavery was not exclusively racial, since whites captured in war were also sold. But since there were no whites native to West Africa, the overwhelming majority of slaves were black. Some slaves were sold to owners in Islamic cities in Spain and Portugal during the medieval period, but slaveholding never spread to the rest of Europe. In contrast, it was widely practiced in Islamic lands. Only with Europe's discovery of the Americas in the late fifteenth century did slavery become a race-based global phenomenon.

Trans-Saharan trade urbanizes West Africa

Finally, the trans-Saharan traffic urbanized West Africa and transformed clusters of villages into centralized kingdoms. African merchant families served as middlemen between Muslim traders and African mine owners. These merchants opened caravanserais (*care-ah-VAN-sair-ās*), complexes of inns and markets where camel merchants could sleep, care for their animals, refresh themselves, and conduct their business. Shops and services expanded in these complexes, and urbanization quickly followed. Between the ninth and thirteenth centuries, the populations of cities such as Kumbi (*KOOM-bē*),

Djenné (*jen-NĀ*), and Timbuktu, in what would later be known as Mali, grew to exceed 10,000 inhabitants each. What had been tiny kingdoms expanded as well, as Africans learned more about the sophisticated political systems of the larger Islamic world and adapted some of its features.

West African Kingdoms: Ghana and Mali

The expansion of trade stimulated by the camel caravans enhanced the wealth of West Africa. Its rulers used much of that wealth to construct extensive empires on the foundations of what had been small kingdoms. Two of those empires, Ghana and Mali, provided centralized government and economic organization to a region previously divided along clan and tribal lines.

The Conversion of Ghana

The kingdom of Ghana (not to be confused with the modern republic of the same name) was located in the area north of the Niger and Senegal Rivers (Map 13.3). It was founded by the Sondinke (*sahn-DIN-kā*) people between the second and fourth centuries of the Common Era. By 800, Muslim traders were calling it "the land of gold," and it began

Map 13.3 West Africa, 800–1400

The trans-Saharan trade connected West Africa to the Islamic world. Observe, both here and on Map 13.1, that trans-Saharan trade routes connected West Africa to the commercial highways of the Mediterranean Sea. Kingdoms such as Ghana and Mali emerged to organize traffic in salt, gold, and slaves. In addition to money and goods, what did Islamic traders supply in return?

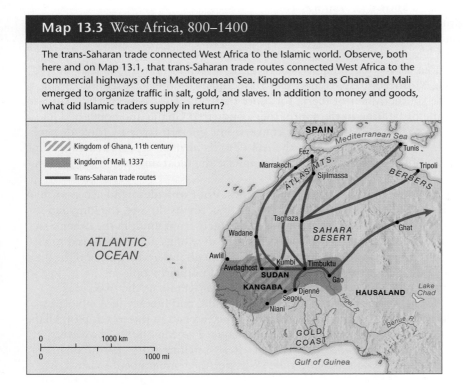

appearing on their maps in 833. Ghana was a prosperous kingdom, located between major sources of gold and salt. Its rulers did not control the gold mines, which were located in a southern forest belt that they could neither penetrate nor influence for long. But they did control the transport of gold from south to north, an extraordinarily profitable trade that made them rich.

Gold and salt make Ghana a powerful kingdom

At the same time, Berber tribesmen known as Sanhaja (*san-HAH-yah*) conducted a valuable salt trade from north to south. Salt was essential to life in a prerefrigeration age, as it offered an effective method of preserving meat. The continual exchange of salt for gold was carried out in Ghana's capital city of Kumbi, where a swarm of royal officials collected tribute, customs duties, taxes, and revenues.

The Sanhaja brought Ghana not only salt and manufactured goods but Islam. The ruling elite learned Arabic and accepted Muslim aid in organizing an efficient bureaucracy. Few Ghanaians (*GAHN-ē-ans*) converted at first, however. Because the king's authority was religious as well as political, he was reluctant either to convert personally or to urge spiritual changes on his people, most of whom continued to practice animism.

Kumbi.

By the tenth century, however, Ghana's kings had become wealthy enough to expand their domain northward until the kingdom dominated an area nearly as large as Texas. In the process they took control of the salt trade routes from the Sanhaja, who simultaneously were being squeezed out of their trans-Saharan trade routes by competition from Berbers to the north. Irritated by these events, the Sanhaja found solace and inspiration in a militantly puritanical sect of Islam called *al-Mirabitun* (al *mē-RAH-bih-TOON*), whose followers were known as **Almoravids**.

Almoravids convert Ghana to Islam

The Almoravids believed that to be successful in a war against unbelievers, the faithful Muslim must first conduct an inner struggle to purify his soul against the remnants of unbelief. This Berber movement, considered unorthodox by most Muslims, inspired the religious fervor the Sanhaja needed to fight back. In the 1050s they moved north, conquering Morocco in 1070. Between 1086 and 1106 they crossed into Spain and controlled the southern half of Iberia for more than a century. And in 1076, after more than a decade of fighting in the south, they conquered Ghana and converted its people to Islam. Historians debate whether conversion came primarily by force or persuasion. Available evidence indicates that the Almoravids blended trade, preaching, and military intimidation in a successful effort to Islamicize the most important kingdom in West Africa.

Ghana's conversion roots Islam in West Africa

Ghana's conversion altered its society and politics. Prior to widespread acceptance of Islam, the capital city of Kumbi was actually two distinct towns. In one, the king and his people lived and held court in buildings constructed largely from mud; in the other, Sanhaja traders lived and conducted their business in stone dwellings. Kings, believed to exercise divine powers, were considered holy persons, although not gods. Their political authority was grounded in the sense of awe they inspired in their people.

With the coming of Islam, mosques were built all over Kumbi as the two cities merged into one. Stone houses replaced those built of mud, and literacy in Arabic grew dramatically. The sacred role of the king gradually vanished before the worship of Allah, while Islamic prayer and ritual replaced Ghanaian magic. The Almoravids, however, were based to the north and presided over trade routes stretching from central Spain to the Niger River, and they possessed neither the skills nor the temperament to centralize such far-flung holdings. Having undermined the authority of the king, they substituted nothing for it. Their camels, sheep, and goats devoured Ghana's pastures and wrecked its agricultural base. As the Almoravids paid more and more attention to their territories in Spain, the Sondinke reasserted their leadership in Ghana itself.

For a time in the twelfth century Ghana seemed to be returning to its former greatness, but the bases of its power had been fractured. Kings, no longer seen as holy men, could not lead their people on the basis of their sacred powers. In addition, Ghana's agriculture never recovered from the Almoravid occupation, and its trade routes had been severely disrupted. Political uncertainty and the failure of the Almoravids to restore central authority prompted trans-Saharan caravans to bypass Ghana. Such routes were less convenient but also less troubled, and this shift in commerce proved fatal to Ghana's prosperity and power.

Trade begins to bypass Ghana

Islamic Mali, 1200–1450

The alteration of trade routes worked to the advantage of the Mandinke (*man-DIN-kā*) people, who had converted to Islam but had not been subjected to the Almoravids. Living close to the Niger in a region more suitable for agriculture than Ghana's northern areas, they controlled the more lengthy central trade routes and seized the opportunity to break free of Ghanaian control. In 1235, following a lengthy struggle among Mandinke tribes, a king named Sundiata (*soon-JAH-tah*) emerged victorious and began to construct a successor state to the ruined kingdom of Ghana. This new state, known as Mali, became even more influential.

The Mandinke people, who were linguistically tied to the Sondinke and who had been part of the kingdom of Ghana, built their successor state on the upper Niger River. Constructed on lines similar to those of Ghana, this new kingdom of Mali enjoyed a rich agricultural base. Rainfall in this sector of West Africa was more abundant in the twelfth century than it is today, and temperature ranges appear to have been less severe. A secure food supply combined with Ghana's traditional position astride the gold-salt trading route ensured population growth and employment opportunities necessary for success.

Mali emerges as Ghana's successor

All that was needed was capable leadership, and the Mandinke were fortunate to have the dynamic Sundiata, who ruled Mali from about 1235 until 1255. Sundiata was one of 12 royal brothers who together were heirs to the throne of the tiny West African kingdom of Kangaba. A neighboring king, Sumanguru, overran Kangaba early in the thirteenth century and murdered 11 of the brothers, sparing only Sundiata, a sickly child who was not expected to live to adulthood.

But Sundiata survived, grew into a strong warrior, and in 1235 defeated Sumanguru in battle. Within a few years Sundiata's forces made Mali the clear winner of the struggle among the Ghanaian successor states. Sundiata's capital in the Niger River town of Niani (*nī-AH-nē*) became both a base for military conquest and a vibrant commercial center. Sundiata's fame spread across Africa, and his immediate successors continued his expansionistic policies and consolidated Mali's wealth. Sundiata's son, Mansa (or "Emperor") Uli (1255–1270), was secure enough to leave his kingdom and become the first of his line to make the pilgrimage to Mecca.

Sundiata builds a powerful kingdom in Mali

Uli achieved that level of security through his consolidation of Mandinke control of the Songhai (*sahn-GĪ*) people and the central Saharan trade routes. Building on Mali's power and prosperity, Kankan Musa (*MOO-sah*), monarch from 1312 to 1337, eventually ruled almost twice the amount of territory once controlled by Ghana. Like rulers in France and China, he selected provincial administrators from within the ranks of his own family, assuring himself of their loyalty and centralizing control more tightly. Those men governed an empire that now commanded the only approaches to the salt deposits in the north, the gold mining district in the south, and the copper mines to the east. Mansa Musa, at the height of his powers, was the most formidable and wealthy ruler in the recorded history of West Africa, before or since.

Mansa Musa put Mali on the map, both literally and figuratively, during his pilgrimage to Mecca in 1324. Passing through Cairo on his way to Arabia, the emperor visited the sultan of Egypt. His caravan of thousands of camels, one hundred elephants, a vast number of servants and courtiers, and an incredible quantity of gold (which he lavished on innkeepers, camel tenders, and princes alike) made a powerful impression on the Arab world. Muslims in southwest Asia marveled at a visit from a monarch whose holdings were equivalent in size to all of Arabia. For his part, Musa learned about the Mediterranean world and Islam's role in it. His pilgrimage was glorified in song and story for centuries.

Mansa Musa connects Mali to Southwest Asia

Mansa Musa's caravan aimed to do more than enable a West African emperor to make the pilgrimage to Mecca and thus fulfill one of the five pillars of Islam. The spectacle must have been intended to strengthen Mali's connections to the principal cities of the Middle East. Indirect evidence indicates that Mansa Musa succeeded. A dormitory was established in Cairo for students from West Africa, and on his return to Mali, the emperor set about making Timbuktu into a center of learning and culture. Poets, mathematicians, astronomers, and theologians came to Mali from across the Arab world, drawn by the prospect of riches and the excitement of building a new empire of knowledge in yet another desert. Aided by an architect from al-Andalus, Musa built new mosques in Timbuktu and Gao (*GAOW*), along with flat-roofed houses in the Mediterranean style. Having become a renowned center of Islamic scholarship, Timbuktu attracted not only permanent residents but also North African visitors such as Ibn Battuta (*ibn bah-TOO-tuh*), who traveled through Mali in 1352–1353.

Mansa Musa on pilgrimage.

Ibn Battuta left a written record of an impressively sophisticated civilization (see "Ibn Battuta's Travels in West Africa"). He found the roads and cities clean and safe. The emperor, he wrote, was a just judge, quick to punish wrongdoers in accordance with Islamic law; and scholars, poets, and scientists made Mali an intellectual oasis. But other accounts suggest that Ibn Battuta, who spoke no African languages and could communicate only with the Arabic-speaking elites, overestimated both the sophistication of Mali and the extent of its practice of Islam. Mansa Musa apparently told visitors in the 1330s that he was reluctant to force the Mandinke to surrender their animist beliefs in spirits and magic. His own authority was derived in large measure from his status as a sacred person, and to disturb animist beliefs might jeopardize the regular mining of gold. A modern view of fourteenth-century Mali might characterize it as a pyramid, Islamic at the apex but animist at the base.

Mali was ruled by a Muslim emperor who claimed to be partly divine and whose immense wealth permitted him to employ a standing army of nearly 100,000 men. That sort of force bought a great deal of social control in West Africa. It did not, however, ensure a long life for Mali. By 1400 the Songhai tribe, which had been subdued by Mansa Uli, was reasserting itself, reviving its long-lost monarchy and pressing for independence.

Document 13.1 Ibn Battuta's Travels in West Africa, 1352

Ibn Battuta spent three decades during the fourteenth century traveling across the Islamic world. This excerpt from his account of his journeys illustrates the challenges of mining salt in West Africa.

From Marrákesh [in Morocco] I traveled with the suite of our master [the Sultan] to Fez, where I took leave of our master and set out for the Negrolands. I reached the town of Sijilmása, a very fine town, with quantities of excellent dates . . . At Sijilmása I bought camels and a four months' supply of forage for them. Thereupon I set out [in 1352] with a caravan including, amongst others, a number of the merchants of Sijilmása. After twenty-five days we reached Tagházá, an unattractive village, with the curious feature that its houses and mosques are built of blocks of salt, roofed with camel skins. There are no trees there, nothing but sand. In the sand is a salt mine; they dig for the salt, and find it in thick slabs, lying one on top of the other, as though they had been tool-squared and laid under the surface of the earth. A camel will carry two of these slabs. No one lives at Tagházá except slaves, who dig for the salt; they subsist on dates, camels' flesh, and millet imported from the Negrolands. The negroes come up from their country and take away the salt from there . . . The negroes use salt as a medium of exchange, just as gold and silver is used [elsewhere]; they cut it up into pieces and buy and sell with it. The business done at Tagházá, for all its meanness, amounts to an enormous figure in terms of hundredweights of gold-dust.

We passed ten days of discomfort there, because the water is brackish and the place is plagued with flies. Water supplies are laid in at Tagházá for the crossing of the desert which lies beyond it, which is a ten-nights' journey with no water on the way except on rare occasions . . . We passed a caravan on the way and they told us that some of their party had become separated from them. We found one of them dead under a shrub, of the sort that grows in the sand, with his clothes on and a whip in his hand. The water was only about a mile away from him.

SOURCE: Ibn Battúta, *Travels in Asia and Africa 1325–1354* (1929) 317–318.

Between 1464 and 1492 the Songhai king, appealing to animism against Islam despite his own status as a Muslim, carried on a relentless military campaign that eventually destroyed the Mali empire. In its place the Songhai king Ali erected a new realm that dominated the region for most of the next century.

The Songhai defeat Mali and create a successor state

Ethiopia's Christian Kingdom

Islam's expansion in Africa was neither steady nor consistent. Unqualified success in converting the north did not guarantee anything more than partial victory in the west. In the northeast, Muslim intentions to expand southward from Egypt and southwestward from Arabia were blocked not by traditional animists but by Christians in Ethiopia.

Human remains at least 1.5 million years old have been found in Ethiopia, and Egyptian writings speak of a civilization there nearly 2,000 years before the Common Era. The Jewish Scriptures record the visit of the Ethiopian Queen of Sheba to King Solomon of Judaea in the tenth century B.C.E. Apparently she came bearing great riches and irresistible charms, for the legend says that after she returned home she bore a son, through whom all

Map 13.4 Ethiopia and the Red Sea Region, 632 C.E.

Ethiopia was converted to Christianity during the earliest days of the Christian faith. It maintained trade relations with various Arabian kingdoms across the Red Sea. Notice Ethiopia's strategic location at the junction of the Gulf of Aden and the Red Sea. What aspects of Ethiopia's location and topography protected it against Islamic incursions after 632 C.E.?

future kings of Ethiopia claimed descent from Solomon. These references to Ethiopian civilization are, of course, indirect. Direct evidence of Ethiopian culture dates from the sixth century B.C.E., recorded in inscriptions and monuments unearthed by archeologists. These indicate settlement by southern Arabians who blended with the African population to create a hybrid Arab-African culture centered on the city of Axum (*ahk-SOOM*) (Map 13.4).

Like other African societies at this time, this civilization practiced a religion based on polytheism and animism. But its religious practice changed between 320 and 340 C.E., when the Ethiopian king Ezana (*eh-ZAH-nuh*) made Christianity the state religion. Converted by Byzantine Monophysite priests from Egypt, Ezana consecrated polytheist temples to the worship of Christ and created a Christian commonwealth in sub-Saharan Africa.

Ethiopia enjoyed abundant rainfall and rich soil, and Axum became a major participant in Red Sea trade. A favorable combination of commerce, agriculture, and cattle-raising enabled this Christian land to prosper despite its isolation from surrounding polytheist communities. Ethiopia's resources were sufficient to encourage its Christian rulers to project Axum's power across the Red Sea into southern Arabia. Thus Ethiopia became involved in Arabian tribal conflicts. In the early seventh century, Arabians periodically crossed the Red Sea to invade Ethiopia, without notable success.

In 615, several of Muhammad's followers who had fled Mecca arrived in Axum, where they were treated with great courtesy. Their presence in Ethiopia improved Axum's relations with Arabia, and they informed Muhammad of Ethiopia's friendship. The Muslims observed that the early forms of Christian ritual still practiced in Ethiopia were in some ways compatible with rules in the Qur'an, but the Prophet instructed the Muslims not to attempt conversions. To this good will was added Ethiopia's military and naval strength, which made it a discouraging target for invasion.

Ethiopia resists the expansion of Islam

But eventually Islamic expansion cut Christian Ethiopia off from the Red Sea trade and, after Muslims conquered Egypt in 642, from any consistent contact with the Byzantine Empire. Still, surrounded by Islam, Ethiopia for centuries maintained both its political independence and its Christian faith. Rumors of its continued existence fascinated twelfth-century European crusaders. They spread stories of a legendary ruler named Prester John, whose Christian kingdom in East Africa might assist Europeans in seizing the Holy Land from Islamic control. Though the crusaders made no connections with Ethiopia, the land retained its Christian heritage and its strong monarchical rule into the twentieth century.

The City-States of East Africa

Organized settlement along the East African coast is less than two thousand years old. A few small tools dating to 500 B.C.E. have been discovered, but these seem to have been used by small nomadic bands of foragers. These hunters traded with Greeks and Romans, furnishing them with African products such as ivory, rhinoceros horns, fragrant spices, and black slaves, but they built no permanent ports. Persians and Chinese certainly knew of East Africa, but they showed no more interest than the Greeks or Romans in colonizing it. No organized coastal settlements traceable to pre-Islamic times have been found. The history of East Africa changed, however, as first the Bantus and then the Muslims arrived and blended their cultures with those of the local foragers, as well as with each other.

Development of a Bantu-Arab Culture

When people arrived in East Africa to settle rather than forage, they appear to have come from two different directions: overland as part of the Bantu migrations from the west and across the Indian Ocean from Muslim lands. The Bantu came first, arriving from central Africa with cattle, kings, and castes of both warriors and priests. They also brought their Bantu language, which eventually combined with Arabic elements and script to develop into modern-day **Swahili**, a term designating not only the language but also the entire Bantu-Islamic East African culture. The first recognizable ruins in East Africa date from the ninth century C.E. and are clearly Bantu, consisting of small agricultural communities of huts and mud houses, with an occasional stone structure that was probably a religious shrine.

East Africa develops on a Bantu foundation

The Muslims came next, down the coast ("Swahili" means "coasters" in Arabic) from Egypt and Arabia in small, swift boats called dhows (*DOWS*), settling along the Somali shoreline and on the Indian Ocean island of Zanzibar. Islamic settlements, usually beginning as Muslim quarters in existing Bantu towns, began in earnest after 1100. The Arabs turned Bantu towns such as Kilwa, Mombasa, and Malindi into ports attracting oceangoing commerce. This trade in turn encouraged the creation of a series of East African city-states (Map 13.5).

An Arab dhow.

Muslim expansion into India, the extension of Egyptian influence southward from the Red Sea, and the conversion of Indonesians to Islam all encouraged the development of an Indian Ocean community of states and peoples. African traders sailed across the Indian Ocean not only to India but also to Indonesia, and the traffic flowed in both directions: Indians settled all along the East African coast, while Indonesians, accustomed to living on islands, preferred the huge offshore island of Madagascar, which they named Malagasy.

As Islam spread throughout the area, the East African city-states built an Islamic culture upon Bantu agricultural foundations. In the thirteenth and fourteenth centuries, great mosques were built at Kilwa, Mombasa, and Mogadishu (*mō-gah-DĒ-shoo*). Ibn Battuta, visiting the coast in 1331, described Mogadishu as a bustling port filled with wealthy Muslim merchants and a highly ritualized court life. Recent excavations at Kilwa have uncovered the foundations of an imposing royal palace, probably built in the Abbasid Islamic style in the early fourteenth century.

East Africa, like Greece, develops city-states

This Swahili East African culture suggests the power exerted by connections among differing civilizations. East Africa's strength and prosperity emerged not from

Map 13.5 City-States of East Africa, 1500

East Africa's city-states used the Indian Ocean as a highway across which to market products from the interior of Africa. This connected them to the Muslim-dominated Indian Ocean commercial network and turned their political and mercantile elites Islamic. In southern Africa, Great Zimbabwe developed as the center of an empire built on agriculture, animal husbandry, metalworking, and trade in gold, using Sofala as a port. Note that the trade routes hug the African and Asian coastlines. Why would mariners be reluctant to sail directly across the Indian Ocean, for example, from Goa to Kilwa?

the Bantu or Islamic traditions alone but from their blending, a synthesis that existed nowhere else on earth.

East and West Africa Compared

The societies of West and East Africa were both influenced by the Bantu, but they evolved in very different ways. In economic structure, commercial relations, political organization, and contact with non-African cultures, their differences were more pronounced than their similarities.

East African city-states, located on the coast, were oriented toward oceangoing trade. They depended on inland regions for food, which, given the ample rainfall and fertile soil of the East African savanna, was abundant. In West Africa, by contrast, cities were located inland, in the midst of agricultural regions, rather than on the coast. The Atlantic was uncharted and not usable for trade. West African trade was land-based, traversing the Sahara, while East Africa used the Indian Ocean—charted and easily navigable—as a commercial highway.

East and West Africa develop differently

In West Africa, this inward-looking organizational structure led eventually to the creation of extensive empires like Ghana, Mali, and Songhai. Each East African city-state, in contrast, had its own council, headed by a king or sheikh, and was jealously protective of its own rights and distinctive trading networks. While West African empires produced gold, salt, and copper, each East African city-state developed a specialty. One produced tools, another cotton goods, and a third perfumes. Some produced gold, but others did not.

In East Africa, the slave trade was not as profitable as it was in the west. But in both east and west, Muslims expanded that trade, shipping black captives to Arabia, Iraq, Persia, India, and China. In India and China, however, the demand for African slaves was limited by the large size and pervasive poverty of native populations, while in southwest Asia Muslims found it easier to get slaves from West Africa, by means of the trans-Sahara trade routes. Slavery nonetheless persisted in East Africa, where slaves were used to provide heavy labor and to transport goods.

Slavery becomes important to West Africa

The Bantu Connection: Central and Southern Africa

Of all the regions of Africa, the central and southern zones were least affected by the outside world before the fifteenth century C.E. The spread of Islam, which had such an important impact on other parts of the continent, had minimal influence in the center and south. Instead it was the long-enduring Bantu migrations that provided these regions with some degree of ethnic and linguistic cohesion.

The Bantu Influence

Central Africa consists primarily of tropical woodlands and grassy plains, ideal environments for bands of hunter-gatherers, including the diminutive peoples once referred to as Pygmies but known among themselves by such names as Mbuti. Central Africans such as these lived in the rain forests in groups without formal chiefs, moving from camp to camp to secure food. Farming and herding apparently came to this region with the Bantu migrations. Linguistic evidence indicates that people speaking Bantu languages migrated out of the West African savannas and into Central Africa. Archeological evidence suggests that this migration took place over many centuries, primarily between 700 B.C.E. and 800 C.E.

Bantu influence Central Africa

The Bantu brought herds of livestock, iron-making skills, and experience in raising crops such as millet and yams, which unfortunately did not grow as well in the tropical forests as they did in the savanna. Eventually the Bantu began to depend on bananas, the cultivation of which spread, in the fourth and fifth centuries C.E., from Indonesia through Madagascar and to Central Africa. Many Bantu remained in the region, interacting and intermarrying with its native peoples, while others moved on to the east and south.

Settlements in Central Africa, as elsewhere on the continent, were organized along village lines, with several villages sometimes combining to form a chiefdom and several chiefdoms occasionally constituting a kingdom. Several Bantu states had developed by the thirteenth century, including the kingdom of Kongo, which covered a large area around the Congo River. Within these realms, each village or group of villages was led by a hereditary chief, and the king was typically selected from among the chiefs by a group of electors. Elsewhere in the region, however, the people continued to live in stateless societies, without creating central governments.

For the most part, Central Africa remained agricultural and maintained only limited contact with peoples and civilizations from other parts of the continent. The dense rain forests and woodlands, the intense equatorial heat, and the presence of dozens of tropical diseases, such as encephalitis and yaws, ensured the region's isolation.

Farther south, however, the climate is variable and temperate, free from most of the parasites and insect-borne diseases that plague much of the continent south of the Sahara. The Bantu arrived there in the eighth century C.E., bringing with them their knowledge of ironworking and their agricultural skills. They developed a society in relative isolation. Southern Africa's remoteness from Arabia and Europe protected it from incursion and invasion until the sixteenth century.

Mining dominates the economies of early Southern African societies

Beginning in the twelfth century, governmental systems in Southern Africa appear to have become more sophisticated than those of their predecessors, characterized by more elaborate social stratification and increasing interest in the mining of gold and copper. Numerous prehistoric mines have been located in present-day Zimbabwe (*zim-BAHB-wā*) and in the Transvaal (*TRANZ-vahl*) region of South Africa. At least some of this gold reached the Indian Ocean trade through the East African city-state of Kilwa. The towns and trading centers of southern Africa never attained any degree of political unity, although they were influenced to some extent by Swahili culture. They also maintained commercial connections with an Islamic world that seems to have had little interest in venturing inland to convert their inhabitants.

Great Zimbabwe

The most fascinating of the southern African kingdoms is the unnamed one that built the imposing stone-building complex known as Great Zimbabwe. Although more than 150 stone ruins have been discovered in an area extending from southwestern Zimbabwe into Mozambique, most are fragmentary. But the ruins of Great Zimbabwe, an impressive set of buildings northeast of Johannesburg, South Africa, are comparable to no other ancient sites in Africa. Their rounded stone towers, walls, and battlements suggest raw power similar to that conveyed by the fortifications of medieval Europe.

Great Zimbabwe creates a Southern African empire

Great Zimbabwe was constructed over several centuries. Its earlier, less complex structures date from the eighth century, while the most recent buildings were erected between 1700 and 1750. This complex served as the political and ceremonial hub of a far-flung southern African empire, possibly as large as Mali. Like Ethiopia, this empire's prosperity rested upon a combination of agriculture, cattle raising, and commerce; unlike Ethiopia, however, its trade was based on gold. Abandoned gold mining sites abound throughout the region. Regrettably, we know almost nothing of this state's culture, religion, or political organization, since neither the people who built it nor the local Arab and African traders left any written records. In the nineteenth century the ruins of Great Zimbabwe were explored and mapped by a German geologist, who promptly but mistakenly declared that one of its buildings was a copy of King Solomon's temple. Today we know that Great Zimbabwe was built by south Africans from local granite without reference to Solomon's temple or any other non-African architectural achievements. But we know nothing beyond what archeological analysis can suggest.

Great Zimbabwe.

Chapter Review

Putting It in Perspective

Throughout most of their early history, African societies developed largely in isolation from each other, separated by distance, desert, forest, and heat. Two major developments, however, helped to foster connections among the continent's cultures. One was the great Bantu migration, a process lasting many centuries, which spread herding, farming, and ironworking across Africa's sub-Saharan lands and created some ethnic and linguistic links among their assorted peoples. Another development that built connections was the spread of Islam, which came about much more quickly and brought to Africa's northern, western, and eastern regions both a militant new religion and a common written language. Through Islam, these regions were connected to a vast commercial and cultural network that ranged from Spain to South Asia.

Neither of these developments, however, did much to intrude on the dramatic diversity that has continuously characterized the African continent. Indeed, in many ways, they added new elements to its rich and diverse history. Early Africa was influenced by many different peoples: Arab, Bantu, Berber, Mandinke, Mbuti, Sondinke, Tuareg, and numerous others. Today we enjoy only limited knowledge of the accomplishments of these peoples, and Africa's past is still inadequately understood. Archeology, anthropology, and oral tradition can only supplement the scant written record.

Reviewing Key Material

KEY CONCEPTS

Bantu, 302
animism, 304
Fatimid, 308

Isma'ilis, 308
Almoravids, 312
Swahili, 317

KEY PEOPLE

Sundiata, 313
Mansa Uli, 313

Mansa Musa, 314
Ibn Battuta, 314

ASK YOURSELF

1. Why were the Bantu migrations so important to the cultural development and cohesion of early African civilizations?
2. How did the arrival of the Muslims change North Africa?

3. How did the trans-Saharan trade change both West Africa and the Islamic world?

4. How did the Indian Ocean community affect the economic and political development of East Africa?

GOING FURTHER

Bovill, E. *The Golden Trade of the Moors: West African Kingdoms in the Fourteenth Century.* 1995.

Brooks, George. *Landlords and Strangers: Ecology, Society, and Trade in Western Africa, 1000–1630.* 1993.

Bulliet, Richard. *The Camel and the Wheel.* 1975.

Davidson, Basil. *The Lost Cities of Africa.* 1987.

Ehret, Christopher. *The Civilizations of Africa.* 2001.

Harris, Joseph. *Africans and Their History.* 1998.

Horton, M., and J. Middleton. *The Swahili.* 2000.

Iliffe, J. *Africans: The History of a Continent.* 1995.

Khapoya, V. *The African Experience: An Introduction.* 1994.

Levtzion, Nehemia. *Ancient Ghana and Mali.* 1973.

Marcus, Harold. *A History of Ethiopia.* 1994.

Mbiti, John. *African Religions and Philosophy.* 1990.

Middleton, John. *The World of the Swahili: An African Mercantile Civilization.* 1992.

Pouwels, Randall. *Horn and Crescent: Cultural Change and Traditional Islam on the East African Coast, 800–1900.* 1987.

Reader, J. *Africa: A Biography of a Continent.* 1997.

Sellassie, S. *Ancient and Medieval Ethiopian History.* 1972.

Shillington, Kevin. *History of Africa.* 1995.

Trimingham, J. *A History of Islam in West Africa.* 1970.

Trimingham, J. *Islam in East Africa.* 1974.

Vansina, Jan. *Paths in the Rainforest: Toward a History of Political Tradition in Equatorial Africa.* 1990.

Key Dates and Developments

?3000 B.C.E.– 700 C.E.	The Bantu Migrations
320–340	Establishment of Christianity in Ethiopia
639–642	Islamic conquest of Egypt
700–1750	Construction of Great Zimbabwe
702	Islamic conquest of the Berbers
711	Islamic conquest of Spain
800–1100	Zenith of the Kingdom of Ghana
929	Establishment of the Caliphate of Córdoba in Spain
969	Establishment of the Fatimid Caliphate in Egypt
1050–1100	Rise of the Almoravids in Morocco and Spain
1085–1492	The Reconquest in Spain
1100–1800	City-states in East Africa
1235	Sundiata founds the Kingdom of Mali
1324	Pilgrimage to Mecca of Mansa Musa
1352–1353	Ibn Battuta visits Mali
1433	Sack of Timbuktu by the Tuaregs

The Evolution and Expansion of East Asian Societies, 220–1240 C.E.

Buddhist Mandala

In the third through seventh centuries C.E., aided by increased connections among Indian, Central Asian, and East Asian societies, Buddhism emerged as East Asia's main belief system. This Buddhist diagram from ninth-century Japan, depicting numerous holy figures, is called a mandala and used as a focus for prayer and meditation.

Although revered as the father of Japanese culture, Prince Shotoku (*shō-TŌ-koo*), regent of Japan from 593 to 622, borrowed many ideas from neighboring China. He actively promoted Buddhism, which recently had spread from China to Japan. He sent Japanese missions to the Chinese mainland, brought Chinese artisans and artists to Japan, and adopted the Chinese calendar for Japanese use. To strengthen his government, he instituted a bureaucratic system based on the Chinese model. He even asserted equality with the Chinese emperor, sending him a letter addressed "from the ruler of the land of the sunrise to the ruler of the land of the sunset." According to Chinese sources, the emperor was not impressed—his reply was haughtily addressed "the emperor speaks to the prince."

East Asian Societies

Shotoku's story illustrates several important aspects of East Asian history in the centuries following the collapse of China's Han dynasty in 220 C.E. (Chapter 4). One decisive development was the expansion of Buddhism. In the third through sixth centuries, as the Chinese endured a prolonged era of disunity, Buddhism spread from India through Central Asia to China, eventually becoming China's main faith. From China it spread to Korea and Japan, where it was incorporated into the cultures and used by leaders such as Shotoku to enhance their authority.

Another key feature of East Asia in this era was the preeminence of China, reflected in Shotoku's borrowing of Chinese ideas and in the Chinese emperor's refusal to address Japan's prince regent as an equal. In the late sixth century, reunited and reinvigorated after centuries of chaos, China re-emerged as one of history's most powerful and prosperous empires. For the next seven centuries, its cohesion, commerce, technology, and influence were unsurpassed in East Asia. So successful was the Chinese system, and so strong was the Chinese state, that neighboring countries, including Prince Shotoku's Japan, often found it advantageous to imitate Chinese ways. Even the nomadic warriors from the north, who conquered much of northern China in the twelfth and thirteenth centuries, adopted many features of Chinese society.

A third key East Asian reality, embodied in Shotoku's assertion of equality with the Chinese emperor, was the ability of China's smaller neighbors to preserve their cultural autonomy in the face of Chinese preeminence. Vietnam, Korea, and Japan adopted Chinese concepts and conventions but altered them to fit their own cultures, creating in the process their own unique variants of East Asian civilization. And the northern nomadic invaders, after conquering parts of China, used Chinese methods and ideas to organize, govern, and exploit the lands that they had conquered. Connections and conflicts with neighboring peoples thus not only promoted China's preeminence but also in time helped these neighboring peoples hold their own against China.

China's Age of Disunity, 220–589

The foundations of Chinese preeminence had been laid by the end of the Han Empire (206 B.C.E.–220 C.E.), which rivaled the concurrent Roman Empire in size, population, and influence. After the fall of the Han, however, China endured an Age of Disunity (220–589 C.E.) that was in some ways similar to Europe's Early Middle Ages. As in the West, the Chinese Empire was torn apart by internal divisions and nomadic invaders. As in the West, the collapse of imperial authority was followed by a general decline in learning and commerce. And as in the West, where people in these troubled times sought comfort in Christianity, East Asians likewise found a new faith, turning to Buddhism for consolation in the midst of chaos.

The Three Kingdoms Era

The fall of China's Han dynasty in 220 C.E. resulted in the creation of three separate kingdoms in the north, south, and west, none strong enough to defeat the others (Map 14.1). Dominated by powerful families and warlords, these kingdoms engaged each other in an endless series of brutal battles. For most of the century, China was torn apart by civil wars and ravaged by diseases and natural disasters. By the year 280 the population, which had approached 60 million at the height of the Han dynasty, had declined to only 16 million by official counts. It was a terrifying time.

Civil war and devastation mark the Three Kingdoms Era

Despite all the devastation, however, the Chinese later came to see the era as exciting and heroic, full of great exploits and adventures. The *Romance of the Three Kingdoms*, China's most beloved epic tale, was told, retold, and embellished over the ages until it was finally published in its modern form in the sixteenth century. For countless generations, people in China have thrilled to its stories of three heroic blood brothers who, in the declining years of the Han dynasty, joined in the famous "Oath of the Peach Garden" to fight together for their country (see "Excerpts from *Romance of the Three Kingdoms*"). At times they managed to outwit their mortal enemy Cao Cao (*TSOW-TSOW*), a character based on a real Chinese general who seized power in northern China at the end of the Han era. In the long run, however, the three heroes failed to reunite China or preserve the Han dynasty.

The actual Three Kingdoms era (220–280) was disastrous for China. For decades descendants of the real Cao Cao fought against descendants of his foes, wreaking widespread havoc. By 280 a general from the north had managed to conquer the south and west, briefly reuniting the realm under the short-lived Jin (*JĒN*) dynasty. But after he died a decade later his 25 sons vied for power, dividing the domain into numerous warring states. Then one of them unwisely asked for assistance from the **Xiongnu** (*shē-ONG NOO*), warlike Turkic nomads from the Central Asian steppes who had long threatened China from the north. This request gave the Xiongnu, many of whom had entered the empire during its years of division, a new opportunity to overrun northern China. And they did so with a vengeance. By 317 the Xiongnu had laid waste to northern China's great cities, destroyed the imperial library at Chang'an, and driven the Jin emperors out of the north. The Xiongnu rulers also claimed the Mandate of Heaven, thereby asserting that they had divine approval to rule over China (Chapter 4).

Nomadic Xiongnu overrun northern China in early 300s

FOUNDATION MAP 14.1 China's Age of Disunity, 220–589

With the fall of the Han Dynasty, China experienced a long age of disunity, beginning with the Three Kingdoms Era (220–280), depicted in Map A. Notice that, after splintering into numerous small states in the Sixteen Kingdoms Era (304–439), shown in Map B, northern China was reunified under Toba (Northern Wei) rule from 439 to 534 (Map C) but again divided by the mid-500s (Map D), while southern China endured a succession of short-lived regimes known as the Six Dynasties. How did this age of disunity affect China's culture and religion?

Division, Invasion, Adaptation, and Migration

For the next century the Yellow River region, birthplace of Chinese culture, endured further ruin as Xiongnu chieftains and other tribal leaders ravaged the land and warred among themselves. This era was known in the north as the time of the Sixteen Kingdoms (304–439) for its rapid succession of short-lived regimes, most of which failed to establish any dynastic continuity. The era finally ended in 439 when the Toba (*TŌ-BAH*), a Mongolian nomadic tribe, gained control over the entire northern region (Map 14.1).

Document 14.1 Excerpts from *Romance of the Three Kingdoms*

Told and retold over the centuries until published in its modern form, Romance of the Three Kingdoms is China's most beloved epic tale. In the following excerpts from early in the story, its three heroes meet, agree to fight as one, and together take the "Oath of the Peach Garden" swearing brotherhood and mutual fidelity.

Empires wax and wane; states cleave asunder and coalesce . . . The rise of the fortunes of Han began with the slaughter of the White Serpent. In a short time the whole Empire was theirs and their . . . heritage was handed down until the days of Kuang-Wu . . . A century later came to the throne the Emperor Hsien, doomed to see the beginning of the division . . . known to history as the Three Kingdoms . . .

The Government went quickly from bad to worse, till the country was ripe for rebellion . . .

Yüan-tê was twenty-eight when the outbreak of the rebellion called for soldiers. The sight of the notice saddened him and he sighed . . . Suddenly a rasping voice behind him cried, "Noble Sir, why sigh if you do nothing to help your country?" Turning quickly he saw standing there a man . . . with a bullet head like a leopard's, large eyes, a pointed chin, and a bristling moustache. He spoke in a loud bass voice . . . "Chang Fei is my name . . . I live near here where I have a farm; and I am a wine-seller and a butcher as well. And I like to become acquainted with worthy men . . ."

Yüan-tê replied, "I am of the Imperial Family, Liu by name, and my distinguishing name is Pei. . . . I would destroy these rebels and restore peace to the land, but alas! I am helpless."

"I am not without means," said Fei. "Suppose you and I raised some men and tried what we could do."

. . . The two betook themselves to the village inn to talk over the project. As they were drinking, a huge, tall fellow appeared pushing a hand cart . . . He had eyes like a phoenix and fine bushy eyebrows like silkworms. His whole appearance was dignified and awe-inspiring. "I am Kuan Yü" said he; ". . . I have been a fugitive . . . for five years because I slew a ruffian who . . . was a bully. I have come to join the army here.

Then Yüan-tê told him his own intentions and all three went away to Chang Fei's farm . . . Said Fei, "The peach trees in the orchard behind the house are just in full flower. Tomorrow we will institute a sacrifice there and solemnly declare our intention before Heaven and Earth . . ."

All three being of one mind, the next day they prepared the sacrifices, a black ox, a white horse, and wine for libation. Beneath the smoke of the incense burning on the altar they bowed their heads and recited this oath: "We three, Liu Pei, Kuan Yü and Chang Fei, though of different families, swear brotherhood, and promise mutual help to one end. We will rescue each other in difficulty, we will aid each other in danger. We swear to serve the state and save the people. We ask not the same day of birth but we seek to die together. May Heaven, the all-ruling, and Earth, the all-producing, read our hearts, and if we turn aside from righteousness or forget kindliness may Heaven and man smite us!"

SOURCE: Lo Kuan-Chung, *Romance of the Three Kingdoms* (Tokyo: Charles E. Tuttle Company, 1959) I: 1, 2, 4–6.

Then, as so often happened after such conquests, the victors adopted features of the conquered society, thus connecting and combining the cultures. To strengthen and sustain their rule, for example, the Toba established a Chinese-style administrative system, staffed it with Chinese officials, and created a new dynasty called the Northern Wei (*WAY*) that restored to northern China a semblance of stability for most of the next century. In the 490s they even moved their capital to Luoyang, which had also been the capital during the Later Han, and made Chinese the official language of their realm.

Nomadic conquerors
adopt Chinese ways,
creating internal strife

In time these cultural adaptations helped to produce new conflicts. The adoption of the Chinese language created serious strife among the Toba warriors, many of whom resented the submersion of their own Mongolian language. Their resentment fueled internal strife, and by the 530s northern China was once again divided into different domains and dynasties.

Turmoil in north
prompts mass migration
to south

Meanwhile, China's ongoing turmoil had prompted a mass migration. As chaos enveloped the north in the third through sixth centuries, thousands of wealthy and educated Chinese families fled to the south. As a result this region, long accustomed to domination from the north, gradually emerged as China's cultural center as well as its most populous and prosperous zone. Largely spared the ravages that befell the north, southern China nonetheless experienced recurrent power struggles throughout the Age of Disunity as six successive short-lived regimes, later called the "Six Dynasties," sought but failed to achieve a long-lasting reign.

Central Asian Connections and the Arrival of Buddhism

During these tumultuous times, a new religion began to flourish in China. Founded in northern India in the sixth century B.C.E. by the man later called the Buddha, Buddhism was based on the belief, embodied in his Four Noble Truths, that one could best avoid life's pain by curbing desire and living righteously. After spreading throughout India, it was later adopted by the Kushans (*koo-SHAHNZ*), who ruled the region to India's northwest from roughly 50 to 240 C.E., and who fostered the Buddhist faith in many Central Asian towns and cities (Chapter 3).

Buddhism spreads to
China from India via
Asian trade routes

By this time there was regular contact between Central Asia and China. Most of the connections were commercial, as merchants traded along the Silk Road established in the early Han dynasty. But over time the trade routes conveyed not just goods but ideas, including religious beliefs. Promoted in Central Asia by the Kushans, Buddhist ideas spread from there along the Silk Road to China, arriving in the Later Han dynasty (Map 14.2).

Buddhism, meanwhile, had split into two branches. Theravada (*ter-ah-VAH-dah*) Buddhism, prevailing in Sri Lanka and Southeast Asia, largely remained true to the simple beliefs originally advanced by the Buddha. But Mahayana (*mah-hah-YAH-nah*) Buddhism, the branch that came to China through Central Asia, had all the trappings of an established religion, with priests, sects, monasteries, convents, and bodhisattvas (*bō-dih-SAHT-vuhz*). Said to be former mortals who had earned the endless peace called nirvana but postponed it to help others get there, bodhisattvas were revered as saviors by Mahayana Buddhists, who sought to follow their examples of mercy, hope, and love.

Statue of the Buddha
from Central Asia, Third
Century C.E.

Mahayana Buddhism fits
with Chinese traditions

Mahayana's features coincided with certain aspects of the Confucian and Daoist traditions, long prevalent in China. Its stress on charity, compassion, and good works, for example, paralleled the Confucian ethic of benevolence, civility, and public service. At the same time, its basic Buddhist emphasis on meditation and curbing desire concurred with Daoism's focus on silence and passivity. Furthermore, like Mahayana Buddhism, Daoism had evolved over time into a complex religion with numerous devotions and divinities, a hierarchical structure of priests and officials, and a network of monasteries and convents. In fact, although Daoism and Buddhism retained their separate identities, to the common people of China they were often indistinguishable from each other. Chinese people could thus adopt Buddhism without forsaking their traditional beliefs.

Map 14.2 Buddhism Spreads to East Asia, Second Through Sixth Centuries C.E.

In the early centuries of the common era, Buddhism expanded from its origins in India throughout the eastern part of Asia. Notice that, while Theravada Buddhism spread across Southeast Asia, Mahayana Buddhism expanded through Central Asia to China, where it took hold during the Age of Disunity (220–589), and eventually spread from there to Korea and Japan. What factors and conditions facilitated Buddhism's spread?

The Spread of Buddhism in China

Initially Buddhism did not make much of an impact in China. As long as the Han dynasty flourished, Confucianism reigned as the official philosophy, and the Confucian bureaucrats who ran the country enjoyed great prestige as preservers of stability and order.

Foreign religions such as Buddhism, dismissed by Confucians as alien cults, attracted little following.

Instability and disunity aid Buddhism's spread

In the Age of Disunity, however, the cultural climate changed. As nomadic invasions and civil wars shattered China's stability, the prestige of the Confucians declined, and Chinese cultural confidence gave way to confusion and anxiety. People began to look for relief in creeds such as Buddhism and Daoism, which promised inner peace and relief from life's burdens.

In the fourth century, then, in the chaotic conditions of northern China, Buddhism began to thrive. With its emphasis on avoiding desire and ambition, the faith was actively fostered by Xiongnu warlords, who hoped to keep power by promoting passivity among the people. Buddhism's premise that life was painful reflected the people's perceptions, while Buddhism's promise of escape from pain consoled them. The faith offered hope of salvation from suffering and the prospect of attaining nirvana, perpetual peace. Buddhism's numerous shrines and temples gave Chinese artists and sculptors opportunities to express creativity, while its monasteries and convents, like the ones in Christian Europe, provided a refuge for those who felt called to a life of contemplation and devotion. By 400 C.E. most of northern China had accepted the new faith.

Buddhist temple in north-western China.

Buddhism comes to southern China from India and from the north

By this time Buddhism had also begun to penetrate the south. Partly it came from northern China, where it was already established, and partly it arrived over land and sea routes from India and Southeast Asia. From 399 to 414 a Chinese Buddhist monk named Faxian (*FAH shē-YAN*) made a historic pilgrimage from China to India, crossing treacherous mountain passes on foot. After spending a decade in India, visiting Buddhist shrines and talking with Indian Buddhists, he returned by sea to southern China with hundreds of Indian Buddhist texts, which he painstakingly translated into Chinese. During the rest of the fifth century, his efforts and those of other monks and missionaries helped make Buddhism increasingly popular in southern China, where it attracted both leaders and common folk. Finally, in 517, it was proclaimed the official religion there by Liang Wudi (*lē-AHNG WOO DĒ*), the so-called Bodhisattva Emperor, a ruler so devout that, much to his advisors' dismay, he twice gave up his throne to become a Buddhist monk. By 589, when China re-emerged as a unified empire, the entire land had become a bastion of Buddhism.

China's Age of Preeminence, 589–1279

History does not repeat itself, but similar patterns do at times recur. There are, for example, striking parallels between China's initial unification in the third century B.C.E. (Chapter 4) and its reunification in the sixth century C.E. In both instances a ruler from the north united the realm after centuries of chaos, establishing a powerful but brief regime that paved the way for a far more eminent, enduring dynasty. In the third century B.C.E., the First Emperor ended the Warring States Era by conquering all of China, founded the short-lived Qin dynasty, and opened the way for four centuries of Han dynastic rule. In the sixth century C.E. a northern general named Yang Jian (*YAHNG jē-AHN*) ended the Age of Disunity by conquering all of China, founded the short-lived Sui (*SWAY*) dynasty, and opened the way for six centuries of Chinese preeminence under the Tang (*TAHNG*) and Song (*SŌNG*) dynasties.

China Reunited: The Sui Dynasty, 589–618

Yang Jian, a general with both Chinese and Toba ancestry, emerged as China's dominant force through crafty opportunism. First he married a wealthy noblewoman, whose status helped him become the main advisor to a northern emperor; then he wed his daughter to that emperor. When that emperor died soon after she bore him a son, Yang Jian arranged to have himself named regent for his own grandson, the infant who inherited the throne. Then, in 581, he deposed the boy monarch and claimed Heaven's Mandate for himself, starting a new dynasty called the Sui. Using skillful propaganda, carefully cultivated Buddhist support, and a well-planned river and land campaign, he conquered one-by-one the several weak states that had survived in the south. By 589, for the first time in centuries, one man ruled all of China.

Yang Jian conquers and reconnects China, initiating Sui dynasty

Yang Jian, who reigned from 581 to 604 as Wendi (*WUN-DĒ*), proved a resourceful emperor. He devised a nationwide law code and restored the civil service system begun by the Han dynasty. He centered his government at Chang'an, earlier the Han capital, and built it into one of the world's great cities. He also began construction of the Grand Canal, a thousand-mile waterway linking the Yellow River in the north with the Yangzi River in the south. Henceforth, since China's great rivers flow from west to east, the canal played a crucial role in connecting the north with the south, transporting troops and grain, and thereby combining the north's military might with the south's agricultural prosperity.

Central rule is restored as Grand Canal links north and south

Yang Jian's son and heir, however, was a disastrous ruler. Yangdi (604–618) has gone down in Chinese annals as a despot who reportedly poisoned his father to hasten his own rule, then alienated his people by imposing harsh taxes and sacrificing millions of laborers' lives to erect an extravagant palace, complete the Grand Canal, and rebuild the Great Wall. He also launched a series of disastrous wars that ruined the economy and prompted widespread rebellions. Then he abandoned his armies and fled to the rural south where he lived in luxuriant debauchery until he was murdered in 618. That same year the powerful Duke of Tang, one of Yangdi's most effective governors and generals, declared himself emperor and assumed the Mandate of Heaven, thereby putting an end to the Sui dynasty.

The Grand Canal.

China Triumphant: The Tang Dynasty, 618–907

The seizure of power by the Duke of Tang ushered in a new regime known as the Tang dynasty (618–907). Under its dominion, China attained new heights in political stability, economic prosperity, military expansion, cultural sophistication, and technological innovation.

The new Tang Dynasty builds on Sui foundations

The Tang era's most successful ruler was Li Shimin (*LĒ SHUR-MIN*), son of the Duke of Tang. After persuading his reluctant father to claim the throne, the 18-year-old Li led a series of skillful campaigns against numerous revolts while holding back the northern nomadic invaders. Then, after ambushing and killing his two older brothers, he forced his father to abdicate and assumed the throne himself at age 26. Bold and energetic, Li then reigned from 626 to 649 as the Emperor Taizong (*TĪ-ZŌNG*).

Nothing seemed impossible to Taizong. He forced the northern nomads to become his vassals and allies, then with their help invaded Central Asia and conquered Turkestan (Map 14.3). He even sent an army to India to arrest a local ruler who had insulted his ambassador. In China he promoted education, patronized the arts, and revitalized the

Map 14.3 China Under the Tang Dynasty, 618–907

Under the Tang Dynasty, China expanded into Central Asia, reopening trade routes and cultural ties with its various neighbors. Observe that the Grand Canal, constructed under the Sui Dynasty (589–618) and expanded under the Tang, linked the Yellow and Yangzi Rivers and the port of Hangzhou, expediting commerce and communication between China's north and south. How did good internal connections contribute to the Tang Empire's power and wealth?

civil service. Although a Confucian, he promoted religious toleration and devotion among the Buddhist and Daoist masses. Revered as a hero, he attained a legendary status among the Chinese people.

Another notable Tang-era leader was Wu Zhao (*WOO-JOW*), later known as Empress Wu. According to traditional accounts, in her youth she was one of Taizong's many concubines and was obliged to enter a Buddhist convent after he died. But she was only 24 and reportedly a reluctant nun. When the new emperor visited her convent, the accounts assert, she seduced him and won his heart. She became his full-time consort and

Wu Zhao rises from concubine status to become Empress Wu

then his official empress. In 660, when his eyesight failed, she took over as informal regent and skillfully ruled the realm, staffing the government with her supporters and killing those who got in her way. In 683, when the emperor died, she had their sons locked in the palace and ruled as regent until 690, when she formally claimed the throne for herself. Finally, in 705, a palace coup forced the aged Empress Wu to abdicate the throne and resume her long-lost calling as a nun.

Although disgruntled male Confucian historians later denounced her as a brutal and shameless opportunist, Wu Zhao actually accomplished a great deal. During her long period of power she granted tax relief, improved the civil service system, decreased the power of the old nobility, fostered military expansion, and promoted economic prosperity.

Empress Wu.

Not long after Wu Zhao's removal, one of her grandsons took the throne as Emperor Xuanzong (*shu-WAHN ZŌNG*), reigning from 713 to 756. His early reign was a time of peace, prosperity, and cultural achievements, the age of China's most beloved poets and a high point of Chinese art. The emperor himself patronized the arts, lengthened the Grand Canal, reformed the bureaucracy and coinage, and maintained a magnificent court. But in his later years, after falling madly in love with a concubine called Yang Guifei (*YAHNG GWĀ-FĀ*), he neglected his duties and let her relatives run the country. In 751, as the empire drifted without strong direction, its armies were driven from Central Asia by Islamic forces. In 755 a massive revolt led by An Lushan (*AHN LOO-SHAHN*), a Chinese general of Turkish descent, forced the emperor and Yang Guifei to flee from the capital for their lives. Thus began a civil war that brought about the strangling of Yang Guifei, the abdication of Xuanzong, and the devastation of China.

The Tang dynasty survived the An Lushan revolt, but it never regained its earlier domination. Local warlords took advantage of the turmoil to reassert their power, while the palace eunuchs guarding the emperor's concubines came to dominate the court. Religious strife broke out as Confucian civil servants came to resent the untaxed wealth of Buddhist monasteries, some of which had acquired vast riches through generous donations. In the mid-800s, as Confucian civil servants worked to suppress Buddhism as a "foreign cult," a Daoist emperor who hated all things foreign ordered thousands of Buddhist shrines and monasteries destroyed. Later that century a famine in eastern China sparked a mass rebellion and convinced many that the Tang regime had lost Heaven's Mandate. Finally in 907, as local warlords carved up the country, one of them overthrew the dynasty, leading to a new age of disunity.

Revolts, religious strife, and famine destroy the Tang dynasty

China in Turmoil: Ten Kingdoms and Five Dynasties, 907–960

Fifty-three years of dynastic disruption followed the end of the Tang era. The south was partitioned into warring states, later called the Ten Kingdoms. The north retained a measure of unity under a string of brief regimes called the Five Dynasties but also lost a number of border provinces to the Khitans (*KĒ-TAHNZ*), a people from Manchuria who emerged as a new nomadic threat. Establishing a capital at what is now Beijing (*BĀ-JĒNG*), the Khitans created an expansive domain called the Liao (*lē-OW*) Empire,

Nomads again move into northern China during turmoil

Map 14.4 Song China and the Khitan Liao Empire, 960–1125

Under the Song Dynasty (960–1279), China enjoyed a renewed era of stability and prosperity. Notice, however, that the northernmost part of China was controlled by the Khitans, a nomadic people from the northeast, whose Liao Empire (907–1125) also ruled much of what is now Manchuria and Mongolia. How did the Song approach to northern nomadic peoples differ from that of the Tang?

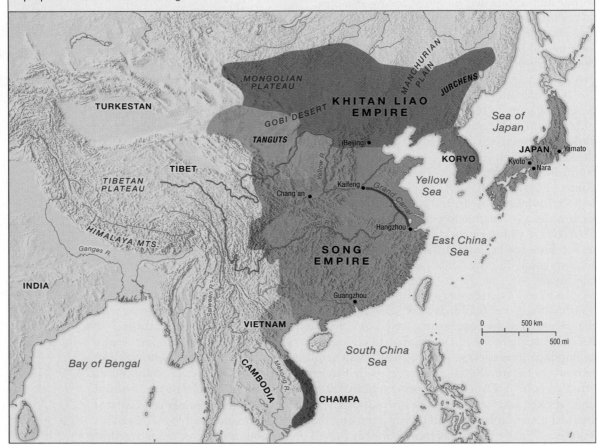

which for the next few centuries ruled Manchuria, Mongolia, and parts of northern China (Map 14.4).

Meanwhile, in 960, a Chinese general named Zhao Kuangyin (*JOW KWAHNG-YIN*) began the reunification of the rest of China. He overthrew the last of the north's Five Dynasties at the urging of his troops, who proclaimed him emperor and pledged him their absolute allegiance. Once they had done so, he compelled his key officers to retire, thus preventing their emergence as warlords and ensuring that none of them could threaten his rule. He then annexed most of the south's Ten Kingdoms, exploiting their peoples' hunger for unity and peace.

China Resurgent: The Song Dynasty, 960–1127

In the process of reunifying China, Zhao Kuangyin founded the Song Dynasty, which lasted from 960 until 1279. In its later years, however, it ruled only the south, and it never matched the size or military success of the Han and Tang dynasties. But it was second to none in political and economic vitality.

Zhao Kuangyin, who reigned from 960 to 976 as Emperor Taizu (*TĪ-DZUH*), took a series of decisive steps. He restored and strengthened the Confucian civil service, promoting professional governance. He banned court eunuchs from holding high state office, preventing conflicts between them and the civil servants. He centralized control over the army, reducing the influence of local nobles and warlords. Toward the end of his life he decreed that he would be succeeded, not by his young son, but by his talented brother, who then completed the conquest of the south to consolidate dynastic control.

Unlike their predecessors, however, the Song rulers made little attempt to conquer or control foreign lands, judging that such ventures in the past had drained the country's resources. In 1004, for example, after a futile effort to subdue the Khitans and win back the border provinces they ruled, the Song made peace and agreed to pay them a large annual tribute. Similar settlements, far less costly than conquest and control, were also arranged with other peoples on China's borders. This policy reversed China's age-old practice of making weaker neighbors pay tribute, but it did enable China to buy peace with tribute in silver and silks.

The Song regime placates neighbors rather than fighting them

Instead of expanding outward, the dynasty focused its energies on controlling China itself. To stop the rise of local warlords and prevent armed revolts, it tightly managed the army, frequently rotating commands among generals to keep them from turning the forces they led into their own personal armies. To limit the power of aristocratic families that had often dominated regional affairs, it enticed some of them to move to the new capital at Kaifeng (*KĪ-FUNG*), where they lived in splendor but had little local power.

The Song regime reduces the power of generals and nobles

To administer the empire, the Song regime consolidated the Confucian civil service bureaucracy. **Civil service exams**, established initially in the Han dynasty and revived under the Sui and Tang, were now standardized and strengthened, requiring of applicants comprehensive knowledge of the Confucian classics. Potential state bureaucrats were required to pass a series of extremely rigorous exams, first on the regional and then on the national level. So competitive were the tests that not even 1 percent of the candidates actually became state officials. Those who did, once in office, had to earn their promotions through performance. As a result, their loyalty was largely to those who had the power to promote them—that is, to the emperor and central government, which hence became more autocratic than ever.

The Song regime strengthens the civil service and exam system

Chinese civil servants typically were quite conservative. Trained in the ancient classics, which many had learned by heart, Confucian bureaucrats were steeped in tradition and devoted to the system that reinforced stability, fostered civility, and brought them great power and prestige. Most came from wealthy families, since they could send their sons to schools or hire tutors to prepare them for the civil service exams. To ensure they had the means to do so, families of state officials often intermarried with those of wealthy landowners. This practice over time helped create a Confucian **scholar gentry**—an educated elite class supported by both official state posts and large rural estates—that tended to be self-perpetuating and resistant to change.

Confucians thwart efforts to reform Chinese economy

As the Song regime searched for ways to cover the costs of its vast army and bureaucracy, however, a key civil servant decided that change was needed. From 1069 to 1085 a reforming official named Wang Anshi (*WAHNG AHN-SHUR*), as the emperor's main advisor, sought to boost state revenues by increasing the wealth of the farmers and merchants who paid the state taxes and duties. He intervened in the economy, establishing price controls and government monopolies, introducing a graduated land tax that increased with the soil's productivity, and providing low-interest loans to peasants so they could increase their harvest by buying seeds and tools. He engaged the state directly in commerce, acquiring products in one area and selling them elsewhere at a profit. He even tried to open up the civil service exams to more talented young men. But his actions horrified other civil servants, who, as members of the Confucian elite, looked down upon merchants, had little use for commerce, and feared that his reforms would upset their domination of the social order. When floods, droughts, and famine, sparking widespread unrest, seemed to show that Heaven did not favor Wang Anshi, his enemies managed get him dismissed and undo most of his reforms.

Commerce makes Song China an economic giant

Wang's enemies could not, however, undo the growing influence of the commercial class. Although Confucians ranked merchants as nonproducers at the bottom of the social scale, merchants helped to bring about huge advances in money and banking, trade and transport, manufacturing, and technology, fostering a Chinese commercial revolution. Combined with vast increases in agricultural output, these advances also promoted urbanization. By the twelfth century the empire had at least fifty large cities, each with hundreds of thousands of inhabitants. With abundant capital and resources, expanding foreign and domestic markets, many miles of roads and canals, merchant ships, textile mills, printed books, advanced military technology, flourishing farmlands, and thriving cities, Song China appeared to have all that was needed for sustained economic and industrial growth, and perhaps even global domination.

China Divided: Jurchens and Southern Song, 1127–1279

Warlike nomads again overrun northern China

In the twelfth and thirteenth centuries, however, China's growth was disrupted again by nomads to the north. In 1114 the Jurchens (*JUR-chenz*), warlike pastoral nomads from Manchuria, staged a massive rebellion against the Khitans and their Liao Empire. Seeing this rebellion as an opportunity to win back for China the northern border provinces under Khitan control, the Song emperor allied with the Jurchens. The result was disaster for the dynasty. In the 1120s, after totally crushing the Khitans, the Jurchens turned violently against their Chinese allies. By 1127 the Jurchens had overrun all of northern China, plundered the capital at Kaifeng, and driven the Song armies deep into the south (Map 14.5).

The Song regime eventually rallied, but it never regained control of the north, where the Jurchens ruled for the rest of the century. The Song rulers could do little more than secure and stabilize the south. Establishing a new capital in 1138 at the bustling

Map 14.5 The Jurchens and the Southern Song, 1127–1279

After overthrowing the Khitan Liao Empire in the 1120s, the Jurchens, nomadic warriors from the Manchurian Plain, attacked the Song Dynasty and overran all of northern China. Note, however, that the Song Dynasty, now called the Southern Song (1127–1279), continued to govern the south, where it ruled over a prosperous realm with thriving commerce until the Mongol invasions of the thirteenth century. How did southern China continue to prosper despite the loss of the north?

eastern port of Hangzhou (*HAHNG-JŌ*), they maintained their regime in southern China until 1279.

During this era, known as the Southern Song, the regime ruled only half the country. But the half it ruled was probably the most prosperous place on earth. Agriculture and technology continued to advance and flourish; cities and commerce continued to grow and thrive. Although substantially reduced in its size and power, the realm was as rich as ever. Nonetheless, despite its great wealth and technical sophistication, it could not survive the great challenge of the thirteenth century, when first the Jurchens and later the Song fell to the Mongol conquests (Chapter 15).

The Song regime survives and thrives in south until the Mongol conquest

Highlights and Hallmarks of Chinese Society

From the sixth through twelfth centuries, during the Tang and Song dynasties, China may well have been the world's most prosperous and cosmopolitan culture. The empire had extensive trade; innovative technology; inspiring poetry and art; robust religious institutions; large, vibrant cities; and intense intellectual creativity. But many Chinese people, including most peasants and women, derived little benefit from their country's commercial and cultural preeminence.

Commercial and Technological Innovations

Stability, security, roads, and waterways strengthen Chinese commerce

China's commercial preeminence was based on such factors as effective governance, agricultural abundance, and creative innovation. The Tang and Song regimes, with their capable civil servants and soldiers, typically provided the internal stability, effective law enforcement, and security from foreign threats needed for commerce to thrive. They also constructed and maintained the thousands of miles of waterways and highways, including the bustling Grand Canal and the tree-lined roads alongside it, that connected China's productive farmlands with its urban commercial economy.

Government-forged connections also contributed to China's agricultural abundance. Tang and Song domination of northern Vietnam, for example, introduced farmers in southern China to new strains of fast-growing rice developed in the region of Champa (now central Vietnam). Since Champa rice matured in three months, rather than in five like other strains, farmers could double their output by growing two crops in succession, rather than one, each year. Other agricultural innovations, including the use of animal-powered pumps and waterwheels to bring new lands under irrigation, added substantially to China's food supply.

Terraced rice fields in southern China.

Farming advances in turn helped sustain China's growing population, which rose from under 50 million in the seventh century to over 100 million in the twelfth, and contributed to the rise of commercial farming. As cultivating rice took up less of their time, Chinese farmers additionally produced and sold marketable goods such as silk, cotton, and tea, a distinctive Chinese drink that emerged in the Age of Disunity and later gained global popularity. Most important, perhaps, the growing food supply supported large numbers of merchants, manufacturers, artisans, and inventors, some of whom developed innovations that would transform the world.

Farming advances increase population and commerce

Some innovations improved domestic commerce. As copper and silver grew scarce, for example, and as the coins made from them proved cumbersome for interregional trade, enterprising Tang era merchants introduced "flying cash" (mobile money)—paper notes that could be bought in one region and redeemed for face value in another. These notes in turn prepared the way for the use of checks, credit certificates, and government-issued paper money during the Song era. The invention and use of the abacus, a computing device with sliding counters grouped in multiples of ten, also greatly aided commercial calculations.

Giant ships and magnetic compasses enhance international trade

Other innovations enhanced international trade. As bandits and brigands made land trade dangerous along the Central Asian Silk Road (Chapter 4), especially after Tang armies lost control of that region in 751 C.E., Chinese merchants increasingly transported their silks, ceramics, tea, and other goods by sea. Giant ships, sailing from Chinese ports, were equipped by Song times with multiple masts, watertight compartments, and magnetic compasses. The compass was especially influential, enabling ships to stay on course while traveling great distances with no land in sight. Adopted from the Chinese by Arab sailors, and later used by European explorers, the compass eventually helped open an era of global trade and travel.

Additional Chinese innovations also had global impact. Gunpowder, which eventually revolutionized warfare around the world, was originally used in Tang China for fireworks, then by Song armies in grenades, flame-throwers, and crude early cannons. Coal was first used in northern China as fuel, and was later used to smelt iron and make steel, eventually resulting in sturdier weapons and farm tools the world over. Song-era China also developed, among other things, a mechanical clock and cotton textile mills centuries before other societies.

China's most influential invention, however, may have been the printing process. The printing of books, using blocks of wood that were carved for each page and brushed with ink to make impressions on paper, began in Tang China and improved during Song times. Song-era printers also experimented with moveable type, using small blocks of print for each character, but since Chinese writing employs thousands of characters, most Chinese printers found it more efficient to simply make a block for each page. Printing eventually spread westward from China to the Muslim and Christian worlds, sparking a global revolution in information and learning.

Gunpowder and other Chinese innovations will have a global impact

Early carved woodblock used for Chinese printing.

Spiritual, Intellectual, and Cultural Creativity

In China itself, printing was used first to publish Buddhist scriptures and later to record the works of religious thinkers, scholars, philosophers, and poets. By providing writers, artists, and artisans with security and food so they could specialize in diverse pursuits, Tang and Song stable governance and agricultural abundance also contributed to China's flourishing intellectual and cultural life.

Stability and prosperity foster cultural creativity

In the early Tang era, while Buddhism enjoyed broad support from the people and their rulers, several innovative Buddhist sects became very influential. One was **Pure Land Buddhism**, which claimed that humans could not achieve enlightenment by their own works and instead preached salvation by faith in the Buddha of Infinite Light who ruled the Western Paradise, or "Pure Land." Another was **Chan (*CHAHN*) Buddhism**, known in Japan as **Zen**, which taught that meditation was the only path to enlightenment, and stressed love of nature, simplicity of life, and individual self-discipline.

In the late Tang era, as noted above, Confucian officials began suppressing Buddhism as a "foreign cult," bringing about both a Buddhist decline and Confucian revival that continued into the Song era. But the "neo-Confucianism" that emerged triumphant was far more complex and theoretical than the simple, pragmatic ethical system devised by Confucius and his followers over a millennium earlier. Responding to the challenge of Buddhism and Daoism, neo-Confucian thinkers grappled with such concepts as the nature of reality and the meaning of life. In contrast to the Buddhists and Daoists, however, neo-Confucians concluded that reality is understood through education and reason rather than through meditation, and that life derives meaning from action and involvement rather than withdrawal. By the twelfth century, when the great philosopher

Confucianism rebounds and synthesizes learning and tradition

Zhu Xi (*JOO-SHĒ*) created a neo-Confucian synthesis stressing tradition, education, and personal morality, neo-Confucianism reigned supreme among the educated elite. Buddhism retained a following but ceased to be China's main faith, while Daoism continued to thrive among peasants, poets, artists, and others who had close connections with nature.

Chinese poetry flourishes in the Tang era

China's most beloved poets, Li Bai (*LĒ-BĪ*) and Du Fu (*DOO-FOO*), flourished in the early Tang era. Li Bai (701–763) was a homeless wanderer and Daoist free spirit, undisciplined and romantic, a lover of nature and wine. He wrote more than 20,000 poems, including the haunting "Drinking Alone by the Moonlight," which contains the following lovely but lonely lines:

> A cup of wine, under the flowering trees;
>
> I drink alone, for no friend is near.
>
> Raising my cup, I beckon the moon to join me;
>
> For he, with my shadow, will make three men . . .

According to legend, Li Bai's career ended during a drunken nighttime boat ride, when the sentimental poet drowned while trying to embrace the moon's reflection on the water.

Although a great friend and admirer of Li Bai, Du Fu (712–770) was a more refined and sober poet who wrote in structured verse and was known for his Confucian compassion and strong social conscience. Having failed the civil service exams as a young man, he lived for years in poverty and endured many hardships. Some of his poems contrast the wasteful indulgence of the rich with the sufferings of the common people, as reflected in these famous phrases:

> Inside the red gates the wine and meat go to waste;
>
> On the roadside lie the bones of men who died from cold . . .

Turning away from Confucianism, a system that stamped him a failure, Du Fu became a Buddhist and spent his last years as an impoverished pilgrim. On one of his journeys he met a government official who had read and appreciated his poetry. The delighted official took the poet home, wined and dined him, and gave him his own bed to sleep in. Du Fu died the next morning.

Arts and crafts thrive in Tang and Song eras

Chinese arts and crafts likewise flourished in the Tang and Song eras. Tang sculptors produced splendid Buddhist statues to adorn many temples as well as lifelike figures of horses and soldiers to guard the emperors' tombs. Other skilled artisans fashioned fine porcelain vessels and glazed pottery statuettes. Song-era painters refined the technique of working with a flexible brush on silk, creating naturalistic masterpieces ranging from magnificent vistas and landscapes to exquisite studies of birds, insects, bamboo sprigs, and flowers.

Glazed pottery horse from the Tang era.

Urban and Rural Society

China's commercial, cultural, and intellectual life was centered mainly in the cities, especially the imperial capitals, which ranked among the world's largest and busiest metropolitan areas. While urban dwellers enjoyed abundant goods and cultural activities, however, village farmers, who made up most of the population, lived in stark simplicity. Women of all classes were typically subordinate to men.

Chang'an, China's capital during the Tang dynasty, was that era's grandest city, with an overall population of almost two million, half of whom lived within its walls. It was laid out as a rectangle, roughly five by six miles, with wide north-south and east-west boulevards connecting its main gates and other avenues dividing it into a huge grid (Map 14.6). The city was dotted with Buddhist and Daoist temples and monasteries. Its two large markets boasted goods and visitors from all over Asia, as well as performers, musicians, artists, craftsmen, and fashionably dressed shoppers. The emperor's palace sat in the north, behind the Imperial City, a section of Chang'an that served as government headquarters.

Kaifeng and Hangzhou, the Song era capitals, strove to imitate Chang'an's size and splendor. Kaifeng, located near where the Grand Canal connected with the Yellow River, was a commercial hub that had shops, warehouses, shipyards, restaurants, and hotels

China's great cities provide extensive commerce and diverse activities

Map 14.6 Chang'an: China's Imperial Capital, 589–907

Chang'an, the imperial capital of China during the Sui and Tang Dynasties, featured rows of blocks and boulevards in a symmetrical rectangular layout. Observe that its city walls, within which lived up to a million people, also encompassed markets, temples, monasteries, gardens, lakes, and government facilities. What other features and diversions did this great city provide?

▲ Buddhist monasteries
● Daoist monasteries
□ Manichean, Christian, Zoroastrian temples
▬ Gates in the city walls

0   2 km
0   2 mi

Imperial Park

IMPERIAL PALACE

IMPERIAL CITY

ADMINISTRATIVE CITY

West Market

East Market

Hibiscus Garden

Serpentine Lake

but lacked the elegant symmetry of Chang'an. Hangzhou, situated south of the Yangzi River at the canal's other end, was a striking seaport brimming with bridges and waterways, merchants and shops, cabarets and tea houses, entertainers and artisans, public baths and brothels. In the thirteenth century, long after Hangzhou had passed its prime, European observer Marco Polo nonetheless described it as the world's "finest and noblest city."

The peasants, who made up most of China's population, knew little of this urban elegance. Dwelling in rustic rural villages, they rarely traveled farther than the nearest market town. The young men worked the fields around the village, and the elder males reigned as family patriarchs. But women typically ran the household, preparing meals, raising children, tending the chickens and silkworms, and helping in the fields when needed.

Patriarchal Chinese society subjects women to men

No matter what class they belonged to, women were subject to men: first to their fathers, then to their husbands, and finally (if widowed) to their sons. Parents arranged marriages as compacts between families, often engaging in complex negotiations to decide such matters as the size of the dowry to be supplied by the bride. Society demanded virginal brides and faithful wives, but placed no such requirements on men, who might have mistresses or concubines if they could support them. Property and inheritance laws favored men, as did the education and civil service systems. A few women, such as Empress Wu and Yang Guifei, did exercise great influence, but even they achieved their goals mainly by working through men.

Parents sometimes bind girls' feet to help attract wealthy husbands

Women of means, whose lives were not burdened by physical labor, sometimes paid a painful price for this exemption. Starting in Song times, many girls from urban and well-off rural families underwent **foot binding**, a process in which their feet were tightly wrapped with strips of cloth for years, beginning in early childhood. Foot binding was designed to restrict the foot's growth and achieve a "lily-foot" effect, with toes and heels pointed downward to resemble the bell-shaped lily flower. Since many Chinese men considered women with tiny feet sexually attractive, and since men of means saw it as a sign of wealth and status to have a wife with feet so dainty that she could not work, mothers often bound their daughters' feet to help them attract wealthy husbands. But the process was extremely painful, and the resulting deformation frequently made it hard for the woman to walk without a cane. Foot binding thus became an indicator of social status, distinguishing idle upper class ladies from hardworking peasant women.

Foot reshaped by foot binding compared to normal foot.

Vietnam and the Chinese Impact

Overshadowed by China's vast size and wealth, the lands on its borders often served as its colonies or tribute-paying vassals, while their societies broadly imitated Chinese ideas and ways. China's neighbors nonetheless managed to preserve key elements of their traditional cultures and even, in time, to secure their political autonomy. Especially successful in these endeavors were the Vietnamese.

Vietnam Under Chinese Dominion

Vietnam occupies the easternmost part of the huge Southeast Asian peninsula, which extends out from southwestern China, west of the South China Sea (Map 14.7). A lush subtropical region with abundant sunshine, rainfall, mountains, forests, rivers, and plains,

Map 14.7 Early Vietnam and Its Expansion in the Tenth Through Fifteenth Centuries

Throughout most of its history, Vietnam was linked with China by strong political, cultural, and commercial connections. Notice, however, that after gaining political autonomy from China in the mid-900s, Vietnam expanded its rule southward in ensuing centuries over the region of Champa. What distinctive social and cultural patterns developed in Vietnam that distinguished it from China?

it was one of Asia's first agricultural areas, with early farmers raising yams, rice, chickens, and pigs. In what is now northern Vietnam, a thousand miles from the early centers of Chinese society, people produced fine works of bronze, traded throughout Southeast Asia, and developed a distinctive culture centered on village societies in which women played a leading role.

In 218 B.C.E. this region was conquered by China's Qin dynasty. Although Qin rule ended with the dynasty's demise in 206 B.C.E., the Han Martial Emperor (Wudi) reconquered the Red River valley in 111 B.C.E. For much of the next millennium the region was ruled by the Chinese, who imposed on it their language, writing system, Confucian ideals, and bureaucratic structures. It briefly regained independence under the legendary Trung Sisters, who reportedly rebelled and reigned as independent queens from 39 to 41 C.E., and later during China's Age of Disunity (220–589), when the region was divided, like China itself, among local warlords. It again came under Chinese rule during the Sui dynasty (589–618) and throughout the Tang era (618–907).

Various Chinese dynasties rule northern Vietnam

Vietnam blends Chinese beliefs and ways into its own culture

Thus, unlike the rest of Southeast Asia, which was heavily influenced by India's culture, northern Vietnam was overlaid with Chinese ideals and institutions. While Theravada Buddhism spread through the rest of Southeast Asia, for example, the Vietnamese adopted from China the Mahayana branch of that faith, combining it with Confucianism and Daoism to form a blended belief system called the **Three Religions**. Vietnam also adapted various aspects of Chinese education, urban life, architecture, and administration to fit traditional Vietnamese culture.

Vietnamese women retain a distinctive role and status

As a result of this adaptation, Vietnam retained distinctive social and family patterns, which gave women a relatively prominent role. Among both rural villagers and urban dwellers, Vietnamese women enjoyed a higher status than women in China. A Vietnamese woman, for example, could take an active part in selecting her spouse, receive from his family a wedding endowment rather than giving him a dowry, and have him come to join her family's household rather than going to join his. Thus supported by ongoing connections with their families of origin, Vietnamese women apparently could also seek and obtain divorces, inherit and bequeath family wealth, and even keep their own family names after marriage. These practices, which predated the imposition of Chinese culture, were never completely eradicated by it.

Vietnamese Autonomy

Vietnam becomes autonomous in the 900s

With its distinctive social structure and distance from China's power centers, Vietnam maintained its own cultural identity throughout the many centuries of Chinese rule. Finally, in 939, during the chaotic decades following the fall of the Tang, the Vietnamese managed to regain their political autonomy. Then, in 968, a legendary leader named Dinh Bo Linh (*DIN-BŌ-LIN*), having defeated the other warlords and unified the realm, proclaimed himself Vietnam's first emperor.

Henceforth Vietnam was ruled mostly by native regimes rather than by outsiders, but this autonomy did not mean the end of Chinese influence. Indeed, as China regained its unity and strength under the Song dynasty, Dinh Bo Linh and his successors found it advisable to recognize Song rulers as official overlords and pay them tribute. In response China's rulers largely left the Vietnamese alone, free to develop their own institutions and policies. But Vietnam's rulers continued to imitate practices that had proven successful in China. Borrowing ideas from the great empire to their north, the Vietnamese formed a stable state with its capital at Hanoi, developed a Chinese-style bureaucracy, and eventu-

Vietnam expands southward along Southeast Asian coast

ally even experienced their own succession of dynastic cycles. They also began gradually expanding to the south, incorporating over the next five centuries the various kingdoms that made up the region called Champa, whose culture had hitherto been influenced by India. This process eventually brought the whole eastern coastline of Southeast Asia under Vietnamese rule (Map 14.7).

Korea and the Chinese Impact

China's influence was also felt in Korea, the large peninsula that extends from Manchuria toward Japan, across the Yellow Sea from northeast China. Like the Vietnamese, the Koreans developed a distinctive language and culture, then came under Chinese rule in the second century B.C.E. Also like the Vietnamese, the Koreans adapted Chinese ideas and institutions to their local culture. Eventually the Koreans, too, regained their political autonomy, but for centuries they continued to pay tribute to China's emperors.

Early Chinese Influence in Korea

Chinese influence in Korea dates from the third and fourth centuries B.C.E., when refugees from China's Warring States Era migrated to the Korean peninsula, bringing Chinese farming and writing techniques. Later, in 109–108 B.C.E., Han China's Wudi conquered northern Korea, only a few years after he had conquered the Vietnamese. As in Vietnam, he and his Han successors imposed in Korea their Confucian cultural values and administrative system.

Korea is influenced by Chinese migrations and conquest

Also as in Vietnam, the collapse of China's Han dynasty in the third century C.E. brought to the Koreans both autonomy and division into warring states. Eventually, in the disarray of the fourth century C.E., three rival kingdoms emerged in the Korean peninsula: Silla (*shē-ILL-ah*) in the southeast, Paekche (*PĪK-chā*) in the southwest, and Koguryo (*kō-GOOR-yō*) in the north (Map 14.8). During the next few

Three kingdoms emerge in Korea during China's Age of Disunity

Map 14.8 Early Korea and Its Kingdoms in the Fourth Through Tenth Centuries

Korea's culture, commerce, and beliefs were strongly influenced by its connections with China. Observe that, after gaining autonomy from China in the third century C.E., Korea was divided into three rival kingdoms from the fourth through seventh centuries. Then, with Chinese help, Silla emerged predominant until the tenth century, when Koguryo gained control of the peninsula, ruling as the Kingdom of Koryo. In what ways was Korean culture influenced by connections with China? How did Korean society and governance differ from that of China?

centuries, as these three realms fought each other for supremacy, new waves of refugees arrived from China's Age of Disunity, spreading their Buddhist beliefs among the Koreans.

After China was reunified in 589 C.E., both the Sui and the Tang rulers made repeated efforts to reconquer the Koreans but were rebuffed by Koguryo's rugged resistance. In the 660s, however, aiming to dominate all of Korea, Silla joined forces with China to conquer Paekche and Koguryo. Then, having unified Korea with Chinese help, Silla used its united forces to resist full Chinese control, agreeing instead to pay tribute to the Tang regime.

Korea blends Chinese ways and beliefs into its own culture

For the next few centuries Silla ruled Korea as a semi-autonomous tributary of China, broadly imitating its society and culture. During this era Korea, like Vietnam before it, adopted China's writing system, imitated its architecture, and sought to replicate its great cities and civil service bureaucracy. Mahayana Buddhism, with monasteries, temples, statues, shrines, and sects similar to those then flourishing in Tang China, spread across the peninsula. Koreans copied Chinese customs and commodities and even produced ceramics and porcelain ware superior to China's.

In several respects, however, the administrative and social structure of Korea differed from that of China. Governmental posts in Korea remained under the control of local aristocratic families, rather than being staffed through a system of civil service exams. Despite the outward appearance of a Confucian civil service bureaucracy, Korea's regions and provinces continued to be governed mostly by warlords rather than scholar-officials, and its peasants remained in a status similar to serfdom.

Korean porcelain vase from the Kingdom of Koryo.

The Kingdom of Koryo, 935–1392

During the ninth century the deterioration of the Silla regime, accompanied by the decline of China's Tang dynasty, gave the kingdoms of Paekche and Koguryo a chance to reassert their autonomy. But eventually Wang Kon (*WAHNG-KŌN*), a wealthy northern merchant who became a military officer, seized control of Koguryo and reunited Korea by conquering Silla in 935 and Paekche in 936. He then shortened the name of his kingdom to Koryo (*KOR-yō*), from which comes the name Korea, and established a dynasty that lasted until 1392.

Koryo was even more imitative of China than Silla had been. It set up a new capital at Kaesong (*KĪ-SŌNG*), modeled after the great Chinese city of Chang'an, with a similar gridlike pattern and impressive imperial palace. Koryo established a Confucian-style administration with its own civil service exams—but the old aristocracy nonetheless maintained its monopoly of the major posts. And in the eleventh century, after experiencing several invasions by the Khitans, Koryo even built its own version of the Great Wall across the northern part of the peninsula.

Like Vietnam, then, Korea blended Chinese ways with its own distinctive culture. In the meantime, across the sea to Korea's east, another East Asian society adopted Chinese ideas, then diverged from them to become more distinctive from China than Vietnam and Korea.

The Emergence of Japan

Of the various East Asian peoples, Japan's were among the last to develop a complex culture based on farming settlements. Living mostly on four main islands, more than a hundred miles east of the Korean coast, the early Japanese were largely isolated from outside influence (Map 14.9). With a mild climate, abundant rainfall, a scenic mountainous terrain, and ready access to the sea, they lived for centuries on hunting, fishing, and gathering wild food. Rice farming began by the third century B.C.E., along with the use of bronze and iron. By 300 C.E. the land was dominated by native warrior clans called uji (*OO-JĒ*).

A distinctive religion emerged, based on the worship of divine spirits called kami (*KAH-MĒ*), which included not only gods and goddesses of the sun, moon, and earth but also the spirits of ancestors, animals, and natural objects such as rocks, trees, and waterfalls. Worship centered on fertility and purification rites, often performed in a festival atmosphere. Originally nameless, this nature-based Japanese religion was later called **Shinto** (*SHĒN-TŌ*), the "way of the kami."

By 500 C.E. the Yamato (*YAH-MAH-TŌ*) uji, a powerful warrior clan, had brought approximately two-thirds of Japan under its control, thereby establishing itself as the ruling dynasty. Tracing their descent from the Shinto sun goddess, the Yamato emperors

Japan develops a distinctive religion worshipping spirits in nature

Yamato clan forms a dynasty that claims divine status

Map 14.9 Japan Emerges as an Island Nation in the Sixth Through Twelfth Centuries

Although it borrowed many ideas and features from China, Japan developed as an independent nation with a distinctive culture. Notice that Japan, endowed with a mild climate and mountainous terrain, is located on islands over a hundred miles from the Asia mainland. Nara and later Heian (eventually called Kyoto) served as the early capitals and homes of Japan's emperors, even as others exercised real power in their name. How did Japan's society and governance differ from that of China?

claimed a divine status that helped perpetuate their position. Although others have often ruled in their name, the Yamato heirs have persistently maintained the imperial title, and they still reign today as history's longest enduring dynasty.

Early Borrowing from China

In the mid-sixth century, a new religion came to Japan from China by way of Korea. Buddhism, promoted in Japan by the Soga clan as a compelling new faith from the mainland, was rejected by other clans as an alien cult, eventually resulting in warfare. In 587 the Soga won and later installed their own Prince Shotoku as regent to the Yamato ruler.

Shotoku promotes Buddhism and Chinese ways in Japan

Prince Shotoku, whose exploits are highlighted at the start of this chapter, directed affairs from 593 until his death in 622. Determined to learn from China's experience and to borrow concepts useful for Japan, he sent at least four large missions to China for trade and cultural exchange. He instituted in Japan a Chinese-style bureaucracy, based on ranks that were assigned by merit rather than uji status, thus improving government effectiveness and strengthening the central state at the expense of the warrior clans. He further promoted Buddhism—building temples, supporting monasteries, and issuing precepts urging adherence to Buddhist ideals—so effectively that he would later be revered as a bodhisattva.

Thus began an era of extensive borrowing from China. Over the next two centuries, the Japanese adopted China's writing system and imitated Chinese literature, poetry, philosophy, art, and architecture. The Fujiwara clan, which came to dominate the Japanese court in the 640s, surpassed the Soga in copying China's laws, taxes, roads, and civil service. The city of Nara, erected in 710 as Japan's new capital, was modeled after Chang'an, and Japan's Nara Period (710–784) was marked by imitation of Chinese ways.

Ancient Buddhist temple near Nara, Japan.

The Heian Era: Divergence from China

By 794 a new capital, even more imitative of Chang'an than Nara, was constructed at Heian (*HĀ-YAHN*), later called Kyoto (*kē-YŌ-TŌ*), where the emperors would reside for more than a thousand years. During the Heian Period (794–1185), Japan gradually stopped imitating China, developing instead a distinctive new culture that blended Japanese and Chinese ways.

Japan develops a distinctive culture blending Japanese and Chinese ways

Emperor Kammu (*KAH-MOO*), who built the new capital during his reign (781–806), sought to unite his realm religiously by blending Buddhism, the faith imported from China, with Japan's native Shinto beliefs. He thus promoted various sects that accepted conflicting beliefs as different levels of truth or that depicted Shinto as an early revelation of Buddhist beliefs in Japan.

Japanese women develop a distinctive literature

In the ninth century, a new writing system developed called **kana** (*KAH-NAH*), which used simplified Chinese characters to create a phonetic Japanese alphabet. By 1000 C.E., while men in Japan still struggled to write Chinese, which they considered a superior language, Japanese women, typically denied an education in Chinese, were using kana to produce Japanese prose classics. The most famous is *The Tale of Genji* (*GEN-jē*), a subtle, sensitive portrayal of the refined court life at Heian and the romantic

Document 14.1 Excerpts from *The Tale of Genji*

Murasaki Shikibu's classic tale portrays in exquisite detail the lives and loves of an emperor and his court. These excerpts describe the emperor's love affair with Genji's mother, the birth of Genji, the death of his mother, and the emperor's abiding love for them both.

In a certain reign there was a lady not of the first rank whom the emperor loved more than any of the others. The grand ladies with high ambitions thought her a presumptuous upstart, and the lesser ladies were still more resentful. Everything she did offended someone. Probably aware of what was happening, she fell seriously ill . . .

It may have been because of a bond in a former life that she bore the emperor a beautiful son, a jewel beyond compare . . .

With the birth of the son, it became yet clearer that she was the emperor's favorite. The mother of the eldest son began to feel uneasy. If she did not manage carefully, she might see the new son designated crown prince . . .

When the young prince reached the age of three, the resources of the treasury . . . were exhausted to make the ceremonial bestowing of trousers as elaborate as that for the oldest son. Once more there was malicious talk, but the prince himself, as he grew up, was so superior of mien and disposition that few could find it in themselves to dislike him . . .

In summer the boy's mother, feeling vaguely unwell, asked that she be allowed to go home . . . The emperor . . . begged her to stay, and see what course her health might take. It was steadily worse . . .

So, in desolation, he let her go. He passed a sleepless night.

He sent off a messenger and was beside himself with impatience . . . The man arrived to find the house echoing with laments. She had died shortly past midnight . . . The emperor closed himself up in his private apartments. He would have liked to keep the boy with him, but no precedent could be found for having him away from his mother's house through the mourning . . .

The months passed and the young prince returned to the palace. He had grown into a lad of such beauty that he hardly seemed meant for this world . . . When, the following spring, it came time to name a crown prince, the emperor wanted very much to pass over his first son in favor of the younger, who, however, had no influential maternal relatives . . .

Lacking the support of maternal relatives, the boy would be most insecure as a prince . . . As a commoner he could be of great service . . . The emperor therefore encouraged the boy in his studies, at which he was so proficient that it seemed a waste to reduce him to common rank. And yet—as a prince he would arouse the hostility of those who had cause to fear his becoming emperor. Summoning an astrologer . . ., the emperor . . . concluded that the boy should become a commoner with the name Minamoto or Genji.

SOURCE: Murasaki Shikibu, *The Tale of Genji*, translated by Edward G. Seidensticker (New York: Alfred A. Knopf, 1978) 1–4, 13, 15.

affairs of a fictional prince named Genji (see "Excerpts from *The Tale of Genji*"). The tale was composed by a court lady known as Murasaki Shikibu (*moo-RAH-sah-kē SHĒ-kē-boo*), who, while vastly enriching Japanese literature, offered the world what may well be its oldest complete novel.

Political changes in Heian Japan brought further divergence from the Chinese model. The powerful Fujiwara clan increasingly dominated the imperial family, first by forcing the emperors to marry Fujiwara women, then by serving as regents for their offspring. As soon as an emperor had a son by his Fujiwara wife, the clan leaders would force that emperor to retire so they could rule as regents for his infant son who became the new emperor. But this farce only weakened the central government because other ambitious clans, deprived of influence at court, built power bases in the countryside, while smaller landowners submitted to their protection to avoid taxation.

The Rise of the Warrior Class

Peasant serfs and samurai warriors embrace new Buddhist sects

By the twelfth century, although the court at Heian continued to claim authority, Japan was actually dominated by local warlords ruling independent estates. Each warlord developed his own army of warriors, later known as **samurai** (*SAH-MOO-RĪ*), who provided military service to their lords. These warriors were often supported by peasant labor on land given them in reward for military service, similar to the manors of medieval Europe (Chapter 9). In time the samurai became Japan's dominant class, with a unique code of conduct. Rejecting the urbane Heian society, which they saw as decadent and weak, the samurai instead adopted an austere rural culture based on courage, honor, discipline, simplicity, and indifference to pain. Supported by foot soldiers and protected by elaborate armor, the samurai fought on horseback, using bows, arrows, and tempered steel swords. Professing total loyalty to their lords, they were trained to value death over dishonor. In a practice called **seppuku** (*SEP-OO-KOO*), also known as hara-kiri, or "belly-cutting," a defeated warrior could restore his honor by taking his own life without showing pain.

Minamoto clan creates a dominant military leader called the shogun

This rise of the samurai reduced the peasants to serfdom, forcing them to work the land in servitude to support the warrior class. For comfort many peasants turned to Pure Land Buddhism, the Chinese creed that promised its faithful salvation in the Western Paradise. The samurai, meanwhile, embraced Zen, Japan's name for China's Chan Buddhism, perhaps because its stress on meditation, discipline, simplicity, and self-understanding seemed akin to their warrior code.

Regional warlords and samurai warriors come to dominate Japan

The rise of the samurai also brought an end to the political power of the Heian court. In 1185, when the Minamoto (*MĒ-NAH-MŌ-TŌ*) clan defeated the forces controlling Heian in a great naval battle, clan leader Minamoto Yoritomo (*YŌ-RĒ-TŌ-MŌ*) emerged as the country's dominant warlord. In contrast to what often happened in such situations in China, however, he did not seize the throne and end the Yamato dynasty, whose emperors were worshipped as descendants of the gods. Instead, in a move that set a precedent for future conquering warlords, in 1192 he assumed a new post called **shogun** (*SHŌ-GOON*), the commander-in-chief of Japan's armed forces and its real ruler. Thenceforth, while the emperors still reigned in Heian (Kyoto) as religious figures, they lacked political power. Minamoto Yoritomo and his successors as shogun actually ruled from the city of Kamakura (*KAH-MAH-KOO-RAH*), which served as Japan's true political center from 1192 until 1333.

Wooden statue of Buddhist monk from Kamakura era.

Chapter Review

Putting It in Perspective

Despite the disasters of the third through sixth centuries, China survived its Age of Disunity, merging its new Buddhist faith with the basic elements of its ancient society and emerging reunited in 589 C.E. Then, for almost seven centuries, under the Sui, Tang, and Song dynasties, China flourished as one of the world's largest and most cosmopolitan societies. Its officials mastered the art of governing an expansive empire, its merchants and manufacturers produced unprecedented prosperity, and its farmers found ways to feed its rural masses and large urban populations. Its poets, artists, inventors, intellectuals, and religious believers created a culture noted for its elegance, complexity, and technological sophistication.

So successful was China's experience that other East Asian cultures often followed its example, sometimes compelled by Chinese conquest, sometimes encouraged by commercial and cultural connections with China. The Vietnamese, Koreans, and Japanese all copied or adapted features of Chinese society, especially its writing system, Buddhist beliefs, Confucian civil service, art, architecture, and urban organization. Thus, through a series of connections and conflicts, Chinese culture dominated most of East Asia.

Conflicts, however, also undermined China's preeminence. For all its power and wealth, China never fully succeeded in subduing the nomads to its north. The Tang dynasty held them off and sometimes even conquered their homelands. But in the tenth century, after that dynasty's fall, tribal Khitan warriors captured some of China's northern provinces and added them to their Liao Empire. Eventually China's Song dynasty, after failing to defeat these warriors, decided instead to pay them tribute. But in the twelfth century the Jurchens, after the Song rulers helped them conquer the Khitans, overran and dominated the whole northern half of China.

This disaster did not mark the end of China's troubles. For in the thirteenth century the Mongols, an even more expansionist group of nomadic invaders from the north, would conquer the Jurchens and then all of China and most of Eurasia as well.

Reviewing Key Material

KEY CONCEPTS

Xiongnu, 325	Three Religions, 344
civil service exams, 335	Shinto, 347
scholar gentry, 335	kana, 348
Pure Land Buddhism, 339	samurai, 350
Chan (Zen) Buddhism, 339	seppuku, 350
foot binding, 342	shogun, 350

KEY PEOPLE

Prince Shotoku, 324, 348	Zhao Kuangyin (Taizu), 334
Cao Cao, 325	Wang Anshi, 336
Faxian, 330	Zhu Xi, 340
Liang Wudi, 330	Li Bai, 340
Yang Jian (Wendi), 330	Du Fu, 340
Yangdi, 331	Trung Sisters, 343
Duke of Tang, 331	Dinh Bo Linh, 344
Li Shimin (Taizong), 331	Wang Kon, 346
Wu Zhao (Empress Wu), 332	Kammu, 348
Xuanzong, 333	Murasaki Shikibu, 349
Yang Guifei, 333	Minamoto Yoritomo, 350
An Lushan, 333	

ASK YOURSELF

1. How and why did Buddhism spread throughout China, emerging as its main religion, during the Age of Disunity? Why did Buddhism decline in China by the middle of the Song era?
2. After China was reunified in 589, what steps did the Sui, Tang, and Song regimes take to maintain its unity and prosperity during the next seven centuries? How did these various regimes respond to the ongoing threat of the northern nomadic peoples?
3. What were the main hallmarks and achievements of Chinese society during the Tang and Song eras? How did the lives of rural peasants differ from the lives of

city-dwellers? How did the roles and rights of women differ from those of men?

4. Why and how did Vietnam, Korea, and Japan emulate Chinese ideas and institutions? How did they blend their own cultures and traditions with ideas and institutions adapted from China?

GOING FURTHER

Adshead, S. A. M. *Tang China*. 2004.

Batten, B. I. *To the Ends of Japan*. 2003.

Benn, Charles. *China's Golden Age: Everyday Life in the Tang Dynasty*. 2004.

Bingham, Woodbridge. *The Founding of the T'ang Dynasty*. 1975.

Cho'e, Yongho, ed. *Sources of Korean Tradition*. 2000.

Davis, Richard L. *Court and Family in Sung China*. 1986.

De Bary, W. T., et al., eds. *Sources of Japanese Tradition*. 2001.

Dien, A. E., ed. *State and Society in Early Medieval China*. 1990.

Ebrey, Patricia Buckley, et al. *East Asia: A Cultural, Social, and Political History*. 2006.

Ebrey, Patricia Buckley. *Inner Quarters: Marriage and the Lives of Chinese Women in the Sung Period*. 1993.

Gernet, Jacques. *Buddhism in Chinese Society*. 1995.

Hymes, R. P. *Way and Byway: Taoism, Local Religion, and Models of Divinity in Sung China*. 2002.

Kim, KiBaik. *A New History of Korea*. 1984.

Liu, J. T. C. *China Turning Inward: Intellectual Changes in the Early Twelfth Century*. 1988.

Mann, S., and Y. Cheng, eds. *Under Confucian Eyes: Writings on Gender in Chinese History*. 2001.

Mason, R. H. P. *A History of Japan*. 1987.

McKnight, B. *Law and Order in Sung China*. 1992.

Nahm, Andrew C. *Introduction to Korean History and Culture*. 1993.

Owen, S. *The Great Age of Chinese Poetry: The High T'ang*. 1981.

Pai, H. I. *Constructing "Korean" Origins*. 2000.

Shaughnessy, Edward, ed. *China: Empire and Civilization*. 2005.

Souryi, P. F. *The World Turned Upside Down: Medieval Japanese Society*. 2001.

Sullivan, M. *The Arts of China*. 4th ed. 1999.

Tao, Jingshen. *Two Sons of Heaven*. 1988.

Taylor, K. W. *The Birth of Vietnam*. 1983.

Temple, Robert. *The Genius of China*. 1989.

Twitchett, D., and M. Loewe. *Cambridge History of China*. Vol. 3. *Medieval China*. 1986.

Varley, H. Paul. *Japanese Culture*. 4th ed. 2000.

Warshaw, Steven. *Japan Emerges*. 1987.

Woodside, A. *Vietnam and the Chinese Model*. 1988

Wright, Arthur F. *The Sui Dynasty*. 1978.

Key Dates and Developments

China

220–589	China's Age of Disunity
300–500	Buddhism spreads throughout China
581–589	Unification of China by Yang Jian
589–618	Sui Dynasty
618–907	Tang Dynasty
626–649	Reign of Taizong (Li Shimin)
660–705	Dominance of Wu Zhao (Empress Wu, 690–705)
713–756	Reign of Xuanzong
720–770	Poetry of Li Bai and Du Fu
755–766	An Lushan revolt
907–960	Fall of the Tang and renewed disunity
907–1125	Khitans rule northern borderlands (Liao Empire)
960–1279	Song Dynasty
960–976	China Reunified under Zhao Kuangyin (Song Taizu)
1069–1085	Wang Anshi Reforms
1127–1206	Jurchens conquer Khitans and rule northern China

Vietnam and Korea

111 B.C.E.	Chinese conquer northern Vietnam
108 B.C.E.	Chinese conquer northern Korea
220–589	Age of Disunity in China, Korea, and Vietnam
300s–668	Korea divided into three kingdoms
668–935	Korea unified under Silla rule
936–1392	Korea unified under Koryo rule
939	Northern Vietnam gains autonomy from China
968	Din Bo Linh unifies northern Vietnam, becomes emperor
1000–1500	Vietnam expands southward into Champa

Japan

by 300	Emergence of Uji warrior clans
by 500	Emergence of Yamato clan as Japan's imperial dynasty
500–600	Buddhism spreads to Japan
592–622	Prince Shotoku guides Japan, emulates Chinese culture
710–784	Nara era: intensive emulation of China
794–1185	Heian era: emergence of the samurai
1000–1010	*Tale of Genji*, by Murasaki Shikibu
1185–1333	Kamakura era: reign of the Minamoto shoguns
1192	Minamoto Yoritomo becomes shogun

Nomadic Conquests and Eurasian Connections, 1000–1400

Temujin Is Proclaimed Genghis Khan

In this fourteenth-century illustration, Temujin is proclaimed Genghis Khan as his sons (on the right) and supporters look on. Genghis Khan and his successors created a vast empire that connected cultures across Eurasia.

Around 1162, in the harsh Mongolian region northwest of China, the wife of a Mongol chieftain bore him a son named Temujin (*TEH-moo-jēn*). About nine years later, when members of a rival tribe poisoned his father, Temujin and his mother were left without status or support. Raising her son in great hardship, Temujin's mother taught him that he was divinely destined to avenge his father and become a great ruler. Later, when captured by foes and confined in a heavy wooden collar, Temujin managed to overpower his guard and escape to a nearby river, where he hid until a friendly tribesman released him from the collar. This incident further convinced the young Mongol that he was destined for greatness.

Turkic and Mongol Empires

Temujin grew to be a formidable warrior, single-minded and opportunistic in pursuing power. Returning to his tribe, he eventually asserted himself as its leader, vanquished its neighbors, and killed his father's murderers. He won battles and forged alliances with other Mongol tribes, overcoming their fierce independence to unite them into a powerful military machine. Then, after they proclaimed him "Genghis Khan" (*JEN-gis KAHN*), or "universal ruler," he led them on a quest to conquer the world.

Genghis Khan and his followers were part of a wide array of nomadic herders who had long lived in Central Asia. For ages these peoples, most of whom spoke Turkic or Mongolian languages, had lived sparse lives tending cattle and sheep, moving about in search of grazing grounds and sometimes raiding or invading settled societies to their east, south, and west.

In the tenth through fourteenth centuries, however, Central Asian nomads made a momentous impact on the wider world. Some took control of northern China, forming empires and dynasties there. Others, known as Seljuk (*SELL-jook*) Turks, conquered Islamic Southwest Asia, embraced the Islamic faith, and sparked a series of consequential conflicts with the Christian world. Then the Mongols, led by Genghis Khan and his heirs, overran much of Eurasia, creating the largest land empire the world had ever seen. In time these conquerors adopted many features of the societies they conquered, while expanding commerce and helping to spread ideas, technologies, weapons, and diseases. By conquering and connecting the cultures of Eurasia, Central Asian nomads changed the course of world history.

The Nomads of Central Asia

By 1000 C.E., agriculture had long since become the way of life for most people on the planet. Although it required tedious, time-consuming labor, farming provided greater stability and much more food than hunting or herding alone. It could thus support far more people than could these other forms of subsistence. Agriculture was the economic foundation of the large, complex, settled societies that had arisen in China, India, Persia, Southwest Asia, Europe, and several parts of Africa (Map 15.1).

FOUNDATION MAP 15.1 Areas of Farming and Herding by 1000 C.E.

By 1000 C.E., settled agricultural societies prevailed in places where climate and soil supported farming. Note, however, that in Central Asia, where climate and soil made farming unreliable, most people lived as pastoral nomads, following their herds in search of grazing grounds, and occasionally interacting with the settled agricultural societies to their east, west, and south, as indicated by the arrows. How did these connections influence the societies of both the settled farmers and the nomadic herders?

Farming societies
Pastoral Nomadic Herding societies
Foraging societies
Pastoral nomadic encounters with settled farming societies

0   1000 km
0   1000 mi

In some areas, however, conditions were not suitable for farming. These areas included the northernmost reaches of Eurasia, where it was too cold; the equatorial rain forests of Africa, where it was too wet; and the arid plains and deserts of Africa and Eurasia, where it was too dry. In these regions, where limited food supplies kept populations low, people lived as nomads, moving frequently and surviving by hunting or herding.

Central Asia connects Eurasian societies

The largest of the regions where nomadic life prevailed was the immense Central Asian expanse, extending for thousands of miles from the semi-arid steppes of southern Russia to the barren Mongolian highlands. Sparsely populated and bleak, battered by harsh winds and brutal winters, Central Asia was both a barrier that separated Eurasia's settled societies and the crossroads of the trade routes that connected them. It thus not only shaped the nomadic lifestyle of its hardy inhabitants but also helped shape the commerce and cultures of the surrounding societies.

Herding and Horsemanship

Herding was the main way of life for most Central Asians. As pastoral nomads—herders who move about in search of fresh grasslands on which to pasture their herds—they set up camps where they found good grounds for grazing, then moved elsewhere when the forage was depleted. The nomads ate mainly meat, milk, cheese, and butter, and clothed themselves largely with fleeces and hides, supplied by their herds. To protect themselves from the winds and rain, they fashioned large tents (known as yurts) from coarse felt made of matted wool and animal hairs. They even collected the animals' manure, using it as fuel for the fires that warmed them and cooked their food.

A Mongol family outside its tent, or yurt.

Some Central Asians raised cattle, many kept goats, and those involved in overland trade used camels, but most of the nomads centered their livelihoods on sheep and horses. Sheep were prized mainly for their meat, milk, and wool, but also because they survived better than cattle on the sparse, coarse vegetation of the steppes. Horses were used for hunting, herding sheep, and pulling carts that carried tents and goods from one campsite to the next. Since mare's milk was preserved by fermenting it into a beverage called kumiss (*KOO-miss*), horses also supplied an important source of sustenance.

Horses were also crucial to the conduct of war. Nomadic life meant frequent movement in search of new pastures, and this movement often led to clashes with neighboring nomads or settled societies. Especially during famines or droughts, when food and adequate grazing grounds were scarce, mounted nomads fought each other for the scarce pasturelands and sometimes traveled into farming regions to raid villages and towns. Survival depended on both mobility and fighting skill.

Nomadic warrior societies depend on horses

Central Asian societies thus were warrior societies. The men spent most of their time in the saddle, learning at an early age to eat, sleep, hunt, herd, fight, and raid on horseback. They trained to ride for days without food or rest, to attack in unison, and to fight with fearless abandon. In these endeavors they were ably assisted by their mounts, sturdy steppe ponies bred and trained for discipline and endurance, with long shaggy hair that protected them from the wind and cold.

The warriors also were greatly aided by the use of stirrups. Developed by Central Asians in the first or second century C.E., these rings that hung from each side of the saddle secured the feet of the riders, allowing them to stand and maneuver while moving at high speed. Mounted warriors could thus load and reload their powerful bows and fire their arrows in any direction with amazing accuracy, even while charging or fleeing at full gallop. Large armies from settled societies, vastly outnumbering the nomadic warriors, might chase them back to the open steppes, only to be annihilated during the pursuit by the well-aimed arrows of the retreating nomads.

Stirrups give Central Asian warriors an advantage

Family and Social Structure

Family and society on the steppes were structured to meet the needs of nomadic life. Gender roles, social status, governance, and religion all showed the stamp of a culture that focused on mobility, resourcefulness, and warfare.

Women played a prominent role in Central Asian societies, managing the camps while men traveled far afield to hunt, raid, and fight. Women tended the campfires and gathered the manure that fueled the flames. They sheared the sheep and goats, and then used the fleeces, along with furs and hides brought back by men from the hunt, to make

Women sustain nomadic societies

essential items such as clothing, mats, rugs, and the large tents called yurts. Women bred the sheep and horses, helped them give birth, milked them, and used the milk to make butter, cheese, and kumiss. And, of course, women bore and nursed the children, caring for and protecting them when the men were gone. Skilled on horseback and adapted to a mobile life, the women could readily move their whole families and households on short notice. Some women on occasion traveled with the men into combat, attending to such necessities as food and other supplies.

Marriages, as elsewhere, were arranged by parents, often to enhance family status or form political ties. As a sign of prestige, prominent warriors typically took several wives, frequently maintaining a separate tent and household for each. The leading warriors also constituted a kind of nobility, but their social status depended more on military prowess than heredity. Status could improve based on acts of bravery or leadership in combat, or decline in the absence of such exploits.

Nomads combine into tribes and federations

Like other nomadic peoples, Central Asians organized into clans and tribes that were small enough to maintain mobility, with no need for complex governance systems. For political and military purposes, however, the nomads sometimes formed larger federations linking many tribes. These federations were typically led by a regional overlord called the **khan**, who exercised broad authority but was expected to consult regularly with a council of tribal leaders and gain its approval for his decisions.

Central Asian spirituality centered for centuries on **shamanism** (*SHAH-mun-izm*), a form of religion in which spiritual leaders called shamans performed elaborate rituals and induced trances in efforts to communicate with spirits, heal the sick, forecast the future, and influence events. Typically consulted by tribal leaders facing major decisions, such as when to do battle or whom to select as khan, shamans often played a crucial role in nomadic cultures. Eventually, however, as Central Asians adopted various forms of Buddhism, Christianity, and Islam through contact with settled societies, shamans lost much of their clout.

Ongons (spirit houses) used by shamans to contact spiritual forces.

Contacts and Conflicts with Settled Societies

Central Asia was bordered on the east, south, and west by the large, complex, settled societies of China, India, Persia, Mesopotamia, Byzantium, and Europe. With numerous farming villages, thriving towns and cities, intricate social structures, organized religions, and sophisticated technologies, these wealthy, populous societies tended to see themselves as "civilized" and the nomads as crude "barbarians." The settled societies, however, often owed their origins, and many of their attributes, to contacts and conflicts with the nomads.

CULTURAL AND COMMERCIAL CONNECTIONS. Over the ages, as noted in earlier chapters, Central Asian nomads had played pivotal roles in forming, connecting, and challenging the settled Eurasian societies. The Indo-Europeans who migrated to India, the Iranian Plateau, Anatolia, and Europe in the second millennium B.C.E. came from Central Asia, imparting and imposing their languages and ways (Map 15.2). So did the Kushans, who ruled northern India from the first to third centuries C.E.; the Xiongnu and other nomads who dominated northern China from the third to sixth centuries C.E.; and the Huns whose attacks on Germans and Romans in the fourth and fifth centuries C.E. foreshadowed the German conquest of the Western Roman Empire. Central Asians over the

Map 15.2 Key Central Asian Nomadic Movements Before 1000 C.E.

Over many centuries, numerous nomadic groups from Central Asia helped to forge Eurasian connections. Observe, for example, that Hittites migrated to West Asia and Aryans to India in the second millennium B.C.E., that Kushans settled in northwest India in the first through third centuries C.E., that Xiongnu penetrated northern China in the third through sixth centuries C.E., and that Huns invaded Eastern and Central Europe in the fourth and fifth centuries C.E. What major impacts did each of these groups have on the development of Eurasian cultures?

centuries had also spread skills such as ironworking and horsemanship, belief systems such as Buddhism, and diseases such as smallpox from one region to another.

Nomadic attitudes toward settled societies were mixed. On one hand, nomads disdained the sedentary lives of settled villagers and townsfolk. Nomads might be poor, and at the mercy of the elements, but from their perspective at least they were unfettered and free, neither bound to the land and a landlord like a typical peasant, nor crammed into a crowded, fetid city like urban artisans and merchants. Rugged, vigorous, and violent, Central Asians centered their lives on their horses and herds, with little desire to imitate their sedentary neighbors.

On the other hand, to enhance their Spartan lifestyle, the nomads often relied on contacts with settled societies. Some nomads bartered with villagers and townsfolk, offering hides, wool, and furs from their herds and hunts in exchange for such goods as flour, grain, cotton, silk, iron, and salt produced by the settled societies. Some nomads even made their livelihoods by facilitating commerce among settled societies, forming and guiding caravans that carried commodities across Central Asia, along the ancient Silk Road and other overland trade routes.

Nomads trade and interact with settled societies

Other nomads, however, coveting the wealth and abundance of the towns and villages, repeatedly raided them and sometimes even carried off their residents for use or sale as slaves. As long as settled societies were united and strong, they were generally able to resist the nomads by beating them in battles, buying them off with tribute, and building barriers such as China's Great Wall. But when settled societies were divided and weak, their thriving towns and fertile farmlands made tempting targets for the nomads, especially when famine or drought drove the nomads to seek new sources of sustenance.

THE NOMADS IN NORTHERN CHINA.   Nowhere was the interaction between nomadic and settled societies more consequential than in northern China. Since around 2000 B.C.E., when horse-drawn chariots and bronze weapons were introduced to this region by nomads from Central Asia, contacts with pastoral peoples had played a crucial role in Chinese history (Chapters 4 and 14).

Examples of this interaction are numerous. In the third century B.C.E., to protect his realm against nomadic raids, China's First Emperor linked his northern fortresses to create the first Great Wall. In succeeding centuries, many nomads served as merchants and guides along the Silk Road, the great cross-Asian trade route opened by China's Martial Emperor by around 100 B.C.E. Later, in China's Age of Disunity (220-589 C.E.), nomadic groups ruled northern China and supported Buddhism, a religion spread from India to China via Central Asian merchants and nomads.

Nomads help sustain the Silk Road and spread Buddhism

In the tenth century C.E., as related in Chapter 14, nomadic Mongols from Manchuria known as Khitans captured several northern Chinese provinces. In the early 1100s, anxious to oust the Khitans, China's Song dynasty aided other nomads called Jurchens, unwittingly enabling them to conquer northern China and rule it for the next century.

Northern China nonetheless remained a settled society. The Khitans at first tried maintaining tribal ways, but in time they created a Chinese-style dynasty called the Liao Empire, complete with a Confucian bureaucracy, civil service exams, and Chinese writing. The Jurchens did likewise, calling their dynasty the Jin and presiding over a populous Chinese realm with a complex economy, cosmopolitan culture, and Confucian administration. In China, as elsewhere, nomads who conquered a settled society tended to embrace its institutions, though they were often still seen as alien barbarians by the people they ruled.

Khitans and Jurchens adopt Chinese ways

The Rise and Fall of the Seljuk Turks

While Khitans and Jurchens penetrated northern China, far to the west and south another nomadic expansion was under way. In the tenth and eleventh centuries, changes in the Central Asian climate, reducing the already fragile food supply, may have pushed some tribes to the brink of starvation. Forced to migrate in search of new food sources, they set in motion a series of chain reactions. When one tribe moved into its neighbors' pasturelands, it often drove them into surrounding regions, where they in turn attacked the local peoples. In time some nomadic groups, compelled by such events to combine with others, began to invade the cities and farmlands of neighboring settled societies.

Driven by such forces, Turkic-speaking tribes from Central Asia infiltrated the Islamic lands of southern Asia. One such group, the Ghaznavids from Afghanistan, penetrated northeastern Persia in the mid-tenth century. By the early eleventh century they were also moving into northwest India, ravaging that region and subjecting it to their rule (Chapter 12). But then they made a monumental mistake: they let another Turkish group from Central Asia move with its herds into Persia.

The Seljuk Conquests

These newly arriving nomads, who would dominate much of Southwest Asia for the next few centuries, were the Seljuk Turks. In the decade following 1025, with Ghaznavid consent, they entered northeastern Persia. Led by heirs of their deceased chieftain Seljuk, they had been chased from Central Asia by other Turkish tribes, who found them too belligerent even for the warlike ways of the steppes. Once in Persia the unruly Seljuks attacked their Ghaznavid hosts, defeating them in 1040 at Dandanqan (*dahn-dahn-KAHN*), a decisive battle that opened southern Asia to waves of Turkish nomads (Map 15.3).

The Seljuks then drove westward, plowing through Persia and into Mesopotamia. Recent converts to Islam, they embraced its dominant Sunni branch and attacked its Shi'ite minority. In 1055 the Seljuks captured Baghdad, claiming to have freed it from the clutches of Shi'ite warlords but actually bringing it under the control of the growing Seljuk domain.

The Great Seljuk Empire

The Great Seljuk Empire, as the new realm came to be known, was consolidated and expanded by Sultan Alp Arslan, who reigned from 1063 to 1072. Bent on extinguishing Shi'ism and reuniting the Islamic world under Sunni sway, he planned to attack the Shi'ite Fatimid Caliphate in Egypt. Seeking first to protect his western flank, however, he came into conflict with the Christian Byzantine Empire, whose armies he defeated in 1071 at Manzikert (Chapter 10). This victory sidetracked the Seljuks, who went on to conquer Syria and Palestine but never made it to Egypt. Instead, with Byzantine lands now vulnerable, the Turks flooded westward into Anatolia, a rich farming region that had been for centuries the heart of the Byzantine Empire.

Seljuks invade Syria, Palestine, and Anatolia

Once in Anatolia, the Seljuks sought to make it a Sunni Muslim stronghold. They restricted Christianity and promoted Islamic immigration from elsewhere in their empire, granting special rights to those who embraced Islam. In the long run these Turkish efforts proved so successful that Anatolia, which had been a Christian bastion for almost a millennium, was transformed into a Muslim land that is today called Turkey.

The Great Seljuk sultans nonetheless centered their empire in Persia. Like others who had earlier ruled this region, the Seljuks fell in love with the Persian culture and adopted many of its features, including its Farsi tongue. Although Arabic was enshrined in the Qur'an and used in Muslim worship, the Seljuk elite communicated in Farsi, while commoners spoke a brand of Turkish peppered with Farsi expressions. Under Turkish and Persian influence, then, Islamic culture continued to evolve away from its Arab roots, while Seljuks were transformed from nomadic marauders into settled rulers of a vast cosmopolitan empire.

Seljuks embrace Persian culture

Thus, rather than ruining Islamic culture, Seljuk rule revitalized it. In this effort the early Seljuk sultans were ably guided by a Persian chief minister, the Nizam al-Mulk (*nē-ZAHM al-MOOLK*), a superb administrator who founded a series of eminent educational institutions and skillfully adapted the structures of the long-dead Persian Empire to meet the needs of the Seljuks. A devout Sunni Muslim, the Nizam also guided Seljuk Sultan Malik Shah (*mah-LĒK SHAH*), who reigned from 1072 to 1092, into unrelenting warfare against Shi'ism.

Fine woven carpet from Seljuk culture.

Map 15.3 Southwest Asia and The Seljuk Turks, 1040–1189

In the eleventh century the Seljuk Turks, nomadic warriors from Central Asia, created a realm they called the Great Seljuk Empire, winning major battles at Dandanqan, Baghdad, and Manzikert. Note, however, that, once the empire began to break apart after 1092, a breakaway Seljuk Sultanate of Rūm ruled eastern Anatolia, the Great Seljuk sultans continued to reign in Persia, and a new sultan in Egypt, Salah al-Din, eventually carved out a realm embracing Palestine and Syria. How did the Seljuks help to revitalize Islamic culture?

	Area of Seljuk rule in 1090s
	Empire of Salah al-Din (Saladin) 1189
⊗	Major Seljuk battles, with dates

The Shi'ite Assassins strike at Sunni leaders

This anti-Shi'ite drive met fierce resistance from a radical Shi'ite sect known as "the self-sacrificers." Founded in 1090 by a zealot called "the Old Man of the Mountain," this group terrorized the Islamic world for almost 170 years, slaying numerous Sunni leaders, including the Nizam al-Mulk. According to legend, at a secret mountain fortress its members used hashish (*hah-SHĒSH*), a mild narcotic, to fortify themselves for murder by providing a foretaste of the pleasures of paradise awaiting them if they were martyred. This sect of Shi'ite killers came to be known in Arabic as hashashin (*hah-SHAH-shēn*), or "hashish users," and hence in the West as the **Assassins**.

The Fragmentation of the Seljuk Realm

The assassination of the Nizam al-Mulk in 1092, followed quickly by the death of Malik Shah, touched off a succession crisis that split the Seljuk realm apart. In the west several smaller states emerged, while in the east the Great Seljuk sultans struggled for the next century to control what was left of their empire.

Seljuks threaten Byzantium; Christians respond with Crusades

The main successor state in the west was the Sultanate of Rūm (ROOM), a break-away Seljuk regime that controlled much of Anatolia. Since the name Rūm ("Rome") asserted a claim to the Roman heritage, and since the realm of Rūm expanded toward Constantinople, the Byzantine ruler, as Eastern Roman emperor, saw the sultanate as a mortal threat. In desperation he sought aid from the Christian West, appealing to the pope in Rome, who responded by launching a Christian holy war, later called the First Crusade (1096–1099), which defeated Islamic forces in Anatolia, Syria, and Palestine (Chapter 16). When the Muslims finally reconquered this territory in the next century, they were led not by Seljuks but by Salah al-Din (sah-LAH al-DEN), a gifted Sunni Muslim warrior also called Saladin (SAH-lah-dēn). He ended Shi'ite rule in Egypt, served as its sultan for two decades (1173–1193), and drove the Christian crusaders out of Palestine. The Seljuk Sultanate of Rum endured in Anatolia, but lost a key battle in 1202 to Georgia, a realm to its northeast skillfully ruled by a talented woman named Tamar.

Tamar, ruler of Georgia, 1184–1213.

The eastern remnant of the Great Seljuk Empire lost power in the 1150s, as its local commanders battled each other for the remains of the realm. In this struggle the commanders of Khwarazm (khwah-RAZ-um), a Central Asian region northeast of Persia (Map 15.3), eventually emerged supreme. Known as Khwarazm Shahs, they created a large but loose-knit empire that included much of southern Central Asia and northern Persia. Profiting from commerce along the Asian trade routes and an extensive irrigation system that sustained farming on the steppes, Khwarazm endured until 1218 when it was confronted by the Mongols, nomadic warriors whose conquests threatened to engulf all Eurasia.

Khwarazm Shahs connect Central Asia and Persia

The Mongol Invasions

In the early thirteenth century, as noted at the start of this chapter, Mongol warriors set out to conquer the world. Genghis Khan and his heirs, leading a coalition of tribes with a combined population of less than two million, terrorized societies from China to central Europe, overrunning realms with far richer resources and many times more people than Mongolia. Although the Mongols did not conquer the whole world, they did conquer much of Eurasia, creating a huge empire that dwarfed all previous realms. In so doing, they forged connections and fostered trade, spreading ideas and technologies that in time enriched and strengthened the conquered settled societies, fortifying them against further nomadic conquests.

The Conquests of Genghis Khan

Beginning in 1206, following the Mongol conference at which Temujin was proclaimed Genghis Khan, he and his armies set out on their campaign of world conquest. First they allied with the Uighur (WE-goor) Turks to their southwest, a people who would later

Map 15.4 Conquests of Genghis Khan, 1206–1227

After Temujin was proclaimed Genghis Khan by the Mongols in 1206, he and his armies set out to conquer the world. Notice that his empire, carved out by conquest over the next two decades, eventually extended from the Sea of Japan in the east to the Caspian Sea in the west, incorporating much of northern China and all of Central Asia. In what ways did he help lay the foundations for enhanced connections across much of Eurasia?

help the Mongols run their realm (Map 15.4). Then the Mongols moved south against the Tanguts (*TAHN-goots*), Tibetan tribes that had formed a regime called the Xi Xia (*SHĒ shēYAH*) Kingdom in northwestern China. By 1209 the Mongols conquered Xi Xia and forced it to pay tribute but did not yet destroy it.

Mongols lay waste to northern China

The Mongols then moved to their southeast, attacking the Jurchen realm that dominated northern China. From 1211 to 1215 they laid waste to this region, reducing some ninety cities to rubble. In 1215 they attacked the Jurchen capital, a well-fortified metropolis at what is now Beijing, and took it after several months of siege. After finally penetrating its walls, they went on a rampage, plundering its riches, killing its residents, and setting its buildings ablaze. The massacres and fires reportedly went on for a month.

Mongols devastate Khwarazm and Xi Xia

Genghis Khan next directed his efforts far to the west and south. In 1218 he sent emissaries and merchants to meet with the Khwarazm Shah, supposedly to seek diplomatic and commercial ties, but also no doubt to scout this realm and perhaps find a pretext for invading it. The pretext was provided when one of the shah's governors, in a reckless act of defiance, robbed and massacred the Mongol merchants. Responding with ruthless fury, from 1219 to 1221 the Mongols devastated the Khwarazm Empire, ruining its agriculture by wrecking the irrigation system, pillaging the towns along the trade routes, demolishing Persian cities that had come under Khwarazm rule, and slaughtering the inhabitants. Then, because the Xi Xia Kingdom in northwest China had refused to help him conquer Khwarazm, Genghis Khan returned in 1226 to obliterate it and its people.

Genghis Khan died in 1227, allegedly falling off his horse in battle. By then, however, his Mongols had defeated numerous armies, plundered hundreds of cities and towns, killed millions of people, and carved out an empire extending from the Sea of Japan to the Caspian Sea (Map 15.4).

Reasons for Mongol Success

Many factors facilitated the Mongols' amazing military success. These factors included their fighting skills and unity, the lack of a united resistance, their use of reconnaissance and terror, their adoption of ideas and techniques from their foes, and their remarkable leadership.

Fighting skills. The Mongols' skilled horsemanship gave them an immense advantage in mobility, enabling them to strike without warning, capitalize on enemy mistakes, and quickly change direction in the midst of battle. With their powerful bows and superb marksmanship they could shoot with deadly precision from several hundred yards away, decimating an opposing force before it could fight back, or fire flaming arrows over the walls of a surrounded city. With their courage and endurance they could swiftly cover great distances, maintain composure in combat, and almost always outfight and outlast their foes.

Unity and discipline. Insisting that his generals renounce tribal ties and demanding total loyalty to himself, Genghis Khan centralized his command and instilled iron discipline in his troops. As a result, even when his forces grew to 200,000 and included thousands of Turks and other non-Mongols, they were still able to fight as one and closely coordinate their actions in the course of combat.

Lack of united resistance. Animosities among his enemies, and the previous breakup of China and Persia through invasions by other nomads, enabled Genghis Khan to attack and destroy his targets one at a time. He was also occasionally aided by his enemies' foes: in northern China, for example, Chinese and Khitan residents who resented Jurchen rule helped the Mongols to end it.

Reconnaissance. Rarely did the Mongols attack until they had thoroughly scouted their adversaries. From spies, traveling merchants, and tortured captives, Mongol leaders learned about the composition of enemy forces, the layout of cities, and the design of defenses. This knowledge permitted them to plan their assaults efficiently and carry them out with overpowering effect.

Terror and intimidation. Almost everywhere they went, the Mongols' reputation preceded them, complete with reports of merciless invaders, leveled cities, and wholesale slaughter. And the Mongols cleverly fostered this fear, sparing some victims so they could spread terrifying tales and using others as human shields in subsequent attacks. Employing such methods, the Mongols sowed discord and panic among their foes. At the same time, by pledging not to kill those who offered no resistance and to protect

A Mongol archer on horseback.

Genghis Khan's armies unite Turks and other non-Mongols

those who had useful skills—such as engineers, artisans, and merchants—the Mongols even got some groups to submit without struggle.

Mongols adopt ideas
and techniques from
allies and defeated foes

Borrowed ideas and techniques. The Mongols were quick to adopt innovations from the cultures they conquered. From Chinese and Turkish siege engineers, for example, the Mongols learned how to build catapults to heave huge rocks and flaming projectiles over fortress walls, preparing the way for assaults on cities and citadels. From their Uighur Turk allies, the Mongols learned to write, adapting Uighur script to express Mongolian words, compile information, maintain records, and communicate over long distances. From Central Asian merchants and Chinese officials, the Mongols learned how to finance and administer an empire. The most eminent such official was Yelü Chucai (*YEH-LOO choo-SĪ*), a Confucian scholar of Khitan heritage who worked for the Mongols and taught them how to govern. In one of history's most astute acts of statecraft, he convinced them that they could make a fortune by exploiting and taxing northern China's cities and farms—thus derailing a proposal to depopulate the region and turn it into grazing grounds for Mongol herds.

Leadership. A final key factor was their leader himself. Genghis Khan was a masterful military strategist, a talented diplomat, a shrewd opportunist, and a superb leader. Believing that he was destined to conquer the world, he inspired his forces to achieve unprecedented feats. Yet he was also a remorseless man who lived to fight and kill and is said to have claimed that a man's greatest joy was to conquer his enemies, plunder their possessions, ride their horses, and ravish their women. History has furnished few other figures so capable and so cruel.

The Mongol Khanates: Conquest, Adaptation, and Conversion

Mongol khanates
connect Eurasian
cultures

The Mongol drive for power did not end with Genghis Khan. After his death, his sons and grandsons continued to seek world domination, expanding Mongol rule across Eurasia. In the process they established four great **khanates**, vast autonomous regions of the Mongol Empire, each ruled by a khan descended from Genghis. These realms included the Khanate of the Great Khan, comprising most of East Asia; the Khanate of the Il-khans, which dominated Persia and Mesopotamia; the Khanate of the Golden Horde, which ruled over Russia; and the Khanate of Jagadai (*JAH-guh-dī*), which controlled Central Asia (Map 15.5). In adapting their rule to these regions, however, the Mongols were themselves transformed, taking on many ways and ideas of the peoples they ruled.

East Asia: Khubilai Khan and His Mongol-Chinese Empire

The richest and most populous khanate was the one ruled by the **Great Khan**. Chosen by tribal council as Genghis Khan's main successor, he was both the direct ruler of all Mongol lands in East Asia and the overlord of the other Mongol realms, whose khans were considered his vassals. As long as the empire remained intact, he was the planet's most powerful person.

Map 15.5 The Four Mongol Khanates Connect Eurasia in the Thirteenth and Fourteenth Centuries

Building on Genghis Khan's conquests, his sons and grandsons further extended Mongol rule, conquering the rest of China, Russia, Persia, and much of Islamic West Asia. Notice that the four huge "khanates" they formed united much of Eurasia, creating and enhancing connections among distant and diverse cultures. How did Mongol rule help to expedite the exchange of goods and knowledge?

Genghis Khan's son Ögödei (*UH-guh-dā*), elected Great Khan in 1229, vastly expanded the whole Mongol realm, sending armies in the 1230s to invade southwest Asia and Russia. In East Asia he completed the conquest of north China, routing the last remnants of the Jurchen realm that had survived his father's devastation. Then he planned to move against the Song regime in southern China. But Ögödei died in a drinking binge in 1241, leaving his successors to continue his work.

Ögödei's most eminent successor, as a warrior and a ruler, was his nephew Khubilai (*KOO-bih-lī*) Khan. After leading Mongol armies against the Song forces during the 1250s, this talented leader, the ablest of Genghis Khan's grandsons, was chosen as Great Khan in 1260. Over the next two decades, he defeated the Song regime and completed the conquest of China. In 1271 he even claimed the Mandate of Heaven, the divine warrant to rule China, installing himself as its emperor and starting a new dynasty called the Yuan (*yoo-WAHN*). By 1279, when the last Song forces were finally crushed,

Khubilai Khan completes the conquest of China

Khubilai was master of East Asia, ruling as both the Mongol Great Khan and the Emperor of China.

Elsewhere Khubilai was less successful. In 1274 and 1281 he launched against Japan two massive naval invasions, with hundreds of ships and thousands of warriors. But these attacks failed due to Japanese resistance and terrible sea storms the Japanese called **kamikaze** (*KAH-mē-KAH-zē*)—"divine winds" they believed the gods had sent to protect Japan. In the 1280s Khubilai sent armies into Southeast Asia, but they were bogged down by the region's dense rain forests, stifling heat, oppressive humidity, and deadly tropical diseases. In 1293 he dispatched a seaborne force to attack the island of Java, but this force was decisively repelled.

Mongol rulers embrace Chinese ways

In China, however, Khubilai reigned supreme. Unlike other Mongols who disdained China's sedentary society, he embraced many Chinese ways. He moved his capital from Mongolia to northern China, ruling his realm from Khanbalikh (*KAHN-bah-LĒK*), the "city of the Khan," today called Beijing. He adopted China's administrative system, adapted to urban life, and spared China's cities from devastation if they accepted his rule. He encouraged commerce, promoted use of paper money, repaired and expanded highways, and fostered the formation of merchant corporations. He extended the Grand Canal from the Yellow River north to his capital, thus securing the transport of grain and goods along an 1100-mile waterway flanked by a paved road. He practiced religious toleration, became a Buddhist, and even took a Christian woman as one of his four main wives.

Chinese Confucians resent Mongol rule

Despite such efforts, Khubilai and his heirs were deeply resented in China. Many Chinese, regarding their culture as the world's most advanced, saw the Mongol rulers as uncouth barbarians. Chinese Confucians were offended by the Mongols' crude cuisine, their refusal to bathe, their tolerance for non-Chinese religions (such as Christianity and Islam), and the relatively high status they accorded to women. But above all, Confucian scholars resented their own loss of status: although the Mongol regime still employed them as administrators, it reduced their privileges and abandoned their civil service exam placement system, while placing Mongols and other foreigners in most important posts. Within several decades after Khubilai's death in 1294, Mongol rule in China was further weakened by struggles among his successors and by deadly natural disasters.

Southwest Asia: Mongol Devastation and Muslim Resilience

In many ways, Islamic Southwest Asia's experience with the Mongols was similar to East Asia's. In both regions, an assault begun by Genghis Khan was resumed and expanded by one of his grandsons. In both regions, the Mongols overcame strong resistance by a wealthy, cosmopolitan society. In both regions, Mongol forces were eventually turned back, but only after carving out an enormous empire. And in both regions, the Mongols adopted beliefs and practices of the peoples they ruled, but continued to be seen by these peoples as alien oppressors.

Mongols invade Persia and Anatolia

THE MONGOL ASSAULTS ON THE MUSLIM WORLD. The Mongol conquest of Southwest Asia started with assaults on Persia. Ravaged during Genghis Khan's assault on Khwarazm in 1219–1221, Persia got a respite when those armies withdrew. In 1230, however, Great Khan Ögödei sent a sizable force there to complete his father's unfinished business.

Later, after routing local armies and overrunning Persia, the Mongols dispatched armed forays into Anatolia, defeating the Seljuk Sultanate of Rūm in 1243. But at the time they lacked sufficient forces to follow up this victory. Nor were they yet ready to invade Mesopotamia, where the Abbasid Caliphs, claiming spiritual leadership of the Islamic world, reigned in the heavily fortified city of Baghdad.

In the 1250s, however, the Mongols decided to resume and expand their Southwest Asian conquests. While Khubilai led armies against China's Song regime, in Mongolia his brother Hülegü (*hoo-LEH-goo*) assembled a huge force, complete with siege equipment and Chinese technicians, to aid in his intended assaults on Muslim cities and citadels. Hülegü arrived in Persia in 1256 and was joined there by other Mongol forces in the region.

Hülegü conquers Islamic Southwest Asia

The Mongol forces first attacked the Assassins, the Shi'ite murder sect, which by this time had established numerous fortresses throughout the rugged mountains south of the Caspian Sea. One by one the Mongols stormed and demolished these strongholds. By the end of 1257, the Mongols had massacred or captured most of the sect's members, thus eliminating the cult of killers that had long terrorized the Sunni Muslim leaders.

Attackers using a catapult against a walled fortification.

But Sunni Muslims had little time to rejoice. Within weeks the Mongols were threatening Baghdad and insisting, as their price for sparing the city, that the reigning Abbasid Caliph offer them homage and tribute. When Islam's spiritual leader refused to submit, the irate Mongols routed his armies and besieged his city. In February of 1258, after holding out for several weeks, Baghdad fell to the invaders, appalling the Muslim world. Hülegü let his men plunder the city and had the captured caliph trampled to death by horses. Thus ignobly ended the once-great Abbasid Empire.

The next year, while Hülegü headed homeward with some of his troops to take part in a Mongol power struggle, the rest of his army moved west into Syria and Palestine. But the Muslim Mamluks who then ruled Egypt, themselves descended from Central Asian Turks, sent a huge force that decisively defeated the Mongols in 1260 in Palestine. Hülegü later returned to Southwest Asia but died in 1265 without regaining the initiative.

THE IL-KHAN CONVERSION AND TRIUMPH OF ISLAM. Hülegü's heirs, a series of Southwest Asian Mongol rulers known as **Il-khans** (subordinate khans), focused mainly on ruling their own realm. But the Khanate of the Il-khans, which stretched from eastern Anatolia to India's Indus River (Map 15.5), faced serious problems. In their campaigns of conquest the Mongols had ravaged the region, destroying its cities and irrigation systems, killing many of its people and wrecking its economy. As their conquests ceased and they lacked new places to plunder, they made things worse by imposing heavy taxes, effectively pillaging their own empire and ruining its recovery. The coexistence of Mongol and Islamic law created legal chaos, and a string of short reigns by inept Il-khans damaged the regime still further. So did the fact that the Mongol rulers were seen by their subjects as alien, barbaric oppressors.

Eventually, however, like countless earlier rulers of Persia and Mesopotamia, the Mongols were converted by the culture they conquered. Enamored by the splendor of Islamic civilization, they fostered trade, patronized science and scholarship, built cities and schools, and gradually forsook their nomadic ways. Many Mongols became Muslims, including the Il-khans themselves.

Il-khans adopt Islamic ways

The ablest Il-khan was Mahmud Ghazan (*MAH-mood gah-ZAHN*), who focused his brief reign (1295–1304) on rebuilding the region. He converted to Islam, instituted fair taxation, repaired irrigation systems, and returned abandoned lands to cultivation. Though a Sunni Muslim, he tolerated Shi'ites, who had been harshly persecuted under the Abbasid Caliphate.

Rashid al-Din combines Eastern and Western learning

Most of what we know of Mahmud Ghazan, and much of our knowledge of this era, comes from Ghazan's prime minister Rashid al-Din (*rah-SHED ahl-DEN*), an eminent example of the cultural connections fostered by Mongol conquests. Born a Jew, Rashid became a Muslim and worked for the Mongols in places from China to Persia. As a physician familiar with Chinese medicine, he helped bring Chinese knowledge of human anatomy to the Muslim world, whence it later spread to Europe. As a historian, Rashid worked with Eastern and Western scholars to produce the first great history of the world, a monumental work with lavish illustrations (see catapult drawing from Rashid's book on page 369). As an economist and government official, Rashid promoted fiscal and administrative reforms, ably guiding the regime of Il-khan Mahmud Ghazan.

Unfortunately for the Il-khans, Ghazan's reign was cut short in 1304 by his death from an illness at age 32. Instead of consolidating his achievements, his successors indulged in the pleasures of their court, letting corrupt officials run the realm. In 1335, when the last of the Il-khans died without an heir, the empire disintegrated into provinces controlled by ambitious warlords.

As the Il-khan Empire became the first Mongol khanate to vanish, it was clear that the Muslim world had weathered the nomadic onslaught. Both Seljuk Turks and Mongols had brought death and destruction to Southwest Asia, but both had also embraced its culture and religion, and for a time provided good governance, until their realms were fragmented by conflicts among the rulers. Both had actually expanded Muslim horizons, the Seljuks by making Anatolia Islamic and using Persian culture to revitalize Islam, and the Mongols by uniting a Eurasian empire that brought East Asian medicine, scholarship, commerce, and technology to the Muslim lands of Southwest Asia.

Russia: Conquest, Tribute, and the Tatar Yoke

Although the Mongol invasion of Russia, like those of China and Southwest Asia, involved the vanquishing of a vast realm by a grandson of Genghis Khan, the Mongol method of governing Russia differed from that employed elsewhere. For one thing, the Mongols ruled Russia indirectly. Withdrawing their forces after ravaging Russia's city-states, the Mongols demanded tribute and made Russian rulers vassals of the Mongol khan. For another thing, the Mongols who ruled Russia did not adopt Russian ways. Rejecting Russia's Orthodox Christianity and settled agrarian society, they lived in the steppes, remained pastoral nomads, and embraced Islam. Still, by aiding the rise of Moscow as Russia's dominant city, Mongol rule in Russia, which lasted more than two centuries, played a key role in Russia's political development.

Batu Khan conquers Russia

The onslaught began in late 1237 when Batu Khan (*BAH-too KAHN*), grandson of Genghis and cousin of Khubilai and Hülegü, stunned northern Russia by attacking in winter, piercing the dense forests by using frozen rivers as highways for his horsemen. In December his Mongols, whom the Russians called Tatars (*TAH-tarz*), overran Russia's

Document 15.1 Russian Chronicle Account of the Mongol Attack on Kiev

In 1240, having earlier overrun northern Russia, Batu Khan and his Mongols, known by the Russians as Tatars, descended upon the great city of Kiev. This account from the Russian chronicles provides a vivid description of the Mongol assault.

In this year [1240] Batu Khan approached and surrounded the city of Kiev with a great multitude of soldiers. The Tatar force besieged it, and it was impossible for anyone either to leave the city or to enter it. Squeaking of wagons, bellowing of camels, sounds of trumpets and organs, neighing of horses, and cry and sobs of an innumerable multitude of people made it impossible to hear one another in the city. The entire country was overflowing with Tatars. . . .

Batu ordered that many wall-destroying rams be brought to Kiev and placed near the Polish Gate, because that part was wooded. Many rams hammered the walls without interruption day and night and the inhabitants were frightened, and there were many killed and blood flowed like water. And Batu sent the following message to the inhabitants of Kiev: "If you surrender to me, you will be forgiven; if, however, you are going to resist you will suffer greatly and perish cruelly." The inhabitants of Kiev, however, did not listen to him, but calumniated and cursed him. This angered Batu very much and he ordered [his men] to attack the city with great fury. And thus with the aid of many rams they broke through the city walls and entered the city, and the inhabitants ran to meet them. It was possible to hear and see a great clash of lances and clatter of shields; the arrows obscured the light and because of this it was impossible to see the sky, but there was darkness from the multitude of Tatar arrows, and there were dead everywhere and everywhere blood flowed like water.... The Tatars took the city of Kiev on St. Nicholas Day, December 6 [1240].

SOURCE: *Polnoe Sobranie Russkikh Letopisei (Complete Collection of Russian Chronicles)*, X, 115–117. Translation by Basil Dmytryshin, *Medieval Russia: A Source Book, 900–1700* (2nd. ed., New York: Praeger Publishers, 1973), 112–113.

major cities, putting people to the sword and buildings to the torch, spreading terror, death, and devastation. In spring 1238, the Mongols arrived at Novgorod ($N\overline{O}V$-*guh-rud*), a prosperous commercial metropolis, but decided not to attack, partly because the spring thaw made the swampy area unfit for a siege, and partly because the city's merchants quickly agreed to pay tribute. The Mongols had learned that they could profit as parasites, not just as plunderers.

Besides, Batu's main aim was to secure his northern flank for an invasion of Europe. In 1240 he began this quest with an assault on Kiev, former capital of Kievan Rus (Chapter 10), sacking the city and leaving behind fields full of skulls and bones (see "Russian Chronicle Account of the Mongol Attack on Kiev"). In 1241 the Mongols moved into Poland and Hungary, where they encountered European knights. Finding arrows useless against the metal armor of these mounted warriors, Batu's marksmen shot the knights' horses out from under them to win several major battles. But early the next year, when Batu learned that Great Khan Ögödei had died, he withdrew his forces to the east to influence the choice of a successor.

Europe thus was spared, but not Russia. Batu and his minions set up a new realm that came to be called the Khanate of the **Golden Horde**. From their capital at Sarai (*sah-RĪ*), amid the steppes and pasturelands north of the Caspian Sea, they commanded a domain that extended from north Central Asia into Eastern Europe. For the next few centuries the Mongols dominated Russia, forcing its city-states to furnish tribute, soldiers, and slaves, while playing their princes off against one another. This era of Mongol domination was known in Russia as the **Tatar Yoke**.

Still, the Tatars largely let the Russians run their own affairs as long as their main leader would travel to Sarai and humbly seek the khan's formal permission to serve as Grand Prince. At first the khans alternated this office among various Russian princes, so none would gain too much power. Eventually, however, the khans entrusted it mostly to the rulers of a rising metropolis called Moscow. Henceforth, by doing the khan's bidding and acting as his agents in repressing other Russians, Moscow's rulers usually maintained the title of Grand Prince. In time this status would help Moscow become Russia's leading city, and eventually grow powerful enough to challenge Mongol rule.

Golden Horde rules Russia indirectly

Central Asia: The Struggle to Maintain the Mongol Heritage

Strife among the Mongols also threatened their empire. Discord stemmed from its size and diversity, which bred conflicts among its various regions, and from its lack of a clear succession system, sparking power struggles among Genghis Khan's heirs. As early as the 1260s, Batu's successors in the Golden Horde clashed with Hülegü's Il-khan regime, while Khubilai fought a four-year battle against a younger brother to prevail as Great Khan.

Khanate of Jagadai seeks to maintain Mongol heritage

In time the struggles among the Mongols tended to converge in Central Asia, in the lands that Genghis Khan had consigned to his second son, Jagadai. Centered among the other three khanates, the Khanate of Jagadai was the empire's hub (Map 15.5). It was also the poorest and least populated khanate, and the one that came closest to maintaining the Mongols' original nomadic warrior lifestyle.

The khanate's devotion to this lifestyle set the stage for conflicts. War and conquest were part of the Mongol heritage, and the empire's expansion had come mainly at the expense of settled societies. But the Khanate of Jagadai, largely surrounded by the other three khanates, could not expand without attacking other Mongols. At first it saw no need to do so and was content to supply the other realms with rugged Central Asian horsemen to sustain their assaults.

Eventually, however, after conquering settled societies, the other khanates adopted new customs and beliefs. The Il-khans embraced Islam, as did the Golden Horde, while Khubilai became a Buddhist, declared himself Chinese emperor, and moved the Great Khan's capital from Mongolia to China. Seeing such changes as a debasement of Genghis Khan's legacy, the rulers of the Central Asian khanate rallied to restore this heritage.

Kaidu combats Khubilai for control of Mongol heritage

Their leader, Ögödei's grandson Kaidu (*KĪ-doo*), was resentful that his branch of the family had lost out in the struggles for succession as Great Khan. In the 1260s he extended his sway over the Khanate of Jagadai, portraying himself as protector of the Mongol traditions. He declared that all true Mongols must live in tents on the steppes and must not degrade themselves by dwelling in cities and towns. Then, in the 1270s, after assembling an army of followers, he attacked the western part of the region ruled by the Great Khan.

Responding swiftly, Great Khan Khubilai sent a strong force to repel the attack. But Kaidu, refusing to admit defeat, stunned the other Mongols in 1277 by invading

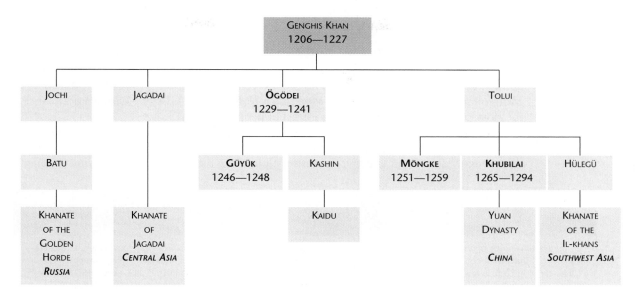

MONGOL RULERS AND KHANATES
GREAT KHANS IN BOLD

Mongolia itself. Although the next year Khubilai's armies drove back the forces of Kaidu, the Great Khan chose to continue his military efforts elsewhere rather than to stop and finish off his upstart relative. So the conflicts continued for a generation, until Kaidu died in 1301. Left without a leader, his followers reluctantly submitted a few years later to Khubilai's successor, but then fought among themselves sporadically for decades. By the 1340s, as a result, the Jagadai Khanate had split into two smaller realms.

The Mongol empire thus began to unravel, but its impact could not be undone. In conquering much of Eurasia, the Mongols wrought massive ruin, but in ruling it they forged connections that had extensive and enduring consequences.

The Mongol Impact: Connections and Consequences

The initial impact of the Mongol onslaught was widespread devastation. Across Eurasia hundreds of cities and towns were leveled, thousands of farmlands were ruined, and millions of people were killed. According to contemporary counts, the population of China dropped by 40 percent, from around 100 million to about 60 million, during the decades of Mongol invasion and rule. Russia's wealth and talent were depleted by two centuries of the Tatar Yoke. Southwest Asia was hit especially hard, pillaged first by the Seljuk Turks and then by the Mongols. Many of the region's great cities were destroyed, and it took decades for its farms to recover from the damage done to irrigation.

In the long run, however, the main impact of the Mongol era was increased Eurasian integration. By connecting distant and diverse regions under a common rule, the Mongols promoted trade and travel from one end of Eurasia to the other, vastly enhancing the exchange of goods, ideas, and technologies—as well as the spread of diseases—among Eurasian societies.

Trade and Travel: *The Pax Mongolica*

Much as Romans had created a Roman Peace, or *Pax Romana*, promoting commercial and cultural exchanges in the first and second centuries C.E., the Mongols produced a Mongolian Peace, later called **Pax Mongolica** (*PAHX mon-GŌL-ih-kuh*), that advanced the flow of goods and ideas among Eurasian peoples (Map 15.6).

Pax Mongolica facilitates Eurasian connections

The *Pax Mongolica* was not just a fortuitous byproduct of the Mongol invasions; it resulted from deliberate policies pursued by Mongol rulers. To manage their vast realm, the Mongols devised an effective administration, using the Uighur Turks' writing system

Map 15.6 Pax Mongolica Enhances Eurasian Connections in the Thirteenth and Fourteenth Centuries

By connecting much of Eurasia in the thirteenth and fourteenth centuries, the Mongols created a Pax Mongolica, a "Mongolian Peace" that enhanced the exchange of goods and knowledge. Note the land and sea routes that linked numerous cultures, carrying cottons from India; spices from Southeast Asia; timber, furs, and slaves from Russia; silks, porcelains, and teas from China; grapes, wines, and olive oils from Europe; and horses, dates, sugar, and slaves from Islamic West Asia and Africa. Along with increasing commerce, what ideas, knowledge, beliefs, and technologies did Mongol rule help to spread?

and often employing the Uighurs themselves as civil servants and scribes. To expedite communication, the Mongols created a long-distance postal system, with an extensive network of relay stations, staffed by thousands of riders and ponies capable of carrying messages 200 miles a day. To secure interregional travel and commerce, Mongol forces protected the trade routes with groups of warriors stationed across Central Asia. To enhance diplomatic relations, Mongol rulers dispatched emissaries to distant realms and welcomed embassies from other lands. The Mongols even supplied traveling merchants and dignitaries with an embossed metal seal that served as an early form of passport, to indicate that the bearer's travel was officially approved (see photo on page 376).

Aided and protected by such policies, growing numbers of traders and travelers transported goods and knowledge across Eurasia. Merchants conveyed and exchanged cottons from India; spices from Southeast Asia; timber, furs, and slaves from Russia; silks, porcelains, and teas from China; grapes, wines, and olive oils from Europe; and

Map 15.7 Travels of Marco Polo, 1271–1295, and Ibn Battuta, 1325–1355

The *Pax Mongolica* enabled travelers such as Marco Polo (an Italian Christian) and Ibn Battuta (a Moroccan Muslim) to visit many distant lands. Note that Marco Polo traveled across Eurasia from Italy to China, where he lived for over seventeen years before returning to Europe, while Ibn Battuta's travels took him to numerous cities and places in Africa and Eurasia. How did their vivid descriptions of their travels, and of the lands they visited, help inspire others to create new connections linking Europe, Africa, Asia, and beyond?

A Mongol "passport."

Travels of Marco Polo and Ibn Battuta enhance cross-cultural connections

horses, dates, sugar, and slaves from Muslim domains in Africa and Southwest Asia. Mongol era travelers also spread knowledge by publishing accounts of their visits to widely varied lands.

One such account was that of Marco Polo, an Italian merchant who claimed to have traveled across Central Asia to China (Map 15.7) and to have worked in Khubilai Khan's service from 1275 to 1292. Later, back in Europe, Polo published *Il milione* (The Million), a book describing an immense Chinese empire with huge, prosperous cities, printed books and paper money, flourishing canals and roads, black rocks (coal) that were used as fuel, great ships in bustling harbors, splendid architecture, and fabulous goods. At first he was dismissed as a liar, and even today some critics contend that his accounts were based not on personal experience but on tales heard from other travelers, amplified by his imagination. Nonetheless, whatever their source, his stories helped inspire a fascination with the East among the peoples of Europe. This fascination, along with accounts of Asian wealth and a growing Western appetite for eastern goods such as spices, ceramics, textiles, and teas, led later Europeans to embark on epic voyages that would transform the world (Chapter 19).

Another influential travel account was the *Rihlah* ("Travels") of Ibn Battuta (*IB'n bah-TOO-tah*), a Muslim from Morocco who between 1325 and 1355 journeyed some 75,000 miles across the Mongol khanates and beyond. He reported visiting the reigning Mongol Il-khan, the Golden Horde headquarters at Sarai, various trading towns on the Silk Road, and numerous other settlements in India, Southeast Asia, China, Europe, and Africa. His detailed recollections, dictated after his return, provided his readers, and subsequent historians, with remarkably accurate descriptions of these diverse regions and societies.

Exchanges of Ideas and Technologies

Mongols help spread religious and scientific ideas

Eager to exploit the talents of their conquered subjects, the Mongols moved people with special skills—such as architects, engineers, miners, metalworkers, and carpenters—all over the empire. Intrigued by the diverse ideas of the peoples they ruled, many Mongol rulers also welcomed travel by scholars and religious figures.

Such practices helped to disseminate ideas and technologies. Buddhist, Muslim, and Christian communities, for example, emerged in many new places, exposing societies all over Eurasia to their religious ideas. Muslim knowledge about mathematics and astronomy spread eastward to China, where Khubilai Khan employed Persian scholars to help build a new observatory, and westward to Europe, where such knowledge eventually helped inspire a scientific revolution. Chinese expertise in medicine and anatomy was likewise spread westward by traveling scholars and officials, most notably Rashid al-Din. From China also came two enormously influential technologies: printing and gunpowder weaponry.

Mongols and Uighur Turks help spread process of printing

By the time of the Mongol conquests, the Chinese technique of printing on paper from carved wooden blocks had spread to the land of the Uighur Turks, in Central Asia southwest of Mongolia. Allied with the Mongols, and employed throughout their empire as artisans, scribes, and officials, Uighurs then helped spread printing westward across Eurasia. Although printing was initially shunned by Muslims, who deemed that sacred texts must be recopied devoutly by hand, Il-khan officials in Persia introduced printed paper money in 1294—then withdrew it when people rioted against what they saw as worthless pieces of paper. In the 1300s, printed playing cards and holy pictures were introduced into Europe, aided no doubt by diplomats and clerics who had seen them in eastern travels during the *Pax Mongolica*. These printed cards and pictures foreshadowed the development in Europe of woodblock artwork and movable-type printing presses during the next century (Chapter 16).

More direct was the Mongol role in proliferating gunpowder weapons. During the Tang dynasty (618–907 C.E.), the Chinese had learned to combine saltpeter (potassium nitrate) with sulfur and charcoal to create a powder that, when ignited, burned very quickly or exploded. This substance, later called gunpowder, soon proved useful in mining, clearing forests, building canals, and staging fireworks displays. Eventually China's warriors also used it in crude arrow weapons and in bombs that were thrown or catapulted in battle. In the 1200s such devices helped China to slow—but not stop—the Mongol assault.

Mongols help spread gunpowder weapons

Asian warriors firing arrows from tubes.

The Mongols quickly saw the value of such weapons. While fighting the Jurchens in north China (1211–1215), Genghis Khan's forces learned from Chinese allies how to build catapults and gunpowder bombs, which later Mongol armies used in their attacks on Islamic Southwest Asia. By the late 1200s, also with Chinese help, the Mongols learned to cast thick metal firepots and then pack them with gunpowder and a large rock or metal ball. Once ignited, the exploding powder propelled the projectile with enough force to smash holes in enemy walls. Thus were born the first cannons.

Others, too, were capable of copying their foes. Battered by Mongol assaults, Muslims soon learned to make gunpowder weapons, and Europeans, experienced in forging metal pots and church bells, were not far behind. By the 1300s both Muslims and Christians were using gunpowder cannons, and by century's end some European armies had handheld firearms.

Although cumbersome and inaccurate, these early cannons and firearms gradually transformed warfare. Initially gunpowder helped nomadic warriors seize the walled cities of settled societies. But guns eventually gave an edge to the settled societies, which had the resources, mines, and artisans to produce them in far greater numbers than could the nomads. In time the use of firearms neutralized the nomads' advantages—their horsemanship, courage, and speed—by enabling enemy armies to shoot at them from a distance. The Mongols thus helped to spread a technology that later contributed to their undoing.

The Plague Pandemic

The Mongols also helped to spread a disease that contributed to their undoing. In the mid-1300s Eurasia was swept by a pandemic of **bubonic plague**, a deadly contagion typically carried from rodents to humans by fleas. Unaware of how it spread, people at the time had little chance to protect themselves from this terrible affliction, which brought painful inflammations followed by chills, vomiting, fever, diarrhea, and delirium—often leading to death in three or four days.

The outbreak began in southwest China (Map 15.8), where rats and people had been beset by the plague sporadically for centuries. In the 1330s and 1340s, probably aided by traveling Mongol soldiers whose supply wagons may have harbored infected rats and fleas, the plague spread to other parts of China, where numerous people had already been weakened by floods and famines.

Mongol connections help spread plague throughout China

Map 15.8 The Plague Pandemic of the Fourteenth Century

In connecting most of Eurasia by conquest and commerce, the Mongols also helped facilitate the spread of disease. Compare this map with Maps 15.6 and 15.7, noting that the plague, having ravaged parts of China, moved westward along trade and travel routes that the Mongols used to connect their vast Eurasian empire. In what ways did the Mongols, and connections they helped develop, contribute to the plague pandemic? How did the plague help to end Mongol rule in China?

Meanwhile, aided by increased caravan traffic promoted by the Mongols, the plague moved westward across Central Asia, spread by fleas that fed on the blood of squirrels, rats, marmots, dogs, and humans. The deadly contagion ravaged not just caravans and towns along the trade routes but also encampments of nomadic herders and Mongol warriors scattered across the steppes.

Mongol connections help spread plague to Egypt and Europe

By 1346, the plague had reached the Black Sea's northern shores, where it afflicted Mongol soldiers besieging the city of Kaffa, a fortified trading port controlled by the Italian Republic of Genoa. According to some accounts, in one of history's earliest attempts at biological warfare, Mongols catapulted corpses of plague victims over the town walls into the surrounded city, evidently intending to infect its defenders. Fleeing Genoese ships, apparently harboring infected rats, carried the plague to Egypt and to Europe, where perhaps a third of the population perished in an epidemic that Europeans called the Black Death (Chapter 16).

The plague pandemic thus ravaged the peoples of Eurasia and northeast Africa, killing tens of millions and leaving behind a trail of death and devastation. It induced widespread panic, disrupted commerce, and created chaotic conditions that contributed to the disintegration of the Mongol Empire.

The End of the Mongol Era

By the 1330s, when the plague pandemic began, the Mongol Empire was already in decline. In Southwest Asia, as we have seen, the Khanate of the Il-khans dissolved after its last ruler died with no heir in 1335. In Central Asia, the Khanate of Jagadai, torn by internal discord, split into eastern and western khanates during the 1330s and 1340s. In China, Mongol rule was beset by dynastic strife: as Khubilai's descendants vied for power, often by intrigues and assassinations, eight different emperors reigned between 1307 and 1333.

Then catastrophe struck China. In the mid-1330s, deluged by crop-destroying floods, northern China endured a calamitous famine. In the 1340s, before the region recovered, another famine ensued. Faced with widespread starvation, the government strove to repair the dikes and dams, only to have them burst again. Meanwhile, huge amounts of paper money printed to finance the repairs deeply debased the currency. In the midst of these disasters came the plague from southwest China, ravaging much of the country and intensifying the crisis. By the 1350s many Chinese were joining mass revolts against the Mongol regime. To them the disasters had an obvious explanation: the Mongol dynasty had lost the Mandate of Heaven.

Mongols lose the Mandate of Heaven

These disasters and this perception bolstered rebel leaders, especially Zhu Yuanzhang (*JOO yoo-wahn JAHNG*), a poor peasant orphaned as a youth when his parents starved to death in a famine. While other rebels looted the countryside, Zhu amassed an army of supporters. In 1356, as China descended into chaos, he captured Nanjing, one of China's largest cities, and made it his capital. During the next decade he defeated other rebels, gaining control of the entire Yangzi valley. Finally he moved north with his huge army to confront the Mongol emperor, who promptly fled to Mongolia. In 1368 Zhu claimed Heaven's Mandate as the emperor Hongwu (*HONG WOO*) and founded a new dynasty called the Ming (Chapter 21). Mongol rule in China thus came to an end.

The Mongol Empire never recovered from its loss of China. In the late 1300s, a Turkic warrior called Timur (*tē-MOOR*) Lenk tried to reunite the Mongol realm, but his ruinous attacks on other Turks and Mongols instead opened the way for new Islamic empires (Chapter 17) and for Russian independence (Chapter 25). For several centuries surviving Mongol khanates would stage sporadic raids on settled societies such as Russia and China. But armed with gunpowder weapons, knowledge of which the Mongols had helped spread across Eurasia, the settled societies with their large armies would increasingly manage to keep the mounted steppe warriors at bay. The age of the great nomadic empires was over.

Chapter Review

Putting it in Perspective

The nomadic invasions of the tenth through fourteenth centuries shook the very foundations of Eurasia's settled societies. In a remarkable series of assaults, the nomads of Central Asia, with small populations and simple societies based on herding and horsemanship, devastated the large armies, fertile farmlands, and cosmopolitan cities of their far more populous and prosperous neighbors. The Khitans, and later the Jurchens, moved into northern China, the cradle of Chinese civilization. The Seljuk Turks overran most of Southwest Asia, seizing the historic heartlands of the Islamic and Byzantine worlds. Then came the Mongols, mightiest of all the nomads, who not only overran the Jurchen and former Seljuk domains, but also conquered all of China and much of Eurasia as well.

In the long run, however, the nomadic conquests transformed the nomads and facilitated the triumph of the settled societies. Over time the victorious nomads adopted many features of the conquered cultures, including governance structures, economic patterns, and religious beliefs. Thus, by the time their empires were finally overthrown, the former nomads had themselves become more settled and cosmopolitan, largely forsaking their original tribal and itinerant ways. Furthermore, by forcibly uniting large parts of Eurasia under their rule, the Seljuk Turks and Mongols fostered connections that in time would strengthen the settled societies. Indeed, by expediting the growth of east-west commerce and the spread of technologies such as gunpowder and printing, the nomadic conquests eventually enhanced the wealth and power of both the Muslim and the Christian worlds.

Reviewing Key Material

KEY CONCEPTS

khan, 358
shamanism, 358
Il-khans, 369
Golden Horde, 371

Assassins, 362
khanates, 366
Great Khan, 366
kamikaze, 368
Tatar Yoke, 372
Pax Mongolica, 374
bubonic plague, 377

KEY PEOPLE

Genghis Khan, 355
Alp Arslan, 361
The Nizam al-Mulk, 361
Salah al-Din, 363
Tamar of Georgia, 363
Yelü Chucai, 366
Ögödei, 367
Khubilai, 367
Hülegü, 369
Mahmud Ghazan, 370
Rashid al-Din, 370
Batu, 370
Kaidu, 372
Marco Polo, 376
Ibn Battuta, 376
Hongwu, 379

ASK YOURSELF

1. Why did the peoples of Central Asia rely mostly on herding and horsemanship rather than on farming? What was the impact of this reliance on their societies and governance?
2. How and why were the Seljuk Turks able to conquer most of Southwest Asia? How were they transformed from destructive marauders into rulers of a cosmopolitan empire?
3. What factors account for the incredible success of the Mongol campaigns of conquest? Why did the Mongols fail to conquer Japan, Southeast Asia, Egypt, and Europe?
4. Why did the nomadic conquerors so often adopt the features, structures, and beliefs of the cultures they conquered?
5. What were the benefits and disadvantages of the *Pax Mongolica*? What were its long term impacts on the Mongol Empire and on the large Eurasian settled societies?
6. How did Mongols compare, in their tactics, policies, and impacts, with earlier rulers of multicultural empires, such as Persians, Macedonians, Romans, Muslim Arabs, and Seljuk Turks?

GOING FURTHER

Adshead, S. A. M. *Central Asia in World History.* 1993.
Allsen, Thomas. *Commodity and Exchange in the Mongol Empire.* 2002.

Allsen, Thomas T. *Culture and Conquest in Mongol Eurasia*. 2001.

Amitai-Preiss, R., and D. Morgan, eds. *The Mongol Empire and Its Legacy*. 2000.

Bartlett, W. B. *The Assassins: The Story of Islam's Medieval Secret Sect*. 2001.

Chase, Kenneth. *Firearms: A Global History to 1700*. 2003.

Dardess, J. W. *Conquerors and Confucians*. 1973.

De Hartog, Leo. *Genghis Khan, Conqueror of the World*. 1989.

De Hartog, Leo. *Russia Under the Mongol Yoke*. 1996.

Farmer, Edward L. *Early Ming Government*. 1976.

Frank, A. G. *Re-Orient: Global Economy in the Asian Age*. 1998.

Golden, P. *Introduction to the History of Turkic Peoples*. 1992.

Grousset, Rene. *The Empire of the Steppes*. 1970.

Khan, Paul, ed. *The Secret History of the Mongols*. 1984.

Martin, H. D. *The Rise of Genghis Khan and the Conquest of North China*. 1971.

Mokyr, Joel. *The Lever of Riches: Technological Creativity and Economic Progress*. 1990.

Morgan, David. *Medieval Persia, 1040-1479*. 1988.

Morgan, David. *The Mongols*. 1986.

Ostrowski, D. *Muscovy and the Mongols*. 1998.

Ratchnevsky, Paul. *Genghis Khan: His Life and Legacy*. 1991.

Rossabi, M. *Khubilai Khan: His Life and Times*. 1988.

Severin, Tim. *In Search of Chinggis Khan*. 1992.

West, Elizabeth E. *Mongolian Rule in China*. 1989.

Key Dates and Developments

1025–1040	Seljuk Turks enter Persia		1255–1260	Mongols invade Southwest Asia, take Baghdad in 1258
1055	Seljuk Turks conquer Baghdad		1274, 1281	Japan rebuffs Mongol invasions with help of storms
1071–1076	Seljuks defeat Byzantines, take Syria and Palestine		1275–1292	Marco Polo reportedly resides in China
1092–1194	Seljuk Empire disintegrates		1279	Khubilai completes conquest of China
1114–1127	Jurchens defeat Khitans and conquer northern China		1325–1355	Ibn Battuta travels across much of Asia and Africa
1206	Temujin proclaimed Genghis Khan		1335	Il-khan regime collapses in southern Asia
1211–1215	Mongols defeat Jurchens and ravage northern China		1340s	Plague pandemic spreads across Eurasia
1219–1221	Mongols conquer Khwarazm and ravage Persia		1368	Mongols ousted from China; Hongwu begins Ming dynasty
1237–1241	Mongols invade Russia and central Europe		1380–1405	Timur Lenk ravages much of Asia

The Resurgence of the Christian West, 1050–1530

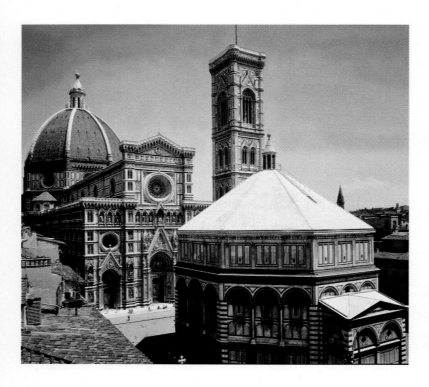

- Conflicts and Connections Between Europe and Islam

- The High Middle Ages

- The Decline of the Middle Ages

- The European Renaissance

- Chapter Review

The Cathedral And Baptistry Of Florence

In the eleventh through sixteenth centuries, the Christian West experienced a political, economic, and cultural resurgence, as reflected in the splendid architecture of Renaissance Florence.

In 1095 the Byzantine Empire, a shrunken remnant of the once-great Roman realm, was in serious trouble. A few decades earlier the Seljuk Turks, after conquering much of Southwest Asia and converting to Islam, had seized the empire's eastern provinces and its most valuable farmlands. The Turks had also overrun Syria and Palestine, conquering a region revered as a Holy Land by Christians, Muslims, and Jews. Seeking to shore up his defenses, the Byzantine ruler, as leader of the Christian East, asked the Christian West for help in fighting the Islamic Turks. It proved to be a fateful request.

Christian West

Crusade Areas

Pope Urban II (1088–1099), as head of the Western Church, responded with a grandiose plan to retake the Holy Land for Christianity. At Clermont, France, in late 1095, he called for Christian warriors to drive out the "accursed" Turks. "Wrest that land from the wicked race," he urged, according to one account of his speech, "and subject it to yourselves." Inspired by religious zeal, dreams of wealth and territory, and a papal promise of "the imperishable glory of the kingdom of heaven," thousands of European Christians heeded his call.

Thus began the crusades, a series of Christian holy wars directed mainly against Muslims, heralding a resurgence of the Christian West. For centuries, captained by feudal warlords and piloted by predatory Church leaders, Western Christians had lagged behind Muslims in power, wealth, learning, and technology. But in the eleventh century, energized by increasing prosperity and reforming popes, the West began to rebound. The crusades not only reflected this resurgence but also enhanced it by bolstering Western commercial and cultural growth.

Europe's High Middle Ages, coinciding with the crusades, witnessed a flowering of the cultural, political, economic, and religious elements that underlie what is now called Western Civilization. Ravaged in the fourteenth century by famines, plagues, schisms, and wars, the West rebounded again. By the fifteenth century, enriched by conflicts and contacts with Muslim societies, it was undergoing a cultural and technological Renaissance and emerging as one of the world's most expansive civilizations.

Conflicts and Connections Between Europe and Islam

The West's resurgence was rooted in conditions that arose in the eleventh century. By then, the Viking and Magyar invasions that plagued Europe in preceding centuries had ceased. Agricultural advances, combined with a warming of the climate, were helping to bring prosperity and population growth. The Great Schism of 1054, by cutting the ties of the Roman popes to Eastern Christianity, freed them to focus on strengthening their supremacy in the West. And a series of ambitious popes began to institute reforms, curtail corruption, and expand the power and prestige of the Western Church.

Seljuk conquest of West Asia leads to Muslim-Christian conflicts

Meanwhile, both the Muslim and Byzantine worlds had problems. In the previous few centuries, the splintering of the Abbasid Empire, and the growth of diverse groups within Islam such as Shi'ites, Sufis, and Almoravids, had undermined Islamic unity. During the 1040s and 1050s, the Seljuk Turks conquered the Muslim heartland, taking Baghdad in 1055 and making the Abbasid caliphs puppets of the Turkish sultan. Although the Seljuks themselves became Muslims, their conquests further fragmented the Islamic world. Then Byzantium made the fateful mistake of engaging the Seljuks in combat, suffering a disastrous defeat at Manzikert in 1071. Within a decade the Turks had taken Palestine, Syria, and eastern Anatolia, opening the way for expanded encounters between Europe and Islam.

Christians and Muslims in Iberia

As Turks took control in the East, Christians were already moving against Muslims in Iberia, the peninsula that now embraces Portugal and Spain, most of which had been under Islamic rule since the early 700s. In the eleventh century, as strife broke out among Iberian Muslims, small Christian kingdoms surviving in the North began working for **Reconquista** (*rā-kahn-KĒS-tah*), or Christian reconquest of Iberia (Map 16.1). In 1063 Pope Alexander II (1061–1074) supported their effort by sending in French and Norman soldiers; he also sanctified it by pardoning their sins, setting a precedent for future popes who would likewise grant spiritual rewards to Christians who fought against Muslims.

Led by Castile and Aragon, Christians expel Muslims from Iberia

Over the next few centuries, forces led by the Spanish Christian kingdoms of Castile (*cass-TĒL*) and Aragon (*AIR-uh-GŌN*) gradually pushed the Muslims back. In 1085, Castile and its allies captured Toledo, an Islamic cultural stronghold in central Iberia. In the Northeast, Aragon captured several Muslim cities, most notably Saragossa in 1118. Fearing that Islam might be pushed out of Europe entirely, Muslims from North Africa intervened in Iberia, but a united Spanish Christian army defeated them in 1212. Christians took Córdoba in 1236, Valencia in 1238, and Seville in 1248, while Portugal freed itself from Islamic rule by 1250. Although Muslims held the southern province of Granada until 1492, by the mid-1200s most of Iberia was under Christian control.

Contacts with Iberian Muslims enhance Western learning and technology

Conquests and connections with Muslims in Iberia brought many benefits to the Christian West. By taking Toledo, a major center of Islamic learning for over three centuries, Christians gained access to its large library of works in Arabic on science and philosophy. Once translated into Latin, these works greatly aided the advancement of Western scholarship. Eventually, Europeans also learned how to make paper and forge fine steel swords through contacts with Muslims in Iberia.

Conquests in Iberia also built Western confidence in religious warfare. Conducting war in God's name, as the Muslims had often done, was now the approach used by Christian crusaders in seeking to take the Holy Land from the Islamic Turks.

The First Crusade: "It Is God's Will!"

Pope wants crusade to take Holy Land and end strife in Europe

In 1095, a decade after the Christian conquest of Toledo, Pope Urban II called for Christian invasion of the Holy Land (see "Excerpts from Pope Urban II's Speech at Clermont, 1095"). Although he was responding to a Byzantine appeal for help, Urban clearly had

FOUNDATION MAP 16.1 Christians Reconquer Spain from Muslims, 1080–1492

From the eighth through eleventh centuries, Muslims ruled much of Spain, building there an impressive Islamic culture. Observe, however, that in the eleventh through fifteenth centuries, supported by the papacy and led by the Christian kingdoms of Castile and Aragon, Spanish Christian forces steadily defeated and drove out the Muslims. What benefits did Christian Europe gain from the legacy of Muslim rule in Spain?

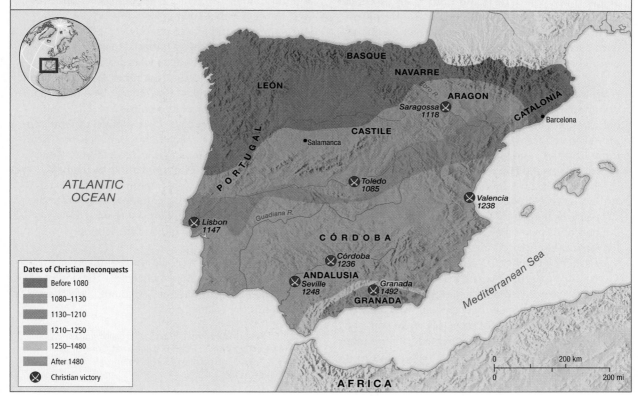

some additional goals. He hoped to bring peace to Europe, ending wars among its peoples by uniting them in a common cause. He wanted to enlarge Christendom through warfare fueled by faith, against the Muslims, who had shown the world how effective that combination could be. He aspired to enhance the papacy's power, and perhaps even restore its leadership over the Eastern Church.

The response to Urban's appeal was dramatic. As he preached his crusade, he was reportedly greeted by shouts of "It is God's will!" Within months, knights and foot soldiers from Italy, France, and Germany assembled into armies and headed for Constantinople, where they converged in 1097 to continue their eastward march.

The First Crusade (1096–1099) was a stunning success for the West. Benefiting from divisions among Muslims and the recent breakup of the Seljuk Empire, Christian warriors conquered the lands around the eastern Mediterranean (Map 16.2), creating four small "crusader states" and even capturing Jerusalem in 1099. But the Christians also engaged

Crusaders conquer Holy Land but also commit atrocities

Document 16.1 Excerpts from Pope Urban II's Speech at Clermont, 1095

In 1095, at the Council of Clermont in France, Pope Urban II issued a ringing call for a great crusade to retake the Holy Land from the Islamic Seljuk Turks, whom he demonized as an "accursed race" and accused of vicious atrocities. He called on Christian warriors to put aside their conflicts with each other and unite in a common cause that would bring them eternal glory.

From the confines of Jerusalem and the city of Constantinople a horrible tale . . . has been brought to our ears, namely, that . . . an accursed race, a race utterly alienated from God, . . . has invaded the lands of those Christians and has depopulated them by the sword, pillage and fire; it has led away a part of the captives into its own country, and a part it has destroyed by cruel tortures; it has either entirely destroyed the churches of God or appropriated them for the rites of its own religion . . . On whom therefore is the labor of avenging these wrongs and of recovering this territory incumbent, if not upon you?

. . . Let the deeds of your ancestors move you and incite your minds to manly achievements . . . Let the holy sepulchre of the Lord our Saviour, which is possessed by unclean nations, especially incite you, and the holy places which are now treated with ignomy and irreverently polluted with their filthiness . . .

Let none of your possessions detain you, no solicitude for your family affairs, since this land which you inhabit, shut in on all sides by the seas and surrounded by the mountain peaks, is too narrow for your large population; nor does it abound in wealth; and it furnishes scarcely food enough for its cultivators. Hence it is that you murder one another, that you wage war, and that frequently you perish by mutual wounds. Let therefore hatred depart from among you, let your quarrels end, let wars cease, and let all dissensions and controversies slumber. Enter upon the road to the Holy Sepulchre; wrest that land from the wicked race, and subject it to yourselves. That land which as the Scripture says . . . was given by God into the possession of the children of Israel . . . is now held captive by His enemies, and is in subjection to those who do not know God, to the worship of the heathens . . . God has conferred upon you above all nations great glory in arms. Accordingly undertake this journey for the remission of your sins, with the assurance of the imperishable glory of the kingdom of heaven.

When Pope Urban had said these and very many similar things . . . , he so influenced . . . the desires of all who were present that they cried out, "It is the will of God! It is the will of God!"

SOURCE: Robert the Monk, *Historia Hierosolymitana* (Medieval Sourcebook: Urban II, Speech at Council of Clermont, 1095), http://www.fordham.edu/halsall/source/urban2-5vers.html

in butchery and bigotry: unruly bands of "peasant crusaders," seeing the crusade as a war against all non-Christians, massacred Jews in Germany, and Christian soldiers pillaging Jerusalem slaughtered defenseless Muslims.

The Muslim Response and the Later Crusades

In time, however, the crusaders' conquests and brutal behavior motivated Muslims to combine their efforts and launch retaliatory attacks. By 1144 they had amassed a large army and reconquered one of the crusader states. Pope Eugenius III quickly authorized a Second Crusade (1147–1149), led by the German Emperor and the King of France. This time, however, the crusaders lost. After almost getting into battle against Byzantines near Constantinople, they were badly beaten by Islamic Turks in Anatolia, and thus failed to recover any lost ground.

Map 16.2 Crusades Create New Connections and Conflicts, 1095–1300

The crusades, which began as bitter conflicts between Christians and Muslims, also involved attacks by Western Christians upon other Christians. Notice that the First Crusade, in which Christians gained control of the Holy Land and set up "crusader states," was followed by others meant to regain control after Muslim-led counterattacks. Note, too, that the Fourth Crusade never made it to the Holy Land; instead its Christian crusaders sacked the great Christian city of Constantinople. How did the Crusades, which ultimately failed to maintain Christian rule in the Holy Land, bolster connections between Muslims and Christian Europeans? What impacts did these connections have on Western culture and commerce?

A few decades later, the West lost even more ground. The brilliant Muslim warrior Salah al-Din, known in Europe as Saladin, founded a new dynasty in Egypt in 1173. He quickly conquered Syria and Arabia, uniting them with Egypt into a formidable realm, and then attacked the remaining crusader states. In 1187 his forces took Jerusalem, refraining on his orders from sacking the Holy City. The work of the First Crusade was thus largely undone: most of the Holy Land was again under Muslim control.

Muslims under Salah al-Din retake most of Holy Land

Salah al-Din (Saladin).

At once Europe's three leading rulers—German Emperor Frederick Barbarossa (*bar-buh-RŌ-sah*), English King Richard I the Lionheart, and French King Philip II Augustus—organized a Third Crusade. The Muslims under Saladin prepared to defend their lands, while Byzantines braced for another threat to their region's stability.

The Third Crusade (1189–1192), planned as a multi-pronged land and sea assault, was a disaster for the West. Frederick, by then in his late sixties, drowned on his way to the Holy Land while crossing a river with his armor on. Richard and Philip quarreled constantly, until the latter, citing his poor health, returned to France in 1191. Richard soldiered on, and even defeated Muslim hero Saladin in several battles, but he failed to retake Jerusalem, which henceforth remained under Islamic control.

Fourth Crusade pillages Constantinople and ousts Byzantine ruler

A decade later, noting weakness and division within the Byzantine Empire, Pope Innocent III (1198–1216) called for a Fourth Crusade (1202–1204), hoping not only to undo the conquests of Saladin, who had died in 1193, but also to reunite Eastern and Western Christianity. Driven more by greed than by faith, however, the Germans, Normans, and Venetians who organized this crusade diverted it against Constantinople. Dismayed at their decision to plunder Christians instead of attacking Muslims, Innocent condemned the crusaders in 1202, but he could not control them. In 1204 they sacked the great city, forcing the Byzantine emperor to flee, and replaced his regime with a Western-dominated Latin Empire that lasted until 1261. The Byzantine realm was then restored and endured until 1453, but it never regained its former size or strength.

Later crusades target other Christians not aligned with Rome

Later crusades, forsaking the original quest for control of the Holy Land, were directed against targets other than Muslims. From 1209 to 1229, for example, crusaders in southern France annihilated Albigensians, radical Christian spiritualists who defied Church teaching by denouncing as evil all aspects of the physical world, including sex and material possessions. In succeeding decades the Teutonic Knights, a military religious order founded by earlier crusaders, conquered surviving pagan lands near the eastern Baltic Sea (Map 16.2) and invaded Russian regions settled by Eastern Christians. By 1291, when Muslims finally captured the last Christian outpost in the Holy Land, the initial crusading ideals had long since disappeared.

Islamic Impacts on Western Commerce and Culture

Crusades ultimately fail to meet original goals

In the long run, then, the crusades were a failure, at least in terms of their original goals. Muslim control of the Holy Land, although interrupted by the early crusaders, was ultimately restored. Europe remained divided into feuding states, whose leaders focused more on fighting each other than on battling Muslims. The split in Christianity widened, as the crusaders' sack of Constantinople, plundering its cathedrals and its great library, bred lasting bitterness toward the West in the Eastern Church. And brutal assaults against Jews in Europe opened the way for centuries of anti-Jewish abuse.

Increased contact with other cultures expands European horizons

But the Christian holy wars had unforeseen consequences for Europe and the world. The crusades spurred the growth of European credit and banking, as popes and rulers borrowed heavily to finance these costly ventures. The crusades boosted Western commerce, helping such Italian states as Genoa and Venice gain greater access to east-west trade, long dominated by Muslims. By exposing Europeans to textiles and spices from China, India, and Indonesia, this trade in time inspired Western voyages of exploration, which led in turn to Europe's exploitation of Africa and the Americas. And by giving

Westerners a taste for cane sugar from West Asia and North Africa, this commerce eventually prompted Europeans to grow their own sugar on plantations worked by slaves, vastly expanding the African slave trade.

The crusades and *Reconquista*, combined with the translation of Arabic works into Latin, also exposed Europe to the ideas of eminent Muslim scholars. From the writings of mathematician al-Khwarizmi, for example, the West was introduced to algebra, Arabic numerals, and Egyptian astronomy, laying the foundations for the later growth of European science. Through the work of physician and philosopher Ibn Sina, known in the West as Avicenna, Europeans learned about Greek and Indian medicine and ancient Greek philosophy, contributing greatly to the development of Western medicine and scholarship.

Exposure to Muslim scholarship advances Western learning

New technologies from the Muslim world also enhanced the West's resurgence. Water mills and windmills, which helped farmers drain swamps and grind grain, came to Europe through Islamic Spain. So did the production of paper, a key component of inexpensive printed books, later developed in Europe. Navigational innovations, such as the triangular "lateen" sail (which could be moved from side to side to let sailors tack into the wind) and the astrolabe (a device for navigating by the sun and stars), were introduced to Europe through contacts with Muslims. So were gunpowder weapons, spread westward from East Asia by Mongols and Turks (Chapter 15). In time such technologies helped European nations become global powers.

Exposure to technologies from Muslims advances Western wealth and power

Thus, for all the atrocities and havoc they produced, the crusades and *Reconquista* enhanced connections that contributed to European growth. The Arabic origins of numerous Western words—including cotton, coffee, sugar, tariff, musket, admiral, algebra, and zero—amply attest to the impact of such connections on European commerce, technology, and science.

Water mills in Islamic Syria.

The High Middle Ages

The era surrounding the crusades, which is known in the West as the High Middle Ages (roughly 1050 to 1300), is often seen as the high point of Medieval European culture. It brought advances in almost every area of European endeavor: agriculture expanded, towns and trade grew, monarchies strengthened, religion thrived, universities emerged, scholarship blossomed, and architecture flourished.

Agricultural Advances

Much of this era's economic growth began with agricultural advances, aided by improvements in climate and adoption of new technologies. Between 1050 and 1200 Europe's climate warmed considerably, creating a longer growing season and shorter, milder winters. Farmers were able to plant more crops and cultivate more land, often by clearing swamps and forests. Heavy plows made of wood and iron, introduced earlier but widely adopted mainly in the High Middle Ages, enabled farmers to turn over the earth instead of just scratching its surface, loosening the soil to vastly improve its fertility. The horse collar, a harness that fit around an animal's shoulders rather than its neck, enabled beasts of burden to pull plows and carts with the full weight of their bodies. Water mills and windmills helped farmers use the forces of nature to grind grain and drain swamplands.

Many Western farming advances were pioneered in Asia and Africa

These innovations were hardly unique to Europe. For centuries the Chinese had used heavy plows and water mills, East Asians and North Africans had employed efficient horse harnesses, and Persians had utilized windmills. But in the High Middle Ages interregional contacts and commerce, enhanced by the crusades and *Reconquista*, helped acquaint Europeans with such devices, which combined with the warming climate to increase the quantity and quality of food. As more food and better diets improved the health of childbearing women and helped more children survive to adulthood, Europe's population grew much larger.

The Growth of Towns and Trade

Increases in food and population help expand towns and trade

As the overall population increased, so did the number of people who lived in towns, often working as artisans or merchants, supported by the growing food supply. Towns had walls to protect them and marketplaces where artisans and merchants could exchange their goods—such as tools, furnishings, pottery, or clothing—for food brought in by local farmers. As more towns emerged, interregional trade increased, and a money economy replaced simple barter.

Long distance commerce was also stimulated by the crusades, which expanded European contacts with the East and interest in eastern goods, and by the Mongol conquests, which increased trade and travel across Eurasia (Chapter 15). European seaports, led by Genoa and Venice, imported eastern goods, while banking arose in cities such as Florence to finance commercial ventures. By the thirteenth century, Europe had many urban settlements, ranging from small fortified towns to sizable cities—such as London, Paris, Venice, and Florence—of fifty thousand people or more.

Urban occupations form guilds to protect their interests

In many towns and cities, the people in each occupation—such as merchants, carpenters, masons, shoemakers, or weavers—formed **guilds**, associations to promote their commercial and professional interests. Guilds had long flourished in Chinese and Byzantine cities, but in the West they had largely been absent since the fall of Rome. Their re-emergence in the High Middle Ages reflected not only Europe's increasing economic complexity, but also its growing commercial contacts with eastern civilizations.

Guilds as a rule fixed prices, wages, and standards, thereby protecting their members from competition while assuring their customers of quality. Guilds also provided training, as masters in each craft took on young apprentices. Apprentices typically worked with their masters for several years to learn the trade, then became journeymen who labored for wages, and perhaps eventually masters with their own shops or businesses. Some merchant guilds became so influential that they virtually controlled their towns.

Medieval towns were often unpleasant places. They were typically filled with vermin and waste, which served as breeding grounds for disease, and often torn by strife between merchants selling goods from other places and local craft guilds seeking to shield their members from such competition. Apprentices were often exploited, and sometimes even cruelly abused, by their masters. Women were frequently confined to occupations, such as clothes making and domestic service, that were far less prestigious and profitable than crafts and guilds controlled by men.

Medieval walled town.

The Rise of Royal Authority

As towns grew in power and wealth, they sought freedom from the local warlords, who over the centuries had developed into a landed nobility. Some towns strove to assert their own autonomy, while others allied with kings who, eager to expand their power by reducing that of the nobility, were often willing to work with townsfolk against local nobles. The kings issued charters, granting towns the right to establish their own governments and law courts. In return, instead of paying dues to the local noble warlord for protection, these towns now paid taxes to the king, enabling him to hire officials and soldiers so he could rely less on nobles to administer and defend the realm. Under royal protection, the towns also often became havens for peasants escaping their noble landlords, further undermining the influence of the landed nobility.

Towns help strengthen monarchs over landed nobles

The crusades and other foreign wars also motivated monarchs to increase their authority. To organize and finance such complex, costly ventures, kings found it useful to centralize their administrative and tax-collecting systems. In so doing, they not only made their governments more effective, but also made themselves more powerful and wealthy.

Different monarchs used different means to centralize their power. In France, for example, King Philip II Augustus (1180–1223) expanded his control by appointing for each province officials called baillis (*bī-YĒ*) to exercise authority and collect taxes in the name of the king. To ensure their loyalty, he made sure that the baillis had no ties to the provinces they governed and were paid good salaries directly by him. In England, King Henry II (1154–1189) focused on law and order, creating an extensive judicial system that was run by the central government rather than by local lords, thereby enhancing justice, stability, and royal authority.

Monarchs gain power by controlling courts and local officials

Other rulers were hampered by strong opposition from nobility. Henry's son King John (1199–1216), for example, having fallen deeply in debt, was forced in 1215 to accept the **Magna Carta**, a "Great Charter" that affirmed the nobles' rights, placed the king firmly under the law, and barred him from raising new taxes without their consent. In Germany, Emperor Frederick Barbarossa (1152–1190) had to concede broad political and military autonomy to the local princes in return for their recognition of him as overlord.

The general trend of governance in the High Middle Ages was nonetheless toward centralized monarchies. The growth of European populations and economies increased not only the size of royal treasuries and budgets but also the need for more powerful and effective central governments, strengthening the authority of the kings.

The Revitalized Roman Church

Despite the growing power of the monarchs, the Roman Church continued to thrive as Europe's central institution. As Pope Urban II had hoped, his leadership in launching the crusades enabled his successors for the next few centuries to act as political overlords as well as spiritual leaders. Furthermore, since most western Christians saw the Church as the key to their salvation, many donated lands and riches to it in hopes of gaining God's favor. Church wealth and power reached a peak under Pope Innocent III (1198–1216), the initiator of the Fourth Crusade. With huge revenues and a powerful bureaucracy, he crushed heresies, meddled freely in politics, arranged royal marriages, and decided disputes among rulers.

Roman Church and papacy dominate medieval Europe

Map 16.3 Europe in the High Middle Ages, 1050–1300

Europe's High Middle Ages, lasting from roughly 1050 to 1300, witnessed the emergence of cities, universities, and monarchies in Western and Central Europe. Note that the Holy Roman Emperors, whose realm looks impressive on the map, did not manage to fully centralize their power, so the empire was home to many small states that exercised considerable autonomy, while recognizing the emperor as their nominal overlord. How did the growth of cities, commerce, learning, and monarchies help to transform Europe in the High Middle Ages?

New religious orders also revitalized the Church. The Cistercians, founded in 1098 in what is now eastern France, set up monasteries in remote woods and wastelands to avoid worldly corruption. Under the dynamic leadership of Saint Bernard of Clairvaux (*clār*-VŌ) (1090–1153), who promoted the Second Crusade, the Cistercians acquired vast influence; by 1200 they had more than 500 monasteries. The Dominicans, founded in 1215 in southern France by Saint Dominic (1170–1221), took a different approach: rather than withdrawing from society as monks, they instead became *friars*, living in the world as beggars and becoming Europe's great preachers and teachers.

Another famous order of friars was founded by the era's most beloved Christian saint. After a dissolute youth as the son of a wealthy merchant, Francesco Bernadone (*bār-nah-DŌN-ā*) (1182–1226) had a radical change of heart. He gave up his possessions, dressed in rags, and lived in stark simplicity, ministering to the poor and outcast, and even to animals and birds. His Christ-like compassion attracted many followers, including the future Saint Clare, who started an order of Poor Sisters. He also won the trust of Pope Innocent III, who in 1209 approved what became the Franciscan order: a community of preachers, missionaries, and teachers devoted to the ideals of gentle, faithful Francesco, later revered as Saint Francis of Assisi (*ah-SĒ-zē*).

Cistercians, Dominicans, and Franciscans revitalize Roman Church

Yet the Church's wealth and power also attracted ambitious men who engaged in rampant corruption, and the use of crusaders to fight the Church's foes set a precedent for the use of force against other groups. Jews, for example, forbidden to own land in many countries, frequently worked in towns and cities as artisans, bankers, and merchants. Although they contributed greatly to medieval commerce, their efforts often drew abuse from their Christian competitors and neighbors, many of whom believed false rumors that Jewish religious rites used the blood of young Christians. Christians who dissented from Church teachings, denounced as heretics by Church leaders, typically faced violent suppression, sowing the seeds for great religious conflicts in the sixteenth century (Chapter 20).

European Christians persecute Jews and dissenters

Intellectual and Cultural Developments

Also sown in the High Middle Ages were seeds of scholarship and learning. Confucian academies had long prepared young men in China for civil service, and Muslims had set up learned academies that gathered great scholars in one place. Building on such ideas, Europeans in the High Middle Ages developed the **university**, an educational institution in which scholars from various fields helped students become experts and then granted them degrees to certify their expertise. A university typically consisted of several colleges, each of which served as a sort of educational guild, providing training, setting standards, and accrediting those who mastered their field.

Universities emerge as centers of medieval learning

Medieval European universities started in various ways. In 1088 some students in Bologna (*buh-LŌN-yah*), an Italian town that had become a center for the study of Roman law, formed an association to hire and set standards for teachers. In Paris, around 1170, teachers at the cathedral school formed an instructor's guild and later organized into faculties of arts, law, medicine, and theology. Thus began the Universities of Bologna and Paris; others soon arose at Oxford and Cambridge in England, Naples in Italy, and Salamanca (*sah-lah-MAHN-kah*) in Spain (Map 16.3).

Paris, meanwhile, became a center of **scholasticism**, a system of study combining Christian faith with ancient Greek philosophy, especially that of Aristotle. Contacts with the Muslim world acquainted Paris scholars not with only the works of al-Khwarizmi and Ibn Sina but also with the works of such intellectual giants as Ibn Rushd (Averroes), the great Spanish Muslim thinker, and Moses Maimonides (*mī-MAH-nuh-dēz*), the noted Jewish philosopher who was also Saladin's court physician (Chapter 12). Building on their work, which reconciled Aristotle's pagan philosophy with Muslim and Jewish monotheism, Thomas Aquinas (*uh-KWĪ-nuss*) (1225–1274), a Dominican teacher at the

Medieval scholasticism is based on Greek and Muslim thinking

University of Paris, synthesized Aristotle's ideas with Christian theology. Arguing that scholars must use both faith and reason to learn about God and the world, Thomas became medieval Europe's dominant thinker. His writings, especially his monumental summary of theology, the *Summa Theologica* (*SOO-mah thā-uh-LŌ-jē-kah*), served for centuries as the main foundation of Western thought.

Gothic churches arise as the dominant medieval architecture

As Thomas used reason to reveal God's truth, the French monk Suger (*soo-ZHĀ*) used architecture. As head of a monastery at Saint-Denis (*san-duh-NĒ*) near Paris from 1122 to 1151, Suger constructed a new church, developing a new architectural style soon copied across much of Europe. Earlier churches were bulky and dark, their heavy roofs supported by thick stone walls with round arches and small windows. But the new **Gothic architecture** produced soaring churches with pointed arches and towering walls, braced by external support beams called flying buttresses, which freed vast expanses of wall for stained glass windows that bathed church interiors in radiant light. Cities and towns spent fortunes and decades erecting these majestic cathedrals, which embellished and transformed the European landscape.

Gothic cathedral of Notre Dame in Paris.

Exaltation of Women and Marriage

Cathedral construction in the twelfth and thirteenth centuries coincided with a growing devotion to the Virgin Mary, mother of Jesus Christ. Mary emerged as the Church's foremost saint, revered as the mother of God and honored by festivals, prayers, paintings, statues, and shrines. Many Gothic churches, including famous French cathedrals at Paris, Chartres (*SHART*), and Reims (*RĒMZ*), were named Notre Dame (*nō-truh-DAHM*) ("Our Lady") in her honor.

The cult of Mary in turn reflected an idealization of women. Among knights a code of chivalry extolled gallantry and loyalty to one's lady as well as one's lord. Male poets and minstrels called troubadours praised women as wondrous beings who inspired their men to feats of ardor and courage, while a new literature called "romance" exalted courtly romantic love on the part of men toward their ladies.

Medieval Church idealizes women and marriage

Marriage, too, was exalted, defined by the Church as a sacrament, a vehicle of God's grace, and carefully protected by Church law. Marriage to close relatives was banned, as were divorce and remarriage; children born outside of marriage were deemed "illegitimate" and barred from entering the priesthood or receiving their parents' inheritance. Women were expected, like the Virgin Mary, to be loyal wives and mothers, devoted to the service of husband and family.

Some women, in this service, acquired substantial influence. Wives of nobles, for example, frequently managed their estates, as the men were often away on military duties. And royal women at times exercised real power: Eleanor of Aquitaine (*AK-wih-tān*) (1122–1204), having gone on crusade as wife of French King Louis VII, later governed England during the absences of her second husband, King Henry II, and crusading son, Richard the Lionheart.

Such women, however, were exceptions. Lower-class women played important roles—brewing ale, baking bread, making clothes, raising children, caring for the sick, and helping with the harvest—but socially and legally they were subject to men. And the institutional Church, despite its exaltation of womanhood and marriage, was entirely run by celibate males.

The Decline of the Middle Ages

By 1300, the basic structure of Western civilization, with its thriving commercial cities, maturing national monarchies, powerful Christian Church, and Christian-centered intellectual and social institutions, was firmly in place. But in the years that followed this structure was badly shaken. Battered by Church decline, famine, plague, and constant warfare, Europe's medieval civilization started to unravel, creating a climate of foreboding and fear.

The Avignon Popes

The deterioration of medieval Europe began with the decline of the Church. As national monarchs increased in power and wealth, they were much less willing to accept papal dominance. A crisis began in 1294 when France's King Philip IV the Fair (1272–1307), on the verge of war against England, imposed heavy taxes on the French clergy. Pope Boniface VIII (1294–1303), forbidding him to do so without papal consent, ordered the priests not to pay. But the king struck back, suspending all shipments of church revenues to Rome. Faced with this resistance, the pope for a time backed down.

In 1302, however, Boniface renewed the conflict by issuing an edict declaring that all rulers, indeed all humans, are subject to the pope. Philip retaliated by sending his agents to kidnap the pope, thereby shocking all Europe. The aged and ailing Boniface was soon freed by supporters, but died the next year a broken man.

Clash between pope and king of France creates crisis

The Church's crisis nonetheless continued. In 1309 a new pope, pressured by Philip the Fair, moved from Rome to Avignon (*AH-vēn-YŌN*), a papal enclave bordering southern France. Thus began a long period (1309–1377), often called the Church's Babylonian Captivity (recalling the Biblical Jewish exile in Babylon), during which eight popes in succession lived at Avignon rather than Rome. Although not under direct French control, they were clearly under French influence, undermining their credibility and offending most of Europe.

Famine, Plague, and Social Unrest

While thus deprived of effective spiritual leadership, Europeans were hit with several horrific disasters. A changing climate, marked by colder weather and heavier rains, wreaked havoc with the food supply, already endangered by population growth. Catastrophe struck in 1315–1317, when floods in the North led to deadly famine in which tens of thousands died, while others ate farm animals and seed crops to survive. Further crop failures in 1333, 1337, and 1345–1347 left the population weak, malnourished, and susceptible to disease.

A plague victim.

Then, in fall 1347, a merchant ship returning to Genoa from Kaffa on the Black Sea landed in Sicily with a deadly cargo. In its hold were rats infested with the plague that had recently ravaged much of Asia (Chapter 15). Carried by fleas from rats to humans (bubonic plague), or spread by the coughing of afflicted people (pneumonic plague), the disease devastated Europe from 1347 through 1351. Death toll estimates range from 25 to 45 million people, roughly 30 to 60 percent of Europe's population. Since victims, who often died in three to five days, were covered with dark swellings, the plague at the time was commonly called the "Black Death."

Commerce helps spread bubonic plague from Asia to Europe

Map 16.4 Europe Ravaged by Plague Pandemic, 1347–1351

Known in Europe as the "Black Death," the plague pandemic killed perhaps 30–60 percent of Europe's people, depopulating cities, disrupting commerce, and traumatizing European society. Compare this map with Map 15.8, observing that the plague, having swept westward across Eurasia thanks to Mongol-developed connections, spread from the Black Sea port of Kaffa by ship through Constantinople to Sicily and southern Italy in 1347, then ravaged much of the rest of Europe during the next few years. What key impacts did the plague pandemic have on European society?

The plague, spread by fleas on rats, kills millions in cities and towns

The cities, where people were crowded together and streets were full of sewage and rats, were hit especially hard (Map 16.4). Victims, whose bodies gave off a vile stench, often were left uncared for, as others refrained from assisting them for fear of catching the disease. Hoping to save themselves, thousands fled the cities, helping to spread the plague to the countryside.

Unaware of what caused the disease, many people saw it as divine punishment for the sins of Church and society. Some joined groups of flagellants (*FLAJ-uh-luntz*), people who whipped themselves with chains and leather straps in hopes of gaining God's mercy. Others, however, assuming their time was short, indulged in the pleasures of food, drink,

Document 16.2 Excerpts on the Plague from Boccaccio's *Decameron*

The Decameron, an entertaining literary work by early Renaissance author Giovanni Boccaccio, is a collection of tales supposedly told by people who had fled from Florence to a nearby villa while the plague was ravaging that city in 1348. At the start of his narrative, Boccaccio provides a graphic description of the plague and its impact on the people of Florence.

In the year 1348 . . . , that most beautiful of Italian cities, Florence, was attacked by a deadly plague. It started in the East either through the influence of the heavenly bodies or because God's just anger with our wicked deeds sent it as a punishment to mortal men; and in a few years killed an innumerable quantity of people . . . The symptoms were not the same as in the East, where a gush of blood from the nose was the plain sign of inevitable death; but it began both in men and women with certain swellings in the groin or under the armpit. They grew to the size of a small apple or egg, more or less, and were vulgarly called tumours. In a short space of time these tumours spread . . . all over the body. Soon after this the symptoms changed and black or purple spots appeared on the arms or thighs or any other part of the body . . . These spots were a certain sign of death . . . most people died within about three days . . .

The violence of this disease was such that the sick communicated it to the healthy who came near them . . . To speak to or go near the sick brought infection and a common death to the living . . .

From these . . . occurrences, such fear and fanciful notions took possession of the living so that almost all of them adopted the same cruel policy, which was entirely to avoid the sick and everything belonging to them . . .

Some thought that moderate living and avoidance of all superfluity would preserve them from the epidemic. They formed small communities, living entirely separately from everybody else. They shut themselves up in houses where there were no sick . . . Others thought just the opposite. They thought the cure for the plague was to drink and be merry, to go about singing and amusing themselves . . . , laughing and jesting at what happened. They . . . spent day and night going from tavern to tavern . . .

Others again held a still more cruel opinion . . . They said that the only medicine against the plague stricken was to go right away from them. Men and women, . . . caring about nothing but themselves, abandoned their own city, their own houses, their dwellings, their relatives, their property, and went abroad or at least to the country around Florence . . .

Thus a multitude of sick men and women were left without any care . . . Owing to the lack of attendants for the sick and the violence of the plague, such a multitude of people in the city died day and night that it was stupefying to hear of, let alone to see.

SOURCE: Giovanni Boccaccio, *The Decameron,* translated by Richard Aldington, 1949, 1–4.

and sex. Some tried witchcraft or magic; others secluded themselves from human contact (see "Excerpts on the Plague from Boccaccio's *Decameron*"). Still others attacked the Jews, blaming them for the tragedy.

Even when the plague was gone, its impact remained. Trade was disrupted, as ports turned away ships and towns excluded outsiders. With few workers left to till fields, farms often went untended. Grotesque folk art showed skeletons doing a "Dance of Death," reflecting a general sense of doom.

The plague disrupts trade and farming and fosters a sense of doom

The shortage of workers forced employers to pay higher wages, leading many landlords to let peasants own some land to keep them from leaving the manor for better pay elsewhere. Some nobles tried passing laws to keep wages down and the peasants in place, only to have these efforts spark rebellion. French peasants, often called "Jacques" (*ZHAHK*) by their lords, went on a rampage called the Jacquerie (*zhah-KRĒ*) in 1358, looting and burning manor houses and killing a number of nobles. The lords responded ruthlessly, slaying some 20,000 rebels. In England, villagers and townsfolk alike joined a 1381 Peasants' Revolt led by a rebel called Wat Tyler, who demanded equality for all, claiming God had not created a privileged class of "gentleman" nobles. "When Adam delved and Eve span," asked the rebels, recalling the Bible's first humans, "who was then the gentle man?" Although these and other similar revolts were crushed, the labor shortage improved workers' wages and helped many peasants escape serfdom.

The Great Western Schism

The Church divides, with two and later three competing popes

Compounding Europe's chaos, the Church's ongoing crisis got even worse. In 1377, aiming to end the scandal, the reigning pope moved back from Avignon to Rome, then died the following year. Intimidated by a Roman mob, the cardinals elected in his place an Italian, Pope Urban VI, who boldly attacked Church abuses. Threatened by his reforms, a number of cardinals, most of them French, later reconvened and declared his election invalid. They chose as their pope the French king's cousin, who set himself up at Avignon. But Urban VI in Rome refused to step down, so now there were two competing popes. This Great Western Schism (1378–1417) scandalized all Europe, dividing it between supporters of Avignon and Rome. Hoping to resolve the crisis, in 1409 a council at Pisa deposed both popes and chose a new one, but the other two defied it, producing a three-way split.

Finally, a Council at Constance (1414–1418) ended the schism by persuading two of the three popes to step down and resume their former status as cardinals. The third, unreconciled, fled to a Mediterranean island, from which he excommunicated the rest of the Christian world. Despite this lonely defiance, a newly-chosen pope called Martin V (1417–1431) was able to rule from Rome with general support. But by then the papacy's status had been badly damaged.

Europe in Disarray

In the midst of all these crises, France and England added to the chaos by fighting a series of conflicts called the Hundred Years War (1337–1453). It began with a dispute over who should be king of France and was fought mainly on French soil. Gunpowder cannons and firearms, knowledge of which by then had reached Europe through the Mongols and Muslims, were forged and used by both sides in this conflict, adding to the devastation.

By the 1420s, after winning some substantial victories, the English held large parts of France and seemed on the verge of triumph. But the tide turned in 1429 when a French teenager named Joan of Arc, believing God had summoned her to drive the English from France, inspired French soldiers with a new sense of purpose and pride. As a result, although the English later got hold of Joan and executed her as a heretic, when the war finally ended in 1453 they had lost almost all their possessions in France.

Political conflict also troubled Central Europe. Its nominal overlords, the Holy Roman Emperors, failed to centralize their power, leaving Germany divided into numerous small states while five great families competed for the position of emperor. The Golden Bull, an edict issued in 1356 by Emperor Charles IV, provided some stability by designating seven

An English longbow, as used in the Hundred Years War.

key regional leaders as electors who would choose each new emperor by majority vote. But it also recognized the autonomy of the various local rulers, leaving the empire still divided and weak. In 1438 the electors chose as emperor the head of Austria's Habsburg (*HAHPZ-boork*) family, beginning a succession of Habsburg rulers who held the imperial title almost continuously until 1806. The Habsburgs increased their possessions through strategic marriages, but failed to create a centralized German state.

The European Renaissance

During the fourteenth century, even as Europe was racked with disasters, foundations were laid for a cultural revival, known as the Renaissance ("rebirth"), which lasted until the sixteenth century. It began in Italy, where growing commercial wealth amid ruins of Roman grandeur inspired efforts to restore the culture of the classical age. Based initially in Florence, an Italian city-state and wealthy banking center, the Renaissance eventually brought a new vitality to culture and society throughout Europe.

In the Renaissance, as in the High Middle Ages, connections with other cultures were crucial to European cultural renewal. The Renaissance was rooted in Europe's rediscovery of ancient Greek and Roman art and thought, advanced by contacts with Islamic and Byzantine artists and scholars. It was funded largely by wealth acquired through commerce with Eastern cultures and by the banking system that supported such trade. And it was enhanced by technologies such as paper and printing, developed in China and spread westward through the Muslim world.

Contacts with Muslims, Byzantines, and Asians help enhance Renaissance

In the Renaissance, as in the High Middle Ages, religious themes and the Church played a central role. But the Renaissance focused on life in this world rather than life after death.

Roots and Attributes of the Renaissance

Early in the fourteenth century, Florence produced two pivotal figures who helped lay the foundations for the Renaissance. One was the painter Giotto (*JAW-tō*) (1267–1337), whose portrayals of saints and biblical scenes pioneered **artistic realism**. He created portraits that were lifelike, showing detail, depth, and perspective, overcoming the flatness and stylized rigidity of earlier medieval art. The other was the writer Dante Alighieri (*DAHN-tā ah-lig-YĀ-rē*) (1265–1321), whose poetic masterpiece, the *Divine Comedy*, portrays him as a pilgrim traveling through hell, purgatory, and heaven. Full of Christian devotion, the work also uses biting satire, mocking many popes and rulers by depicting them in hell. Composed in Italian rather than in Latin, it pioneered **vernacular literature**, written in the everyday spoken language of the common people.

Crucifix painted by Giotto.

A generation later, Florence supplied the two great writers who began the Renaissance. Scorning medieval European culture as Germanic and crude, Francesco Petrarch (*PĀ-trark*) (1304–1374) worked to revive the literature of ancient Rome. He collected ancient Latin texts, wrote letters to famous ancient Romans, composed accounts of their lives, and even penned a Latin epic poem. Yet he also used the vernacular, writing beautiful love sonnets in Italian to a woman named Laura who perished in the plague. Petrarch's contemporary, Giovanni Boccaccio (*bō-KAH-chō*) (1313–1375), likewise wrote in Italian vernacular. Boccaccio is best known for *The Decameron* (*dē-KAM-uh-ron*), a collection of 100 stories

Petrarch and Boccaccio begin literary Renaissance

told by ten people to amuse themselves while secluded in an estate outside Florence to escape the plague (see "Excerpts on the Plague from Boccaccio's *Decameron*," page 397). Witty, racy, and bawdy, dealing with intrigue, adventure, and sex, the stories are designed to entertain, not to enlighten. Boccaccio depicted people as they really *were*—charming, crude, and corrupt—not as they *should be*.

Vernacular literature spreads from Italy to northern Europe

Soon engaging vernacular literature also appeared in the North. In English verse, Geoffrey Chaucer (1340–1400) wrote the *Canterbury Tales*, an assortment of lively, earthy stories told by thirty people from all walks of life traveling together on pilgrimage. In French, Christine de Pisan (*pē-ZAHN*) (1363–1430) wrote biographies, poems, and works about women, challenging her era's gender barriers. Many Latin texts were also translated into French, German, English, and Czech.

Classicism, secularism, and individualism characterize Renaissance humanism

Another key feature of Renaissance culture was **humanism**, an outlook emphasizing the value of humans and their activities. Renaissance humanism incorporated *classicism*, *secularism*, and *individualism*. Spurning as Germanic the culture of the Middle Ages, it revered the classical culture of ancient Greece and Rome. Altering the medieval focus on faith and spirituality, it celebrated secular ideals and worldly beauty, even when dealing with religious themes. Rejecting the medieval emphasis on humility and community, it stressed individual pride and achievement.

The Italian Renaissance

In fifteenth-century Italy the Renaissance expanded and flourished. Remains of the ancient Roman world, which surrounded Italians, sustained their desire to revive their region's past glory. The wealth of merchants and city-states, acquired mainly through commerce, enabled them to enhance their prestige by patronizing the arts. And an influx of artists and scholars from the Byzantine Empire, which fell to the Turks in 1453, added to the depth and diversity of Italy's cultural renewal.

Renaissance Italy was politically divided, with the Kingdom of Naples in the South, the Papal States (lands ruled by the pope) in the center, and various independent city-states in the North. The leading city-states—Venice, Milan, Genoa, and Florence—were wealthy commercial centers that ruled the lands around them (Map 16.5). Although organized as republics, each was run from behind the scenes by prominent wealthy families. To gain

Map 16.5 Political Divisions in Fifteenth-Century Italy

During the Italian Renaissance, Italy was distinguished by artistic expression and by political disunity. Note Italy's division into a variety of city-states, duchies, republics, and kingdoms, with the Papal States in the center, ruled by the pope in Rome. How did commercial and cultural competition among these small states help to bolster the Italian Renaissance?

prestige and enhance civic pride, these families promoted art and culture, often competing to outdo each other.

Byzantine artists and Italian commerce advance the Renaissance

RENAISSANCE FLORENCE. Florence again led the way. For much of the fifteenth century it was dominated by the Medici (*MED-ih-chē*), a rich banking family that used its fortune to fund the creation of paintings, sculptures, palaces, and churches by the great masters of the day. Many wealthy merchants did likewise, while guilds held contests to decide which artists, sculptors, and architects to commission for major projects.

In 1401 a contest was held to decide who would design the bronze doors of the Florence Baptistry (page 382), a chapel used mainly for baptisms. The winner, Lorenzo Ghiberti (*gē-BAR-tē*) (1378–1455), spent decades creating two sets of majestic doors, made up of panels depicting Biblical scenes, sculpted and cast in bronze. The loser, Filippo Brunelleschi (*broo-nuh-LESS-kē*) (1377–1446), went on to gain fame as an architect, designing chapels and cathedrals for the Medici, the city's cloth merchants, and other wealthy Florentines. Models of perspective and symmetry, his works are relatively small, constructed on a human scale in the spirit of the Renaissance, unlike the towering medieval Gothic churches built for exaltation of God.

Florence produces outstanding sculptors, architects, artists, and writers

Donatello (*dō-nah-TELL-ō*) (1386–1466), a student and rival of Ghiberti, emerged as the city's leading sculptor. A master of anatomy, Donatello created the West's first major nude statue since Roman times, depicting the Hebrew hero David in bronze. His starkly realistic works also included a monumental equestrian bronze sculpture of a Venetian warrior, capturing the power and dignity of horse and rider, and a marvelous wooden statue of a gaunt and aging Mary Magdalene, a friend of Jesus believed by some to have been a repentant prostitute.

The standard for Florentine painting was set by Masaccio (*mah-SAH-chō*) (1401–1428), a youthful artist who improved on the realism of Giotto. Masaccio used perspective, shadows, and light to create a three-dimensional effect, conveying his subjects' personalities through striking stances and expressions. He also mastered the art of **fresco**, or painting on walls when the plaster was still wet so the colors would penetrate it. Later Sandro Botticelli (*bō-tih-CHELL-ē*) (1445–1510), not satisfied merely to depict reality, sought to transcend it by creating beauty, using bright colors, fanciful themes, and sensuous depictions of female anatomy in works such as *Spring* and *Birth of Venus*.

Renaissance Florence also produced several outstanding writers. One was Leon Battista Alberti (*al-BAIR-tē*) (1404–1472), whose treatises *On Building* and *On Family* set the era's standards on architecture and virtue. A multi-talented architect, athlete, scholar, sculptor, and statesman, he embodied the ideal of the well-rounded Renaissance man. Another was Niccolo Machiavelli (*MAH-kē-uh-VELL-ē*) (1469–1527), whose classic work, *The Prince*, devised as a ruler's guidebook for unifying Italy, separated politics from ethics. Focusing not on how statesmen *should* act but on how they *do* act, and not on what is *right* but on what *works*, *The Prince* pragmatically advises rulers to use deceit and violence when necessary to achieve their goals.

Donatello's Mary Magdalene

THE HIGH RENAISSANCE. In the early 1500s, envious of Florence's success, ambitious popes such as Julius II (1503–1513) and Leo X (1513–1521) hired prominent artists, architects, and sculptors to help restore Rome as Christendom's greatest city. Thus began the Roman or High Renaissance, an era dominated by three great figures: Leonardo, Raphael, and Michelangelo.

Sixteenth-century popes sponsor Renaissance in Rome

Sketch for a helicopter by Leonardo da Vinci.

Leonardo da Vinci emerges as universal genius

Raphael expresses female beauty and classical harmony

Michelangelo displays superhuman talent as a sculptor and artist

Leonardo da Vinci (1452–1519) started as a painter in Florence, but clashed with the Medici and left in 1482 for Milan, whose ruling family gave him greater freedom of expression. There he produced his first masterpiece, *Virgin of the Rocks*. In this portrait of a serene mother and children among plants and boulders, Leonardo displayed a gift for depicting both nature and human psychology. While in Milan he also painted on a convent wall his monumental *Last Supper*, an emotional drama that peers into the apostles' hearts as each reacts to Jesus's disclosure that "one of you will betray me." Leaving Milan in 1499, Leonardo traveled about Italy, spent time in Rome, and then settled in France under royal patronage. In 1503–1506 he created the world's most famous portrait, a beguiling psychological study of *La Gioconda* (*lah jō-KON-dah*), better known today as *Mona Lisa*.

Considered one of history's greatest artists, Leonardo was also a scientist, sculptor, naturalist, engineer, musician, and inventor. Possessing boundless curiosity, he studied plants, anatomy, optics, mathematics, currents, clouds, and birds' wings. He sketched plans for devices, such as helicopters, submarines, and tanks, whose actual invention lay centuries in the future. He was a visionary and universal genius.

Raphael (*RAH-fī-EL*) (1483–1520), most beloved of Renaissance painters, was known for his exquisite madonnas (portraits of the Virgin Mary) and depictions of female beauty. Born in Urbino, he spent time in Florence before 1508, when Pope Julius II brought him to Rome to decorate the papal palace, known as the Vatican because it sits on Vatican Hill. Raphael's *School of Athens*, a huge fresco mural in the Vatican study, is a full expression of the Renaissance spirit. It depicts classical Greek philosophers, some of them painted in the likeness of Renaissance figures, in a setting of harmony and symmetry. In the center are Plato, flanked by theoretical philosophers and pointing upward toward idealism and inspiration, and Aristotle, flanked by logicians and rationalists, with his arm outstretched downward toward realism and moderation.

If Raphael captured the Renaissance spirit, Michelangelo (1475–1564) transcended it. Raised and trained as a sculptor in Florence, he moved to Rome at age 21 and soon caused a sensation with his *Pietà* (*pē-ā-TAH*), a magnificent marble statue of the Virgin Mary cradling the dead body of her son Jesus. In 1501 Michelangelo was called back to Florence to create a statue of David, the Biblical giant-killer, to symbolize the city's resistance to tyranny. In three years he produced a work of superhuman proportions, an imposing 17-foot likeness of a muscular youth, giant, defiant, and nude.

With singular audacity, in 1508 Pope Julius II summoned the great sculptor to Rome and hired him to paint the ceiling of the Vatican's Sistine Chapel. Lying on his back atop scaffolding near the ceiling, Michelangelo labored four years to produce in fresco a work of colossal genius, an immense set of murals depicting Bible scenes from *Creation* to the *Flood*. In 1536 he added another fresco, the somber and imposing *Last Judgment*, on the chapel's altar wall. In his later years, as he continued to create masterpieces of sculpture, Michelangelo also served as chief architect for Saint Peter's Basilica in Rome, a monumental edifice whose construction had begun in the reign of Julius II.

Politically, the High Renaissance was a time of turmoil and foreign intervention in Italy. Trouble began in 1494 when Milan, on the verge of war against Naples and Florence, asked France for help. Seizing the opportunity, the French invaded and conquered much of Italy, leading the pope to seek assistance from Spain. The next three decades were marked by foreign intervention and internal war, culminating in 1527, when Rome

Michelangelo's David.

was sacked by foreign forces supposedly sent to help the pope. After this attack the Italian Renaissance subsided. As the Spanish opened the Atlantic, eroding Italy's commercial leadership, and as the Protestant movement challenged Rome's religious primacy, Italians lost their undisputed leadership of Western fortune, faith, and culture.

The Northern European Renaissance

Northern Europe, meanwhile, had its own Renaissance, which differed from the Italian in several key respects. First, it was less classical: northerners studied Greco-Roman classics but did not try to imitate ancient culture. Second, it was less secular: it promoted Christian morals, studied early Church fathers, criticized abuses in the Church and society, and abhorred the worldliness of Renaissance popes. Third, it built upon medieval culture rather than rejecting it. Finally, it was less lavish and more practical, partly because northerners had less wealth, and partly because they were offended by Italian extravagance and indulgence.

The northern Renaissance proves less classical and worldly than the Italian

FOUNDATIONS OF THE NORTHERN RENAISSANCE. In the 1400s, two key figures laid the foundations for the northern Renaissance. One was Jan van Eyck (*YAHN van ĪK*), the first in a series of superb artists from Flanders, a region (now part of Belgium) where commercial towns such as Bruges (*BROOZH*), Ghent, and Antwerp enjoyed prosperity and civic pride like that of northern Italy. Van Eyck (1395–1441) mastered the use of oil paints, which produced vivid colors and dried slowly, giving the artist time to paint with patience and precision. He also perfected the realism introduced by Giotto, meticulously portraying the appearances and lifestyles of his subjects. His masterpieces, including the Arnolfini portrait and the Ghent altarpiece, display unsurpassed attention to detail and light.

Northern artist Jan van Eyck perfects realism, perspective, and detail

The other founding figure of the northern Renaissance was the German inventor Johannes Gutenberg (*GOO-ten-berg*) (1400–1468), who began a communications revolution. European books had long been copied by hand onto costly animal-skin parchment, making them expensive and rare. The use of paper and printing from carved wooden blocks, developed initially in China, had spread to Europe in the 1300s by way of the Mongols and Muslims. But this printing process still involved much time and expense, since a whole block had to be carved for each page. In the 1450s, however, Gutenberg began making books by using **movable type**, small metal blocks for each letter, arranged in a frame to print one page and then rearranged and reused to print others. Multiple copies of each page were made by inking the type and pressing it on paper, using a **printing press** similar to the presses used to crush grapes for wine. The use of the movable type printing press spread quickly, vastly increasing the number of books and decreasing their cost. It thereby advanced the spread of ideas and knowledge, at first among the educated elite, but eventually among the masses too.

Gutenberg's movable-type printing press fuels communication revolution

An early printing press.

NORTHERN WRITERS AND ARTISTS. In the early 1500s, as the Renaissance moved north, the printing press helped spread the views of several outstanding writers. One was Dutch humanist Erasmus (*ih-RAZZ-muss*) (1466–1536), the era's most influential thinker. After leaving the monastery where he spent his younger years, Erasmus lived and wrote in various places, winning universal respect as a man of insight, tolerance, and honesty. Dismayed by the Church's elaborate ritualism and scholasticism's rigid formalism, he promoted instead a simple, humane piety called the "philosophy of Christ." His works included *Handbook of the Christian Knight* (1503), a guide to moral living in a corrupt

Northern writers criticize corruption; artists stress innovation

society, and *The Praise of Folly* (1509), a witty, stinging satire that ridiculed the hypocrisy of monks, bishops, lawyers, and scholars.

Another key writer of the northern Renaissance was Erasmus's friend Thomas More (1478–1535), a prominent English lawyer, statesman, and humanist. In 1516 More published *Utopia* ("nowhere"), a fictional journey to an imaginary island where people held property in common, worked together for the common good, and avoided poverty and war by using good sense and reason. By thus portraying his vision of an ideal society, More implicitly criticized by contrast the violence, corruption, and injustice of the society in which he lived. A man of talent and conviction, he later served as Lord Chancellor, England's highest official post, and eventually died a martyr for refusing to forsake the Roman Church.

Many northern artists were influenced by van Eyck's realism and use of oil paints, the style and technique of Italian painters, and the development of printing. One was Hans Holbein (*HŌL-bīn*) the Younger (1497–1543), a German portrait painter who worked in Switzerland and England, producing lifelike portrayals of such figures as Erasmus and More. Another was Albrecht Dürer (*DOOR-ur*) (1471–1528), son of a German goldsmith, who became Germany's most innovative artist. Inspired by visits to Italy, he combined Italian techniques of proportion and perspective with a northern talent for detail similar to van Eyck's, creating such paintings as *Adoration of the Magi* and *The Four Apostles*. But Dürer is best known for his woodcuts (carvings on wooden blocks) and engravings (etchings in copper), used to print multiple copies of the same work. These were then either sold as separate prints or used to illustrate books, making his art available to ordinary people. Although they lacked color, prints such as *The Four Horsemen of the Apocalypse* and *Knight, Death and the Devil* were genuine artistic masterpieces.

The Four Horsemen of the Apocalypse.

Social and Political Effects

The Renaissance was mainly an urban phenomenon, affecting primarily the cities, where three distinct social groups emerged. At the top were the patricians, wealthy merchants and bankers who dominated urban politics, lived in conspicuous extravagance, and hired artists and architects to exalt their status. In the middle were artisans and shopkeepers, typically members of guilds, who lived in reasonable comfort and often had some education. At the bottom were paid laborers, who subsisted on irregular wages, and the unemployed, who lived in dire poverty. Many cities were great centers of culture, but crowded conditions and lack of sanitation also made them breeding grounds for filth, squalor, stench, and disease.

Renaissance transforms warrior nobility into a cultured upper class

In the countryside, the Renaissance had less of an impact. Still, the landed nobility, originally a crude warrior class, began to assume a sense of refinement and gentility. According to the *Book of the Courtier* (1528), by Baldassare Castiglione (*kah-stēl-YŌ-nā*), the ideal gentleman should be classically educated, widely read, accomplished in arts and music, eloquent in speech, dignified in manner, and graceful in style. Ladies too might exhibit these traits, as education for noble and patrician women became increasingly common. But women were still largely excluded from public affairs, expected instead to be capable household managers and charming hostesses with good social skills.

Peasant life remains harsh, but serfdom declines

Although peasants, who still made up about 90 percent of the population, were affected least by the Renaissance, they did experience some important changes. The labor shortages created by fourteenth-century famines and plagues, along with growing opportunities and attractions in the cities and towns, helped to improve the lives of the common people. Many landlords sought to keep their peasants from leaving by granting them their own land, or by replacing compulsory labor with rent payable in cash. As a result, during the Renaissance serfdom declined, especially in Western Europe. In time, the increased availability of printed books also promoted growing public awareness and literacy among the lower classes.

Politically, the Renaissance advanced the formation of strong national monarchies (Map 16.6), as capable rulers increased both their own power and the unity of their

Renaissance monarchs further consolidate power

Map 16.6 Europe in the Late Fifteenth Century

During the fifteenth century, while the Renaissance engulfed Italy and spread to the rest of Europe, monarchs continued to consolidate their realms and expand their powers. Note, for example, that the marriage of the rulers of Castile and Aragon, and their completion of the *Reconquista* by ousting the Muslims from Granada, would lay the basis for a united Spain, soon to emerge as Europe's wealthiest power. How did growing commercial connections, and the growing strength of European monarchies, help to bolster Europe's power and wealth, despite its political divisions?

realms. In France, King Louis XI (1461–1483) imposed heavy taxes on the peasants and townsfolk, enlarged the royal army to avoid reliance on the nobles, and extended his direct control over various lands in the North, East, and South. In England, King Henry VII (1485–1509) put an end to three decades of dynastic strife, built up the royal treasury by managing his income frugally, and used his royal council to impose justice and control unruly nobles. In central Europe, Emperor Maximilian I of Habsburg (1493–1519), although unable to centralize control of the Holy Roman Empire, vastly expanded his family's domains by arranging astute marriages for himself and his son.

Castile and Aragon united; Spanish Inquisition and sea voyages begin

But the biggest political success came in Spain, a land long divided into separate states and ravaged by the *Reconquista*. Here the marriage of two monarchs, Isabella of Castile (1474–1504) and Ferdinand of Aragon (1479–1516), linked the two largest realms. To consolidate control and enforce Christian rule they used the Spanish **Inquisition**, a judicial institution that prosecuted people it identified as heretics—including many Jews and Muslims who outwardly converted to Christianity but privately practiced their old faith. In 1492 Isabella and Ferdinand completed the *Reconquista* by conquering Granada, the last Muslim outpost in Spain, and expelled most Jews from their domains. That same year a sea admiral named Columbus, sailing in Isabella's service, embarked on the first in a series of voyages that eventually gave Spain the world's largest empire, made it Europe's greatest power, and altered the course of world history.

Chapter Review

Putting It in Perspective

The West's resurgence was partly due to developments in Europe. The warming of its climate, the ingenuity of its farmers and artisans, and the ambition of its merchants and bankers all contributed to Europe's economic expansion, which supplied the resources to fund expensive enterprises. Energetic popes who reformed and revived the Roman Church, and determined monarchs who turned weak regimes into strong central governments, provided the leadership and stability needed for cultural growth. Talented scholars, artists, architects, and writers splendidly nourished this rebirth. Even the disasters of the fourteenth century, although they disrupted the West's resurgence, failed to derail it for long.

Europe's revitalization, however, also resulted from its contacts and conflicts with Islamic peoples, and its willingness to adopt from them whatever it found useful. From the Muslims, for example,

Europe borrowed the concept of combining warfare with religious zeal, launching its own set of Christian holy wars, or crusades. From Islamic scholars, Europe became acquainted with its own Greco-Roman legacy, and learned to combine its Christian faith with this classical heritage. Through Mongols and Muslims, Europe learned about gunpowder, paper, and printing, Chinese inventions that added greatly to Western power and influence. And it was also through the Muslims that Europe acquired a taste for the fine goods of the East and the wealth to be gained through eastern commerce. These tastes in time sent Europeans on great sea voyages aimed at taking control of this trade from the Islamic world.

But Europe's resurgence was not a sign of Muslim weakness. Indeed, the Muslim expulsion of Christian crusaders from the Holy Land and Western adaptation of Muslim innovations attested to Islamic preeminence. And, as we shall see in the next chapter, while Europe was having its Renaissance, Muslims were conquering Constantinople, rebuilding Persia, and subduing the Indian subcontinent, creating three great empires of their own.

Reviewing Key Material

KEY CONCEPTS

Reconquista, 384
guilds, 390
Magna Carta, 391
university, 393
scholasticism, 393
Gothic architecture, 394
artistic realism, 399

vernacular literature, 399
humanism, 400
fresco, 401
movable type, 403
printing press, 403
Inquisition, 406

KEY PEOPLE

Pope Urban II, 382, 384
Salah al-Din (Saladin), 387
Emperor Frederick
    Barbarossa, 388
King Richard I the
    Lionheart, 388
King Philip II Augustus,
    388
Pope Innocent III, 388
King Henry II, 391
Saint Bernard of
    Clairvaux, 392
Saint Dominic, 392
Saint Francis of Assisi,
    393
Thomas Aquinas, 393
Suger, 394
Eleanor of Aquitaine, 394
King Philip IV the Fair,
    395
Pope Boniface VIII, 395
Wat Tyler, 398
Joan of Arc, 398
Giotto, 399
Dante Alighieri, 399
Petrarch, 399

Boccaccio, 399
Chaucer, 400
Christine de Pisan, 400
Ghiberti, 401
Brunelleschi, 401
Donatello, 401
Masaccio, 401
Botticelli, 401
Alberti, 401
Machiavelli, 401
Pope Julius II, 401, 402
Leonardo da Vinci, 402
Raphael, 402
Michelangelo, 402
Jan van Eyck, 403
Gutenberg, 403
Erasmus, 403
Thomas More, 404
Hans Holbein, 404
Albrecht Dürer, 404
Castiglione, 404
Emperor Maximilian I
    of Habsburg, 406
Isabella of Castile, 406
Ferdinand of Aragon, 406

ASK YOURSELF

1. Why did Pope Urban II initiate the First Crusade? Why were the later crusades undertaken? What benefits and damages did Europe incur as a result of the crusades and *Reconquista*?

2. What factors contributed to Europe's political, economic, and cultural development during the High Middle Ages?

3. What factors led to the disasters and crises of fourteenth-century Europe? What were the social, economic, cultural, and political repercussions of these disasters and crises?

4. What were the main characteristics of the Renaissance? How did the spirit of the Renaissance differ from that of the High Middle Ages? How did the Northern European Renaissance differ from the Italian?

5. In what specific ways did contacts with the Muslim world influence Western commerce, culture, learning, and technology during the High Middle Ages and Renaissance?

GOING FURTHER

Asbridge, Thomas. *The First Crusade: A New History.* 2004.

Bartlett, Robert. *The Making of Europe, 950–1350.* 1993.

Brotton, J. *The Renaissance Bazaar: From the Silk Road to Michelangelo.* 2002.

Burke, P. *The European Renaissance: Centres and Peripheries.* 1998.

Cantor, Norman. *In the Wake of the Plague: The Black Death and the World It Made.* 2001.

Cohn, Samuel. *The Black Death Transformed.* 2003.

Curry, A. *The Hundred Years' War.* 1993.

Finucane, R. C. *Soldiers of the Faith.* 1983.

Gottfried, Robert S. *The Black Death.* 1983.

Hale, J. R. *The Civilization of Europe in the Renaissance.* 1994.

Hay, D., and J. Law. *Italy in the Age of the Renaissance.* 1989.

Herlihy, D. *The Black Death and Transformation of the West.* 1997.

Holmes, George. *Europe: Hierarchy and Revolt, 1320–1450.* 2000.

Jardine, L. *Worldly Goods: A New History of the Renaissance.* 1996.

Jordan, W. C. *Europe in the High Middle Ages.* 2003.

Kedar, Benjamin Z. *Crusade and Mission: European Approaches Toward the Muslims.* 1988.

Kelly, John. *The Great Mortality: An Intimate History of the Black Death.* 2005.

King, Margaret L. *Women of the Renaissance.* 1991.

Madden, Thomas. *A New History of the Crusades.* 2005.

Mollat, M., and P. Wolff. *The Popular Revolutions of the Late Middle Ages.* 1973.

Mundy, J. H. *Europe in the High Middle Ages, 1150–1309.* 3rd ed. 1999.

Nauert, C. G. *Humanism and the Culture of Renaissance Europe.* 1995.

Oakley, F. P. *The Western Church in the Later Middle Ages.* 1980.

O'Callaghan, Joseph F. *A History of Medieval Spain.* 1975.

Phillips, J. R. S. *The Medieval Expansion of Europe.* 1988.

Powell, James M. *Innocent III: Vicar of Christ or Lord of the World?* 2nd ed. 1994.

Renouard, Y. *The Avignon Papacy, 1305–1403.* 1970.

Riley-Smith, J. *The Crusades: A Short History.* 1987.

Rosenwein, Barbara. *A Short History of the Middle Ages.* 2002.

White, John. *Art and Architecture in Italy, 1250–1400.* 3rd ed. 1993.

Key Dates and Developments

1070s	Seljuk Turks defeat Byzantines and conquer Holy Land	1378–1417	Great Western Schism divides Western Church
1085	Spanish Christians capture Toledo from Muslims	1430s	Jan van Eyck flourishes in Flanders
1096–1099	First Crusade	1434–1492	Medicis rule Florence: height of Florentine Renaissance
1144	Suger begins first Gothic church at Saint-Denis	1453	Fall of Constantinople; end of Hundred Years War
1147–1149	Second Crusade	1456	Gutenberg publishes Bible printed with movable type
1189–1192	Third Crusade	1492	Spanish Christians take Granada; Columbus's First Voyage
1202–1204	Fourth Crusade	1503–1506	Leonardo da Vinci creates the *Mona Lisa*
1267–1273	Thomas Aquinas writes *Summa Theologica*	1508	Pope Julius II brings Raphael and Michelangelo to Rome
1309–1377	Popes reside at Avignon	1513–1516	Machiavelli's *The Prince* and More's *Utopia* published
1310–1320	Dante composes the *Divine Comedy*	1527	Sack of Rome by German and Spanish troops
1337	Hundred Years War begins		
1347–1351	Black Death devastates Europe		
1348–1353	Boccaccio composes *The Decameron*		

Culture and Conflict in the Great Islamic Empires, 1071–1707

- The Conquests of Timur Lenk

- The Cosmopolitan Ottoman Empire

- Safavid Persia: A Shi'ite State

- The Mughal Empire: A Muslim Minority Rules India

- Chapter Review

Ottoman Compass Points

A sixteenth-century Ottoman illustration of the 32 points of the compass. At that time the great Islamic empires still dominated trade routes across the Indian Ocean, but Europeans were challenging them for commercial control (page 420).

Mughal India

Safavid Persia

The Ottoman Empire

The morning of May 29, 1453, dawned overcast and warm on the outskirts of Constantinople, the capital of the Byzantine Empire. Shortly after sunrise, the Ottoman Turkish sultan, Mehmed II, ordered his Muslim troops to storm the city. A large cannon made for the sultan by a Hungarian metallurgist pounded away at the city's thick walls. Shortly before noon a hole was torn in one of the walls, and jubilant attackers piled through the breach into Constantinople. The last Byzantine emperor died in hand-to-hand combat, and by early afternoon Mehmed's forces were in possession of a Christian city that Muslims had sought to conquer for more than eight centuries.

As the battle raged around him, Mehmed II calmly rode his horse into the Hagia Sophia (*Hā-jē-ah sō-FĪ-ah*), the Church of the Holy Wisdom, and claimed it for Islam as a mosque. According to legend, the Orthodox Christian priests chanting divine services at the time quickly gathered up the sacred objects on the altar and vanished into the marble walls of the church's sanctuary, from which they will return to finish the services when the Muslims are expelled from Constantinople. Oblivious to this possibility, Mehmed surveyed his conquest, gave orders to limit the looting and pillaging, and contemplated the collapse of the last outpost of Christendom in the old Roman East.

All three of the great Islamic empires of the fifteenth through seventeenth centuries—the Ottoman, the Safavid (*SAH-fah-vid*), and the Mughal (*MOO-gull*)—were created through conflict, but they were connected to each other in many ways. Each was established by nomadic Turks from Central Asia. Each dynasty constructed its new empire on the foundations of existing Asian civilizations, adapting its previously nomadic life to the framework of settled agricultural urban societies. Each empire was spiritually and culturally Islamic. And each was influenced profoundly by a Turkish empire that rose and fell with astonishing speed: the empire of Timur Lenk.

The Conquests of Timur Lenk

Timur was born in 1336 into a Muslim family of Turks in Central Asia. His father, a mid-level government official in the service of the Mongols, claimed descent from Genghis Khan. Timur, who limped from wounds received in battle as a young man, was contemptuously called Timur Lenk, "Timur the Lame," by the Persians he conquered. Europeans corrupted this nickname to Tamerlane (*TAM-ur-lān*). Considering himself a worthy heir to Genghis Khan, Timur set out to conquer Asia, and in the process connected several parts of it, although his lack of patience for administration ensured that his empire would not survive him for long.

Timur's Strengths and Good Fortunes

Timur followed his father by serving the Mongols, although as a cavalry captain rather than as a government official. Charismatic and cruel, he compensated for his limp by turning himself into a master horseman and soon won the allegiance of the Turkish mercenaries with whom he rode. The Mongol leadership of the Jagadai Khanate in Central Asia was torn apart by rival factions, and Timur skillfully allied with one and then the other, pretending to serve each of them while actually serving only himself. By 1360 he had gained control over the lands between the Oxus (*OX-us*) and Jaxartes (*jacks-AR-tēz*) rivers in Central Asia (Map 17.1). Over the next three decades he mobilized a fearsome

FOUNDATION MAP 17.1 The Empire of Timur Lenk, ca. 1405

The extent of Timur's conquests, undertaken in a time without electronic communication or rapid transit, suggests the difficulty of ruling such vast and varied domains. Compare the location of Timur's empire with the Persian Empire of Cyrus and Darius I (Map 6.3). Then remember that nearly two millennia earlier, Darius had ruled even more extensive lands effectively through satraps. Why didn't Timur institute the sort of efficient administration that characterized the Persian Empire?

force of mounted cavalry in a series of campaigns designed to conquer every region he could reach.

Timur owed his military successes in part to his personal abilities, in part to the quarrels and weaknesses of his enemies, and in part to luck. Some of that good fortune was an ongoing shift in weather patterns, beginning decades before his birth, that brought ample rains to areas of Central Asia which had previously been arid. New and extensive pasturelands supported the horses and livestock of Turkish nomads who, under Timur's leadership, went from there to conquer large parts of Asia.

Timur Lenk conquers large parts of Asia

In 1370 Timur established his capital in the Central Asian city of Samarkand (*sahmur-KAHND*), from which the Mongol Khanate of Jagadai had controlled the region. In 1380 Timur's forces descended upon Persia and ravaged the countryside. They then crossed the Iranian plateau and subdued Baghdad. This conquest took 13 years, largely because Timur himself was, for most of that time, in Central Asia, consolidating his base with decisive victories over the Mongols in their own heartland. By the final decade of the fourteenth century he was poised to move further.

In 1395 Timur's mounted archers invaded the region of the lower Volga, destroying the Khanate of the Golden Horde within 18 months. The Mongols thereupon surrendered an empire stretching from the Caucasus Mountains northeastward to Siberia. Two years later Timur turned toward India, devastating the Punjab in the West and sacking Delhi. He enslaved numerous Indians to build him a great mosque at Samarkand, while behind him he left desolate cities stalked by hunger and disease. The severed heads of Hindus were piled into immense towers as testimony to his visit, but Indian Muslims fared no better: some were among the 100,000 prisoners he massacred after capturing Delhi. As the fourteenth century drew to a close Timur marched to the eastern Mediterranean, where he encountered the Ottoman Turks.

Attack on the Ottomans

The Ottoman Turks, successors to the Seljuks in the Balkans, were at that point planning what they hoped would be a decisive assault on the Byzantine Empire. Sultan Bayezid (*BĪ-yeh-zēd*) I, who considered himself the heir to the Great Seljuk Empire, had worked for a decade to consolidate the Ottoman realm, and, using the Balkans as his base, he hoped to join Europe with Asia by taking Constantinople and western Anatolia. His plans alarmed Christian Europe at his back, but he had not reckoned on Timur's presence on the Byzantine Empire's eastern frontier. Suddenly it seemed that the potential confrontation would involve three enemies, not just two. When King Charles VI of France emerged from one of his intermittent bouts of insanity to send messengers urging Timur to save Constantinople by striking at Bayezid's Ottomans from the East, Timur needed no further encouragement. He moved against Bayezid, who led his forces into battle near Ankara (*AIN-kah-rah*) in 1402.

Timur's attack diverts the Ottomans from Constantinople

The battle of Ankara was disastrous for the Ottomans. Timur's well-disciplined, carefully integrated armies routed Bayezid's powerful but poorly organized troops. The sultan himself was captured by Timur and treated with contempt. Timur used Bayezid as a footstool and made Bayezid's favorite wife strip naked to serve midday and evening meals to the conqueror's entourage. Imprisoned in a cage so small that he could not stand, sit, or lie down, Bayezid soon died.

Constantinople had been saved from Ottoman assault, but Timur's victory gave no comfort to the Christians. Who or what could stop Timur from turning his attentions on Europe? As it turned out, only his own restless nature. He had taken every acre of land once owned by the Mongols who had ruled him—except China. There the Ming dynasty had claimed the Mandate of Heaven and ousted the Mongol Yuan dynasty in 1368. Timur moved east to prepare his forces for the largest invasion of his career, but while doing so he drank much more wine than his 69-year-old constitution could absorb, and he died of alcohol poisoning in 1405.

Timur as Warrior and Administrator

In many respects, Timur Lenk was an impressive figure. Illiterate but not ignorant, his insatiable curiosity led him to surround himself with scholars with whom he debated questions of religious doctrine, natural science, and history. A skillful chess player, he was also in real life a master of both battle and diplomacy, employing every means imaginable to defeat his opponent. His nomadic upbringing provided him with a flexibility of perspective that enabled him to seize the most favorable opportunity, whenever it presented itself. Timur's reputation for ferocity terrified everyone in his path and proved useful in securing his remarkable sequence of victories. Yet Timur presented himself as a unifier who attacked only those who had been disloyal to Islam.

Some of the very qualities that made Timur a magnificent warrior also made him a poor statesman. The tactical flexibility that served him well in battle equipped him poorly for administration. He never cared to rule the lands he conquered, appointing his sons and grandsons as provincial governors while setting forth at once in search of more military glory. His governors were supposed to act only in Timur's name, but because he was almost never in contact with them they were forced to act on their own. This prevented the creation of durable institutions that might have helped his empire endure.

Timur might have been a builder as well as a destroyer, but his temperament inclined him in other directions. He beautified Samarkand but spent almost no time there, preferring his tents and the back of his horse. His atrocities sealed his reputation. When he died, nothing could hold his lands together. Like a powerful windstorm from the steppes of Central Asia, he leveled everything in his path and then vanished, leaving others to rebuild what he had destroyed.

The interior of the chapel at the tomb of Timur Lenk in Samarkand, in present-day Uzbekistan.

Timur is unable to consolidate his empire

The Cosmopolitan Ottoman Empire

Like the rest of Asia, the Muslim world had been badly battered by the nomadic invasions of the eleventh through fourteenth centuries. The Seljuk Turks, the Mongols, and Timur Lenk had brought war and destruction, but none proved able to hold their huge empires together. Even though they conquered Islam, they were also assimilated by it.

Islam appealed strongly to these nomads. The simplicity of its monotheism, the hope of paradise offered by its five pillars, and the rigor and consistency of its legal code all resonated with tribal peoples uninterested in the sort of complex doctrinal disputes that fascinated Byzantines. The nomads were accustomed to settling quarrels directly, physically, and permanently.

Islam appeals to nomadic civilizations

Consequently, although nomadic rule in southern Asia could be exploitative and devastating, it did not destroy Muslim culture. Mahmud of Ghazni's conversion to Islam could not save the Il-Khan Empire from dissolution in 1335, but it did perpetuate the hold of the Islamic faith. Timur conquered in the name of Islam, not as its enemy. And Mongol advances in southwest Asia were stopped by Egypt's Muslim Mamluk rulers, who in turn were conquered by invaders from Anatolia known as the Ottoman Turks.

Ottomans and Byzantines

In the late thirteenth century, a Turkic-speaking nomadic group led by a man named Osman (*oz-MAHN*) arrived in Anatolia, fleeing westward from the Mongols. They came as polytheists but were eventually converted to Sunni Islam by the Seljuk Turks, who granted them lands in Anatolia along the Byzantine frontier. These grants placed the Ottoman Turks, so named because they were followers of Osman, in an advantageous position that they were quick to exploit. When the Seljuk state collapsed and the Mongols withdrew, the Ottoman Turks took over as champions of the Muslim cause against the Byzantine Empire.

The Ottomans oppose the Byzantine Empire

That once-great realm was now in ruins. Even after 1261, when the Byzantines recaptured their capital from the Western Crusaders, they were beset by insurrections and civil wars, and they never managed to recover their Balkan provinces of Bulgaria, Serbia, and Macedonia, which the Bulgars had taken. Their glorious capital of Constantinople was in decline, its wealth squandered and its trade with the East having passed into the hands of the Italian commercial republics of Venice and Genoa.

The real winners of the Fourth Crusade were the Ottoman Turks, who had stood by while Christians killed one another. Early in the fourteenth century, in an effort to recover its Balkan possessions from the Bulgars, Byzantium decided to ally with the Turks. Thus Turkish forces, rather than having to fight their way into Europe, came as invited guests. Then they quickly took advantage of Byzantine weakness to construct a network of vassal principalities in the Balkans. When the Serbs and Bosnians rose up against Ottoman rule in 1387, the capable Sultan Murad (*MEW-rahd*) I defeated the rebels at the Battle of Kosovo (*KŌ-sō-vō*) in 1389. This outcome provoked the Europeans to mount a multinational anti-Islamic crusade, which the Ottomans defeated seven years later.

The Pax Ottomanica stabilizes southwest Asia and the Balkans

These Balkan victories gave the Ottomans a territorial base in Europe and allowed them to consider their strategy for administering the area. Murad, who had led them into Europe, was an exceptional ruler who refused to impose Islamic or Ottoman forms of government in the Balkans. He was convinced that new systems must be developed that would take into account local conditions and cultures and permit daily life to continue as it had. With this conviction he laid the foundation of a religiously and ethnically pluralistic society that would create a stable *Pax Ottomanica*, or "Ottoman peace," similar in some ways to the *Pax Romana* created centuries earlier by the Roman Empire. Like the Romans, Murad granted citizenship to all foreigners who were willing to work for his administration.

The primary concern of Murad and his successors, however, was to advance Islam. Several Ottoman officials once told a Byzantine visitor that the westward expansion of the faith had been ordained by Allah, and the Ottomans were the "sword" of that advance. The Byzantine Empire could continue to exist, if its citizens converted to Islam.

The Ottoman goal was not to destroy that empire but to assimilate it into Islamic civilization. In reality, of course, the Byzantine realm had been decaying for centuries, so its absorption into the Muslim world would be of far less value than Murad had hoped.

Murad was slain by a Serb at Kosovo in 1389, and succeeded by his son Bayezid I, who possessed few of his father's leadership abilities. Bayezid continued Murad's policy of granting citizenship to able foreigners, but in other respects he was a warrior, not a statesman. By early 1402 he was ready to besiege Constantinople, but just as his armies were preparing to move, he had to send them back to Anatolia to deal with a momentous threat from the East: Timur Lenk.

Timur's defeat of the Ottomans at Ankara saved the Byzantine Empire, but only temporarily. Once Timur was gone, the Ottomans regrouped. Two successive sultans tried to capture Constantinople and failed. But eventually the Ottoman Turks succeeded and went on to absorb Byzantium into their own immense cosmopolitan empire, one that spanned three continents and endured for more than 400 years.

Timur's attack on the Ottomans eases the pressure on Byzantium

Mehmed the Conqueror

The final conqueror of Byzantium was a new sultan named Mehmed (*MEH-med*) II who came to the Ottoman throne in 1451, determined to take Constantinople. By May 29, 1453, he had succeeded, as this chapter's opening story describes (see "Mehmed the Conqueror Takes Constantinople, 1453"). Changing the name of the Byzantine capital from Constantinople to Istanbul, he claimed it for the Islamic faith. The Byzantine Empire had been replaced by an Islamic Ottoman realm.

Constantinople's fall threw Western Christendom into despair. Europe was now threatened directly by the Ottoman Turks from the Southeast, and the flow of east-west commerce was completely in Islamic hands. For Mehmed the Conqueror, however, the events of 1453 fulfilled the will of Allah, who had ordained that His sultan rescue the Roman Empire from unbelievers. Mehmed was now both the legitimate Roman emperor and successor to Constantine the Great, and Ottoman *Padishah* (*PAH-dih-sha*), a Persian word meaning "God's deputy on earth" and used by the Ottomans to mean "imperial sovereign." The Byzantine tradition of caesaropapism, in which the same man exercised both political and religious authority, was of great use to Mehmed and his successors.

Mehmed II.

The ambitious Mehmed sought to make the Byzantine Empire part of an Ottoman Empire and a platform for Islam's conquest of all Europe and Asia. This was a tall order, but Mehmed saw himself as selected by Allah to achieve the worldwide unity of Islam. He expanded the administrative policies of Murad I, transforming the Ottoman state into a powerful empire prepared to draw on the talents of all its citizens, regardless of their attitudes toward Islam.

Mehmed II intends to restore the Roman Empire

The Ottoman State and Society

Having destroyed the last vestige of Imperial Rome, the Ottoman Empire evolved from an Asian-based Turkish political and social system into a multi-ethnic, intercontinental state. In doing so, it combined previously unrelated administrative methods derived from

Document 17.1 Mehmed the Conqueror Takes Constantinople, 1453

Kritovoulos, a Greek, was not present at the siege of Constantinople, but soon thereafter visited it and entered the service of Mehmed II, who eventually appointed him governor of the island of Imbros. "He admired the Sultan's military prowess and ability, even while mourning the loss of the City and the downfall of the last vestige of the Byzantine Empire (page viii)." His description of the conquest of Constantinople is based on the personal testimony of hundreds who took part in it.

Sultan Mehmed, who happened to be fighting quite near by, saw that a palisade and a part of a wall that had been destroyed were now empty of men and deserted by the defenders . . . He shouted out, "Friends, we have the City! We have it! They are already fleeing from us! They can't stand it any longer! The wall is bare of defenders! It needs just a little more effort and the City is taken! Don't weaken, but on with the work with all your might, and be men and I am with you!"

So saying, he led them himself. And they, with a shout on the run and with a fearsome yell, went on ahead of the Sultan, pressing on up to the palisade . . . Now there was a great struggle there and great slaughter among those stationed there . . . There the Emperor Constantine, with all who were with him, fell in gallant combat . . . Then a great slaughter occurred of those who happened to be there . . . men, women, and children, everyone, for there was no quarter given. The soldiers fell on them with anger and great wrath. For one thing, they were actuated by the hardships of the siege. For another, some foolish people had hurled taunts and curses at them from the battlements all through the siege. Now, in general they killed so as to frighten all the City, and to terrorize and enslave all by the slaughter . . .

After this the Sultan entered the City and looked about to see its great size, its situation, its grandeur and beauty, its teeming population, its loveliness, and the costliness of its churches and public buildings and of the private houses and community houses and those of the officials . . . When he saw what a large number had been killed, and the ruin of the buildings, and the wholesale ruin and destruction of the City, he was filled with compassion and repented not a little at the destruction and plundering. Tears fell from his eyes as he groaned deeply and passionately: "What a city we have given over to plunder and destruction!"

SOURCE: Kritovoulos, *History of Mehmed the Conqueror,* translated by Charles T. Riggs (Princeton: Princeton University Press, 1954) 70–77.

Turkish, Persian, and Byzantine traditions into a new governing form connecting aspects of three of the dominant cultures of Asia.

THE OTTOMAN GOVERNMENT'S UNIQUE SYNTHESIS. Ottoman government was based on the sultan's exclusive right to rule, a concept drawn from Persian tradition and amplified after 1453 by Byzantine caesaropapism. The sultan was supported in this effort by the four "pillars of empire," a Turkish image taken from the four poles that had traditionally held up the sultan's tent. The first pillar of the government was the **grand vezir** (*veh-ZĒR*), chief minister to the sultan; the second pillar was the judiciary; the third was the treasury; and the fourth consisted of administrators who drew up the sultan's edicts. These pillars existed to enhance the sultan's authority, not to limit it.

The Ottomans blend diverse traditions into a new governing system

But Mehmed II and his successors were not entirely free to rule as they wished. As a Muslim, the sultan was required to conduct himself in accordance with the Shari`ah or Islamic law, based upon the Qur'an, Islamic custom, and the sayings of the first four caliphs. In significant political decisions, he was expected to seek a **fatwa** (*FAHT-wah*), a legal opinion from the highest Islamic legal authority, sanctioning his course of action. Yet seventh-century Islamic law was not always applicable to issues arising in a fifteenth-century Muslim state.

Turkish tradition proved helpful in resolving this problem. The sultan in his role as Padishah enjoyed the right to issue commands and regulations on ordinary governmental matters without interference from the Islamic legal establishment. These state laws, called **urfi** (*UR-fē*), could be shaped in response to modern issues and problems that the Shari`ah could not possibly have foreseen. Urfi could, for example, be used to authorize the lending of money at interest despite religious objections to the practice. In one form or another, the Turkish principle that state law takes precedence over religious law remained in use for centuries in most Islamic nations.

This practical synthesis of diverse concepts meant that the Ottomans behaved differently from other Islamic states. First, their approach to their enemies was shaped by practical considerations rather than by religious zeal. Living side by side with Greeks in the Balkans convinced them of the essential humanity of their opponents and the impracticality of dealing with them harshly. Ottoman willingness to blend governmental traditions enabled them to develop a hybrid system well suited to ruling the assorted cultures and ethnic groups that made up their diverse domain.

Second, the Ottoman system of landholding differed significantly from both Arab and European practice. The nomadic origins of many Islamic societies lived on in the high value placed on land as belonging to the tribe, and the low value placed on individual ownership. European societies, in contrast, placed a high value on individual land ownership, and medieval systems of inheritance encouraged the development of landed nobilities. In Ottoman territory, however, all land belonged to the state. Newly conquered land was distributed by the sultan to his soldiers as a reward. These land grants promoted the growth of a professional standing army. But the land grants could not be handed down from father to son; upon a soldier's death, his land reverted to the state. This system prevented the creation of a landed aristocracy that could challenge or even rival the sultan himself. Instead, what evolved was a meritocracy, in which each succeeding generation was rewarded according to the value of its service to the state.

Ottoman law book.

OTTOMAN SOCIETY. The Ottoman state apparatus was thus a unique blend of Turkish, Persian, Byzantine, and Islamic influences. Unique as well was the society on which it rested. The Ottoman ruling class of about 350 people was composed exclusively of slaves belonging to the sultan. Almost all of them were former Christians who converted to Islam. This elite status was also nonhereditary; these slaves and their descendants could never become a more formal and permanent nobility that might one day rival the sultan. Promotion was based solely on merit and demotion was possible in cases of poor performance. Parallel to this ruling class was the corps of **Janissaries** (*JAN-is-sair-ēz*), a ten thousand–member infantry, also composed of slaves who were Christian-born converts to Islam and totally dependent on the sultan. Armed with gunpowder weapons, the Ottoman armies were superior to all they encountered until the late seventeenth century.

Janissaries help Ottoman armies dominate southwest Asia

In Ottoman society, as in Ottoman governance, privilege was thus based on performance, not ancestry. A household servant might rise to the rank of grand vezir, while a vezir might fall to the status of a blacksmith, all without any loss of dignity. Since all were slaves of the Padishah, all served at his imperial pleasure in whatever post it pleased

Flexibility is a feature of Ottoman society

him to place them. This arrangement was a Turkish-Persian-Islamic hybrid, which at its height proved remarkably effective.

For the sultan, the arrangement carried with it a flexibility that proved particularly useful in a multiethnic empire. Ottoman rule did not depend on overwhelming military force to keep conquered peoples in line. Instead, subject peoples might join and move up in Ottoman administration. This possibility minimized internal unrest. The adaptability of these political and social structures helps explain why the Ottoman Empire survived into the twentieth century.

Suleiman the Magnificent

Selim I claims the title of Caliph

Mehmed the Conqueror lived up to his name, solidifying Ottoman control over Anatolia and moving northwest from Istanbul deeper into southeastern Europe. The next two sultans, Bayezid II (r. 1481–1512) and Selim (*seh-LĒM*) I "The Grim" (r. 1512–1520), concentrated on warfare in the East and South. Selim ruled for only eight years, but in that time he managed to conquer Syria, Palestine, Egypt, and North Africa, defeating the Mamluks in Egypt and beginning a series of attacks on Persia's new Safavid regime. He also improved the Ottoman navy, which now threatened Christian shipping in the Mediterranean. Most significant, he claimed the title of Caliph, vacant since 1258, thereby completing the transfer of Islamic leadership from Arabs to Turks (Ottoman sultans remained Caliphs until 1924). By the end of Selim's reign, the Ottomans ruled about two-thirds of the territory of the old Eastern Roman Empire. All that was left for them to conquer was central and western Europe.

THE OTTOMAN EMPIRE AS A FORCE IN WORLD AFFAIRS. Selim was succeeded in 1520 by his 26-year-old son Suleiman (*SOO-lē-mahn*). Islamic seers, pointing to the sacred number ten, predicted glorious victories for the new ruler: Suleiman was the tenth Ottoman sultan, and he began his reign at the start of the tenth century after Muhammad's move to Medina in 622. Suleiman was also an intellectual, eager to absorb Turkish, Persian, and Byzantine culture and to participate in the European Renaissance's revival of Greek and Roman learning. Suleiman saw himself as a unifier, the leader who could unite East and West under the banner of the Prophet. His 46-year reign extended Ottoman power into central Europe and across the Mediterranean, terrifying Christian Europe and establishing the Ottoman Empire as a decisive force in international affairs (Map 17.2).

Suleiman moves against Europe

The Ottomans struck first into Hungary, slaughtering Hungarian forces at Mohács in 1526. But Suleiman's resources were inadequate for the permanent governance of a hostile country so far from Istanbul, on the other side of the rugged and treacherous Balkan peninsula. Selim had been able to control southwest Asia and North Africa with relative ease, as the inhabitants of those areas had been Muslims for centuries. But central Europe was intensely Christian and unwilling to submit to Islamic rule. Suleiman burned Budapest and marched his armies home for the winter, leaving Hungary open to the influence of the Austrian Habsburgs. That Catholic royal family immediately began to fortify central Europe against the Turkish threat.

Three years later, in May 1529, Suleiman led an immense army to attack Vienna. But the rains were so persistent that summer that the Turks could not bring up their heavy siege artillery over Austria's primitive roads. In October, as winter approached and the

Map 17.2 The Ottoman Empire in 1566

Comparison with Map 17.1 indicates that the Ottoman Empire at the death of Suleiman the Magnificent was much larger than that of Timur Lenk. Notice that the Ottoman Empire connected parts of three continents and included ethnic groups as diverse as Egyptians, Syrians, Mesopotamians, Turks, Greeks, and Bosnians. What methods did the Ottomans develop to rule such far-flung domains and so many distinct peoples?

cavalry could not feed its horses, Suleiman returned to Istanbul in frustration. In 1532 he tried again, this time failing even to reach Vienna because of poor weather and Hungarian and Croatian resistance. Now, at one of history's turning points, Suleiman concluded that, given distance, weather, terrain, and the hostility of the population, Vienna and central Europe lay beyond the reach of military conquest launched from Istanbul.

Grudgingly, Suleiman turned his attention toward the East. Over the next three decades he fought Safavid Persia for possession of Mesopotamia, sent his powerful navy to raid the eastern Mediterranean, and periodically returned west to extend his control

Suleiman turns eastward

further into Hungary. He also played a major role in European affairs, allying with France against the Habsburgs and supporting Protestants against Catholics during the Reformation. In 1566, on his seventh campaign into Europe, he died in his tent, having failed to unify East and West but having succeeded in making the Ottoman Empire a world power.

SULEIMAN THE LAWGIVER. Despite his constant campaigning, the Sultan was often at home; and if to Europeans he was "Suleiman the Magnificent," to his subjects he was "Suleiman the Lawgiver." Like western monarchs, he was not above the law but subject to it, although his exalted status allowed him a considerable range of action. Given the centrality of the Shari`ah within Islamic culture, he could not have created a new legal structure, but he did adapt the law to the conditions of his immense multi-ethnic empire. His subjects lived on three continents and were free to profess non-Islamic faiths, and while not all of them were subject to the Shari`ah, all were accountable under the urfi, which the sultan alone could declare.

Suleiman adapts Islamic law to Ottoman needs

Suleiman.

Suleiman worked diligently to guarantee that laws would apply equally to all. Corporal punishment was replaced by a system of fines, although forgers and perjurers might still have their right hands cut off. The Sultan also strengthened mechanisms for the enforcement of Islamic law, viewing the church-state relationship as one in which two complementary strands reinforced royal authority—a typically caesaropapist perspective.

Was Suleiman the Magnificent an absolute monarch in the sense of having unlimited power? Certainly his authority, dignity, and legal status would seem to fit this description. But Suleiman himself would probably have seen absolutism as a curious contrivance of nonbelievers, of little use to an Islamic sovereign. He was Allah's deputy on earth, the Ottoman Padishah, a ruler for whom the distinction between spiritual and political authority was not a source of tension but of power. Clearly superior, in his own mind, to any monarch in the West, Suleiman would have been unlikely to consider their forms of governance applicable to his lands.

A Faltering Empire

Europeans challenge the Ottomans economically

After the death of Suleiman, Ottoman fortunes remained favorable for a time. Although in 1571 a multinational European navy demolished the Turkish fleet at the Greek strait of Lepanto (*leh-PAHN-tō*), the vessels were quickly rebuilt, and the Turks continued to dominate the eastern Mediterranean (see page 409). More worrisome in the long run was the takeover of the Indian Ocean spice trade by the Dutch and French in the seventeenth century, costing Istanbul dearly in terms of lost customs duties. That shortfall could not be made up: Ottoman revenues could be expanded only by conquering additional territory, and the empire's failure to advance into Europe meant that its income would stagnate during a period of rapid inflation fueled by gold and silver shipments from the western hemisphere.

This fiscal challenge might have been addressed by competent leadership, but that was in short supply. Suleiman had been trained as a soldier and as a governor of a province before becoming sultan, but his successors had no such experience; they were brought up in the harem to protect them from rivals. Bred to luxury and debauchery, they often became alcoholics and drug addicts. The grand vezirs took over to keep the empire running, but since they governed at the sultan's pleasure, one gesture from him could end either a career or a life.

Poor decisions hurt the empire tremendously. For example, in 1683 the grand vezir Kara Mustafa (*KAH-rah moo-STAH-fah*) led an immense army to once again besiege Vienna, in an effort to accomplish what Suleiman had already concluded was impossible. The Turks were again defeated, this time by a multinational Christian force led by King Jan III Sobieski (*YAHN sō-B'YEH-skē*) of Poland. Istanbul was forced in 1699 to sign the Peace of Karlowitz, recognizing that Hungary and Transylvania belonged to Austria. For the first time Ottoman expansion had been not only stopped but rolled back. The defeat suggested an uncertain future for the empire, especially as its failure to overcome Christian Europe was paralleled by failures to meet challenges to its leadership within the Islamic world from empires farther east.

The Ottoman Empire declines and is unable to respond to Europe's military challenges

Safavid Persia: A Shi'ite State

Ethnic, linguistic, religious, and geographic diversity characterized the Islamic empires from Istanbul to Delhi. Yet Islam provided a powerful faith-based appeal that helped unify its followers. The five pillars offered each Muslim a framework for living a righteous life. The Qur'an, amplified by the sayings of the Prophet, guided the faithful to a deeper understanding of Allah's will. Islamic law, as developed in the Shari'ah, was interpreted differently in different states but furnished a common code of conduct in civil and criminal matters. Mosques and minarets were found in all Islamic communities, although built in various architectural styles. And while Sunni observances differed from Shi'ite services, Islam offered a common tradition that enabled Muslims of all lands and ethnicities to transcend their differences. Nowhere was this more apparent than in Persia.

A late seventeenth-century Islamic map of the world.

Shi'ite Islam as a Unifying Force

The Iranian plateau had for centuries endured the ravages of raiders and nomads from Central Asia, but the combination of Genghis Khan and Timur Lenk brought devastation on a scale previously unknown. Invading armies obliterated towns, erecting huge columns of skulls to mark their former sites. All told, the population of Persia was reduced by 90 percent. Both Genghis and Timur were accompanied by large bands of Turks, who converted to Islam upon arrival in Persia and who eventually rebuilt it once the Mongols had moved on to other conquests.

The rebuilders, who called themselves the Safavid movement, were established by a Kurd named Safi al-Din (*SAH-fē al-DĒN*), who lived from 1252 to 1334. Claiming descent from the fourth caliph, Ali, and through him from the Prophet Muhammad, Safi founded an order of Turkish Sufi mystics who believed that post-Mongol Persia must be rebuilt on a foundation of purified Islamic devotion and militancy. In opposition to the turmoil and exploitation of Mongol conquest, the Safavid movement preached a positive message of rededication and strength. The order spread across Persia, quickly becoming the most powerful spiritual force in the land.

The Safavid movement rebuilds Persia

Map 17.3 The Safavid Empire in Persia, 1600

A shared Islamic faith connected the peoples of southwest Asia, but differing brands of Islam and other areas of conflict divided them. Notice the geographic location of the Safavid Empire, positioned as a buffer state between the Ottoman Empire (to its west) and the Mughal Empire in India (to its east). The Safavids' adoption of Shi'ite Islam separated Persia from both its Sunni Muslim neighbors, while the natural barriers of the Zagros Mountains and the Hindu Kush discouraged those neighbors from interfering in Safavid affairs. What commercial advantages might this central location have offered the Persians?

After Timur Lenk ravaged Persia late in the fourteenth century, many survivors looked to the Safavids as the most cohesive opposition force. When Timur's empire broke up early in the fifteenth century, Safavism turned from preaching to political action. In 1501, forces led by Safi's descendant Ismail (*IS-mah-ĒL*) conquered the Persian city of Tabriz (*tah-BRĒZ*) (Map 17.3). Ismail proclaimed himself **shah** (or king) of Persia, a position he held until his death in 1524. He also proclaimed Shi'ite Islam the state religion of Persia.

Safavids use Shi'ism to unify Persia

Ismail's 1501 proclamation was highly significant. Persia had been nothing more than a geographic expression, without any independent political identity, since the Arab conquest had reduced it to dependent status. As the Abbasid Caliphate disintegrated, Persia had been torn by the ambitions of warlords and invaders. Now Ismail, by establishing Shi'ism, gave his subjects a new sense of identity and unity that distinguished Persia from its cosmopolitan, Sunni Ottoman neighbor and created what would later be known as the modern state of Iran.

Ismail's accession to the throne was noted immediately in Istanbul. A revived Persian Empire would have been dangerous enough for the Ottomans, but the Safavids were also Shi'ites. Shi'ite Muslims believe that Ali was the legitimate successor to the Prophet and that his murder in 661 constituted a wrong that has never been avenged. Sunni Muslims, who have been in the majority in the Islamic world since that time, are in Shi'ite eyes usurpers who have no right to guide the faithful.

Shi'ism divided Persia from its Sunni neighbors east and west. Its rituals underscored that division. Regular commemorations of Sunni persecutions of Shi'ites are important parts of the Shi'ite Muslim calendar, and they intensify with a two-week observance of the murder of Ali's son Hussein by Sunni assassins in 680. Then as now, pilgrims marched tearfully through the streets, whipping themselves and chanting dirges in honor of the martyr.

A Safavid battle tunic.

Developments in Persia were profoundly disturbing to the Sunnis who ruled the Ottoman Empire. They worried that hundreds of thousands of Shi'ites living under Ottoman rule might be sympathetic to the Safavids. In addition, the Safavid dynasty was of Turkish origin and commanded considerable support in Anatolia. For their part, the Safavids were similarly worried about possible Ottoman intervention, especially because many Persians—perhaps a majority—were Sunnis. Open warfare broke out when Selim I became Ottoman sultan in 1512. Two years later the Ottomans defeated the Persians and occupied Tabriz, but were unable to force the Safavids from power. The attack initiated a bitter, centuries-long struggle during which Sunnis were persecuted in Iran while Shi'ites were hunted down in Anatolia. The animosity between the two Islamic factions deepened.

Sunnis worry about the attractiveness of Safavid Shi'ism

At one point it appeared that Shi'ism might prevail. Shah Abbas (*ab-BAHS*), who reigned from 1587 to 1629, developed a modern army on the Ottoman model. After defeating the Central Asian Uzbeks (*OOZ-becks*), a nomadic people who had occupied portions of eastern Persia, the shah turned against the Ottomans and captured Baghdad. He also allied with the English, who helped his army expel the Portuguese from the Persian Gulf port of Hormuz (*hōr-MOOZ*) in 1622. Commercial rivalries between European powers enabled the shah to shrewdly play one against another. By the end of the shah's reign, Shi'ite Persia seemed to have little to fear from either Europeans or Ottomans.

Persia avoids dependence on either Europe or the Ottoman Empire

Shah Abbas was also sensitive to the need for a strong economy. He encouraged the rapid expansion of trade in both carpets and tiles, items of exquisite beauty soon prized around the world. Transferring his capital to the centrally situated city of Isfahan (*ISS-fah-hahn*), Abbas gained freedom from persistent Ottoman raids and was able to rebuild the city into a commercial center and an architectural wonder. Isfahan's every detail was meticulously planned, from the enormous central square (used for polo matches, festivals, and ceremonies) to the exquisite royal mosque and the luxurious summer palace. The shops in the royal bazaar were centrally located for ease of taxation. Isfahan's grandeur and beauty enhanced Safavid legitimacy and epitomized the validity of Shi'ite Islam.

The Shah Mosque in Isfahan, considered by experts to be the supreme perfection of Islamic architecture.

Following the death of Shah Abbas in 1629, Safavid fortunes declined rapidly. He was succeeded by incompetent, pampered rulers who were unable to defend an empire that needed cleverness to survive. While the Ottomans reconquered Baghdad, Afghans and Uzbeks seized large regions of Persian territory in the East, and Russian Cossacks began to press the empire from the North. Persia remained independent not through its own strength, but because the Ottoman and Mughal Empires were declining as well.

Regional and Islamic Influence on Family and Gender Roles

In Safavid Persia, as in the Ottoman and Mughal empires, societies were shaped as much by regional customs as by Islamic ideals. In each society, for example, practices affecting family and gender, such as the seclusion of women in the home, were often rooted in regional rather than Islamic traditions.

The Qur'an had established family and gender roles in Islamic Arabia (Chapter 11), strengthening the patriarchal nature of Arabian society but also enhancing the status of women. Both genders were entitled to human dignity and personal privacy. Women were granted explicit property rights and were protected from impoverishment in case of divorce. These rights and protections had not previously been available to them.

As Islam spread beyond Arabia, however, the status of women was impaired by local customs that often overrode Qur'anic requirements. In Persia, for example, male domination and female seclusion had for centuries been embedded in legal and cultural systems. Marriages were arranged by the fathers or male guardians of the brides-to-be. Brides lived with their husband and his relatives, an arrangement that gave them little security should the marriage fail. Persian men, citing local practice, frequently refused women their rights as Muslims to inherit property left them by previous husbands or other relatives. The Shari`ah allowed women to buy and sell property, but in Persia these actions could be taken only through male agents. Although the Qur'an spelled out certain rights for women, these were limited, and in some cases canceled, by Persian traditional practice.

The seclusion of women and their segregation from public life must be placed in context, however. In traditional family-based Islamic societies, the private sphere was typically much more important than the public. Girls could not be educated *outside* the home in Safavid Persia, but *inside* it they were taught the Qur'an and the sayings of the Prophet, at least in middle- and upper-class families. Most economic activity involved the family, and here women exercised considerable influence away from public view. In the Ottoman Empire, women could hold business partnerships and employ tax collectors. In Mughal India, unlike Safavid Persia, women played the primary role in arranging the marriages of their daughters. Men were clearly dominant, but women in the Islamic empires did not define themselves as a separate interest group. They played an indispensable role in family life, in societies in which the family was the center of almost all activity.

Local practices negatively affect the status of women in Islamic countries

Persian women.

The Mughal Empire: A Muslim Minority Rules India

East of Persia, other Muslims struggled to extend their dominion over India and its Hindu population. In the northern part of the subcontinent, the main Islamic rulers were the Delhi sultans, who had established their regime in 1206. For the next few centuries, while the Mongols overran most of the rest of Asia, these sultans tried to spread their control across the Indian subcontinent. Although they ultimately failed, the third of the great Islamic empires was eventually constructed on foundations they laid.

The Delhi Sultanate in India

In the 1220s Genghis Khan complicated the Delhi sultans' situation by chasing Central Asian tribes out of their homelands and into northern India. The reigning sultan, Iletmish (*ill-LET-mish*), prudently refused the refugees' offers of alliance and encouraged them to turn westward into Persia. He thus prevented a Mongol invasion of India. By the time of his death in 1236 Iletmish had consolidated all of north India under the Delhi Sultanate (Map 17.4).

A sensible and enlightened ruler, Iletmish did what he could to reconcile India's Hindu majority to Islamic rule. He left the Hindu rajahs alone as long as they paid tribute on time and supported him against the Mongols. He also proved to be a good judge of talent, openly preferring his daughter Radiya (*rah-DĒ-yah*) as his successor because she was clearly more capable than his sons. But when Iletmish died in 1236, her succession was opposed by her brothers and by a group of influential military officers. Radiya battled against this coalition but finally lost in 1240 and died at the hands of Hindus while fleeing Delhi.

Radiya's defeat plunged the Delhi sultanate into a series of coups and intrigues that ended in 1266 with the assumption of power by the Mamluk slave Balban (*bahl-BAHN*), who had been one of the sultanate's most effective generals. He reorganized the army and government in an effort to hold off the persistent Mongols. Balban's death in 1287 was followed within a decade by the rule of Sultan Ala al-Din (*AH-lah-al-dēn*), an imaginative, skillful, and ruthless leader who expanded the sultanate southward, both to extend its holdings and to raise the money and troops required to defend the North against the Mongols. In 1298 he captured the west Indian state of Gujarat and its vast treasury enriched by the Arabian Sea trade. Then he crossed the Deccan plateau into southern India and managed to occupy the tip of the subcontinent. India, it seemed, had at last been united under Muslim control.

But Ala al-Din's unifying rule did not last. His successors proved capable of organizing victories over the Mongols but not of holding India together. The subcontinent was simply too large and too diverse, linguistically, culturally, and geographically, to be consolidated by groups with considerable talent for warfare but little for administration.

Ala al-Din temporarily unites all of India

The Sultanate's authority crumbled rapidly. In 1338, a Sufi sect contributed to the defection of the northeastern state of Bengal from orthodox Muslim rule. In 1347, Muslim nobles formed an independent kingdom on the Deccan plateau. In South India, the Hindu states that Ala al-Din had conquered broke away to form the Vijayanagar (*vē-jā-YAH-nah-gahr*) Empire, and in 1390 Gujarat in West India left as well. These losses weakened Delhi so profoundly that it was unable to resist the catastrophic invasion of Timur Lenk.

Following Timur's atrocities in the late fourteenth century, what remained of Indian unity collapsed. The Delhi sultanate was reduced to the status of a North Indian

Timur Lenk destroys Indian unity

Map 17.4 The Delhi Sultanate in India, 1236

The Delhi Sultanate was India's best hope for defense against the Mongols. Observe that the Sultanate stretched from the banks of the Indus River eastward across the Himalaya Mountains, thereby blocking Mongol penetration of the Indian subcontinent. What factors eventually undermined the regime and opened the door for Mongol invasion?

principality, and several of its former tributaries now became powerful in their own right. In the fifteenth century, no single state dominated. In 1405 Timur's son established the Timurid (*tee-MOOR-id*) dynasty in India, but it lacked the organized military force necessary for effective imperial rule, and the states of northern India generally ignored it.

Sikhs attempt to blend Hinduism with Islam

Further fragmenting the Indian subcontinent was the emergence of a new **Sikh** (*SĒK*) religion in the late fifteenth century. In the Punjab, centuries of conflict between Hindu and Muslim had deeply scarred the population. There a Hindu mystic named Nanak (*NAH-knock*), inspired by a spiritual experience, worked to develop a synthesis of the two antagonistic religions. Impressed by Islamic monotheism, he accepted the idea of the unity of God, blended it with the Hindu mystical notions of samsara, dharma, and karma, and rejected the Hindu caste system in favor of the Islamic principle of the equality of all believers. Nanak's synthesis, known as Sikhism, still thrives in the Punjab, centered on its holiest site, the Golden Temple at Amritsar (*ahm-RIT-zar*). But his dream of reconciling Hinduism with Islam failed. Rejected by most members of these two opposing creeds, Sikhism became yet another force working against the unity of India.

The Golden Temple.

Babur: Founding the Mughal Empire

India in 1500 was a land in turmoil, divided by religion, culture, and politics. Into this situation came a Muslim invader from Kabul, Babur (*BAH-boor*), whose name means "the Panther," a Turkish-Mongol descendant of both Timur Lenk and Genghis Khan. His ancestry alone was enough to make him feared throughout the subcontinent. Calling himself "the Mughal" (Mongol), Babur committed himself to conquest. In 1524 he was invited into the Punjab by a faction seeking his help in overthrowing the local sultan. Babur accepted the invitation and then quickly overran the Punjab and appointed his own officials to rule it. His Indian allies promptly broke ties with him, but Babur secured pledges of cooperation from a number of noble families in Delhi and advanced on that city in the spring of 1526, intent on overthrowing its sultan.

Babur creates the Mughal Empire

On April 21, 1526, Babur's forces faced the spears and elephants of Sultan Ibrahim (*ib-rah-HĒM*) of Delhi at the battle of Panipat (*PAH-nē-paht*). Although his troops were outnumbered by about two to one, his horsemen were more mobile than the infantry of his opponents, and his cannon blew sizable holes in the elephants. By noon he had won the battle and founded what would be named, after him, the Mughal Empire, the greatest Islamic state in Indian history (Map 17.5).

Four years later, Babur died. His son Humayun (*hoo-MAH-yoon*) proved to be a useless leader, more interested in casting horoscopes and indulging in opium than in ruling an empire. Babur's Afghan generals were dissatisfied, and one of them, Sher Khan Sur (*SHĒR KAHN SOOR*), challenged the new emperor and defeated him in 1539 and 1540. But Sher Khan died young in 1545, and Humayun seized this opportunity to regain the power that had never much interested him. By 1555 he was once again in command of northern India. The following January, however, after smoking at least one opium pipe too many, Humayun slipped on the steps of his private observatory and fractured his skull. This accident left the Mughal Empire in the hands of his 13-year-old son Akbar (*OCK-bar*), whose name in Arabic means "great." As matters turned out, he deserved the title.

Akbar's Reign of Cultural Accommodation

Akbar remained under the tutelage of regents until taking control of his empire at age 20. He was an active man, a formidable hunter and fighter, but illiterate throughout his life. He is reported to have advised others that since the Prophet himself could neither read nor write, it would be a good idea for each family to raise at least one illiterate son. In addition to his total lack of formal education, he appears to have been an epileptic, suffering from seizures and dramatic mood swings that baffled his courtiers. None of these conditions, however, prevented his becoming one of history's finest rulers.

Akbar could not read, but he could learn from the past. He understood not only that India was huge and incurably pluralistic, but also that no government could endure without the cooperation of the Hindu majority. Accordingly, Akbar initiated a program that would reconcile his Islamic regime with the Hindu population. Beginning with a personal gesture, he sent an unmistakable signal by marrying a Hindu princess, who bore him three sons. In 1562 he prohibited the enslavement of prisoners of war and their families, as well as all efforts to forcibly convert them to Islam. One year later he abolished all taxes levied on Hindus making pilgrimages to shrines and temples. In 1564 he canceled a tax imposed on non-Muslims. After fewer than three years of formal rule, Akbar had shown himself to be uncommonly generous, tolerant, and sensible. He was the first Muslim ruler to win significant support from Hindus throughout the subcontinent.

Tolerance and conciliation were not, of course, the only tactics Akbar employed. He also used force to solidify his power. Under Akbar the Mughal Empire tripled in size. Its land mass was one-third that of the Ottoman Empire, but its population of 150 million was six times as large. Yet full integration of southern India proved impossible. Akbar could win battles in the South, but once he returned to the North, southern opposition surfaced and reversed his achievements.

In the rest of India, however, Akbar was master of a competent bureaucracy that administered the Mughal Empire. He divided his domain into 12 provinces, subdividing each into districts. Each province was ruled by a governor directly accountable to the emperor. Akbar himself selected the highest officials, a majority of whom were Muslims born outside of India, but a large minority were drawn from other religious, ethnic, linguistic, and regional groups (15 percent, for example, were Hindus). In addition to demonstrating tolerance and inclusiveness, this policy brought the best qualified Indians into his service, giving them responsible roles in the Mughal Empire as an alternative to leading rebellions against it.

Akbar provides an administrative structure for the Mughal Empire

This bureaucracy also collected taxes. Most Indians were peasants, paying taxes not in money but in produce and livestock. Tax collection was handled at the local level,

Map 17.5 The Mughal Empire in India, 1690

Building on the foundations laid by the Delhi Sultanate, the Mughals dominated northern and northwestern India, but the size and topography of the subcontinent prevented them from extending their control further. Note that the central Deccan Plateau, a center of resistance to Muslim rule, sealed the Mughals off from southern India's coast until the late seventeenth century. What weaknesses in Mughal rule made this formidable-looking empire vulnerable to eventual foreign incursions?

▨	Mughal Empire at death of Akbar (1605)
▨	Territory added to Mughal Empire by 1690

where the revenue agents, following Akbar's orders, could assess local agricultural conditions. In years in which the harvest was ruined by insects or bad weather, or in which animals were afflicted by outbreaks of disease, agents were directed to use tax revenues for humanitarian relief. Since the highest-ranking tax collectors were Hindus sympathetic to the peasants, the emperor's wishes were unfailingly carried out. Moreover, in legal disputes involving Hindus on both sides, Hindu rather than Islamic law was used, and the decisions of Hindu courts were final unless the losing party appealed to the throne.

Akbar's tolerant policies trouble orthodox Muslims

These policies meant that Hindus were not only better off under Akbar than under any previous Muslim ruler, but also better off than many would be in centuries to come. Indeed, the emperor's tolerance of Hindus began to worry orthodox Muslims. When, after 1581, Akbar put down several revolts in Muslim regions in the North, he increased his popularity among the Hindu majority. Akbar himself practiced Sufi rituals, with additional practices adapted from Hindus, Jains, Sikhs, and Christians.

Under Mughal rule India's culture became increasingly Persian. Akbar made Farsi the language of administration and Islamic law, offending orthodox Muslims who believed that Arabic, the language of worship, should also be the language of state business. Akbar also encouraged the creation of poetry and literature in the Farsi, Urdu (*UHR-doo*), and Hindi (*HIN-dē*) languages, rather than insisting on the exclusive use of Arabic or Turkish. In addition, Sufism, the basis of Akbar's ritual observances, was essentially a Persian doctrine, and fashions and etiquette at the Mughal court also owed more to Isfahan than to Baghdad or Delhi.

Akbar was not typical of sixteenth-century Islamic rulers. In some ways he resembled an absolute monarch; in others, an enlightened despot—one whose absolute rule is tempered by learning and a commitment to the service of his subjects. In his willingness to incorporate aspects of other cultures into a Mughal synthesis, Akbar can with some justice be called modern. But the end of his reign was troubled by a vicious struggle for succession. Akbar's son Salim (*sah-LĒM*) rebelled in 1601, and after four years of turmoil the emperor died, probably a victim of poison. The impatient Salim then became emperor of the most powerful empire in the history of India, and one of the most formidable in the entire world.

The Great Mughals

Prince Salim's reign ushered in the era of the Great Mughals. With much of South Asia unified under their control, there seemed to be no threats to the empire. Salim celebrated his coronation by taking the name Jahangir (*zhah-hahn-GĒR*)—"World Seizer"—and by continuing his father's efforts to create in India a new unified civilization with Islamic, Hindu, and Persian components.

NUR JAHAN AND SHAH JAHAN: LIGHTING THE WORLD. In 1611 the Persian strand became dominant as Jahangir married a 34-year-old widow from Persia whom he renamed Nur Jahan (*NOOR jah-HAHN*), "Light of the World." She was quick-witted and politically skilled, and since Jahangir possessed neither of these attributes, she quickly became the true sovereign. Through her and her Persian relatives, Safavid style and culture left an enduring mark on India.

Nur Jahan saw to it that her father became Jahangir's chief minister and arranged for the marriage of her niece, Mumtaz Mahal (*MOOM-tahz mah-HAL*), to Shah Jahan ("Emperor of the World"), Jahangir's son by an earlier marriage. She then supported Shah Jahan for the imperial succession. Jahangir, preferring to spend his time drinking wine, making love, and writing Persian poetry, was more than willing to turn military affairs over to his crown prince. By 1622, however, Nur Jahan had become jealous of her stepson, and when she ordered him to undertake a risky expedition to Kabul, he refused and rose in revolt. When Jahangir died in 1627, Shah Jahan exiled Nur Jahan to Lahore, where she lived out her life on a sizable pension.

Nur Jahan becomes the real ruler of the Mughal Empire

That solution was typical of Shah Jahan, who seldom hesitated to spend money. He lavished gifts on his harem of 5,000 women and on Mumtaz Mahal, his wife, who bore him 14 children prior to her death in childbirth at the age of 39. Inconsolable, Shah Jahan immortalized her with the construction of her magnificent tomb, the Taj Mahal (*TAHZH mah-HAHL*), a masterpiece fusing Persian artistic form with Indian craftsmanship and materials. He also built the Pearl Mosque at Agra (*AH-grah*), a sparkling jewel of white marble and a monument to Muslim rule in northern India.

But for all his spendthrift ways, Shah Jahan was not generous to his subjects. Rather than suspending taxation to ease famine and the burden of natural disasters, as Akbar had done, Shah Jahan grudgingly passed out a handful of rupees. This policy prompted recurring revolts on the central Deccan plateau, an area inhospitable to agriculture and a never-ending drain on money and manpower for the Great Mughals. Instead of relief efforts, Shah Jahan sent armies, causing additional resentment.

Shah Jahan builds monuments but neglects his subjects

In the early 1640s Shah Jahan began construction of a new capital at Delhi, the seventh and last such city to be built on that site, which he immodestly named Shah Jahanabad (see "François Bernier Comments on Conditions in Delhi"). The city was laid out on an immense scale and included two spectacular building complexes, the Red Fort and the Jama Masjid (*JAH-mah mahs-JĒD*) Mosque. All this construction required enormous sums of money, which Shah Jahan obtained by increasing tax rates by 50 percent. Thus although he left an architectural legacy that dazzles visitors to the present day, he was neither popular nor competent in his own time, and when he fell ill in 1657, his sons saw their opportunity. They intrigued against each other for a year, and in 1658 the winner was the militant orthodox Muslim Aurangzeb (*ore-RAHNG-zebb*), who ruled as Alamgir (*AH-lahm-gēr*) I ("World Conqueror") for 49 years.

The Taj Mahal.

AURANGZEB'S REIGN: REBELLION AND DISUNITY. Aurangzeb's combination of cunning, ruthlessness, piety, and administrative brilliance made him the most formidable of the Great Mughals. Joyless and puritanical, he spent many hours in prayer and ended the extravagant ways of his father, both in architecture and in the harem. He also ended Akbar's policy of tolerance for non-Muslims, increasing their taxes, denying them building permits for temples, and requiring Hindus to pay double taxes for food. Those who protested these harsh measures were trampled by elephants. As taxes increased and starvation threatened, revolts broke out in various parts of the empire.

Aurangzeb reverses Akbar's policy of tolerance

Under Aurangzeb's tyranny, Sikhs in the Punjab transformed their peace-loving faith into an instrument of rebellion and evolved into a militant community, the "army of the pure." All Sikh males were baptized with the surname Singh (*SĬNG*), or "Lion." Sikh men vowed to wear beards and carry sabers for mutual recognition. Easily outnumbering them,

Document 17.2 François Bernier Comments on Conditions in Delhi

François Bernier, a French traveler in India in the mid-seventeenth century, commented upon the suitability of Indian buildings to the tropical climate.

In treating of the beauty of these towns . . . I have sometimes been astonished to hear the contemptuous manner in which Europeans in the Indies speak of [Delhi] and other places. They complain that the buildings are inferior in beauty to those of the Western world, forgetting that different climates require different styles of architecture; that what is useful and proper at Paris, London, or Amsterdam, would be entirely out of place at Delhi; insomuch that if it were possible for any one of those great capitals to change place with the metropolis of the Indies, it would become necessary to throw down the greater part of the city, and to rebuild it on a totally different plan . . .

The heat is so intense in [Delhi] that no one, not even the King, wears stockings; the only cover for the feet being slippers, while the head is protected by a small turban, of the finest and most delicate materials. The other garments are proportionately light. During the summer season, it is scarcely possible to keep the hand on the wall of an apartment, or the head on a pillow. For more than six successive months, everybody lies in the open air without covering—the common people in the streets, the merchants and persons of condition sometimes in their courts or gardens, and sometimes on their terraces, which are first carefully watered. Now, only suppose the streets of [Paris] transported hither, with their close houses and endless stories; would they be habitable? or would it be possible to sleep in them during the night, when the absence of wind increases the heat almost to suffocation? Suppose one just returned on horseback, half dead with heat and dust, and drenched, as usual, in perspiration; and then imagine the luxury of squeezing up a narrow dark staircase, there to remain almost choked with heat. In the Indies, there is no such troublesome task to perform. You have only to swallow quickly a draught of fresh water, or lemonade; to undress; wash face, hands, and feet, and then immediately drop upon a sofa in some shady place, where one or two servants fan you . . .

SOURCE: François Bernier, *Travels in the Mogul Empire, A.D. 1656–1668*, translated by Archibald Constable (Delhi: S. Chand, 1968) 240–241.

Mughal armies held them off, but the Sikhs retained their hatred for Islamic political authority and remained a dangerous force.

Aurangzeb encountered further opposition from Hindus on the Deccan plateau, where Shivaji Bonsle (*shē-VAH-jē BAHNS-lē*) founded the Hindu **Maratha** (*mah-ruh-TAH*) nationalist movement to resist Mughal rule. Shivaji was a pioneer in **guerrilla warfare**—raids by small roving bands of warriors that aim to disrupt armies rather than defeating them in open battle. He once killed an opposing Muslim general during apparent surrender talks. Irreconcilable to the Mughal Empire, the Marathas' ferocious Hindu nationalism represented exactly the sort of reaction that Akbar's policy of tolerance and respect had been designed to avoid.

At enormous cost, Aurangzeb unifies India

Aurangzeb reacted vigorously, realizing that the many different forces arrayed against him were as suspicious of one another as they were of Mughal rule. His armies isolated the Sikhs in the Punjab and plundered the Deccan. By 1700 Aurangzeb had unified India to an extent undreamed of even by Ashoka. But his was a grim victory, costing more than two million lives, wasting tremendous sums of money, and despoiling virtually the entire subcontinent. His armies left behind empty cities and devastated farmlands, dooming central India to famine and disease for years to come.

Few mourned Aurangzeb when he died in 1707. His ill-conceived policies had created a vast empire while at the same time impoverishing it, and the opposition his brutality had provoked actually strengthened Indian regionalism and disunity. These developments occurred just as India began to notice the danger posed by visitors from Europe.

Chapter Review

Putting It in Perspective

From the thirteenth through sixteenth centuries, the Islamic world underwent two profound transformations. In the thirteenth it was devastated and divided by Mongol conquests. In the fourteenth, when it seemed to be recovering from these onslaughts, it was hit by a new wave of invaders led by Timur Lenk. Once again the Islamic world was shattered; once again it was rebuilt.

Those who led this second period of rebuilding—the Ottomans, Safavids, and Mughals—were themselves the descendants of Mongolian and Turkish nomads from Central Asia, and thus relative newcomers to the regions they ruled. With the flexibility of outsiders, they were able to combine cultures, creating hybrid systems that drew from various traditions. Consequently, by the sixteenth century, the realms that their descendants ruled were among the most powerful and prosperous on the planet. But these empires also faced dangers that became apparent in the next century.

One danger came from within. The size, multiethnicity, and religious diversity of their domains bred tensions and conflicts that challenged both state and society. Exceptional rulers such as Suleiman and Akbar were able to balance competing interests and treat all subjects fairly, thus maintaining broad support. Other rulers, however, far less talented and tolerant, either sought to impose uniformity by force or withdrew into the pleasures of royal palaces and ignored the needs of their realm. Either way, the results were often mass discontent, and sometimes regional rebellion.

Another threat came from outside. The Europeans, having adopted ideas and technology from the Chinese and Muslims, were searching for new sea routes to connect the East and West. This largely commercial quest led them to engage the Muslim world in a long and bitter conflict over commerce. It also brought them in contact with some extraordinary empires that had arisen in the Americas, in total isolation from the rest of the world.

Reviewing Key Material

KEY CONCEPTS

Pax Ottomanica, 414	shah, 422
grand vezir, 416	Sikh, 426
fatwa, 416	Maratha, 430
urfi, 417	guerrilla warfare, 430
Janissaries, 417	

KEY PEOPLE

Mehmed II, 410	Radiya, 425
Timur Lenk, 410	Ala al-Din, 425
Bayezid I, 415	Nanak, 426
Murad I, 415	Babur, 426
Selim I, 418	Akbar, 426
Suleiman I, 418	Jahangir, 428
Kara Mustafa, 421	Nur Jahan, 428
Jan III Sobieski, 421	Mumtaz Mahal, 429
Safi al-Din, 421	Shah Jahan, 428
Shah Ismail, 422	Aurangzeb, 429
Shah Abbas, 423	Shivaji Bonsle, 430
Iletmish, 425	

ASK YOURSELF

1. What blended features made Ottoman government and society unique? Why were these features developed?
2. How did the Safavids use Shi'ite Islam as a governing tool in Persia?

3. How did the Mughals manage to rule India despite their status as members of a religious minority? What did Akbar do to reconcile his Islamic regime to the Hindu population?

4. In what ways did each Islamic empire blend Islamic practices with the cultures of the people under its rule? How were social structures, family, and gender roles influenced by this blending?

GOING FURTHER

Basham, A. *A Cultural History of India.* 1975.

Chandler, Neelan. *Socio-Economic History of Mughul India.* 1987.

Etil, Esin. *The Age of Sultan Suleyman the Magnificent.* 1987.

Faroqhi, Suraiya. *The Ottoman Empire and the World Around It.* 2004.

Goffman, Daniel. *The Ottoman Empire and Early Modern Europe.* 2002.

Golden, Peter. *An Introduction to the History of the Turkic Peoples.* 1992.

Goodwin, Jason. *Lords of the Horizon: A History of the Ottoman Empire.* 1999.

Hansen, W. *The Peacock Throne: The Drama of Mogul India.* 1972.

Ikram, S. *History of Muslim Civilization in India and Pakistan.* 1989.

Imber, Colin. *The Ottoman Empire, 1300–1650.* 2002.

Itkowitz, Norman. *The Ottoman Empire and the Islamic Tradition.* 1980.

Kafadar, Cemal. *Between Two Worlds: The Construction of the Ottoman State.* 1995.

Keyvani, Mehdi. *Artisans and Guild Life in the Later Safavid Period.* 1982.

Kunt, Metin, and Christine Woodhead, eds. *Süleyman the Magnificent and His Age.* 1995.

Lambton, Ann. *Continuity and Change in Medieval Persia.* 1988.

Marozzi, Justin. *Tamerlane.* 2004.

Monshi, E. *History of Shah Abbas the Great.* 2 vols. 1978.

Richards, John. *The Mughul Empire.* 1996.

Savory, Roger. *Iran Under the Safavids.* 1980.

Soudawar, A., and M. Beach. *The Art of the Persian Courts.* 1992.

Wheatcroft, A. *The Ottomans.* 1993.

Key Dates and Developments

1206–1397	The Delhi Sultanate
1360–1405	Conquests of Timur Lenk
1389	Battle of Kosovo; Ottoman Rule in the Balkans
1453	Constantinople falls to Mehmed the Conqueror; end of the Byzantine Empire
1501	Shah Ismail proclaims Shi'ism in Safavid Iran
1526	Ottoman victory at Mohaćs (Hungary) Battle of Panipat; Mughal Empire begins in India
1529	Suleiman fails to take Vienna
1556–1605	Akbar rules Mughal India
1571	Ottoman fleet defeated at Lepanto
1587–1629	Rule of Shah Abbas in Iran
1605–1707	The Great Mughals in India
1683	King Jan III Sobieski defeats Ottomans at Vienna
1699	Peace of Karlowitz

The Aztec and Inca Empires, 1300–1550

Machu Picchu

In the fifteenth century C.E., the Inca Empire constructed this fortress city of Machu Picchu, high in a remote area of the Andes Mountains. The Inca overcame this formidable terrain to create an empire extending for more than 3,000 miles north to south (page 441).

Throughout the city, the women arose before dawn. They laid fresh wood on the fires and warmed up a simple meal of tortillas stuffed with beans. Then they awakened their husbands and children for breakfast. The sun was just barely above the horizon when the men left to work in the fields or started their work at home, making weapons, tools, or goods to be offered for sale. After cleaning the family's dishes and utensils, the women left to sweep the streets and to collect the neighborhood's garbage and waste. At mid-morning they would carry the refuse to the water's edge, where it would be loaded into canoes and transported to the mainland. Perhaps some of them would pause to talk among themselves, or simply to gaze out over the placid surface of Lake Texcoco toward the mountains in the distance.

The Inca Empire

The Aztec Empire

These were the women of Tenochtitlán (*teh-nōsh-tit-LAHN*), capital of the Aztec Empire and one of the most unusual cities of the world. Built on a group of islands within a lake in the Valley of Mexico, eight thousand feet above sea level, Tenochtitlán was the center of a civilization that by 1500 was less than two centuries old. Its women worked diligently to keep the city clean, a critical task in a tropical metropolis surrounded by fungus-bearing water. They raised the children and maintained the households for their husbands, most of whom worked as farmers or artisans for eight months and devoted the remaining four to military combat on behalf of the empire. As farmers, the Aztecs cultivated a wide variety of nutritious crops; as artisans, they created quetzal-feather mosaics of exceptional beauty; as warriors, they constructed a powerful state that awed and intimidated all other Amerinds who knew of its existence. Yet within a generation, the realm in which these Aztecs lived and worked was invaded and conquered, not by other Amerind peoples but by a foreign people from another hemisphere.

The Great Amerind Empires

In 1500 C.E., the Amerind civilizations were very new and very isolated. Their newness was due to the relative lateness of the Amerinds' transition from hunting and gathering to agriculture. Before the development of agricultural and urban economies, there had been no need for governments and states with the power to organize labor for public works, such as draining swamps and building walls around cities. All these processes had happened earlier in the river civilizations of ancient Asia and Africa. Also delaying the development of Amerind social organization was the scarcity of large four-footed mammals that could be domesticated for meat and—more important to the economy—for work in pulling plows or heavy loads. These kinds of animals had lived in the Americas before humans arrived, but most had been hunted to extinction shortly thereafter. These and other factors meant that in 1500 early American societies were in earlier stages of development than those inhabiting the Eurasian landmass.

Amerind societies were also isolated compared to Eurasian societies, which had both suffered and benefited from extensive connections among cultures. The economic and technological advantages enjoyed by Europeans in 1500 had been copied or adapted from Persia, Greece, Carthage, Arabia, India, and China—societies that Amerinds did not know existed. European social and governing structures had been influenced by Greece, Rome, the Germanic invasions, and institutionalized Christianity. In contrast, the Aztec and Inca Empires had developed in isolation, cut off not only from any knowledge of the older societies of the eastern hemisphere but also from each other. Because of this isolation, Amerinds lacked immunity to Eurasian diseases, familiarity with Eurasian technology, and acquaintance with Eurasian governing structures.

Isolation delays the development of early America

Three Amerind civilizations, however, had evolved more rapidly than others, despite their isolation. They had created class systems that proved capable of technological innovation, including the construction of cities more extensive in scope and more refined in conveniences than most cities in Asia and Europe. The oldest of the three, the Maya culture of what are now Mexico and Guatemala, had achieved substantial complexity before 800. But a combination of undetermined circumstances had first weakened and then destroyed this civilization in the next few centuries. By 1500 millions of Maya were living in extremely primitive conditions in the rain forests. Their great cities had long been abandoned, and even the ruins remained unknown until the nineteenth and twentieth centuries.

The other two cultures had achieved significant cultural complexity only one or two centuries before 1500. In central Mexico, the Aztec people organized themselves around a warrior elite, conquered neighboring tribes through intimidation or force, and built the spectacular city of Tenochtitlán to serve as their empire's capital. Farther south, the Inca people of Peru pieced together an empire that stretched thousands of miles from north to south, linked by an intricate network of roads and bridges crossing the Andes mountains. They had assimilated other ethnic groups using techniques like those practiced in earlier millennia by Persia and Rome.

The Aztec and Inca empires each considered itself the greatest on earth, a claim attributable at least in part to its complete lack of knowledge of comparable societies. Eurasian and African societies could learn from each other, but the Aztecs and Inca never had that opportunity. Europeans could, by contrast, learn of Chinese inventions such as gunpowder and paper and adapt them to their own purposes, but Amerind societies could not. Their newness and their isolation constituted fatal disadvantages early in the sixteenth century, when European invaders suddenly arrived by sea.

Aztec and Inca empires develop in relative isolation

The Aztec Empire

According to the Aztecs' own creation story, they originated on an island called Aztlán (hence the name *Aztecs*) off the Pacific coast of Mexico, but left that island in 1111 to search for the land promised them by their most important god, Huitzilopochtli (*hwē-tsē-lō-PŌSH-tlē*), or Southern Hummingbird. From 1270 until 1319 they occupied Chapultepec (*chah-PULL-tā-peck*) Hill on the western fringe of what is today Mexico City. By 1325 they had moved onto an island in Lake Texcoco (*tesh-KŌ-kō*), on which Huitzilopochtli had told them they would find an eagle perched on a cactus and devouring a snake—the

An Aztec representation of the founding of Tenochtitlan in 1325 C.E.

The Aztecs' creation
story portrays them as
a wandering people

symbol in the center of the modern Mexican flag. The Aztecs, who called themselves Mexica (*mē-SHĒ-kah*), named the valley surrounding Lake Texcoco after themselves, calling it the Valley of Mexico. On the islands in the lake they built Tenochtitlán.

Tenochtitlán: City in the Lake

The Aztecs quickly recognized the advantages of building a city on islands. The lake was full of fish and birds to eat, and Aztecs used its waters to cultivate their crops. Instead of irrigating, they layered mud and lake plants to build large, latticework platforms, called **chinampas** (*chē-NAHM-pahs*), on which they planted their crops. Then they floated the entire structure on the surface of the lake. Nourished by the mud and plant matter, the roots of the crops sucked up the lake water and produced huge quantities of fruits, vegetables, and grains. Chinampas could be strung together to form rectangles of land on the lake, complete with intersecting waterways. With inexhaustible moisture and a tropical climate, conditions that permitted the cultivation of two successive crops each year, the chinampa system proved capable of sustaining a large population at high levels of nutrition.

The Aztecs build their
capital in a lake

Building a city in the middle of a lake carried with it two additional benefits. First, cargo could be moved by canoe, both within the city on canals and between the city and the mainland. Since Mexico lacked wheeled carts (and the large animals required to pull them), water transport was quicker and less exhausting than packing loads on the backs of people. Second, the location provided valuable strategic protection for an assertive, ambitious people who made enemies easily. The city was connected to the shores by three causeways, each 25 to 30 feet wide, separated at intervals by drawbridges that could be raised to cut off the advance or retreat of hostile forces. To invade Tenochtitlán successfully, an enemy would need to construct a fleet of canoes on the lakeshore. The only other way to penetrate the city was to be invited in.

As a location for a city-state, therefore, Lake Texcoco was an unusual but not irrational choice. Nor were the Aztecs alone in their new surroundings: about a dozen other Amerind towns sprang up along the shoreline, and three of them extended into the lake. By 1500 there were some 50 cities in the Valley of Mexico.

Few cities anywhere in the world could compare with Tenochtitlán. Its center was dominated by a great double temple dedicated to Huitzilopochtli and Tlaloc (*TLAH-lock*), the god of rain. Its many canals were spanned by sturdy bridges. In contrast to other cities of the time, it was also immaculate: there was good drainage, sewage and garbage were hauled away in barges, and every day a crew of a thousand women swept down and washed public streets. Estimates of its population range from 80,000 to 250,000, but even at 80,000, it would have been one of the largest cities in the world. By contrast, in 1500 Seville, the most populous city in Spain, contained 40,000 people.

Exploitation and Human Sacrifice

Tenochtitlán was also the heart of one of the world's most oppressive realms. Following a succession of capable and aggressive leaders, the Aztecs established an empire in 1468 under Motecuzoma I (*mō-teh-koo-ZŌ-mah*), whose name was later corrupted into Spanish as Montezuma. Although destined to last only half a century, this empire (Map 18.1) was hated profoundly by all neighboring tribes for its ruthlessness.

FOUNDATION MAP 18.1 The Aztec Empire in 1519

Notice the empire's location, west of the old Mayan city-states. The Aztecs were a subgroup of the Chichimec tribe of northern Mexico, and their empire represents an intrusion of the Chichimecs into the fringes of the Mayan homelands. Notice also the existence of connections between central Mexico and the Mayan homelands three hundred years before the arrival of the Aztecs, who built trading relationships on preexisting networks. How would the compactness of central Mexico and the Yucatan Peninsula have contributed to contacts between Aztec and Maya?

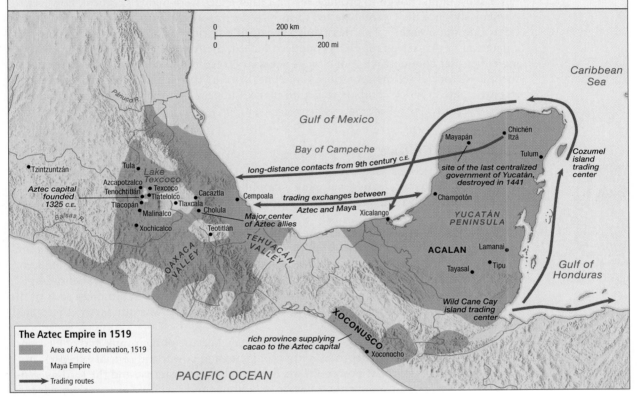

Aztec ruthlessness derived from a **cosmic mission theory** that justified a program of human sacrifice. According to this theory, the sun, the source of all heat and light and therefore of all life, grows weary during its journey across the heavens. It must be sustained by the repeated offering of a life-giving elixir, found only in beating human hearts. For this purpose, human beings were sacrificed on a regular schedule, their hearts torn from their bodies by priests and offered to the sun while still beating. Failure to perform this essential ritual was believed to doom the entire world to perpetual darkness and extinction. Human sacrifice was practiced by other early Amerind cultures, but usually only on important ceremonial occasions or in dire emergencies, such as drought or earthquake. For the Aztecs, human sacrifice was a routine program that allowed elites to legitimize their position and ensure social control.

Aztec religion provides a mechanism of social control

The cosmic mission
theory justifies Aztec
expansion

The cosmic mission theory was, in fact, a political and religious hoax devised by the ruling elite of the Aztec Empire. Warriors and priests both had a stake in it: warriors obtained prisoners of war for the slaughter, while priests sacrificed the victims in the proper manner. Both classes used the theory as a mechanism of social control, employing it to keep Aztec commoners subservient to the regime and to terrorize subject peoples. If ordinary Aztecs doubted its validity (and there is no reason to assume that they did), their doubt was never substantial enough to produce revolt. Other tribes were highly skeptical, however, particularly since they were expected to furnish the prisoners of war, but they could do little to alter the situation. This theory also provided a spiritual justification for the perpetual expansion of the Aztec Empire by conquest. Indeed, the Aztecs had so terrorized neighboring tribes that conquest was not always necessary to secure prisoners of war. The tribes themselves, out of self-preservation, sometimes selected the victims, who were then forced to participate in mock combats staged to make it appear that they had been captured by Aztec warriors.

Society and Culture

The Aztec Empire was founded on blood. But this obsession with human sacrifice did not prevent the Aztecs from developing a carefully stratified society with a standard of living that many throughout the world would have envied.

Human sacrifice.

SOCIAL CLASSES AND GENDER ROLES. At the top of Aztec society was the ruling class, or *Tecuhtli* (*teh-COOT-lē*), drawn from the leading generals, high officials of Tenochtitlán, chiefs of outlying districts, judges in the capital, and priests. This class elected the emperor, a nonhereditary position. The emperor was almost always a distinguished warrior; only once was a priest elected, and even he had been a general too. Thus, although sons of the *Tecuhtli* were nobles by right of birth, leadership in the empire was ultimately determined by success in warfare.

The lords of Mexico were wealthy men, but only because of their rank and obligations. Aztec society considered riches to be a result of increasing power and official expenses, not a method of obtaining that power. Priests lived in chilling austerity, and the leading generals and political officials spent money on everything and everyone except themselves. This meritocracy offered the chance for social mobility. Commoners could rise into the *Tecuhtli* through exceptional skill in combat, while nobles could descend to common status just as readily through incompetence or cowardice. And the empire paid a great deal of attention to the training of both its leaders and its workers: no Mexican child, whatever his or her rank or wealth, was denied an education.

The love of profit for its own sake that was rejected by the nobility was embraced by the *Pochteca* (*pōsh-TECK-ah*), the merchant caste. Utterly inbred, with marriage restricted to those within the caste and with fathers passing businesses on to their sons, the merchants spent their lives on the road selling manufactured goods and luxury items throughout Mexico and Central America. On their continuous journeys they dispensed justice within their own ranks, defended themselves against bandits without the help of warriors, and prayed without the intercession of priests. They sold jewelry, household implements, and elegant mosaics made of quetzal feathers. The Aztec Empire relied on the Pochteca for its material needs and left them alone.

Below the Pochteca were the *Tolteca* (*tōl-TECK-ah*), a caste of artisans practicing trades such as goldsmith, jeweler, salter (a specialist who preserved food by salting it), and quarryman. Here too skills remained within families. This caste had its own chiefs, who represented Tolteca interests within the highest councils of the empire.

Most Mexica were commoners, or *Macehualtin* (*MAH-sā-wahl-tēn*). Full citizens of the Aztec Empire, they enjoyed certain civil rights. Men could own land, send their children to school, share in the spoils of conquest, vote for local chiefs, and if they were intelligent and courageous, rise out of their class to become honored and wealthy. On the other hand, if a *macehual* did nothing to distinguish himself in the first years of his adult life, he was subject to weighty obligations, including communal labor and the payment of taxes (from which nobles were exempt).

At the bottom of the social structure were the *Tlatlacotin* (*TLA-tla-cō-tēn*), or slaves. They were owned by others, but were housed, clothed, and fed like ordinary citizens. They could sell their labor in their spare time, accumulate savings, buy land or houses, or even buy slaves for their own service. Marriage between a slave and a free person was permitted, and all children of such unions were born free. Unlike the Atlantic trade that later enslaved Africans, slavery as practiced in the Aztec Empire was based not on race but on bad conduct. Enslavement was a punishment for certain crimes or for chronic indebtedness. It also served as a form of welfare: people who were unsuited by temperament to earning a living, who drank too much, or who were mentally or emotionally unstable could sell themselves into slavery in order to obtain food, clothing, and shelter. Giving up the rights and duties of freedom, they were able to survive.

> Slavery in Aztec Mexico had no racial basis

While men in Aztec society engaged in the governance of the empire and its expansion through battle, women were almost completely confined to domestic roles. The remarkable cleanliness of Tenochtitlán and other Aztec cities was largely women's responsibility. Women also wove the elaborate costumes, cotton armor, and everyday clothing worn throughout central Mexico. Marriage and childbearing were expected and were welcomed with joyful festivities. An unmarried woman was an oddity attributable to some sort of mental or emotional defect. Some women served as physicians and accumulated extensive knowledge of herbal remedies and medical procedures.

LAW, HEALTH, AND DEATH IN AZTEC MEXICO. Governing this complex society was a highly effective legal system. There were no lawyers; judges examined defendants directly and used a wide variety of methods to determine the truth. Judges were drawn from the finest graduates of Aztec schools and took up their posts after years of success as warriors.

In keeping with a society that used the cosmic mission theory as a form of social control, punishment for offenses was harsh. Acts considered serious crimes, such as treason, homicide, espionage, adultery, and homosexuality, were punishable by death, a sentence that was carried out immediately. Minor crimes such as theft were punishable by slavery or mutilation. A judge found to have delivered a false verdict based on bribes or favoritism would be executed. No citizens could take the law into their own hands; nor was there any need to do so, since the administration of justice was so swift and severe. The Aztec Empire wanted to control its people, not rehabilitate them, and it succeeded.

> Aztecs develop a legal system based on punishment

Despite its harshness, life under the Aztecs had its advantages. Cleanliness was a cultural expectation, people bathed several times a week, and Aztec medical practices were advanced for their era. Healers knew how to set broken bones and treat dental cavities.

> Aztecs practice sophisticated medical procedures

The Aztec goddess
Coatlicue.

*Aztec concepts of the
afterlife reinforce the
cosmic mission theory*

Occasionally they even performed brain surgery. Like their medical counterparts else-where, they did not understand the causes of diseases, but they developed effective cures and medicines, many of which are still used in Mexico today.

But no medicine, however effective, could stave off death indefinitely, especially in a society so obsessed with hurrying it along through war and sacrifice. When the end arrived, all Aztecs understood that it was ordained by fate, part of an unavoidable pattern of birth, death, and afterlife. Warriors who fell in battle were reborn as colorful hummingbirds; women who died in childbirth were transformed into goddesses. The hummingbirds escorted the sun from its rising to its zenith, while the goddesses accompanied it from its zenith to its setting. Farmers who were struck by lightning or drowned (the latter a frequent occurrence in a city built in the midst of a lake) were led by Tlaloc, the god of rain and water, to a paradise of flowers, springs, and gardens. These beliefs mirrored the cycles of nature itself: the sun comes up each morning after passing the night in the Underworld; corn dies in autumn and is reborn in spring; the luxuriant wild plants of Mexico do the same.

For those unfortunates who died an ordinary, undistinguished death, however, the out-look was much less attractive. Their destination was Mictlan (*MICK-tlahn*), the Under-world, presided over by the god and goddess of the dead. This ghoulish couple ruled a cold, dark realm of dust and bones, seated on thrones surrounded by spiders and owls. The prospect of this afterlife made death in battle welcome rather than something to be feared. In contrast, the sacrificial victims, whose beating hearts nourished the sun, became one with it and lived forever as part of the source of heat and light that made life on earth possible.

The Inca Empire

The Inca civilization of western South America developed even later than Aztec society. Covering a much larger range of territory than Aztec Mexico, the Inca Empire extended from what is today northern Ecuador into central Chile, some three thousand miles from north to south. It also differed from the Aztec realm in many other ways since, although these two empires existed at the same time in the same hemisphere, the barriers to travel between them were so great that they developed in isolation from one another.

A Unified Empire

*The Inca's creation story
portrays them as a
people emerging from
the earth*

*The Inca create an
extensive empire in
difficult terrain*

The Inca creation story asserts that the Inca people emerged around the year 1200 from three caves 18 miles southeast of the city of Cuzco (*COOZ-kō*), Peru. Other Amerind peoples lived in the region, including the Huari, the Chanca, and the Chimú. The Inca did not at first challenge any of them, gradually building Cuzco and developing their po-litical and social institutions. During this time the Inca were apparently ruled by seven legendary emperors, about whom nothing can be known with certainty. But the eighth ruler, Viracocha (*vē-rah-KŌ-chah*) Inca, laid the foundations of an empire. Between 1400 and 1438 he expanded Inca control over a 25-mile radius from Cuzco, reaching as far south as Lake Titicaca (*tih-tē-KAH-kah*) (Map 18.2).

Viracocha was followed by two remarkable rulers who enlarged the small Inca do-main into one of the world's biggest empires. Pachacuti (*pah-chah-COO-tē*), who ruled from 1438 to 1471, gave the realm its official name, **Tahuantin-Suyu** (*tah-wahn-tin*

SOO-yoo), the Empire of the Four Quarters. He also made his native language, Quechua (*KEH-chwah*), the language of official business and organized the administrative structure of what was becoming a very large state (see page 433). By the time of his death in 1471 the Inca ruled all of present-day Peru. Then Topa Inca Yupanqui (*TŌ-pah IN-kah yoo-PAHN-kwē*), who ruled from 1471 to 1493, extended the empire to the north and south, defeating the Chimú kingdom in Ecuador and conquering the northern half of Chile. Together, given the territory they amassed, he and Pachacuti are ranked with Alexander the Great and Genghis Khan among history's great empire builders.

The Inca conquered in an unusual way, always announcing their attacks in advance and never using force except when persuasion failed. Once defeated, a conquered population was assimilated into the empire through the process of **mitima** (*mē-TĒ-mah*), or resettlement and integration. Within a generation, families resettled in Inca towns had lost their original cultural identities and become Inca, a transition made smoother by the complete absence of discrimination against them.

In 1493 a new ruler, Huayna Capac (*HWAH-nah KĀ-pack*), consolidated Inca gains and focused on the administration of the empire. Further territorial advance was blocked—to the East by the Andes mountains and the dense rain forests of their eastern slopes, and to the South by the Mapuche (*mah-POO-chā*) Amerinds, warlike and hostile to outsiders. Still, at the beginning of the sixteenth century the Inca Empire, just one hundred years old, encompassed a great expanse of land and a great many peoples, much like ancient Rome and the concurrent Ottoman Empire.

Society and Economy

Inca society contained fewer distinct social classes than did Aztec society. At the top of its political pyramid stood the emperor, called the **Sapa** (*SAH-pah*) **Inca**, a man who claimed to rule by divine right because of his direct descent from the sun god, Inti (*ĒN-tē*). He was worshiped as divine during his lifetime; after death he was carefully embalmed and mummified, and became a god like his ancestor, Inti. Because he claimed divinity, the Sapa Inca was compelled to keep the royal line pure; he could not defile it through marriage to a mortal. Thus he always chose one of his full sisters as his principal wife. From among her sons, he chose his heir. The practice usually brought the most competent son to power but also set

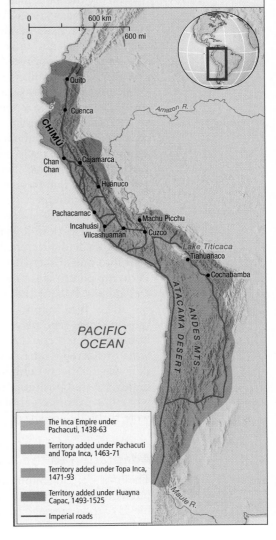

Map 18.2 The Inca Empire, 1438–1525

The Inca Empire of Tahuantin-Suyu was carved out of the Andes Mountains between the highlands of Quito and the Atacama Desert. Note the empire's shape, dictated by Andean geography: it was three thousand miles north to south at its longest point, but only four hundred miles east to west at its widest. The Aztec Empire enjoyed the advantage of compactness (Map 18.1), while the Inca Empire struggled successfully with geographic disadvantages. How did the Inca overcome those disadvantages?

brothers against one another. When the Sapa Inca died suddenly without designating a successor, a brutal power struggle followed.

The Sapa Inca's authority was so great that some of it actually survived him. After death, the emperor's body was embalmed with fragrant resins and dried in the sun in the arid highlands around Cuzco. Then his mummy was enshrined in one of the palaces in which he had lived. Servants attended the mummies of each successive Sapa Inca, deciding when to offer him food and drink, occasionally taking one mummy to visit another or to visit living people in their homes. On great ceremonial occasions, or if the empire faced challenges or dangers, all the mummies would be assembled in the great squares of Cuzco. People would pay them homage, and the ruling Sapa Inca would formally consult them, asking their advice on affairs of state. Thus the emperors were revered after death as living spirits equal to most of the other gods of the empire.

Below the Sapa Inca, the empire was governed by a two-class nobility, the Inca Caste and the Curacas (*coo-RAH-kahz*). The Inca Caste was composed of blood relatives of the Sapa Inca, usually numbering several hundred people. Curacas were all other governmental officials and their families. Both components of the nobility were exempt from taxes and were supported by produce from government-owned fields tilled by commoners. Sons of the nobility were the only Inca subjects to be educated, in contrast to the Aztec practice of universal education for boys and girls. Since there was no written language, instruction was entirely oral.

Beneath the Sapa Inca and the nobility, all were commoners and all were free; slavery was unheard of in Tahuantin-Suyu. Commoners provided all the labor for public works. Since no money existed and payments in kind were unknown, commoners paid taxes through labor service. This duty furnished recruits for the army, laborers in mines and on public works, and messengers who traveled the remarkable system of imperial roads.

Most commoners were farmers, and Inca agriculture was highly advanced, benefiting from centuries of development by earlier societies in the region, and supported by extensive irrigation. Peasants grew a wide variety of crops, most significantly the potato, which they had developed through selective breeding from a hard, unappetizing nut-like root into one of the world's most nutritious foods. Later, after the Spanish conquest of Peru, the potato was taken to Europe, where it became the staple crop of areas such as Ireland and Poland and was eventually grown almost everywhere.

In the Inca Empire, as in Aztec Mexico, most men spent their days farming, while most women, who played exclusively domestic roles, spent their days doing farm chores, housework, and cooking. Married life was the normal state, and the raising of children was considered woman's sacred task. Sexual intercourse before marriage for both genders was relatively common and not frowned upon, although some women selected for highly favored positions at Inca religious shrines remained virginal for life. These virgins wove the elaborate garments worn by Inca idols, swept and beautified the shrines, and were forbidden to speak to men.

Adaptation to the Andes

The Inca were ingenious in adapting to their physical environment and in keeping the empire connected. The extensive network of roads and bridges that they built made it possible to carry a message from one end of the empire to the other in about 12 days. Since the

Margin notes:

The Sapa Inca exercises enormous power, even after death

Inca nobility dominates a free people

The Inca base their society on agriculture

The Inca connect their empire by a network of roads and bridges

Sapa Inca ruled from the centrally located capital of Cuzco, he rarely had to wait more than six days for the latest news from outlying areas. The roads were smoothly paved with great blocks of stone and lined with retaining walls. Even in the narrowest mountain passes, a dozen men could walk along them side by side. Across the dizzying gorges formed by swiftly flowing Andean rivers, the Inca threw suspension bridges made of thick fibers and secured at each end by stone pylons. In a kind of postal system, a succession of sure-footed runners traveled these roads and bridges. The messages they carried, in the absence of writing, were composed of a series of knots in cords dangling from a piece of wood called a **quipu** (*KĒ-pooh*).

Physically, the Inca had evolved over the years to meet the demands of their harsh environment. To handle the stress caused by the lack of adequate oxygen at high elevations in the Andes, their lung capacity was 40 percent greater than that of sea-level dwellers, with much denser capillary beds. Their bodies also contained 25 percent more blood of very high viscosity, with a far greater number of oxygen-carrying red corpuscles. To handle that sort of load, their hearts were enlarged by 40 percent, and their bodies tended to be short and compact, with low centers of gravity. These characteristics are still found today in the Andean peoples of Ecuador, Peru, and Bolivia.

A Quipu.

Governance and Religion

Politically, Tahuantin-Suyu was the product of centuries of South American cultural development. Before the Inca became the dominant force in Peruvian life, Peru had experienced a long tradition of centralized political control that made possible extensive public works, road-building, and intervalley irrigation systems. Ceramics and metallurgy were mastered, and commercial relations linked the farthest reaches of the Pacific coast. On this foundation the Inca built new concepts of military organization, colonization, and total state control. Their well-trained ruling class possessed the foresight and skill needed to manage so extensive an empire.

The Inca Empire was divided into four provinces (the "four quarters"), each ruled by a governor from the noble Inca Caste. Each significant city was ruled by a lieutenant who reported directly to the provincial governor. Below these leaders were hereditary governing positions filled by Curacas. These local officials, the basic governing personnel of the empire, handled matters such as taxation, public works, minor crimes, complaints, and institutions such as the imperial mass marriage, announced periodically by the Sapa Inca in order to ensure a ready supply of children for the empire. During this ceremony, all single men and women would line up opposite each other, after which the Curaca assigned mates on the basis of physical condition. For obvious reasons, the day before the imperial mass marriage was usually filled with weddings.

The Inca centralize their far-flung empire

Tahuantin-Suyu's division into four provinces somewhat reduced the imperial power of the Sapa Inca. Although this power was theoretically absolute, in practice it was exercised by many governors and local officials. These men were given considerable latitude in the interpretation and execution of imperial commands, provided that their loyalty was beyond dispute. To guarantee that loyalty, the Sapa Inca occasionally sent from Cuzco a special official known as the *Tocoyricoc* (*tō-COY-rē-cōke*), or "he who sees all." This official was actually an informer charged with reporting on the loyalty and competence of the governor and on the general state of affairs within the province. He was

Inca buildings in the former imperial capital of Cuzco. Stones were fit together with such precision that mortar was unnecessary.

usually a close relative of the Sapa Inca, fearless and incorruptible, and the ever-present possibility of his arrival helped keep administrators honest.

Inca religion is polytheistic and tolerant

Inca religion, like Aztec religion, was founded on sun worship. It combined nature worship and magic, all centered on Inti, the sun god. Behind the sun, and indeed behind all things, stood Viracocha, Creator of the Universe; but he was invisible to men and women, while Inti appeared in the heavens every day. The Inca worshiped other deities, too, such as the Storm God. Like the ancient Persians and Romans, they tolerated the gods of those they conquered, insisting only on a place of honor for Inti in all rites and festivals. Such tolerance was essential to the practice of mitima.

These gods were believed to be pleased by sacrifice, usually of food, coca leaves (later to become the base for cocaine), and animals. In serious emergencies, such as drought or earthquake, or on important occasions, a pure white llama or a beautiful child might be killed to win the gods' favor. But the Inca never developed any equivalent of the Aztec Empire's "cosmic mission theory" to justify human sacrifice.

Aztec and Inca on the Eve of Invasion

Aztec and Inca political systems develop similarly to those of Europe

For all their differences, the Aztec and Inca Empires had in common certain institutions that affected their encounters with Europeans. First, authority resided in an emperor whose power was absolute. No assemblies or councils existed to restrict his decisions, and unquestioning obedience to the emperor was demanded. Theoretically, the emperor could respond quickly to emergencies, and at the head of an army of dedicated warriors, he would be difficult to defeat. But if either empire were ever defeated, the stress on unquestioning obedience to leaders would make it easier for the conqueror to rule. Unconditional obedience was readily transferable from one set of masters to another.

Second, in considering the clash of civilizations that began with the European invasions, the youth and isolation of the Aztec and Inca Empires proved to be disadvantages. The invaders came from societies whose extensive intercultural contacts had furnished them with methods, technologies, animals, and immunities unknown in the Americas. It was not a fair contest. The early American civilizations, remarkably rich in their cultural development in comparison with other cultures in the hemisphere, were about to meet their match. No one can say how the Aztec and Inca societies, so highly developed in comparison with other cultures in the western hemisphere, might have evolved had Europeans never arrived.

The Invasion and Conquest of Mexico

Montezuma II (1502–1520), emperor when the Spanish arrived, was the first priest to rule the Aztec Empire. Thirty-four when elected, he was a valiant warrior as well as a pious man. He was fascinated by magic and omens, or signs about the future, and by 1519 had come to prefer contemplation and diplomacy to action. These priestly tendencies did not, however, make him gentle: he terrified both his court and the general public and was the most feared ruler in the history of Tenochtitlán. His commitment to consolidating his empire rather than continuing to expand it was based not in weakness but in realistic calculation.

Unlike the Inca, the Aztecs had never attempted to integrate conquered peoples into their culture. Their empire was held together by coercion and fear, not by any form of assimilation that might have developed loyalty in the defeated. Therefore it was not surprising that during the reign of Montezuma II two inferior but significant regional powers challenged the supremacy of Tenochtitlán. In the west, the Tarascan (*tah-RAHS-cahn*) Empire united several ethnic groups hostile to Aztec expansion into a small but heavily fortified realm defended by skilled archers. In the east, the **Tlaxcallan** (*tlash-CAHL-lahn*) **Confederacy** knitted together several city-states that spoke Nahuatl (*na-WHA-tl*), the language spoken by the Aztecs and some of their neighbors, into a potent alliance that could have badly injured the Aztec Empire in an all-out war. Cautiously, Montezuma II encircled both sets of enemies as part of a long-range strategy that would yield results in decades rather than years. By 1519 the Aztecs had made substantial progress on both fronts, despite a persistent series of omens that worried their ruling elite and left the emperor perplexed.

The Aztecs base their rule on coercion

The Arrival of the Spaniards

In 1517 disturbing events took place in Mayan territory well to the East of Tenochtitlán. Bearded men with white skin, riding in what appeared to be mountains floating on the sea, began to come ashore on the Yucatan peninsula. More such events took place the following year, accompanied by omens in Tenochtitlán itself. A comet streaked across the sky at midday, temples burned for no apparent reason, and an invisible wailing woman cried out every night. These events were mysterious and unsettling to a people accustomed to searching for messages from the gods. As the Aztecs eventually learned, the strangers in floating mountains were Spaniards in sailing ships following those who had first come to the Caribbean 25 years before, looking for a sea route from Europe to Asia.

Aztecs are perplexed by the arrival of the Spaniards

The Spaniards who came in 1517, however, were no longer looking for Asia; instead they were inspired by tales of gold and glory to be found in Mexico itself. Their leader, Hernán Cortés, was an ambitious Spanish lawyer who left Spain to seek his fortune in the Caribbean. Fifteen years later, in 1519, Cortés accepted a commission from the governor of Cuba to lead an expedition to Mexico to determine the location and strength of a large and reportedly fabulously wealthy empire. He sailed for Mexico with 550 men, including a number of Africans and Cuban Amerinds, and 16 horses.

In the early spring of 1519, as Cortés was arriving in Mexico, the reports reaching Montezuma became more precise and factual. From the Gulf of Mexico, peasants reported sighting white men catching fish with nets and rods. Montezuma and his advisors decided to have the coast and the strangers watched; in the meantime, their arrival was kept secret from the people.

In the summer of 1519, news arrived that the strangers were moving inland. Aztec officials met them and spoke with them through a 15-year-old Mayan girl whom the Spaniards had baptized Marina and who spoke both Nahuatl and Spanish. The Spaniards rode on huge animals and carried and dragged long-barreled sticks that could be made to explode, discharging fire and noise. At this point the ruling elite began to consider the possibility that these people, or at least their leaders, might be gods.

Aztec legend stated that Toltec god-king Quetzalcóatl (*kwet-zahl-KŌ-ah-tul*), expelled from Tula (Chapter 5), had vowed to return one day from his eastern exile and

Dona Marina and Cortes.

The legend of
Quetzalcóatl affects
the Aztec view of the
Spaniards

reclaim Mexico for himself. He and his forces would appear in boats in the guise of light-skinned men. Given the apparently supernatural capabilities of these strangers' boats, animals, and weapons, the possibility that Quetzalcóatl was returning could not be ruled out. Even if they were mere mortals, their arrival could not be prevented: their boats could land anywhere without warning, and their weapons seemed deadly. Under such unprecedented circumstances, watchful waiting seemed the only sensible course.

The Spaniards insisted on meeting with Montezuma. In response, the emperor sent them more than a hundred porters carrying luxurious gifts normally sacrificed to gods. Included with these presents was Montezuma's order that the Spaniards remain in the East and advance no farther inland. The Aztec emperor was trying either to gain favor with a vengeful god or to deal with powerful invaders in a way that would ensure the survival of Aztec power. In either case, the empire was clearly in danger.

Spaniards exploit Aztec
perplexity

Cortés knew nothing of the legend of Quetzalcóatl, but, upon listening to Marina's translations and advice, he realized that Montezuma considered him some sort of god and feared him. He also interpreted the emperor's gifts as an offer of vassalage and therefore a sign of weakness. In Europe, vassalage involved an oath of personal loyalty that gave the lord contractual rights over the actions of the vassal. In Mesoamerica, however, vassalage involved the payment of tribute in return for being left alone. This was a very significant distinction. By interpreting Montezuma's actions in a European context, Cortés seriously underestimated the power of the empire he would encounter. He ignored Montezuma's instructions, accepted the gifts, and pressed on.

Encounter Between Aztecs and Spaniards

Cortés moved his forces west and concluded alliances with peoples such as the Totonacs (tō-TŌ-nacks) and Tlaxcaltecs (tlocks-CAHL-tecks), who paid tribute to the Aztec Empire. These Amerinds believed Cortés' promises of liberation from Aztec dominance and sent thousands of warriors to accompany the Spaniards inland. In Tenochtitlán, warriors were still engaged in the harvest; otherwise Montezuma would have had hundreds of thousands of warriors ready to defend the empire. Instead, Montezuma arranged for the Spaniards to be escorted into the city, where, without their allies, they would be far more vulnerable.

A 1524 map of
Tenochtitlan.

Tenochtitlán's size
intimidates the
Spaniards

Nothing had prepared the Spaniards for what they saw on November 8. The road to Tenochtitlán was straight, 11,500 feet above sea level, flanked by two immense active volcanoes; the altitude, solitude, and strangeness of it all began to unnerve the Spaniards. But even this impression paled when compared to the sight of the city itself. Not only was it spectacularly beautiful, it was colossal, with at least 80,000 inhabitants, the capital of an empire of more than a million people. Cortés suddenly realized the magnitude of his miscalculation. He had dismissed as exaggerations Amerind stories of the size and glory of Tenochtitlán, interpreting them in the contexts of his familiarity with Europe and of the modest size of the Mexican towns he had encountered thus far. Now he stood before an Amerind metropolis significantly larger than anything he had ever imagined, at the head of an army of a few hundred men. The success of his mission and the lives of his men hung by threads (see "Entry of the Spaniards into Tenochtitlán, November 8, 1519").

Document 18.1 Entry of the Spaniards into Tenochtitlán, November 8, 1519

Bernal Díaz del Castillo, one of the men who accompanied Cortés to Mexico, wrote an eyewitness account of that expedition fifty years after it occurred. Here he describes what the Spaniards saw and felt as they entered Tenochtitlán, which he refers to as "Mexico" or "the city of Mexico."

Early next day we left Itzapalapa with a large escort . . . and followed the causeway, which is eight yards wide and goes so straight to the city of Mexico that I do not think it curves at all. Wide though it was, it was so crowded with people that there was hardly room for them all . . . and we could hardly get through the crowds that were there. For the towers and the passages were full, and they came in canoes from all parts of the lake. No wonder, since they had never seen horses or men like us before!

With such wonderful sights to gaze on we did not know what to say, or if this were real that we saw before our eyes. On the land side there were great cities, and on the lake many more. The lake was crowded with canoes. At intervals along the causeway there were many bridges, and before us was the great city of Mexico. As for us, we were scarcely four hundred strong, and we well remembered the . . . many other warnings we had received to beware of entering the city of Mexico, since they would kill us as soon as they had us inside. Let the interested reader consider whether there is not much to ponder in this narrative of mine. What men in all the world have shown such daring? . . .

When we came near to Mexico, at a place where there were some other small towers, the great Montezuma descended from his litter . . . many more lords walked before the great Montezuma, sweeping the ground on which he was to tread, and laying down cloaks so that his feet should not touch the earth. Not one of these chieftains dared to look him in the face. All kept their eyes lowered most reverently . . . And as they accompanied their lord we observed them marching with their eyes downcast so that they should not see him, and keeping close to the wall as they followed him with great reverence. Thus space was made for us to enter the streets of Mexico without being pressed by the crowd.

Who now could count the multitude of men, women, and boys in the streets, on the roof-tops and in canoes on the waterways, who had come out to see us? It was a wonderful sight and, as I write, it all comes before my eyes as if it had happened only yesterday . . .

So, with luck on our side, we boldly entered the city of Tenochtitlán or Mexico on 8 November in the year of our Lord 1519.

SOURCE: Bernal Díaz del Castillo, *The Conquest of New Spain*, translated by J. M. Cohen (London: Penguin Publishers, 1963) 216–219.

Operating in Cortés' favor, however, was Montezuma's behavior. Meeting the Spaniards face to face should have convinced the emperor that they were men, not gods. But even after they entered the capital, in the narrow streets where they could have been trapped, the emperor publicly embraced Cortés and continued to lavish gifts upon him. In the next months, the Aztec military elite pressed for the destruction of the strangers, but Montezuma's subservience prevented any such action. Cortés recognized that he held the advantage, and he soon placed the emperor under a form of house arrest in his own palace.

Montezuma's acceptance of this treatment remains inadequately explained. Some historians assert that he continued to believe that Cortés was divine, but the Spaniards did not behave like servants of a Mexica god. They were horrified at the practice of human sacrifice, especially the Aztec custom of presenting their guests with delicious food liberally sprinkled with human blood. They smashed images of Aztec gods and generally behaved in a manner indicating their complete disgust with Mexican culture. This was a strange way for gods to behave. Other historians speculate that Montezuma may have been clinging to whatever measure of power he could still exercise while hoping that events would turn out in his favor. Had he refused to cooperate with the Spaniards, he would have been taken by force, the imperial elite would have split among potential successors, and the Aztec empire would be leaderless in its hour of maximum danger. This explanation is more likely than that he still considered Cortés to be Quetzalcóatl.

The Aztecs finally fight the Spaniards

But if Montezuma hoped to preserve his authority by cooperating with the Spaniards, he was soon disappointed. His subservience to Cortés eroded his support among both the elite and the common people. It vanished completely in May 1520, when the Aztecs took the offensive at last. They surrounded the Spaniards in central Tenochtitlán, and Cortés proved unable to negotiate his way out of the city. Cortés then ordered Montezuma to direct the Aztecs to stop fighting. Cortés did not understand that the emperor ruled *with*, not *over*, the nobility that was now attacking the Spaniards, and could not simply tell his nobles what to do. Montezuma tried anyway but was killed as he attempted to address Aztec forces from the roof of a palace, apparently by a rock thrown by one of his own people.

The End of the Aztec Empire

Denied food and water, under assault from every side, the Spaniards eventually broke out of Tenochtitlán at midnight on June 30, 1520, during a heavy downpour. Some were killed by Aztecs attacking from canoes, but Cortés escaped with most of his men. The Spaniards fought their way through the neighboring hostile regions to Tlaxcaltec lands, which gave them refuge and an opportunity to regroup.

Smallpox cripples the Aztecs

Aztec forces did not launch a full-scale attack against the retreating invaders, in part because their armies were not at full strength due to agricultural duties, but primarily because of political instability. During the fighting in Tenochtitlán, the imperial elite replaced Montezuma with his younger brother Cuitlahuac (*quit-LAH-wock*), who had argued from the first that the invaders must be killed. But within three months Cuitlahuac was dead of smallpox. An infected Spanish soldier carried the disease, and because the peoples of the western hemisphere had never been exposed to European diseases and had no immunity to them, this smallpox outbreak killed more than a third of the population of central Mexico in less than a year.

Smallpox is a disease that kills through high fever, dehydration, and debilitation. The dying suffer terribly, and the survivors often are disfigured by scarring from pustules. The Aztecs concluded that this unknown plague was either a sign of the wrath of their gods or a punishment sent by the gods of the Spaniards. Certainly, since the strangers did not suffer from the disease (having survived it in childhood, they had immunity), their gods were protecting them. In any case, to the Aztecs the epidemic clearly demonstrated Spanish superiority. It also, of course, killed many warriors and made others unfit for battle.

The Aztecs find a strong leader in Cuauhtemoc

In February 1521, however, Cuauhtemoc (*kwow-TĀ-mock*), the son of a former emperor, succeeded Cuitlahuac and rallied his forces to attack the Spaniards. The Aztecs fought in closely packed ranks, using archery, spears, and swords with edges of polished

Document 18.2 Two Elegies on the Fall of the City of Tenochtitlán

Immediately after the fall of Tenochtitlán to the Spaniards, the surviving Aztecs reacted with shock and grief. Both emotions are vividly captured in these excerpts from two elegies, or memorial poems, written by survivors.

FIRST ELEGY

Broken spears lie in the road;
we have torn our hair in our grief.
The houses are roofless now, and their walls
are red with blood.

Worms are swarming in the streets and plazas,
and the walls are splattered with gore.
The water has turned red, as if it were dyed,
and when we drink it,
it has the taste of brine.

We have pounded our hands in despair
against the adobe walls,
for our inheritance, our city, is lost and dead.
The shields of our warriors were its defense,
but they could not save it.

SECOND ELEGY

Our cries of grief rise up
and our tears rain down,
for Tlatelolco [*tlah-tā-LAHL-kō*, a city adjacent to
Tenochtitlán] is lost.
The Aztecs are fleeing across the lake;
they are running away like women.

How can we save our homes, my people?
The Aztecs are deserting the city:
the city is in flames, and all
is darkness and destruction.

Weep, my people:
know that with these disasters
we have lost the Mexican nation.
The water has turned bitter,
our food is bitter!
These are the acts of the Giver of Life.

SOURCE: Miguel Leon-Portilla, editor, *The Broken Spears: The Aztec Account of the Conquest of Mexico,* translated from Nahuatl into Spanish by Angel Maria Garibay K., and from Spanish into English by Lysander Kemp (Boston: Beacon Press, Little, Brown, 1962).

obsidian. The Spaniards countered with cannon, muskets, and swords fashioned from Toledo steel. Their metal armor was much more protective than Aztec armor made of cotton, and their horses terrified Aztec foot soldiers.

Spanish firearms killed 25 Aztecs for every one Spaniard killed by the Aztecs, but with more than one hundred thousand warriors in his armies, Cuauhtemoc's forces could sustain such losses. The Aztecs won a number of engagements and sacrificed captured Spaniards, but in late July Cortés received reinforcements from Cuba. The Aztecs' desperate subjects, now believing that the Spaniards would win, flocked to their ranks by the tens of thousands.

Cuauhtemoc requested peace talks in early August, seeking to learn how much tribute the Spaniards would demand as the price of surrender. But it quickly became apparent that Cortés was interested only in total victory, not in turning the Aztecs into vassals of the Spanish Empire. Trapped in the midst of the lake, the Aztecs fought to the end. They finally surrendered the ruins of Tenochtitlán on August 13, 1521. The Spanish invaders took possession of the city and buried the dead. The most powerful empire in the history of Mesoamerica had been destroyed (see "Two Elegies on the Fall of the City of Tenochtitlán").

Spanish firepower.

Reasons for the Spanish Victory

Several factors account for Spain's victory

Spain's victory in this epic confrontation of European and Mesoamerican civilizations can be explained by a number of factors. First, the Toltec legend of Quetzalcóatl distracted and confused the Aztecs before Cortés entered Tenochtitlán. Second, the Spaniards arrived in early November, when many warriors, who might have been able to hold off the invaders, were busy with the harvest. Moreover, Spanish military technology was clearly superior and, together with European tactical insights, gave the invaders a significant, although not decisive, advantage. Smallpox proved even more significant. This contagious disease weakened the Aztec population and nearly eliminated its elite, but had no effect on the Spaniards. As it also killed most of the political elite of the Spaniards' native allies, it gave Cortés the opportunity to name loyal commanders in their place. Cortés' leadership tactics were also important, especially compared to the indecisiveness of Montezuma. And although each side misinterpreted the actions and motives of the other, Aztec misinterpretations proved the more serious and weakened their resistance.

All of these factors gave the advantage to the Spaniards. Overriding them all, however, was the Aztec policy of enslaving, persecuting, and sacrificing the people it conquered. Had the Aztecs assimilated those they defeated and sought to gain their loyalty, Cortés would never have been able to enlist more than one hundred thousand Amerind warriors as his allies, and without them he could not have conquered the Aztec Empire.

Smallpox victims.

The Invasion and Conquest of Peru

The collapse of the Aztec Empire, a momentous event in Mexico, went unnoticed in Peru. The Inca, unaware of Mesoamerican civilizations, would have been more surprised by news of the existence of the Aztecs than by their defeat.

Upheavals Among the Inca

Europeans begin to encounter the Inca Empire

Huayna Capac, who became Sapa Inca in 1493, at first concentrated on consolidating his empire. Then in the early 1520s he began to extend Inca control into northern Ecuador. While fighting there, he received word that a raiding party of Amerinds had crossed into present-day Bolivia in search of tools and jewelry. Huayna Capac sent a detachment of soldiers to drive the raiders back into what is now northern Argentina and fortify the frontier. He did not know that their war leader was a Portuguese adventurer named Aleixo (*ah-LĀ-shō*) García. Had he known, he would not have understood what the arrival of Europeans signified.

The Sapa Inca continued his campaign in Ecuador. Several months later, in 1526, he received terrifying news: an unknown plague was sweeping through Cuzco, killing the strong and weak alike. By forced marches he returned to his capital and soon fell ill himself. The plague, the symptoms of which suggest smallpox, may have been introduced into Tahuantin-Suyu by merchants from Colombia, who had been exposed to Europeans, or by soldiers fighting the raiders from Argentina, who had taken in Europeans like García. Whatever its source, it killed the Sapa Inca and threw his entire empire into disarray.

Before he died, Huayna Capac had time to consider two matters of supreme importance. First was a series of disturbing reports from the coast. Bearded men were floating southward on the waves, riding in a house of gleaming white. Huayna Capac believed that these visitors, together with the unexplained plague, foretold great trouble for the empire. Second, he changed his mind about which son should succeed him. His principal wife being childless, he had originally designated Huascar (*WHASS-car*), a son by one of his other wives, as his successor. But when the fever came upon him, Huayna Capac selected another son, Ninan Cuyochi (*NĒ-nahn coo-YŌ-chē*). The Sapa Inca soon died, and a few days later Ninan Cuyochi died as well. Huascar now claimed the throne, but the fact that his dying father had passed him over emboldened yet another brother, Atahuallpa (*ah-tah-WHALL-pah*), to contest his right to rule. Huascar seized power in Cuzco, while Atahuallpa did the same in Quito, the empire's second largest city. Tahuantin-Suyu descended into civil war.

Smallpox throws the Inca Empire into disarray

Huascar was tactless, willful, and immature, and he alienated so many in Cuzco that the empire's capital gradually lost the will to defend him. Atahuallpa, by contrast, earned the allegiance of the two foremost war chiefs of the realm and conducted himself in battle with dignity and courage. The rugged terrain ensured a long, difficult struggle, but when conflict ended early in 1532 the empire was in the hands of Atahuallpa. One year earlier he had first learned of an actual landing by the Spaniards, who followed the orders of a man named Francisco Pizarro (*pē-ZAH-rō*). Pizarro, a Spanish adventurer, had set sail from Panama in 1531 with about 180 men to conquer what they had heard was a rich land to the South.

Atahuallpa wins the civil war and becomes Sapa Inca

Encounter Between Inca and Spaniards

When Pizarro's forces reached the Inca city of Tumbez, they seized it and learned at once that the Inca Empire had been torn by civil war for four years. The Spaniards, unlike the Inca, understood clearly what smallpox was and knew that they had little to fear from it. They also understood that a physically weakened population distracted by internal turmoil was exactly what Cortés had encountered and conquered in Mexico in 1521.

Spaniards understand the usefulness of smallpox in conquering Amerinds

Atahuallpa reacted to the seizure of Tumbez with a mixture of caution and interest. He concluded, incorrectly, that the newcomers were interested in taking sides in the civil war; if so, they might be worth meeting. After he captured Huascar and ended the civil war, he sought information concerning the invaders.

Unlike the Aztecs, the Inca had no Quetzalcóatl legend to distract them, and the fact that several Spaniards had been killed at Tumbez indicated that they were not gods but humans. The Sapa Inca sent an envoy to assess the situation. This man reported that Pizarro had landed with a very small number of men, that his horses were nothing more than large dogs, that his soldiers lacked fighting spirit, and that he himself could defeat them with two hundred warriors. Now feeling that he could easily rid his domain of these outsiders, Atahuallpa sent them several virgins, escorted by a war chief who promised them silver and gold if they agreed to return home.

Atahuallpa underestimates the Spaniards

In the eyes of the Inca, Pizarro reacted strangely. He accepted the women but declined to leave, marching inland instead. At Tumbez he had killed the governor and other high officials, replacing them with Inca who swore loyalty to him. Yet he continually sent messages to Atahuallpa acknowledging the latter's rights as ruler of

Map 18.3 Pizarro's Third Expedition to Peru, 1531–1533

Pizarro did not simply invade the Inca Empire without familiariz-ing himself with the terrain and its inhabitants. He was well aware of the imposing size of the empire and the challenging terrain his soldiers would have to cross. Observe that the length of his route was nearly fifteen hundred miles, forcing him to expose his forces to the possibility of hostile assault over a distance four times the width of the Iberian Peninsula, where he was born. His third expedition placed his forces unexpectedly in the midst of an Inca civil war. How did Pizarro use that conflict to disrupt the Inca Empire?

Tahuantin-Suyu. The Sapa Inca sent word to Pizarro of his recent victory over Huascar and pointed out that the visitors were far from home in a foreign and hostile land. Still the Spaniards con-tinued inland by a route leading to the provincial city of Cajamarca (*kah-yah-MAR-kah*), populated by several thousand Inca and guarded by a large fortress. Pizarro hoped to capture or kill the Sapa Inca and take over the Inca Empire without engag-ing in a long military campaign like the one Cortés had waged against the Aztecs.

Cajamarca and the End of the Inca Empire

Atahuallpa's attitude and tone differed substan-tially from Montezuma's approach to Cortés in Mexico. However, the Sapa Inca was no less con-fused about the Spaniards' intentions than Mon-tezuma had been, and he held a much lower estimation of their military potential. Still, the Spaniards might be useful as allies in pacifying the areas previously held by Huascar, and their recognition of his authority suggested that they could become his vassals and eventually be assim-ilated into the empire through mitima. In any event, they could not be allowed to march around the countryside unsupervised. Atahuallpa re-solved to go to Cajamarca (Map 18.3) and see them for himself.

Atahuallpa arrived ahead of the Spaniards, residing at a compound built around warm springs a short distance from the city. On November 15, 1532, the Spanish entered Cajamarca. The Sapa Inca and his courtly entourage entered the city the following afternoon, as two thousand Inca swept the road before him. Carried on a litter, he was greeted by a single black-robed Spanish priest, who directed him to submit to two men called Jesus Christ and the King of Spain. Declaring that there was only one god in the heavens and that all Inca idols were to be destroyed, the priest presented Atahuallpa with a small black book of Christian devotions. The emperor examined it curiously, but since no one in a culture lacking writing could interpret the symbols on its pages (or even realize that they were intended to be read), he assumed the book was a flimsy idol and threw it on the ground. The priest then retrieved it and fled toward one of the houses surrounding the square, calling out in Spanish.

Document 18.3 An Inca Account of the Conquest of Peru

Diego de Castro Titu Cusi Yupanqui, the son of Manco Inca and the nephew of Atahuallpa, was born in 1530, two years before Pizarro's victory over Atahuallpa at Cajamarca. Titu Cusi became Sapa Inca of the unsubdued state of Vilcabamba in 1560. In 1570, he dictated to a Spanish missionary this account of the conquest.

At the time when the Spaniards first landed in this country of Peru and when they arrived at the city of Cajamarca, my father Manco Inca was residing in the city of Cuzco. There he governed with all the powers that had been bestowed upon him by his father Huayna Capac. He first learned of the Spaniards' arrival from certain messengers who had been sent from there by one of his brothers by the name of Atahuallpa, who was older but a bastard . . . They reported having observed that certain people had arrived in their land, people who were very different from us in custom and dress, and that they appeared to be Viracochas (this is the name that we used to apply to the Creator of All Things). They named the people as such because they differed very much from us in clothing and appearance and because they rode very large sheep with silver feet (by which they meant horseshoes). Another reason for calling them so was that the Indians saw them alone talking to white cloths as one person would speak to another, which is how they perceived the reading of books and letters . . .

When my uncle [Atahuallpa] was approaching Cajamarca with all of his people, the Spaniards met them at the springs of Conoc, one and a half leagues from Cajamarca . . . After having heard what they had to say, my uncle attended to them and calmly offered one of them our customary drink in a golden cup, but the Spaniard poured it out with his own hands, which offended my uncle very much. Having seen how little they minded his things, my uncle said, "If you disrespect me, I will also disrespect you." He got up angrily and raised a cry as though he wanted to kill the Spaniards. However, the Spaniards were on the lookout and took possession of the four gates of the plaza where they were, which was enclosed on all its sides.

The Indians were thus penned up like sheep in this enclosed plaza, unable to move because there were so many of them. Also, they had no weapons as they had not brought any, being so little concerned about the Spaniards . . . The Spaniards stormed with great fury to the center of the plaza, where the Sapa Inca's seat was placed on an elevated platform . . . After they had taken everything from him, they apprehended him, and because the Indians uttered loud cries, they started killing them with the horses, the swords or guns, like one kills sheep, without anyone being able to resist them. Of more than ten thousand not even two hundred escaped . . .

SOURCE: Titu Cusi Yupanqui, *An Inca Account of the Conquest of Peru*, translated by Ralph Bauer (Boulder: University Press of Colorado, 2005).

Atahuallpa instructed his entourage to punish the Spaniards. But just then musket fire burst forth from the houses, and great numbers of Spaniards, some on horses but most on foot, poured into the square. The perplexed Inca elite stood transfixed until the Spaniards fell upon them with swords and began cutting off their arms and heads. Then the panicked survivors tried to escape, but the Spaniards killed freely, as none of the Inca in the imperial entourage were armed. After the Inca guarding his litter were killed to the last man, Atahuallpa was taken prisoner. Learning what was happening in Cajamarca, the thousands of armed Inca warriors outside the city, who could certainly have intervened, fled in terror (see "An Inca Account of the Conquest of Peru").

The Spaniards attack the Inca at Cajamarca

Pizarro deceives
Atahuallpa

Having learned from his envoys that the Spaniards lusted for gold and silver, Atahuallpa offered at once to pay a huge ransom for his freedom. Pizarro demanded that two large rooms be completely filled with precious objects, one room with silver and the other with gold. He was soon presented with an amazing treasure: 26,000 pounds of pure silver and 13,420 pounds of 22-carat gold. To make this plunder portable, the Spaniards melted down priceless Inca artworks of great beauty and value, turning them into bars of gold and silver. But Atahuallpa had erred in assuming that he could trust Pizarro. Once the ransom was paid, the Sapa Inca was tried on charges of raising armies to overthrow Spanish rule, murdering his brother Huascar, and marrying his own sister. He was strangled in 1533.

In deciding to kill the Sapa Inca, Pizarro had reasoned treacherously but well. The Inca Caste, after so many years of infighting, was profoundly divided. Civil war, smallpox, and the Cajamarca ambush had killed most of the experienced leaders of the empire. By 1535 the conquest was complete. The Inca Empire had offered no significant resistance.

Reasons for the Spanish Victory

Spain's victory in this confrontation with this greatest of all Amerind empires can be explained by a number of factors. First, the demonstrated success of Spanish weaponry and tactics in Mexico, coupled with Inca ignorance of what had taken place there, gave Spain a decisive advantage at Cajamarca in 1532. As in Mexico, smallpox proved advantageous, killing the Sapa Inca in 1527 and touching off a civil war over the succession that Pizarro interpreted accurately and exploited skillfully. Third, Atahuallpa underestimated the Spanish, especially following the mistaken reports of his envoy. Then, after Cajamarca, the Inca practice of mitima worked to Spain's advantage, as the Inca, assuming the Spaniards would assimilate them as equals, did not resist. Most significant, perhaps, was Pizarro's deception. Pizarro led Atahuallpa to believe he would be freed upon payment of a huge ransom, and so the Sapa Inca did not order his massive armies to attack the invaders. When the extent of this deception became obvious, the Spaniards had been heavily reinforced.

In Peru as in Mexico, Spanish greed for gold and silver led bold men to take risks that, in retrospect, seem incredibly dangerous. But the invaders capitalized on every advantage that came their way, destroying the two greatest Amerind empires in the western hemisphere. On the ruins of those empires, other Spaniards would build a European empire of their own.

Chapter Review

Putting It in Perspective

The civilizations built by the Aztecs and Inca developed in distinctive environments, totally isolated from each other and from the eastern hemisphere. Both were based on political hierarchies headed by emperors and dominated by warrior elites, settled economies balanced between agriculture and trade, and polytheistic religions. These two civilizations created large cities, extensive transportation networks, and intricate social structures. Neither had yet completed its second century of existence when the Spaniards arrived.

Aztec Mexico was clearly the more coercive of the two. Raising human sacrifice to the level of a divine obligation and conducting it with mechanistic efficiency, Tenochtitlán terrified all those who lived in central Mexico. Disdainful of other Amerind cultures, the Aztecs sought not to govern them but to dominate and exploit them. Many of their vassals welcomed the prospect of Spanish rule. The possibility that the Spanish could be more oppressive than the Aztecs seems not to have occurred to the elites of central Mexico.

Tahuantin-Suyu was no less ruthless in its expansion than Tenochtitlán, but it developed into a militaristic empire that aimed to gain the loyalty of conquered peoples rather than slaughter them. The Inca practice of mitima gave subject peoples a stake in the empire. Human sacrifice, while not unknown, was practiced primarily during emergencies or on important occasions.

When Atahuallpa was captured at Cajamarca, the Spaniards found it easy to rule the general population of the empire. Most Inca appear to have believed that the newcomers would integrate all peoples into their new empire with some degree of equality. Like the Aztecs, however, the Inca interpreted new experiences in terms of old customs and were mistaken regarding the conquerors' intentions. They faced a situation completely unlike anything they had ever imagined: conquest by aliens from another world.

Reviewing Key Material

KEY CONCEPTS

chinampa, 436
cosmic mission theory, 437
Tahuantin-Suyu, 440
mitima, 441

Sapa Inca, 441
quipu, 443
Tlaxcallan Confederacy, 445

KEY PEOPLE

Montezuma I, 436
Viracocha Inca, 440
Pachacuti, 440
Topa Inca Yupanqui, 441
Huayna Capac, 441
Montezuma II, 444

Hernán Cortés, 445
Cuitlahuac, 448
Cuauhtemoc, 448
Huascar, 451
Atahuallpa, 451
Francisco Pizarro, 451

ASK YOURSELF

1. How did the cosmic mission theory shape Aztec society?
2. How did the Inca and Aztec empires differ in their attitudes toward conquered peoples?
3. In the encounters between Europeans and Amerinds, what difference did it make that Amerind civilizations had developed more recently than European civilization?
4. How did Aztec and Inca ignorance of the existence of European civilization handicap them in responding to European invasion?

GOING FURTHER

Bankes, G. *Peru Before Pizarro.* 1977.
Berdan, Francis. *The Aztecs.* 1989.
Cameron, Ian. *Kingdom of the Sun God.* 1990.
Canseco, Maria. *History of the Inca Realm.* 1999.
Caso, Alfonso. *The Aztecs: People of the Sun.* 1988.
Clendinnen, Inga. *Aztecs.* 1991.
Conrad, Geoffrey, and Arthur Demarest. *Religion and Empire: The Dynamics of Aztec and Inca Expansionism.* 1984.
Davies, Nigel. *The Aztecs.* 1989.
Day, Jane. *Aztec: The World of Montezuma.* 1992.
Disselhoff, Hans. *Daily Life in Ancient Peru.* 1967.
Fagan, B. *The Aztecs.* 1984.
Gillespie, S. *The Aztec Kings.* 1989.

Haas, Jonathon, et al. *The Origin and Development of the Andean State.* 1987.

Hassig, Ross. *Aztec Warfare: Imperial Expansion and Political Control.* 1988.

Henning, E., and J. Raney. *Monuments of the Inca.* 1982.

Leon-Portilla, Miguel. *The Aztec Image of Self and Society.* 1992.

Lockhart, J. *We People Here: Nahuatl Accounts of the Conquest of Mexico.* 1993.

Mason, J. Alden. *Ancient Civilizations of Peru.* 1988.

McIntyre, Loren. *The Incredible Inca and Their Timeless Land.* 1978.

Metraux, Alfred. *The History of the Incas.* 1970.

Murra, John. *The Economic Organization of the Inca State.* 1980.

Padden, R. C. *The Hummingbird and the Hawk.* 1967.

Silverblatt, Irene. *Moon, Sun, and Witches: Gender Ideologies and Class in Inca and Colonial Peru.* 1987.

Soustelle, Jacques. *Daily Life of the Aztecs on the Eve of the Spanish Conquest.* 1955.

Sullivan, W. *The Secret of the Incas: Myth, Astronomy, and the War Against Time.* 1996.

Townshend, Richard. *The Aztecs.* 1992.

van Zantwijk, Rudolf. *The Aztec Arrangement: The Social History of Pre-Spanish Mexico.* 1985.

Key Dates and Developments

ca. 1111	The Aztecs move into central Mexico
ca. 1200	Inca ascendancy begins in the central Andes
1325	Foundation of Tenochtitlán
1400–1438	Inca expansion under Viracocha Inca
1438–1471	Pachacuti founds Tahuantin-Suyu
1440	Aztecs dominate the Valley of Mexico
1471–1493	Topa Inca expands the Inca Empire
1502–1520	Reign of Montezuma II
1519	Cortés leads an expedition from Cuba to Mexico
1521	Fall of Tenochtitlán
1527	Death of Huayna Capac; civil war in Tahuantin-Suyu
1531	Pizarro leads an expedition from Panama to Peru
1532	Capture of Atahuallpa at Cajamarca

Global Exploration and Global Empires, 1400–1700

Portuguese Claims
In Africa And Brazil

A sixteenth-century map shows Portugese claims in Africa and Brazil. Few would have predicted that tiny Portugal would lead the way in European exploration of the globe (see page 459).

- The Iberian Impulse
- The Portuguese Seaborne Empire
- The Spanish and Portuguese Empires in America
- Amerinds and Europeans in North America
- The Columbian Exchange
- Chapter Review

Morning dawned foggy and damp, but by 8 AM the Portuguese sun was burning off the mist. Already merchants, artisans, vendors, and shoppers were moving toward the docks in Lisbon. It was a typical day in early September 1600, and a fleet had arrived the previous evening from the Indian Ocean. Now its ships were being unloaded and the docks stacked with exotic plants, animals, minerals, and manufactures. Those who arrived early would have first pick from the cargoes.

Cramming the docks of Lisbon was a staggering variety of commodities from four continents. From Europe itself came wheat, wool, brassware, glass, weapons, tapestries, and clocks. North Africa provided dates, honey, barley, and indigo, as well as ornate metalwork. West Africa contributed gold, ivory, musk, parrots, and slaves. East Africa sent ebony, coral, salt, and hemp. Arriving from India were calico, pepper, ginger, coconut oil, cinnamon, cloves, and nutmeg. Southeast Asia furnished sandalwood, resins, camphor, and saffron. From Macao came porcelains, silks, and medicinal herbs. Finally, Brazil supplied sugar, brazilwood, and monkeys from the Amazon. Lisbon in 1600 was the commercial focus of Europe, a cosmopolitan connector of products and peoples from throughout the world.

Lisbon's prosperity was a relatively recent development. Prior to 1453, world trade focused on the Mediterranean, where Italian city-states like Venice and Genoa competed with Muslim merchants for cargoes and profits. But Mehmed the Conqueror's dramatic victory at Constantinople, which at first appeared to expand Islamic wealth and power significantly, actually weakened existing Muslim trade networks. By stimulating Europeans to seek overseas routes to the Indies and the Spice Islands, the fall of Constantinople reoriented European trade in a westward direction, to the eventual benefit of the eager buyers who swarmed over the Lisbon docks in 1600.

The Portuguese Empire

The Spanish Empire

The Iberian Impulse

The Iberian interest in sea voyages is largely anti-Muslim

Portugal was an unlikely location for a commercial nexus. The Iberian peninsula, home to Spain and Portugal, sits at the far southwestern edge of the Eurasian landmass, separated from the rest of Europe by the Pyrenees mountains. From the eighth through twelfth centuries most of Iberia was linked to the Islamic world by Muslim rule. By the mid-1200s, however, fired by an anti-Muslim crusade called the *Reconquista*, the Christian kingdoms of the North had retaken most of the region. In 1479 the two main Spanish kingdoms, Aragon and Castile, were linked by the marriage and joint rule of their respective monarchs, Ferdinand and Isabella, laying the basis for a united Spain. By 1492, when they finally expelled the Muslims from Granada in the South, this couple ruled most of Iberia— except for the kingdom of Portugal along the Atlantic coast.

By this time both Spain and Portugal, far from Europe's centers of commerce and wealth, were embarking on great sea voyages that would soon enlarge European ideas about the geography of the globe. Determined to bypass the Muslims, who controlled the land links and profitable trade with East Asia, both Iberians and Italian city-states searched for an all-water route to India, the Spice Islands, and China, regions that Europeans called collectively the East Indies. The Portuguese, who had been exploring southward along the Atlantic coast of Africa since the early 1400s, finally found a sea route in 1498, arriving in India by way of the Indian Ocean after sailing around Africa. Six years earlier the Spanish had funded an ill-conceived effort to reach East Asia by sailing west across the Atlantic. In the process, and by accident, they discovered what seemed to them a "New World," and they went on to create a western hemispheric empire that rivaled even that of the Mongols in size and significance.

Like the Mongols, the Iberians had a warrior culture, bred by centuries of *Reconquista*. Like the Mongols, they used technologies adopted from other civilizations, such as gunpowder weapons and navigational tools from Asia. Like the Mongols, they killed untold thousands through combat, slaughter, and the spread of infectious diseases, gaining wealth and power by exploiting and enslaving millions. And like the Mongols, they created conflicts and connections among cultures.

Iberians and Mongols share more similarities than differences

Unlike the Mongols, however, the Iberians zealously imposed their faith on the people they ruled. And unlike the Mongols they created new societies, destined to endure even after the Iberian empires were gone.

Portuguese Overseas Exploration

Given the small size and relative poverty of Portugal, it is surprising that this kingdom started the European drive for overseas exploration (page 457). But the forces it set in motion had an immense impact.

Like other European nations, Portugal suffered a drastic fourteenth-century population decline from the Black Death and the famines and epidemics associated with it. Depopulation of villages and poorly producing farmland left much of the landed nobility seriously short of revenue. Some tried to compensate for these shortages by turning to plunder. In 1415 Portuguese raiders captured the Moroccan seaport of Ceuta (*THĀ-oo-tah*), but Portugal's small population and limited resources made it impossible for it to conquer all of Morocco in a land war.

Portugal initiates seaborne exploration

The sea offered an alternative route to plunder, however. Portugal was a nation of farmers and fishermen with a lengthy Atlantic seacoast. Following the conquest of Ceuta, Prince Enrique (*awn-RĒ-kā*), the third son of the king of Portugal and therefore unlikely to inherit the throne, decided to pursue his own interests by organizing maritime expeditions to chart the western coast of Africa. Starting in 1418, these expeditions sought to determine how far south Muslim rule prevailed in Africa and where the Christian faith could be advanced at the expense of Islam (Map 19.1). The Portuguese also wanted to develop trade relations with African Christians, including the mythical Christian kingdom of Prester John, sought by Europeans since the crusades. Slowly, Portuguese explorers and traders moved ever farther south along Africa's west coast. They covered fifteen hundred miles, reaching as far as present-day Sierra Leone by the time Prince Enrique died in 1460. Later generations called him Prince Henry the Navigator.

Henry the Navigator initiates Portuguese expansion

When the Ottoman Turks had taken Constantinople, they had stunned Christian Europe and disrupted its merchants. The Muslims were now in control of the eastern Mediterranean, the meeting point of three continents and the focus of world trade for centuries. While they had no intention of closing the traditional land-sea trade routes to Christians, they intended to raise the fees for safe passage to levels that would enrich the

FOUNDATION MAP 19.1 European Global Exploration Routes, 1415–1522

Note the principal voyages of European exploration, all undertaken for differing reasons. Vasco da Gama's journey to India built on several decades of Portuguese exploration of the western coast of Africa. Columbus's westward expedition was designed to reach first Japan and then the Spice Islands by a route that Columbus believed to be shorter than sailing around Africa. Magellan's circumnavigation of the globe was intended to demonstrate that Columbus could have established a commercially viable connection to Asia had America not been in his way. Why did that conclusion prove incorrect?

Constantinople's fall intensifies Portugal's maritime quest

Ottoman Sultan and cut deeply into European profits. Their middlemen squeezed European merchants even more by marking up the prices of spices and luxury items as much as 1,000 percent. These burdens were enough to convince several Western nations to search for alternative routes to the East Indies.

Because of Henry's expeditions, Portugal had a sizable lead in this search. Its ships reached the equator in 1471 and discovered that, contrary to legend, the ocean there did not boil. They also found that the heat decreased as they sailed farther south. In 1487, Portugal's King João (*ZHWOW*) II dispatched a land expedition across Africa to search for Prester John and for a connection to the Indian Ocean and a sea expedition to search for a route around Africa. The land expedition failed to find Prester John but did reach India. The sea voyage, commanded by Bartholomeu Días (*DĒ-ahz*), rounded the Cape of Good Hope at Africa's southern tip and could have gone on to India had not the sailors insisted on returning home. When Días sailed into Lisbon in 1489, he reported that Portugal had found a way to undercut the Muslim traders, since cargoes could be shipped by sea for a fraction of the cost by land. Present in Lisbon when Días arrived was a Genoese navigator named Cristóbal Colón, whose proposal for a voyage to find a route to the Indies by sailing westward across the Atlantic had been previously rejected by João II. The Latinized version of this navigator's name was Christopher Columbus.

Columbus's Enterprise of the Indies

An experienced mariner and cartographer, Columbus knew that the earth was round, and he calculated the distance from Portugal to China at fewer than 5,000 miles. He was right about the shape of the earth but wrong about its size. His calculations of one degree of longitude at the equator were off by 15 miles, a mistake that caused him to think that the circumference of the earth was 18,750 miles rather than 25,000. His sources for the size and locations of Asian lands were also inaccurate. But he was able to make a plausible argument that Europeans could reach East Asia by sailing west, across the Atlantic, on voyages that would be shorter than those Europeans had already sailed and less expensive than going around Africa to the Indies. Moreover, since the journey would be east to west instead of north to south, the winds, currents, and climatic changes encountered along the way would be less troublesome. In 1484 Columbus presented his **Enterprise of the Indies**, a detailed plan for a westward maritime expedition, to João II, and asked for Portuguese financial support.

Columbus's errors lead to unwarranted optimism

João referred this request to a committee of experts, who agreed with Columbus that the world is round—a well-known fact by 1484—but considered his estimate of the earth's circumference ridiculously small. This committee projected the distance from Portugal to Japan at 13,100 miles, a highly accurate prediction that placed East Asia well beyond the range of any expedition that expected its sailors to carry their own food and drink. Rather than reconsider his estimate, Columbus tried his luck with King Isabella of Castile (although female, Isabella was officially a *king*, and she insisted on being called by that title). She established a similar committee that reported similar findings. Columbus was about to try the Portuguese court again when Días returned to Lisbon in 1489 with good news about the route around Africa. Recognizing that Portugal would pursue that route for trade, Columbus sought support from Venice and Genoa. But these city-states, with established interests in existing routes through the eastern Mediterranean, turned him away.

Still convinced that his calculations were right, Columbus went back to Isabella in 1492 and was rejected again. However, as he was preparing to leave for Paris to try to interest the French, he was called back to Isabella's court. Her finance minister, Luís de Santander (*loo-ĒSS dā sahn-tahn-DARE*), had scolded his sovereign for lack of imagination and offered to finance the Enterprise himself by loaning funds to Isabella. If Columbus were mistaken, Santander argued, he would die on the voyage and a small investment would be lost; but if, against the odds, he turned out to be right, Castile would have a more direct route to the Indies than either Portuguese or Islamic merchants.

Isabella now gave the Enterprise more careful thought. She and her husband Ferdinand, kings of Castile and Aragon respectively, hoped to instill a militant, crusading Catholicism in all the Spanish kingdoms and unite them under the rule of their daughter Juana. A new route to the Indies would not only make this unified Spain rich, they reasoned, but also make it possible to convert hundreds of millions of Asians to their faith. They decided that the potential rewards were worth the risks. Isabella accepted Santander's offer,

Isabella finances Columbus's gamble

Document 19.1 Columbus Describes His First Encounter with People in the Western Hemisphere, 1492

The Enterprise of the Indies sighted land before dawn on October 12, 1492, and Columbus went ashore after dawn broke. He recorded the events in his own words, including his assumption that his expedition was then very close to Asia.

As I saw that [the native people] were very friendly to us, and perceived that they could be much more easily converted to our holy faith by gentle means than by force, I presented them with some red caps, and strings of beads to wear upon the neck, and many other trifles of small value, wherewith they were much delighted, and became wonderfully attached to us. Afterwards they came swimming to the boats, bringing parrots, balls of cotton thread, javelins and many other things which they exchanged for articles we gave them, such as glass beads, and hawk's bells; which trade was carried on with the utmost good will. But they seemed on the whole to me, to be a very poor people. They all go completely naked, even the women, though I saw but one girl. All whom I saw were young, not above thirty years of age, well made, with fine shapes and faces; their hair short, and coarse like that of a horse's tail, combed toward the forehead, except a small portion which they suffer to hang down behind, and never cut. Some paint themselves with black, which makes them appear like those of the Canaries, neither black

nor white; others with white, others with red, and others with such colors as they can find. Some paint the face, and some the whole body; others only the eyes, and others the nose. Weapons they have none, nor are acquainted with them, for I showed them swords which they grasped by the blades, and cut themselves through ignorance. They have no iron, their javelins being without it, and nothing more than sticks, though some have fish-bones or other things at the ends. They are all of a good size and stature, and handsomely formed. I saw some with scars of wounds upon their bodies, and demanded by signs the cause of them; they answered me in the same way, that there came people from the other islands in the neighborhood who intended to make them prisoners, and they defended themselves. I thought then, and still believe, that these were from the continent [of Asia]. It appears to me, that the people are ingenious, and would be good servants; and I am of opinion that they would very readily become Christians, as they appear to have no religion. They very quickly learn such words as are spoken to them. If it please our Lord, I intend at my return to carry home six of them to your Highnesses, that they may learn our language.

SOURCE: Christopher Columbus, *Journal of the First Voyage to America* (New York: A. and C. Boni, 1924) 24–26.

Columbus's first encounter with Indians.

gave Columbus letters of introduction to the Emperor of China, and sent him on his way with three ships, the *Niña*, the *Pinta*, and the *Santa Maria*. Columbus sailed from Palos (*PAH-lōs*), Spain, on August 3, 1492, and made landfall on an island, most likely in the Bahamas, in what is today the Caribbean Sea on October 12 (see "Columbus Describes His First Encounter with People in the Western Hemisphere, 1492"). It was a voyage of fewer than three thousand miles.

Columbus assumed that he had reached islands off the eastern coast of Japan, but the inhabitants did not wear Japanese clothing (indeed, they wore no clothing at all), did not speak Japanese, and did not seem to know anything about Japan. The plant and animal life was unlike anything seen in Asia, and when Columbus returned to Spain in 1493 with samples of what he had found, the general conclusion was that he had landed in an unknown part of the world. Columbus, however, did not agree. He mounted three more expeditions in search of Japan, dying in Spain in 1506 without ever knowing what part of the world he had reached.

Columbus may have been mistaken concerning the nature of the lands he encountered, but Isabella was not. She repaid Santander handsomely and made the discoveries her personal property. Then she appealed to Pope Alexander VI for recognition of Castile's claims to the Indies and its exclusive right to the westward passage. In Christian Europe at that time, such matters were routinely referred to the Vatican. Alexander, a Spaniard, divided the entire world known to Europeans between the two Iberian nations, drawing an imaginary line from pole to pole 450 miles west of the Azores and the Cape Verde Islands (though they are not at the same longitude). Ignoring the rights of the inhabitants whose lands he gave away, he granted everything east of the line to Portugal

Map 19.2 The Treaty of Tordesillas and the Line of Demarcation, 1494

Observe that the line drawn by the Treaty of Tordesillas not only divided the western hemisphere between Portugal and Spain; it went around the world and bisected the eastern hemisphere as well. One can only imagine the reactions of the Japanese and Chinese emperors and the various rulers of India, had they known that their lands had been assigned to two European nations by a treaty of whose very existence they knew nothing. Europe had progressed from exploring the world (Map 19.1) to dividing it. Why did Europeans believe they had a right to divide the world in this way?

and everything west to Castile. The Portuguese, who had not yet actually sailed all the way to India, were outraged and threatened war.

    Subsequent negotiations between Portuguese and Spanish in 1494 resulted in the **Treaty of Tordesillas** (*taur-dā-SĒ-yahss*), an agreement that drew the Line of Demarcation 1,675 miles west of the Cape Verde Islands (Map 19.2). Both sides pronounced themselves reasonably dissatisfied but proceeded to claim their halves of the world. The other European powers, not having been consulted, saw no need to comply; nor did Muslims, who paid no attention to the pope. Still, although the Europeans did not yet know about South America, the treaty's main effect would be to give most of it to Spain, while leaving to Portugal the large eastern section later known as Brazil.

Pope Alexander VI divides the world between Portugal and Spain

Portugal and Spain claim the entire world

The Voyage of Magellan

The Spanish followed up on the voyages of Columbus by creating an American empire, first colonizing several Caribbean islands and later conquering the Aztecs in Mexico and the Inca in Peru (Chapter 18). Some, however, continued to believe that profitable trade routes to Asia could be found by sailing westward from Spain.

    Thus, while Cortés was conquering Mexico, a Portuguese mariner known as Ferdinand Magellan (*mah-JEL-lin*), sailing in the service of Spain, was finally accomplishing what Columbus had set out to do. By now it was obvious that the Americas were not part of Asia: in 1497 and 1498 English expeditions had explored the coast of North America, and in 1513 a Spaniard named Balboa had seen another great ocean on the far side of the American continents. But although ancient Polynesians knew the width of the Pacific, no European yet knew this, and the dream of sailing westward from Europe to reach the riches of Asia lived on.

Magellan proves it impractical to sail west from Europe to the Spice Islands

In pursuit of this dream, Magellan set out from Spain in 1519 with five ships and about 280 men. They headed for South America, where for a year they probed the coast for a passage, finally sailing through what is now called the Straits of Magellan in November 1520. For the next four months, with only three ships left, they crossed the seemingly endless Pacific, eating leather and ship rats once supplies ran out. In March 1521, the near-starving survivors reached the Philippines. They claimed the islands for Spain, but the next month Magellan and many of his men were killed in a conflict with the Filipino peoples.

Eventually, in September 1522, one ship with 18 men made it back to Spain, having sailed around the globe. Their voyage had proven that it was indeed possible to reach Asia by sailing west from Europe. But it had also revealed that the trip was three times the distance Columbus had calculated, and that given the distance and dangers involved it was not really worth the trouble.

Magellan's circumnavigation of the globe.

The Portuguese Seaborne Empire

The Portuguese, meanwhile, were finding that using their new sea routes was very much worth *their* trouble. The Treaty of Tordesillas granted half the world to Portugal, and Lisbon set out to make the most of it. Portugal's kings soon placed its new oceanic empire on firm foundations: knowledge of currents, winds, and coastlines; superb sailing vessels; and first-rate seamanship. The curiosity of Prince Henry the Navigator turned out to have tremendous commercial benefits.

Empire in the Atlantic Ocean

Vasco da Gama connects Portugal to India

A generation after Prince Henry's death, King João II authorized the establishment of a fortress and trading post in the Gulf of Guinea in 1482. The next year a Portuguese explorer named Diogo Cão (*COWM*) found the mouth of the Congo River, eventually establishing good relations with the Kongo Kingdom (Chapter 23). Other Portuguese pressed on toward India, as King Manoel (*mahn-WELL*) I commissioned a mariner named Vasco da Gama to sail all the way around Africa to India. In 1497 da Gama left Lisbon, reaching the Cape of Good Hope after 93 days, then rounding it and sailing up Africa's east coast and across the Indian Ocean to India (see "Vasco da Gama's Expedition Observes the Spice Trade, 1498"). This was the greatest seafaring feat in European history to date. As a follow-up, King Manoel dispatched a 12-ship fleet under the command of Pedro Alvares Cabral (*PĀ-drō AHL-vah-rez kah-BRAHL*) in 1500. Blown off course by a violent storm, Cabral made landfall on an "island" in the western Atlantic, naming it the "Isle of the True Cross" and claiming it for Portugal before continuing on to India. It was not an island at all—it was Brazil.

Portuguese sailors bump into Brazil

Manoel decided to assess the value of Brazil as an intermediate base for future voyages to India. In 1501 he sent a three-ship expedition to the new land, with Amerigo Vespucci (*ah-MARE-ih-gō vess-POO-chē*) aboard as cartographer and chronicler. In this capacity on a future trip Amerigo named the entire hemisphere after himself: America. The expedition explored two thousand miles of coastline, leading Manoel to suspect that

Document 19.2 Vasco da Gama's Expedition Observes the Spice Trade, 1498

Vasco da Gama's first voyage to India enabled the Portuguese to observe the nature and extent of the spice trade. This excerpt from the journal of one of the sailors charts the course of that commerce. Notice the emphasis placed on the dangers of overland travel, the frequent payment of customs duties, and the enormous income the Sultan of the Ottoman Empire derived from those duties. All of these facts led the Portuguese to seek a sea route to the Indies in the first place.

From this country of Calecut, or Alta India, come the spices which are consumed in the East and the West, in Portugal, as in all other countries of the world, as also precious stones of every description. The following spices are to be found in this city of Calecut, being its own produce: much ginger and pepper and cinnamon, although the last is not of so fine a quality as that brought from an island called Ceylon, which is eight days journey from Calecut . . . Cloves are brought to this city from an island called Malacca. The Mecca vessels carry these spices from there to a city in [Arabia] called Jiddah, and from the said island to Jiddah is a voyage of fifty days sailing before the wind, for the vessels of this country cannot tack. At Jiddah they discharge their cargoes, paying customs duties to the Grand Sultan. The merchandise is then transshipped to smaller vessels, which carry it through the Red Sea to a place . . . called Tuuz, where customs duties are paid once more. From that place the merchants carry the spices on the back of camels . . . to Cairo, a journey occupying ten days. At Cairo duties are paid again. On this road to Cairo they are frequently robbed by thieves, who live in that country, such as the Bedouins and others.

At Cairo, the spices are embarked on the river Nile . . . and descending that river for two days they reach a place called Rosetta, where duties have to be paid once more. There they are placed on camels, and are conveyed in one day to a city called Alexandria, which is a seaport. This city is visited by the galleys of Venice and Genoa, in search of these spices, which yield the Grand Sultan a revenue of 600,000 cruzados in customs duties . . . [about $15 million in 2006 dollars].

SOURCE: *A Journal of the First Voyage of Vasco da Gama, 1497–1499*, translated by Eric Axelson (Cape Town: Stephan Phillips Ltd., 1998) 77–78.

---

this was not an island after all. It also brought back samples of a type of brazilwood, a tree whose wood could be used to produce a red dye for textiles. This wood gave Brazil its name and Portugal a reason to explore the area further, since it was really too far west to be of any use as a way station en route to India. Later, the Portuguese learned that they could make a fortune growing sugar in Brazil, provided they settled it with colonists and African slaves. But for the moment, the eastern hemisphere seemed far more attractive.

Empire in the Indian and Pacific Oceans

The Treaty of Tordesillas, amplified by a papal edict of 1514 forbidding other European powers to interfere with Portuguese possessions, enabled Portugal to avoid European competition in the eastern hemisphere for most of the sixteenth century. Its superior gunnery, vessels, and seamanship held off its occasional Asian enemies. But the Portuguese seaborne empire was less an empire than a network of commercial ports and fortifications, designed not for settlement but for trade.

Vasco da Gama's voyage to India opened the Indian Ocean to Portuguese traffic. In 1500, after Cabral bumped into Brazil, one of his ships located Madagascar. The Portuguese established trading posts in India and connected them with their newly founded station at Kilwa in East Africa.

Portugal builds an empire based on commerce

In 1505 the first Portuguese **viceroy**, or vice-king, arrived in India, and beginning in 1510 the second viceroy, Afonso de Albuquerque, began developing the system of fortified posts at strategic locations that guaranteed Portuguese domination of Indian Ocean trade. Albuquerque conquered Goa in 1510 and made it Portugal's headquarters in Asia. During the next five years his forces took Malacca, the Moluccas, and Hormuz. Portuguese seamen reached China shortly thereafter, and in 1557 they established a trading post at Macao.

Albuquerque's strategy helps Portugal dominate the Indian Ocean

Goa became the principal port of western India. The Portuguese controlled the Persian Gulf from Hormuz, and their installation at Malacca dominated the passageway from the Indian Ocean to the South China Sea. Fortified Portuguese trading posts were located all along the East African coastline and the seacoasts of India and Ceylon.

Portugal's Commercial Empire in 1600

The Portuguese created their far-flung empire skillfully, employing their navigational expertise to master the seas and sail them at will. They guarded their knowledge jealously, refusing to share it with competitors. They carefully selected important strategic locations that would help them dominate Indian Ocean trade, and occupied those locations through a combination of diplomacy and intimidation. Once installed there, they protected their positions by negotiating trading rights in contracts that benefited local merchants as well as themselves, giving those merchants a stake in Portuguese success. This strategy enabled a nation with a tiny population of less than two million people to develop a commercial network that spanned the entire globe.

Portuguese ships carry goods across enormous distances

The Portuguese were responsible for establishing regular oceanic trade across vast spaces: between the Atlantic and Indian oceans, between West Africa and Brazil, between southwest Europe and West Africa, and between the north and the south Atlantic (Map 19.3). These sea routes regularized connections between these regions and enhanced commercial and cultural contacts between societies.

Portuguese vessels carried spices from the Indian Ocean to Europe, and while this was a valuable trade route, Portuguese shipping lanes from one part of Asia to another were even more profitable. The Portuguese sold Chinese silk not only in Europe but also in India, the Moluccas, Borneo, Timor, and Hormuz. Cloth from India, spices from the Moluccas, minerals from Borneo, and sandalwood from Timor were distributed throughout the Portuguese empire, as Portuguese ships connected these sites not only to Lisbon but to one another.

A modern-day replica of a Portuguese caravel.

In addition to goods, Portuguese sailors and merchants also carried diseases from one region of the world to another. Malaria spread rapidly across the tropics as mosquitoes bred prolifically in the water carried on Portuguese ships. Asians and Africans, because of prior contact with Europeans, were generally immune to the most drastic effects of Old World diseases, but the Amerinds of Brazil were devastated by smallpox, influenza, and measles. More than a century after Cabral reached Brazil, smallpox remained lethal enough to wipe out the entire Amerind population of Sao Luís in northern Brazil in 1621.

Portuguese commerce connects Asia to Europe

In addition to the transmission of germs, goods, and people, the Portuguese also spread European culture and practices throughout their empire, and scattered bits of information about Asian, African, Amerind, and Brazilian cultures everywhere they went. Building and artistic materials such as rare woods, gems, dyes, and metals were shipped from Asia, Africa, and Brazil to Europe, where they were used in churches, libraries, jewelry, paintings, and furniture. The Portuguese built European-style churches in India and churches with Asian motifs in Brazil. Amerind art was widely sold in Brazil, Africans purchased colorful

Map 19.3 The Flow of Commerce in the Portuguese World, ca. 1600

The Portuguese impulse to expand overseas created commercial connections linking four continents. Note that a bewildering variety of goods, some of which are depicted in the chapter opener, flowed into Lisbon from across the globe. Customs, rituals, languages, clothing, and ideas moved not only to and from Lisbon, but between each of the ports depicted on the map. The result was a vast increase in cosmopolitanism and knowledge from one end of the Portuguese world to the other. Why did this Portuguese challenge worry the Islamic world?

Amerind textiles, and Brazilian-inspired furniture graced parlors in Portuguese homes. The Portuguese seaborne empire facilitated widespread transmission of styles and tastes.

This transmission operated in several directions simultaneously. European clothing was introduced in Africa and Brazil, with sometimes comical results: top hats were widely worn by foremen of labor gangs in Rio de Janeiro, and for a brief period, Portuguese-style baggy pants were all the rage in Nagasaki. Brazilian tobacco was smoked in Portugal and coveted in Africa, where *arrobas*, bundles of tobacco twisted into ropes and soaked in molasses, became so popular that they were used as currency. West African foods and words entered the culture of eastern Brazil, and the African slaves transported to Brazil by the Portuguese became devoted converts to Portuguese Catholicism while retaining many rituals and songs from their African religions. The cross-fertilization of cultures produced by the Portuguese seaborne empire was as stimulating, and penetrating, as the connections generated by conflict and conquest among the many great land-based empires of previous centuries.

The Spanish and Portuguese Empires in America

Once the great Amerind empires had fallen to the Spaniards, Spain began to consolidate what had become the largest territorial possession in human history. From California to the tip of Cape Horn, Spain controlled everything except Portuguese Brazil (Map 19.4). Subduing Mexico proved relatively easy after the conquest of Tenochtitlán. In Peru, however, the Inca found ways to neutralize Spain's mounted cavalry, and although they were unable to expel the invaders, they created an independent Inca kingdom high in the Andes that lasted until 1572. Elsewhere the weaker, less centralized Amerind cultures, including the vestiges of the once-imposing Maya civilization, offered only occasional resistance to their new masters.

Iberia colonizes America

At the same time, the Portuguese began to recognize the economic potential of Brazil. Their eastern seaborne empire involved cooperation and profit-sharing with Muslim traders, but Brazil was entirely theirs, and they used it to profit from the growing European taste for sugar. Unlike Spanish America, with its centralized Amerind societies, Brazil was home to native cultures that lived in the inaccessible interior and had not developed central institutions. These cultures fled from the Portuguese rather than resisting them, but could not provide the labor required for sugar cultivation. Nor, given their small population, could the Portuguese.

The Amerind Foundation

Spain, in contrast, was able to construct its empire on the foundations of Amerind societies. Particularly helpful to the Spanish effort was the hierarchical structure of the Aztec and Inca Empires. It proved relatively easy for the Spaniards to substitute the king of Spain for the Aztec or Inca emperor at the top of the hierarchy and to expect that the king's orders would be obeyed without hesitation.

Iberians build empires on existing Amerind societies

Aztec and Inca polytheism also contributed to this submission. Accustomed to a large array of gods, the conquered peoples interpreted their defeat as indicating that their own gods were weaker than those of the Spaniards. It seemed logical to worship the gods who were stronger. The Spaniards, noting this tendency, did nothing to discourage Inca and Aztecs from considering Catholic saints and angels as powerful gods. Mary, the mother of Jesus, actually had a parallel in Aztec religion, in which one female goddess was the mother of all the gods. Through this blending of Christian and Amerind traditions, the defeated societies were encouraged to accept their fate and embrace the new European faith.

Slave Labor

Once Mexico and Peru had been pacified, Spaniards began arriving steadily from the mother country, drawn to the Americas by the prospect of wealth in gold and silver or in sugar production. For labor in the mines and the fields, they expected to use Amerinds, but Amerinds were not easily enslaved for these purposes. First, smallpox and other European diseases to which Amerinds had no acquired immunity killed large numbers of them. Moreover, those who survived had greatly reduced life expectancies, either owing to Spanish cruelty or because they simply found unrelenting labor unendurable in the absence of the religious significance it had had under the Aztec and Inca Empires. Third, many Catholic missionaries to the Americas, particularly the Franciscans and the Jesuits,

Map 19.4 The Iberian Empires in the Western Hemisphere, 1750

Spain and Portugal, two small countries on the Iberian Peninsula on the southwestern fringe of Europe, constructed enormous empires in the western hemisphere. European languages, customs, and products spread throughout these empires, while American, African, and Asian resources, customs, and cultures moved through Iberia into Europe. But notice that large portions of South America—the Amazon basin, the interior of Brazil, and Patagonia—remained untouched by Europeans. Why?

Legend:

- Aztec Empire, 1519
- Inca Empire, 1525
- Spanish settlement to 1640
- Spanish settlement to 1750
- Spanish frontier lands to 1750
- Portuguese settlement to 1640
- Portuguese settlement to 1750
- Portuguese frontier lands to 1750

protested strongly against the enslavement of Amerinds. They argued to the king that Amerinds were people with souls, not draft animals.

Spaniards replace
Amerind labor with
African slaves

The missionaries' genuine concern for the well-being of the Amerinds, however, did not extend to Africans, many of whom were soon imported as slaves. With Amerind workers unavailable, the American colonies needed a labor force accustomed to tropical conditions. There were not enough men in all of Iberia to supply this labor force, and if there had been, few could have survived manual labor in tropical climates for very long.

Here the Portuguese took the lead. Having experienced serious labor shortages in Brazil, they imported slaves from trading posts that they had established along the west coast of Africa. Spain followed, and before long Portuguese and Spanish ships were carrying human cargoes from West Africa, thousands upon thousands of slaves to be sold at auction in the port cities of Central and South America. Iberian America quickly became a mixed society of people of Amerind, European, and African descent who produced a physical and cultural blending unlike anything in the eastern hemisphere.

Government and Administration

Governing such diverse and distant empires required new strategies. At first Isabella of Castile, who owned Spanish America outright by virtue of Santander's financing and the Treaty of Tordesillas, simply appointed her chaplain to administer the entire area. When this overworked priest died in 1503, one year after Isabella herself, her husband Ferdinand established a Board of Trade to oversee the increasingly profitable transatlantic commerce. After the final unification of Spain in 1516 under Carlos I (who three years later also became Holy Roman Emperor Charles V), the Americas were governed through councils. Rather than delegate responsibility to a number of ministries or departments (as was done in France and England), authority was assigned in 1524 to a single board, the **Council of the Indies**.

The Council of the Indies supervised every aspect of governance in Spanish America, including legislative, judicial, commercial, financial, military, and religious matters. It approved all significant expenditures, decided which Spanish laws should apply unchanged in the New World, drafted revisions for those that required adjustment, and advised the king on everything pertaining to colonial affairs. Meeting in Seville between three and five hours daily, it was a hardworking body with extensive authority. Formal votes were not unheard of, but usually the Council reached agreement on important matters before submitting its unanimous recommendations to the king for review.

But distance proved to be the most significant difficulty facing those who tried to govern the western hemisphere. Sailing from Portugal to Brazil took an average of seventy to one hundred days; from Spain to Panama, about seventy-five. Troublesome winds and currents made the return trip even longer. Atlantic crossings were always unpleasant, often dangerous, and occasionally fatal. Ships from the Americas, laden with treasure and exotic goods, were frequently set upon by pirates, although convoys protected by warships eventually reduced this danger. Royal messages and orders, as well as colonial reports, took months to cross the Atlantic and were often lost altogether.

The empires thus could not be run from Iberia. Kings and councils might issue laws and edicts, but who would enforce them in America? Clearly agents of unquestionable loyalty were required, men who would know the royal will instinctively, without having to ask questions at every turn. The rulers found such agents in their viceroys, or "vice-kings."

Viceroys were responsible for the execution of the king's orders on virtually every aspect of colonial administration. Until 1717 there were two viceroyalties in Spanish America: New Spain (from California south to Panama, including the Caribbean), and Peru (from Panama south to Cape Horn). In the eighteenth century Peru was subdivided into two additional viceroyalties because of its overwhelming size.

Portuguese America developed in a less centralized fashion. King João III in 1534 divided the eastern seaboard into 12 hereditary captaincies, varying in width between 100 and 270 miles and extending indefinitely into the uncharted interior. The proprietors were responsible for the recruitment of settlers and the economic development of their captaincies. The system never worked effectively, and in 1549 João III placed Brazil under the direct administration of a governor-general, whose duties were similar to those of a Spanish American viceroy. This action accelerated development and attracted thousands of Portuguese settlers to Brazil.

Whether Spanish or Portuguese, these vice-kings were men of talent and expertise, but the principal qualification for the post was loyalty to the king. They had to make decisions in the king's best interests even when the king's orders might be impractical or irrelevant to conditions in the New World. Under such circumstances, the Spanish viceroy could delay implementation or initiate a reassessment of the situation by invoking the Spanish legal maxim, "I obey but I do not enforce." Portuguese governors-general acted similarly, but without the maxim. A wise monarch would consider such an opinion carefully before overruling his representative.

But the kings of Spain and Portugal were customarily suspicious, and viceroys, like the officials who served under them, were always subject to the *residencia* (*rez-ih-DEHN-sē-ah*). This was a thorough audit of all the appointee's dealings during his term of office. It was conducted by a royal bureaucrat sent from the mother country, and it restrained those who might otherwise have been tempted to engage in illegal activity or abuse of power.

All authority came from the king. Neither Spanish nor Portuguese America contained any broadly based institution providing representation within the government for ordinary people. Spain itself had such a body, called a *cortés*, but because it was a representative institution that restricted royal power, Spanish kings refused to introduce it into the New World. The only truly representative body in the Spanish Empire was the town council, which maintained roads, policed the streets and markets, and regulated local affairs. Only through the town council could the residents of these empires play any role in their own governance. But the authority of town councils was limited to the towns themselves. The extensive centralized powers exercised by the Iberian kings over their American empires helped them hold those distant territories for more than three centuries.

Spain and Portugal find different ways to administer their empires

Viceroys and governors-general administer in the king's name

The Plaza de Armas in Cuzco, Peru, displays sixteenth-century Spanish colonial architectural style.

The Colonial Church

Iberian expansion was driven not only by a quest for gold and glory, but also by the desire to save the souls of New World peoples, who had never before heard the message of Jesus Christ. That ambitious goal was pursued by the Spanish and Portuguese branches of the Roman Catholic Church.

Ferdinand and Isabella, calling themselves "the Catholic kings," had completed the *Reconquista* by 1492 and had made Catholicism an element of Spanish nationality that helped bring unity to their diverse kingdoms. In the New World Catholicism would

Iberian empires are shaped by Catholicism

help assimilate conquered peoples into either Spain's or Portugal's colonial order. The pope supported this effort, granting the Iberian monarchs extensive rights over the appointment of bishops, the activities of religious orders, and the organization of all Catholic undertakings in the western hemisphere. In return, the kings assumed responsibility for supervising the Church in its evangelical, educational, and charitable efforts overseas.

At first these efforts were directed by the Franciscan, Dominican, and Augustinian religious orders. They concentrated on converting the Amerind chiefs, who then saw to it that their people would be baptized. To preach to the newly converted and teach them the elements of the faith, the friars learned native languages and promoted the widening use of dominant Amerind languages as a means of centralization.

The Amerinds reacted to conversion in a variety of ways. Some were enthusiastic, eager to worship the new gods who had proven themselves stronger than the old. Others converted for practical reasons, considering it both wise and useful to adopt the belief system of the conquerors. Still others rebelled, like the Inca of the central Andes, who objected to the destruction of their mummies and idols. Considering this destruction to be sacrilegious, bringing natural disasters and diseases, these Inca rebels returned to their ancient beliefs in the 1560s. Their action provoked a stern response from the viceroyalty of Peru, which worked vigorously over the next decade to eliminate the movement.

A Spanish American catechism from the colonial period.

By 1549 in Brazil and 1572 in Spanish America, priests from the Jesuit order arrived in the New World, and they quickly became the most influential of all. They soon dominated the conversion campaigns, emphasizing similarities between native belief systems and Catholicism, and bringing Amerinds together in settlements to permit mass conversion. They also defended their native followers against many who wished to enslave them. As did the other orders, the Jesuits grew prosperous through their access to native labor. The Church thus became wealthy, but it earned the resentment of colonial elites. In a land without a banking system, the Church became the principal source of funds for agricultural or commercial investment. It also became the largest property owner in the New World and a powerful manufacturer of pottery, fabrics, and leather goods.

The Catholic Church dominates commerce and education

Education in the colonies was handled exclusively by the Church. It operated all primary and secondary schools, educated Amerinds as part of the conversion process, and founded institutions of higher education such as the Universities of Mexico (Mexico City) and San Marcos (Lima), both established in 1551. In Brazil, however, the Portuguese Church did not establish a university until the nineteenth century. Before that, Brazilians seeking a university degree had to pursue it in Europe.

Religious orders for women expanded during the colonial period and played a major role in social and economic life. Convents attracted Spanish women who wanted to manage their own affairs, obtain a good education, and live lives of piety and service. Some women entered convents in order to escape the burdens imposed by husbands and children, or to lead well-protected lives. Most, however, took their vows seriously and contributed greatly to colonial life. Much more important in Spanish than in Portuguese America, convents owned substantial properties, provided funds for investment, and cultivated literary and artistic pursuits. Through its male and female orders, its strong belief in the importance of its work, and its active involvement with the Amerinds, the colonial Church exercised a powerful influence over Iberian America.

Society in the Iberian Empires

The people of Spain and Portugal were predominantly white, although there were a few people of African descent. But Spanish and Portuguese America contained a great many racial and ethnic groups, and in the New World a new social order emerged.

A Spanish American family of mixed races. The man is European, the wife is African, and the child is mestizo.

THE IBERIAN-AMERICAN SOCIAL HIERARCHY. At the top of the social ladder were white Spaniards and Portuguese, who tended to consider free people of other races as undesirable **mestizos** (*mes-TĒ-zōs*). Mestizos were people of mixed descent, often the result of unions between the invading Iberians—almost all of whom were male—and Amerinds or Africans. Only 5 percent of these unions were marriages, and children born outside of marriage were discriminated against. In Spanish America, whites excluded such people from artisan guilds in the 1540s, from the priesthood in 1555, and from any position carrying with it the possibility of social advancement. After 1550 the government discouraged interracial relationships, with little effect. Mestizos were not, of course, exclusively the product of Iberian-Amerind or Iberian-African unions; Amerinds and Africans interacted as well. The result has been a racial mixture found nowhere else on earth.

As time went on, increasing numbers of Africans were imported to make up for the high death rate among slaves. The Spanish and Portuguese did not encourage slave family formation, as it proved far less expensive to buy and transport Africans than to raise African children from infancy to adulthood. Male and female slaves were customarily housed separately. Slaves performed all sorts of physical labor and menial services, ranging from domestic chores and handicrafts to the difficult and life-shortening occupations of miner and field hand.

Iberia had long had slaves, both from Islamic areas and from sub-Saharan Africa, and neither Spaniards nor Portuguese considered black Africans a slave race. For Iberians, enslavement was a matter of social class or wartime misfortune, and it was thus possible for slaves to purchase their freedom. Still, slavery was a brutal, degrading institution, and even those able to buy their way out of it found their lives severely restricted. Many officials and most Iberians treated all Africans as slaves, even if they were legally free.

Africans, whether free or unfree, lived on the margins of society in the Iberian empires, as did Amerinds. Africans were subjected to a superficial assimilation, and they hid their own culture and customs away from the view of white people. Amerinds converted to Catholicism in large numbers, but most proved less adaptable than Africans to the Iberian colonial way of life. Thus many Spaniards and Portuguese valued Africans over native peoples as workers.

In their own villages, however, Amerinds maintained independent, largely self-sufficient lifestyles. They kept their traditional social structures, permanently distinct from those of their Iberian conquerors. Spaniards and Portuguese forced Amerinds to work through labor exchanges, in which Amerind villages were compelled to provide a specified number of adults for forced labor for a specified number of days each year. The Amerinds adapted themselves to market structures and unwillingly interacted with the Iberian agricultural world. But they played little or no role in colonial town or city life, leaving skilled labor to mestizos and free Africans.

Social class in Iberian America was not based primarily upon skin color, although race was certainly an important factor. Portuguese and Spanish societies were organized according to a European structure of three estates: clergy, nobility, and commoners. The

Race mixing shapes Iberian colonial societies

Africans and Amerinds occupy inferior social positions

Iberian colonial societies are organized according to European structures upper levels were reserved for high-ranking bishops and nobles, although Spanish colonial nobles tended to be lower-ranking dignitaries who had earned their ennoblement through military service during or after the Spanish conquests in America. The highest-ranking Spanish nobles had no motivation to go to America, except occasionally as a viceroy or general.

Colonial nobles distinguished themselves from commoners largely by their ownership of great estates. On those lands the nobles built lavish manor houses and presided over large numbers of laborers, servants, and slaves. Most Spaniards in America, of course, were commoners, and they earned their livings as shopkeepers, clerks, overseers, doctors, lawyers, notaries, accountants, merchants, craftsmen, or manual laborers. Some were wealthy, others were poor, but all were European in origin.

Mestizos, excluded from many lines of work, often had to make their living by their wits and skills. By the early 1600s many had found niches as silversmiths, wheelwrights, tailors, and carpenters, but most worked as servants or unskilled laborers. Free Africans and Amerinds were even less fortunate. Constrained by descent and skin color, they could never move into the commoner class.

Iberian whites dominate colonial societies

Among whites of Iberian descent, one additional distinction was made—between peninsulares (*pehn-ihn-soo-LAH-rāz*) and criollos (*crē-YŌ-yōs*). **Peninsulares** were white people born in the Iberian peninsula (hence their name). They monopolized the highest offices in church and state and looked down on **criollos**, white people who had been born in the western hemisphere. The names of these groups varied in Portuguese America, but the principle remained the same. The distinction arose with the efforts of Iberian kings to fill the most important positions in their empires with men of social stature whom they knew well. But over time, peninsular status came to be required even for mid-level colonial positions, and eventually the poorest Iberian-born newcomer considered himself the social superior of people whose families had been born and prospered in America for generations. This unfair treatment angered criollos, alienating many who might otherwise have remained loyal to their king but who later gladly joined independence movements.

Women play significant economic roles in the Iberian empires

THE ROLE OF GENDER. Gender distinctions were particularly evident in the Iberian colonial economy. Elite white women usually married, raised large families, and as widows administered the estates of their late husbands. But they could not engage in professional or commercial activity, and those who were frustrated by patriarchal restrictions frequently entered convents in order to gain at least limited autonomy. Middle- and lower-class white women worked at a wide variety of occupations, including spinning thread, taking in laundry, sewing, peddling goods, selling food, and serving as free domestics in the homes of the elite. Amerind women dominated the town marketplaces as sellers of fruits, vegetables, fish, and meat. Free African women were restricted to domestic service and cooking in inns and marketplaces. Most free women performed some type of paid labor during much of their lives. Survival in Iberian America below the level of the elites was not easy, and women's incomes, however meager, were badly needed.

Amerinds and Europeans in North America

Before the sixteenth century, the peoples of North America were largely isolated from the rest of the world. Influenced only by occasional trade with the Mesoamerican cultures that flourished to their south, the numerous tribes and nations of North American

Amerinds had over the ages developed their own distinctive cultures, values, beliefs, and institutions, without having to deal with outside interference (Chapter 5).

Then, in the sixteenth century, explorers from Europe began to map the continent's coastlines and rivers, looking for gold and a passageway to Asia. In the seventeenth century, having found neither, Europeans started settling in North America, exploiting its resources and farming its lands. In the process, the intruders from abroad displaced the Amerinds, whose numbers were already diminished by European diseases.

Coalitions and Contacts

North America lacked large empires like those that existed in Mexico, Peru, and throughout the eastern hemisphere. Most North Americans lived in village-based societies that typically included no more than a few thousand people, and even the larger nations probably numbered only in the hundreds of thousands. Usually these societies were ruled by powerful kings or chiefs who exercised both religious and political authority. They presided over rituals aiming to establish harmony with the spirits of nature, and also over councils made up of prominent warriors and advisors.

Occasionally some societies combined for protection, but rarely did they surrender their autonomy. In the 1500s, for example, the Haudenosaunee (*HOW-din-ō-SAW-nā*) people of what is now upstate New York organized themselves into a League of Five Nations, later called the Iroquois (*EAR-uh-kwoy*) Confederacy. According to oral tradition, a legendary figure called the Peacemaker, along with a mighty chief known as Hiawatha, persuaded regional leaders to end their constant warfare and join together for the common good. But the League, despite an intricate governance system, was more of an alliance than a union: each of its five members (Seneca, Cayuga, Onondaga, Oneida, and Mohawk) remained a sovereign nation.

The Haudenosaunee create an alliance of Amerind nations

The North American Amerinds were thus politically divided and culturally diverse, but they were not isolated from each other. Using the continent's extensive river systems, they could attack their enemies, travel to distant hunting and fishing grounds, conduct long-distance trade, and maintain a network of contacts with other societies.

North American Amerinds preserve their autonomy

Through contacts with Mexico, some North Americans knew that there was a powerful and wealthy empire to their south. They could not know, however, that there also existed across the ocean mightier and wealthier empires, whose warriors carried weapons against which the Amerinds had no defense and diseases against which they had no immunity. They did not anticipate the catastrophe to come.

The Coming of the Europeans

Not long after the first voyage of Columbus, Europeans looking for a new route to Asia began arriving in North America. In 1497 Italian mariner Giovanni Caboto explored the northeast coast, staking a claim for his English employers, who called him John Cabot. In 1500 Portuguese explorers reached Newfoundland; soon fishermen from Portugal, England, and France were fishing the cod-rich waters off the northeastern banks. They also made contact with the coastal Amerinds, who proved willing to trade their food and furs for European trinkets and tools.

In the following decades, while the Spanish conquered the Aztecs and built an empire in Mexico, French and English explorers farther north found neither gold nor a climate in which sugar would grow. Lacking such financial incentives, Europeans in the sixteenth century made little effort to colonize the north.

A 1607 map of the northeast coast of North America, drawn by the French explorer Samuel de Champlain.

Map 19.5 European Exploration and Colonies in North America, 1607–1763

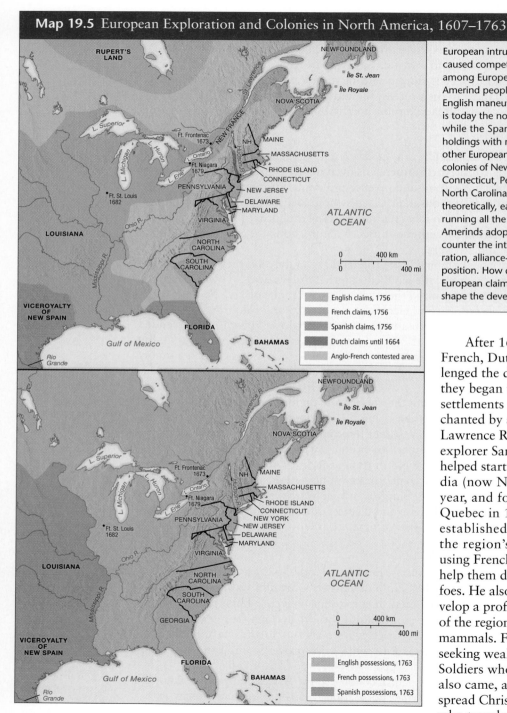

European intrusion into North America caused competition for territory, both among European nations and with Amerind peoples. The French, Dutch, and English maneuvered for advantage in what is today the northeastern United States, while the Spaniards amassed massive holdings with minimal opposition from other Europeans. Note that the English colonies of New Hampshire, Massachusetts, Connecticut, Pennsylvania, Virginia, and North Carolina had no western borders; theoretically, each of them claimed land running all the way to the Pacific Ocean. Amerinds adopted a variety of strategies to counter the intrusions, including collaboration, alliance-building, and outright opposition. How did these conflicting European claims and Amerind strategies shape the development of North America?

After 1600, however, as the French, Dutch, and English challenged the dominance of Spain, they began to establish permanent settlements in North America. Enchanted by a voyage up the Saint Lawrence River in 1603, French explorer Samuel de Champlain helped start a small colony in Acadia (now Nova Scotia) the next year, and founded a settlement at Quebec in 1608. Eventually he established good relations with the region's Huron Amerinds, using French forces and firearms to help them defeat their Iroquois foes. He also helped the Hurons develop a profitable trade in the furs of the region's many fur-bearing mammals. French traders followed, seeking wealth from the fur trade. Soldiers who fought the Iroquois also came, as did Jesuits who spread Christianity, and explorers who traveled the Great Lakes and down the Mississippi River. By the century's end the French had claimed these regions as a colony called New France (Map 19.5), based mainly on the fur trade with the Amerinds, most of whom were unaware that their lands were now supposedly subject to someone called the King of France.

Meanwhile other Europeans were arriving. In 1607 about a hundred hearty Englishmen, searching for gold and adventure, founded an outpost called Jamestown (named for King James I) in a region they knew as Virginia (named for Elizabeth I, the "Virgin Queen"). In 1609 an explorer named Henry Hudson, sailing in the service of the Dutch, traveled up the great river that now bears his name, seeking a new passage to Asia. He found no such route but did discover a region rich in furs. In the 1620s the Dutch founded the colony of New Netherland, which four decades later was seized by the English and renamed New York. In 1620 about fifty self-styled "Pilgrims" and fifty other English voyagers arrived at a place they named Plymouth, in a region soon called New England. Within a few decades thousands of other English Puritans, seeking religious freedom, had joined them in forming a Massachusetts Bay Colony. Other English religious groups followed: Catholics created a Maryland colony in the 1630s, and Quakers founded Pennsylvania in the 1680s. By 1700 there was a string of English colonies along the Atlantic coast.

Europeans establish colonies in North America

Disease and Demographic Decline

The coming of the Europeans brought disaster to the North American Amerinds. Like their Spanish rivals to the South, the French, Dutch, and English brought deadly diseases to which the Amerinds had no immunity. The European colonists also brought agricultural techniques involving large farm animals, metal tools and plows, and crops that required the clearing of huge tracts of forest. With a concept of possession that let individuals claim land parcels as their property and exclude all others, they constantly expanded the amount of land under cultivation. Over time these practices, combined with growing numbers of European immigrants, destroyed the Amerinds' way of life.

At Jamestown, for example, the colonists at first related well to the local Powhatan (*POW-uh-TAHN*) peoples, who provided the newcomers with corn, meat, and fish that helped the colony survive. But as more settlers arrived from England and the Powhatans were ravaged by European diseases, the relationship changed. The peoples clashed, the Amerinds attacked, and the English responded by seizing Powhatan lands. Then, rather than planting food, the colonists grew tobacco, which the Amerinds had taught them how to cultivate, and shipped it for sale to England, where smoking became the rage. Within decades the whole region was covered by tobacco plantations, and the surviving Amerinds were forced off their lands.

European diseases devastate Amerind societies

At Plymouth the colony initially survived with the aid of Massasoit (*mass-uh-SŌ-it*), chief of the Wampanoag (*wahm-puh-NŌ-ug*) nation, who in 1621 agreed to help the Pilgrims if they would support his people in battles against tribal foes. Soon, however, clashes occurred between the disease-ravaged Amerinds and growing English communities, which rapidly claimed increasing amounts of land for farms and used firearms when necessary to enforce their claims. In 1675, desperate to save the Wampanoag way of life, Massasoit's son Metacom (*MEH-tuh-kahm*), whom the colonists called King Philip, attacked the Europeans. A brutal war followed, during which the English slaughtered thousands of Amerinds and sold the survivors into slavery. After Metacom was captured and beheaded in 1676, the Plymouth colonists displayed his head on a pole for 25 years. "King Philip's War" effectively ended Amerind resistance, leaving most of New England in European hands.

The English Captain John Smith is condemned by a Powhatan chief.

To the West, the Dutch and English settlers brought both tragedy and triumph to the Iroquois Confederacy. On one hand, as elsewhere, the colonists brought disease, such as a smallpox epidemic that killed perhaps half of the Iroquois population in the 1630s. On the other hand, the Dutch and English gave the Iroquois firearms to help them fight the Hurons and the French, enabling the Confederacy to carve out an empire extending from the Hudson River to the Great Lakes.

In contacts between Europeans and Amerinds, the Amerinds are at a disadvantage

Elsewhere along the coast, similar events occurred. Sometimes Europeans allied with Amerinds to fight common foes, and sometimes Europeans slaughtered Amerinds or drove them off their lands. Sometimes the Amerinds held off the Europeans for awhile, but in the long run their way of life collapsed in the face of European diseases, European weapons, and the spread of European settlement.

The Columbian Exchange

The initial contact between European and American civilizations involved not only conflict and conquest but connection. Since the two hemispheres had been separated from each other since the submersion of the Bering land bridge more than ten thousand years earlier, many varieties of living things had developed in each hemisphere that were totally unknown in the other. The eastern hemisphere had wheat, grapes, horses, cows, sheep, goats, and pigs; the western hemisphere had potatoes, tomatoes, maize, cacao, and tobacco. When people from the two hemispheres encountered one another, their connections involved an interchange of crops and animals. In reference to Christopher Columbus, scholars call this process the Columbian Exchange.

The Columbian Exchange brings benefits as well as devastation

Some exchanges of crops improved the quality of life in both hemispheres. The impact was immediately obvious in the western hemisphere. Before long wheat and grapes were being grown for the first time in the New World, to make the bread and wine that were central to the European diet and religion. Farm animals brought in by the Iberians provided transport, labor, and food, and they flourished in the Americas.

For the eastern hemisphere, corn (maize), potatoes, tomatoes, peanuts, and manioc (*MAN-ē-ok*)—a starchy root plant, now grown widely in Africa and Brazil, also called *cassava* or *tapioca*—proved hardy and rich in nutrients. Eventually becoming staples in Europe, Africa, and Asia, they later helped foster a global population explosion. Other American plants, like cacao (the basis for chocolate) and, particularly, tobacco, were also sought by people around the world.

African women preparing manioc.

Microorganisms were an additional part of the Columbian Exchange. Syphilis, for example, a debilitating venereal disease that first showed up in southern Europe in the 1490s, was probably introduced by sailors returned from the New World. But the exchange of diseases proved far more devastating for the Amerinds. Smallpox, measles, and chicken pox, to which most Europeans had been subjected as children and thus developed immunities, ran rampant through unprotected Amerind populations. About 30 percent of children who came down with smallpox died, and 90 percent of adults. As a result, Amerind farming was interrupted, social structures shattered, villages depopulated, and entire regions abandoned. Smallpox weakened Aztec and Inca resistance to the Spaniards. Throughout the Spanish possessions in the western hemisphere, smallpox and measles ravaged Amerind communities off and on throughout the sixteenth century, reducing those communities by as much as 90 percent.

There are no reliable statistics on pre-1492 Amerind populations, but scholars estimate that the Americas contained between 15 million and 125 million people. In 1600, Spanish estimates indicated a population of one million Amerinds in the viceroyalty of New Spain (Mexico, Central America, and the Caribbean islands). It is clear that European diseases destroyed the overwhelming majority of the Amerind peoples in the greatest demographic catastrophe in history.

Chapter Review

Putting It in Perspective

Tremendous consequences flowed from the Iberian overseas expansion of the fifteenth century. Under different circumstances, China might have discovered a sea route around Africa, or Japanese mariners might have sailed east and found the Pacific coastline of North America. But it was the Europeans whose curiosity and seamanship broadened human geographic knowledge and extended the horizons of the entire world. When they found previously unknown lands, they conquered and exploited them, motivated by a combination of greed and religious faith.

The clash of civilizations in the New World changed forever societies that had previously been isolated from outside influences. Amerind societies largely collapsed in the face of conquest and disease. In their place the Iberians imposed new governance systems, religious beliefs, and social structures. They created a new economy, based on the cultivation of cash crops by imported slave labor. Finally, they transplanted their whole way of life, bringing plants, animals, foods, and diseases common in Europe but hitherto unknown in the Americas.

The political and economic impacts were immense. The Spanish and Portuguese, and later the French, Dutch, and English, were set on a course to become world powers, surpassing the great Asian and Islamic empires. The Atlantic Ocean soon replaced both the Indian Ocean and the Mediterranean Sea as the center of world commerce. Eventually, Europe led the world in power and prosperity, in large part due to its exploitation of Africa and the New World.

But the most direct Iberian legacy was the new culture created in the conquered lands. The Spanish and Portuguese empires ended in the early 1800s, but their legacy lives on today. Though modern Latin American societies remain intensely hierarchical, the peoples of these societies, displaying a broad variety of outlooks and customs, celebrate this cultural synthesis as their unique contribution to the human experience.

Reviewing Key Material

KEY CONCEPTS

Enterprise of the Indies, 461	*residencia*, 471
Treaty of Tordesillas, 463	mestizos, 473
viceroy, 466	*peninsulares*, 474
Council of the Indies, 470	*criollos*, 474

KEY PEOPLE

Prince Henry the Navigator, 459	Manoel I, 464
João II, 460	Pedro Alvares Cabral, 464
Bartholomeu Días, 460	Amerigo Vespucci, 464
Christopher Columbus, 461	Afonso de Albuquerque, 466
Isabella of Castile, 461	João III, 471
Luís de Santander, 461	John Cabot, 475
Ferdinand of Aragon, 461	Samuel de Champlain, 476
Pope Alexander VI, 463	Henry Hudson, 477
Ferdinand Magellan, 463	Massasoit, 477
Vasco da Gama, 464	Metacom, 477

ASK YOURSELF

1. Why did Portugal take the lead among European nations in promoting overseas expansion?
2. Why did the Iberian nations enslave Africans and transport them to their empires in the western hemisphere?

3. In what ways did the Spanish and Portuguese empires differ from each other? In what ways were they similar?
4. How did the conflicts between Iberian and American civilizations forge connections that changed them all?

GOING FURTHER

Boorstin, Daniel. *The Discoverers*. 1985.
Boxer, C. R. *The Portuguese Seaborne Empire*. 1971.
Burkholder, Mark, and Lyman Johnson. *Colonial Latin America*. 2000.
Burns, E. Bradford. *A History of Brazil*. 1998.
Callaway, Colin. *New Worlds for All: Indians, Europeans, and the Remaking of Early America*. 1997.
Crosby, Alfred. *The Columbian Exchange: Biological and Cultural Consequences of 1492*. 1972.
Diffie, W., and G. Winius. *Foundations of the Portuguese Empire, 1415–1580*. 1979.
Liss, Peggy. *Mexico Under Spain*. 1984.
Lockhart, James, and Stuart Schwartz. *Early Latin America*. 1982.

Parry, J. H. *The Discovery of South America*. 1979.
Pearson, M. *The Portuguese in India*. 1987.
Pescatello, Ann. *Power and Pawn: The Female in Iberian Families*. 1976.
Ramírez, Susan. *The World Upside Down: Cross-Cultural Contact and Conflict in Sixteenth-Century Peru*. 1996.
Russell-Wood, A. J. R. *The Portuguese Empire, 1415–1808*. 1998.
Scammell, Geoffrey. *The First Imperial Age: European Overseas Expansion, 1400–1700*. 1989.
Schaeffer, Dagmar. *Portuguese Exploration in the West and the Formation of Brazil, 1450–1800*. 1988.
Schnaubelt, Joseph, and Frederick van Fleteren. *Columbus and the New World*. 1998.
Smith, Roger. *Vanguard of Empire: Ships of Exploration in the Age of Columbus*. 1993.
Stern, Steve. *Peru's Indian Peoples and the Challenge of Spanish Conquest*. 1993.
Tracy, J. *The Rise of Merchant Empires: Long-Distance Trade in the Early Modern World, 1350–1750*. 1990.

Key Dates and Developments

1415	Portugal captures Ceuta from the Muslims
1415–1460	Expeditions financed by Prince Henry the Navigator
1489	Bartholomeu Días rounds the Cape of Good Hope
1492	Christopher Columbus reaches the Caribbean islands
1494	Treaty of Tordesillas divides the world between Portugal and Spain
1498	Vasco da Gama reaches India
1500	Pedro Alvares Cabral lands in Brazil
1516	Carlos I becomes King of Spain
1519–1521	The Cortés expedition overthrows the Aztec Empire
1519–1522	The Magellan expedition circumnavigates the globe
1524–1532	Pizarro's three expeditions to Peru
1524	Establishment of the Council of the Indies
1532	Capture of Atahuallpa at Cajamarca, Peru
1549–1572	The Jesuits arrive in the New World

The West in an Age of Religious Conflict and Global Expansion, 1500–1650

- The Protestant Reformation

- The Catholic Counterreformation

- Religious and Political Strife in Europe

- The Globalization of Western Christianity and Commerce

- Western Society in an Age of Religious and Economic Change

- Chapter Review

Executing A Peasant Rebel

In the sixteenth century, while Western nations forged global connections, Western society was wracked by divisive religious and social rebellions. Here a leader of the German Peasants' Revolt is shown being burned at the stake.

On April 18, 1521, the Imperial Diet, an assembly of the Holy Roman Empire's leading princes and nobles, met at the bishop's palace in the German town of Worms (*VOHRMSS*). There, on the previous day, the Diet had ordered a monk named Martin Luther to retract his writings, which defied the authority of the Roman Catholic Church. Now, in the emperor's presence, the Diet reassembled to hear Luther's response. His bold reply, delivered that day, echoed throughout Europe for decades: "Unless I shall be refuted by . . . the scriptures or by manifest reason (for I believe in neither the Pope nor in the Councils alone . . .) I am not able to retract . . ."

European Colonies and Claims

The Christian West

Angered by this defiance, Holy Roman Emperor Charles V, then barely 21 years old, issued a stinging rebuke. A single monk must not be allowed to deny what Christianity had held for more than a thousand years. To defend the Catholic faith, Charles declared, he was prepared to use "all my possessions, my friends, my body, my blood, my life, and my soul." Thus were drawn the battle lines of a great religious conflict that divided the Western world for centuries.

At first this conflict was mainly a struggle among European Christians. Backed by Germans who feared imperial power and resented Church corruption, Luther boldly defied both emperor and pope. His success led others to do likewise, creating new religions and sparking revolts that fragmented Western Christendom.

Soon, however, the struggle was entwined with developments worldwide. In 1521, even as Charles vowed at Worms to defend the Catholic cause, his subjects were conquering distant lands such as Mexico and the Philippines, laying the foundations of a global Spanish empire. In ensuing decades, as officials and religious orders spread Catholicism throughout that empire, Charles and his heirs exploited its wealth to fight their European foes.

The result was a century of religious strife, accompanied by zealotry and witch hunts. But these conflicts were also accompanied by increased global trade, new kinds of commerce and production, expansion of learning and literacy, and changes in family life. By the seventeenth century, although Europe was still torn by religious and political strife, its monarchs, missionaries, and merchants had extended their reach around the world.

The Protestant Reformation

In the early 1500s almost all Western Christians still belonged to the Catholic Church. Headed by the pope in Rome and administered by a hierarchy of bishops and priests, the Church had long been a source of authority and unity in the West. Soon, however, this authority was challenged, and this unity shattered, by religious rebellions that divided Western Christendom into differing denominations. Collectively these rebellions are called the Protestant Reformation.

Roots of the Reformation

The Reformation of the sixteenth century was rooted in two key concerns. One was corruption in the Roman Catholic Church, the institution most Europeans looked to for salvation. The other was political unrest in the Holy Roman Empire, an assortment of central European states, loosely united by their rulers' recognition of its emperor as their overlord (Map 20.1).

Renaissance Europe had sophisticated culture, but death and disease still surrounded its people, whose main concern was thus eternal salvation: When they died would their souls go to heaven or hell? Most believed that the Catholic Church held the keys to eternal salvation, providing the rules and rituals they needed to make it to heaven. Chief among the rituals were the **sacraments**, sacred rites believed to bestow the graces needed for salvation.

The most important sacraments were baptism, Eucharist, and penance. To make it to heaven, one first had to undergo baptism, the ritual use of water that brings membership in the Church. Then one had to lead a virtuous life, doing good works and avoiding serious sins. Those who committed such sins and died with them unforgiven were damned

Church corruption and political unrest help spark the Reformation

FOUNDATION MAP 20.1 Europe in the Sixteenth Century

From 1519 to 1556, Europe's most powerful ruler was Holy Roman Emperor Charles V, heir to the Habsburg family's many possessions. Note that these possessions included Spain, Austria, the Netherlands, and much of Central Europe and Italy, as well as a growing Spanish American empire. Who were his major friends and enemies in the rest of Europe? Why did the Protestant Reformation pose a threat to his power?

Sketch of Friar John Tetzel selling indulgences.

Sale of indulgences and other abuses increase Church corruption

Scandalous Renaissance popes discredit papacy

to eternity in hell. But through Eucharist (also called Communion), the consumption of consecrated bread and wine, believed by the faithful to be Christ's body and blood, Christians could gain grace to avoid sin. And through penance, the confession of one's sins with sincere repentance to a priest, Christians could have their sins forgiven.

After that, however, sinners still had to atone for the wrong they had done. If they died without doing so, the Church taught, they would have to endure **purgatory**, a place of suffering that purified the soul so it could enter heaven. But people could also atone for their sins while still alive. Through certain prayers and sacrifices, such as fasts, pilgrimages, and charitable works, a person could earn an **indulgence**, a remission of the punishment still due for sins that had been forgiven through penance, to reduce or eliminate suffering in purgatory. Eventually, when popes started granting indulgences for *financial* sacrifices, such as donations to the Church, it began to look as if people could buy their way into heaven.

This sale of indulgences was one of several abuses that contributed to Church wealth and corruption. Others included simony (*SIH-muh-nē*), the sale of Church offices and benefits, and pluralism, the practice by which some clerics held multiple church offices, typically to enhance their income. Furthermore, while high Church officials such as popes and bishops lived lavishly in sumptuous palaces, poorly educated parish priests were often neither sober nor chaste.

Over the years, various individuals had dared to condemn such abuses. One was John Wyclif (*WICK-liff*) (1330–1384), theology professor at England's Oxford University, who denounced the sale of indulgences and Church offices. Asserting that the Church must set an example of poverty and piety, he called on civil rulers to reform it and seize its possessions. He also declared that divine authority resided in the Bible, not the Church. His followers, called Lollards, were vigorously suppressed, and some were even burned to death as heretics. Another Church critic was John Hus (1369–1415), rector of Prague University, who promoted similar ideas in Bohemia (now the Czech Republic). In 1415 he was invited to a Church council with a promise of safe conduct, but then convicted of heresy and burned to death at the stake. For the time being, the Church thus silenced its dissidents.

In time, however, Renaissance popes supplied a new set of scandals. Pope Sixtus IV (1471–1484), for example, sold Church offices to enrich his family and imposed heavy taxes on the Papal States. He also proclaimed that living people could gain indulgences for souls already in purgatory. Pope Alexander VI (1492–1503), having gotten his post through bribery, used Church wealth to indulge his illegitimate children, including a daughter with whom he was alleged to have had sexual relations and a son who used the papal armies in an effort to create his own kingdom. The next pope, Julius II (1503–1513), a vain and violent man, led wars to enlarge the papal domains and sold indulgences to finance extravagant projects—including the construction in Rome of a grandiose new church, Saint Peter's Basilica, replacing an ancient one built by Constantine that Julius had torn down.

Political unrest in Central Europe, the Reformation's other root cause, had meanwhile spread among the German people. Irked by Italians who saw themselves as culturally superior, many Germans also resented the use of money collected in Germany, through indulgence sales and other Church payments, to fund the costly wars and ventures of the Renaissance popes. Devout Germans, such as those belonging to the Brethren of the Common Life, a lay movement stressing piety and simplicity, were also dismayed by Church wealth and worldliness.

Furthermore, the heads of Germany's numerous states were anxious to protect their local autonomy against the ambitions of their overlords, the Holy Roman Emperors. Austrian Archduke Maximilian of Habsburg, elected emperor in 1493, seemed intent on ending this autonomy by transforming the empire into a centralized monarchy. By arranging favorable marriages for himself and his son, he also assured that his grandson, the future Emperor Charles V (1519–1556), would inherit not only Austria, the Netherlands, Sicily, Sardinia, and much of Central Europe and Italy (Map 20.1), but also Spain (where he was King Carlos I) and its American empire. Alarmed, many German princes and nobles resolved to resist any further Habsburg ambitions.

The Lutheran Revolt

Statue of Martin Luther in Wittenberg, Germany.

Into these troubled waters waded Martin Luther (1483–1546), a devout German monk obsessed with fears of death and eternal damnation. As a young man he had prepared to study law but, when caught in a violent storm, vowed instead to enter a monastery if God let him survive. He lived to join the Augustinian order and became an exemplary monk, repeatedly fasting, praying, and confessing his sins. But he still felt unworthy of salvation and feared he was doomed to hell. A 1510 trip to Pope Julius II's Rome only intensified his fears: how could a Church so worldly and corrupt help him save his soul? In confronting this question, Luther plunged Western Christendom into turmoil.

At the University of Wittenberg (*VIT-in-bărg*), in the central German state of Saxony, Luther studied scripture and became a doctor of theology, finally developing a doctrine that eased his torment. No one, he concluded, is worthy of salvation. It is not something one can *earn* by doing good works. It is rather a *gift* from God, who freely bestows his saving grace on those who have faith in him. We do not gain grace by doing good, reasoned Luther; we do good because we have grace. We are "justified," in Luther's words, not by our deeds but by God's grace, which we receive through faith.

The doctrine of "justification by faith alone," which Luther grounded on the writings of Saint Paul, implicitly threatened the Catholic Church. For if faith alone brought salvation, who needed sacraments and indulgences? Indeed, who needed the Church?

Luther asserts that faith alone, not the Church, brings salvation

Trouble arose in 1517 when a friar named John Tetzel traveled through Germany selling indulgences to help build the new Saint Peter's in Rome and pay the debts of a corrupt archbishop who had purchased his post. The crafty friar, assuring donors that coins put in his coffer would earn indulgences to ease the suffering of their departed loved ones, allegedly used slogans like "As soon as the coin in the coffer rings, the soul from purgatory springs!" Appalled, on October 31 Luther responded by issuing his **Ninety-five Theses**, a set of propositions challenging the Church's power to forgive sins and grant indulgences. Legend says he posted his theses on the Wittenberg castle church door.

The theses circulated widely, winning Luther fame and support among disgruntled Germans and religious reformers, while evoking Rome's anger. In a 1519 debate he defended the views of John Hus and denounced the Church for Hus's execution. In 1520 Luther published an *Address to the Christian Nobility of the German Nation*, urging German nobles to cast off Rome's control and seize Church property, artfully appealing to their Germanic pride and zest for wealth and power. The pope responded with a papal *bull* (edict) condemning Luther's views as heresy.

Luther urges German nobles to reform the Church and seize its property

Undeterred, Luther burned the papal bull and continued his assault. God's truth was found, he said, not in Church teachings but only in the Bible, which people must read and interpret themselves. He denied all sacraments except baptism and Communion, finding no biblical basis for the rest. He renounced not just indulgences but also belief in purgatory, pilgrimages, fasts, papal authority, and even monastic life. Proclaiming a "priesthood of all believers," he rejected priestly celibacy and encouraged clergymen to marry.

In truth, then, Luther was not just a reformer who attacked *abuses* the Church could conceivably correct, but also a rebel who denounced *doctrines* the Church regarded as inspired by God. Luther essentially denied the authority and divine mission of the Church. And this no pope could accept.

The Rising Tide of Rebellion

Soon Charles V, the new Holy Roman Emperor, grew alarmed about the danger Luther posed to both Church and empire. In 1521 he summoned Luther to face the Imperial Diet. Ordered to repudiate his views, as noted at the start of this chapter, the religious rebel held firm. Then, denounced by the emperor as a heretic, he was secretly taken to the castle of Saxony's ruler, Frederick the Wise, a German prince dismayed by Church corruption and determined to resist the emperor's growing power. There Luther hid for a year and began translating the Bible into German.

The printing press and German nobles help spread Luther's ideas

Aided by the new printing press, developed by German inventor Johannes Gutenberg in the 1450s (Chapter 16), and by German nobles eager to expand their wealth and power at Church expense, Luther's ideas spread quickly. Central Europe was soon divided between Lutherans, who adopted these new ideas, and Catholics, who remained loyal to the emperor and pope.

The situation quickly became more complex. By denying the Catholic Church's authority and urging people to interpret the Bible on their own, Luther opened the way for others to dissent, further fragmenting Christendom into additional sects. In 1522, for example, a dissident priest named Huldrych Zwingli (*TSVING-lē*) began his own movement in Zurich, Switzerland. More extreme than Luther, he rejected anything not literally found in the Bible, including the belief that Christ is present in Communion bread and wine. Soon zealots called *Anabaptists* (or Rebaptizers), since they baptized adults (rather than infants) as a sign of conscious faith commitment, split with Zwingli and started communities throughout central Europe.

Other religious rebels called for radical social reforms, helping to inspire a violent Peasants' Revolt against German nobles in 1524–1525. Although Zwingli supported this uprising, Luther did not. Heavily reliant on noble support, and anxious to keep his religious movement from becoming a social rebellion, Luther urged the authorities to "smash, strangle, and stab" the rebels, who were thenceforth slaughtered by the thousands.

Diverted by other conflicts, emperor and pope cannot stop "Protestants"

Meanwhile neither emperor nor pope could stem the Lutheran tide. Charles V was resisted by an alliance of German Lutheran princes, called "Protestants" after 1529, when they formally protested his efforts to curb their religion. He was also diverted by wars against the Ottoman Turks, who conquered much of Hungary in 1526 and besieged Vienna in 1529 (Chapter 17), and even the Catholic French, who so greatly feared his power that they sided against him with the Protestant German princes and Islamic Turks. Several successive popes, faced with calls for a Church council that could work at resolving the religious issues, resisted convening one for fear that it might also act to reduce papal powers. And a growing conflict with England's king further hampered the papacy.

Henry VIII and the English Reformation

England's Reformation, unlike Luther's, was rooted in royal affairs, not doctrinal disputes. John Wyclif, it is true, had earlier sown seeds of religious unrest in England, and Luther's ideas attracted much interest there. But English humanist Thomas More, though critical of Church corruption, explicitly condemned the Lutheran creed. And King Henry VIII (1509–1547) was a staunch Catholic who in 1521 issued a *Defense of the Seven Sacraments*, for which the pope proclaimed him "Defender of the Faith." England seemed safely within the Roman Catholic fold.

But things began to change in 1527, when Henry aspired to end his long marriage to Catherine of Aragon, a Spanish princess by birth. She had borne him six children, but only one, their daughter Mary, survived. As he and his wife got older, Henry feared he would have no male heir, leaving the realm in crisis after he died. Besides, he had fallen in love with youthful Anne Boleyn (*boo-LIHN*), one of his wife's attendants.

Anne Boleyn.

The Church did not permit divorce, but it could grant an annulment, a ruling that the marriage was never valid. Since Catherine had first wed Henry's older brother and then had married Henry after his brother died, and since the Bible stated that a man who took his brother's wife would die childless (Leviticus 20:21), Henry saw his lack of a son as a sign that God disapproved of his marriage to Catherine. He thus appealed to Rome to have the union annulled.

The request put Pope Clement VII (1523–1534) in a difficult bind. He did not want to anger Henry and risk losing England from the Church. But Catherine was the aunt of Emperor Charles V, whose soldiers occupied Rome, and whose help the Church sorely needed against Luther and the Turks. And Charles opposed the annulment: Catherine's marriage was his family's link to England, which he hoped to strengthen by wedding his son Philip to Henry's daughter Mary, who would one day be queen if there were no male heir. Besides, since a prior pope (Julius II) had permitted Henry to wed his brother's widow, an annulment would admit that popes erred, as Lutherans asserted. So Clement delayed his decision.

As Henry's case moved slowly through the papal courts he grew increasingly impatient. By 1533, his mistress Anne was pregnant, so Henry could wait no longer. In order to legitimize his expected heir, he promptly married Anne and got the Archbishop of Canterbury (England's highest cleric), a Lutheran sympathizer named Thomas Cranmer, to annul Henry's marriage to Catherine without waiting for Rome. Anne was then crowned queen, and a few months later gave birth: not to the desired son, but to a girl who was named Elizabeth.

Having acted on his own, in defiance of the pope, the king now completed the break. In 1534 he persuaded Parliament to pass an Act of Supremacy, naming the monarch "supreme head of the Church of England" and cutting all ties with Rome. Then, over the next five years, he closed the English monasteries and seized their property, selling much of it to local nobles. Henry thus solidified his support, since to keep their new lands the nobles would have to back him against the pope. But he also disbanded eminent institutions that had served as centers of learning and charity for centuries.

The English ruler becomes head of the "Church of England"

Henry's legacy was further tarnished by several other events. In 1535, his former friend Thomas More, the highly respected humanist, was beheaded for refusing to support the Act of Supremacy. In 1536 the unfortunate Anne, having twice failed to produce a son, was accused of adultery and likewise beheaded. A third wife finally bore Henry a boy but perished while giving birth. The king went on to wed three more times before dying in 1547.

Despite his break with the Roman Church and attacks on its English supporters, Henry VIII was not a religious rebel. He remained true to most Catholic teachings, and resisted adopting the new practices promoted by Luther and other Protestants. Not until after Henry's death did the Church of England undergo significant doctrinal change.

Calvin and the Elect

In Switzerland, a new religious rebel expanded the Reformation. John Calvin (1509–1564), raised in France and trained as both a lawyer and a theologian, was initially attracted by Lutheran ideas. But in 1533 he reportedly had a conversion that crystallized his views in a flash of light. He concluded that faith, for Luther the key to salvation, was a gift that God gave only to certain people. And he concluded that the Catholic Church was not just a corrupt institution that needed reform, but an evil institution that should be destroyed.

Calvin settles in Geneva, which becomes key Protestant center

In 1536, having earlier fled to Switzerland to escape a crackdown on Protestants by French authorities, Calvin published the *Institutes of the Christian Religion*, soon the central work of Protestant theology. That same year he agreed to settle in the Swiss town of Geneva, which under his influence soon became the center of the Protestant world.

Calvin's teachings focused on **predestination**, the notion that God long ago decided each person's eternal fate. Some are destined for heaven, others are doomed to hell, no matter what they do. Earlier Church thinkers such as St. Augustine had promoted predestination, but had not gone as far as Calvin in dismissing free will and personal choice. Like Luther, Calvin believed that no one could earn salvation, but unlike Luther he concluded that God saved only **the elect**—those God had chosen beforehand for salvation.

John Calvin.

Although God alone knew who the elect were, Calvin's followers assumed that people like themselves, who led lives of faith and virtue, were among the elect. But for them faith and virtue were *results* of their salvation, not causes. Unlike Catholics, who led good lives in order to save their souls, Calvinists led good lives as a sign that they were already saved. For Catholics salvation came *after* one's life and was based on how one had lived; for Calvinists salvation came *before* one's life and determined how one would live.

Calvinists were also **puritanical**, promoting a strict moral code and "pure" religious practices. They held simple worship services, focused on sermons and Bible readings rather than elaborate rituals, in unadorned buildings rather than grandiose churches. Calvinists abhorred the ornate altars, vessels, statues, and stained-glass windows that adorned Catholic churches.

Calvin's Geneva becomes model of Protestant Christian community

The Calvinist model of a Christian community was Geneva, widely seen as the Protestant answer to Rome. Reformers came from all over Europe to take part in Geneva's religious life and learn from Calvin himself. A religious commission, under Calvin's influence, supervised moral behavior, prohibiting offenses such as gambling, dancing, and drinking. Graver crimes, such as blasphemy, adultery, and witchcraft, were punished by secular leaders, who sometimes used torture and executions. Geneva thus became a very sober and austere community.

The Spread of Protestantism

Geneva also served as a Reformation headquarters, sending disciples hither and yon to spread the Calvinist creed, which took root in parts of Northern and Central Europe. Lutheranism, meanwhile, spread from Germany to Scandinavia, and the Church of England eventually embraced many Protestant beliefs (Map 20.2).

One of Calvin's followers was John Knox, who spent several years in Geneva and then took the new faith home to Scotland, where it later became Presbyterianism. Communities of Calvinists likewise emerged in Bohemia, Hungary, and Poland; in the Netherlands, where they constituted the Dutch Reformed Church; in France, where they were called Huguenots (*HYOO-guh-notz*); and in England, where they were known as Puritans. Calvinist churches were largely independent of each other: rejecting the authoritarianism of popes and bishops, they formed no centralized international institution like the Catholic Church.

Lutherans and Calvinists form smaller churches, not a large centralized church

Nor did the Lutherans develop a single centralized church; instead, they relied on secular rulers to adopt the new faith and impose it on their domains. Many rulers did so, not only because they liked Luther's ideas but also as a way to confiscate the property of the Catholic Church and gain control of religion in their realms. Supported by such rulers, Lutheranism spread quickly across northern Germany and Scandinavia, becoming the main faith throughout the Baltic region.

The Church of England, too, was controlled by the monarchs, who after the death of Henry VIII eventually made it more Protestant. Under Henry's sickly son, King Edward VI (1547–1553), Archbishop Cranmer brought in Protestant theologians,

Map 20.2 Sixteenth-Century Reformation Divides Europe Along Religious Lines

By the late 1500s, thanks to the Protestant Reformation and the Catholic response, European Christians had divided into rival denominations. Note that Protestantism had taken hold in northern and central Europe, while elsewhere Catholicism remained the dominant faith. What factors contributed to Protestantism's spread and Europe's religious fragmentation?

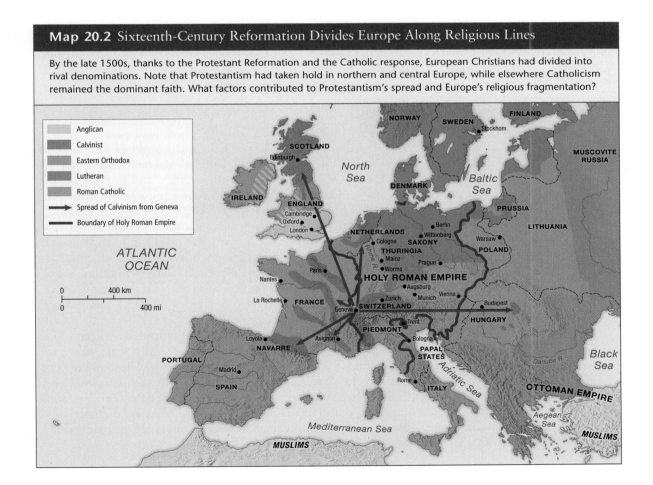

simplified liturgies, allowed priests to marry, and imposed his own *Book of Common Prayer* as the norm for church services. Queen Mary (1553–1558), the Catholic offspring of Henry's first marriage, tried to restore full Catholicism, executing Cranmer and several hundred Protestants. But her efforts were undone by Queen Elizabeth I (1558–1603), the Protestant daughter of Henry's second marriage. Determined to secure her throne by avoiding religious strife, Elizabeth pursued a middle path that aimed at satisfying most of her subjects. The English (or Anglican) Church thus combined Catholic-style liturgies and rituals performed by bishops and priests with the Protestant theology introduced under Cranmer.

By the 1560s, then, Protestantism in various forms had spread throughout northern and central Europe and into parts of France and Eastern Europe (Map 20.2). But by then the Catholic Church, which still prevailed in the South, had launched an effective counterattack and extended its influence far beyond Europe.

The Catholic Counterreformation

In the 1540s, after several decades of inability to stem the Protestant tide, Rome finally mounted a vigorous response. Pope Paul III (1534–1549), the earnest successor to the hapless Clement VII, called a general council to initiate Church reforms, authorized tribunals to prosecute Protestants for heresy, and approved new religious orders that reinvigorated the ancient Church. He thus began an era of Church reform and revitalization, often called the Catholic Reformation, but also labeled by Church foes as the Counterreformation, since it involved a counterattack against Protestantism.

The Council of Trent

The Council of Trent reaffirms Catholic teachings and sacraments

In 1545, after years of pressure from Emperor Charles V, Paul III convened a great council of Catholic bishops and other Church leaders. The Council of Trent, which met in 1545–1547, 1551–1552, and 1562–1563, shaped Catholic doctrine and worship for the next four hundred years. Although Charles V wanted it to compromise with Lutherans, and some bishops hoped it would limit papal power, the council instead went the other direction. It affirmed many things that Protestants denied, including indulgences, papal supremacy, priestly celibacy, the Latin Mass, and the Church's power to forgive sins. It insisted that salvation was based on *both* faith *and* good works, not on faith alone. It declared that divine revelation was found in *both* the Bible *and* Church tradition, not in scripture alone. It reasserted the Church's stance that there were seven sacraments, not just the two (baptism and Communion) that Luther recognized. And to reinforce Church unity, the council affirmed the pope's preeminence.

The Council of Trent also enacted some reforms. Although it affirmed indulgences for pious deeds and prayers, for example, the council forbade their *sale*, the practice that had triggered Luther's revolt. To eliminate pluralism, the council allowed each bishop only one diocese, or administrative district, in which he must reside. To improve the quality of clergy, it ruled that each diocese must have a *seminary*, a training school for priests. These reforms did not win back the Protestants, but that was not their intent. They were designed to purify and strengthen Catholicism for battle against Protestantism, a struggle that lasted far longer than anyone at Trent could foresee.

The Roman and Spanish Inquisitions

The Counterreformation's tactics were sometimes extreme. In central Italy and Spain, where Catholics were in control, they employed Inquisitions, church tribunals mandated to investigate, arrest, and prosecute people suspected of heretical beliefs. In Rome the Inquisition operated under the Holy Office, a council of six cardinals formed in 1542 by Pope Paul III. It was authorized to fine, imprison, and sometimes even execute people it convicted of promoting false doctrines. Starting in 1559, it also published an *Index of Forbidden Books*, a list of works that Catholics were forbidden to read without special permission. Officially designed to protect the faithful from heresy, the *Index* in time banned many works, including even novels such as *Les Miserables* and *The Hunchback of Notre Dame* (Chapter 27), perceived as offensive by the Church.

The Spanish Inquisition, which functioned largely under the rulers of Spain, had been set up in 1478 to investigate Jews and Muslims who had outwardly converted to Catholicism. Now it also targeted people suspected of Protestant views. To extract confessions, inquisitors sometimes used tortures such as the rack, which stretched the victim's body, and the thumbscrew, which crushed the victim's thumbs. Those found guilty of heresy were often burned to death.

Using closed trials, secret informers, tortures, and executions, the Inquisitions enforced Catholicism and virtually eradicated Protestantism in Italy and Spain. But elsewhere their main effect was to increase anti-Catholic hostility among Protestants, who sometimes employed similar methods against their religious foes.

Spanish Inquisition persecutes Muslims, Jews, and Protestants

New Religious Orders

Amid this tumult, the Catholic Church enjoyed a spiritual revival, led by dynamic individuals and new religious orders. Even before the Reformation, the Brethren of the Common Life, an association of devout laypersons and clergy who led simple lives in imitation of Christ, had spread through northern Europe. In Italy, a similar group called the Oratory of Divine Love stressed works of charity and devotion as antidotes to worldly corruption. In the 1530s an Italian woman named Angela Merici (*muh-RE-che*) created the Ursuline (*UR-suh-lin*) order, a community of nuns who educated Catholic girls throughout Italy, France, and the Americas. But the most influential new order was begun by a Spanish nobleman named Ignatius Loyola (1491–1556).

An heir to Spain's crusading tradition, Ignatius was a soldier until 1521, when he was crippled in battle by a cannonball. During a long, painful recovery he read books about Christ and Christian saints. Deeply inspired, he then embarked on a spiritual crusade. He withdrew to a cave, where for months he prayed and lived alone in great austerity, depriving himself of all physical comforts. There he developed the Spiritual Exercises, a four-week regimen of prayer and meditation designed to prepare one for selfless discipline in service to God and Church.

After a pilgrimage to the Holy Land and brushes with the Spanish Inquisition, in 1528 Ignatius enrolled at the University of Paris, where he attracted a group of like-minded men. In 1537 they formed a "Company of Jesus," and in 1540 Pope Paul III formally approved them as the Society of Jesus.

The Jesuits, as they were soon known, became Catholicism's most zealous champions. Highly selective, they accepted only men of talent and discipline. Organized on military

Ignatius of Loyola.

lines, they vowed strict obedience to their superiors and the pope. Refusing to withdraw and live as monks or beggars, they served in the world as educators, missionaries, preachers, and political advisors.

Jesuits work to globalize and strengthen Catholicism

As educators, the Jesuits combined Renaissance humanism (Chapter 16) with Catholic ideals, promoting both secular learning and religious faith, while creating a network of schools and universities that eventually became a worldwide educational system. As missionaries, they worked tirelessly to convert the peoples of the Americas, Africa, and Asia to Catholicism, helping to transform their European faith into a global religion. As preachers to European Christians and political advisors to Catholic rulers, they led an intensive anti-Protestant campaign, helping to stem the Protestant tide and even restoring parts of Central Europe to the Catholic fold. They gained a reputation for both eloquence and political intrigue, making many enemies and adding to the climate of religious and political strife.

Religious and Political Strife in Europe

In the wake of the Reformation, Europe was ravaged by a century of religious and political conflicts. Bolstered by the riches of their Spanish overseas empire, the Catholic Habsburgs strove to impose their power and faith by force on Protestant regions. The Protestants, however, staunchly defended their new religions and political autonomy, perpetuating the fragmentation of Western Christianity.

The Spanish Catholic Crusade

In 1556 Emperor Charles V, longtime Catholic champion and ruler of the Habsburg realms, retired to a monastery. Deeming his domains too vast for one ruler, he split them between his brother and his son. His brother Ferdinand received the Habsburg lands in Austria, Bohemia, and Hungary, and succeeded Charles as Holy Roman Emperor. His son Philip got the rest, including Spain and its American empire, the Netherlands, Sardinia, Sicily, and parts of Italy. As King Philip II he ruled these lands from 1556 to 1598.

The wealth of its American empire makes Spain a global power

By this time Spain was Europe's mightiest country, owing largely to its American empire. The conquest of the Aztecs and Inca, with their enormous riches (Chapter 18), had been followed in 1545 by the discovery of vast silver deposits near Potosí ($p\bar{o}$-$t\bar{o}$-$S\bar{E}$), in what is now Bolivia. These immense resources, exploited by Spaniards using Amerind (American Indian) and African slaves, soon supplied Spain's king with almost limitless wealth. And Philip was determined to use this fortune to further the Catholic cause.

A zealous Catholic, he launched a crusade to reinforce his religion throughout his realms and win back for his Church the lands it had lost. In Spain he used the Inquisition to suppress Protestantism. In America he used missionaries to foster his faith and officials to enforce it; so successful were they that Spanish America became a Catholic stronghold. In the Mediterranean he used his navy to challenge the Ottoman Turks, joining forces with Venice and the pope to defeat the Turkish fleet near the coast of Greece at the Battle of Lepanto in 1571. Elsewhere, however, Philip ran into problems.

Philip's first setback came in England, where he was wed to the Catholic Queen Mary. With her help he hoped to bring England back to Catholicism, and perhaps into his empire. But in 1558 she died in a cholera epidemic, and her Protestant successor Elizabeth, spurning his marriage proposals, soon became a formidable foe.

His next setback was the Dutch Revolt, a rebellion in the Netherlands against his heavy-handed rule. In 1566, alarmed that he might impose the Inquisition on them, Dutch Calvinists rebelled, attacking Catholic churches, smashing sacred vessels, statues, stained-glass windows, and artwork. Enraged by this "Calvinist fury," Philip tried to reassert control by executing rebels and confiscating lands of Calvinist nobles. By 1579 he had sub-dued the Netherlands' southern Catholic provinces, which henceforth became the Spanish Netherlands (and today constitute Belgium). But the northern Protestant provinces then declared independence as the United Provinces of the Netherlands. This new nation, often called Holland (after its main province), continued to fight Spain for a generation.

English and Dutch combat Spain's anti-Protestant campaign

In 1585, fearing that Spain might prevail and then use the Netherlands as a base from which to attack her country, England's Queen Elizabeth sent money and troops to aid the Dutch. Philip, in turn, prepared to invade England. Tension increased in 1587, when Elizabeth approved the execution of her cousin Mary Stuart (Mary Queen of Scots), the Catholic claimant to the English throne. The next year Philip dispatched the Invincible Catholic Armada, a fleet of 130 huge ships, with orders to land in the Netherlands and escort the Spanish army to England to begin the assault.

Its ships emblazoned with crosses and Catholic banners, the Armada set sail in May 1588. In July it met the English fleet in the English Channel. The result was a disaster for Spain. The English, whose ships were smaller and faster, harassed the Armada's huge vessels and kept them from landing. A fierce gale, which the English dubbed the "Protestant Wind," blew the Spanish ships off course, and further storms did even more damage as the Armada's remnants, trying to return to Spain, sailed around Scotland and Ireland. Some survivors, shipwrecked in Ireland, were killed; others settled there and married Irish women.

The defeat of the Spanish Armada in 1588 by no means ended the fighting, which con-tinued until 1604. But it did help the English and Dutch to foil Philip's Catholic crusade, to continue their Protestant course, to challenge Spain for control of the seas, and hence to found their own colonies in North America.

English ships confront the Spanish Armada.

The Wars of Religion in France

From 1562 to 1594, as Catholic Spain battled Dutch and English Protestants, France was torn by internal conflicts called the Wars of Religion. By then, although France remained mostly Catholic, about 7 percent of its people—including about 40 percent of its nobles—had become Calvinists. Known as Huguenots and led by the Bourbon family, they fought Catholic factions in a complex struggle for religious and political power. Catherine de Medicis (*MED-ih-chē*), the influential mother of three Catholic kings who reigned from 1559 to 1589, tried to preserve her family's power by reconciling hostile factions. In 1572, however, fearful of growing Protestant strength, she helped plot the massacre of several thousand Huguenots gathered in Paris for a wedding. But even this atrocity could not save Catherine's clan. In 1589, following her death and the murder of her last royal son, the head of the Huguenot Bourbons inherited the throne as King Henri IV.

The struggle nonetheless continued. French Catholics, refusing to accept a Protestant king, blocked Henri's efforts to enter Paris and assume the throne. So Henri, pragmatically concluding that "Paris is worth a Mass," formally became a Catholic in 1593, thereby gaining acceptance in Paris as king in 1594. Betrayed by their champion, the Huguenots resisted Henri's rule until 1598, when he won them over with religious toleration, issuing the Edict of Nantes (*NAHNT*). This historic document gave French Protestants full civil

Calvinist King Henri IV becomes Catholic and enforces toleration

rights, the freedom to hold worship services in their own manors and towns, and the right to fortify these towns with their own troops. It also helped make Henri IV, already known for his charm and dashing demeanor, one of France's most popular kings. But Henri's tolerant edict did not please everyone: in 1610 he was murdered by a fanatical Catholic. Religious animosities did not die easily in France.

The Thirty Years War

Nor did they die easily in Germany, birthplace of the Reformation, where Lutherans and Catholics had for decades observed an uneasy truce. In 1608 the Calvinists, having made inroads in parts of the Holy Roman Empire, joined with Lutherans in an alliance called the Protestant Union. The next year the Austrian Habsburgs, backed by the wealth of their Spanish cousins, created a rival coalition called the Catholic League, setting the stage for a calamitous conflict known as the Thirty Years War (1618–1648).

Catholic Habsburg rulers battle Central Europe's Protestant nobles

This conflict began in 1618 with an incident called the "Defenestration of Prague" (*dē-FEN-ih-STRĀ-shun*: the act of throwing someone out a window). Protestant nobles in Bohemia, angered by Habsburg efforts to restrict their rights, threw two imperial agents out of a high palace window. Despite their survival—credited by Catholics to divine intervention and by Protestants to the fact that they landed in a dung heap—the fragile peace was shattered. Emperor Ferdinand II (1619–1637), aided by the Catholic League and his Spanish relatives, crushed the Bohemians and other Protestant forces, moving steadily to bring all Germany under Catholic control. By 1629 he was on the verge of triumph, and the Protestant cause seemed lost.

Then, however, two powerful outside forces intervened on the Protestant side. One was Gustavus Adolphus (*gus-TAH-vus ah-DOLL-fus*), Sweden's Lutheran king, who feared for his country's safety should northern Germany come under Catholic control. A talented warrior, he defeated the Habsburgs in several key battles before dying in combat in 1632. The other force was Cardinal Richelieu (*RISH-lih-YOO*), France's chief minister, who first supplied aid to the Protestants, and then had his country join the war on their side in 1635.

As a cardinal in the Catholic Church, Richelieu seemed an unlikely supporter of German Protestants. But his main loyalty was to France, which already faced Habsburg Spain to its South and the Spanish Netherlands to its North. Bent on blocking Habsburg unification of Germany to the East, he aided Protestants as a way to keep Germany divided and weak.

The last phase of the war, from 1635 to 1648, resulted in mass devastation. France and Spain, both deeply involved in the German conflict, battled each other as well. Armies crisscrossed central Europe, assaulting each other and brutalizing the people, while disease and famine stalked the land. The German population was greatly diminished, and wolves roamed the streets in desolate towns and villages.

Although France and Spain fought on until 1659, the German nightmare ended in 1648 with the Peace of Westphalia (Map 20.3). Each German state remained virtually independent, with rulers free to conduct their own diplomacy and decide whether their realms should be Catholic, Lutheran, or Calvinist. The Holy Roman Empire was left with only nominal authority, and it no longer included the Dutch, the Swiss, or the Italians. The Habsburgs remained emperors in name, but their efforts to unify Germany and restore Catholicism throughout Europe had failed. After decades of destructive warfare, Europe remained divided along religious lines.

Map 20.3 Peace of Westphalia Leaves Central Europe Divided, 1648

In 1648, at the end of the Thirty Years War, the Peace of Westphalia left Europe divided along religious lines, while the various states in the Holy Roman Empire retained and enhanced their autonomy. Notice the empire was also diminished by the loss of Switzerland, the Dutch United Netherlands, and the northwest Italian states. Why did the Habsburgs fail in their efforts to unite Central Europe under Catholic Habsburg rule? How did this failure bolster the power of France?

The Globalization of Western Christianity and Commerce

Europe's fragmentation was, paradoxically, accompanied by global expansion. In the sixteenth and seventeenth centuries, as Europe was torn by ruinous religious and political strife, European Christianity and commerce spread across the globe, aided by enterprising missionaries, officials, and merchants.

Catholicism's Global Expansion

Catholics at first took the lead, based on the efforts of empire builders and religious orders. The Spanish and Portuguese, who justified imperial expansion by claiming they were carrying Christ's message to distant lands, systematically imposed their faith on the people they conquered (Chapter 19). Thus in the American colonies, where Iberian Catholics controlled governance and commerce, and where Catholic priests and nuns ran numerous missions and schools, most people adopted the religion of their rulers through coercion, convenience, or conviction.

Jesuits and other orders work to convert Asians to Catholicism

The Jesuits, joined and often rivaled by other Catholic orders, including Franciscans and Dominicans, also strove to implant Catholicism in Asia. Their work was begun by Francis Xavier (*ZĀ-vē-ur*), one of the first Jesuits, a former Paris roommate of Ignatius Loyola. Arriving in India on a Portuguese ship in 1542, Xavier worked for several years among that country's poor pearl fishers, then traveled to Malaya and the Spice Islands, founding various missions before returning to India. From 1549 to 1551 he lived in Japan, whose culture he greatly admired, and converted thousands to the Catholic faith. In 1552 he set out to begin the conversion of China but grew ill and died on an island off the Chinese coast.

Jesuits gain some success by adapting to Asian cultures

Xavier's deep respect for Asians, and his tireless efforts to understand their languages and cultures, set an example for thousands of Jesuits who followed in his footsteps. Jesuits learned local languages, adapted local customs, and blended Catholic teachings into local cultures, rather than simply seeking to impose European ways. Their success in Asian countries was nonetheless often limited by resistance from local religions and rulers. Still, spread by the Jesuits and their fellow missionaries, preachers, and teachers, Catholicism became a global faith, with thousands of missions, parishes, and schools, and millions of followers, around the world (Map 20.4).

Merchant Capitalism and Global Trade

As some Europeans globalized their religion, others were transforming the global economy. Western merchants, eager to enhance their incomes, worked to gain control over the production of goods and to establish worldwide trading networks. European governments, seeking to increase state wealth, encouraged the growth of overseas commerce and the exploitation of colonies.

For many centuries, Chinese, Muslim, and European merchants had conducted interregional trade, engaging in many practices—such as credit, banking, and marketing of goods—later associated with **capitalism**, an economic system based on competition among private enterprises. But merchants usually did not manufacture the goods they sold. These goods were typically produced by artisans, who owned their own tools and workshops, purchased raw materials such as metals, leather, wool, wood, and wax, and used their labor and skill to make these materials into finished products. The artisans then sold the finished goods to customers or merchants, often at prices fixed by artisans' guilds. Merchants were mostly middlemen: traders who bought goods in one place, took them to another place, and sold them at a profit.

European capitalists increasingly control both production and commerce

From the fifteenth century onward, however, European merchants increasingly sought to enhance their profits by gaining control of production. They bought mines, woodlands, and herds of sheep and cattle, thereby acquiring their own raw materials. They also bought tools and equipment, then hired their own workers so as not to be dependent on artisans and guilds, many of whom in turn organized their own enterprises. Thus arose a dynamic new class of capitalists: entrepreneurs who created and ran enterprises that produced and sold their own goods.

In this system, later called merchant capitalism, the merchant entrepreneur owned the means of production—tools, machines, and raw materials—and decided how much to produce and to charge for finished goods. The producer worked for the merchant and was paid a fixed wage or a prearranged price for each piece made. The finished products were thus owned by the entrepreneur, who arranged for their transport and sale, setting

Map 20.4 Globalization of Western Christianity and Commerce, 1500–1750

While Europe was torn apart by religious conflict, Europeans were extending their sway over the Americas and parts of Africa and Asia. Note that Europeans not only helped connect these regions by commerce, but also spread their Christian religions, with the Spanish, French, and Portuguese imposing Catholicism, the Dutch and English promoting Protestantism, and the Russians fostering their Orthodox faith in expanding across northern Asia. How did the spread of Christianity and commerce help to bolster Europe's wealth and power?

prices so as to be competitive in a free market based on supply and demand. Over time, independent artisans were largely replaced by wage laborers, employed and paid by wealthy merchant capitalists.

In expanding production and trade, merchant capitalists often found allies in their national monarchs. Rulers increasingly realized that, as commerce grew, so did their revenues from taxes and tariffs. They could then use these revenues in hiring armies to fight their wars and officials to administer their realms, thus expanding the power of their government. Rulers therefore instituted policies, later referred to as **mercantilism**, that aimed to create a favorable balance of trade, a condition in which a country's trading exports exceeded its imports in value. Since the nation as a whole would thus sell more than it bought, fortune supposedly would flow into the realm, and into the royal treasury.

Mercantilist policies typically included government support of enterprises engaged in overseas trade. In the fifteenth and sixteenth centuries, Portuguese voyagers backed by the government set up numerous trading posts on African and Asian coasts, creating a commercial empire that made one of Europe's smallest kingdoms into one of its richest (Chapter 19). By 1600, eager to gain some of this wealth, England and the Netherlands had begun to follow suit.

In these countries, and later in France, government support for overseas trade was provided through **charter companies**, trading associations protected by royal monopoly. Since overseas trade involved risks and expenses beyond what one investor could bear, merchants in these countries pooled their resources to form a large company in which many owned shares. To support the company and protect it from competition, the country's ruler then issued a charter giving the company a monopoly of trade between that country and a specified region.

English and Dutch East India Companies dominate east-west trade

Especially notable were the English East India Company, which monopolized commerce between England and India starting in 1600, and the Dutch United East India Company, founded two years later, which dominated trade between the Netherlands and the East Indies. For the next two centuries, these companies and others, with large fleets of merchant vessels, maintained profitable trading posts in various parts of the world, gaining vast riches for themselves and their rulers. Global trading networks supplied European consumers with products from distant lands, such as silks, spices, sugar, coffee, tea, and tobacco, while the revenues this trade produced helped European monarchs centralize their governments and increase their royal powers.

Colonies, Commerce, and Religion

Overseas colonies also enhanced a country's commerce and power. The foremost example was Habsburg Spain, which used silver from its American colonies to buy luxury goods in Asia for resale elsewhere, and to finance its powerful armies and navies, making it sixteenth-century Europe's richest and mightiest realm. Another example was Portugal, which gained wealth in that same century through the sale of sugar, grown in Brazil and other colonies using African slaves.

French Jesuit baptizing Amerind convert.

Other Europeans, seeing these successes, imitated the Iberians. Hence, in the seventeenth century, the French, Dutch, and English established North American colonies. The French set up trading posts in eastern Canada and the Mississippi Valley, bartering with Amerinds for animal furs that sold for a fortune in Europe, and the Dutch did likewise in the Hudson Valley of what is now New York State. The English established a Virginia colony that prospered in time from tobacco, a crop that Amerinds taught them to grow, which was sold in Europe for a big profit. The French, Dutch, and English also set up colonies on Caribbean islands that, imitating the Spanish West Indies and Portuguese Brazil, profited greatly from production and sale of slave-grown sugar. By the late 1600s, bolstered by wealth from their commerce and colonies, England, France, and the Netherlands had replaced Spain and Portugal as Europe's dominant political and economic powers.

The French, Dutch, and English impose their religions in their colonies

These developments also had profound religious implications. France, like Spain and Portugal, promoted Catholicism in its colonies, aided by Jesuits and other French priests who worked among French settlers and Amerinds. Dutch Calvinists established settlements in the Hudson River region, while English Calvinists known as Puritans, fleeing persecution in their native land, moved in large numbers to what became New England starting in the 1620s. English Catholics colonized Maryland in succeeding decades, while Anglicans and other English Protestants populated additional new English North American colonies. By the mid-1600s, like Europe itself, North America had a variety of Christian denominations (Map 20.4).

Western Society in an Age of Religious and Economic Change

As Europeans spread their creeds and commerce to diverse lands and peoples, religious divisions and global expansion were transforming Europe's society. On one hand, religious strife led to suffering and fear; on the other hand, global expansion helped foster growing prosperity.

Warfare, Disease, and Witch Hunts

The era of religious upheaval brought hardship to many Europeans. Religious leaders and warriors, fueled by righteous fury, engaged in persecutions and bloodshed, claiming they were doing God's will. Bands of armed fighters, feeding on the chaos of religious conflict, often roamed the countryside, looting, pillaging, and raping at will. Dislocation and devastation frequently followed in their footsteps.

Adding to anxieties in the sixteenth century was a pandemic of syphilis, a sexually transmitted disease whose victims initially suffered sores and rashes, and later often blindness, insanity, and death. Some experts think syphilis was a virulent form of an earlier European ailment; others assume that European sailors brought it from the Americas after contracting it from Amerinds. Either way, it spread misery and fear in Europe, where it was called the great pox (to distinguish it from smallpox) or the "French disease" (as it was often blamed on French soldiers).

War and global contacts help produce syphilis pandemic

Even more unsettling were the witch hunts of the sixteenth and seventeenth centuries. During this era, over a hundred thousand Europeans, most of them women, were placed on trial for witchcraft, supposedly for using supernatural powers to make evil things happen. Perhaps fifty thousand people were executed for this alleged crime.

Various factors contributed to the witch hunts. One factor was the Reformation, which led Catholics and Protestants alike to persecute heretics and to accuse dissenters of doing the devil's work. Luther, Calvin, and the Catholic Church all favored burning witches. A second factor was the misery bred by religious war, leading many to seek scapegoats for the suffering. A third factor was the syphilis pandemic, causing miscarriages, stillbirths, blindness, and insanity, easily ascribed to satanic influence.

Disease, devastation, and religious conflict help to promote witch hunts

A fourth factor was a pamphlet called *Malleus Maleficarum* (*MAH-lā-oos MAH-lā-fē-CAH-room*), "The Hammer of the Wicked." First published by two Dominican friars in 1486, and circulated widely over the next two centuries, it sought to supply an explanation of witchcraft. It alleged that witches made pacts with the devil, sealed by sex with him, which empowered them to make evil things happen to others. Although witches could be male or female, this book portrayed them mainly as women, whom it considered weaker than men and more easily won over to evil. Witches were said to meet their devils at assemblies called synagogues or sabbaths, thereby indirectly linking witchcraft to Jewish worship.

Those accused of witchcraft were usually women, typically single or widowed, aging, and poor, who often had no family to protect them and thus were easy targets. Older women, beyond childbearing age, were sometimes seen as burdens on society and accused of erratic behavior. Aging might bring on deeper voices and a haggard appearance, leading fearful neighbors to label them "hags." Women's customary roles as midwives and healers also left them open to blame when infants or sick people died. Such circumstances, and depictions of women as tools of the devil going back to the biblical Eve, reinforced the tendency to associate witchcraft with women.

Women accused of witchcraft being hanged.

Document 20.1 Excerpt from a Witchcraft Trial

Witchcraft trials were held throughout European countries and their colonies in the sixteenth and seventeenth centuries. In the seventeenth-century indictment excerpted below, couched in the formal legal language of the day, a woman named Rose Cullender is charged with using "incantations" and "enchantments" to harm a certain Ann Baldinge. Rose is identified as a widow, and Ann is identified as spinster, a term commonly used for women who never married, since many earned their living by spinning thread.

The King's sworn officers maintain upon their oaths that Rose Cullender, late of Lowestoft in the aforesaid county, on the 1st day of February in the 14th year of the reign of our lord Charles . . ., being a common witch and "enchantress" and not having God before her eyes but moved and seduced by the instigation of the Devil did . . . violently, unlawfully, diabolically, and feloniously use, practice, and employ certain evil and diabolical "fascinations"—in English "witchcrafts"— and "incantations"—in English "enchantments"—on one Anne Baldinge, spinster, then and there living in the peace of God . . ., and by the aforesaid evil and diabolical witchcraft and enchantments then and there did feloniously bewitch and enchant her, by which evil and diabolical witchcraft and enchantments . . . the aforesaid Ann Baldinge from the . . . 1st day of February of the above mentioned year to the day of the holding of the inquisition at Lowestoft . . . has languished and languishes still and is greatly wasted in her . . . body and is consumed to the injury of the same Anne Baldinge and in the breach of peace of the said lord King . . . and also in breach of peace of the form of the state given forth and provided for such cases.

SOURCE: Gilbert Geis and Ivan Bunn, *A Trial of Witches: A Seventeenth-Century Witchcraft Prosecution* (London and New York: Routledge, 1997) page 39.

Women depicted as witches were blamed for numerous misfortunes, such as accidents, illnesses, sudden deaths, bad weather, infertility, and sexual impotence. Charges were typically brought by someone who had suffered a loss or by professional witch hunters who made a career of identifying witches (see "Excerpt from a Witchcraft Trial"). Many of the accused were tortured, often until they confessed or implicated others to save themselves. The convicted might be burned to death, hanged (in England), banished, or imprisoned. Some of them may actually have tried witchcraft, but most were no doubt innocent victims of fear, superstition, and witch hunts.

Social Effects of Economic Expansion

Urban middle classes benefit from global commerce

Less dramatic, but far more enduring, were changes wrought in Western society by capitalism and global trade. The main beneficiaries were the growing middle classes who lived in towns (burgs) and cities, and hence were called *burghers* or *bourgeoisie* (*boorzh-wah-ZĒ*). They included merchants and bankers who profited from increased trade; doctors, lawyers, and others who prospered by serving wealthy people's needs; and artisans and manufacturers who raised prices on their products as more wealth became available.

Global trade helped prosperous townsfolk live well, enjoying cottons, furs, tea, coffee, sugar, spices, and later tobacco and chocolate, imported from the Americas and Asia. Towns and cities sported rows of tidy townhouses, along with markets, plazas, taverns, inns, banks, and shops. Wealthy bourgeois even challenged nobles for social and political preeminence. But many wage laborers were hurt by rising prices that increased faster than their incomes. And the urban poor, roughly half the townsfolk, lived in squalid slums full of vermin, beggars, criminals, prostitutes, drunks, and gangs.

The nobles, descendants of medieval lords and owners of rural estates, also were affected by the changing economy. Many came to live in cities, where they dwelt in elegant townhouses and enjoyed luxuries provided by global trade, while leaving hired stewards to manage their estates. To enhance their incomes some nobles even invested in commercial concerns or married their children to sons and daughters of wealthy bourgeois parents. In Western Europe, where access to the sea trade enhanced the size and wealth of the bourgeoisie, the nobles' power declined as monarchs and merchants shaped strong political and economic institutions. In Central and Eastern Europe, however, where lack of access to such commerce kept the urban middle classes small and weak, the nobles remained the dominant political and economic force.

Initially the peasants, some 80–90 percent of the population, were little affected by the economic changes. They lived in isolated villages, with little access to the wonders of the wider world. Occasionally they might travel to a town to visit its markets or attend an annual fair. As a rule, however, they rose with the sun, worked the fields by day, and retired to their villages after dark. In Eastern Europe most peasants were still serfs, bound in service to their landlords; but even in the West, where most were legally free, peasants were subject to burdensome taxes and dues.

By the 1600s, however, capitalist commerce was beginning to affect many peasants. To get around dealing with town artisans and guilds, merchants started lending, or "putting out," equipment and raw materials (such as weaving looms and wool) to peasant families, who used them to make products (such as clothing) in their own huts and cottages. The merchant capitalist paid them a fixed price for each item produced and then sold these items at a lower cost than guild artisans charged for such products. This "putting out" system, later called **cottage industry** or the "domestic system," not only lowered merchants' costs and the price of goods produced but also increased peasant incomes, further reducing the landlords' leverage over local villagers.

New "cottage industries" tie rural villagers into global economy

Family, Gender, Education, and Diet

Religious and economic change also affected family patterns, gender roles, education, and diet. Arising in the 1500s, these effects became increasingly visible in the following century.

In the 1500s, as in eras past, the basic unit of Western society was the patriarchal family, headed by men regarded as masters of their households. Noblemen acted as lords of the family estate and often also as military officers or government officials. Middle class men ran the family business or practiced the family trade, while peasant men farmed the strips of land allotted to their family in fields around their village. As household heads and providers, men expected to be waited on by their wives and to make key decisions for their children, including assignment of family duties and selection of spouses.

Although thus considered subservient to men, women played central roles in family life. They raised children, baked bread, prepared meals, and made clothes, often joining in social circles to support and learn from other women. Women also functioned as midwives and caregivers, delivering babies and treating illnesses with folk remedies passed on from previous generations. Lower-class mothers breast-fed their own infants, while wealthy women often hired a "wet-nurse" to breast-feed theirs. Peasant women sustained their families mainly on dark bread and soups made from peas, beans, cabbages, and carrots, supplemented sometimes by eggs, butter, and cheese. Meat meals, white bread, and sweet pastries, standard fare in the upper classes, were rare among the common people.

Peasant couple at market (engraving by Albrecht Dürer).

Women typically have
little freedom or choice

Yet women had little control over their own lives. Parents arranged their marriages, often with more concern for enhancing family status than for their daughters' happiness. Women who wound up with drunken, abusive, or unfaithful husbands had little choice but to endure their plight. Since childhood diseases killed 20–30 percent of all children, women commonly bore at least six or seven children to ensure that some would survive to adulthood.

By the 1600s, despite considerable continuity, some basic family patterns were changing. Increased incomes from commerce and cottage industry, for example, helped many married couples maintain separate households, rather than living as in the past with their extended families. **Nuclear families**, made up of only parents and children, gradually became the norm. And, although their parents still had to approve their marriages, young people increasingly chose their own spouses, often after years of courtship, waiting to wed until their mid-twenties when they could support themselves. Divorce and remarriage, banned by the Catholic Church, were often allowed among Protestants, especially in cases of adultery or abuse.

Printing press and
religious schools boost
literacy and learning

Learning and literacy, too, were becoming more common. The great increase in the number of books produced by the printing press, combined with the Protestant emphasis on individual reading of the Bible, accelerated the spread of education. Protestant pastors and Catholic religious orders set up schools to teach reading and writing, not only to the offspring of merchants and nobles but also to growing numbers of lower-class children. Although such schools were intended mainly for males, prosperous parents increasingly managed to educate their daughters too, enabling them in time to play a larger role in social and cultural life.

Diets are enhanced by
new foods such as
potatoes from the
Americas

European diets also evolved as new foods from the Americas were added. In the seventeenth century, European farmers began growing crops developed by Amerinds, such as corn (maize), which originated in Mexico, and potatoes, which came from Peru. Potatoes proved especially useful, since they took less space to cultivate than grain crops such as wheat or rye, were easier to preserve, and could feed more people. Europe's global expansion thus enhanced not only its prosperity but also its food supply.

Changes in the Role of Religion

Religion's role was likewise altered in the age of religious conflict. Before the Reformation, since most Europeans sought salvation through the Church, religion was central to society. The Church provided sacraments and religious education, collected and distributed donations for the poor, and kept records of births, deaths, baptisms, and marriages. It also offered festival occasions, including baptisms, weddings, and holy days such as Christmas and Easter. It even condoned midwinter Carnival festivities—also called Shrovetide, Mardi Gras (*MAR-dē GRAH*), or Fasching (*FAH-shing*)—during which people dressed in costumes and ate and drank excessively in preparation for Lent, a 40-day period of fasting and sacrifice leading up to Easter.

After the Reformation, changing outlooks slowly started altering religion's role. Since Protestants needed no Church for salvation, their faith was often private and plain, marked by Bible reading in the home and simple Sunday services. Their sober moral code also frowned on such excesses as Catholic pre-Lenten festivities, while their certainty of salvation removed the need for Lenten fasts and sacrifices.

Religious wars, witch
hunts, and economic
change diminish
religion's role

Religious wars and witch hunts also provoked disenchantment with religion, while growing prosperity left Europeans less focused on death and salvation. In Protestant areas, and even Catholic lands, the saints, shrines, monasteries, pilgrimages, and fasts that earlier meant so much grew less important. Freed by Luther and Calvin from the need to earn salvation, many Protestants focused their energies on material success—and many ambitious Catholics did too.

Most people continued to worship and pray, but their lives were less centered on religion than before and they were less inclined to look to religious leaders for guidance. Europe's age of religious upheaval, begun by efforts to enhance religion and diminish the wealth and worldliness of the Roman Church, instead diminished the role of religion and enhanced the wealth and worldliness of European society.

Chapter Review

Putting It in Perspective

In the early sixteenth century, hoping to reform the Catholic Church, reduce Church corruption, improve public morals, and strengthen piety among the people, religious reformers started a rebellion known as the Protestant Reformation. They were supported in their efforts by many political leaders, alarmed at the growing power of the Habsburg family, and by numerous other people who resented the extravagance of popes and bishops, financed by the donations of the faithful.

But the Reformation's outcome was not what its originators intended. Europe's religious unity was shattered, generating all sorts of new beliefs and competing Christian churches, as religious strife and religious zeal fueled wars, inquisitions, persecutions, and witch hunts. Central Europe was left divided and weak, thwarting Habsburg efforts to transform the Holy Roman Empire, including Germany and much of Italy, into a centralized state. And Europe as a whole was left divided among diverse states, each with its own religious institutions and issues.

Despite this destruction and division, however, Europe's wealth and influence expanded. The worldwide spread of Western Christianity, the growth of global commerce and capitalism, the exploitation of the Americas, the flourishing of the bourgeoisie, and advances in literacy and learning all boded well for Europe, especially for European countries that bordered the Atlantic. By the late seventeenth century, profiting from connections created by global expansion, the West was emerging from its religious strife more prosperous and powerful than ever.

Reviewing Key Material

KEY CONCEPTS

sacraments, 483	puritanical, 488
purgatory, 484	capitalism, 496
indulgence, 484	mercantilism, 497
Ninety-five Theses, 485	charter companies, 498
predestination, 488	cottage industry, 501
the elect, 488	nuclear families, 502

KEY PEOPLE

Martin Luther, 485	John Knox, 489
Emperor Charles V, 485	King Edward VI, 489
John Wyclif, 484	Queen Mary, 490
John Hus, 484	Queen Elizabeth I, 490
Pope Sixtus IV, 484	Pope Paul III, 490
Pope Alexander VI, 484	Angela Merici, 491
Pope Julius II, 484	Ignatius Loyola, 491
Maximilian of Habsburg, 485	King Philip II, 492
Friar John Tetzel, 485	Mary Stuart (Queen of
Frederick the Wise, 486	Scots), 493
Huldrych Zwingli, 486	Catherine de Medicis, 493
King Henry VIII, 487	King Henri IV, 493
Catherine of Aragon, 487	Emperor Ferdinand II, 494
Anne Boleyn, 487	King Gustavus Adolphus, 494
Pope Clement VII, 487	Cardinal Richelieu, 494
John Calvin, 488	Francis Xavier, 496

ASK YOURSELF

1. Why did Martin Luther challenge the authority of the Catholic Church? Why did his challenge become a revolt against the Church, rather than a reform movement within the Church?

2. Why did Luther's challenge result in the formation of many new Christian sects? How did the challenges of John Calvin and Henry VIII differ from Luther's challenge?

3. How did the Catholic Church respond to the Protestant challenge? Why were the popes and the Habsburg rulers unable to crush the Protestants?

4. What circumstances led to the globalization of Western Christianity and commerce? What roles did missionaries, merchants, and monarchs each play in this process?

5. What factors account for the economic and social changes in Europe during the age of religious upheavals? Why were women, especially aging women, so often the targets of witch hunts?

GOING FURTHER

Asch, Ronald. *The Thirty Years' War*. 1997.

Bainton, R. *The Reformation of the Sixteenth Century*. Rev. ed. 1985.

Barstow, A. *Witchcraft: A New History of European Witch Hunts*. 1994.

Braudel, F. *Capitalism and Material Life, 1400–1800*. 1973.

Brendler, G. *Martin Luther: Theology and Revolution*. 1991.

Brodrick, James. *The Origin of the Jesuits*. 1971.

Cameron, E., ed. *Early Modern Europe: An Oxford History*. 1999.

Davidson, Nicholas S. *The Counter-Reformation*. 1987.

Dunn, R. S. *The Age of Religious Wars, 1559–1715*. 2nd ed. 1979.

Duplessis, R. *Transitions to Capitalism in Early Modern Europe*. 1997.

Holt, M. P. *The French Wars of Religion, 1562–1629*. 1995.

Kamen, H. *Empire: How Spain Became a World Power*. 2003.

Kittelson, J. M. *Luther the Reformer*. 1986.

Levack, Brian. *The Witch-Hunt in Early Modern Europe*, 2nd ed. 1995.

Lindberg, C. *The European Reformations*. 1996.

MacCulloch, Diarmaid. *The Reformation: A History*. 2005.

Mattingly, Garrett. *The Armada*. 1959, 1988.

McGrath, A. *A Life of John Calvin*. 1990.

Oberman, Heiko A. *Luther: Between God and the Devil*. 1989.

Olin, J. C. *The Catholic Reformation: From Savonarola to Loyola*. 1993.

O'Malley, J. W. *The First Jesuits*, 1993

Ozment, Steven. *Protestants: The Birth of a Revolution*. 1992.

Parker, G. *The Thirty Years War*. 2nd ed. 1997.

Parker, T. H. L. *Calvin: An Introduction to His Thought*. 1995.

Pettegree, A., ed. *The Early Reformation in Europe*. 1992.

Thomas, Keith. *Religion and the Decline of Magic*. 1971.

Warnicke, R. *Women of the English Renaissance and Reformation*. 1983.

Wier, Allison. *The Life of Elizabeth I*. 1999.

Wiesner, M. E. *Women and Gender in Early Modern Europe*. 2nd ed. 2000.

Key Dates and Developments

1517	Luther's Ninety-five Theses initiate Reformation		1545	Pope Paul III convenes Council of Trent
1519	Charles V becomes Holy Roman Emperor		1556	Charles V retires; Philip II becomes King of Spain
1521	Luther appears before Diet of Worms		1562–1594	Wars of Religion in France
1525	German nobles crush Peasants' Revolt		1566	Dutch Revolt begins
1527	King Henry VIII begins to seek annulment		1588	Spanish Armada defeated
1529	Ottoman Turks besiege Vienna		1598	Edict of Nantes in France
1533	Henry VIII defies Rome and marries Anne Boleyn		1600	English East India Company founded
1534	Parliament makes Henry VIII head of English Church		1602	Dutch United East India Company founded
1536	Calvin publishes Institutes of the Christian Religion		1618	Defenestration of Prague begins Thirty Years War
1540	Pope Paul III approves Society of Jesus (Jesuits)		1648	Peace of Westphalia ends Thirty Years War

Ahimsa Nonviolence toward all living things, a principle followed by the Jains of India.

Almoravids Berber followers of a militantly puritanical sect of Islam who believed that in order to conduct successful wars against unbelievers, Muslims must first purify their own souls.

Amerinds Anthropological term for American Indians, used to distinguish them from the Indians of South Asia.

Ancestor worship Veneration of a family's departed relatives and forebears, originally practiced in ancient China.

Animism The belief that spirits exist that can either help or harm human beings.

Archaic Period An era in ancient Greece, from 700 to 500 B.C.E., during which city-states matured and population growth resulted in a shortage of farmland, leading Greeks to develop colonies around the Mediterranean world.

Aristocracy Rule by a class of well-born families.

Artistic realism An artistic style pioneered by Giotto, emphasizing detail, depth, and perspective to replace stylized rigidity with lifelike portraits.

Asceticism The practice of extreme self-denial and renunciation of all possessions.

Assassins A Shi'ite sect of killers known as *hashashin*, or "hashish users."

Augustus One who rules with majesty and grandeur; a title Rome conferred on Octavian.

Bantu The West African word for "people"; a group of related languages; tribes of West Africans who migrated throughout much of Africa over a number of centuries.

Bishops Christian Church officials presiding over districts known as dioceses.

Bubonic plague A deadly contagion typically carried from rodents to humans by fleas.

Caesaropapism The vesting of all spiritual and political authority in a single person in the Byzantine Empire.

Caliph Successor of Muhammad, the Messenger of God.

Capitalism An economic system based on competition among private enterprises.

Castes Exclusive and restrictive hereditary occupational groupings, based on birth and ranked in hierarchical order.

Celibacy Abstinence from marriage and sex.

Chan (Zen) Buddhism A belief system teaching that meditation is the only path to enlightenment and stressing love of nature, simplicity of life, and individual self-discipline.

Charter companies Trading associations protected by royal monopoly.

Chinampas Large latticework platforms of layered mud and lake plants floating on the surface of a Mexican lake and designed for cultivation of crops.

Chosen People The belief that the Jewish people were chosen by the one true God to be His people.

City-States Independent urban political domains that controlled the surrounding countryside.

Civil Service exams Chinese examinations requiring applicants for the state bureaucracy to demonstrate comprehensive knowledge of the Confucian classics.

Civilizations Very large complex societies, or regional groups of complex societies, with widely shared or similar customs, institutions, and beliefs.

Classical Period The era from 500–338 B.C.E., in which classical Greek philosophy, art, and drama flourished.

Concubines Women who are not the main wife of a man (commonly a ruler) but are kept by him for sexual purposes.

Confucianism A system of thought in China based on humane conduct and familial respect.

Cosmic mission theory The Aztec theory that the sun must be nourished with an invisible elixir found only in beating human hearts.

Cottage industry A system under which peasants would make products in their own cottages and sell them to merchant capitalists.

Council of the Indies A board established by King Carlos I of Spain in 1524 to supervise every aspect of government in Spanish America.

Covenant A binding agreement between the God of Israel and his chosen people.

Criollos White people of European ancestry born in Spanish America.

Cultural adaptation   The process by which hominids used their intellectual and social skills to adjust to their surroundings and improve their chances for survival.

Cultures   Unique combinations of customs, beliefs, and practices that distinguish societies from each other.

Cuneiform   Wedge-shaped writing developed by the Sumerians.

Daoism   A naturalistic Chinese philosophy calling on people to live in harmony with nature.

Democracy   Rule by the entire body of citizens.

Dharma   The faithful performance of the duties pertaining to one's caste or station in life; such performance determines one's fate in the next life.

Dictator   Originating in Rome, a term to characterize a tyrant.

Dowry   A bridal endowment of money or property.

Dynastic cycle   A four-phase cycle in China during which a dynasty emerges, rules well for a time, then rules poorly and is overthrown by a new dynasty.

The elect   In Calvinist Christianity, people chosen beforehand by God for salvation.

Enterprise of the Indies   Columbus's detailed plan for a westward maritime expedition to discover a shorter route from Europe to East Asia.

Eunuchs   Castrated men who ran the ruler's palace and guarded his concubines.

Farming villages   Small settlements of homes in a compact cluster, surrounded by lands on which the villagers raised food.

Fatimid   An Egyptian Shi'ite dynasty that broke away from Abbasid rule and established a separate caliphate along the Nile River in 929.

Fatwa   A legal opinion from the highest Islamic legal authority.

Five Pillars   The basic religious tenets of Islam.

Foot binding   A process in which the feet of Chinese girls were tightly wrapped with strips of cloth to make them sexually attractive to men.

Foragers   Those who subsist by gathering wild plant foods and hunting wild animals.

Fresco   Painting on walls when the plaster was still wet so the colors would penetrate it.

Golden Horde   A large Mongol khanate that ruled over Russia and part of Central Asia in the thirteenth and fourteenth centuries.

Gothic architecture   A style of European church architecture that produced impressive churches with pointed arches, towering walls, and stained glass windows.

Grand vezir   Chief minister to the sultan of the Ottoman Empire.

Great ice age   An immense stretch of time marked by frigid glacial stages when enormous ice masses called glaciers spread across much of the globe.

Great Khan   The main successor of Genghis Khan, direct ruler of all Mongol lands in East Asia and overlord of all other Mongol realms.

Greco-Roman culture   A blending of Roman culture with that of the Greeks.

Guerrilla warfare   Raids by small roving bands of warriors that aim to disrupt armies rather than defeating them in open battle.

Guilds   Associations formed to promote the commercial and professional interests of a particular occupational group, such as merchants, shoemakers, or weavers.

Hammurabi's Code   A compilation of early Mesopotamian laws.

Hellenic   The culture developed by Greeks.

Hellenistic   The culture resulting from the blending of Greek, Persian, Egyptian, and Indian customs and societies.

Heresy   A religious opinion contrary to accepted Christian Church doctrine.

Hieroglyphics   Ancient Egyptian writing system based on pictographs.

Hominid   A term scientists apply to human beings and their two-legged pre-human predecessors.

Homo sapiens   "Wise human," a term designating the species that includes all modern people.

Humanism   An outlook emphasizing the value of humans and their activities rather than focusing on faith and spirituality.

Iconoclasm   The destruction of religious images known as icons in the Byzantine Empire.

Il-Khans   Southwest Asian Mongol rulers or "subordinate khans."

Indo-European   A family of languages from India, Iran, and Europe that share many common features.

Indulgence In the Christian Church, a remission of the punishment due for sins that were sacramentally forgiven; designed to reduce or eliminate suffering in purgatory.

Inquisition A judicial institution within the Christian Church that prosecuted people it identified as heretics.

Isma'ilis A branch of Shi'ite Islam claiming direct descent from Isma'il, the last publicly seen imam.

Janissaries Ottoman infantry composed of slaves who were Christian-born converts to Islam and were totally dependent on the sultan.

Jatis Regional subcastes in India, each identified with a certain trade, a specific locale, and often a particular god or goddess.

Jihad In Arabic, a "struggle" or "striving" by Muslims to uphold, defend, or spread their faith.

Kamikaze "Divine winds," storms that sunk Mongol invasion fleets that attacked Japan in 1274 and 1281.

Kana A writing system using simplified Chinese characters to create a phonetic Japanese alphabet.

Karma One's fate or destiny in the next incarnation, as determined by performance of dharma in this life.

Khan A Central Asian regional overlord who exercised broad authority but was expected to consult regularly with a council of tribal leaders and gain its approval for his decisions.

Khanates Vast autonomous regions of the Mongol Empire.

Kinship group An extended family comprising grandparents, parents, siblings, aunts, uncles, cousins, and other relatives.

Knights Armed mounted warriors whose code of conduct entailed strict devotion to their overlords and to the Christian Church.

Legalism A Chinese philosophy advocating strict enforcement of stringent laws by a powerful authoritarian state.

Long count calendar A complex calendar used by the Olmec and Maya peoples to date events according to cycles.

Magna Carta The "Great Charter" issued by King John of England in 1215, affirming nobles' rights and placing the king firmly under the law.

Mahabharata The world's longest epic poem, telling of a legendary war between related families in ancient India.

Mandate of Heaven A Chinese ruler's right to rule, provided that he governed justly and humanely.

Manors Large European landed estates owned by nobles and worked by peasant farmers.

Maratha A Hindu nationalist movement founded to resist Mughal rule in India.

Medieval Referring to the Middle Ages, the period from the fall of Rome through the fourteenth century in Europe.

Mercantilism A policy designed to create a condition in which a country's trading exports exceeded its imports in value.

Mesoamerica Territory that comprises Mexico and northern Central America.

Mestizos People of mixed descent in Iberian America.

Mitima The Inca practice of integrating conquered peoples through resettlement.

Moksha Liberation from the cycle of death and reincarnation in Hinduism.

Monarchy Rule by one person.

Monasticism A religious movement in which especially devout men and women withdrew from secular society to live in religious communities, where life was characterized by prayer and self-denial.

Monotheism Belief in a single god.

Mosque An Islamic house of worship.

Movable type A method of printing using small metal blocks for each letter, arranged in a frame to print one page and then rearranged and reused to print other pages.

Mummification An elaborate process for preserving the bodies of prominent people after death.

Mystery religions Southwest Asian belief systems that addressed directly the problems of human weakness, divine redemption, and eternal life.

Nation A political community united by its people's sense of common heritage and culture.

Natural law A Roman vision of legal principles applicable to all societies regardless of time or circumstances.

Neanderthals An extinct group of large-brained hominids whose remains were first discovered in 1856 in Germany's Neander Valley.

Neolithic The period between 10,000 and 3,000 B.C.E., during which people developed better tools, domesticated plants and animals, cultivated crops, herded livestock, and established permanent settlements; also known as the New Stone Age.

Ninety-five Theses A set of propositions challenging the Christian Church's power to forgive sins and grant indulgences; issued by Martin Luther in 1517.

Nirvana A state of infinite tranquility and peace.

Nuclear families Families made up only of parents and their children.

Oligarchy Rule by a select few.

Paleolithic The period of the earliest and longest stage of human cultural development; also known as the Old Stone Age.

Papal primacy The doctrine that the pope has authority over the entire Christian Church.

Pastoral nomads People who raise livestock for subsistence and move occasionally with their herds in search of fresh grazing grounds.

Patriarchal A type of society dominated by males who served as heads of households and as community leaders.

Pax Mongolica The "Mongolian Peace" that advanced the flow of goods and ideas among Eurasian peoples.

Pax Ottomanica "Ottoman peace," the stability, prosperity, and peace that accompanied Ottoman rule.

Pax Romana "Roman peace," a time of stability and prosperity beginning in the reign of Caesar Augustus.

Peninsulares White residents of Spanish America who had been born in Spain.

People of the Book Islamic term for Jews and Christians, peoples who possess their own scriptural texts.

Polis The Greek word for city-state.

Polygyny The practice by which a man took more than one wife.

Polytheistic The practice of worshiping more than one god.

Pope The bishop of Rome, who headed the Christian Church and claimed to be the vicar, or agent, of Christ on earth.

Predestination The belief that God long ago decided everyone's eternal fate.

Printing press A machine used to print pages set in movable type.

Purdah The seclusion of married women through their confinement to certain rooms of the house.

Pure Land Buddhism A belief system that claimed that humans could not achieve enlightenment by their own efforts and must rely instead on faith in the Buddha of Infinite Light who ruled the Western Paradise, or "Pure Land."

Purgatory In Christian belief, a place of suffering that purified the soul so it could enter heaven.

Puritanical Referring to people who uphold an austere moral code and simple religious practices.

Quipu A piece of wood with knotted cords dangling from it that served the Inca as a means of sending messages.

Qur'an The holy book of Islam.

Race A concept that divides human beings into categories based on external characteristics, especially skin color.

Ramayana A great Indian epic poem based on Vedic oral traditions.

Reconquista The Christian reconquest of Iberia from the Muslims.

Republic A flexible form of government by elected representatives.

Residencia A thorough audit of a Spanish colonial official's conduct during his term of office.

Sacraments In the Christian Church, sacred rites believed to bestow the graces needed for salvation.

Samsara The belief that each being has an eternal spiritual core which is reborn, or "reincarnated," into a new body after the old one dies.

Samurai An army of Japanese warriors which provided military service to their lords and eventually became Japan's dominant class.

Sapa Inca The Inca emperor, who claimed to rule by divine right because of his direct descent from Inti, the sun god.

Sati A practice in India whereby a widow cremated herself on her dead husband's funeral pyre.

Satrapy One of twenty provinces of the Persian Empire.

Schism A division of the Christian Church into separate, competing churches.

Scholar gentry An educated Confucian elite class supported by both official posts and large rural estates.

Scholasticism A system of study combining Christian faith with ancient Greek philosophy, especially that of Aristotle.

Sea Peoples Assorted marauders of unknown origins who ravaged eastern Mediterranean lands in the thirteenth and twelfth centuries B.C.E.

Semitic A language family that includes Arabic, Hebrew, and the languages spoken by ancient Akkadians, Babylonians, and Phoenicians.

Seppuku The practice of ritual suicide by which a defeated samurai warrior in Japan could restore his honor.

Serfs Peasants bound to the manor and under the control of its lord.

Shah The Persian word for king.

Shamanism A form of religion in which spiritual leaders called shamans performed elaborate rituals to communicate with spirits, heal the sick, forecast the future, and influence events.

Shari`ah The holy law of Islam.

Shi'ites The minority of Muslims, following the "Party of Ali" (*Shi'at Ali*).

Shinto The "way of the kami," a nature-based Japanese religion.

Shogun The commander-in-chief of Japan's armed forces and the real ruler of the nation.

Sikh An Indian belief system that blends and synthesizes Hindu and Islamic elements.

Silk Road A network of trade routes named for the precious Chinese fabric it conveyed.

Simony The sale of offices in the Christian Church.

Socratic dialogue Rigorous questioning and analysis of ethical issues, as practiced by the Greek philosopher Socrates.

States Territorial entities ruled by a central government.

Struggle of the Orders A bitterly divisive social contest between patricians and plebeians in the Roman Republic.

Stupa A massive domed edifice constructed of stone, used as a temple for Buddhist pilgrimage and worship.

Sufism A mystic strain of Islam that advocates direct union with God through prayer, contemplation, and religious ecstasy.

Sunni The majority of Muslims, claiming to follow the Sunna, the traditional practices of the Prophet.

Swahili A language widespread in East Africa; the name of Bantu-Arabic East African culture.

Tahuantin-suyu "Empire of the Four Quarters," the official name of the Inca Empire.

Tatar yoke The era of Mongol domination of Russia.

Three Religions A Vietnamese belief system blending Mahayana Buddhism, Confucianism, and Daoism.

Tlaxcallan Confederacy An alliance of several city-states opposed to the Aztec Empire.

Treaty of Tordesillas A 1494 agreement between the Portuguese and Spanish designed to divide the world between them.

Tribes Large associations of villages, bands, or clans that share a common language and often a common leader.

Tyranny The illegal seizure of power by someone who had no right to exercise it.

Umma A purely Islamic community.

University An educational institution in which scholars from various fields helped students become experts and then granted them degrees to certify their expertise.

Upanishads Philosophical and religious texts composed by learned writers over many centuries, beginning in late Vedic India.

Urfi State laws used by the Ottoman sultan without restriction from Islamic legal authority.

Varnas Classes in Aryan Indian society, based on the functions fulfilled by their members.

Vassals Subordinate warlords who swore allegiance and pledged military service to a higher lord.

Vedic The culture of Aryan India.

Vernacular literature Literature written in the everyday language spoken by common people.

Viceroy "Vice-king," an official responsible for the execution of the monarch's orders in a large subdivision of the empire or realm.

Xiongnu Warlike Turkish nomads from the Central Asian steppes who threatened China from the north.

Yin and yang A Chinese principle emphasizing the balancing and blending of natural forces.

Yoga A school of classical Hindu philosophy emphasizing meditation and self-knowledge.

Zen (Chan) Buddhism A belief system teaching that meditation is the only path to enlightenment and stressing love of nature, simplicity of life, and individual self-discipline.

Ziggurats Massive brick towers that ascended upward in a series of tiers, typically topped by shrines that could be used for religious ceremonies.

Zoroastrianism A Persian belief system including the concepts of free will and a Last Judgment.

Cover

Sequoyah (1770–1843) and his Cherokee alphabet, Courtesy of the Library of Congress; Islamic calligraphy, Patrick Ben and Luke Snyder/Lonely Planet Images; El Castillo Pyramid Chichen Itza, Yucatan, Mexico, Peter Adams/JIA/CORBIS; Buddha Sakyamuni, The Art Archive/Musée Guimet Paris/Dagli Orti; D'Espanol y Mulata produce Morisca/Breamore House, Hampshire, England; Tomb of Nebamun, © Copyright The British Museum/Art Resource, NY; Tondo of St. Mamai, c. 1000/Courtesy of the Library of Congress; The NEMESIS destroying Chinese war junks in Anson's Bay, The Art Archive/Eileen Tweedy; Rhinos in Chauvet Cave, French Ministry of Culture and Communication, Regional Direction for Cultural Affairs—Rhone-Alps, Regional Department of Archaeology. International Space Station, NASA; "Parade on Tsarina's Meadow", Vsesoiuznyi Muzei A.S. Pushkina; Bronze head, Kim Sayer © Dorling Kindersley; Spanish Civil War poster, Courtesy of the Library of Congress.

Chapter 1

p. 1, Chauvet cave paintings: horses, Ministere de la Culture et de la Communication. Direction Regionale des affaires Culturelles de Rhone–Alpes, Service Regional de l'Archeologie; **p. 4**, Representative hominid tools, Howard S. Friedman/Pearson Education/PH College Corbis/Bettman; **p. 9**, Venus of Willendorf, © Archivo Iconografico, S.A./CORBIS; **p. 15**, Indians plant corn, Courtesy of the Library of Congress; **p. 18**, Potters and pottery, EMG Education Management Group.

Chapter 2

p. 23, Sumerian Ziggurat, World Tourism Organization: Iraq; **p. 25**, Assyrian King Sargon and a high official, John Serafin/ Pearson Education Corporate Digital Archive; **p. 28**, Clay tablet, Courtesy of the Library of Congress; **p. 34**, Assyrian warrior, EMG Education Management Group; **p. 36**, The hanging gardens of ancient Babylon, EMG Education Management Group; **p. 39**, Mummy Case of Lady Takhenmes, Peter Anderson © Dorling Kindersley, Courtesy of the Bolton Metro Museum; **p. 42**, Sphinx and Cheops Pyramid at Giza near Cairo, Egypt/Egyptian Tourist Authority; **p. 43**, Statues of Ramses II at Abu Simbel, Dominique Roger/Egyptian Tourist Authority; **p. 44**, Wall painting showing Nubians presenting gifts and food offerings, © The British Museum; **p. 48**, A recreation of the ancient walled city of Jerusalem, Israel Ministry of Tourism, North America.

Chapter 3

p. 54, Early Indian sculpture, Andy Crawford © Dorling Kindersley, Courtesy of the National Museum, New Delhi; **p. 58** (top), General view of Mohenjodaro, Embassy of Pakistan; **p. 58** (bottom), Seal of Mohenjodaro, Embassy of Pakistan; **p. 59**, Dancing girl, Mohenjodaro, Embassy of Pakistan; **p. 63**, Two relief panels from the stupa of Bharhut, Courtesy of the Library of Congress; **p. 65**, Vishnu and Lakshmi, Courtesy of the Government of India Tourist Office, New York; **p. 75**, The Great Stupa at Sanchi, Dale William/Government of India.

Chapter 4

p. 80, Cross-section illustration of the tomb of Qin Shihuangdi showing the Terra Cotta Army, Richard Bronson, © Dorling Kindersley; **p. 83** (top), China, Ningxia, Shapotu, Yellow River/Eddie Gerald, © Dorling Kindersley; **p. 83** (bottom), Yangshao pottery from Banpo, China/Courtesy of the Library of Congress; **p. 85**, Chariot burial from the royal Shang tombs near Anyang/National Archives and Records Administration; **p. 86**, Chinese writing on a piece of bone, Laurence Pordes, © Dorling Kindersley/Courtesy of The British Library; **p. 89**, Bell from Zhou Dynasty, Alan Hills, © The British Museum; **p. 90**, Confucius surrounded by his disciples, Courtesy of the Library of Congress; **p. 96**, China's Great Wall, Jupiter Images; **p. 97**, Cave 323, Mogao Grottoes, Dunhuang, China./© www.dunhuanghun.com Dunhuang Academy. All rights reserved. **p. 101**, Model of a Han era house, Courtesy of the Library of Congress; **p. 104**, Bactrian camel, camelus bactrianus/ Dave King, © Dorling Kindersley.

Chapter 5

p. 107, Pueblo Bonito, Chaco Canyon, New Mexico/ Courtesy of the Library of Congress; **p. 109**, Clovis points from sites New Mexico, Arizona, and Colorado/National Archives and Records; **p. 112**, Totem Park, Brockton Point, Gunter Marx, © Dorling Kindersley, Courtesy of Stanley Park, Totem Park, Vancouver, British Columbia; **p. 114**, Ancient Ruins in the

Canyon de Chelly, Arizona/Timothy O'Sullivan, National Archives and Records Administration, Presidential Library; **p. 115,** Monk's Mound in Cahokia, Otis Imboden, Jr./NGS Image Collection; **p. 118,** Colossal Olmec, Demtrio Carrasco © CONACULTA-INAH-MEX. Authorized reproduction by the Instituto Nacional de Antropologia e Historia; **p. 121,** Venus calendar, Sachsische Landesbibliothek; **p. 122,** Pyramid of the Moon, Mike Peters/Pearson Education Corporate Digital Archive; **p. 124,** Atlantis de Tula, Hidalgo/Andrew Sacks, Embassy of Mexico; **p. 129,** Chimu society woven polychrome textile panel, © Judith Miller/Dorling Kindersley/Arte Primitivo.

Chapter 6

p. 133, Frieze showing Persian palace guard/© The British Museum; **p. 139,** Clay cylinder with text, Alan Hills and Barbara Winter/© The British Museum; **p. 143,** Iran, Persepolis: Eugene Gordon, Dorling Kindersley Media Library; **p. 144,** Silver goat from 5th century B.C., Alan Hills and Barbara Winter/© The British Museum; **p. 145,** Ruins of the entrance to the palace of Darius, Iranian Embassy; **p. 151,** Part of a mosaic illustrating the Battle of Issus, Soprintendenza alle Antichita della Campania, picture by Raymond V. Schoder.

Chapter 7

p. 156, Greek athletes on a glazed Athenian vase, National Archives and Records Administration; **p. 159** (top), Fresco from the Palace of Knossos, Crete/Hirmer Verlag/Pearson Education U.S. ELT; **p. 159** (bottom), Agamemnon's mask, Prentice Hall School Division; **p. 163,** Ancient Greek figurine of a warrior, Nick Nicholls/© The British Museum; **p. 164,** Pericles; Statesman of Greece, Courtesy of the Library of Congress; **p. 166,** The Parthenon; Acropolis, Athens/Raymond Schoder, Pearson Education U. S. ELT; **p. 167,** Scene showing chariot race, Michael Holford/Pearson Education U. S. ELT; **p. 171,** Ancient Greek image of women filling jugs from well, Nick Nicholls/© The British Museum; **p. 172,** Asklepios, the Greek god of medicine/Pearson Education U.S. ELT; **p. 173,** Coin with the head of Alexander the Great, Pearson Education U. S. ELT; **p. 179,** Sculpture of Mithras slaying the sacred bull, © The British Museum.

Chapter 8

p. 182, Romulus and Remus/James McConnachie/© Rough Guides; **p. 191,** Mosaic of Roman pupils with their teacher, Raymond V. Schoder/Musea Provinciale Campano, Capua; **p. 193,** Tombstone of a Roman soldier, Celerinus/Romisch-Germanisches Museum der Stadt Koln/Rheinisches Bildarchiv; **p. 195,** Caesar Augustus, Emperor of Rome/Courtesy of the Library of Congress; **p. 196,** Roman aqueduct in Segovia, Spain/Spanish National Tourist Office; **p. 198,** Relief from the Ara Pacis, Italian Government Tourist Board; **p. 199,** The excavations of Qumran, Israel Ministry of Tourism, North America; **p. 202,** Tondo of St. Mamai (Georgia), c. 1000/Courtesy of the Library of Congress; **p. 204** (top), Roma: II Colosseo/Courtesy of the Italian Government Travel Office (Los Angeles); **p. 204** (bottom), Appian Way, Italian Government Tourist Board.

Chapter 9

p. 207, Statue of Emperor Constantine/John Heseltine, © Dorling Kindersley; **p. 210,** Ostrogoth brooches, Christi Graham and Nick Nicholls/© The British Museum; **p. 213,** Night view of the Arch of Constantine/Italian Government Tourist Board; **p. 220,** Baptism and Victory of Cloves/Courtesy of the Library of Congress; **p. 221,** Abbey of Monte Cassino, Italian Government Tourist Board; **p. 222,** Charlemagne's chapel at Aachen, French Government Tourist Office; **p. 224** Oseberg burial ship/Universitets Oldsaksamling, © Dorling Kindersley; **p. 227,** German peasant women/Courtesy of the Library of Congress.

Chapter 10

p. 234, Interior of St. Sophia Mosque, Istanbul/Turkish Tourism and Information Office; **p. 239,** Empress Theodora/The Art Archive/Dagli Orti; **p. 242,** Byzantium and its neighbors/Dorling Kindersley Media Library, Pearson Education/PH College; **p. 244,** Ayasofya Muzesi, Istanbul (Museum of Santa Sophia)/Turkish Tourism and Information Office; **p. 245** (top), St. Michael in the Byzantine Museum in Athens, Greece/Dorling Kindersley, © Archaeological Receipts Fund (TAP); **p. 245** (bottom), Ruins of the fifth-century walls of Constantinople/Turkish Tourism and Information Office; **p. 246,** Byzantines fighting the Bulgars, Courtesy of the Library of Congress.

Chapter 11

p. 257, The Great Mosque, Al Masjeed Alharam/Elkoussy, India Government Tourist Office; **p. 259**, Tuaregs/Eugene Gordon, Pearson Education/PH College; **p. 263** (top), Islamic text, Pearson Education/PH College; **p. 263** (bottom), Qur'an, Courtesy of the Library of Congress, African and Middle Eastern Division; **p. 267**, The Ka'ba in Mecca, Courtesy of the Library of Congress; **p. 273**, The Dome of the Rock, Israel Ministry of Tourism, North America; **p. 275**, Salat, ritual worship or prayer, sequence of movements/Courtesy of the Library of Congress.

Chapter 12

p. 278, Angkor Wat, Cambodia/Andrew Gunners, Getty Images; **p. 283**, Baghdad city plan, © Dorling Kindersley; **p. 284**, Islamic science and alchemy, Courtesy of the Library of Congress; **p. 285**, Suwar-al-Kawakib, Courtesy of the Library of Congress, Near Eastern Section, African and Middle Eastern Division; **p. 287**, The Mosque of Ibn Tulun, Cairo/Jon Spaull, © Dorling Kindersley; **p. 288**, Islamic schematic world map, Courtesy of the Library of Congress; **p. 292**, Water cave, Elephanta/Courtesy of the Library of Congress; **p. 293**, Quwwat-ul-Islam Mosque, Ram Rahman, © Dorling Kindersley; **p. 296**, Relief sculpture at Borobodur in Central Java, © Wolfgang Kaehler/CORBIS, All Rights Reserved.

Chapter 13

p. 299, Ife figure, South African Tourism Board; **p. 303**, San people of the Kalahari, South African Tourism Board; **p. 304**, African fertility symbol, Akuba doll. Ghana, ca 1970's/Courtesy of the Library of Congress; **p. 305**, Grass-skirted spirit masks of the Kuba of Zaire, Ellen Howdon, © Dorling Kindersley, Courtesy of the Glasgow Museum; **p. 307**, Court of the Lions, Pearson Education Corporate Digital Archive; **p. 309**, Al-Azhar Mosque, Cairo/Courtesy of the Library of Congress; **p. 312**, Map of town near Kumbi-Saleh, Pearson Education/PH College; **p. 314**, Mansa Musa on Pilgrimage/Prentice Hall School Division; **p. 317**, Arab dhow vessel, Brian Delft, © Dorling Kindersley; **p. 321**, Conical Tower, Great Zimbabwe/National Archives of South Africa.

Chapter 14

p. 323, Womb Wold mandala/Benrido, Japan; **p. 328**, Gandhara sculpture of Maitreya/Amit Pashricha © Dorling Kindersley, Courtesy of the Indian Museum, Kolkata (Calcutta), India; **p. 330**, Bingling Si (Bright Spirit Temple)/Eddie Gerald, © Dorling Kindersley; **p. 331**, Wu Men Bridge/Linda Whitwam, © Dorling Kindersley; **p. 333**, Empress Wu, Courtesy of the Library of Congress **p. 338**, Longji Titian/Nigel Hicks, © Dorling Kindersley; **p. 339**, Early carved woodblock, Courtesy of the Library of Congress **p. 340**, Shanghai Museum, polychrome glazed pottery horse/Chen Chao, © Dorling Kindersley; **p. 342**, A bound foot, Houghton Mifflin Company; **p. 346**, Korean inlaid celadon porcelain double gourd vase, Koryo Dynasty/© Judith Miller/Dorling Kindersley/Sloan's; **p. 348**, Five-story pagoda at Horyuji Temple complex, Hong Kong Tourist Association; **p. 350**, Kosho, "Kuya Preaching"/Asanuma Photo Studios, Kyoto, Japan.

Chapter 15

p. 354, Bibliotheque Nationale, Paris, France/The Bridgeman Art Library; **p. 357**, Nomads outside yurt, Courtesy of the Library of Congress; **p. 358**, Ongons/Oggshot, © The National Museum of Denmark, Ethnographic Collection; **p. 361**, Seljuk carpet, Tony Souter/© Dorling Kindersley; **p. 363**, Queen Tamar, Charles Cavaliere; **p. 365**, Mongol archer on horseback, Victoria & Albert Museum, London, UK/The Bridgeman Art Library; **p. 369**, Page from Hashid's History of the Worlds, Edinburgh University Library; **p. 376**, Mongol "passport," Bequest of Dorothy Graham Bennett, 1993/The Metropolitan Museum of Art, New York, NY, U.S.A. Image copyright © The Metropolitan Museum of Art; **p. 377**, Ancient warriors, Mark Franklin, © Dorling Kindersley.

Chapter 16

p. 382, Firenze-Battistero-Duomo e Campanile di Giotto/Courtesy of the Italian Government Travel Office (Los Angeles); **p. 388**, Saladin, Courtesy of the Library of Congress; **p. 389**, Syria, Hama, detail of wooden water wheels/Alistair Duncan, Dorling Kindersley Media Library; **p. 390**, Aigues-Mortes, French Government Tourist Office; **p. 394**, Notre Dame, French Government Tourist Office; **p. 395**, Plague victim, Courtesy of the Library of Congress; **p. 398**, Model dressed as archer with long bow, Geoff Dann © Dorling Kindersley; **p. 399**, Giotto crucifix, James McConnachie, © Rough Guides; **p. 401**, Donatello's Mary Magdalene, Alison Harris, © Dorling Kindersley; **p. 402** (top), da Vinci's sketch of a helicopter, Courtesy of the Library of Congress; **p. 402** (bottom), Replica statue of David by Michelangelo, John Heseltine, © Dorling Kindersley; **p. 403**, Renaissance print shop, Courtesy of the Library of Congress; **p. 404**, Albrecht Durer, Four Riders of the Apocalypse/Courtesy of the Library of Congress.

Chapter 17

p. 409, Ottoman compass points, Courtesy of the Library of Congress; **p. 413**, Tomb of Tamerlane in Uzbekistan, Glen Allison, Getty Images; **p. 415**, Muhammad II Ottoman Sultan of Turkey, Courtesy of the Library of Congress; **p. 417**, Ottoman law book, Courtesy of the Library of Congress; **p. 420**, Suleiman, © Dorling Kindersley; **p. 421**, Medieval Islamic map of the world, Courtesy of the Library of Congress; **p. 423** (top), Shiite battle tunic, Courtesy of the Library of Congress; **p. 423** (bottom), Masjed-e-Emam (Shah Mosque), Christopher and Sally Gable, © Dorling Kindersley; **p. 424**, The Fainting of Laylah and Majnun, Courtesy of the Library of Congress; **p. 426**, Amritsar, B. P. S. Walia, © Dorling Kindersley; **p. 429**, Taj Mahal, India Government Tourist Office.

Chapter 18

p. 433, Machu Picchu, Pearson Education Corporate Digital Archive; **p. 435**, Facsimile of the Codex Mendoza, Courtesy of the Library of Congress. Berkeley University of California Press, 1992. General Collections; **p. 438**, Sacrificio humano en Tenochititlan, Courtesy of the Library of Congress; **p. 440**, Coatlicue, Mexican National Tourist Council; **p. 443** (top), Quipa, Incan counting device/© Dorling Kindersley, Courtesy of the Museum of Archaeology and Anthropology, Cambridge; **p. 443** (bottom), Calle Triunfo in Cuzco, James Sawders, The Workshop; **p. 445**, Dona Marina, Courtesy of the Library of Congress; **p. 446**, Map of Tenochtitlan, 1524/ Courtesy of the Library of Congress; **p. 449**, Spanish firepower, Courtesy of the Library of Congress; **p. 450**, Codex Florentino: 111/Courtesy of the Library of Congress.

Chapter 19

p. 457, 16th century map of Portuguese claims in Africa and Brazil, Courtesy of the Library of Congress; **p. 462**, Columbus's first meeting with Indians, Courtesy of the Library of Congress; **p. 464**, Portolan atlas of nine charts and a world map, Courtesy of the Library of Congress; **p. 465**, Replica of caravela, Paul Bernhardt/© Dorling Kindersley; **p. 471**, Plaza de Armas, Cuzco Peru/ Courtesy of the Library of Congress; **p. 472**, First book, Courtesy of the Library of Congress; **p. 473**, D'Espanol y Mulata produce Morisca/Breamore House, Hampshire, England; **p. 475**, Samuel de Champlain's map of the northeast coast of North America, 1607/Courtesy of the Library of Congress; **p. 477**, King Powhatan condemns John Smith, Courtesy of the Library of Congress; **p. 478**, Woman preparing manioc, Courtesy of the Library of Congress.

Chapter 20

p. 481, Ektachrom von "Hinrichtung des Jaklein Rohrbach," Courtesy of the Library of Congress; **p. 484**, Johann Tetzel, Courtesy of the Library of Congress; **p. 485**, Copy of Schadow's Martin Luther, Dorota and Mariusz Jarymowicz, © Dorling Kindersley; **p. 487**, Anne Boleyn, Courtesy of the Library of Congress; **p. 488**, Portrait of John Calvin, Courtesy of the Library of Congress; **p. 491**, Ignatius of Loyola, Courtesy of the Library of Congress; **p. 493**, Fleet of English ships, Brian Delft, © Dorling Kindersley; **p. 498**, French Jesuit performing baptism, Courtesy of the Library of Congress; **p. 499**, Witches being hanged, © Dorling Kindersley; **p. 501**, Albrecht Duerer's "Peasants at Market," Courtesy of the Library of Congress.